T0389525

Étienne Pasquier, *The Jesuits' Catechism or Their Doctrine Examined* (1602)

Jesuit Studies

MODERNITY THROUGH THE PRISM OF JESUIT HISTORY

Editor

Robert A. Maryks (Independent Scholar)

VOLUME 33

Anti-Jesuit Literature

VOLUME 1

The titles published in this series are listed at *brill.com/js*

Étienne Pasquier,
The Jesuits' Catechism or Their Doctrine Examined (1602)

Translated by

Patricia M. Ranum

Edited by

Robert A. Maryks
Jotham Parsons

BRILL

LEIDEN | BOSTON

Cover illustration: Étienne Pasquier. Engraving by Thomas de Leu (1560–1612).

Library of Congress Cataloging-in-Publication Data

Names: Pasquier, Etienne, 1529–1615, author. | Maryks, Robert A., editor. |
   Parsons, Jotham, editor. | Ranum, Patricia M., translator.
Title: Étienne Pasquier, The Jesuits' catechism or their doctrine examined
   (1602) / translated by Patricia M. Ranum ; edited by Robert A. Maryks,
   Jotham Parsons.
Other titles: Catéchisme des Jésuites. English | Jesuits' catechism or
   their doctrine examined (1602)
Description: Leiden ; Boston : Brill, [2021] | Series: Jesuit studies :
   modernity through the prism of Jesuit history, 2214–3289 ; volume 33 |
   Includes bibliographical references and index.
Identifiers: LCCN 2021033313 (print) | LCCN 2021033314 (ebook) | ISBN
   9789004149366 (hardback) | ISBN 9789004164062 (ebook)
Subjects: LCSH: Jesuits—Controversial literature.
Classification: LCC BX3705.A2 P3713 2021 (print) | LCC BX3705.A2 (ebook)
   | DDC 271/.53—dc23
LC record available at https://lccn.loc.gov/2021033313
LC ebook record available at https://lccn.loc.gov/2021033314

Typeface for the Latin, Greek, and Cyrillic scripts: "Brill". See and download: brill.com/brill-typeface.

ISSN 2214-3289
ISBN 978-90-04-14936-6 (hardback)
ISBN 978-90-04-16406-2 (e-book)

Contents

Étienne Pasquier
The Jesuits' Catechism or Their Doctrine Examined

Book 1

Book III

Acknowledgements

Étienne Pasquier's use of a broad range of sources and his references to numerous protagonists and events in his work required consultations with a number of specialists. We would like to acknowledge therefore the assistance of several colleagues of ours, including Christopher Francese, Paul Gwynne, Thomas M. McCoog, s.j., John W. O'Malley, s.j., Joseph A. Munitiz, s.j., and Orest Ranum.

Historical Introduction

Jotham Parsons

Étienne Pasquier's *Jesuits' Catechism* is excessively long, erudite to the point of pedantry, often boring, and almost always tendentious. It is sustained by some humor and a good deal of passion, but for the most part it shows its author's literary gifts in a poor light. The main reason anyone today would want to read it is its historical significance; that, however, is substantial. The culmination of the author's lifelong and somewhat obsessive dedication to opposing the most important new institution of the post-Reformation Catholic Church, it crystallized and then served as a reference point not just for anti-Jesuitism but for an entire approach to religion and politics in France. This approach and the partisan causes it served—in different times and contexts it can be labeled Gallican, historicist, *politique, parlementaire,* Jansenist, patriot—constituted much of the opposition to the absolutism of France's Bourbon kings, already under construction as Pasquier wrote. Towards the end of the eighteenth century, it substantially triumphed as the Jesuits were first expelled from France and then dissolved by the papacy, even if the Enlightenment was the main beneficiary of that triumph. And then, in the summer of 1789, the old world was swept away. Die-hard absolutists (and some ex-Jesuits) could and did defy the revolutionary tide, becoming reactionaries, biding their time, re-emerging as fortunes changed, perhaps learning nothing but certainly forgetting nothing. Not so those who trod in Pasquier's path. The Revolution fundamentally changed what opposition would mean in the modern world, and those texts it did not incorporate soon became dead letter, but not before they had done much to shape the modern world.

Pasquier was above all a lawyer—his English biographer gives him the somewhat clunky but appropriate epithet of "the versatile barrister of sixteenth-century France"—but he lived at a time when the law was at the crossroads of political and intellectual life.[1] Thus, his avocations as a poet, a historian, or a political activist flowed as naturally from his legal formation as did his work as a bureaucrat. The *Catechism* brought together all these elements of his formation, making a more complex a text but also supplying a window into the culture of the day. Its contents can be traced back to anti-Jesuit legal briefs that Pasquier wrote at the beginning of his career, continually fertilized

---

1   Dorothy Thickett, *Estienne Pasquier (1529–1615): The Versatile Barrister of Sixteenth-Century France* (London: Regency Press, 1979).

by work that made him one of the leading experts on the history of France, continually reshaped by his occasional work as a political pamphleteer, and ultimately recast into its final literary and polemical form.

The *Catechism* was also very much the product of a single historical moment. It came after the end of a long and brutal civil war, at a time when the new regime of the Bourbon dynasty and King Henri IV (r.1589–1610) was quite self-consciously laying the foundations of a new political (and social, and religious) order in the kingdom. The immediate question Pasquier addressed was whether the Jesuits, who had at least officially been banished to the geographical margins of France following a 1594 assassination attempt against Henri IV, would be returned to their former status.[2] Behind this there lurked larger issues about the nature of French Catholicism, how the newly established religious peace might be maintained, and above all who had the authority to determine French cultural and legal norms. Pasquier's answers to these questions did not necessarily carry the day, but they were very influential.

Despite Pasquier's efforts, the Jesuits returned to France and remained there for another century and a half. In that time, though, their enemies only multiplied. For reasons both doctrinal and political, conflicts between the friends and the enemies of the Society of Jesus were one of the structuring elements of French politics through the seventeenth and most of the eighteenth century. The *Catechism* was, well, the catechism of this movement. Not only was it read and reprinted, but—along with a few other texts of its time and milieu—it was a nucleus around with accreted vast collections of erudition and invective, designed to write into being a certain vision of a stable, aristocratic France free from the arbitrary actions of king and pope alike and a Catholic Church restored to a deeply idealized version of its ancient rigor. Between 1764, when the Jesuits were finally expelled from France, and 1789, when the Estates General seemed for a moment to herald an ancient constitution reborn, this vision had a startling level of success: but it did not really survive its own triumph. In the wake of the Revolution there were a few attempts to revive Pasquier as a model of statesmanship suitable to a constitutional monarchy, but like constitutional monarchy itself they did not last. Rome successfully revived the Jesuits in 1814. But while history is written by the winners it is not only about them, and there is still much to be learned from the *Catechism*.

❧

---

2 On that issue, see Eric W. Nelson, *The Jesuits and the Monarchy: Catholic Reform and Political Authority in France, 1590–1615* (Aldershot: Ashgate, 2005).

Pasquier always identified himself as a Parisian, in an age when that was much rarer than it is now.[3] He was born in the city on June 7, 1529 (or possibly 1528), and died there at a ripe old age on September 1, 1615. Though he traveled around France for professional reasons—he certainly knew the kind of journey that frames the *Catechism* from personal experience—his career was also almost entirely based in the French capital. His family belonged to an educated professional bourgeoisie that used Renaissance humanism, which at his birth was in its first generation in France, to advance socially and politically. His uncle by marriage Adrien Turnèbe (1512–65), for example, was one of the leading classicists of the time; as royal lecturer in Greek, he helped pave Etienne's way into the world of the University of Paris, in whose satellite colleges he began his education.[4]

The university, though, had never taught civil law. As late as the beginning of the sixteenth century the study of canon law could prepare a man for a successful career in the Parisian legal world, but the changing political, religious, and intellectual climate had made that a much less viable path.[5] So after his undergraduate studies Pasquier left town for law faculties in Orleans, Bourges, Toulouse, and Italy. There, he was at the heart of an intellectual revolution: the so-called *mos gallicus* (French way), a study of Roman law based on the deep understanding of the Latin language and Roman political and institutional history obsessively developed by the humanist movement over the previous century. The great men of this movement, two of whom, Jacques Cujas (1520–90) and Andrea Alciato (1492–1550), were Pasquier's teachers, were fundamentally antiquarians. Cujas, it was said, replied to questions about contemporary political or religious issues, "that has nothing to do with the Praetorian Edict," referring to one of the foundations of the legal system in the Roman Republic.[6] Pasquier, though, along with a number of his contemporaries, soon came to the realization that the *mos gallicus* could be equally well applied to Gallic as to Roman law: in other words, that intensive study of French language and history since the fall of the Roman empire could

---

3   Currently, close to twenty percent of the population of France lives in the Paris metropolitan area; in the sixteenth century, the corresponding figure was perhaps one percent.

4   Pasquier wrote the first serious history of the University of Paris, in Book VIII of his *Recherches de la France*.

5   See Tyler Lange, *The First French Reformation: Church Reform and the Origins of the Old Regime* (Cambridge: Cambridge University Press, 2014).

6   Jean Papire Masson, *Jacobi Cuiacii iureconsulti vita* (Basel: Konrad Waldkirch, 1591), 12: "quanquam de Theologicis quaestionibus interrogatus, respondere solitus erat, *Nil hoc ad edictum Praetoris*."

be a starting place for understanding, and maybe for reforming, French law and politics.

This belief is the key to understanding Pasquier's varied career after he completed his legal studies. Above all he was a lawyer, in private practice for many years and then as a public prosecutor attached to France's main fiscal court, the Chambre des comptes of Paris. But alongside that practice, and in the intervals of leisure provided by underemployment, illness, civil disturbance, and eventually retirement, he was a poet, historian, and political pamphleteer. As a poet he was a pleasant and competent mediocrity and never really pretended to be anything else, but in his other avocations he was a major figure. His most important historical work was a series of essays on mainly medieval French literary and institutional history, the *Recherches de la France* (usually translated "Researches on France," but "In Search of France" might convey the meaning better), published in installments between 1560 and 1596.[7] In its methodology, its command of the sources, and its historical sensitivity it truly broke new ground. Pasquier and his friends built much of the foundations of modern historical scholarship, in Donald Kelley's words, and a glance at the *Catechism* shows that their views of and arguments about religion and politics were essentially historical.[8] Pasquier believed that one could and should determine how rules and institutions ought to work by examining how they had worked in the past. Inherent to this method, though, was a sometimes sincere, sometimes willful blindness to present realities and norms—for just this reason, working lawyers quickly abandoned the historical school in which Pasquier had been trained.

Both the positive and the negative aspects of this perspective are visible in the *Catechism* and its later history. Its essential conservatism hampered the creation of a positive program, or any real appreciation of, for example, where the appeal of the Jesuits might lie. But its historical foundations were genuinely solid, and that gave it lasting appeal and prestige. In the *Catechism*, Pasquier insisted that his argument was rigorous, scholarly, and amply supported by the texts, while that of the Jesuits very much was not. Thus, as Luce Giard notes in a recent study, "Pasquier insists on the seriousness of his documentation; thus, to prove the ignorance and theological incompetence of the first Jesuits he has to show [e.g.] that their studies at Paris were brief and incomplete," a

---

7   There is a modern edition: Étienne Pasquier, *Les Recherches de la France*, ed. Marie-Madeleine Fragonard and François Roudaut, 3 vols. (Paris: Honoré Champion, 1996).

8   See Donald Kelley, *Foundations of Modern Historical Scholarship: Language, Law and History in the French Renaissance* (New York: Columbia University Press, 1970).

line of attack that would long outlive its author.[9] Pasquier's reputation as a historian and particularly the enduring success of the *Recherches* significantly reinforced that claim. In fact, as we shall see, the *Catechism* and the *Recherches* complemented each other down the decades, one emphasizing the polemical and one the scholarly side of an argument in which the two were inseparable.

In one respect, though, Pasquier was distinct from the rest of his intellectual milieu. He had a deep commitment to vernacular literature, not just as an avocation but as a key to understanding France, past and present. "To him," said Donald Kelley, literary "style was not merely a standard of taste or even a tool of analysis," though it was both of those things, "but also a means of identifying the peculiarities of local and national character."[10] Consequently, his attempt to mend French institutions and society by conforming them to their past would also involve understanding and cultivating France's literary tradition—though he was far more open to progress and innovation in literature than in politics or religion. The *Recherches* was, among other things, the first serious work of French literary history and the way it blended the political and the literary in its account of French identity would remain influential through the classical era and the Enlightenment. Pasquier also practiced what he preached, publishing some poetry, but more significantly, a collection of personal letters modeled loosely on those of Cicero (106–43 BCE).[11] Readers of the *Catechism* were generally aware of this side of his work, but not much of the author's literary flair comes through in the polemic: the dialogue format mostly drops out early on and the most ambitious *jeu d'esprit*, the discourse of the statues in Book III, ch. 20, seems to me to fall entirely flat.[12] In

9   Luce Giard, "Le *Catéchisme des Jésuites* d'Étienne Pasquier, une attaque en règle," in Antoine Fabre and Catherine Maire, eds., *Les Antijésuites: Discours, figures et lieux de l'antijésuitisme à l'époque moderne* (Rennes: Presses Universitaires de Rennes, 2010): 73–90, https://books.openedition.org/pur/110462 (accessed April 8, 2021): "Pasquier insiste sur le sérieux de sa documentation. Ainsi, pour prouver l'ignorance et l'incompétence théologique des premiers jésuites, il lui faut montrer que leurs études à Paris furent brèves et incomplètes." Compare *Catechism*, Book I, chs. 11–12.

10   Kelley, *Foundations*, 279.

11   Almost all of Pasquier's literary output has received modern editions: a testament, depending on how you look at it, to his importance or to the excess productive capacity of French literary studies. See *Ordonnances generalles d'amour*, ed. Jean-Pierre Dupouy (Paris: Classiques Garnier, 2018); *Les jeux poétiques: 1610*, ed. Jean-Pierre Dupouy (Paris: Honoré Champion, 2001); *Lettres familières*, ed. Dorothy Thickett (Geneva: Droz, 1974); *Le Monophile*, ed. E. H. Balmas (Varese: Cisalpino, 1957).

12   The chapter is inspired loosely by a story in the prologue to François Rabelais's (d.1553) *Quart livre*, where Jupiter petrifies Pierre de la Ramée (Petrus Ramus; 1515–73) and Pierre de Galland (Petrus Gallandius, 1510–59), both professors of the arts at the University of Paris who had been notable in promoting the suit against the Jesuits, along with Pierre de

fact as in form, in the *Catechism* it is Pasquier the lawyer who does almost all
the talking.

Pasquier set up shop as a lawyer in 1549 (though, typically for the time, he
did not get his first case until 1556) and he retired to his country house in 1604.
For almost the entire long intervening period of his professional life, France
was wracked by civil war. Paris itself was besieged twice; in 1572, it was at the
center of an enormous massacre; and it was shaken by uncountable outbreaks
of violence on a smaller scale. Recounting the generation-long Wars of Religion
would be both tedious and depressing, but for Pasquier and almost all his
contemporaries they overwhelmed all other political issues. In principle the
conflict was between Calvinist Protestants and the Catholic majority, which
(with one brief exception) included the king of France. In practice things were
much more chaotic. On the one hand, in a pattern that had roots deep into the
Middle Ages, shifting coalitions of powerful noble magnates and their clients
faced off against each other and often against the monarch, sometimes only
loosely aligned by religion. This was distressing but, in some sense, normal. On
the other hand, and more ominously, alongside that violence an intensifying
ideological conflict over the very nature of religion and monarchy grew ever
more acute, calling into question the foundations of France itself: faith, the
king, and the law that derived from the cooperation of king and church.[13] All of
Pasquier's historical and political writing, the *Catechism* very much included,
was an intervention in that ideological struggle.

His first political pamphlet appeared at the very beginning of the civil
conflict. The *Pourparler du prince* (Discussion with the prince, 1560) was published over a year before the actual outbreak of hostilities.[14] While its approach
remained very general, his *Exhortation aux princes et seigneurs du conseil privé
du roy pour obvier aux seditions* (Exhortation to the princes and lords of the
king's privy council for avoiding sedition) a year later was much more explicit.
An early statement of what would come to be called the *politique* (purely
political) view, it argued for religious toleration, a crackdown on seditious

---

Cognières (or Cuignières, d.1345) as a makeweight. To be fair, imitating Rabelais is a task
at which far better writers than Pasquier have failed.

13   Nancy Lyman Roelker, *One King, One Faith: The Parlement of Paris and the Religious
Reformations of the Sixteenth Century*, ed. Barbara Diefendorf (Berkeley: University of
California Press, 1996) gives a good account of how, for magistrates like Pasquier, the classic trio of "one king, one faith, one law," directly challenged by the civil conflicts, became
ever more central to their understanding of French identity.

14   This appeared with the first installment of the *Recherches*. There is a modern edition
that includes two later companion pieces: *Pourparlers*, ed. Béatrice Sayhi-Périgot (Paris:
Classiques Garnier, 2007).

preaching, and (in an odd but prophetic development) a healthy fear of fanatical assassins.[15] Pasquier believed that religious repression was un-Christian, but in keeping with his stance of political realism he also argued that getting rid of Protestants would be a herculean task because they had a real point: the Catholic Church was corrupt, its pastoral mission enervated by wealth and privilege. This was a problem with deep historical roots (for Pasquier, everything was), but the biggest offender was an overweening papacy that set a bad example, sheltered the guilty, and sent troublemakers loyal to itself, like the Franciscans and Dominicans, into the pastoral vacuum it had helped create. This argument evolved over the succeeding forty years, but in its outline, it is the one he was still making in the *Catechism*.

The biggest change happened quickly. By the time Pasquier began dabbling in political pamphleteering the new Society of Jesus, which had its roots in a group of students who met in the 1530s during Ignatius of Loyola's (c.1491–1556) studies in Paris, had returned to the city in a sustained way. The Jesuits naturally became involved in the ongoing religious disputes—at the Colloquy of Poissy, in 1561, they opposed the exact policy of coexistence that Pasquier supported. But their main interest, as in many other places, was education. With the help of a bequest from Guillaume du Prat (1507–60), bishop of Clermont-en-Auvergne, they set up a college and began offering their typical low-cost, high-quality education. Many in the University of Paris were inclined to see them as both interlopers and competitors, which gave rise to a dispute that simmered for a while before breaking out, in 1565, into legal warfare. Already inclined to view the Jesuits with suspicion and closely connected to influential members of the university faculty, Pasquier was chosen to argue for the closing of the Jesuits' college, which he did with great vigor. The suit itself did not achieve its goal and was eventually suspended, leaving the Jesuit college and the university to coexist in uneasy hostility, but Pasquier's plea for the university became (at least for him and his friends) a kind of instant classic of legal-historical analysis. The *Catechism* both refers to and draws from it extensively.[16]

From the time of the suit against the Jesuits, Pasquier became ever more convinced that deep-seated Catholic corruption, with many roots in Rome, and arrogant Calvinist innovation were not the only factors destabilizing French

---

15   See *Exhortation aux princes et seigneurs du conseil privé du roy pour obvier aux seditions qui occultement semblent nous menacer pour le fait de la Religion* (Lyon: Jean Saugrain, 1561), 38–43. He pays particular attention to the Old Man of the Mountain and the Assassin cult, which recur in the *Catechism*, Book III, ch. 1.

16   As he mentions in the *Catechism*, Pasquier inserted the plea verbatim into later editions of the *Recherches de la France*, at Book III, ch. 44.

religion and, hence, politics. Increasingly, he worried about the arrogant innovations of *Catholics*—and though his theological conclusions were debatable,
his historical sense was not deceiving him. In fact, as scholars now agree,
European Christianity as a whole, Catholic and Protestant, was going through
a major transformation.[17] The Catholic Church in general was changing rapidly
and nowhere was this truer than in France, a phenomenon that both encouraged and was catalyzed by the increasing radicalism of the Catholic side in
the Wars of Religion (1562–98). New forms of public and private devotion,
new modes of Catholic education (particularly for the elites to which Pasquier
belonged), and new leaders emerging from religious orders old and new as
well as from the parish clergy fueled conflict and outraged *politique* tradition-
alists.[18] The Jesuits provided, if nothing else, a convenient synecdoche for a
process in which they certainly played a prominent role. Their unusually close
ties to the papacy fit in to a broader thesis that Pasquier and his historically-
minded friends had been developing: namely, that this was just the latest and
worst in a long string of corrupt novelties that had been foisted on the church
by Rome and other foreign actors and, for the most part, heroically resisted in
France.[19] Deeply informed by the legal humanist historicism of erudite writers like Pasquier, this conviction, a species of what historians generically call
"Gallicanism," fundamentally shaped not just the *Catechism* but the way it was
subsequently received and preserved.

The latter stages of the Wars of Religion certainly did much to confirm
Pasquier and his fellow Gallicans in that view. King Henri III's (r.1574–89)
decisive break with the organization that by then united France's more radical Catholics, the Catholic League, in 1588, his extrajudicial execution of its
leader, Henri I de Lorraine, duke de Guise (1550–88), and his assassination
by a Dominican friar the following year made it clear that Catholic zeal and
royal authority could be in serious conflict.[20] Following his 1593 conversion from
Protestantism to Catholicism the succeeding king, Henri IV, was able to restore

---

17   See the classic, brief account of John W. O'Malley, *Trent and All That: Renaming Catholicism in the Early Modern Era* (Cambridge, MA: Harvard University Press, 2000).

18   On the overall development of French Catholicism from the period of the Wars of Religion, see Joseph Bergin, *Church, Society and Religious Change in France 1580–1730* (New Haven: Yale University Press, 2009).

19   See Alain Tallon, *Conscience nationale et sentiment religieux en France au XVIᵉ siècle: Essai sur la vision gallicane du monde* (Paris: Presses Universitaires de France, 2002); and on the erudite construction of a Gallican Catholic history, Jotham Parsons, *The Church in the Republic: Gallicanism and Political Ideology in Renaissance France* (Washington, DC: Catholic University of America Press, 2005).

20   Garrett Mattingly, *The Armada* (Boston: Houghton Mifflin, 1949) gives a thoughtful and compulsively readable account of these events in their European context.

the bond between Catholic belief and the monarchy, but the process was slow and difficult.[21] Many Jesuits could be found among the opportunists and true believers who opposed Henri IV, and while they were far from the most prominent group in that coalition the *politiques* singled them out for both rhetorical and legal attacks. Most importantly, in early 1595, following a pair of assassination attempts over the previous year and a half in which some Jesuits were ambiguously and peripherally involved, the Parlement of Paris (one of several bodies that served as high courts in France and the same one that had heard the university's suit thirty years before) expelled the order from its jurisdiction, which covered about half of the kingdom.[22] By the end of the decade fighting had died down and Henri IV, now reasonably secure in his position, began to ponder the outlines of a more permanent settlement. In his relations with the Protestants this took the form of the famous 1598 Edict of Nantes, which restored the toleration they had enjoyed, off and on, since 1561.[23] His relationship with the new Catholicism proved more fraught.

Ultimately, Henri IV needed the new-style Catholics, who made up a solid plurality of France's political classes. While a few ultras went into exile, negotiations with the papacy and the judicious distribution of jobs, favors, and bribes brought around most of the *dévots*, as they were starting to be called. The status of the Jesuits quickly emerged as a key sticking point in these negotiations: the papacy and the *dévots* supported them and wanted them back in the jurisdiction of the Paris Parlement, something the *politique* contingent strongly opposed.[24] This was the immediate context of the *Catechism*: as the Translator's Preface explains in more detail, it was part of a series of pamphlet exchanges hoping to influence the royal decision. In the short term, Pasquier

---

21   See Michael Wolfe, *The Conversion of Henri IV: Politics, Power, and Religious Belief in Early Modern France* (Cambridge, MA: Harvard University Press, 1993).

22   To be specific the first would-be assassin, Pierre Barrière (d.1593), may have consulted with the rector of the Jesuit college at Paris, though the king would later suggest that it was also a Jesuit who revealed his plot. The second, Jean Chastel (1575–94), had been a student at the Jesuit college and shared its political outlook, but an extensive investigation produced no hard evidence that the Jesuits had known of or directly encouraged his attempt. See Roland Mousnier, *L'assassinat d'Henri IV: Le problème du tyrannicide et l'affermissement de la monarchie absolue* (Paris: N.R.F./Gallimard, 1964), 197–212, who however somewhat overstates the Jesuits' case. At the least, the Jesuits were no more pro-League or pro-assassination than many other religious orders.

23   For an English translation of the text of the edict, see Richard L. Goodbar, ed., *The Edict of Nantes: Five Essays and a New Translation* (Bloomington, MN: The National Huguenot Society, 1998), 41–70. In his confrontations with the Parlement of Paris, which opposed both initiatives, Henri IV explicitly equated the Edict of Nantes and the readmission of the Jesuits.

24   See, as noted above, Nelson, *Jesuits.*

probably did his cause more harm than good by structuring his argument as he did, making it an attack on all aspects of the new dispensation of the Catholic Church and the very idea of religious innovation. The ex-Protestant Henri IV had no personal attachment to Pasquier's idealized traditions, and French Catholics as a whole were quite enthusiastic about the new ways. Unsurprisingly, after a conspicuous show of support for Henri and the monarchy, the Jesuits were allowed back to Paris. When the king died (victim of an ultra-Catholic assassin) in 1610, they even got his heart, which was interred at their college of La Flèche in the Loire valley. For Henri and his successors, both the process of overriding opposition to the Jesuits' presence and the very modern kind of spectacular, personalized display that the heart at La Flèche exemplified seemed like excellent ways to underline their own absolute power while they balanced religious factions.

Still, in France, no issue is ever truly settled. If the political project that, for Pasquier, had culminated in the *Catechism* appeared stalled by the time of his death in 1615, the larger intellectual and scholarly project to which it was attached continued. For a century and a half after the publication of the *Catechism*, a seemingly endless succession of sometimes manufactured crises kept opposition to the Jesuits and to the elements of early modern Catholicism that Pasquier had associated with them on the boil; this in turn kept the *Catechism* relevant. In the immediate term, it excited some interest beyond the borders of France. Pasquier himself prepared a Latin translation, which seemingly never made it out of manuscript.[25] Printed translations did appear in English, German, and Dutch.[26] This early burst of Protestant interest was part of an urge to understand and if possible encourage divisions within the Catholic camp; Elizabeth I's (r.1558–1603) government had already fished in those troubled waters in the so-called "archpriest controversy," to which

---

25   The manuscript is now at the Bibliothèque Sainte-Geneviève, Paris, ms. 1409.

26   *The Iesuites catechism, or Examination of their doctrine. Published in French this present yeere 1602 and nowe translated into English. With a table at the end, of all the maine poynts that are disputed and handled therein*, trans. William Watson (London: James Roberts, 1602); *Catechismus oder gründlicher Bericht von der Lehr und Leben der Jesuiten: Erstlich in Frantzösischer Sprach beschriben, nun aber auß guthertziger Meinung meniglichen zur Nachrichtung verdeutschet* (Freystatt, 1603); *Spieghel der Iesuyten, ofte catechismus van der Jesuyten secte ende leere, waerin seer naect eñ grondelijck ontdeckt worden de ontallicke gruwelen die so vanden beginne onder dese secte in swanck zijn gheweest, als daernae vande selve niet alleen tot onderganck veler zielen, maer ooc tot verwerringe eñ verderf veler landen, conincrijcken, ende gemeynebesten alomme bedriven*, trans. Johannes Bogerman (Amsterdam: Jan Evertsz. Cloppenburch, 1608).

Pasquier devoted the last chapter of the *Catechism*, and James I (r.1603–25) made something of a specialty of such tactics in the early years of his reign.

Back in France, there was an important sequel to Pasquier's exchange with the Jesuit Louis Richeome (1544–1625). Twenty years later, and thus well after Pasquier's death, another Jesuit, François Garasse (1585–1631), published an attack on the *Recherches de la France*, but also on the *Catechism* and other anti-Jesuit publications.[27] Garasse was something of a professional troll, and though Pasquier's Gallicanism and anti-Jesuitism may have first attracted his ire, he immediately broadened his scope to attack his target's "libertinism." By this he meant in general an insufficiently narrow adherence to the partisan spirit and decorum of the Catholic Counter-Reformation, but more specifically the broad and tolerant literary culture that had been Pasquier's calling card. Thus the "four evangelists" of his libertinism were "Rabelais, Marot, Clopinel, and Pathelin": that is, the satirist François Rabelais, the poet Clément Marot (1496–1544), the medieval allegorist Jean de Meung (*c*.1240–*c*.1305), and the author of the farce of Maître Pathelin (1457), constituting a nice cross-section of French literature.[28] This attack provoked a reaction sponsored by Pasquier's sons, but it was soon subsumed into a larger controversy.[29]

For a year later Garasse vastly expanded his attack on "libertinism" with a work called *La doctrine curieuse des beaux esprits de ce temps, ou prétendus tels* (The curious doctrine of the great wits of this time, or so they claim). Pasquier was still in Garasse's sights: his recent editor has counted thirty-six mentions in the *Doctrine curieuse*.[30] But this time the main target was more purely literary: a poet named Théophile de Viau (1590–1626). What followed was a complex

---

27   François Garasse, *Les recherches des Recherches et autres œuvres de M^e. Estienne Pasquier, pour la defense de nos roys, contre les outrages, calomnies, et autres impertinences dudict autheur* (Paris: Sébastien Chappelet, 1622). Garasse had previously attacked Pasquier's fellow lawyer and Gallican, Louis Servin: *Le banquet des sages, dressé au logis et aux despens de Me Louys Servin, auquel est porté jugement tant de ses humeurs que de ses plaidoyés, pour servir d'avant-goust à l'inventaire de quatre mille grossières ignorances et fautes notables y remarquée* (n.p., 1617).

28   Garasse, *Recherches*, 715: "Or Pasquier ayant humé cet esprit [de libertinisme] par la lecture de Rabelais, de Marot, de Clopinel, de Patelin, qui sont ses quatre Evangelistes." Pasquier mentioned all of those authors favorably in the *Catechism*.

29   Antoine Remy, *Deffence pour Estienne Pasquier, vivant conseiller du Roy, et son advocat general en la Chambre des comptes de Paris, contre les impostures et calomnies de François Garasse* (Paris: Thomas de la Ruelle, 1624). This text was reprinted several times in the succeeding years, in the context of the *Doctrine curieuse* controversy, under the less specific title *Anti-Garasse*.

30   See François Garasse, *La doctrine curieuse des beaux esprits de ce temps, ou prétendus tels*, ed. Jean Salem (Paris: Les Belles Lettres, 2009), 957.

and not very edifying literary, political, and legal conflict that stretched out over several years.[31] The Parlement of Paris put Théophile on trial for blasphemy, imprisoned, and then exiled him. He defended himself vigorously in court, through his aristocratic connections, and in print. It would not be quite right to say that he had the better of the conflict—he died in 1626 while the controversy was ongoing—but Garasse clearly had the worst of it. He accumulated enemies at an impressive clip. They naturally included literary and philosophical writers sympathetic to de Viau (traditionally labeled "libertines," though this is not a term they generally embraced). Gabriel Naudé (1600–53) produced their most impressive manifesto in his *Apologie pour tous les grands personages qui ont été faussement soupçonnés de magie* (Apology for all the great men falsely accused of magic, 1625).[32] The opinion of Naudé's employer was more immediately influential, though: Armand-Jean du Plessis, Cardinal de Richelieu (1585–1642), newly installed as first minister of Louis XIII (r.1610–43), found the libertines useful and was in competition with the circle around the Queen Mother, Marie de Médicis (1573–1642), which was Garasse's main source of support. He also believed, or professed to believe, that Garasse was writing pamphlets in opposition to him, though that was not in fact the case.

At the same time, he was attacked for his rhetorical faults, including many of the same ones of which he had accused Pasquier, most importantly in a pamphlet by François Ogier (1597–1670), the *Jugement et censure du livre de la Doctrine curieuse* (Judgment and censure of the book of the *Curious Doctrine*).[33] Despite the title, Ogier was also concerned to refute the *Recherche des Recherches* and to defend "the late Maître Étienne Pasquier, most worthy Attorney General in the Chamber of Accounts, good servant of the king, good Frenchman, who was never a Huguenot or a Leaguer."[34] Garasse, Ogier

---

31   For a reasonably comprehensive account of the affair, see Stéphane van Damme, *L'épreuve libertine: Morale, soupçon et pouvoirs dans la France baroque* (Paris: CNRS Éditions, 2008).

32   Gabriel Naudé, *Apologie pour tous les grands personnages qui ont esté faussement soupçonnez de magie* (Paris: François Targa, 1625). Naudé served as librarian to Cardinal Richelieu.

33   Ogier was a priest and a man of letters, the son of a lawyer, and a friend of the prose stylist Jean-Louis Guez de Balzac (1597–1654) who also took part in the controversy. On this episode, see Marc Fumaroli, *L'âge de l'éloquence: Rhétorique et "res literaria" de la Renaissance au seuil de l'époque Classique* (Geneva: Droz, 1980), 326–34.

34   François Ogier, *Jugement et censure du livre de la Doctrine curieuse de François Garasse* (Paris, 1623), sig. Rii v.: "feu Me Estienne Pasquier, tres-digne Avocat general de la Chambre des Comptes, bon serviteur du Roy, bon François, qui ne fut jamais ny Ligueur, ny Huguenot." The pamphlet was successful enough that Ogier had to take legal action against piracy: see *Copie de l'extraict des registres de la chambre civile du Chastellet ... qui a esté publié et signifié à tous les libraires de Paris.* (*Défenses à Mathieu Le Blanc et à tous autres d'imprimer le livre de François Ogier, intitulé: Jugemens et censure du livre de*

claimed, was guilty of grave sins against *decorum*, the rhetorical principle that one must suit one's style to one's subject and audience. Endless jokes, insults, *ad hominem* attacks, and silly stories might be appropriate in a farce or even a political polemic (like the *Catechism*), but not in work treating literally deadly serious theological issues—blasphemy and atheism were capital crimes. Just as important was what Garasse lacked: solid learning and its rhetorical concomitant, citations of historians, philosophers, theologians, or legal documents. All this, of course, Pasquier had in spades, even in his most facetious moments. Ogier's shaft clearly struck home. Garasse arranged a forced reconciliation with him and tried to cover his theological flanks with a popular, French-language *Summa*.³⁵ This backfired even more spectacularly, attracting censure from the entire Paris Faculty of Theology and a blistering attack from one of the most respected religious thinkers in France, Jean Duvergier de Hauranne, Abbé de Saint-Cyran (1581–1643).³⁶ This early enmity with the Jesuits and alignment with Pasquier and his legacy was particularly significant for a man who went on to become the hero of the nascent Jansenist movement. Garasse, for his part, thwarted on the literary, theological, and political fronts, left Paris and dropped from public view.

If we have followed these slightly obscure events from a decade or more after Pasquier's death in considerable detail, it is because they did a great deal both to illuminate and shape what his work would mean from then on. His anti-Jesuit polemic remained relevant even after the readmission of the Jesuits became an established fact, not least because the Jesuits themselves would not let it go. Conflicts between the Jesuits and French Catholics with a different vision of the church were beginning to move onto theological terrain entirely foreign to Pasquier the legist and historian, but Pasquier's work came along for the ride. Richelieu continued the dance between cultivating and rejecting both the Jesuits and their opponents, and thus Pasquier's legacy, that Henri IV had

---

la Doctrine curieuse de François Garasse, sans la permission de l'auteur.) (n.p., n.d. [Paris, 1623]).

35   See *Lettre du Père François Garassus, de la Compagnie de Jésus, à M. Ogier, touchant leur réconciliation, et response du sieur Ogier sur le mesme sujet* (Paris: Sébastien Chappelet, 1624). In this odd publication Garasse works very hard to cite Scripture, philosophy, and the church fathers, while Ogier attempts as a rhetorical exercise to identify the minimum amount of contrition that can be spread over twenty pages.

36   See François Garasse, *La Somme théologique des veritez capitales de la Religion chrestienne* (Paris: Sébastien Chappelet, 1625); Jean Duvergier de Hauranne, *Somme des fautes et faussetez capitales contenues en la Somme théologique du Père Garasse*, 3 vols. in 2 (Paris, Joseph Bouillerot, 1626); *Censure de la sacrée Faculté de Theologie de Paris, contre un livre intitulé* La Somme Théologique des veritéz capitales de la Religion chrestienne (Paris, 1626).

already begun and that would continue with decreasing success into the reign of Louis XV (r.1715–74). More directly, Garasse's attack on Pasquier's literary character helped link literature, Gallicanism, and anti-Jesuitism, while the way that the emerging "classical" tradition of literary criticism leapt to Pasquier's defense brought him into the mainstream of French cultural nationalism. Finally, there was tacit agreement that Pasquier was correct in his view that historical scholarship and an understanding of the past that could smother the novelties of the age was indispensable to French Catholicism.

So it was that while this controversy was playing out, Pasquier's scholarly successors were continuing with ever greater fervor and sophistication the project of documenting and explicating what they took to be the now-faded antique glories of the Catholic Church, and of the Gallican liberties that had long been its ornament. This vast movement had a number of branches. Some remained in the realm of almost pure erudition with only modest political or ecclesiological implications; in such studies the Jesuits themselves were prominent players. Thus, beginning at the turn of the seventeenth century (and continuing to today) the Brussels-based Bollandist fathers worked to edit the corpus of hagiography systematically.[37] Working throughout the reign of Louis XIII, the French Jesuit Jacques Sirmond (1559–1651) produced a widely admired edition of the early councils of the church of Gaul, as well as editing the works of several medieval writers, all of which were of great interest to Gallican theorists.[38]

If the philological study of the Christian past remained neutral territory with respect to the Jesuits at least through the first half of the seventeenth century, the same could not be said of its theological counterpart. By far the most important development here took place at the University of Leuven, in the Spanish Netherlands. There, a group led by Michel de Bay (Latinized as Baius; 1513–89) and Cornelius Jansen (Latinized as Jansenius; 1585–1638) sought to build an alternative to the dominant neo-Scholastic theology by returning to the work of St. Augustine of Hippo (354–430). This burst on the European

---

37   The first volume of their *Acta sanctorum*, edited by Jean Bolland, s.j., and based on the long-running work of earlier Jesuits, appeared in 1643.

38   Jacques Sirmond, ed., *Concilia antiqua Galliæ, tres in tomos ordine digesta, cum epistolis pontificum, principum constitutionibus, et aliis gallicanæ rei ecclesiasticæ monumentis, quorum plurima vel integra, vel magna ex parte nunc primum in lucem exeunt,* 3 vols. (Paris: Sébastien Cramoisy, 1629). Sirmond's very moderate Gallicanism and talent for keeping a low profile endeared him to both Louis XIII, whom he served as confessor, and Richelieu, whom his nephew Jean served as a pamphleteer. He thus smoothed over the damage Garasse (and his more serious colleague Nicolas Caussin [1583–1651]) had done to Jesuit relations with the royal court.

scene in the form of Jansenius's posthumously published and instantly controversial *Augustinus* (1640). As in Paris, the Jesuits maintained an independent school outside of the university at Leuven, and Jansenius had clashed with them there—partly for institutional reasons, but also because Jesuits like Luis Molina (1528–81) and Francisco Suárez (1548–1617) were the most prominent exponents of the neo-Scholasticism and the associated penitential theory of probabilism that Jansenius opposed.

At any rate, as the controversy over the *Augustinus* came to a head the man who emerged as Jansenius's most tenacious defender was a Paris theologian named Antoine Arnauld (1612–94)—whose father of the same name had been a close associate of Pasquier's and had argued for the University in the 1595 revival of Pasquier's 1565 suit against the Jesuits. Part of the appeal to Arnauld of a theology based on the fourth- and fifth-century Fathers must have been its consonance with the Gallican idealization of that period of church history. At any rate, technical disputes over the orthodoxy of the *Augustinus* quickly metastasized into the most ferocious dispute the Catholic Church had seen since the outbreak of the Protestant Reformation, as an often reluctant papacy and an often over-eager French monarchy were drawn into condemnations of what came to be called "Jansenism."[39] In the minds of the "Grand Arnauld" and his disciples, Jansenius's archaicizing theology combined with the ongoing philological recovery of Christian antiquity and with the erudite Gallican project, in which Pasquier and the elder Arnauld had played such important roles, of defending the pure, traditional practice of Catholicism from corruption and innovation via the defense of the liberties of the Gallican church. This formed for them a coherent whole, a vision of ancient, rigorous, uncorrupted Christianity defended by a learned and virtuous few and attacked by the worldly and ambitious everywhere—and above all by those most worldly and ambitious men, the Society of Jesus.

Pasquier's historicist, Gallican anti-Jesuitism thus lay near the heart of Jansenism, and the *Catechism* continued to be read and to be influential into the eighteenth century. In fact, its greatest historical impact may have come from the role it played in inspiring another, infinitely more subtle and readable anti-Jesuit polemic: Blaise Pascal's (1623–62) Jansenist classic, the *Lettres provinciales* (Provincial letters, 1657).[40] Though Pascal largely replaced Pasquier's

---

39   The literature on Jansenism is huge. A reasonable starting place in English is William
      Doyle, *Jansenism: Catholic Resistance to Authority from the Reformation to the French
      Revolution* (London: Palgrave Macmillan, 2000).

40   Blaise Pascal, *The Provincial Letters*, trans. A. J. Krailsheimer (Harmondsworth: Penguin,
      1967).

law and history with ethics and theology, he retained the basic structure of
a conversation between an intelligent layman armed with endless damning
quotes from Jesuit sources and a (less intelligent) Jesuit who in fact hardly says
anything. He also, through sheer literary virtuosity, completed a process that
had already been underway when Garasse attacked Pasquier: he made the
Jesuits appear as the enemies not just of the French church but of French wit
and eloquence, an achievement that was now essentially permanent.[41]

This was, generally speaking, the context for the first reedition of the
Catechism in 1677.[42] More specifically it may have been triggered by an incident that year in which two Jansenist bishops appealed to the pope against
Louis XIV's right to collect revenues called the *droit de régale* (regalian rights)
from their dioceses.[43] That dispute spiraled over the next few years, culmi-
nating in a dramatic break between France and Rome in 1682 when the king
encouraged the French clergy to adopt four "Gallican articles" restricting papal
authority.[44] While Louis XIV quickly backpedaled on this confrontation, it
served to cement the importance of another tradition to which Pasquier had
greatly contributed and in which the *Catechism* was embedded: that of the
Gallican liberties. Already in Pasquier's lifetime the project of collecting and
publishing both documentary support for the legal claims of the liberties of
the Gallican church and argumentative briefs in their favor was a major preoc-
cupation of historically minded jurists. These were increasingly collected into
massive volumes; the brothers Pierre (1582–1651) and Jacques Dupuy (1591–
1656), who among other things were the royal librarians, set the standard in
this department with their 1639 *Traités* (Treatises) and *Preuves des droits et
libertés de l'église gallicane* (Proofs of the rights and liberties of the Gallican

---

41   See Fumaroli, *L'âge de l'éloquence*, 327: "Cette Querelle de la 'raillerie' chrétienne ne
      cessera plus de se ranimer au XVIIe siècle, et les *Provinciales* de Pascal en sont l'étape
      majeure."

42   It was under the same title as in 1602, with the same false imprint (Villefranche: Guillaume
      Grenier).

43   For an exhaustive account of the affair, see Marc Dubruel, "Un épisode de l'histoire de
      l'Église de France au XVIIe siècle: Nicolas Pavillon, évêque d'Alet, et Etienne de Caulet,
      évêque de Pamiers." *Recherches de science religieuse* 7 (1917): 52–92 and 255–88 and 8
      (1918): 78–101 and 222–49; and Dubruel, "La cour de Rome et l'extension de la régale,"
      Revue d'histoire de l'église de France 43 (1923): 161–84 and 465–92. This followed an earlier
      blow-up over the authority of one of the appellant bishops, Caulet, over the Jesuits of
      his diocese. See Dubruel, "Hiérarchie gallicane et Religieux exempts: Un épisode de leurs
      relations au XVIIe siècle; Caulet et les Jésuites," *Recherches de science religieuse* 9 (1919):
      324–68 and 10 (1920): 55–91.

44   The best account of genesis of the Four Articles is still Aimé-Georges Martimort, *Le gal-
      licanisme de Bossuet* (Paris: Éditions du Cerf, 1953).

church), which were periodically reissued with various emendations for almost two centuries.[45] While Pasquier was not much present in these collections his *Recherches* stood alongside them. Editions appeared in 1621 (the one that provoked Garasse), 1633, 1643, and 1665, all of which included his political *Pourparlers*. A 1723 edition of the complete works added his letters and literary efforts, important in a France that by now defined itself largely by its *belles lettres*—but not the *Catechism*.[46] Never officially issued under his name and too overtly partisan to be part of the legal-erudite Gallican project it maintained a shadowy presence, revealing to those who sought it out the practical implications of the massive theoretical apparatus.

By the time the complete works appeared there had been another edition of the *Catechism*, though, printed in 1717.[47] The circumstances of the new century once again made both the *Catechism* and the rest of Pasquier's work appear in a new but no less urgent light. In 1713, at Louis XIV's urging, Pope Clement XI (r.1700–21) had issued the bull *Unigenitus*. It condemned a work of a theologian and protégé of Arnauld's who, not entirely coincidentally, bore the name Pasquier Quesnel (1634–1719). This bull, and the king's strenuous efforts to enforce it, brought about a new and severe crisis in the Jansenist controversy, which had been relatively quiescent for a generation. Two years later the Sun King died, leaving France substantially weakened by military defeat, fiscal chaos, and internal dissent. And in this febrile atmosphere, evidently, French readers turned again to the vision of Étienne Pasquier.

---

45   *Traitez des droits et libertez de l'Église gallicane* and *Preuves des libertez de l'Église gallicane* (n.p., 1639). On the fraught publication history of these volumes, see Gabriel Demante, "Histoire de la publication des livres de Pierre Dupuy sur les libertés de l'Église gallicane," *Bibliothèque de l'École des Chartes* 5 (1843–1844): 585–606.

46   *Les œuvres d'Estienne Pasquier, contenant ses Recherches de la France, son Plaidoyé pour M. le duc de Lorraine; celuy de Me Versoris, pour les jésuites, contre l'Université de Paris; Clarorum virorum ad Steph. Pasquierium carmina; Epigrammatum libri sex; Epitaphiorum liber; Iconum liber, cum nonnullis Theod. Pasquierii in Francorum Regum icones notis; ses lettres; ses œuvres meslées; et les lettres de Nicolas Pasquier, fils d'Estienne*, 2 vols. (Amsterdam: Compagnie des libraires associez, 1723).

47   *Recueil de pièces historiques et curieuses, contenant: 1 ° Le Manifeste de Pierre Du Jardin, Sr de La Garde, sur la mort d'Henry IV. 2 ° Le Manifeste de la Damoiselle d'Escoman, sur le même sujet. 3 ° L'Apologie pour M. le président de Thou, sur son Histoire. 4 ° Epist. Jac.-Aug. Thuani P. Janino. 5 ° Le catéchisme des Jésuites, par Estienne Pasquier*, 2 vols. (Delft: Isaac Vorburger, 1717). The imprint was again false; the *Catechism* is split between the volumes with Book III making up the entire second volume. Each volume also has a preliminary title page saying simply *Le catéchisme des Jésuites, par Estienne Pasquier*, so Pasquier was clearly the main selling point of this rather odd production.

In fact, as Dale Van Kley has demonstrated in a series of magisterial studies, over the first half of the eighteenth-century Jansenism and Gallicanism developed into a powerful political and ecclesiastical movement that seemed for a while on the verge of implementing the full program of restoring (what it believed to be) traditional church organization, the old, austere theology, freedom of Catholic monarchs from (by now largely imaginary) papal interference, and the suppression of much Tridentine innovation, notably including the Jesuits.[48] Van Kley has given this tendency the name "reform Catholicism." Its tentacular struggles, which extended over three quarters of a century and much of the globe, defy summary, and certainly in the space available here. Two aspects of it, however, are particularly relevant to Pasquier's legacy. First, the program of collecting and publishing documents relevant to the reform movement and providing them with historical interpretation not only continued but took on new vigor. Well into the eighteenth century much of this was animated by Jansenist clergy: Louis Thomassin (1619–95), Louis Ellies Dupin (1657–1719), and Claude Fleury (1640–1723) were among the most prominent historical voices.[49] The context of the *Unigenitus* controversy kept Pasquier's historical perspective relevant, but also subordinated it to more purely theological and ecclesiological issues. Still, the old erudite collections of treatises and proofs of the Gallican Liberties continued to be reprinted and reedited as long as the Society of Jesus endured.[50] Towards the middle of the century the Gallican struggle was taken up by circles in the sovereign courts and the bar association of Paris, reinvigorated under the relatively light-touch regime of Louis XV. The leader of that movement was a Jansenist lawyer named Louis-Adrien le Paige (1712–1803), the leading spirit of the bar association, who

48   For our purposes the essential works are Dale Van Kley, *The Jansenists and the Expulsion of the Jesuits from France* (New Haven: Yale University Press, 1975); and Van Kley, *Reform Catholicism and the International Suppression of the Jesuits in Enlightenment Europe* (New Haven, CT: Yale University Press, 2018), though he has published several other books and numerous articles on related subjects.

49   Thomassin was influential through his personal connections and manuscripts, as well as works like *Traitez historiques et dogmatiques sur divers points de la discipline de l'Église et de la morale chrestienne* (Paris: F. Muguet, 1691). On Dupin's career, see Jacques Grès-Gayer, "Un théologien gallican, témoin de son temps: Louis Ellies Du Pin (1657–1719)," *Revue d'histoire de l'Église de France* 72 (1986): 67–121. Fleury published an *Histoire ecclésiastique* in twenty volumes, starting in 1691; continuators eventually added another 36.

50   The last major edition of the eighteenth century was Pierre Toussaint Durand de Maillane et al., *Les libertez de l'Église Gallicane: Prouvées et commentées suivant l'ordre et la disposition des articles dressés par M. Pierre Dupuy*, 5 vols. (Lyon: P.B. Ponthus, 1771). It is probably not coincidental that such editions ceased with the papal suppression of the Jesuits.

certainly considered himself the Pasquier of his day.[51] In Pasquier's footsteps, he advanced historical arguments for the central role of the law courts in the French constitutional order; and like Pasquier, he used historical and legal erudition and the Gallican historical tradition to inspire and coordinate action against his opponents within the church, and especially against the Jesuits.[52] None of these writers, it must be said, were scholars or historical thinkers of Pasquier's caliber. Still powerful, his tradition was showing some signs of decadence.

The second, equally decadent aspect was a kind of mania for forcing the ongoing conflict with the Society of Jesus into the categories Pasquier had created. This appeared most clearly in responses to two assassination attempts against European monarchs: that by Pierre Damiens (1723–90) against Louis XV of France in 1757 and that of an unknown assailant against José I (r.1750–77) of Portugal in 1758. Links to the Jesuits—which consisted entirely of the quite Jansenist Damiens having briefly worked as a servant at the Jesuit college in Paris—were laughably tenuous, but anti-Jesuit propaganda immediately framed the French incident as another Jesuit regicide, while in the propaganda that the anti-Jesuit Portuguese minister, Sebastião José de Carvalho e Melo, later Marquis of Pombal (1699–1782), produced around the 1758 incident, "derivative form overwhelmed current content," with a very healthy dose of the *Catechism*.[53] A pamphlet from le Paige discussing both assassination attempts even concluded with a long development on the Old Man of the Mountain, a clear tribute to Pasquier.[54] If the *Catechism* was not reprinted after 1717 it was because it had become part of the vernacular of anti-Jesuit propaganda. And two years later, as a complex series of legal maneuvers led up to the Parlement of Paris definitively condemning the Constitutions of the Society of Jesus and dissolving it in France, the magistrates (again briefed by le Paige) extensively recycled Pasquier's arguments about the nature, history, and legal status of the Jesuits. In effect they re-litigated the 1565 suit, this time providing the outcome Pasquier had wanted almost two hundred years before.

---

51   On his legal career, see David A. Bell, *Lawyers and Citizens: The Making of a Political Elite in Old Regime France* (New York: Oxford University Press, 1994), esp. 112–28.

52   His most important publications along these lines were *Lettres historiques sur les fonctions essentielles du parlement, sur le droit des pairs, et sur les lois fondamentales du royaume*, 2 vols. (Amsterdam, 1753–54); and, with Christophe Coudrette, *Histoire générale de la naissance et des progrès de la Compagnie de Jésus et analyse de ses constitutions et privileges*, 5 vols. (Paris, 1762–63). The latter was very much the culmination of the *Catechism*'s anti-Jesuit tradition.

53   Van Kley, *Reform Catholicism*, 163–64.

54   Louis-Adrien le Paige, *Réflexions sur l'attentat commis le 3 septembre 1758 contre la vie du Roi de Portugal* (n.p., 1759), 33 ff. On this trope in Pasquier see above, n. 15.

For the Jesuits matters went from bad to worse: in 1773 a relentless lobbying campaign of and by the various Bourbon monarchies, in which French war-horses like le Paige continued to play a prominent role, culminated when Pope Clement XIV (r.1769–74) capitulated and, by the brief *Dominus ac redemptor*, dissolved the entire Society of Jesus.[55] From that point on, Pasquier's anti-Jesuitism was formally anachronistic. There were subsequent attempts to reform the Catholic Church that at least used the rhetoric of ancient forms and historical constitutions, but they took place in a world so different from Pasquier's as to render his thought almost irrelevant. The power of Enlightened despots and totalizing revolutionaries was out of all proportion to that of Renaissance monarchs, and Enlightenment ideals of liberty, patriotism, philanthropy, and family were even more remote from the conceptual world of the Reformation era than many of their supporters realized. Nor were attempted reforms notably successful: Joseph II of Austria (r.1765–80) was already reversing many of his changes before his death, while the 1790 Civil Constitution of the Clergy, the French Revolution's initial attempt to implement a truly Gallican Catholicism, ran into the buzzsaw of revolutionary politics, torn apart by radicals on one side and reactionaries on the other. Napoleon (1769–1821) abandoned it unceremoniously.[56]

But once Napoleon fell in 1814 and the Bourbons returned to France, Pasquier reemerged for a strange and ghostly afterlife. The post-Napoleonic settlement, such as it was, left the French with a multitude of options as to how to define themselves, their politics, and their culture, but with no consensus as to how this should be done—indeed, the matter was periodically fought out with guns on the streets of Paris. Almost everyone looked to the political and cultural figures of the old regime as keys to understanding what was truly French, in a way that the Pasquier of the "Search for France" would certainly have appreciated. And to a certain section of opinion, particularly on the center-right that supported monarchical government but wanted to avoid extra-legal despotism or the "throne-and-altar" fundamentalism of Joseph de Maistre (1753–1821) and

---

55   There is an English translation available online: Boston College Portal to Jesuit Studies, "Dominus ac redemptor (1773)," https://jesuitportal.bc.edu/research/documents/1773_dominusacredemptor/ (accessed April 10, 2021).

56   On Josephism, see most recently Derek Beales, *Joseph II*, vol. 2: *Against the World, 1780–1790* (Cambridge: Cambridge University Press, 2009), who is somewhat more sanguine about the religious reforms than many commentators. For a survey of the revolutionary period, see Nigel Aston, *Religion and Revolution in France, 1780–1804* (Washington, DC: Catholic University of America Press, 2000).

his ilk, Pasquier himself was an attractive if minor exemplar. One prominent statesman, though, made him central to his career and self-image.

Duke Étienne-Denis Pasquier (1767–1862) lived even longer than his name-sake.[57] The exact place of the original Étienne Pasquier in his family is slightly obscure, but by the end of the eighteenth century Étienne-Denis's father, also named Étienne, was well enough established in the nobility to die as a victim of the Terror; Étienne-Denis, who had entered the Parlement of Paris imme-diately before its revolutionary dissolution, followed a fairly typical noble trajectory of imprisonment, then lying low before rallying to the Napoleonic regime, under which he gained the important office of prefect (chief adminis-trative and law-enforcement officer) of the Paris region. After Waterloo (1815) he became a pillar of the restored Bourbon monarchy as a minister in several governments and, after the July Revolution of 1830 that brought the Orléanist branch of the family to the throne, as president of the Chamber of Peers, the upper house of the legislature. For this post King Louis-Philippe revived the title of chancellor, which under the old regime had been the chief judicial offi-cer and one of the great offices of the crown—a good index of Étienne-Denis's own self-image.

Something of a man of letters himself—his membership in the Académie Française was largely but not entirely political—he held a belief as sincere as it was self-serving that the heritage he represented of a scholarly nobility and the ancient legal traditions of France offered a way forward for the nation, and for this his predecessor was a model and an inspiration. He published a manuscript of Étienne Pasquier's, a commentary on the Roman law, that had remained in the family and generally promoted his memory.[58] He also held tightly to the family tradition of support for the liberties of the Gallican church, a position in which he was joined by his counterpart in the lower chamber, André Dupin (1783–1865), who had one last go at editing the documentary cor-pus that went back to the sixteenth century.[59] And the duke was also an enemy of the Jesuits. For in 1814, Pope Pius VII (r.1800–23) had celebrated Napoleon's

---

57   The only modern study of the Duke is James Kieswetter, *Étienne-Denis Pasquier, the Last Chancellor of France* (Philadelphia: American Philosophical Society, 1977).

58   Étienne Pasquier, *L'interprétation des Institutes de Justinian: avec la conférence de chasque paragraphe aux ordonnances royaux, arrestz de parlement et coustumes générales de la France*, ed. Étienne-Denis Pasquier and Charles Giraud (Paris: Videcoq aîné and Durand, 1847).

59   André Dupin, *Libertés de l'Église gallicane suivies de la déclaration de 1682* (Paris: Baudouin frères, 1826). Dupin was president of the Chamber of Deputies from 1832 to 1839, a posi-tion he reprised under the Second Republic. Between these two men, attachment to old-regime Gallicanism went all the way from the right end to the left end of the Orléanist coalition.

defeat by reviving the Society, which had continued a shadow existence in the territories of the Russian empire.[60] And once again those who valued the ancient order of the French Church could turn to the *Catechism* for guidance. At least for a moment.

With the duke's wind behind him, Étienne Pasquier appeared in systematic attempts to create a usable literary history for France, including the definitive efforts of Charles-Augustin Sainte-Beuve (1804–69).[61] His most prominent academic champion was Léon Feugère (1810–58), a pillar of the mid-century Establishment who taught at the Lycée Louis le Grand—the former Jesuit Collège de Clermont. He was both a scholar of Renaissance literature and, it would seem, close to the Orléanist royal family.[62] Having begun by editing the faintly republican Étienne de la Boëtie (1530–63), he turned to the safer Pasquier with an *Essai sur la vie et les ouvrages* (Essay on the life and works) and an *Œuvres choisies* (Selected works).[63] He collaborated on this work with the chancellor, and his Pasquier was a model of the learned statesman: devoted to king and country, above partisan faction, working to create a glorious literary past and a glorious literary future for his country. His devotion to the law and to the Gallican church were entirely laudable.

But when Feugère came to discuss the *Catechism* (which he did not include among his selected works), his tone became profoundly elegiac. The passage is worth quoting at length:

> These polemical monuments that breathe the passions of our fathers have the same interest for us as those aged pieces of armor whose engravings we enjoy examining and whose temper we like to study. We look above all for the image of the past, which is reflected there more vividly than in any other production of the time. Still, though the *Jesuits' Catechism* was more a religious and political manifestation than a work of spirit, an action more than a book, it is far from lacking importance from the literary point of view [...]. Here the weapon of sarcasm is wielded with

---

60   See Robert Maryks and Jonathan Wright, eds., *Jesuit Survival and Restoration: A Global History, 1773–1900* (Leiden: Brill, 2015).

61   In Charles-Augustin Sainte-Beuve, *Causeries de lundi*, 3 ed., vol. 3 (Paris: Garnier, 1868): 249–69, originally published January 6, 1851. This is essentially a review of Feugère's *Œuvres choisies*, discussed below. Sainte-Beuve was also the first major historian of the Jansenist movement.

62   See the biographical notice by E. J. B. Rathery prefacing Léon Feugère, *Les femmes poètes du XVIᵉ siècle* (Paris: Didier et co., 1860).

63   Léon Feugère, *Essai sur la vie et les ouvrages d'Étienne Pasquier* (Paris: Firmin Didot, 1848); and Étienne Pasquier, *Œuvres choisies*, ed. Léon Feugère (Paris: Firmin Didot, 1849).

dexterity. Happily stolen from the divine Plato, this adroit dialectic [...] will soon pass into an immortal creation of the seventeenth century. It is no small glory for Pasquier to seem to have blazed the path for Pascal.[64]

For Feugère published his essay in 1848, the revolutionary year that in France saw the end of the July Monarchy and the beginning of the Second Republic. As the last Bourbon stepped down from the throne of France, as Étienne-Denis Pasquier adjourned for the last time a senate he had imagined might revive the sovereign courts of Paris, and as the restored Jesuits continued to advance in a Catholic Church building towards the papalist crescendo of the First Vatican Council (1869–70), the *Jesuits' Catechism* passed finally into history. And there we find it today.

---

64   Feugère, *Essai*, 175–76: "Ces monuments de polémique, où respirent les passions de nos
      pères, ont pour nous le même intérêt que ces armures vieillies dont on se plait à consi-
      dérer les ciselures et à étudier la trempe. On y cherche avant tout l'image du passé, qui
      s'y reflète plus vivement que dans aucune autre production contemporaine. Cependant,
      bien que le *Catéchisme des Jésuites* ait été plutôt une manifestation religieuse et politique
      d'une œuvre d'esprit, une action plutôt qu'un livre, il est loin, au point de vue littéraire, de
      manquer d'importance.... L'arme du sarcasme y est maniée avec dextérité. Heureusement
      dérobée au divin Platon, cette dialectique adroite [...] passera bientôt dans une création
      immortelle du dix-septième siècle. Ce n'est pas une petite gloire pour Pasquier de paraitre
      avoir frayé la route à Pascal."

Translator's Preface

Patricia M. Ranum

1   **Guests at a French Country House: Étienne Pasquier's *Catéchisme des jésuites* (1602)**

It is the spring of 1600. The scene is a country house in northern France. Six weary travelers have been offered rest and hospitality by the gentleman who resides there. Among these guests are a disguised Jesuit, an ebullient lawyer who talks continually, and a narrator who calls himself "I."

   This last guest is a multi-faceted person. Sometimes he simply narrates, as he does in the opening paragraph of *The Jesuits' Catechism*. Sometimes, he reveals a detail about himself. For example, he refers to things he has written.[1] If one takes him at his word, one must conclude that this narrator is none other than Étienne Pasquier, the *avocat général* of the Chamber of Accounts of Paris, lawyer, historian, poet, and author. At other times it seems possible, albeit far from certain, that the excitable lawyer is Pasquier. In the end, how much difference does it make? The travelers seem to know one another (or know about one another), and they share similar religious and political concerns.

   We too are travelers: time-travelers. We have hidden in a small service room adjacent to the large reception room of the house. Putting our ears to the door, we learn what élite male society was like at the dawn of the seventeenth century. But above all, we learn about the issues that were preoccupying many Frenchmen: the imminent return of the Society of Jesus to France, and the assassination attempts that have been troubling France for a decade.

   The ebullient lawyer is travelling with a saddle bag full of books and documents about the Jesuits. He turns out to be a committed anti-Jesuit. For the next few days, he lectures his housemates, reads aloud excerpts from Jesuit publications, and quotes from papal bulls and police reports. Sometimes his approach is bi-lingual: he reads from a Latin document, then immediately provides a translation into French, for he is aware that Latin is no longer the universal language it once was. Or as the lawyer put it: "Perhaps there are some among us who don't understand Latin: that's why, this censure document being the foundation of my discourse, I'll dress it in French fashions so that everyone will understand." French was essential, if everyone was to grasp the

---

1   "My *Recherches* on France, which includes my *Plaidoyer*," says the narrator, Book II, ch. 19. Both publications were written by Étienne Pasquier.

point being made. To keep his captive audience from falling asleep, the lawyer lards his serious presentation with poems, classical references, historical anecdotes, puns, and word-play.

The gentleman who is their host realizes that his guests risk drowning in this flow of words. Fortunately, his social rank permits him to impose his will on his visitors. He orders them to go to bed, to attend Mass, to walk in the gardens of the manor house. In other words, we time-travelers witness social behavior among unpretentious noblemen: meals, walks, and conversations, with each man showing his wit by puns, his intellect by anagrams, his artistry and declamatory skills by reciting poems, and his learning by citing classical sources.

As it turns out, the gentleman will inspire the title of Pasquier's new book, *Le Catechisme des jésuites ou examen de leur doctrine* (The Jesuits' catechism or an examination of their doctrine). The gentleman, conversing with the Jesuit, says:

> Please let's clear the table and, after thanking God for what it has pleased him to give us each day, continue our discussion. [...] [The gentleman] begged the Jesuit not to disapprove if, as with the catechisms of our faith, the child be allowed to enter and question his schoolmaster, in order to learn the basic fundamentals. He did the same with the Jesuit, asking to be informed about the principal points of his order. The Jesuit freely agreed.[2]

A long chapter follows, during which the gentleman asks rather long questions. The Jesuit generally replies quite succinctly. In other words, chapter 2 is, properly speaking, the "catechism." During it, the Socratic method is employed, to permit the gentleman "to draw out what he was seeking."[3]

Like all good things, the visit, and the three books that form *The Jesuits' Catechism*, come to an end. The narrator prepares to leave the manor house:

> Having dined, and our horses being bridled, we thanked the gentleman for the fine food he had been pleased to offer us, and he thanked us for the honor he claimed to have received from our visit [...]. There were six of us in our group: he kept the lawyer at his house, saying that he wanted to pay a debt that he owed him, having not tended to it for a long while. As for the other five travelers, after crossing the mountains, three of them

---

2   See the final paragraph of Book I, ch. 1.
3   Book I, ch. 1.

took the road to Venice, intending to sail to Jerusalem, in order to fulfill a vow to visit the Holy Sepulcher. The Jesuit and I set off for Rome.[4]

2   "This Great World-Stage"

The Jesuits' Catechism begins as a "dialog"[5] between two persons. The dialog was a familiar literary genre. Each speaker was identified when he began talking. These speakers were not real people, however; but strictly speaking they were not allegorical figures either. Rather, they were stock figures whose capitalized name shows that they are generic: the Jesuit, the Gentleman, the Lawyer.[6] A dialog could be carried on by a half-dozen characters. Pasquier's dialog did just that: as chapter after chapter flowed from his lively mind and into his quill pen, the number of characters increased, miniature plays become nestled into the larger work. Indeed, at times the dialog approaches theater.

Throughout the book, Pasquier alludes to the stage and to actors. Indeed, the opening chapters of Book I are typeset as if for a printed play: the character's role is specified, sometimes as an abbreviation, sometimes written in full. Then come the actor's lines. However, as Book II progresses, Pasquier seems to forget the initial format: the character's name now begins to appear within parentheses. Gone is succinctness: one or another character may give a very long speech. These speeches intermingle with the briefer comments of one character or another. In the *Catechism*, the lawyer is especially prone to giving a tirade. Indeed, the core of the book presents his arguments. Book III brings a different approach. Conversations heard in dreams are reproduced: Saint Peter, Ignatius of Loyola, a cluster of school boys, and a marble statue known as "Pasquino."

---

4   Book III, ch. 27.
5   Pasquier himself uses that term, Book III, ch. 28.
6   I have tacitly given names to a few characters. The one called "I" in the original book becomes "the Narrator." Or "I, the Narrator." Names that were abbreviated in the original have been expanded throughout this translation. My decision to treat names in this manner is influenced by Louis Richeome's *La chasse du renard Pasquin, découvert et pris en sa tannière* (The hunt for Pasquin the fox, discovered and caught in his lair) (Villefranche: Le Pelletier, 1603), which is a reply to Pasquier's *Catéchisme*. Published under the pseudonym "Foelix de la Grâce, *gentilhomme françois*," the book replies to Pasquier's criticisms of the Society of Jesus in the *Catéchisme* (1602). Among Richeome's characters are Pasquin, Félix de la Grâce, the Theologian, the Seigneur, the Master of Requests, the Author.

Pasquier doubtlessly knew that his "dialog" would be read aloud before the fire, as books and plays often were at the time.[7] A skilled reader would have known how to modify his voice, in order to breathe life into a character. In such a context, the word-play, the puns, the anecdotes, the soliloquy-like intervals, the dream scene, and the encounter with the stones take on a new meaning.

As the number of characters increased, and as Pasquier's manuscript became thicker, the "stage" on which these characters were exchanging ideas expanded, until it included Rome, England, Scotland. As Pasquier put it in the penultimate paragraph of the book:

> Where was this fierce tragedy performed? On the stage of the Catholic Church of England [...]. Who wrote the plays? Our holy and devout Jesuits, the sole resource of our Catholic Church. What was the plot being proposed?[8]

The content may be political, but the presentation is literary. Pasquier notes that "each prince plays his character on this great world-stage."

Was it the lawyer who read aloud? It seems likely, for he is described as being weary from having talked so much. In fact, with the start of chapter 3, the catechism is pushed into the background. The lawyer talks incessantly from then on. The formatting of the pages begins to change: the initials that identified the Jesuit and the gentleman are replaced by brief parenthetical indications that blend into the text: "(said the lawyer)," or "(the Jesuit said to him)."

In the end, the lawyer says far more than any other character, but that is not always obvious, because Pasquier frequently neglects to label the passages uttered by the lawyer. To confuse readers still more, the lawyer tends to go on

---

7 Several times in the book, the lawyer alludes to having read something aloud to the other guests.

8 Pasquier frequently returns to the theme of the stage. See for example Book I, ch. 1, final sentence: "by playing the role of Socrates, he got the other to play the Platonic role"; Book I, ch. 2, final sentence: "the Lawyer entered the jousting field"; Book I, ch. 19, final sentence: "let's watch him come on stage and act his character"; Book II, ch. 5: "this devout comedy" [comédie, that is, "a staged play"]; Book II, ch. 17: "Each prince plays his character on this great world-stage"; Book III, ch. 9: "no subject should attack his prince, no matter what character he is playing"; Book III, ch. 20: "each of us began to act as if he were flabbergasted"; Book III, ch. 21: "I praise your inventiveness at having that person play the roles of stones"; Book III, ch. 28: "I call him Personatus, for he's the person who played as many different characters in England as there are religions"; Book III, ch. 28, penultimate paragraph: "Where was this fierce tragedy performed? On the stage of the Catholic Church of England [...]. Who were their playwrights? Our holy and devout Jesuits, the sole resource of our Catholic Church. What was the plot being proposed?"

talking for several chapters, almost without stopping for breath, and without always being identified.

3   Some Visual Clues

The form in which we have received it, makes both the *Catéchisme* and the *Catechism* visually daunting. For example, the paragraphs are very long and very dense to the eye.[9] Was it the printer's decision? Be that as it may, I, the translator, had to push aside a major temptation. That is to say, an editor would have every reason to propose that, for the *Catechism*, each of those mammoth paragraphs be subdivided into several smaller ones. This option had to be ruled out, and for a very telling reason. More than one reader will want to compare the first printed French edition of the *Catéchisme* (or Claude Sutto's modern recreation of it) with Patricia Ranum's translation, the *Catechism*. Or the reader might want to locate sources that are cited in the footnotes of Sutto's edition, but not in the English translation. That sort of comparison would be close to impossible if the paragraphs of the French edition did not coincide with the paragraphs of the translation. That is to say, if a reader is prevented from moving his eye quickly from paragraph to paragraph, in both versions of the book, he will have considerable difficulty locating a specific sentence. If, however, he knows that the sentence he is looking for is in the fifth paragraph of Book II, chapter 8, he can make his way to the fifth paragraph of that chapter. *Voilà*, a comparison becomes possible, if not always easy.

Another sort of visual aid seemed indispensable. That is to say, the names of the stock characters tend to blend into the dense paragraphs. Consequently, the reader must thumb back and forth, in an attempt to discern who is speaking in a specific paragraph, or in an entire chapter. To help readers, identification tags have been tacitly added to the first line of every chapter: they make it immediately clear who is talking as that chapter begins. These tags are set entirely in capital letters that attract the eye: THE LAWYER, THE GENTLEMAN, and so forth. The same sorts of tags have been added throughout the text proper, permitting the eye to locate, with relative ease, the place where a different character begins speaking.[10] These in-the-text tags replace Pasquier's abbreviated names or parenthetical identifications, thereby creating a homogeneity,

---

9   These formatting decisions are inspired by my year-long struggle to locate specific sentences, and my repeated thumbing through chapters in order to discern who is speaking.

10   On a few occasions the capital letters direct the eye to a stage instruction: a character rises, stops talking, and so forth.

and an ease of recognition, that is absent from the original book and from Sutto's edition.

Pasquier occasionally drops a hint about a character's personality. For example, the Jesuit is described as speaking "with such grace." In addition, "his way of talking" is so distinctive that the gentleman quickly realizes that one of his house guests is a Jesuit.[11] By contrast, the lawyer struggles with "these violent passions of the mind" that beset him. In fact, a bit later the lawyer, "appearing very upset at heart, was going to continue his angry words" when he was interrupted by the Jesuit.[12]

Could these personality traits be woven into this translation? I found a solution that I hope readers will find useful, especially if they decide to imitate the lawyer and read this translation aloud. Rhetoric handbooks of the period emphasize that a slow and even speech rhythm (or heartbeat) reveals a speaker's calm, his self-control. This speech rhythm is especially calming and majestic when it is expressed in poetic feet where three-syllable feet predominate. By contrast, irritation gives rise to irregular speech rhythms (or heartbeats).[13] To suggest this contrast between calm and animation, I have used contractions throughout the lawyer's monologs, to suggest his haste and his drive to convince the other guests: "isn't," "they're," "won't," and so forth. These contractions complement the exclamations that the lawyer strews throughout his discourse. I have made the Jesuit avoid these contractions.[14] Nor does he exclaim, as the lawyer does. It doubtlessly is because his speech is so controlled that the gentleman immediately recognizes him for what he is: a Jesuit in disguise.

I have assumed that initially all the guests were quite restrained. To suggest this restraint, they articulate quite carefully on the first evening; but as they begin to relax, contractions creep in. As for the lawyer, I gave him only a few contractions at first; but as he increasingly gives vent to his emotions, contractions stud his remarks. The gentleman is warm and welcoming, using

---

11   Book I, ch. 1.

12   Book I, ch. 9.

13   See Patricia M. Ranum, *The Harmonic Orator* (Hillsdale, NY: Pendragon Press, 2001), 146–52, 184–86, 417–19, 425–26, 407–11.

14   Pasquier's version of the comments about the grace of the Jesuit's speech mimics the sort of declamation for which Jesuits were renowned. Poetic scansion reveals the underlying rhythm of the Jesuit's statement (S = short and L = long: SSL SSL SSL SSL *Ig-nace*, SSL SSL *de notre religion* SSL *mais* SSSL *ordinairement que Dieu* SSSL SSSL). This long flow of three-syllable units is perceived as expressing calm and majesty. The words that briefly interrupt that flow of sound are key words: "Ignatius," "of our religion"; then comes some four-syllable units, interrupted by "but ordinarily," and "God." Concocting a sentence like that is more difficult that it might seem.

just enough contractions to make people feel relaxed. French speakers do not, of course, use contractions: they express anger or irritation by shortening syllables and speaking quickly, like a machine gun.

It would, of course, be totally inappropriate to use contractions in translations of papal bulls or other documents, or in excerpts from Richeome (that is, from books by "Montaignes" or "René La Fon").

4   Pasquier's Style

Pasquier's sentences can be convoluted. They often lack a subject or a verb. It is as if he were taking notes in the courtroom.[15] He sometimes tucks redundant words into a statement, as if the redundancy would strengthen his point: "in the future [...] he will henceforth"; or "Now [...] and at this time." His use of the present or the future tense of a verb does not always fit the chronology he is depicting. In fact, he often can be caught talking about a specific event and using both the past tense and the present. He can be redundant. But he can also be witty, weaving puns and word-play into his narratives. He invents words and applies them mockingly to Jesuits.

The punctuation has been reworked, redundant adverbs and conjunctions have been removed, endless sentences have been shortened, and indications of what a "he" or a "she" (both of which can, of course, become "it") might be referring to, have been tacitly inserted. When there was sufficient evidence about the antecedent of a vague pronoun, the pronoun has tacitly been replaced by a noun.

The punctuation rules observed by writers and printers in 1602 do not match today's rules, where commas show supplementary items, colons show that a thought is not yet complete, semicolons subdivide a long and complex sentence into several units, and a period mark signals the end of the statement. In Pasquier's day, punctuation suggested either breathing places or subdivisions in the long flow of words that constituted a sentence. For example, colons seem to have been just another sort of comma for Pasquier; and semicolons were rarities.

The vocabulary of a lawyer during the first decade of the seventeenth century may surprise someone who reads the text in the early twenty-first century. Pasquier had a large vocabulary. Approximately half of it was the vocabulary

---

15   See the style of the choppy excerpts from court records that Pasquier quotes in Book III, ch. 20: "Questioned whether [...], Inquired whether he had been [...], Once again questioned [...]."

employed in courts where he practiced law. The meaning of those words is provided in footnotes or, if a word is used frequently, it is explained in the Glossary. The other half of his vocabulary was popular parlance of the late-sixteenth century. Pasquier rarely employed words that would be defined in the dictionary of the French Academy, 1694 (cited in this translation as "DAF 1694"). Rather, his vocabulary is that of Randle Cotgrave's *Dictionarie*, 1611. In short, Pasquier seems to have been conservative about his vocabulary, just as he was conservative and affectionate about "this France," and the "Catholic, Roman, and Apostolic Gallican Church" that he loved so dearly. At one point or another during the process of translating Pasquier, virtually every word of the *Catechism* was checked against Cotgrave, to ascertain what Pasquier probably meant. Once that meaning had been determined, simply inserting Cotgrave's word into the sentence usually did not work. The effect tended to be unbearably quaint. In the end, I used Cotgrave's English word when I could; but more often than not, I searched for a modern word that would capture Pasquier's wit and verve.

Pasquier's original quotation marks have been respected, because they mark the start and finish of quoted material.[16] He italicized his Latin quotations; thus they are italicized in this translation. The quotations from Latin documents provided by Pasquier appear to be based on actual documents. The capitalization and the punctuation have therefore been respected. In like manner, when he provides a document in French, his capitalization, punctuation, and accents (or lack of them) have been respected.

Another problem cried out for a solution: Pasquier is giving his own personal rendering of the Latin texts. More often than not it proved anachronistic to search out a modern English translation that could be inserted into this English edition. Where Pasquier neglected to provide a French version of a Latin document, an English translation has been provided. The goal has been to make these translations, and these re-translations of Latin documents, follow Pasquier as closely as possible.

5   **Pasquier's Printed Version of *Le Catéchisme des Jésuites***

The first printed version of Pasquier's *Catéchisme des Jésuits* ("Villefranche": Guillaume Grenier [that is, Jérôme Haultin], 1602), is available as a Google

---

16   I initially followed the Chicago rules for double and single quotes. By the time I reached the end of Book II of my translation, I realized that this simply would not do. It was no longer possible to distinguish the original from the editorial. I therefore went back to page one, removed the anachronistic quotation marks, and inserted Pasquier's own marks.

Book. It was used for the critical edition by Claude Sutto, *Le Catéchisme des Jésuits* (Sherbrooke, Quebec: University of Sherbrooke Press, 1982), abbreviated throughout my translation as "Sutto."

The present translation used Sutto's edition as a point of departure. Readers are referred to Sutto's bibliography and notes. His notes reveal just how intensive Sutto's work was: he was striving to find the texts that Pasquier had consulted. (By contrast, the notes to this English translation identify people whom Pasquier mentions, evoke France in 1602, and explain some of Pasquier's humor.) I have cited some of Sutto's identifications, as a gesture of solidarity with a scholar who collected all that information in a pre-Google era. Sutto's citations of sources were intended for specialists of sixteenth-century religious issues. Consequently, his footnotes provide a reader with abundant sources (generally in French) for further research.

Unless otherwise stated, Biblical texts in English come from *The New American Bible, Revised Edition* (2011).

•••

1   Two Related Books

Two related books were published in 1602. The first was written by a royal legal official named Étienne Pasquier. In this preface, it is called *The Jesuits' Catechism*—or simply *The Catechism*. The second book was by a Jesuit named Louis Richeome. It is called *The Hunt for Pasquin the Fox*—or, for brevity, *The Hunt*.

These books permit modern time-travelers to take the pulse of two early seventeenth-century authors. Both authors are wrapped up in religious issues. We can chuckle at their witticisms, admire their education, glower at some of the extreme religious positions they are espousing, and eavesdrop when they read their works aloud.

Let us examine the two title pages.

2   The Jesuits' Catechism

Étienne Pasquier's *Le Catéchisme des jésuites ou examen de leur doctrine* (The Jesuits' catechism, or an examination of their doctrine) was purportedly printed at one of the many French towns called Villefranche (free city). The printer was said to be Guillaume Grenier, that is, William Granary; but in reality, that first edition was typeset by Jérôme Haultin, a Protestant printer at La

Rochelle.[17] The author's name was not provided on the title page, nor does the book bear a royal printing privilege.[18]

The notes for the present English translation identify persons whom Pasquier mentions; they call attention to passages that shed light on France in 1602; or they explain some of Pasquier's humor—several examples of which can be discerned in the first pages of his books. Indeed, shop names suggest to potential purchasers that the book contains at least a few comic passages.

Later in this preface, we shall learn more about Father Richeome and his reply to Étienne Pasquier's *The Jesuits' Catechism*.[19]

3   The Hunt for Pasquin the Fox

The full title of the second book, which replies to Étienne Pasquier's *Catechism*, is *La chasse du renard Pasquin, descouvert et pris en sa tannière du libelle diffamatoire faux-marqué, Le Catéchisme des jésuites* (The Hunt for Pasquin the Fox, discovered in his den; the defamatory book falsely called *The Jesuits' Catechism*). The title page claims that, like *The Catechism*, it was published in 1602, at a real or false place called Villefranche; but although the place probably was the same "Villefranche" as for *The Catechism*, on this occasion the purported printer was named after Saint Hubertus, the patron saint of hunters. To this information was added a family name that likewise was connected to hunting: *Le Pelletier* (the furrier). The print shop was allegedly situated on the *rue de la Vénerie,* Kennel Street, at the sign of the *Lévrière,* The Greyhound Bitch. The title page claims that the author is *Sieur Foelix* (or *Félix*) *de la Grâce,*

---

17   *The Hunt*, 14.

18   A facsimile of the 1602 version is available as a Google Book. A copy of that first edition was used for the critical edition by Claude Sutto, *Le Catéchisme des Jésuits* (Sherbrooke, Quebec: University of Sherbrooke Press, 1982), abbreviated throughout this translation as "Sutto." Since the present translation into English took Sutto's edition as a point of departure, readers are referred to his bibliography and to his notes, which reveal just how thorough Sutto was in his search for texts that Pasquier had consulted. Sutto's citations of sources were intended primarily for specialists of sixteenth-century religious issues. In fact, his footnotes provide the reader with abundant sources (usually in French) for further research.

19   The two biographies that follow focus upon the first half of each author's life. Those were the years that prepared the two men for the books they would write in 1602. The brief biographies of Étienne Pasquier and Louis Richeome, below, were constructed by paraphrasing articles in general reference books, and in Sutto's 110-page Introduction. Unless otherwise stated, biblical texts in English come from *The New American Bible, Revised Edition* (2011).

gentil-homme François, seigneur dudict lieu (Sir Happiness in Grace, a French gentleman who is the lord of the said place). It is not always easy to distinguish Félix de la Grâce from "le seigneur," that is, the lord of the manor; but since Father Louis Richeome put that name on the title page, as a pseudonym for himself, one can presume that Félix is in the main synonymous with *le seigneur,* and that when Félix or *le seigneur* talks, it may well be Richeome who is speaking.

4   A Brief Biography of Étienne Pasquier

Etienne Pasquier was born in 1529 into a well-off Parisian family. After studying law with several of France's greatest jurisconsults,[20] he pleaded his first case in 1556.

Ill health made Pasquier's law career grind to a halt for several years (he blamed some poisonous mushrooms); but by 1564, he was well enough to represent the Sorbonne[21] in a lawsuit before the Parlement that pitted the Society of Jesus against the theologians at the university, reinforced for that important event by powerful bishops. The brilliance of the Jesuit colleges had cast a shadow over the university, which was struggling to preserve its monopoly over the education of youths. Hence the lawsuit.

Pasquier and Antoine Arnauld (1560–1619)—the latter was one of the greatest lawyers of his day—argued for the university; Pierre de Versoris (1528–88), a lawyer in the Parlement of Paris, represented the Jesuits. Pasquier, who gave a brilliant plea (*plaidoyé*), won the attention of the public and the esteem of his colleagues; but the Jesuits won the lawsuit, despite their adversaries' powerful rhetoric.

His lack of success in the law courts did not keep Pasquier from other interests. Over the years, he wrote poems, corresponded with some of the most illustrious persons of his time, and researched old documents that he eventually published. Concurrently with these activities, he began an innovative project that would keep him busy until his death in 1615. He called the project *Les Recherches de la France* (Researches on France). The project nourished his curiosity about the past—especially the French past: Joan of Arc, the Gauls, medieval poems from southern France, Nostradamus and his prophecies, the origins of the French language, and so forth. The first volume of *Researches,*

---

20   Among them were François Baudoin (1520–73), François Hotman (1524–90), and Jacques Cujas (1522–90).

21   "La Sorbonne" was another name for the Faculty of Theology of the University of Paris.

published in 1560, was dedicated to the powerful Cardinal of Lorraine.[22] Despite some errors, this masterful volume bears witness to the breadth of Pasquier's knowledge about the history of French monarchical institutions and about French literature and culture.

That same year saw the publication of a dialog[23] by Pasquier: *The Pourparler du Prince* (The Discussion with the prince). In it, some friends are discussing the best forms of government. The Student views literature as a necessity for kings, who must control their passions; and literature likewise is a necessity for developing society. The Courtier is entrusted with wielding sword and laws, but although he helps administer the kingdom, much of his contribution is flowery speech. The last to speak is the *Politique,* that is, the Political Man, who asks the sovereign to reconcile freedom with power, as is being done in France. He should temper his power by calling assemblies of estates, and by remembering that the common people are not made for the king, kings are made for the people. This *Politique*[24] is Pasquier himself.

Over the years, Pasquier carried out the duties of his legal calling, but this did not protect his family from the horrors of civil war. His wife and a son were slaughtered by the ultra-Catholic Holy League. Pasquier survived. Ennobled by King Charles IX (r.1560–74) in 1585, he was granted the office of *avocat général* in the Chamber of Accounts in Paris.

The final years of the century found Pasquier exchanging information with Louis Richeome, a Jesuit with whom we shall soon be better acquainted. From approximately the final months of 1599 and on into late December of 1602, Richeome seems to have been scouring Paris for copies of famous French legal pleas (*plaidoyés*), especially pleas in the Parlement involving the Society of Jesus.[25] The final pages of Richeome's *Hunt*—they are quoted at the end

---

22   Charles de Lorraine (1524–74), known as the cardinal de Lorraine, was a member of the powerful house of Guise and was a protector of the Jesuits. See Book 1, ch. 4 below.

23   For dialogs, see especially Colette H. Winn, "The Dialogues of Louis Le Caron, 1544–1556," in Colette H. Winn, ed., *The Dialogue in Early Modern France, 1547–1630* (Washington, DC: The Catholic University of America Press, 1993). See also Nancy Struever, "Pasquier's *Recherches de la France*: The Exemplarity of His Medieval Sources," *History and Theory* 27 (1988): 57–59.

24   The term *"Politiques"* denoted French moderates who, during the religious conflicts of the sixteenth century, held national unity to be more important than the absolute predominance of a single religion, and who advocated religious tolerance as government policy.

25   Pasquier is mentioned on the title page of another book by Richeome, who was using another of his pseudonyms, "René de La Fon": *Response de René de La Fon pour les Religieux de la Compagnie de Jésus au plaidoyé* de Simon Marion en l'arrest donné contre iceux le 16 octobre 1597 avec quelques notes sur le *Plaidoyé* et autres subjets des Recherches d'Estienne Pasquier (Reply by René de La Fon on behalf of the Religious of the Society of

of this preface—prove that the two men were exchanging ideas, and perhaps even texts, and that Pasquier's *Catechism* was the fruit of these encounters. The same pages prove that Pasquier remained in touch with Richeome throughout 1602, when both *The Catechism* and *The Hunt* were being written and printed.

In sum, we know for a fact that the two men were acquainted, even though the circumstances under which they met are not clear. Perhaps this brief biography of Pasquier—or the even briefer biography of Richeome that will be available later in this preface—will shed some light on that mystery. Perhaps those biographies will even permit us to deduce the favorable opinions (and the unfavorable ones) that readers might have exchanged before setting off for an afternoon walk—as we shall soon do during our visit to a French country house.

In 1604, Pasquier resigned his prestigious position as *avocat général* to his surviving son. He died in 1615.

5   Pasquier Recounts a Weekend at a Country House

We will recall that Pasquier's *Catechism* is set in a country house, where six travelers have been offered hospitality by the gentleman who resides there. We will also recall that the guests include a disguised Jesuit, an ebullient lawyer who talks continually, and a narrator who calls himself "I." This lawyer proves to be Étienne Pasquier, the *avocat général* of the Chamber of Accounts of Paris, lawyer, historian, poet, author.

We too are travelers: time-travelers. We have hidden in a small service room adjacent to the large reception room of the house. Putting our ears to the door, we learn what élite male society was like at the dawn of the seventeenth century. But above all, we learn about two issues that were preoccupying many Frenchmen: the imminent return of the Society of Jesus to France, and the assassination attempts on kings that have been troubling France for a decade.

Jesus to the *Plaidoyé* of Simon Marion in the decree issued against them on October 16, 1597, along with some Notes on the *Plaidoyé* [of Étienne Pasquier] and other subjects from Étienne Pasquier's *Researches*). That book purportedly had been printed in 1599 at Villefranche by Guillaume Grenier. (The same imaginary printer appears on the title page of Pasquier's *Catechism*.)

6   Some Entertainments

We will also recall that the lawyer's baggage is crammed with books and documents relative to the Society of Jesus. For the next few days, he lectures his
housemates, reads excerpts from Jesuit publications aloud, and quotes from
papal bulls and police reports. Sometimes his approach is bilingual. That is,
he reads from a Latin document, and then he immediately provides a translation into French, for he is aware that Latin is no longer the universal language
it once was. Or as the lawyer himself put it: "Perhaps there are some among
us who don't understand Latin: that's why, this censure document being the
foundation of my discourse, I'll dress it in French fashions so that everyone
will understand."[26] To keep his captive audience from falling asleep, the lawyer
lards his serious presentation with poems, classical references, historical anecdotes, puns, and word-play.

The gentleman who is their host realizes that his guests risk drowning in this
flood of words. Fortunately, his social rank permits him to impose his will on
his visitors. He politely orders them to go to bed, to attend Mass, to walk in the
gardens of the manor house. In other words, we time-travelers are witnessing
social behavior among unpretentious noblemen: meals, walks, and conversations, with each man showing his wit by puns, his intellect by anagrams, his
artistry and his declamatory skills by reciting poems, and his learning by citing
classical sources.

As it turns out, the gentleman will inspire the title of Pasquier's latest book,
The Jesuits' Catechism. Conversing with the Jesuit, the gentleman issues a
polite order for the afternoon: "Please let's clear the table,[27] and after thanking

---

26   Richeome later mocks Pasquier's fixation on using the vernacular: "I laugh when I read
      one of the letters he sent to Turnebus, where he tried to prove that the sciences should
      be expressed in our vulgar tongue, and that foreigners will one day beg us for it," *The
      Hunt*, 182.

27   Shortly after the publication of Pasquier's *Catechism*, and perhaps basing his remarks on
      Pasquier's own words, Richeome recounted his version of how the idea of writing a "cat-
      echism" came to Pasquier. "It was conceived during a supper, although I [Pasquier, going
      by the sobriquet *Pasquin*] spent a long time shaping it. [...] Since then, I've spent many
      hours among the pots and the cups, writing down what we said" (*The Hunt*, 12). Indeed,
      Pasquier did not say grace with the other guests. Instead, he went to the kitchen. When he
      emerged, he said to his host: "I have the most agreeable and well-made thing one can find:
      The Jesuits' Catechism. In it I've made three fine persons speak: a Jesuit, a gentleman, a

God for what it has pleased him to give us each day, continue our discussion." The gentleman begs the Jesuit not to disapprove if, "as with the catechisms of our faith, the child be allowed to enter and question his schoolmaster, in order to learn the basic fundamentals. He did the same with the Jesuit, asking to be informed about the principal points of his order. The Jesuit readily agreed."[28] A long chapter follows, during which the gentleman asks rather lengthy questions. The Jesuit usually replies quite succinctly. During this question time, the Socratic method is employed, to permit the gentleman "to draw out what he was seeking."[29]

Approximately a year later, Pasquier, using the sobriquet *Pasquin*, would share with some acquaintances his definition of what was implied by the term "The Jesuits' Catechism": "It does not deal with the faith [...]. It contains the finesses, the subtleties, and the craftiness of the Jesuits, in order to enthrone themselves in the world, to get a confirmation from the pope, to be received in France and in other places, to supplant the universities, to shake the obedience of bishops and curates, to accumulate wealth, strip lofty families of their inheritances and take them to their *meuse* or their great kettle, take children from their fathers, who steal, stir rebellions in cities and kingdoms, cause the common people to rise up against princes and kings and take physical control of them."[30]

Like all good things, the visit, and the three books that form *The Jesuits' Catechism*, come to an end. The narrator prepares to leave the manor house: "Having dined, and our horses being bridled, we thanked the gentleman for the fine food he had been pleased to offer us, and he thanked us for the honor he claimed to have received from our visit [...]. There were six of us in our group: he kept the lawyer at his house, saying that he wanted to pay a debt that he owed him, having not tended to it for a long while. As for the other five travelers, after crossing the mountains, three of them took the road to Venice, intending to sail to Jerusalem, in order to fulfill a vow to visit the Holy Sepulcher. The Jesuit and I set off for Rome."[31]

---

lawyer, and a few others whom you will meet." Then, speaking through Father Richeome, Pasquier adds a detail about the theater: "And I played my role as a lawyer, as the dialog required," *The Hunt*, 12.

28   See the final paragraph of *The Catechism*, Book I, ch. 1.

29   *The Catechism*, Book I, ch. 1.

30   See, for example, *The Hunt*, 10. *Meuse* appears to be a printer's error rather than an archaic word.

31   *The Catechism*, Book III, ch. 27.

7   "This Great World-Stage"

The Jesuits' Catechism begins as a "dialog" between two persons.[32] In the early seventeenth century, the dialog was a well worked-out genre that was often both political and literary. Each speaker was identified when he began talking. These speakers were not real people, however; but strictly speaking they were not allegorical figures either. Rather, they were stock figures whose capitalized names show that they are generic: the Jesuit, the Gentleman, the Lawyer.[33] A dialog could be carried on by a half-dozen characters. Pasquier's dialog did just that. As chapter after chapter flowed from his lively mind and into his quill pen, the number of characters increased and miniature plays became nestled into the larger work. At times the dialog approaches theater.

Throughout his book, Pasquier alludes to the stage and to actors. In fact, the opening chapters of Book I are typeset as if for a printed play: the character's role is specified, sometimes as an abbreviation, sometimes written in full. Next come the actor's lines. However, as Book II progresses, Pasquier seems to forget the initial format: the character's name begins to appear within parentheses. Gone is succinctness: one or another character may give a very long speech. These speeches intermingle with the briefer comments of one character or another. In *The Catechism*, the lawyer is especially prone to giving tirades. Indeed, the core of the book presents his arguments. Book III brings a different approach. Conversations heard in dreams are reproduced: Saint Peter, Ignatius of Loyola, a cluster of school boys, and a marble statue who is known as "Pasquino" in Italy and "Pasquin" in France.

Pasquier doubtlessly knew that his "dialog" would be read aloud before the fire, as books and plays so often were.[34] A skilled reader would have known how to modify his voice, in order to breathe life into a character. In such a

---

32   Pasquier himself uses that term, Book III, ch. 28. See Winn, *Dialogue in Early Modern France*.

33   I have tacitly given names to a few characters. The one called "I" in the original book becomes "the Narrator." Or "I, the Narrator." Names that were abbreviated in the original have been expanded throughout this translation. My decision to treat names in this manner is influenced by the formatting of Richeome's *Hunt*. Among his characters are Pasquin the Buffon, a theologian, the lord of the manor, and a *maître des requêtes*. At one point (*The Hunt*, 12), Richeome has Pasquin refer to the three principal characters in *The Catechism*: a Jesuit, a Gentleman, "and I [Pasquin] was the third [*sic*] person, playing the part of the Lawyer as persons do in a dialog."

34   Several times in the book, the lawyer alludes to having read something aloud to the other guests.

context, the word-play, the puns, the anecdotes, the soliloquy-like intervals, the dream scene, and the encounter with the stones take on a deeper meaning.

As the number of characters increased, and as Pasquier's manuscript became thicker, the "stage" on which these characters were exchanging ideas expanded, until it included Rome, England, Scotland. As Pasquier put it in the penultimate paragraph of *The Catechism*: "Where was this fierce tragedy performed? On the stage of the Catholic Church of England [...]. Who wrote the plays? Our holy and devout Jesuits, the sole resource of our Catholic Church. What was the plot being proposed?"[35] The content may be political, but the presentation is literary. Pasquier notes that "each prince plays his character on this great world-stage."

Was it the lawyer who read aloud? That seems likely, for he is described as being weary from having talked so much. He does indeed talk incessantly! The formatting of the pages begins to change: the initials that identified the Jesuit and the gentleman are replaced by brief parenthetical indications that blend into the text: "(said the lawyer)," or "(the Jesuit said to him)."

In the end, the lawyer says far more than any other character; but that is not always obvious, because Pasquier frequently neglects to label the passages uttered by the lawyer. To confuse readers still more, the lawyer tends to go on talking for several chapters, almost without stopping for breath, and without always being identified.

8   Some Visual Clues for Reading Cheaply Printed Dialogs

In the form in which we have received it, *The Catechism* can be visually daunting. For example, the paragraphs are very long and very dense to the eye. Was that the printer's decision? Be that as it may, I, the translator, had to push aside a major temptation. That is to say, an editor would have every reason to propose

---

35   Pasquier returns frequently to the theme of the stage. See also *The Catechism*, Book I, ch. 1, final sentence: "by playing the role of Socrates, he got the other to play the Platonic role"; Book I, ch. 2, final sentence: "the Lawyer entered the jousting field"; Book I, ch. 19, final sentence: "let's watch him come on stage and act his character"; Book II, ch. 5: "this devout comedy" [*comédie*, that is, a staged play]; Book II, ch. 17: "Each prince plays his character on this great world-stage"; Book III, ch. 9: "no subject should attack his prince, no matter what character he is playing"; Book III, ch. 20: "each of us began to act as if he were flabbergasted"; Book III, ch. 21: "I praise your inventiveness at having that person play the roles of stones"; Book III, ch. 28: "I call him *Personatus*, for he's the person who played as many different characters in England as there are religions"; Book III, ch. 28, penultimate paragraph.

that, for *The Catechism*, each mammoth paragraph should be subdivided into several smaller ones. But this option had to be ruled out, and for a very telling reason. More than one reader of this translation will want to compare the first printed French edition of *Le Catéchisme* (or Claude Sutto's modern re-creation of it) with Patricia Ranum's translation, *The Catechism*. Or the reader might want to locate sources that are cited in the footnotes of Sutto's edition, but not in the English translation. Making comparisons would be close to impossible if the paragraphs of the French edition did not coincide with the paragraphs of the translation. That is to say, if a reader is prevented from moving his eye quickly from paragraph to paragraph, in both versions of the book, he will have considerable difficulty locating a specific sentence. If, however, he knows that the sentence he is looking for is in the fifth paragraph of Book II, chapter 8, he can find his way to the fifth paragraph of that chapter. *Voilà*, a comparison becomes possible, if not always easy.

Another sort of visual aid seemed indispensable. The names of the stock characters tend to blend into the dense paragraphs; consequently, the reader must thumb back and forth, in an attempt to discern who is speaking in a specific paragraph, or in an entire chapter. To help readers, identification tags have been tacitly added to the first line of every chapter: they make it immediately clear who is talking when that chapter begins. These tags are set entirely in capital letters that attract the eye: THE LAWYER, THE GENTLEMAN, and so forth. The same sorts of tags have been added throughout the text proper, permitting the eye to locate, with relative ease, the place where a different character begins speaking. These in-the-text tags replace Pasquier's abbreviated names or parenthetical identifications, thereby creating a homogeneity and an ease of recognition that are absent from the original book and from Sutto's edition.

Pasquier occasionally drops a clue to a character's personality. For example, the Jesuit is described as speaking "with such grace." In addition, "his way of talking" is so distinctive that the gentleman quickly realizes that one of his house guests is a Jesuit. By contrast, the lawyer struggles with "these violent passions of the mind" that beset him. In fact, a bit later the lawyer, "appearing very upset at heart, was going to continue his angry words" but was interrupted by the Jesuit.

Could these personality traits be woven into this translation? I hope readers will find my solution useful, especially if they decide to imitate the lawyer and read this translation aloud. Rhetoric handbooks of the period emphasize that a slow, even speech rhythm (roughly a heartbeat) reveals a speaker's calm self-control. This speech rhythm is especially calming and majestic when it is expressed in poetic lines where three-syllable feet predominate. By contrast, irritation gives rise to irregular speech rhythms that are provoked by erratic heartbeats. To suggest this contrast between calm and animation, I have used contractions throughout the lawyer's monologs, to suggest his haste and his drive to convince the other guests: "isn't," "they're," "won't," and so forth. These contractions complement the exclamations that the lawyer strews throughout his discourse. I have made the Jesuit avoid these contractions. Nor does the Jesuit exclaim, as the lawyer does. It doubtlessly is owing to his self-control that the gentleman immediately recognizes him for what he is: a Jesuit in disguise.

I have assumed that initially all the guests were quite restrained. To suggest this restraint, they articulate quite carefully on the first evening; but as they begin to relax, contractions creep in. As for the lawyer, I gave him only a few contractions at first; but as he increasingly gives vent to his emotions, contractions stud his remarks. The gentleman of the manor is warm and welcoming, using just enough contractions to make people feel relaxed. Generally French speakers do not, of course, use contractions: they express anger or irritation by shortening syllables and by speaking quickly, like a machine gun.

It would, of course, be totally inappropriate to use contractions in translations of papal bulls or other documents, or in excerpts from Richeome (that is, from books by "Montaignes" or "René La Fon").

9   Pasquier's Style, through Twenty-First Century Eyes

Pasquier's sentences can be convoluted. They often lack a subject or a verb. (Is he attempting to capture oral speech on paper?) It is as if he were taking notes in a courtroom. He sometimes tucks redundant words into a statement, as if the redundancy would strengthen his point: "In the future he will henceforth"; or "Now and at this time." His use of the present or the future tense of a verb does not always fit the chronology that he is depicting. In fact, he can often be caught talking about a specific event and using both the past and the present tenses. He can be redundant. But he can also be witty, weaving puns and word-play into his narratives. He invents words and applies them mockingly to Jesuits.

The punctuation has been reworked, redundant adverbs and conjunctions have been removed, endless sentences have been broken up, and indications of what the pronoun "he" or "she" (either of which can, in French, become "it") might be referring to, have been tacitly inserted. When there was sufficient evidence about the antecedent of a vague pronoun, the pronoun has tacitly been replaced by a noun.

The punctuation rules observed by writers and printers in 1602 do not match today's rules, where commas show supplementary items, colons show that a thought is not yet complete, semicolons subdivide a long and complex sentence into several units, and a period mark signals the end of the statement. In Pasquier's day, punctuation suggested either breathing places or subdivisions in the long flow of words that constituted a sentence. Colons seem to have been just another sort of comma for Pasquier; and semicolons were rarities.

The vocabulary of a lawyer during the first decade of the seventeenth century may surprise someone who reads that text in the early twenty-first century. Pasquier's vocabulary was large. Approximately half of it consisted of words employed in the courts where he practiced law. The meaning of those words is provided in footnotes or, if a word is used frequently, it is explained in the Glossary. The other half of his vocabulary was popular parlance of the late sixteenth century. Pasquier rarely employed words that would be defined in the dictionary of the French Academy, 1694 (cited in this translation as "DAF 1694"). Rather, his vocabulary is that of Randle Cotgrave's *Dictionarie*, 1611. In short, Pasquier seems to have been conservative about his vocabulary, just as he was conservative and affectionate about "this France," and the "Catholic, Roman, and Apostolic Gallican Church" that he loved so dearly. At one point or another during the process of translating Pasquier, virtually every word of *The Catechism* was checked against Cotgrave, to ascertain what Pasquier probably meant. Once that meaning had been determined, simply inserting Cotgrave's word into the sentence did not always work. The effect tended to be unbearably quaint. In the end, I used Cotgrave's English word when I could; but more often than not, I searched for a somewhat more modern word that would capture Pasquier's wit and verve.

Pasquier's quotation marks have generally been respected, because they mark the start and finish of quoted material. He italicized his Latin quotations; they therefore are italicized in this translation. The quotations from Latin documents provided by Pasquier appear to be based on actual documents. The capitalization and the punctuation have therefore been more or less respected. In like manner, when he provides a document in French, Pasquier's capitalization, punctuation, and accents (or lack of them) have in the main been respected.

Another editing problem cried out for a solution: Pasquier supplied his own personal translations of the Latin texts. More often than not, it proved anachronistic to search for a modern English translation that could be inserted into this English edition. Where Pasquier neglected to provide a French version of a Latin document, an English translation has therefore been provided. The goal has been to make these translations, and these re-translations of Latin documents, follow Pasquier's text as closely as possible.

10   A Brief Biography of Louis Richeome

Louis Richeome (1544–1625) was born at Digne, a city perched high above Cannes, in the mountains of southern France. He studied in Paris under Juan Maldonado (1533–83), who was teaching at the Jesuits' Collège de Clermont. In 1565, when Richeome was twenty-one, he entered the Society of Jesus. In 1580, he was appointed rector of the student residence at the university of Pont-à-Mousson which Charles, cardinal of Lorraine, had established in 1572.

The new university grew rapidly. Soon there were some two thousand students drawn from across western and central Europe and studying in four faculties: theology, the arts, law, and medicine.

In 1604, the Jesuit colleges that had been expelled from France owing to Jean Châtel's (1575–94), attempt to assassinate King Henri IV (r.1589–1610) in 1595, were permitted to return to France. Father Richeome negotiated the reopening of the Jesuit house in Bordeaux.

Richeome's contemporaries called him "the French Cicero." He formed a trio with the leading French Catholic controversialists of his age: Cardinal Jacques Davy du Perron (1558–1618), a converted Protestant, and the Jesuit Pierre Coton (1564–1626), who was the king's confessor. The trio drew heavily on arguments against Protestant doctrine compiled by Robert Bellarmine (1542–1621). Each man developed a distinctive style with which to go through the points he was making. Richeome's speciality lay in his appeal to visual media, a strategy he laid out in 1601 in his *Tableaux sacréz des figures* (Sacred illustrations of figures), which was reedited many times.

Between 1595 and 1600, Richeome published a book each year, most of them under one or another of his pseudonyms: "François des Montaignes," "René de La Fon," and, in 1602, "Foelix de la Grace" for *The Hunt*, which is a reply to Pasquier's *Catechism*, published earlier that year. As the final pages of this preface will show, Richeome and Pasquier were in touch with one another from approximately 1599 to 1602. Several of Richeome's books are especially revealing about their researches: not only is Pasquier mentioned in one or another book or title page, but he quotes from some of those books in his *Catechism*.

During the final years of the century, Richeome taught at Bordeaux and Dijon. In 1605, he was appointed superior provincial for the province of Lyon, and, from 1608 to 1616, he was in Rome, as assistant to Superior General Claudio Acquaviva (in office 1581–1615). In other words, by 1608, his contacts with Pasquier had largely been severed.

Louis Richeome died at Bordeaux on September 15, 1625.

11   The Hunt for Pasquin the Fox

We are nearing the end of *The Catechism*, but this is not the end of Pasquier's story. Indeed, Richeome appears to have viewed the book as incomplete. For example, readers seem to have been asking him about the symbolism of the title and the different characters. Then too, the book scarcely paints an impartial tableau of the Jesuits' position on many issues. Did a disguised Jesuit prop up *The Catechism* on the table before him, and create a word picture and a dialog that parodied Pasquier's? (He says that he later was given a copy and read all of it.)[36]

Let us therefore set off for another country house where a foxhunt has been planned. Along the way we should have plenty of time to examine briefly a few texts that shed light on Pasquier, as he was viewed by Richeome and his followers during the final months of 1602, and as the Jesuit preserved Pasquier's doings in *The Hunt*.

> To the Reader[37]
>   *Reader Friend*
>   *If I learn that this Hunt for Pasquin the Fox has been both useful and pleasant, his skinning is ready to be shown to you this very day. That will conclude the entire book, until there is a second and more ample edition, should someone want it. You may take the whole thing, which I offer you without hesitation. I pray that God will preserve you.*
>   Skinning a fox? That sounds ominous.

Earlier in this preface, we learned that a book called *La Chasse du Renard Pasquin* (The hunt for Pasquin the fox) was printed late in 1602, under the pseudonym "Foelix (or Félix) de la Grâce." We also learned that the author was a Jesuit in disguise: his real name was Louis Richeome.

The brief summary that follows, sketches the contents of *The Hunt*, translates a few paragraphs of Richeome's text, and casts some light on the fox's rather unusual name: *Pasquin*. It soon becomes clear that Richeome's *Hunt* not only mimics Pasquier's *Catechism*, it also takes Pasquier to task for aiming a foul "libel" at the Society of Jesus.[38] In short, *The Hunt* offers us a glimpse of

---

36   *The Hunt*, 42.

37   Set in the same italic font as the final pages, this message remains anonymous; but judging from the titlepage, it is the work of Richeome.

38   The Theologian tells Pasquin that "there are two things that offend me and all honorable men: One is that this Pasquin gave his defamatory libel the title *The Catechism* and *The Jesuits' Catechism*."

how Pasquier's contemporaries received the anti-Jesuit remarks he published in *The Catechism*.

12   A Visit to Another Country House

Imitating Étienne, Richeome begins his book with a visit to a country house that is considerably more splendid than the one depicted by Pasquier. Everything—the meals, the gardens, the entertainments, the music—seems more enchanting.

Also, in imitation of *The Catechism*, a "dialog" about "The Jesuits' Catechism" will be performed. The characters appear to be the same three that Pasquier had depicted several months earlier, but this time they will be depicting the three "estates" of France.[39] The clergy, that is, the "first estate," is portrayed by a theologian from the Sorbonne; the nobility, known as the "second estate," is incarnated in the lord of the manor; and the *maître des requêtes* embodies the countless commoners and officials who make up the "third estate.'"

The discussion of Pasquier's *Catechism* continues. The nobleman promises that the fete will involve not only a fox but also "some very serious people."[40] This courteous conversation is interrupted by a bizarre figure who has just arrived from Paris.

13   Enter Pasquin

The *seigneur*'s valet usually can identify an individual's estate, but this time he fails to guess the visitor's social rank, because the interloper seems to bear the marks of each of the three estates. "He seemed to be an *avocat*, and he was followed by a basket-bearer from the *Palais*, with packets of almanacs, songs, and little books tucked under his arms."[41] He turned out to be *Pasquin the Bouffon*, otherwise also known as Étienne Pasquier, "the author of *The Jesuits' Catechism*".[42] This is the first time in *The Hunt* that a character is robbed of

---

39   *The Hunt*, 3, 9–10. It is not clear whether the planned "dialog" to be performed by the three estates of the realm is a new one written by Richeome, or whether Pasquier's dialog was going to be performed a second time. The performances almost certainly were literary, not real.

40   *The Hunt*, 9.

41   *The Hunt*, 5.

42   From this point on, this preface will go into greater detail, the better to capture the events surrounding the different Pasquins. On the other hand, most of the page numbers for the

his name, but it is not the last time. Indeed, Pasquin and Pasquier intermingle with one another all the way to the final pages of the book. And their names change frequently. For example, Pasquier is sometimes Pasquin the Fox and sometimes Pasquin the Bouffon. Sometimes another identity is fleetingly suggested: Pasquin the Rabbit, Pasquin the Wolf, Pasquin of Rome. But occasionally Pasquier is called *Pasquier* or *Monsieur Pasquier*. None of them makes an important point, however: Pasquier has lost his respected family name, which has been replaced by a word that suggests that he is given to libel.[43]

Pasquier explains that he prefers to be called *Pasquin*, to honor his hoary ancestor, a damaged marble statue that sits in the Piazza Navona in Rome.[44] The lord of the manor assumes that the Bouffon will be surprised at hearing himself called *Pasquin*, when his true and honorable name is *Pasquier*. But in the end the floating labels pose no great problem: *Pasquin* turns out to be the preferred name because, just like Étienne Pasquier (the author of *Researches of France*), Pasquin of Rome collects memoranda from all over the world and then peddles his wares in the Piazza Navona of Rome. And Pasquin the Parisian Bouffon, writes his discoveries (his *"Researches"*) on paper and sells them in the law courts, the marketplaces, and the fairs of France. However, Pasquin of Rome does not write: he merely displays insulting verse.[45]

That is how Richeome depicts Pasquier (who appears to be playing the characters called *Pasquin the Bouffon* and *Pasquin* of Rome (the decrepit marble statue) as they go about their Researches: "The Roman picks up all the little notes and memos and papers that he is sent from everywhere in the East, West, South, North, and his head, neck, shoulders, back, and ribs are so coated that he is often out of breath, and looks as if he will collapse. In short, he carries the bundles for every novelty. [...] As for me, I gather memoranda and research on every side. I have so many things to say that I am fit to burst. [...] Pasquin the Roman brings his items to the Piazza Navona, but I sell my stories in the Palais."[46]

---

snippets of text quoted in that final part of the book have been omitted. (They are scattered through pages 117–86.) The page numbers of a few especially pertinent pages are, however, provided.

43   For showing deference by the way one addresses a person of merit, see *The Hunt*, 35.

44   The mystery of Pasquin's appearance in the stone skit of *The Catechism* is perhaps solved: Pasquin is Pasquier himself.

45   *The Hunt*, 6–7.

46   *The Hunt*, 6.

The host decides that the Bouffon will be permitted to join the other guests, as long as he promises not to speak ill of someone. This is convenient for us: as time-travelers, we can eavesdrop on the theologian and the *maître des requêtes*.

The conversation eventually centers on Pasquier's *Catechism*, which, as Félix puts it, is filled with "atrocious insults" aimed at the Jesuits. By contrast, Pasquin emphasizes that his book is "strewn, nay stuffed with gallant dreams, pleasant reveries, allusions, illusions, poems." He implores the nobleman to read the book.

Pasquin undergoes a sort of interrogation by the guests who are curious about the book.[47] The *maître des requêtes* and Félix offer their views on what Pasquin is saying about the state and about rulers around the world. Indeed, Richeome puts words into Pasquin's mouth, and these words almost seem to come from Pasquier himself. Without being actual quotations, could these remarks be based upon Richeome's recollections of a written or spoken exchange between the two men? (This cannot be ruled out, for the final few pages of *The Hunt* reveal unequivocally that they were in contact as early as the 1590s, and on until 1602.)

The guests continue asking questions. For example, did Pasquin himself actually write the book? Pasquin replies with a witticism based on the visit to the manor house that spring. "It was conceived during a supper, although I spent a long time (three years) shaping it."[48] His thoughts then move to the dialog with the three principal characters in his book: "a Jesuit, a Gentleman, and I was the third person, playing the part of the Lawyer as persons do in a dialog. Since then, I've spent many hours among the pots and the cups, writing down what we said."[49] (This witticism provides evidence about writing *The Catechism*: Richeome is implying that during the visit to the first country house, a good part of the Lawyer's role was based upon actual conversation. Pasquin then adds: "Don't be surprised that I wrote that kind of book: my principal craft is to beat with my pen those whom I think are harmful to the public. And is there any subject more noble than the Jesuits, whom all good folks hate? When I have publicly discredited such a lofty order, I will have triumphed over a thousand individuals who belong to it, and whom I hate in general and in detail. And I do this as a man of honor and a conscience for the public."[50]

---

47   *The Hunt*, 11, 12, 13.
48   *The Hunt*, 13.
49   *The Hunt*, 12–13.
50   *The Hunt*, 11–12.

For whom did he write the book? "For the public," replies Pasquin. What public? "Honorable folk, and people who love the liberties of France," says Pasquin.[51] This makes the theologian grumble: "That is bad jargon: *the liberties of France*. By that he means that good Frenchmen don't want to be listened to." Asked why he has brought up the subject now, when peace is returning, Pasquin replies: "The time to give birth had arrived, I had been pregnant for more than three years, and I had conceived it at supper."[52] In other words, Richeome is saying that Pasquier got the idea of writing *The Catechism* in 1598 or 1599, perhaps during a shared meal.

"But, Pasquin," the lord continues, "we want something from you that is not so lofty, so facile, so joyous: we want something about the soul."[53] Pasquin replies that he does not talk about that in his book; he talks about the "finesses, the subtleties, and the craftiness of the Jesuits, so that they may be enthroned in the world, and be approved by the pope." Having promised this, he begs the guests to at least read *The Catechism*.[54]

Things do not go as well as anticipated, however. During the hunt, for which he was one of the main entertainments offered to the lord's guests, Pasquin is chased through the woods and has to hide in the undergrowth, like a fox. He was apprehended and tried by the theologian for heresy (which the fox symbolizes), for libel (*pasquin, pasquille*), and for "atrocious insults." *The Catechism* is examined point by point; and Pasquin is censured every time.

If Pasquin is treated that way it is because he is, for awhile at least, *Pasquin the Fox*. The theologian does not mince words: "My sentence against you is that, in addition to being a buffon, a position that is fully acquired and assured for you, you are a fox, which is an evil animal covered by the skin of a buffon,[55] which is a private and domestic animal and which defames all sorts of honest folks or spreads the venom of heresy or even of atheism. You will not deny that you are a calumniator: your book [*The Hunt*] provides us with all too many proofs that you are not content to wound the fine renown of the Jesuit reverend fathers."[56] For these sins, Pasquin the Fox will pay dearly.

As it turns out, Richeome had definitely been in touch with Pasquier. Indeed, the two men seem to have debated the issues for three years. That is, Richeome

---

51   *The Hunt*, 13. Compare this allusion to the so-called "Gallican liberties" and Pasquier's very
      Gallican comments that are scattered throughout Book I of *The Catechism*.

52   *The Hunt*, 13.

53   *The Hunt*, 10.

54   *The Hunt*, 10.

55   This paragraph calls to mind the "skinning" promised in the ominous poem addressed to
      Richeome's readers.

56   *The Hunt*, 42.

asks Pasquier "not to wait three years, as you did with your *Catechism*, before you reassure me of your intentions."[57] Indeed, Richeome clearly was so familiar with Pasquier's views that he dared to put words in Pasquier's mouth. Some of these tidbits seem to be recollected comments that had been sent Pasquier's way while he was working on *The Catechism*—or else immediately after the book was published. In short, these comments appear to be passing remarks that the Jesuit attributes to Pasquin and that shed light on the creation of Pasquier's *Catechism*.

14   Pasquin's Trial

As if they were flipping through the pages of the *Catechism*, the characters who are performing the dialog discuss one chapter or another in Pasquier's book. Gradually the mood turns ugly. The theme of the fox hunt returns. Pasquier is pursued. He hides.

Beginning on page 48, and continuing on until the end of the trial, the man who was sometimes called "Pasquin" and sometimes "Monsieur Pasquier" receives tongue lashings for things he wrote in *The Catechism*. A few of the jabs directed at him by the theologian from the Sorbonne reveal how irritated Richeome and his associates are. These "libels," this "heresy," has stuck in their craw.

This is the theologian's opinion: "In this very house I read your book. I judged that, in addition to acting the bouffon, which you do very well and with great confidence, you are a fox, a malign animal who is private and domesticated, who defames all sorts of honest persons, or who spreads the venom of heresy, or even of atheism. You do not deny that you are a calumniator, for your book provides many proofs of it [...], and you are not content to injure the good reputation of the Jesuit reverend fathers:[58] "By what right does Pasquin, as secretary in heaven, interpreter of God's will, counselor in God's private Council, dare to propose?" asks the theologian, "Monsieur Pasquier would do better to confine himself within the boundaries of his profession." "Pasquin, your foxiness, your error, your heresy, are gradually becoming manifest." "Why then, Pasquin, do you want to tie the Holy Father's hands?" And on and on. The theologian repeatedly attacks him and is heard saying: "Pasquin, you are

---

57   *The Hunt*, the farewell letter, no pagination. Following p. 86. This provides strong proof that Richeome and Pasquier were in touch with one another from 1599 to 1602 and that they exchanged ideas during the three years evoked by Richeome.

58   *The Hunt*, 42.

not an Abelardist, you are a great babbler, and you who call René de La Fon[59] 'Master,' are, along with Pasquier, an arch master-fool, a natural fool, a fool by sharps, a fool by flats, a fool with triple soles, a double-dyed fool tinted with scarlet, a fool in all sorts of foolishness. I'm not saying this to wound you, but to sympathize with your hurt."[60]

Pasquin, who is described as "the great calumniator of illustrious cardinals, princes, archbishops, bishops and generally all sorts of persons,"[61] is then censured (and found guilty) by the *maître des requêtes*, "with a plenary absolution and a justification of the Jesuits." The censure centers on Jesuit activities, about which "Pasquin is careless and contradicts himself," "is guilty of secret collusion with the enemies of religion," "is guilty of several atrocious calumnies about the Jesuits." For example, he accuses the Jesuits of "perturbing the state." And when Pasquin's book is scrutinized, it becomes clear that all his accusations against the Jesuits were false.

15   Pasquier Is Declared Guilty of Libel

The *maître des requêtes* issues a decree against Pasquin, who is duly convicted of "atrocious insults and false calumnies against all sorts of persons, particularly the Jesuits. In addition, he is a very bad Frenchman, and is in general the enemy of all Christian states. He teaches very pernicious things to children, whom he wants to deprive of Christian piety and doctrine, and of knowledge, both secular and sacred. In a word, he is diametrically opposed to the good of souls. For that reason, everything he has copied will be confiscated by the lord of this place and will be burned in the large public square by the executioner. As for the person called *Pasquin*, he will be sent before the judge of the criminal court and will make the appropriate amends."[62]

The lord of the manor thanks the court (156) for all the trouble they have taken to rid the countryside of evil-doing beasts: the wolf and the wily fox. "But," he continues, "no one has given as much joy and pleasure as the joy you gave to Foxy Pasquin, the old fox, the furry fox, the white-headed fox, the gray-furred fox, the fox who is bald on part of his body, the fox who stinks and who wets everything with his stinky urine. [...] I beg two things of you. The first is

---

59   A reminder: this is Richeome's sobriquet.
60   *The Hunt*, 57.
61   *The Hunt*, 117.
62   *The Hunt*, 156.

for you, cousin. [...] It involves the bulls that approve the Jesuits, to which I beg you to add the forceful refuting of the invectives hurled at the blessed Ignatius and his nine companions, with which Pasquin has stuffed his bookish head, as the asp and the viper stuff themselves with venom. The second thing involves [...] judging Pasquin's written style. For although every upright man criticizes its content, some praise its form and style; but they are vulgar fellows."[63]

16   Richeome's Verdict about Pasquier's Writing Style

What was the verdict about Pasquin's style or, if you will, Pasquier's style? Félix de la Grâce (that is, Richeome, the author of *The Hunt*) states his opinion: "Pasquin gave me a copy last night and I spent most of the night reading it.[64] [...] There is some fluidity, but I need some eloquence. [...] Sometimes he seems to want to weave some in; but he suddenly falls back and puts his nose to the ground. In other words, his pen is short and feeble on the one hand, it being incapable of attacking, shocking, pressing his enemy. On the other hand it is base, humble, unable to soar high, always crawling and tumbling on the ground. [...] Gentlemen, in your learned and serious speeches, you do not commit that sort of error. [...] I thought all of you had been warned about this, so that you would not judge Pasquin to be more eloquent than he really is. I do not know whose style I should compare to Pasquin's, other than the style of Master Étienne Pasquier [...]; and I have noticed that Pasquin used a lot of texts written by Pasquier. [...] Pasquier is incapable of erasing the blot of frivolity with which he has burdened his fame. I hope he will pardon me for saying this, for it is true. [...] In vain does Pasquier nourish his fame to make it last as long as possible; the fame of that sort of man will be perpetually attached to the blot of frivolity. Pasquin has followed in Pasquier's footsteps, and has borrowed from him, word for word, several entire compound sentences that are injurious to the Jesuits. [...] And what I said about Pasquin's style applies to Pasquier's. [...] I laugh when I read one of the letters he sent to Turnebus, where he tried to prove that the sciences should be expressed in our vulgar tongue[65] and that foreigners will one day beg us for it. He is so caught up in himself and his capabilities that he thinks he is a past-master at this sort of writing. [...] We honor him, but we censure him as a writer. He does not merit

---

63   *The Hunt*, 156.
64   *The Hunt*, 179.
65   For Turnebus and writing in French, see Pasquier's *Catechism*, Book II, ch. 6.

a pardon, because he wrote so much to the detriment of the church, of France, and of a holy order in religion. Yet Pasquier and Pasquin will be warned in the future not to take on impudently the honor and praise of the language and of the French pen. [...] Someone like Father Richoeme,[66] rich in his manly eloquence, rich in beautiful conceptions, pious inventions, and delicious comments about nature. [...] In the name of God, and for their honor, let Pasquier and Pasquin be quiet and hide. To conclude on this point, we shall say: *Whover does not hate Pasquin, loves Pasquier*."[67]

Everyone accepted Félix de la Grâce's decision. And the *maître des requêtes* gave an order: To serve as an example, Pasquin the calumniator should be made to feel the rigors of justice. The bouffon should be chased from the gentleman's house and from all his lands, and on his head should be placed a hat of yellow feathers as in a rooster's tail, and a scepter in his hand. To which the gentleman added: "Let us go and eat a wretched noonday meal, and may Pasquin dine in the scullery, so that he can't claim that he left my house hungry."

The End[68]

---

66   In other words, Lord Félix de la Grâce appears be praising himself, Father Richeome. Note also the repeated adjective "rich," which creates a pun based on the Jesuit's name, Richeome (pronounced "reesh omme"). We encountered this very sort of pun throughout *The Catechism*, and it is likely that this particular pun prompted Richeome to assert, in his closing *Letter to Pasquin*, that he was only resorting to such puns in order to "please and content" Pasquier.

67   *The Hunt*, 178.

68   This is not, however, the end of the book. This very revealing *Letter to Pasquin* follows it: "Pasquin, several persons of renown having come running when they learned about the discourses and arguments you had some days ago with a *maître des requêtes* and a doctor of the Sorbonne, and having hoped in vain to be present when this debate ends they have begged me to write down everything that happened in order to inform the public. The benefits derived from it for you and for the reader made it easy to pick up my pen. For the reader will doubly profit. First, he will be instructed about the points that stirred up the Jesuits: an important thing at this time, when the heretic and the false Catholic, his little falcon, are warring against them. Second, he will feel pleasure and contentment at this blend of witticisms that are interwoven with serious subjects. For although the bouffonesque air that abounds in you and in your work never pleased me very much, I did not in the least want to break with your literary style, since you chose that sort of weapon. Indeed, I only wanted to temper it in the manner of those who are preparing poisonous helleborus. As for you, you will receive two conveniences from it. First, since you are very old and on the brink of your tomb, what I am bringing up-to-date will, after your death, take the place of the best funeral oration possible, to honor your glorious memory, by which everyone will recognize what you were. Second, in the short time you have to live, it will be the consolation of your venerable and final old age. There you will read yourself, you will see yourself, admire yourself, contemplate yourself, as livelier and more natural than if painted by an idiotic painter, and also with greater contentment. If you pity yourself because some details are missing from this portrait that I have drawn of you, blame

my lack of time, for I only had two months of leisure. [In other words, Richeome's *Hunt* was dashed off in roughly two months, that is, during the early autumn of 1602. A bit farther down the page we learn that Pasquier worked on *The Catechism* for three years. Reading between the lines, one can surmise that Pasquier was in touch with Richeome during some or all of that time.] But if you give me to understand that I am adding those details here, I will be faultless. A few days ago, I received some very fine and very special pigments. I shall grind them as soon as I hear from you, and on your behalf, I shall willingly mix them with the best ship-oil. I ask only two things of you. The first is not to wait three years, as you did with your Catechism, before you reassure me about your intention. For if you were to die in the meantime, I would lose my opportunity, and not without regret, to do you an agreeable service. The second is not to forget your name this time, as you did in the Catechism. Those long voyages that are mentioned in it, and others that I am debating about writing, have greatly debilitated your memory and your brain, owing to several illnesses and unfortunate catarrhs: yet they have not reduced you, along with that Roman, to having forgotten your name. I see, by your writings, that the name Pasquin pleased you greatly; if you were telling the truth. As for me, I am speaking as truly as I can: but because others may claim to be interested, I am of the opinion that you should not, in the future, take any name but your antique and ordinary one. Assured as I am that you will grant me my request, I thank you for your good wishes."

Glossary of Terms

Amende honorable (honorable amends)   A form of punishment that required the offender, barefoot and stripped to his shirt, to be led into a public square with a two-pound candle in his hand. Around his neck was a rope held by the public executioner. On his knees, the offender begged to be pardoned by God, by his king, and by the courts. See also *Question*.

Ancient (*ancien*)   Something that has been there a long time. It is often used for contrasts: the opposite of new and modern. Ancient Greece, Ancient and modern Rome. In this book, *ancien* is primarily translated as "ancient," and somewhat less frequently as "old."

Antique (*antique*)   Very old: Antique coins, antique statue. It is the opposite of modern.

Appel comme d'abus (appeal as from an abuse)   A procedure used by the monarchy to assert its authority over ecclesiastical courts. It took the form of an appeal to a superior royal court, usually the Parlement, against usurpation by the church of the rights of civil jurisdiction, and against judgments by a church court that plaintiffs deemed unjust.

Appoint (*appointer*)   A term used in the law courts of the *Palais* (q.v.). It refers to a matter that was being pleaded there but that could not be given a hearing, either because there were too many cases waiting, or because the case was too complex. The judges therefore ordered the parties to produce a written document.

Avocat (lawyer)   An *avocat du roi* is the king's counsel in a court. He is responsible for conducting prosecutions. At the Parlement (q.v.) there were also two *avocats généraux*. See also *Lawyer*.

Censure (*censure*)   Corrections, reprehensions, or "ecclesiastical" censures such as excommunications, interdicts, and suspensions of the perquisites of one's position or benefice. Censure can also denote judging and condemning a book: for example, a censure by the Sorbonne. (Note: "censure" is not synonymous with "censor.")

Church (*église*)   The church in general, and in this specific case, the Roman Catholic Church. However, Pasquier draws a distinction for the church in France. For him, "the church" is the Catholic, Apostolic, Roman Church, which he also calls "our antique Gallican Church." He contrasts the Catholic Church of Rome with this "Gallican" church, situated in "our France." The Gallican Church sought strength in the actions and writings of the church fathers: early conciliar decrees and papal decisions, especially on spiritual matters.

College (*collège*)   A secondary school where letters, sciences, and classical languages were taught to students who were still in their teens. Classes were typically taught by "regents." The Jesuits were famed for their excellent colleges. In this translation, the word does not have the grave accent unless a specific school is being named.

Constitutions (*Constitutions*)   The word is used in general to denote *ordonnances* (q.v.), laws, and rulings that together make the legal foundations of a religious order. This general sense of the word appears rarely in Pasquier's text; when it does, the translated word is not capitalized: constitutions. On the other hand, the Constitutions of the Society of Jesus are mentioned frequently; and Pasquier's printer usually capitalized the word: Constitutions. The term is not italicized in this translation, the only exception being a reference to a specific printed version of the Constitutions: *The Constitutions*.

Decree (*décret*)   An order issued by a magistrate that usually stipulated the seizure of a person or his property.

Fact (*fait*) and **law** (*droit*)   The distinction between "fact" and "law" was central to Roman legal procedure, which drew a distinction between establishing facts and evaluating a juridical proceeding. The juridical code is therefore independent of facts. Indeed, to be universally valid, law cannot be based on fact. What goes on in the facts does not determine what should go on in law, except in cases before a court.

Family (*famille*)   Pasquier often described the Jesuits as a "family." In almost every instance, he is talking about a religious house and its inhabitants. Pasquier's use of this term is echoed in the dictionary of the French Academy (DAF), 1694: "all the persons who live in the same house, administered by the same head of the household."

Fulmination (*fulmination*)   An action by which certain formalities are made public. The word is used exclusively for ecclesiastical matters: fulminations of bulls, the fulmination of an ecclesiastical decision.

Gallican (*Gallicane*)   Gallicans such as Pasquier held that the French monarch's authority over the church was, in many respects, like that of the pope in the Roman Church, except on spiritual matters. Gallicans were also anti-ultramontanist, that is, they did not desire to strengthen papal powers in France. Gallicanism became particularly strong among legal professionals in the fourteenth and fifteenth centuries, as a result of the attempts by church councils to stop, if not decrease, papal powers over nominations to benefices in France, and contestations over jurisdictions between ecclesiastical courts in France and papal courts in Rome. For a detailed presentation of Gallicanism, see Jotham Parsons, *The Church in the*

Republic: Gallicanism and Political Ideology in Renaissance France (Washington DC: The Catholic University of America Press). See also J. H. M. Salmon, "Clovis and Constantine: The Uses of History in Sixteenth-Century Gallicanism," *The Journal of Ecclesiastical History* 41 (1990): 584–605, for Pasquier's perspective as a historian (and a Gallican).

Grève, place de   An open area between the Hôtel de Ville of Paris and the Seine River. Public executions were held there.

Indult (*indult*)   A gift from the pope, by which he grants a grace, especially an expectative grace, that is, a benefice that will be granted in the future.

Induce, induction (*induction*)   To instigate or impel someone to do something. To bring forward separate facts or instances, so as to prove a general statement; and therefore, reasoning from particular facts to a general conclusion.

Inquiry (*informations, informer*)   In legal terminology, it means to make an inquiry. It is almost exclusively used about criminal issues. To collect information about someone, that is, to conduct an inquiry into an assassination.

Institute (*Institut*)   In the Catholic Church, an institute of consecrated life is an association of the faithful that was erected by canon law and whose members profess chastity, poverty, and obedience. The most numerous type of religious institute is characterized by the public profession of vows, life in common as brothers or sisters, and a degree of separation from the world. Institutes require the written permission of a bishop in order to operate within his diocese. After consulting the Apostolic See, a bishop can erect an institute in his own diocese.

Lawyer (*avocat*)   A person who defends litigants in the courts. The word is often translated as "barrister," but that term is too lofty to be applied to many French *avocats*, circa 1600. The present translation opts for Randle Cotgrave's translation of 1611: "lawyer," rather than his longer, and more British, "counsellor at law." When Pasquier uses the word in its general sense, *avocat* is translated as "lawyer"; but where the text refers to a specific type of *avocat*, the italicized French word and its modifier is given. See also *Avocat*.

Lettre dimissoire   A letter by which a bishop consented that one of his diocesans should be promoted by another bishop to the clergy or to an order.

Letters-patent (*lettres patentes*)   *Patente* is a term used by the chancellery. It refers to royal letters signed by the king and counter-signed by a secretary of state. They were folded or rolled, and then sealed with small royal seals applied to silk threads. The king would send these letters to his courts concerning the administration of justice. They were not in force until the Parlement had registered them.

Lit de justice   The personal attendance of the king at a solemn ceremony of the Parlement, usually to enforce registration of an edict. Beneath a canopy strewn with golden *fleurs-de-lis*, the sovereign sat on a throne with a large pillow (hence the term "bed of justice"). A *lit de justice* was also a ceremony used to register "constitutional" laws or to declare a regency or a minority.

Obreption (*obreption*)   Reticence about some fact that should have been presented and that makes documents fraudulent or suspicious. It refers to favors obtained by surprise (q.v.), for example, obtaining or attempting to obtain a dispensation from ecclesiastical authority, receiving a gift from the sovereign by fraud. Compare this with *subreption* (q.v.).

Oraison   A prolonged and silent prayer in the presence of God. The human being clings to this presence by a profound act of faith. To make an *oraison* means to humbly open oneself to the mysterious action of God's spirit within the human heart.

Ordinaire (ordinary)   Suggests a position that has nothing special about it, or an event that takes place regularly, as contrasted with something or someone who is *extraordinaire* (extraordinary), that is, who participates in a special event. In Paris, there was a group known as the *ordinaires*, that is, the established secular clergy: the bishop, the curates, and the university of Paris. Pasquier always employs this term in the context of the commitment to respect the jurisdiction and privileges of the *ordinaires*, made by the Jesuits at the assembly of the clergy held at Poissy in 1560.

Ordonnance (ordonnance)   Laws and constitutions issued by one or more persons who had the power to make such a ruling: the king, a sovereign prince, a judge, a bishop. The English word "ordinance" is not synonymous with *ordonnance*.

Palais (palace)   Several French cities had a *palais* where justice was rendered. The principal *palais* of the realm was in Paris: it was a medieval fortress situated on the Île de la Cité, not far from the church of Notre-Dame. It was the residence of the French kings from the sixth to the fourteenth century, at which point it became the seat of the Parlement of Paris (q.v.), the treasury, and the law courts.

Parlement (*parlement*)   A body of high-ranking judges in Paris and in several provincial cities, which typically were referred to as "sovereign courts" (q.v.) Each court legislated in its own right, and, in last resort, heard litigious lawsuits and appeals from lower courts in the king's name. They also reviewed laws for conformity with previous legislation, and oversaw the registration of royal edicts, declarations, and *ordonnances*. Pasquier and his contemporaries often likened the Parlement to the Senate of Ancient Rome.

Penitentiary (*pénétencier*)   A priest assigned by a bishop to absolve reserved cases (*cas réservés*) in sacramental confession. In Rome, there were *pénétenciers* for different nationalities; the *grand pénétencier* was always a cardinal. The Jesuits played a prominent role in the Apostolic Penitentiary of Rome.

Plead (*plaider*)   To present facts and laws appropriate to judging a crime. A plea (*plaidoyé*) was a speech by a lawyer addressed to the court. Although the plea was technically oral, written versions were sometimes printed. Pasquier cites several such *plaidoyers*, especially the published versions of the original pleas by Arnauld, Versoris, and Pasquier himself. In the present translation, *plaidoyé* is reserved for the title of a published plea.

Procureur (*procureur*)   Someone, for example a *procureur* in the Parlement, who acted in court in the name of persons who are pleading (q.v.) in some jurisdiction. A *procureur* drew up the documents, followed the proceedings, and tended to legal formalities, on behalf of the plaintiffs. A *procureur général* was a magistrate who sat on one of the appeals courts. A *procureur général du roi* (general *procureur* for the king) took care of matters that concerned the king or the public, within the confines of a specific jurisdiction. The *procureur général* of the Parlement was an official who held an office in a *bailliage* or a *présidial* (that is, in one of the lower jurisdictions).

Questioning (*question*)   The interrogation of a suspect, sometimes combined with torture. Throughout the jurisdiction of the Parlement of Paris, there were two sorts of questioning: ordinary and extraordinary. The latter involved forcing the suspect to swallow a large amount of water in a short amount of time, and then stretching his legs on a rack.

Rector (*recteur*)   See *Superiors.*

Request (*requête*)   Something one requests by asking submissively. The term denoted certain judicial acts by which one requested something from the judges. For example, one could present a *requête* to the royal council or to the parlement. Masters of requests were judges who presented the requests of individuals before the royal council or the Parlement (q.v.). There was also a tribunal in the Parlement that was called "the requests of the *Palais.*"

Scholar (*écolier*)   Someone who attends a school or a college, or who learns something under a master. A scholar in law, in philosophy, in grammar, in theology, etc. In short, what we today call a student.

Seigneur (*Seigneur*)   Someone who has land or a fief that gives him authority over subjects or vassals. The title *Seigneur* was given to honor a person who has rights and property, owing to his function or his rank.

Sovereign courts (*cours souveraines*)   Under the French monarchy, this was a sovereign jurisdiction without appeal, judging matters assigned to it by the king. Only the king or his council could nullify the judgments or decrees coming from these courts. The parlements were the principal sovereign courts of the realm.

Subornation (*subornation*)   Enticement by which someone causes someone to do something contrary to his duty. For example, one can induce someone to commit an unlawful act such as perjury; or one can conspire to suborn witnesses.

Subreption (*subreption*)   A silence about statements or facts that should have been expressed when applying or petitioning for something. Indeed, canon law requires that the true and just causes that lie behind the motive be stated in every request for a dispensation or grace.

Superiors (*supérieurs*)   The *Catéchisme des jésuites* refers frequently to "superiors" and to the hierarchy within the Society. What follows is very schematic: it focuses on the levels to which Pasquier refers. At the top of the hierarchical pyramid was the "superior general" (known as "the general"); he was elected for life and was the head of the entire Society. Below him came the "provincials," who administered one or another of the "provinces" into which the Jesuit world was divided. There was also the "rector," who supervised a college and carefully watched over each student or an important Jesuit community, like a professed house. Below these administrators came all the Jesuits who were slowly moving up the pyramid: novices; temporal coadjutors who did "low and humble services"; spiritual coadjutors who were devoting themselves to a life of ministry but did not expect to climb to the top of the pyramid; scholastics ("approved students") who were studying and who, depending on their success and the needs of the order, would become either a professed (of four vows) or a spiritual coadjutor (of three vows). This upward motion coincided with the various vows described by Pasquier in Book III, ch. 25.

Surprise (*surprise*)   To do something "by surprise" (*par surprise*) means to deceive someone or lead him into error. Thus one says: "Be suspicious of that man: he will surprise you." Or one says: "It is easy to surprise simple folk." Surprise also means to obtain something fraudulently, by artifice or by unusual ways: "he surprised a permit to print a book."

Troubles (*Troubles*)   A discreet way of referring to the turmoil of the French Religious Wars, especially the time when the Holy League was in power in Paris.

Étienne Pasquier
The Jesuits' Catechism or Their Doctrine Examined

∴

Book 1

CHAPTER 1

Wherein a Gentleman Opens His Country House to a Group of Weary Travelers

I, THE NARRATOR. About two years ago, leaving Paris, we encountered by chance, out in the fields, a group of six persons whom we were guiding, some of them to Rome, and others to Venice. Having journeyed for a week, and our horses being exhausted, one of our traveling companions told us that a gentleman with whom he had developed a friendship long ago resided nearby, and that he was sure the gentleman would consider it a great honor if we went to visit him and took refreshment. At first, some of us could not savor that idea, but it finally received the plurality of votes. We therefore left the road and headed for his house, where he was with several other gentlemen. And having seen his old friend, and having embraced him gaily several times, he spoke to his friend. THE GENTLEMAN. How can it be that I am now so fortunate as to see my other me?[1] You are most welcome here; I am much obliged to you for having unexpectedly laid siege to my house, and for bringing such good company with you. Each of us having thanked him, he ordered our horses stabled; and having drunk some of our wine,[2] he showed us through his house. We spent a delightful time there; and he ordered his domestics to serve supper early, so that we might rest. Meanwhile, we conversed about several things. But just as we usually place our hand on the sorest part of our body, we chiefly talked about the misfortunes taking place in France as a result of religious differences, each of us wanting to emphasize his individual passion, which he called devotion. Among us there was a carefully disguised Jesuit,[3] a man who certainly was very suitably attired; and there also was a lawyer,

---

1 *Un autre moy-mesme* (another myself) that is, a friend whom I love as dearly as myself.
2 Note the role that embracing, sharing wine, and making witty remarks played in early modern male hospitality.
3 Sutto, 85, proposes that Étienne Pasquier himself was the model for the Lawyer, and that Louis Richeome (1544–1625), a powerful Jesuit, was the inspiration for the disguised Jesuit. Richeome did in fact disguise his identity by signing some of his writings with an alias; and his humor made him stand out from other moralists of his day, just as the Jesuit's subtle mind sets him apart from the travelers portrayed here by Pasquier. See Henri Bremond, *Histoire littéraire du sentiment religieux en France, Vol. 1: L'humanisme dévot (1580–1660)* (Paris: Bloud and Gay, 1935), 1:48.

whom I found to be very well-versed about the papal bulls, the Constitutions,[4] and the rules of the Jesuit order. Now, as these comments were being passed from one person to another, the Jesuit put himself forward and led the discussion, showing how obligated our church was to the Society. THE JESUIT. Believe me, Messieurs, if God had not sent us good Father Ignatius and his companions, it would have been the end of our Catholic religion; but it usually happens that God, in order to chastise us for our sins, having afflicted a country with some widespread illness, subsequently sends remedies so that we will not lose after all. Having, therefore, permitted Martin Luther[5] to infect several nations with his venom, God wanted another Daniel[6] in his church, to protect its head from the venomous bites of that monster; and it seems that the name *Ignace Loyhola*[7] was not given to him casually, but miraculously. By changing a *C* into an *R*, posterity knew that, by his coming, he ended the ignorance of Luther and of those on whom that ignorance had subsequently grafted other heresies. *Ignace Loyhola*: *Ignare Loy hola*. This comment made everyone smile, for the Jesuit said it with such grace that no one could be offended, other than Monsieur the Lawyer, who spoke to him haughtily. THE LAWYER. I'll not allow those words to fall to the ground and not pick them up. I'd willingly learn about miracles wrought by the Jesuits, and what sort of plug they used to prevent

---

4   *The Constitutions of the Society of Jesus and Their Complementary Norms* (St. Louis, MO: Institute of Jesuit Sources, 1996). Henceforth, citations of the *Constitutions* will include not only the "part," "chapter," and so forth, but also, in parentheses, the page number in the printed edition.

5   Martin Luther (1483–1546), an Augustinian monk, was excommunicated in 1520. He founded the first major branch of the Protestant church: the "Evangelical" or Lutheran. See *Encyclopaedia Britannica*, https://www.britannica.com/biography/Martin-Luther (accessed February 4, 2021).

6   "Dan shall achieve justice for his people as one of the tribes of Israel. Let Dan be a serpent by the roadside, a horned viper by the path, that bites the horse's hoof so that the rider tumbles backward" (Gen. 49:16–17).

7   Pasquier's wordplay forced him to modify the name of Ignatius of Loyola (*c.*1491–1556), the co-founder of the Society of Jesus, called Ignacio de Loyola in Spanish. *Ignare* means "ignorant person"; *Loy* (pronounced "lwa") is the French word for law; and *Hola* (the letter *H* is silent in French: thus, O-la) is an interjection that is the equivalent to the English exclamation "Hey!" By changing the *C* of *Ignace* to an *R*, one therefore turns "Ignace" into "Ignorance," and Loyola becomes "Hey, law!" that is, "Ignorant Ignatius shouts 'Hey' to stop the law." In addition, the Jesuit emphasizes that Loyola was a nobleman: that is, he was called Ignace *de* Loyhola, not Ignace Loyhola. In reality, his original Basque name was Íñigo and he adopted the name of Ignatius during his studies in Paris. The Latin root of this name comes from "ignis" (fire). Loyola is the name of his noble family's castle in the municipality of Azpeitia. See Gabriel María Verd, "De Íñigo a Ignacio: El cambio de nombre en San Ignacio de Loyola," *Archivum historicum Societatis Iesu* 60 (1991): 113–60.

heresy from pouring out, and what the difference is between the behavior of the one and the other; for if the Huguenots caused Troubles for our France in 1561 by defending themselves,[8] the Jesuits stirred it up among us in 1585 by assailing us,[9] the latter Troubles being far more cruel and ferocious than the former. And as for your new anagram, you're going too far. Ignatius was a gentleman from Navarre,[10] from a good family, and he didn't go by the name Ignace Loyhola: he was Ignace *de* Loyhola, Ignatius *of* Loyola. And so, without any flattery, one could more appropriately call him Ignace de Loy hola. For, being as ignorant as possible, it would have been far more appropriate for him to remain silent than to speak. Wisely realizing this, he never displayed his wit by preaching, teaching, or writing, except in the beginning, when he taught the little children of Rome their *Credo*, as our schoolmasters do in elementary schools. These words stirred just as many chuckles as the first ones had. Our host said that he saw nothing here to laugh about; then he turned to the Jesuit. THE GENTLEMAN. Monsieur, your way of talking leads me to believe that you belong to the Society of Jesus. THE JESUIT replied that he did, and that his order was permitting him to disguise himself, in order to probe one another's humors more easily. THE GENTLEMAN. I'm very relieved about that, and I believe that some good angel brought you to my house; because for a long time, I've been wishing I would find myself in such good company, in order to know how things are going with your order, which I see is balancing equally between being greatly praised by some, and just as greatly blamed by others. But since this is not food for striplings, please let's clear the table and, after thanking God for what it has pleased him to give us each day, continue our discussion. Everyone did as requested; and all the young striplings having left the room, he begged the Jesuit not to disapprove if, as with the catechisms of our faith, the child be allowed to enter and question his schoolmaster, in order to learn the basic fundamentals. He did the same with the Jesuit, asking to be informed about the principal points of his order. THE JESUIT freely agreed. From what I

---

8   Pasquier is alluding to the Colloquy of Poissy, held in September of 1561, and the distur-
     bances connected to it.

9   By the summer of 1585, the League, that is, the Catholic party, had gained sufficient sup-
     port to impose its will on King Henry III (r.1574–89) and involve him in a war against his
     Calvinist successor, Henry of Navarre (r.1589–1610). See Julien Coudy, *The Huguenot Wars*
     (Philadelphia: Chilton, 1969), 261–64.

10   The castle of Loyola in Azpeitia was at that time a part of the Kingdom of Navarre, which
     was a disputed territory between Spain and France. Indeed, Loyola was wounded defend-
     ing Pamplona, its main city, from the French in May of 1521.

could gather from their conversation, THE GENTLEMAN knew as much as the Jesuit did; but by playing the role of Socrates, he got the other man to play the Platonic role, in order to draw out what he was seeking.[11]

---

11   Socrates (*c.*470–399 BCE) was an Athenian philosopher. His principal student was Plato (*c.*428–348 BCE). Socrates taught by means of what is called "Socratic debate," that is, a cooperative but argumentative dialogue between individuals, based on asking and answering questions that stimulate critical thinking and draw out ideas and underlying presumptions. Plato wrote approximately thirty dialogues, in most of which Socrates is the main character: these so-called "Platonic dialogues" became a literary genre. Strictly speaking, the term refers to works in which Socrates is a character. In short, by carefully planned questions, in Chapter 2, the Gentleman plans to draw out the Jesuit's ideas and underlying presumptions. This was not the only time that Pasquier was likened to Socrates. Antoine Loisel honored him by having him play the role of Socrates in the *Dialogue des avocats du Parlement de Paris* (Dialogue of the lawyers of the Parlement of Paris). Disseminated in 1603, Loisel's dialogue purportedly took place on three consecutive Sundays in 1602. It cannot be a coincidence that Pasquier's *Catéchisme* was published in 1602. In short, his aside about Socrates is a response to Loisel's compliment. Antoine Loisel, or Loysel (1536–1617), was a jurisconsult whose research enabled him to set down on paper the general principles of old French common law. For Pasquier, Loisel, Socrates, and the political context, see Nancy Lyman Roelker, *One King, One Faith: The Parlement of Paris and the Religious Reformation of the Sixteenth Century* (Berkeley: University of California Press, 1996), 93, 116, 135.

CHAPTER 2

The Plan of the Society of Jesus, Whom Ordinary Folks Call Jesuits

THE GENTLEMAN. You say that you are Jesuits, that is, a new religious order. THE JESUIT. But it is very old, and it is the cause for which we have taken, as ours, the holy name of the Society of Jesus, as imitators, above all others, of Our Lord Jesus Christ, and of his apostles. THE GENTLEMAN. You preach, and you also teach literature free of charge to any student who wishes to hear you. THE JESUIT. Yes. THE GENTLEMAN. Did the apostles teach youths? THE JESUIT. Nay, nay. THE GENTLEMAN. You therefore have a great advantage over the apostles; and it's not without reason that, disdaining the name Christian, as they called themselves, you have people call you Jesuits. THE JESUIT. If they had taught, as we do, their charity would have accomplished more; and as for the name Christian, we deemed it too lofty. THE GENTLEMAN. In that, you surpass them in charity and humility. Don't you take the three vows: chastity, poverty, and obedience? THE JESUIT. Don't doubt it. THE GENTLEMAN. So, you are monks. THE JESUIT. Not at all, we are religious. THE GENTLEMAN. So, you reside in monasteries. THE JESUIT. Far from it: we call the places we live houses, and in them one finds our churches. THE GENTLEMAN. What sort of special mystery is this, that these messieurs, who take ordinary vows and who officiate like other religious, disdain the holy names of monks and monasteries that venerable antiquity honored so devoutly? To be accurate, you should call your houses God's houses; but I believe you are aware of that, because we use the word hospitals for the houses of God that shelter poor beggars; and if I'm not going too far, you fear nothing as much being poor. Do you at least wear the cowl and dwell in cloisters like other religious? THE JESUIT. We are not familiar with cloisters, and we avoid them like sewers, which we do not want to enter; and we do not dress like monks, but like secular priests. It is true that, in accordance with our first Institute[1] we fastened the collars of our long robes, sometimes with a pointed lacing known as an *aiguillette*, and sometimes with a clip; but we soon gave up that custom, after our cause was pleaded in 1564

---

[1]   *Institut* (institute): manner of living in a religious community according to a certain rule. The constitutions given to a religious order at the time of its establishment, DAF, 1694. For the Jesuit Institute, see *Constitutions*, 3–16.

against the University of Paris.[2] Because the heretics used to say that (like a fishhook) our clip was for catching the belongings of idiot souls; and others were even more insulting, saying that we wore an *aiguillette* like the ladies of the *Castel Vert* in Toulouse.[3] THE GENTLEMAN. For the honor I bear you, I'd like us not to reawaken the memory of your old quarrels. Let's leave those bad remarks to the bad-mouthed, and let's show no ill will[4] about everything that involves your order. For I desire nothing so much as to see you on good terms with everyone; though being in religion, you've given up the monk's habit and everything external about monks; yet as far as the interior is concerned,[5] for example fasting and not eating meat, as other orders do in order to mortify the flesh, I have no doubt that you observe that. THE JESUIT. Just the opposite: our statutes expressly forbid us to mortify the flesh, but it is left to our personal devotions, in which there is great merit.[6] THE GENTLEMAN. That consideration deserves some respect; but believe me, those who leave Lent for each person to arbitrate, would create great inconsistencies. That is why, in other religious groups, the first founders wanted it, judging that the general law was wiser than the individual will of one or another religious. As for the processions that the church has honored ever since Antiquity (for it seems that they were even held in the days of Tertullian[7]), I believe that you want to participate, without fail. THE JESUIT. You are not even close about what we approve; for on the contrary, our Constitutions forbid us to be present at processions, and those Constitutions were later approved by

---

2   Pasquier participated in the pleading of 1564.

3   The *Complainte de l'Université* described Jesuits as "men with clasps, for their clasps will catch your possessions by their subornation." An *aiguillette*, was a shoelace-like cord used to attach one part of a man's garb to another. There is sexual innuendo here: "running the *aiguillette*" meant being a prostitute; impotence was attributed to a tightly-tied *aiguillette*; and the "Green Castle" (*Castel Vert*) was a brothel created by the city fathers of Toulouse; Sutto, 125nn1–3.

4   In this sentence, the Gentleman, via Pasquier, plays with the prefixes *mis-* (or *mes-*), and *mal-*: *mesdisance* (detraction), *malebouche* (dirty mouth) and *maltalent* (ill will).

5   For "exterior" and "interior" among Jesuits, see Louis Lallemant, *Spiritual Doctrine*, ed. and trans. Patricia Ranum (Chestnut Hill, MA: Institute of Jesuit Sources, 2016), espec. 113–15, 171–77.

6   "The chastisement of the body ought not be immoderate or indiscreet in abstinences, vigils, and other external penances and labors which cause harm and prevent greater goods," *Constitutions*, part III, ch. 2 (p. 127).

7   Quintus Septimus Florens Tertullian (*c*.155–*c*.240), known simply as Tertullian, was a prolific early Christian theologian. See *Encyclopaedia Britannica*, https://www.britannica.com/biography/Tertullian (accessed February 4, 2021).

Pope Gregory XIII.[8] THE GENTLEMAN. If I understand correctly, you aren't on the faculty of the University of Paris; but if you had registered in 1564, as you wanted to, would you have failed to attend the rector's processions, in which the four mendicant orders and other religious participated?[9] THE JESUIT. Yes. THE GENTLEMAN. But if some solemn procession had taken place in Paris, as when the reliquary chest of Saint Genevieve[10] is taken down in order to appease God's wrath, and all the parishes and all the monasteries are present, as well as the sovereign law courts followed by an infinite number of people, you wouldn't have attended? THE JESUIT. No. THE GENTLEMAN. Don't you greatly respect the Council of Trent? THE JESUIT. Yes, great respect, for the council confirmed our order despite all its enemies. THE GENTLEMAN. Don't you know that this council states explicitly: *Quod tam clerici seculares, quam regulares, quicumque etiam Monachi, ad publicas Processiones vocati, accedere compelluntur, his tantum exceptis qui strictiore clausura perpetua vivunt.*[11] You aren't included in this exception, for it seems to me that it was written for the Carthusians and the Celestines.[12] THE JESUIT. I realize that: but you must know that we have dispensations that were issued by Gregory XIII in 1576, to the detriment of the Council of Trent, which not only gave us a dispensation

---

8   Gregory XIII (1502–85), born Ugo Boncompagni, was pope from 1572 to his death. He is best known for commissioning the "Gregorian" calendar that was carried out under the leadership of the Jesuit Christopher Clavius (1538–1612). He was one of the more original and constructive popes of the sixteenth century and influenced religious life in Europe and missionary activity overseas. Sympathetic to the Jesuits, he sponsored the Collegio Romano founded by Ignatius, which today bears his name, the Gregorian University. See *Encyclopaedia Britannica*, https://www.britannica.com/biography/Gregory-XIII (accessed February 4, 2021).

9   The participants in such processions included principals, regents, teachers, and recipients of scholarships, plus twelve students selected from each of the colleges of the University of Paris.

10 Genevieve (c.422–512) was patron saint of Paris. In 451, she saved Paris by diverting Attila's Huns away from the city. The principal procession in her honor was held each year on her feast day, October 19, but processions were also organized when calamity threatened. See Moshe Sluhovsky, *Patroness of Paris: Rituals of Devotion in Early Modern France* (Leiden: Brill, 1998), 122–23. Cf. Book III, ch. 20 below.

11 Council of Trent, Session XXV, decree 7: "And all exempted persons whatsoever, as well Secular as Regular clerics, and even monks, on being summoned to public processions, shall be obliged to attend; those only being excepted who always live in more strict enclosure"; http://www.thecounciloftrent.com/ch25.htm (accessed January 25, 2021).

12 Founded in 1264 by Pietro da Morone, born Pietro Angelerio (1215–96) and pope for a few months in 1294 under the name of Celestine V, the austere order known as the Celestines was introduced into France circa 1380. It became extinct in the eighteenth century. See Robert L. J. Shaw, *The Celestine Monks of France, c. 1350–1450: Observant Reform in an Age of Schism, Council and War* (Amsterdam: Amsterdam University Press, 2018).

but also forbade some very specific things. THE GENTLEMAN. Yet you were not there prior to that dispensation. On what do you base your privilege? THE JESUIT. On our being assured that we shall obtain it one day. THE GENTLE-MAN. Spirited horses are always lodged in a separate stable. Are you a religious like that, among other religious? Pray tell me, as if in the confessional: why were you forbidden to do those things? THE JESUIT. Since you conjure up that holy word, the confessional, I shall tell you truthfully. Some of our superiors got someone to insert into Pope Gregory's bulls that it was in order that we not be distracted from our preaching, teaching, and hearing confessions: yet, seeing that the four mendicant orders were preaching and hearing confessions, as we do; that they were teaching their faithful, and were only abandoning that in order to be present at processions, I thought they had come up with a rather inappropriate pretext, a pretext based on some other cause that, according to the ceremonies of our order, would have had us marching at the tail end of the procession. In so doing, we would have done great wrong to the splendor of the Society of Jesus, which we think superior to all the others. THE GENTLEMAN. If that's so, your holy devotion isn't without some heat of ambition. Let's move on. When you say your canonical hours in your churches, don't you sing them aloud in two rows, as we do in ours? Don't you too have a place for your priests who are officiating, a place called the choir that is distinct and separate from the nave where the people must remain in order to say their prayers. THE JESUIT. To that I can reply by heart, reciting the text of our Constitutions: *Non utantur nostri choro, ad horas canonicas, vel Missas, aut alia offica decantanda.*[13] And indeed, if you looked at the church of our Paris house, there was no choir. THE GENTLEMAN. Perhaps your law-giver meant that you were so privileged, that even if your prayers and meditations were done without heart and without devotion, but only as lip-service, they would still be heard by God, in order to annex this privilege to your extraordinary ones. THE JESUIT. You are mocking me. Besides, I'm telling you that as far as the canonical hours are concerned, nothing obliges us to do what others do; but we can say the canonical hours softly, if it pleases us. THE GENTLEMAN. Our ancestors must have been great dunces, since devout souls today celebrate the divine office in a totally different fashion than in the past. And as for anniversaries, do you celebrate them on behalf of the person who gave you some possession as alms? THE JESUIT. We willingly accept the alms given to us, but for all that, we are not obliged to celebrate anniversaries.[14] THE GENTLEMAN. You aren't so foolish.

---

13   "They will not regularly hold choir for the canonical hours or sung Masses and offices," *Constitutions*, part VI, ch. 3, 4 (p. 256).

14   *Constitutions*, part VI, ch. iii, 6 (p. 258).

THE JESUIT. We are very wise and very devout. For we do not want to resemble the others, who undertake to talk so much about it, that they let it pass as a *fidelium*, as the well-known French saying goes.[15] In sum, we would be very conscientious about deceiving our benefactors. THE GENTLEMAN. Here's a new church that is the exact opposite of the ancient one. You told me earlier that you observe the three vows: poverty, chastity, and obedience. That, at least, centers on the many novelties that separate you from us. You have those three vows that are shared by the other religious orders. THE JESUIT. We call the first one a simple[16] vow, and the other two are solemn[17] vows. THE GENTLEMAN. Pray explain your doctrine about this: for to tell the truth, it's High German to me.[18] THE JESUIT. You must understand that, in each of these three vows, we profess poverty, chastity, and obedience, as they do in other orders. True, it is rather special for a first vow: because as much and for as long as we are settled in the order, we can possess temporal goods and can receive inheritances, by either direct descent or collaterally.[19] Moreover, as far as the religious are concerned, they lack the power to leave our Society, even after ten, twenty, or thirty years, or more, or less. Our general is permitted to absolve a religious and send him away, and to have him renounce his vow in order to marry, if he wishes. THE GENTLEMAN. Good Lord! What sort of a vow is that? THE JESUIT. One that Pope Gregory confirmed for us; and I don't find it strange, because Navarrus,[20] the foremost of all the doctors on the subject of canon law, refers to this simple vow and calls it great and marvelous. THE GENTLEMAN. But he should have said that it was quite miraculous, all the more so since it puts wealth and poverty under one and the same subject, something that is impossible according to the common course of nature. And what surprises me

---

15   He seems to be referring to the phrase, *passer par un fidelium* (pass by a *fidelium*) that is, do something quickly. This proverb refers to monks who, unable to carry out all the Masses founded in their church, end with a *fidelium*, which is the last phrase recited for the dead. See *Dictionnaire françois et latin* (Paris: Delaune, 1743), 1761.

16   *Constitutions*, part v, ch. iv (p. 206).

17   *Constitutions*, part v, ch. ii, 3 (pp. 198–200); and part v, ch. iii, 1–6 (pp. 254–58).

18   This is the equivalent of "It's all Greek to me." Indeed, the men participating in Pasquier's imaginary dialog presumably possessed at least a smattering of Greek.

19   *Constitutions*, "General Examen," ch. IV, 3, (pp. 34–35); part III, i, 7–9, pp. 112–15; and part VI, art. ii, 11–12 (p. 236).

20   Martín de Azpilcueta (1491–1586), Francis Xavier's cousin, also known as Doctor Navarrus, was an important Spanish canonist and theologian. See Wim Decock, "Martín de Azpilcueta," in *Great Christian Jurists in Spanish History*, ed. Rafael Domingo and Javier Martínez-Torrón (Cambridge: Cambridge University Press, 2018), 116–32. Azpilcueta's manual for confessors had been very popular among Jesuits and recommended by the official Jesuit *Directory to Spiritual Exercises* of 1599. See Book III, ch. 25 below.

more, is that your general can dismiss that religious when he sees fit. This had never before been practiced in our Christian religion. THE JESUIT. And Jesuits alone are permitted to do this. THE GENTLEMAN. But what is your second vow, the one you call solemn and which is, I think, the first of your two solemn vows? THE JESUIT. We bring nothing new beyond a simple vow, except that once our religious has entered the order, he loses all hope of inheriting and of returning to his family, and he is reduced to being like all other professed religious. THE GENTLEMAN. Before moving on to the great solemn vow, which is the third vow, I want you to tell me about some other peculiarities of your order. You teach humane letters, philosophy, and theology, not only to your brethren but also to all those foreign students who give themselves to you. I've no doubt that everyone who enters your Society is also destined for study. For charity begins at home, and also with making priests: this must be your intention, they must have studied. THE JESUIT. You are exaggerating. We take in an infinite number who do not know how to read or write, who are temporal coadjutors destined to tend to our household work, if need be. THE GENTLE-MAN. Voluntarily, as with Oblates[21] and converted monks from other orders, who are only half-monks and whom the populace calls *boute-culs*, "bump rumps." THE JESUIT. You keep exaggerating. Our temporal coadjutors[22] are true religious who belong to our order, just as the others do who make the simple vow or the first solemn vow. THE GENTLEMAN. And yet they profess to be ignorant, like *gli frati ignoranti* of Italy.[23] THE JESUIT. That is indeed the case. THE GENTLEMAN. What a bizarre order yours is, being composed of so many assorted pieces. Good God, all those good old doctors of theology who in their holiness chat among beatified souls, what would they say if they now had to send people back into the world, and if they saw this family of religious reign in the midst of our church? Now go on! Please talk about that great solemn vow, your final one. THE JESUIT. This one marks the fulfillment of our work; for by this vow, in addition to the three substantial vows of all the other orders, we make a fourth one to the Holy Father, which we call the Mission vow, by which, if it pleases his Holiness to send us to the lands of the Turks, pagans, heretics, schismatics in order to convert them, or reduce them to our Christian faith, we

---

21   Laymen who had withdrawn to a religious community and who ceded their possessions to the community. Many of them were old soldiers who were lodged and cared for at an abbey. See Sutto, 129n23.

22   *Constitutions*, "General Examen," ch. VI, 3–4 (pp. 49–50).

23   This name was given to the Hospitalers of St-Jean-de-Dieu, founded by Saint João de Deus (1495–1550). They would be introduced into France by Marie de' Medici (1575–1642), the wife of Henry IV, in the early seventeenth century. See *Catholic Encyclopedia*, https://www.newadvent.org/cathen/02802b.htm (accessed February 5, 2021).

are obliged to obey him without debating, even without taking gold or silver to defray our journey.[24] THE GENTLEMAN. A beautiful and holy devotion, if it can be put to use: but what trustworthy recollections do you have, to bear sure witness to your exploits? THE JESUIT. It suffices that one be content in Rome. As soon as this great vow is made, which is the final vow, we begin to be called Father. That title is not borne by the others, yet there is so much humility among us that as soon as we are made a father, we adopt a poverty so strict that we cannot possess any real property, either in general or in particular, but are obliged to beg our livelihood at houses, not by the intervention of converse brothers, as other mendicant orders do, but by our most outstanding fathers.[25] THE GENTLEMAN. That's an inimitable vow. In addition, the more you are magnified above your brethren, the more submissiveness and poverty you bring. But you who call yourselves Jesuits, as true imitators of the apostles, do you think that the apostles professed begging? You may think so, but that opinion has been condemned by the church. THE JESUIT. Do you find it blameworthy that, from an abundance of new zeal, we have added something to their ancient charity? THE LAWYER. That question is inappropriate (excuse me for interrupting you), for you've never seen Jesuits carry a beggar's purse in the streets. THE JESUIT. We are in no worse condition than the birds who live by God's grace, God who distributes his manna wherever he pleases, as he did long ago to the children of Israel.[26] THE GENTLEMAN. You pay us in very fine money, and I accept it, since it pleases you. Do you remain within the limits of your three vows: poverty, chastity, obedience? THE JESUIT. Nay, nay. For we do not want, as atheists want, to separate the affairs of state and the affairs of religion; and we think that everything works out for the glory of God and the salvation of our souls, when they are joined together. THE GENTLEMAN. What droll new doctrine are you stating now? For to tell the truth, nothing ever was better: we learn from Optatus[27] that religion was in the state, not the state in religion. Each of us should wish that those who manipulate the reins of the republic will bring religion to it, that is to say, faith and integrity, and will not

---

24   *Constitutions*, part VIII, ch. 1 (p. 316).

25   *Constitutions*, part VI, ch. ii, 3, 4, 5, 10 (pp. 228–34).

26   Exodus 16:13–36.

27   Saint Optatus (*c.*320–392), bishop of Milevis in Numidia, is remembered for his writings against Donatism. The phrase is from "De schismate Donatistarum adversus Permenium," in Jacques-Paul Migne, ed., *Patriologia Latina*, vol. 11 (Paris: Vrayer, 1845), col. 999: "Non enim republic est in ecclesia, sed ecclesia in respublica est, id est, in imperio romano." This maxim was a favorite of Gallican jurists like Pasquier. See Jotham Parsons, *The Church in the Republic: Gallicanism and Political Ideology in Renaissance France* (Washington, DC: The Catholic University of America Press, 2005), 8.

easily amuse their consciences in order to favor their business. But that a religious order might manipulate the affairs of state while praying and meditating,
that is a great irreligion or, to be more accurate, a heresy. THE JESUIT. What
you are saying was Optatus's opinion, not the opinion of our Ignatius. THE
GENTLEMAN. But what is your reply to Saint Paul, when he says: *Nemo militans
Deo, implicat se negotiis secularibus.*[28] Also, if it's done well, why have you, for
the past few years, forbidden your brethren to be more involved in it? THE
JESUIT. It was merely a statute of the time. For in order to return to grace, we
drew up that constitution[29] at the end of 1593, at a time when, counter to our
hopes, all of France was yearning for peace; but don't think that this put us on
a firm footing. For the same Constitutions permit us to believe, individually,
what the occasion makes seem advisable.[30] THE GENTLEMAN. That's a terrifying permission. But what do you understand by the expression affairs of state?
THE JESUIT. The day would not be long enough for me to tell you. Be satisfied
that the greatest and most assured advice that we can follow is our conscience,
which we know is guided by Our Lord's hand. And on that footing, let us sometimes stir up kingdoms, and let us chastise kings and princes who, we think, are
lying in the wrong place, all for the glory and honor of God and of his holy
church. THE GENTLEMAN. All of Christendom is marvelously indebted to you,
and I'm dismayed that you aren't so ungrateful as to have annulled this holy
law. THE JESUIT. It is not paid for in that fashion, it lives only and always in our
souls. During the past three years, we failed to kill the Queen of England and
Count Maurice of Nassau.[31] Those were two coups that unfortunately did not
succeed, and when opportunities present themselves, we are ready to try them
again, there and wherever we choose. THE GENTLEMAN. You therefore mix up
affairs of state, murders and assassinations. Is that what you call joining

---

28   "To satisfy the one who recruited him, a soldier does not become entangled in the busi-
     ness affairs of life" (2 Tim. 2:4).

29   He is alluding to the *Decreta, canones, censurae et praecepta congregationum generalium
     Societatis Jesu*, 2 vols., published much later by François Seguin (Avignon: Ex typographia
     Francisci Seguin, 1838), 1:346–48. At that time, Henri IV converted to Catholicism and a
     general truce was declared.

30   *Constitutions*, part VI, v (p. 268).

31   See Sutto's introduction, 71n277. The target was Maurice of Orange-Nassau (1567–1625),
     the son of William the Silent. It appears that the would-be assassin's correct name was
     Peter Panne. He was a barrel-maker (*tonnellier*) from Ypres. Panne was executed for hav-
     ing plotted an assassination at the instigation of the Jesuits of Douai. See Jean de Serres,
     Inventaire général de l'histoire de France, 2 vols. (Paris: Compagnie des Libraires, 1658), 1:867.
     Cf. Cesare Cuttica, "Tyrannicide and Political Authority in the Long Sixteenth Century,"
     in Henrik Lagerlund and Benjamin Hill, eds., *Routledge Companion to Sixteenth-Century
     Philosophy* (New York: Routledge, 2017), 265–92, here 273. See Book III, ch. 1 and 20 below.

together the state and religion? THE JESUIT. Have you any doubts? Heresy is a sickness on which one must use fire and the iron, just as empirics[32] are used on sick people who are thought to be incurable. THE GENTLEMAN. You couldn't choose more suitable terms than to compare your order with the empiric physicians who've been condemned by the faculty of medicine. Using fire and the iron against a heretic is the duty of the magistrate (in whose hands God placed the sword in order to chastise the punishable), but it's not the duty of you other messieurs the religious, who have another calling. THE JESUIT. And who would the magistrate be, who dares to try kings, if not us, inspired with the grace of the blessed Holy Spirit? THE GENTLEMAN. Is that a part of your first Institute? THE JESUIT. We added it by right of Christian decorum, in order to help our neighbor. And in order to show you how piously we proceed: whenever our holy exhortations win over some good man to carry out our plans, before he leaves we hear his confession and we use a part of the confession to confirm him in that holy undertaking, making him hear Mass devoutly, administering the Blessed Sacrament of the Altar to him, so that he can go straight to heaven. Was there ever a holier and more meritorious way than that? For in the end, it defends and protects our Christian church? THE GENTLEMAN. Oh, truly Christian Society! But I wanted to know why Our Lord Jesus Christ, when arrested, became so bitterly angry with Saint Peter, who had cut off Malchus's ear: for while we are on the subject of the greatest merit, it at first appeared that the sword couldn't be used. THE JESUIT. You are right, but you are forgetting the clever word: Our Lord did not forbid Saint Peter to grasp the sword, but well after the cut, he ordered him to sheathe his sword. THE GENTLEMAN. Excuse me, this reply smacks of Machiavelli.[33] THE JESUIT. In addition, Saint Peter, driven by an indiscreet zeal, wanted to prevent a mystery that should not involve the redemption of mankind; and we use the sword for the

---

32   Empiric medicine was based upon an educated guess rather than a confirmed diagnosis. Empiric physicians abounded in France at the time. See Sutto, 132n36.

33   Niccolò Machiavelli (1469–1527) was secretary in the Chancery of the Republic of Florence, 1498–1512, when the Medici were out of power. He wrote his best-known work, *The Prince (Il Principe)* in 1513, when exiled from city affairs. He described immoral behavior as being effective in politics. Indeed, the book was said to teach evil recommendations to tyrants to help them remain in power. Machiavelli's book gave rise to an "-ism": a negative term that characterizes unscrupulous politicians. In spite of being often charged with Machiavelism, important Jesuits wrote treatises that were anti-Machiavellian in nature, like those by Pedro de Ribadeneyra (1527–1611), Robert Bellarmine (1542–1621), and Giovanni Botero (1544–1617), who left the Society in 1580. See Keith David Howard, *The Reception of Machiavelli in Early Modern Spain* (Cambridge: Cambridge University Press, 2014) and the special issue of the *Journal of Jesuit Studies*, "Jesuits as Counsellors in the Early Modern World," ed. Harald E. Braun, *Journal of Jesuit Studies* 4 (2017): 175–289.

manutention[34] of the church, without which mankind would perish. THE
GENTLEMAN. Oh, beautiful and holy explanation! But is it your opinion that
this way pleases God? THE JESUIT. Only the heretics of our day doubt it. THE
GENTLEMAN. I'm not a heretic, nor have I ever wanted to be one, yet I'm very
dubious. Is there nothing in your statutes that orders you to disregard the contrary opinion? THE JESUIT. Yes. THE GENTLEMAN. And what is it? THE JESUIT.
The general of our order, to whom we vow blind obedience (that is the exact
word employed in our Constitutions),[35] and to whom we are supposed to bind
our consciences; to let ourselves be manipulated by him, like a staff that has no
movement other than the movement given by the persons who are holding it;
to drop everything we are doing in order to obey him, and to recognize in him
the presence of Our Lord Jesus Christ, as if it were his command. THE GENTLE-
MAN. Does that apply to your order? THE JESUIT. Every word is true. THE
GENTLEMAN. Oh, admirable and paradoxical obedience, which conforms to
the obedience of our Abraham![36] THE JESUIT. And it is also the example that
Ignatius always had on the tip of his tongue, teaching us that obedience was
more agreeable to God than a sacrifice. THE GENTLEMAN. Oh, blessed Jesuit
fathers, indeed, true and unique patriarchs of our church! And truly, it's not
without reason that you take the title Father after fulfilling your third vow.
However, if your general ordered you to have someone killed (I won't say a
prince, for I don't believe that you would obey), if the Holy Father ordered it,
would you do it? THE JESUIT. I would ask for a day to think about it. THE GEN-
TLEMAN. If you asked for that, your conscience would no longer be bound to
his: and in addition, your statute robs you of your leisure to think about it.[37]
THE JESUIT. You have caught me unprepared, so at the very least I am asking
to delay my reply. THE GENTLEMAN. Your order being founded on all these
pious and holy resolutions, our church certainly owes you a great deal: I mean
not only the ancient doctors of the church, and the apostles themselves, to
whom you teach what would have come from the abundance of their duty.
What? I'm talking about the apostles. But also, this great seigneur, who should
be the model for all our actions when, contrary to the specific command that
he gave Saint Peter, you want to have kings and princes killed. But what was
your reward? THE JESUIT. Everything we could desire or hope for, because we
are permitted to give absolution for all sins and faults, no matter how

---

34   *Manutention* (manutention): the total conservation of something. It almost always refers
      to moral things: the manutention of decrees, the manutention of privileges, DAF 1694.
35   *Constitutions*, part VI, ch. I (p. 222).
36   This is an allusion to the testing of Abraham, recounted in Gen. 22:1–19.
37   *Constitutions*, part VI, ch. I, I (pp. 220–23).

enormous they may be, even those that are reserved for the Holy See; and for all these results of sentences, censures, ecclesiastical punishments, save for what is included in the papal bull that customarily is read in Rome on Absolution Thursday.[38] And for everything mentioned above, to order whatever penance we please, such as works of piety; pilgrimage vows, except for three places, Jerusalem, Rome, and Santiago de Compostela; singing Mass before daylight as well as after noon, when our superiors find it necessary; confessing and administering the Blessed Sacrament of the Eucharist; building chapels, oratories, churches wherever our general wants them: all of this without asking bishops or curates for permission. Going through the countryside, carrying portable altars in order to celebrate Mass everywhere, even in the places forbidden by the Holy See. No bishop in his diocese can issue a priesthood order to any of our brethren, even though he wears the habit, unless he has *lettres de dimissoire* from our general. We can also dispense forbidden foods without being obligated to appease the bishops and absolve the censures of all those tainted by heresy. THE GENTLEMAN. What a lot of privileges you've been granted, prejudicial, first, to the bishops and then to the curates, and even to the Holy See itself. In addition, all of this has a great charm that attracts the common people to you, and that distracts them from their true, natural, and legitimate shepherds, and which consists of introducing a sort of new schism in our church. THE JESUIT. The person who comes every year to make his devotions in our houses for an entire day will get a plenary indulgence for all his sins, and he merely says an *Our Father* and a *Hail Mary*. THE GENTLEMAN. Another bit of bait for hunting you down. THE JESUIT. We enjoy all the privileges issued to the four mendicant orders. THE GENTLEMAN. They have reason to be angry: you, gorged with possessions up to your ears, benefit from their privileges. THE JESUIT. If that took place, all the other religious orders would have their indults and their grants. THE GENTLEMAN. And yet you are in no way obliged to observe their vows and abstinences. That's putting things out of proportion, for the Lawyer here will tell you that the jurisconsults of yore teach: *Secundum naturam esse, ut quem sequuntur commoda, eundem sequantur*

---

38   He is referring to the bull *In coena Domini*, which contains a series of general excommunications that were fulminated in Rome each year on Holy Thursday, aimed at persons who had committed certain infractions and for which only the pope could give absolution; most European monarchs, even the most Catholic, objected to it as impinging on secular affairs and it was discontinued for that reason in 1770. See the English translation of the bull, https://archive.org/stream/ThePapalBullInCoenaDomini/ThePapalBullInCoenaDomini_ djvu.txt (accessed January 19, 2021).

incommoda.[39] And to tell the truth, it's also a new subject for jealousy and discontent between you and them. THE JESUIT. Everything I stated above concerns the divine service; what I am going to tell you now concerns our colleges and our lectures.[40] It is lawful for our general, or for the person to whom he has given power, to build colleges, create lectureships in the faculty of theology, and in all the other faculties in every city, without the authorization of the bishops; and our brethren can, in the universities or outside them, take bachelor's degrees, licenses, master's degrees, doctorates, having taken the examination and having been deemed capable by two or three persons whom our superiors have assigned, without having to seek out the chancellors or the rectors of the other universities. In stronger terms, we can have entire universities composed solely of our brethren, where there is a chancellor and a rector who are Jesuits, as we see in the city of Pont-à-Mousson. Moreover, we are permitted to practice medicine with the permission of our superiors, if they deem us capable. THE GENTLEMAN. And you have no one but them to vouch for you, although they haven't been brought up to be physicians? THE JESUIT. Nay, nay. THE GENTLEMAN. I supposed that your general had the power to make a Jesuit, but not a physician, and I wouldn't want to put my life in your hands on the basis of that title. This is a terrifying division between you other messieurs and the universities, and even between that great, famous, and ancient University of Paris. THE JESUIT. What else? We can excise, correct, and reform all sorts of books where we find the least suspicion of heresy. THE GENTLEMAN. Even if the faculty of theology didn't? THE JESUIT. Yes. THE GENTLEMAN. I'd always heard that this was their particular prey, and that it didn't belong to anyone else. THE JESUIT. Do you think we should take any of that into account? Long ago, in the infancy of our Society, we learned to scorn it. Then, in 1554, the faculty censured us, just when we were beginning to blossom; but we soon took revenge, because we caused that censure to be censured by the Spanish Inquisition. *Porrò in Hispania* (said one of our courageous historiographers) *quod Sorbonense decretum esset contra sacrosanctam sedis Apostolicae authoritatem, à qua Religio nostra probata et confirmata est, fidei quaesitores, illud*

---

39   A variant of this text reads: *Secundum naturam est, commoda cujusque rei eum sequi, quem sequentur incommoda.* See Sutto, 134n47. The expression, used by lawyers, means that he who has the benefit of the thing should also have the burden.

40   The text refers to *lecteurs*, and *lectures*. The root of these words can refer to either "readers" and "readings," or to "lecturers" and "lectures." Cotgrave's *Dictionarie* of 1611 defined *lecteurs* as "public readers," "professor," while DAF, 1694, indicates that the word denotes "preceptors" or "doctors who teach theology, law and so forth."

tanquam, falsum et quod pias aures offenderet, suo decreto legi prohibuerunt.[41]
THE GENTLEMAN. You say that you subjected to the Inquisition this fair and holy Faculty of Theology of Paris, that old buttress, that moral support, that resource of our Catholic, Apostolic, Roman Church, and you turned it into a trophy! THE JESUIT. Do not be scandalized about that: for if need be, we would attack the pope, if we found him straying ever so little from his ancient duty. Some time after the accession of King Henri IV to the crown (we called him *le Béarnais*, the fellow from Béarn), we were of the opinion that Pope Sixtus V[42] turned away everyone who was in favor of him; and God knowns we spared him in our pulpits, even though some wanted to make people believe that we had given him a poison that was shortening his life. THE GENTLEMAN. You wouldn't pardon the pope? You, who are his creatures, you who get your power from him! If that's the case, I'll quit the whole party and shut up. I'd merely like to have some Gneus Flavius[43] between us, so as to unveil your secrets to France, where another Tacitus wrote about them with the same liberty as you are. The Lawyer had been silent until then, but now he broke his silence. THE LAWYER. You can be as silent as you please; but I, who will be the Gneus Flavius you are hoping for, I won't be silent. For he revealed to the Romans the perfumes that the pontiffs were selling them so dearly: in recognition of which he was made tribune of the people, that is to say, conservator of popular liberty. In like manner I wish to unveil, bit by bit, the doctrine that the Jesuits have previously sold us for its weight in gold. And I'm assured that one day our posterity, which isn't ungrateful, and which will find, written down, the things I'm telling you, will

---

41   "Furthermore, it was decided in Spain that the decree of the Sorbonne was against the holy authority of the Apostolic See, by which our order had been approved and confirmed to faith seekers, this was false and offensive to pious ears by a decree law prevented." Toledo-born Ribadeneyra was admitted to the Society of Jesus in 1540 before he turned fourteen. In his long life, he held important administrative positions and was a very prolific writer. His most important work is his life of Loyola (1572), from which the above citation comes. See *DHCJ*, 4:3345–46.

42   Sixtus V (1521–90), born Felice Piergentile, was elected pope in 1585. As a youth he displayed talents as a scholar and preacher. During his pontificate, he rooted out lawlessness across Rome and launched a costly rebuilding program. He unsuccessfully strove to quash Protestant rulers by means of excommunications. See Casimiro Liborio Tempesti, *Storia della vita e geste di Sisto Quinto: Sommo pontefice dell'Ordine de' minori conventuali di San Francesco* (London: Forgotten Books, 2018).

43   Gnaeus Flavius (*fl.* 4th century BCE), the son of a freedman, rose to the office of aedile in the Roman Republic. As secretary to a powerful consul, he gained knowledge of Roman law and published an account of legal procedures. The Lawyer is equating himself with this Roman of Antiquity. See *Encyclopaedia Britannica,* https://www.britannica.com/biography/Gnaeus-Flavius (accessed February 5, 2021).

consider me the protector of the liberties of our Gallican Church.[44] And subsequently it shall transpire that, just as the Ancients made a proverb about of their Gneus Flavius, saying that *Cornicum oculos confixerat*,[45] they will say of me that I crushed the eyes of the crows who feed on the cadavers and rotting flesh of other animals; and the Jesuits feed not only on carcasses, but on the finest revenue of our families. And in order not to keep you longer in suspense, I say, and I maintain, that no sect ever had a more dangerous effect on our Christian religion than this one. And as such, it was condemned, first in Rome and then in France. But I'll begin with France, to which I think I have more of an obligation, because it produced me. This first step by the Lawyer kept us on our guard; for until then, some of us had been dozing. Having heard this bold promise, the Narrator[46] spoke up. THE NARRATOR. I've been mute until now, when I see you on the point of taking up arms to assassinate this holy Society. The chance to talk comes to me as it did to the son of Croesus, when some persons were trying to murder his father.[47] If you're the Gneus Flavius of the Jesuits, I'll be the Tacitus, and I'll faithfully set down in writing everything I hear you say. I've always believed that the Society was one of the surest bulwarks of our Catholic religion, and to me it seems highly impious to want to

---

44   "Men of letters and savants tended to be Gallican in spirit," notes Robert Schneider, who proceeds to sketch the intellectual circle in which Étienne Pasquier was flourishing: "Gallicanism is probably the most overlooked aspect of the intellectual and religious history of the seventeenth century. Traditional accounts emphasize Gallican elements in the precincts of the university, the parlement, or the clergy, for these were corporate bodies formally threatened by ultramontanism, and in particular by the Tridentine Reforms and the Society of Jesus. But it was the cause of men of letters and savants as well. And for good reason: with their fear of Rome's encroaching influence on French life, especially at the hands of the Jesuits, their concern for ultramontanism can only be compared to the anxieties of the Protestant English about the dreaded and ubiquitous agents of the Counter-Reformation [...]. There were several species of Gallicanism, some quite doctrinaire, some more critical of Rome than others, much of it increasingly erudite. And it was a stance tailor-made for the more discreet, less public orientation that characterized religious discourse in this post-civil war environment. [...] But Gallican sentiments extended beyond this savant circle. Many other *gens de lettres* [literary persons] shared in the general suspicion of the Rome-Hapsburg-Jesuit axis [...]. If they were not card-carrying Gallicans [...], they nevertheless harbored deep concern in the face of these threats both for themselves as *gens de lettres* and *esprits forts* [strong minds], and for their country," Robert A. Schneider, *Dignified Retreat, Writers and Intellectuals in the Age of Richelieu* (Oxford: Oxford University Press, 2019), 14, 22–23, where Pasquier is presented as a Gallican.

45   That is to say, "to deceive the subtlest people." See Cicero, *Pro Murena*, XI, 25.

46   Here "I," that is, the Narrator, speaks to the entire group for the first time.

47   Croesus, king of Lydia (595–c.546 BCE) was famed for his vast wealth. See *Encyclopaedia Britannica*, https://www.britannica.com/biography/Croesus (accessed February 5, 2021).

calumniate it. THE LAWYER. Do you call someone a calumniator when he is telling the truth? As for me, I'll say nothing that I won't set down in writing, and I claim rights over their papal bulls, their Constitutions, and their recognitions and confessions that I've found in a thousand books they've had printed in the last five or six years, and which are only sold owing to the privilege given them by the general of their order. Which any of us who doubts it, can consult, if he so pleases. THE NARRATOR. You promise a great deal. THE LAWYER. I make no promise that I can't keep.[48] At this point, he paused, like someone who was pulling back, the better to jump. I, THE NARRATOR, took out a fresh side from my writing tablets[49] in order to note the passages about which he was making his allegations. I'll tell you about all of that at length; for all of us want the Lawyer to be chastised if he's found to be a liar; and if, on the contrary, he was telling the truth, we can totally drive the Jesuits from our France, without a hope of respite. THE LAWYER, having been silent for a while, entered the jousting field and continued his forward progress as follows.

48   "I" and the Lawyer sometimes appear to be different people, but sometimes they seem to be facets of a single person. From ch. 3 on, the book consists mainly of a long speech by the Lawyer, who recounts from a legal perspective various matters concerning the Society of Jesus.

49   The Narrator imagines that he is taking notes on little wax-covered wooden tablets, on which he scratches with a stylus, as was done in Roman times.

CHAPTER 3

Censure of the Jesuit Sect by the Faculty of Theology of Paris in 1554

THE LAWYER. I see our France taking sides, some persons favoring the Jesuits excessively and others abhorring them. I beg you, Messieurs (for I am addressing the men who, by a scruple of their consciences, are nourishing that Jesuit family in their cities), please listen to me with an attentive ear, and if you find that my statements are false or that I'm driven by a poorly controlled passion, please pardon me. But also, since there's only one truth that rules me, a truth that should center on the edification of us all, do me the favor of not believing your first perceptions until you come up with second ones. You make a great fuss over these messieurs, as if they were the only buttresses of our church. I beg you, let's look at the judgment of the Faculty of Theology of Paris in 1554. At that time, the *parlement*, which was being besieged by the importunities of these new brethren who were the bearers of two papal bulls, one from Pope Paul III and the other from Julius III, sent them back to that faculty to find out whether the new brethren should be received into this kingdom. The faculty replied as follows:

> *Anno Domini 1554, die verò prima Decembris, sacratissima Theologiae facultas Parisiensis, post Missam de S. Spiritu, in aede sacra Collegii Sorbonae ex more celebratam, jam quarto in eodem Collegio, per juramentum congregata est, ad determinandum de duobus diplomatibus quae duo Sanctiss. Domini summi Pontifices, Paulus III.[1] et Julius III.[2] his qui Societatis Jesu nomine insigniri cupiunt, concessisse dicuntur. Quae quidem duo diplomata, Senatus seu Curia Parlamenti Parisiensis, dictae facultati visitanda et examinanda, misso ad eam rem Hostiario, commiserat.*
>
> *Antequam verò ipsa Theologiae facultas, tanta de re, tantique ponderis tractare incipiat, omnes et singuli Magistri nostri, palam atque aperto ore*

---

1 Pope Paul III (1468–1549), born Alessandro Farnese, reigned 1534–49. He formally approved the Society on September 27, 1540 with the bull *Regimini militantis ecclesiae*. See *Encyclopaedia Britannica*, https://www.britannica.com/biography/Paul-III (accessed February 5, 2021).

2 Pope Julius III (1487–1555), born Giovanni Maria Ciocchi del Monte, was pope from 1550 to 1555. He confirmed the Jesuits in 1550 with the bull *Exposcit debitum*. See *Encyclopaedia Britannica*, https://www.britannica.com/biography/Julius-III (accessed February 5, 2021).

professi sunt, nihil se adversus summorum Pontificum authoritatem et potestatem, aut decernere, aut moliri, aut etiam cogitare velle. Imo verò omnes et singuli, ut obedientiae filii, ipsum summum Pontficem, ut summum et Universalem Christi Jesu Vicarium, et Universalem Ecclesiae Pastorem (cui plenitudo potestatis à Christo data sit, cui omnes utriusque sexus obedire, cujus decreta venerari, et pro se quisque tueri et observare teneantur) up semper agnoverunt et confessi sunt, ita nunc quoque sincerè, fideliter et libenter agnoscunt et confitentur. Sed quoniam omnes, praesertim verò Theologos paratos esse oportet ad satisfactionem omni poscenti de his quae ad fidem, mores, et aedificatione Ecclesiae pertinent, dicta facultas, poscenti, mandanti, et exigenti Curiae praedictae satisfaciendum duxit. Itaque utriusque diplomatis, omnibus frequenter lectis articulis, repetitis, et intellectis et pro rei magnitudine, per multos dies, menses, et horas, pro more prius diligentissimè discussis et examinatis, tum demum unanimi consensu, sed summa cum reverentia et humilitate, rem integram correctioni sedis Apostolicae relinquens, ita censuit.

Haec nova Societas, insolitam nominis Jesu appellationem sibi vendicans, tam licenter, et sine delectu quaslibet personas, quantumlibet facinorosas, illegitimas et infames admittens, nullam a Sacerdotibus secularibus habens differentiam in habitu exteriore, in tonsura, in horis canonicis privatim dicendis, aut publicè in templo decantandis, in claustris et silentio, in delectu ciborum, et dierum, in jejuniis at aliis variis ceremoniis (quibus status Religionum distinguntur et conservantur) tam multis, tamque variis privilegiis, indultis, et distinguntur et conservantur) tam multis, tamque variis privilegiis, indultis, et libertatibus donata, praesertim in administratione Sacramenti Poenitentiae et Eucharistiae, idque sine discrimine locorum, aut personarum, in officio etiam praedicandi, legendi, et docendi in praejudicium Ordinariorum, et Hierarchici Ordinis, in praejudicium quoque aliarum Religionum, imo etiam Principum et Dominorum temporalium, contra privilegia Universitatum, denique in magnum populi gravamen, RELIGIONIS MONASTICAE HONESTATEM VIOLARE VIDETUR, studiosum, pium, et necessarium, virtutum abstinentiarum, ceremoniarum, et austeritatis enervat exercitium, imo occasionem dat liberè apostatandi ab aliis Religionibus, debitam Ordinariis obedientiam, et subjectionem substrahit, Dominos tam temporales, quàm Ecclesiasticos, suis juribus injustè privat, perturbationem in utraque Politia, multas in populo querelas, multas lites, dissidia, contentiones, aemulationes, rebelliones, variaque schismata inducit, Itaque his omnibus, atque aliis diligenter examinatis et perpensis: HAEC SOCIETAS VIDETUR IN NEGOTIO FIDEI

PERICULOSA, PACIS ECCLESIAE PERTURBATIVA, MONASRICAE
RELIGIONIS EVERSIVA, ET MAGIS AD DESTRUCTIONEM, QUAM
AD AEDIFICATIONEM.[3]

I don't want to do you a good turn covertly. Perhaps there are some among us who don't understand Latin: that's why, this censure document being the foundation of my discourse, I'll dress it in French clothes so that everyone will understand.[4]

"The year 1554, on the first day of December, the venerable Faculty of Theology of Paris, having attended the Mass of the Holy Spirit[5] celebrated in the chapel of the Collège de la Sorbonne, and an oath having been taken by the faculty, which has already assembled four times in the aforesaid place, in order to reach a conclusion about the two papal bulls that are said to have been decreed by our Most Holy Lords and Popes, Paul III and Julius III, in favor of those who want to be distinct from us, under the name the Society of Jesus, the said two bulls having been sent by the court of Parlement via an usher, to be viewed and examined."

"Now, before turning to such a lofty matter, a matter of such weightiness, each and every one of our masters declared publicly and frankly that they did not intend to issue an opinion or to challenge the authority and power of the Holy See, and that they did not even want to think of such a thing. By contrast, they all, in general and in particular, as obedient children, and as in the past, also want to acknowledge plainly, faithfully, and frankly, that Our Holy Father the Pope is the sovereign and universal vicar of Jesus Christ and the general shepherd of his church, to whom plenary power was given and whose holy decrees each of us, of either sex, should embrace with his or her full devotion. But because all of us, and especially the theologians, should be disposed to

---

3   For this document, see Sutto, 53n189.

4   Pasquier's emphasis upon providing his readers with French translations should be viewed in the context of the *Ordonnance* of Villers-Cotterets (1539), which stipulated that all decrees and other proceedings should be "spoken, written, and given to the parties [concerned] in the French mother tongue, and not otherwise," quoted by Robert A. Schneider, *Dignified Retreat, Writers and Intellectuals in the Age of Richelieu* (Oxford: Oxford University Press, 2019), 43. In the present book, translations into English (rather than into French) come after Pasquier's quotes from the original Latin. Pasquier's translations from Latin to French often weave personal comments into an otherwise relatively close translation. We have opted to enclose the hybrid result in quotation marks, as Pasquier himself did.

5   This Mass is a means of invoking the Holy Spirit for guidance and wisdom throughout the coming months or, in some instances, before making a crucial decision. The so-called "Golden Sequence," that is, the hymn *Veni Sancte Spiritus* (Come, Holy Spirit) is sung during a Mass for the Holy Spirit.

reply to those who want to be enlightened on points of the faith, the behavior, and the edification of the church, it was deemed part of his duty to satisfy what had been asked, ordered, and commanded of him by the said court of Parlement. That is why, having diligently read, reread, and heard all the articles of the two bulls, and owing to the importance of the subject, having maturely thought about it for several months, days, and hours, and finally by common consent (but with all reverence and submission, and turning over to the Holy See the decision on this matter), the court was of the following opinion":

"This new Society, which specifically takes for itself the unaccustomed title of the Society of the Name of Jesus, with much liberty and absence of selection opens the door to all sorts of people, wicked, scoundrels and infamous though they may be, there being on their exterior no difference between their clothes and the clothes of the secular clergy. They have received an infinite number of prerogatives, indults, and exemptions for the tonsure, the canonic hours that the Society says in private or sings publicly in the church, for cloisters, silence, choice of living, days, or fasting, and other laws and ceremonies (by which religious orders are separate and maintained), even in the administration of the sacrament of penance and the Eucharist, and this without regard for places and persons, and also permission to preach, read, and teach, to the detriment of the *ordinaires* and of the hierarchical order, and the other religious orders, or princes and temporal lords, against the privileges of the universities, and finally to the great vexation and disadvantage of the common people, IT SEEMS TO US THAT IT VIOLATES THE HONOR and the discipline of monastic orders, to corrupt pious, holy, and necessary usages, abstinences, and ceremonies and austerities: or to create the opportunity and subject for easily wandering away from other religious orders. Moreover, it takes from the *ordinaires* the obedience that is due them, unjustly deprives seigneurs, be they temporal or spiritual, of their rights, stirs up troubles in one government or another, stirs up a number of quarrels among the common people, a number of debates, brawls, factions, jealousies, rebellions, and diverse schisms. That is why, having examined at length and considered all the above-mentioned particularities, and others as well, WE ARE OF THE OPINION THAT THIS COMPANY IS OF PERILOUS CONSEQUENCE FOR OUR FAITH, BORN TO TROUBLE THE PEACE OF THE CHURCH, TO OVERTHROW THE STATE OF MONASTIC ORDERS, AND IN A FEW WORDS, IT HAS INTRODUCED MORE FOR DESOLATION AND RUIN THAN FOR EDIFICATION."

Was there ever a finer opinion accompanied by a more certain prophesy than that one? And why? At the time, there were no underhanded debates; each person relied on the sincerity of his conscience before God. This was not a tumultuous assembly: it lasted for four whole days, and it involved persons who had been pondering the matter for a long time. Still less did they want to oppose the authority of the Holy See, as we can judge from their humble protests; and that's why the Holy Spirit, devoutly invoked by their sacrifice, spoke through this sacred faculty. I was conceited: and I believed that, for the past thousand years, no work of the Holy Spirit was greater than this censure that was put before us. The Parlement of Paris had sent to the Faculty of Theology, and to it alone, the bulls of Pope Paul III of 1543 and the bulls of Julius III of 1550; the Jesuits had hidden the others away: 1543, 1545, 1546, and 1549. But from these two samples, the faculty, in a holy way, judged just what the duration of the document should be. Simply remember these few lines: *Multas in populo querelas, multas lites, dissidia, contentiones, rebelliones, variaque schismata inducet.*[6] And remember what our Jesuit here told you about his order, and you'll find that this is exactly what the Sorbonne said. The holy service that the Jesuits carry out in their churches is a schism from the service that our priests conduct; their privileges are a schism between the bishops and themselves, between the monasteries and themselves. Still more, their propositions bring a schism between the Holy See and kings. But what maintains them in these privileges? Their colleges, their confessions, their preaching. The colleges are traps to catch young people; confessions are subornations, preaching is charlatanism. If we listen to our Jesuit here, we have no other preachers but them, to sustain our ancient church. They've been afoot for some sixty years. What Jesuit preachers did we have in Paris: Émond Auger[7] and Jacques Commolet;[8] I can't name others for you. On the other hand, how many preachers were produced by the Faculty of Theology of Paris, I mean learned folk who live a holy life and who haven't altered our old ways? Let me add that one never hears a Jesuit, up in his pulpit in the center of the church, decipher a passage of Holy Scripture in order to support the Holy See, or to stamp out the heresies of our day. What do the Jesuits preach about? They declaim against the absent, and they edify those who are present, solely by talking about scandals that involve kings and princes. But what I find most admirable about that censure, is that

---

6   That is, "stirs up troubles in one and another government, stirs up several quarrels among the common people, several debates, brawls, factions, jealousies, rebellions, and diverse schisms."

7   Émond Auger (1530–91), a French Jesuit, founded the Jesuit college at Pamiers. In addition to being a renowned preacher, he was the confessor of King Henri III. See *DHCJ*, 1:268–69. Cf. Book III, ch. 11 below.

8   Jacques Commolet (*c.*1548–1621), was a professor of philosophy at the Collège de Clermont (where his disciple was future cardinal François de La Rochefoucauld) and a renowned preacher. He was also the rector of the Jesuits' professed house in Paris (1587–96) and vice-provincial of France (1591–92). See *DHCJ*, 1:875–76.

our theologians foresaw the rebellion, and that these new Sires would in the future act against our king. If, then, I now embark against them, it's not from temerity, nor from malice, nor from madness, which suits me, for I have before my eyes, like a lamp for navigating, this holy and venerable Faculty of Theology of Paris.

CHAPTER 4

How, When, and by What Artifices, the Jesuits Wormed Their Way into France

THE LAWYER. When God wants to afflict a kingdom, he assembles great and unhoped-for means. That's the very thing encountered in our kingdom. Several years earlier, in 1559, had come the lamentable death of King Henri II.[1] God sent two sects to us in France, one just as dangerous as the other on various questions. There was the Ignatians' sect; they go by the name the Society of Jesus. The other sect is the Calvinists, who claim to belong to the Reformed Religion. Although the one and the other formerly lodged in Paris, which is the capital city of the realm, the Jesuits did their monkey business overtly, and the Calvinists held their assemblies secretly. Now, since the Jesuit sect is a bastard religion, the offshoot of our ancient Catholic, Apostolic, and Roman religion (for to tell the truth, it retains a few traits and characteristics of it, but not what is needed), it was authorized by Messire Guillaume du Prat,[2] bishop of Clermont, the bastard son of Legate du Prat.[3] He lodged them in his Hôtel de Clermont in Paris; and when he died, he willed them more than sixty thousand crowns, or so they say. From there, they advanced and began to lodge more spaciously, buying the Hôtel de Langres in the rue Saint-Jacques, where they created a college and a monastery that were housed under various roofs. They gave public lessons without the approval of the rector of the University of Paris; they administered the holy sacraments of penance and the Eucharist to all comers, without getting permission from the *ordinaires*. In

---

1 Henri II (1519–59) was king of France from 1547 until his death. He was killed in a jousting tournament, leaving three young sons (François II, Charles IX, and Henri III), whose minorities and relatively ineffectual reigns helped spark the Wars of Religion that pitted Catholics against Protestants. See *Encyclopaedia Britannica*, https://www.britannica.com/biography/Henry-II-king-of-France (accessed February 5, 2021). See Book III, ch. 17 below.

2 Guillaume du Prat (1507–60) was the illegitimate son of Chancellor and Cardinal Antoine du Prat. He was named bishop of Clermont in 1529. He not only received Jesuits into his diocese, where they ran two colleges, but he also aided them financially and helped them found the Collège de Clermont in Paris. See Book II, ch. 3 and Book III, ch. 18.

3 Antoine du Prat (1463–1535) became first president of the Parlement of Paris in 1508 and chancellor in 1515, personally negotiating the Concordat of Bologna on behalf of King François I. After his wife's death he became a religious and was created cardinal in 1527. He served as legate *a latere* in 1530. See *Encyclopaedia Britannica*, https://www.britannica.com/biography/Antoine-Duprat (accessed February 5, 2021).

like manner, the Calvinists began to preach and to implement their doctrine, if not completely openly, at least not as covertly as in the past: witness the large assembly that was caught unawares by the Parlement near the Collège du Plessis, where an infinite number of men and women were detained and a lawyer, a pedagogue, and a gentlewoman were subsequently executed.[4] Thus I can assert, as something very true, that clusters of these two sects began to grow vehemently on the rue Saint-Jacques of Paris, in fifteen or twenty adjacent houses. And later, some of them vowed to have Jesus's name stamped on coins[5] while the Jesuits marked it on the doors of their Parisian houses and colleges and put a cross above it to show that they were lodged at the sign of the cross. Let me add that, just as the Calvinists call their religion reformed, the Jesuits glorify themselves for having been in some of the Italian cities, for example Modena, which is called the Reformed. I might add that the Calvinists, whom we call Huguenots, took up arms against France in 1561, in order to defend their religion, just as the Jesuits, envious of them, had recourse to the same weapons in around 1585, in order to increase their religion.

But in order not to leap across time, and not to stray from my goal, let's turn to the death of King Henri II, under whom the Calvinists believed they could forge ahead in the middle of France, without being hindered. This good king had left behind four young princes, his children, in the charge of the queen, their mother. She was a foreign princess[6] in whom the great marriage alliances of France were not evident. She guided her sons. Thus, at one and the same time, the two sects began to grow, one owing to the death of a king, the other owing to the death of a bishop.[7] During the minorities of our kings, the great seigneurs of France donned their ambition and dressed up in the mantle of religion. There were new partisanships among them: some supported the party of the ancient religion and others the party of the new religion; and each

---

4   This took place on September 14, 1557. The three victims were Taurin Gravelle, Nicolas Clinet, and Philippine de Luns de Graverons. See *Histoire universelle de Jaques-Auguste de Thou …*, 2 vols. (La Haye, 1740), 2:531.

5   These coins were minted in Geneva from 1562 into the mid-seventeenth century. On the face of the coin was *Geneva*, followed by the date and the imperial crowned eagle bearing at its heart the Genevan *crown*. On the reverse was the motto *Post tenebra lux* (Light after darkness), and a sun, in the center of which was *IHS*. See Sutto, 142n63.

6   Catherine de' Medici (1519–89) was the daughter of Lorenzo II de' Medici, duke of Urbino. By marrying King Henri II, she became queen of France. After her eldest son's death in 1560, she ruled France as regent for her minor son, King Charles IX (r.1560–74). A younger son, was technically not a minor, though he was not up to ruling, so Catherine was not a regent until his death. See *Encyclopaedia Britannica*, https://www.britannica.com/biography/Catherine-de-Medici (accessed February 5, 2021).

7   This is an allusion to the bequest of Guillaume du Prat, bishop of Clermont, who died in 1560.

followed the judgment of the most clairvoyant, more because it was convenient for their splendor than because of their devotions. Amid this contrast,
the Protestant ministers, who until then had been burned, presented their
request to King Charles IX to be heard in his presence. This was granted to
them quite fecklessly. And to this end, the city of Poissy[8] was chosen. There, on
one side, were several cardinals, archbishops, bishops, and doctors of theology;
and on the other side were several ministers, including Theodore Beza,[9] the
captain, assisted by Peter Martyr,[10] Marlorat,[11] Saint-Paul,[12] and others among
them of a certain rank.

After the Sorbonne's opinion of 1554, our Jesuits found their hopes dashed:
for Master Noël Brûlart,[13] the king's *procureur général* in the Parlement of Paris,
was diligently seeking the most austere life that has ever been led. Seeing this

---

8   For this assembly, see H. Outram Evennet, *The Cardinal de Lorraine and the Council of
     Trent* (Cambridge: Cambridge University Press, 2011), 283–393; and "Poissy, Colloquy of,"
     in *Encyclopedia of the Early Modern World*, 4:494–95. Two prominent Jesuits, Diego Laínez
     (1512–65) and Juan Alfonso de Polanco (1517–76) accompanied the papal legate there, a
     fact Pasquier does not mention. See Mario Scaduto, *L'epoca di Giacomo Lainez, 1556–1565:
     L'azione* (Rome: Civiltà cattolica, 1974), 113–35.

9   Theodore Beza (1519–1605) was a theologian, humanist, and polemicist. In 1561, he repre-
     sented the Evangelicals at the Colloquy of Poissy, eloquently defending the principles of
     the Evangelical faith. As head and advocate for all the Reformed congregations of France,
     he was variously revered and hated. A disciple of Calvin, he succeeded Calvin as spiri-
     tual leader of the Company of Pastors of Geneva, 1564–80. See *Encyclopaedia Britannica*,
     https://www.britannica.com/biography/Theodore-Beza (accessed February 5, 2021).

10   Pietro Martire Vermigli (1500–62), also known as Peter Martyr, was an Italian-born
     Augustinian monk who went over to the Reform. In the 1550s, Vermigli became deeply
     involved in English church politics. He attended the abortive Colloquy of Poissy, which
     was held with the intention of reconciling Catholics and Protestants. See *Encyclopaedia
     Britannica*, https://www.britannica.com/biography/Peter-Martyr-Vermigli (accessed
     February 5, 2021).

11   Augustin Marlorat du Pasquier (1506–62), also known as Augustinus Marloratus, was
     a French Protestant minister and reformer. Shortly after the Colloquy of Poissy, he was
     tried for treason and executed for having supported Protestant plans to capture the city
     of Rouen. See Stephen Mark Holmes, *Sacred Signs in Reformation Scotland: Interpreting
     Worship, 1488–1590* (United Kingdom: OUP Oxford, 2015), 195.

12   François de Saint-Paul was a pastor at Dieppe.

13   Noël Brûlart (?–1582) was the *procureur général* of the Parlement of Paris. Brûlart was a
     hot-headed Gallican (that is, a supporter of the French Catholic Church), and an enemy
     of the Reform. For example, he sought to have the most vituperative preachers disci-
     plined. See Archives Nationales (AN), *Civil Registers of the Parlement,* x^{1a} 1550, fol. 278.
     Speech of Pierre Lizet, as premier président, and procureur général Noël Brulart on cur-
     rent preaching and royal policy (1543), cited in Nancy Lyman Roelker, *One King, One Faith:
     The Parlement of Paris and the Religious Reformations of the Sixteenth Century* (Berkley:
     University of California Press, 1996), 491. See Book III, ch. 18 below.

great assembly gathered at Poissy, those who lost no opportunity to become more powerful promised that they would join the faction. Their agent in Paris at the time was Ponce Cogordan.[14] Charles, cardinal de Lorraine,[15] remarked in conversation that Cogordan was the finest negotiator he'd ever seen, and he'd seen several of them. This man takes the matter in hand, presents his request to the court of the Parlement of Paris, not as the Society of the Name of Jesus, but as the Collège de Clermont, by which all the Jesuits of Paris promised to abjure all their vows; and would they please approve their college? By doing this, at the same time they obtained the approval for their big legacy.[16] With its customary prudence and religiousness, the court sent this request back to the Gallican church (then assembled at Poissy), to issue a decree.

Never was an assembly more specious; and never did an assembly produce so many ills for a state as that one did. There's a placard that I'd hesitate to put into the hands of someone who is writing the history of our time; for without doing so wittingly, it authorizes these two sects. And more amazing still, two great cardinals were the first instruments, cardinals full of understanding and fine zeal, cardinals who were not mere apprentices in either the mysteries of our religion or the affairs of state. For one of them had been employed in the greatest affairs of our kingdom during the reign of the great King François I, and the other during the reign of Henri II. The two cardinals to whom I'm referring were the cardinal de Tournon[17] and the cardinal de Lorraine. The former, who was quite elderly and whose judgment consequently was more solid, maintained that one shouldn't participate in a conference with Protestant ministers; that to do so, was to recognize them as members of our republic (until then we had deemed them to be rotten members). Even when the king was young, which freed him from having to judge those coups. The latter cardinal,

---

14 Ponce Cogordan (1500–82) was a French Jesuit who worked in the Italian Peninsula and France. He flanked Nicolás Bobadilla in his conspiracy against the Jesuit governance after the death of Loyola. See Book III, ch. 26.

15 Charles de Lorraine (1524–74), known as the cardinal de Lorraine, was a member of the powerful house of Guise and was a protector of the Jesuits. He became archbishop of Reims in 1538 and cardinal in 1547. He represented France at the third session of the Council of Trent. See *Encyclopaedia Britannica*, https://www.britannica.com/biography/Charles-de-Lorraine-2e-cardinal-de-Lorraine (accessed February 5, 2021).

16 That is, the huge sum willed them by Guillaume du Prat in 1560.

17 François de Tournon (1489–1562) was archbishop of Embrun, then of Bourges, and finally of Lyon. He received the cardinal's hat in 1530. This put him in a prominent position in the fight against Lutheranism and Calvinism that he perceived as a growing menace to both doctrinal orthodoxy and the social order. He was one of the six cardinals who attended the Colloquy of Poissy. See Alice Saunier-Seïté, *Le Cardinal de Tournon: Le Richelieu de François Ier* (Paris: Éd. des deux mondes, 1997).

who was in the flowering of his years, showed his assured spirit, assisted by two great theologians. Despense[18] and Salignac[19] wanted to be put on view, promising that if he spoke against Beza, he would easily attain his goal. On this matter, the latter man received the plurality of votes. Cardinal de Tournon, seeing that he had been supplanted in people's opinion, began to call attention to the Jesuits. A fine and specious pretext (so it seemed) for combating the new religion. In this he was followed by several other prelates, not that they didn't foresee an infinity of inconveniences that might spring up; rather, they judged that the physicians were purging the poisons by putting them in the presence of another poison.[20] Scaffolds were raised, and cardinal de Lorraine and Beza played their little roles before the young king, in the presence of several great nobles of one party or another. The assembly disbanded; and after that, we openly had three different religions in France: one talked only about Christ in its sermons; the other mentioned Jesus's name in its synagogues; and the third one was us, the ancient Catholics who, in our churches, recognized the merit of our faith by the words of Jesus Christ.

18   Claude Despense, or d'Espence (1511–71), was secretary to the cardinal de Lorraine. He was also a preacher and theologian. See Henry Outram Evennett, "Claude d'Espence et son discours du Colloque de Poissy," *Revue historique* 164 (1930): 40–78.

19   Jean de Salignac was a theologian, linguist, and teacher. He represented the Sorbonne at the Colloquy of Poissy. See H. Outram Evennett, *The Cardinal of Lorraine and the Council of Trent: A Study in the Counter-Reformation* (Cambridge: Cambridge University Press, 2011), 243.

20   He is alluding to a counter-poison, that is, a poison used against another poison and serving as an antidote. See Book III, ch. 20.

Decree of the Gallican Church against the Jesuits at the Colloquy Held at Poissy in 1561

THE LAWYER. Nonetheless, Messieurs, don't think that, amid all that last-mentioned Jesuit poison, our Gallican church didn't bring several imposing ingredients to temper things. For having listed at length, in the decree, all the privileges and indults that had diversely been granted them by Paul III and Julius III, and by some letters-patent that they had obtained; and having discussed the state of the request that had been presented to the court and sent back to those prelates, here at last is the *ordonnance* they saw fit to decree:

> The court of the Parlement of Paris having sent the request back, the assembly received and receives, approved and approves the said society and company, in the form of a society and a college, and not as a newly instituted order, charging them to use a name other than the Society of the Name of Jesus, or Jesuits; and over the said Society and college, the diocesan bishop will have full superintendence, jurisdiction, and can correct by chasing away and removing from the said company, transgressors and persons living an evil life. The brothers of the said company will not undertake or do, in the spiritual or the temporal, anything that is prejudicial to the bishops, chapters, curates, parishes, and universities, nor the other religious orders, and therefore will be made to conform entirely to the disposition of common law, without having any right or jurisdiction, and renouncing in advance and expressly all the privileges named in their bulls, concerning things that are contrary to the above. Otherwise, for failure to do this, or to obtain others in the future, the present bulls will remain null and of no effect and virtue, save the right to hold the said assembly, and the other in all things. Issued at Poissy in the great refectory of the venerable nuns of the said Poissy, under the sign and seal of the most reverend cardinal de Tournon, archbishop of Lyon, primate of France, presiding over the said assembly as principal archbishop of France, and of Reverend Father in God Monsieur the bishop of Paris,[1] reporter for the said request. Signed with the seals of Master Nicolas

---

1 Eustache du Bellay (?–1565) was appointed bishop of Paris in 1551. He attended the Council of Trent and opposed the introduction of the Society of Jesus into his diocese. He resigned

© KONINKLIJKE BRILL NV, LEIDEN, 2021 | DOI:10.1163/9789004164062_006

Le Breton[2] and Guillaume Blanchy, registrars and secretaries of the said
assembly, on Monday, the fifteenth day of December 1561.

Ponce Cogordan, their agent, all dressed up in this holy decree, presents it to
the court of the *parlement*, which effortlessly verifies it. I'll pause here and say
that, if ever they discussed it, if not the whole document then at least the lesser
part of this great decree, I'm ready to beg their pardon, and to be assured that
the same thing will be done by messieurs Marion,[3] Pasquier,[4] Arnauld,[5] and
Dollé,[6] who vowed to wage war against them. But if the request that they presented was really only a pantomime, in order later to make fun of the Gallican
church and the *parlement*, and if they treated what they were ordered to do as
if it were horse manure, they must unanimously agree with me that neither

his bishopric in 1564. See http://www.catholic-hierarchy.org/bishop/bbellaye.html (accessed
February 5, 2021).

2   Nicolas le Breton (1506–74) was the cardinal de Lorraine's private secretary. A humanist, he
loved things Italian. He was a counselor in the Parlement of Paris. See Joachim du Bellay, *The
Regrets with, The Antiquities of Rome, Three Latin Elegies, and The Defense and Enrichment of
the French Language* (Philadelphia: University of Pennsylvania Press, 2006), 108.
Guillaume Blanchy was a secretary of the Parlement in 1561. See *Actes, tiltres et memoires,
concernant les affaires du clergé de France: Recueillis, mis en ordre, & omprimez par comman-
dement de l'assemblee generale, tenuë à Paris és années 1645. & 1646* (n.p.: n.p., 1646), 106.

3   Simon Marion (1540–1605), baron de Druy, was the father-in-law of Antoine Arnauld, *avo-
cat général* in the Parlement of Paris. He was famed as a great jurisconsult. See *Plaidoyez de
M. Simon Marion, Advocat en Parlement de Druy: Avec les arrests donnez sur iceux* (Paris: Chez
Michel Sonnius, 1594).

4   The author of *The Jesuits' Catechism* refers to himself here in the third person. Pasquier studied law under several famed lawyers (Omer Talon, Pierre Ramus, François Hotman, Jacques
Cujas). His law career was slowed by several years of poor health, during which Pasquier
concentrated on history. The first volume of his *Recherches de la France* appeared in 1560. In
1564, he was chosen to plead the University of Paris's lawsuit against the Society of Jesus. His
plea of March 1565 won him the respect of the public and the esteem of his colleagues. In
1585, he became *avocat général du roi* in the Court of Accounts. In 1593, he was appointed to
interrogate Pierre Barrière, accused of having wanted to assassinate Henri IV.

5   Antoine Arnauld (1560–1619), was a lawyer in the Parlement of Paris, a skilled orator, and
a counselor of state under Henri IV. Perhaps his most famous speech was given in 1594, in
favor of the University of Paris and against the Jesuits. See his printed plea: *Plaidoyé […] pour
l'Université de Paris, demanderesse, contre les Jésuites défendeurs* (Paris: Mamert Patisson,
1594); and also *The arrainement of the whole Societie of Jesuites in Fraunce* [*sic*] (London,
Yetsweirt, 1594). He was the father of the Arnaulds of Port-Royal, which would become
the center of Jansenist opposition to the Jesuit moral teaching known as probabilism. See
Robert A. Maryks, *Saint Cicero and the Jesuits: The Influence of the Liberal Arts on the Adoption
of Moral Probabilism* (Ashgate: Aldershot, 2008), esp. 130–31.

6   Louis Dollé (?–1599) was named to the king's council by Catherine de' Medicis. He was also
an intendant of finances. See W. Carlos Martyn, *A History of the Huguenots* (n.p.: American
Tract Society, 1866), 454.

the reply written personally by François des Montaignes,[7] opposing Arnaud's plea, nor the venomous bites of a certain La Fon,[8] against Marion and Pasquier (the former was the *avocat du roi* in the Parlement, and the latter was in the Chamber of Accounts), nor the hypocritical request addressed to the king, in which the author wanted to suppress his name, will ever suffice to have them declared legitimate and natural children of France. When they appeared, the Faculty of Theology declared them schismatics and disturbers of the peace of our church and of monastic discipline. Since then, the Gallican church, in order to cope with this great disorder, has wanted to authorize them, but with the modifications listed above. However, despite the ingredients and the revivals that the church expected would be an antidote for this poison, the venom was stronger. For as soon as they received the decree, they issued an order to have these words put on the entrance door of their college: THE COLLEGE OF THE SOCIETY OF THE NAME OF JESUS. They went back and picked up their first trail, and they continued to follow it, and they will continue to do so as long as they reside in France. Since the Frenchman's nature is to be, in the beginning, warm and stronger than a man, and in the long term colder and weaker than a woman, we therefore finally allowed ourselves to be won over by the stubbornness of these new brethren. If a person is pursued in a lively manner, he drops public affairs, in order to embrace his private ones.

7 François des Montaignes is one of the *noms de plume* of Louis Richeome (1544–1625), a Jesuit theologian and controversialist. He was instrumental in the reopening of the college of Bordeaux in 1603. In 1605, he was appointed provincial for the province of Lyon, and from 1608 to 1616, he was in Rome as assistant to the general, Claudio Acquaviva (in office 1581–1615). Richeome used several other pseudonyms: Franciscus Montanus, Félix de la Grâce, Ludovicus de Beaumanoir, and René de La Fon. Montaignes and La Fon are repeatedly cited by Pasquier. Sutto points out that Richeome was given the heavy burden of shaping not only the role that the Society of Jesus would play in France, but also the future relations between church and state. This task was in part accomplished by the five works he published in the space of seven years: *La Vérité défendue* (1595, by F. des Montaignes); *Très-humble Remonstrance et Requeste* (1598, under Richeome's name); *Response de René de la Fon* (1599, by René de La Fon); *La chasse du Renard Pasquin* (1602, by Félix de la Grâce); *Plainte apologétique au Roy* (1602, under Richeome's name). See Sutto 73n293. Cf. *DHCJ*, 4:3356–57.

8 René de La Fon was a pseudonym of Louis Richeome. Using Félix de la Grâce, another pseudonym, Richeome replied to Pasquier's *Catechism* (see above, "Translator's Preface," part 2).

On the Request Presented to the Parlement by the Jesuits in 1564, to Matriculate at the University of Paris, and How Many Parties Butted Heads with Them

THE LAWYER. On his end, Ponce Cogordan, noting that we'd slowed down in this fashion, didn't slumber; and, judging that he'd won the city, he presented a request to the university in 1564, the gist of which went as follows:

> They beg the principals and the college of the Society of the Name of Jesus, known as the Collège de Clermont, to please incorporate them into the university in order to enjoy its privileges. The university having driven them away, they are having recourse to the *parlement*. Cogordan chose Versoris[1] as his lawyer, and the university chose Pasquier. They pleaded the case, but the case was so beautiful that Pasquier immediately remonstrated that merely reading their request would make them lose the case. All the more so, since the foundation of their case depended on the decree of the Gallican church, which had expressly forbidden them to take the title Society of the Name of Jesus, but which they had nonetheless used for their request. To do that was to aim directly at the visors of their helmets. In this way, they were forced to disavow their actions, and to seek sanctuary and an exemption, when they found themselves in a tight place that was prejudicial toward them. Versoris disavowed the person who had drawn up the request: the style was good. And Cogordan disavowed himself through the lawyer he'd selected. This shows you that, in all their negotiations with us, in order to advance their sect, the ass and the fox had both been riding.[2] A great marvel! And worthy of having

---

1   Pierre Le Tourneur (1528–88), known as Versoris, became an *avocat* in the Parlement of Paris in 1552 and was an important jurist. He was the head of the council of the Guises and the guard of their seals. He represented the Third Estate in the Estates-General of 1576–77. See Bon Louis Henri Martin, *Histoire de France depuis les temps les plus reculés jusqu'en 1789* (Paris: Furne, 1847), 2:225.

2   He is alluding to one of Aesop's fables: "The Lion, the Fox, and the Ass." The lion takes for himself all the food he has hunted. Humph, grumbles the Fox as he walks away with his tail

horns put on the ears of a long posterity.[3] We had been afflicted by the members of the new religion, first in the environs of the city of Amboise,[4] against the seigneurs who at the time controlled young King François II. Then by the Troubles that cropped up at the Colloquy of Poissy and during the Geneva-style preaching that has wormed its way into France. Last, there were surprise attacks on cities, or a bloody battle fought near Dreux,[5] soon followed by an eighteen-month partisan civil war of words coming from papists and Huguenots; which subsequently lulled us by an edict of toleration.[6] Our forearms are still bloody from these Troubles, and scarcely did we have the leisure to draw a deep breath, than this request by the Jesuits was presented to the court of the *parlement*. There were ten lawyers, as messieurs des Montaignes and La Fon admitted in their extravagant texts; and there were ten opposing parties, six of which (says La Fon) "were powerful and muscled corps: the city, the university, the Sorbonne, the mendicants, the hospitalers, and the curates. The four other parties had just as many seigneurs of great authority: the governor of Paris,[7] Cardinal de Châtillon[8] as protector of the university, the bishop of Paris,[9] and the abbot of Saint-Genevieve."[10] Is it possible

---

between his legs; and in a low growl he adds: You may share the labors of the great, but you won't share the spoils.

3   That is, be cuckolded.

4   The Conjuration of Amboise, March 17, 1560, was a failed attempt by Huguenots to gain power by abducting young King François II and arresting François duke of Guise and his brother, the cardinal de Lorraine. It is claimed that more than one thousand people were killed in what came to be called the Tumult, and their drawn and quartered bodies were hung from the city walls. It was one of the events leading to the religious wars that shook France, 1562–98. See Lucien Romier, *La Conjuration d'Amboise: L'aurore sanglante de la liberté de consceince; Le règne et la mort de François II* (Paris: Perrin, 1923).

5   The Battle of Dreux was fought on December 19, 1562, between Catholics and Huguenots. Commanders from both sides were captured, but the French Catholics won this first major engagement of the French Wars of Religion. See *Encyclopaedia Britannica*, https://www.britannica.com/topic/Battle-of-Dreux (accessed February 5, 2021).

6   *Édit de connivance*: an edict of tolerance or dissimulation (DAF 1694).

7   François de Montmorency (1530–79), the eldest son of Anne de Montmorency, was governor of Paris and the king's lieutenant in the Île-de-France, that is, the region around Paris. See Mack P. Holt, *The Duke of Anjou and the Politique Struggle during the Wars of Religion* (Cambridge: Cambridge University Press, 2002), 10.

8   Odet cardinal de Châtillon (1515–71) was Admiral de Coligny's brother. He became a Huguenot. See *The Prelate in England and Europe, 1300–1560*, ed. Martin Heale (York: York Medieval Press, 2014), 86–87.

9   See ch. 5 above.

10   Joseph Foulon (?–1607), abbot of Sainte-Geneviève from 1558 to 1607. See Sluhovsky, *Patroness of Paris*, 125.

that, during these understandings that had taken such a sinister bent, so many communities and seigneurs banded together against them for no reason at all, in a matter of such importance? But what communities? The ones that quite recently had afflicted the Huguenots to the maximum: they'd smashed the benches of *The Patriarch*,[11] and the benches at Popincourt,[12] where they'd carried on their devotions, eagerly pursuing the execution of Gabaston, the city watchman (protector of their undertakings) and the executions of Cagers and his son.[13] So many wise communities, resolute enemies of heresy, became resolute opponents of the Jesuits, for they were still on the outskirts of our civil wars against the Jesuits (say I), who boasted about being the scourges of the heretics. And certainly, all these great personages who undertook this quarrel with them, deem that this sect was infinitely dreadful, not only for the liberties of our Gallican church and the general state of France, but also for all of Christianity. Now, in addition to these two great parties, there was also a stronger and more powerful one: monsieur du Mesnil,[14] *avocat du roi* in the Parlement, who was formally against them.

But despite so many litigants (says the JESUIT), the case was not only judged immediately, it was also sent to the royal council.[15] Which shows clearly that the justice of our good law made every favor sparkle. Poor fool and scholar! If you'd been raised in the brightness of a royal palace, a *lit de justice* of our kings, rather than in the dust of the colleges, you'd know that the sovereign courts don't judge important cases immediately: they never have enough time and leisure to inform their consciences as they ought. And indeed, the same court did that very thing by its decree of July 1594; and that's why Monsieur Marion, pleading a case against the Jesuits of Lyon in 1597, said that, in 1564, a moderate and imperfect prudence had not in the least made the affairs of France degenerate over time, to the worst degree. And as for me, I'll say, more daringly and

---

11   *The Patriarch* was a Protestant meeting place in the faubourg Saint-Marceau, near the church of Saint-Médard. See Sutto, 148n94.

12   The Protestants had a preaching place near Saint-André's gate. It was suppressed in 1562 by Constable de Montmorency, a gesture that won him the nickname Captain Burn Benches (*capitaine Brûle-Bancs*).

13   Pasquier mentions them in a letter. See Sutto, 148n97.

14   Baptiste du Mesnil (1517–69), *avocat du roi* in the Parlement in 1559 and counselor in the Châtelet in 1569. See his *Plaidoié de feu M. l'advocat du Mesnil, en la cause de l'Université de Paris & des jésuites* (Paris, 1594).

15   The Royal Council was the highest court in the realm; no appeal could go beyond it. The suit between the university and the Jesuits was "appointé au conseil," that is, adjourned indefinitely without decision by the Parlement, in 1564.

frankly, that this case was sent to the council in 1564, thanks to man's wisdom; but that this wisdom was guided by the hand of God who, to avenge our sins, wanted to preserve the Jesuit, as a future shelter from the woes of our France.

Why refer to all this? To show you that I detest and abhor the Jesuit sect. I've no small proofs of my opinion. First, there's the censure by the venerable Faculty of Theology of Paris in 1554, where, I assure you, the greatest theologians were present, the greatest ones ever seen in France: Picard,[16] Maillard,[17] Demochares,[18] Perionus,[19] and Ory, the inquisitor of the faith.[20] The first man is that admirable preacher who was laid out in his house after his death as dean of Saint-Germain de l'Auxerrois. The common people of Paris kissed his feet eagerly, because his life had been holy. The four other men were his companions, extreme persecutors of heretics. I have this great and holy decree of 1561, by our Gallican church: the judgment that subsequently was issued. And finally, many noteworthy seigneurs and many communities who opposed them in 1564, some of whom I can tell you, as something very true, and which I believe because I saw it with my own eyes. They were two venerable figures from the past, solicitors for the case: Jean Benoist,[21] the dean, and Courselles,[22] the sub-dean of the Faculty of Theology of Paris. The latter was eighty at the time and the former was seventy-seven. Both were on the verge of justifying their actions in the other world, where the conscience of each person is more

16   François Picard (1504–56) was the dean of the Church of Saint-Germain l'Auxerrois. See V.-L. Bourrilly and N. Weiss. "Jean du Bellay, les protestants et La Sorbonne (1529–1535): Les poursuites – L'affaire Des Placards," *Bulletin de la Société de l'histoire du protestantisme français (1903–2015)* 53, no. 2 (1904): 97–143, here 113.

17   Olivier Maillard (?–1565) taught at the Collège d'Harcourt and was dean of the Faculty of Theology. He represented the college at the third session of the Council of Trent, and at the Conference of Saint-Germain in 1562, Sutto, 149n102.

18   That is, Antoine de Mouchy (1494–1574), manager (*syndic*) of the Faculty of Theology. He was a *commissaire* in the trial of Anne du Bourg in 1559. In 1547, he published a critical edition of Gratian's *Decretum*. See Lyman Roelker, *One King, One Faith*, 237.

19   Joachim Perion, called Perionus (c.1498–1559), was an erudite Benedictine and theologian. In 1542, he published an edition of Aristotle's *Politics*. See Peter Burke, *Languages and Communities in Early Modern Europe (The Wiles Lectures)* (Cambridge: Cambridge University Press, 2004), 20.

20   Matthieu Ory (?–1557), a Dominican, was grand inquisitor in France in 1539. See *The Catholic Encyclopedia*, https://www.newadvent.org/cathen/11333a.htm (accessed February 23, 2021).

21   Jean Benoist (1484–1573), a theologian and exegete, was dean of the Faculty of Theology, 1565–73, and curate of the parish of the Saints-Innocents. See James Knox Farge, *Biographical Register of Paris Doctors of Theology, 1500–1536* (Toronto: Pontifical Institute of Mediaeval Studies, 1980), 37–39.

22   Émery Courselles (c.1477–1560), sub-dean of the Faculty of Theology of Paris and a student of Hebrew. See Knox Farge, *Biographical Register*, 116.

restrained. And with them was Le Fèvre, the syndic of the Faculty of Theology, one of the most sensible men who ever set foot in the Sorbonne.[23] To conclude, let me add Master Noël Brûlard, the *procureur général*, that great Aristides,[24] and the Cato[25] of his day, who since the 1550s had opposed cases that they wanted to try in order to be received.[26] I'm telling you this expressly, in order to show you the extent of the self-assured impostures with which the Jesuits of our day want to remedy the above. For La Fon is so imprudent as to say that Ramus[27] and Mercerus,[28] who have since been recognized by the king's professors[29] as having strayed from our ancient religion, were the solicitors of this case; and that without their wrangling, the Jesuits would have won immediately; but that, in order to avoid sedition, the court was wisely forced to have someone appointed by the council who would talk less haughtily. You're lying, shameless Jesuit, I can't contain my anger. Neither Ramus nor Mercerus stirred. They belonged to the faction, as did their other colleagues, the royal professors, in order not to be separated from the university. And it may appear that the general wills of this great city of Paris metamorphized, in an instant, and espoused the party of two Huguenots, one of whom was Mercerus. He was so distant from the wrangling, that he was acquainted only with his Hebrew

---

23   Jacques Le Fèvre, professor at the Collège de Bourgogne, manager (*syndic*) of the Faculty of Theology.

24   Aristides the Just (*c*.550–*c*.467 BCE) was an Athenian general and politician. The ancient historian Herodotus called him the best and most honorable man in Athens. See *Ancient History Encyclopedia*, https://www.ancient.eu/Aristides/ (accessed February 23, 2021).

25   Cato the Elder (234–149 BCE) was born Marcus Porcius Cato. A Roman senator and historian, he was known for his conservatism and his opposition to Hellenization. See *Encyclopaedia Britannica*, https://www.britannica.com/biography/Marcus-Porcius-Cato-Roman-statesman-234-149-BC (accessed February 23, 2021).

26   A would-be lawyer or judge had to participate in a real trial before he could be "received," just as a carpenter or a silversmith had to make a "masterpiece" to demonstrate his ability to build a staircase or shape a silver urn and therefore be "received" into the guild.

27   Pierre Ramus (1515–72), also known as La Ramée, was a humanist, mathematician, and philosopher. A professor at the Collège Royal, he became Huguenot. Many Jesuits opposed his anti-Ciceronian rhetoric. *Encyclopaedia Britannica*, https://www.britannica.com/biography/Petrus-Ramus (accessed February 23, 2021).

28   Jean Mercier (?–1570), known as Mercerus, was a professor of Hebrew at the Collège Royal. He too was a Huguenot. See François Secret *Les Kabbalistes chrétiens de la Renaissance* (Paris: Dunod, 1964), 208.

29   That is, the professors of the Collège Royal (now called the Collège de France). The college was established by François I. Humanist in inspiration, it promoted such disciplines as Hebrew, ancient Greek, and mathematics. See Guillaume Duval, *Le Collège royal de France, ou Institution, establissement et catalogue des lecteurs et professeurs ordinaires du Roy* ... (Paris: M. Bouillette, 1645).

books, with which he communicated every day without interruption: great and superior in that language according to the judgment of the most learned, having the upper hand over all the Jews in the entire remnant of the affairs of the world, a real cypher. Well what? (It's the Jesuits' privilege to invent new lies to reinforce their calumnies over time.) If Jesuit La Fon dared, he'd willingly say that the city, the university, the Faculty of Theology of Paris, all four of the mendicant orders, and the curates were Huguenots, because they prevented them from matriculating in their holy order; for what other consequence can be named but that one? Oh, singular and admirable impudence! But excusable nonetheless, since it comes from a Jesuit. And nonetheless, in order to show the faith and the integrity with which I intend to confound their lies, in 1594 they printed Versoris's *Plaidoyer*,[30] desiring to turn[31] into envy this great case against the university: puts[32] forward that not Mercerus but, rather, Ramus and Gallandius[33] had become the solicitors of this case; but that was judged to be so far from verisimilitude that it was deemed hyperbole, owing to the open enmity that they continually displayed and which will accompany them to the tomb.[34] An enmity that Rabelais,[35] the Lucian[36] of our century, in the preface to his third book, and later that nice poet Joachim du Bellay,[37] in one of his

---

30 That is, his *Plaidoyer pour les Prêtres et Écoliers du Collège de Clermont contre l'Université* (Plea on behalf of the priests and students of the Collège de Clermont against the university), not published until 1594.

31 There is subtle, though brief word-play here. Versoris's family name was Le Tourneur, "the Turner," that is, the man who turns wooden spindles on a lathe. Versoris is a Latinism: *versor*, means "the turner."

32 There is no subject for this verb. It seems that it should be Versoris. The clause would therefore begin: "he puts forward ..."

33 Gallandius, that is, Pierre Galland (1510–59), professor of eloquence and Greek at the Collège Royal. See Charles B. Schmitt, *Cicero Scepticus: A Study of the Influence of the Academica in the Renaissance* (The Hague: Martinus Nijhoff 1972), 26–27.

34 Pasquier is referring to a quarrel between Galland and Ramus back in 1551. Galland had defended the Ancients, and especially Aristotle, whom Ramus had attacked. See Kees Meerhoff, *Rhétorique et poétique au XVIe siècle en France: Du Bellay, Ramus et les autres* (Leiden: Brill, 1986), 36.

35 François Rabelais (*c*.1494–1553) was a Franciscan monk, a Renaissance humanist, and a writer, physician, and scholar of Greek. He is best known for his *Gargantua et Pantagruel*, bawdy and grotesque tales about two giants. See *Encyclopaedia Britannica*, https://www .britannica.com/biography/Francois-Rabelais (accessed February 23, 2021).

36 Lucian of Samosata (125–180) was a Syrian satirist and rhetorician, best known for his tongue-in-cheek style. See *Encyclopaedia Britannica*, https://www.britannica.com/bio graphy/Lucian (accessed February 23, 2021).

37 Joachim du Bellay (1522–60) was a poet and a member of the literary group known as *la Pléiade* (the Pleiades), which strove to ennoble the French language by imitating

poems, mocked with the special placards that are their finest books. Moreover, Gallandius never belonged to any religion other than the Catholic, Apostolic, Roman one. I've pointed out this particularity in passing, to tell you that in everything, even the smallest things, the Jesuit can't go somewhere without disguises and lies.

the Ancients. See *Encyclopaedia Britannica*, https://www.britannica.com/biography/ Joachim-du-Bellay (accessed February 23, 2021). Cf. Meerhoff, *Rhétorique et poétique*, 109–30.

How the Jesuits Were Refused at the Very Beginning in Rome, and the Artifice Thanks to Which They Were Received

THE LAWYER. Don't think that if they were badly received in France, they must have been more favorably received in Rome, when they first went there. Ignatius and his nine companions, having arrived there, planned to create a new sect in 1539. The members would make the three vows common to other orders, and an additional fourth one involving missions; and they would have a general to whom they would owe absolute obedience, without full knowledge of the facts. I'll report for you, word for word, the conclusion reached by their assembly, and what Maffei,[1] the Jesuit, said in his life of Ignatius, which he dedicated to Acquaviva,[2] his general, printed with the general's permission: *Ergo sine controversia deligendum, cui omnes in terris, tanquam Christo parerent, cujus in verba jurarent, denique cujus sibi nutum ac voluntatem instar cujusdam divini oraculi ducerent.* And having stated, without pausing, that the general would remain in that honored position as long as he lived, he added: *Itemque ut quicumque Societatis instituta profiterentur, ii ad tria solemnia vota, quae nobis cum aliis dicatis Deo familiis fere communia sunt, quartum nominatim adjungret; quascumque ad fidelium vel infidelium terras Christianae rei causa Pontifici maximo ipsos mittere placuisset, eò sine tergiversatione ulla, atque adeo sine ulla non modò mercede, sed ne viatici quidem petitione proficiscendi.*[3] In this first plan, you see no absolute obedience, except in everything that has to do with their general; and, in the case of the pope, it has to do exclusively with missions. I leave you separately the remainder of their rule, which they will

---

1 Giovanni Pietro Maffei (1535–1603), from Bergamo in the northern Italian Peninsula, was a historian and professor of eloquence at the Roman College. He wrote a biography of Ignatius of Loyola, *De vita et moribus divi Ignatii Loiolae* (Douai: Bogardus, 1585), which is quoted throughout Pasquier's work. See *DHCJ*, 3:2466–67.
2 Claudio Acquaviva (1542–1615), a son of the duke of Atri in Abruzzo, provincial of Naples and then of Rome, and superior general, 1581–1615. See *CEJ*, 12–14.
3 "That those who would make their profession in accordance with the rules and in the manner of the Society, through the three solemn vows, which are almost like those of other orders consecrated to God, would expressly add the fourth, which is to go wherever it pleases our Holy Father to send us, to serve God and the Christian religion, be it Christian lands or in the lands of pagans and infidels, and making no excuse and receiving no salary, and also without asking for the things most necessary for the journey." Maffei, *De vita et moribus*, 116–17.

© KONINKLIJKE BRILL NV, LEIDEN, 2021 | DOI:10.1163/9789004164062_008

present to Pope Paul III, for it pleased His Holiness to approve it. He gave it to three cardinals to examine: they were of the opinion that it should be refused, especially Cardinal Guidiccioni.[4] I absolve Ignatius for being one of the most wary and worldly-wise persons of our day, known for having made a childish error; and by this new statute he saw to it that the general would be getting more obedience than the Holy See. That's why he reworked his rule and granted equal obedience to the Holy See and to the general.[5] Ribadeneyra the Jesuit, who likewise wrote a life of Ignatius, says this: *Quorum quidem Religio Clericorum regularium esset, institutum vero ut summo Pontifici ad nutum praesto forent, et omnino ad eam normam, vitam suam dirigerent, quae multo ante meditata, et à se esset constituta: Quod quidem Pontifex, tertio Septembris, Tibure libenter audivit anno 1539.*[6] From this passage you learn that Pope Paul III began to lend a favorable ear to their sudden request to offer absolute obedience in everything. And yet he still had doubts about opening the door entirely: for in 1540 he opened it for only sixty Jesuits, and only since 1543 has he opened the door fully.

---

4   Cardinal Bartolomeo Guidiccioni (1469–1549) was a jurist and played an important role in the Roman Curia under Paul III. In 1529, he was appointed to a committee that studied whether Ignatius and his companions should be permitted to found a new order. See *DBI*, https://www.treccani.it/enciclopedia/bartolomeo-guidiccioni_(Dizionario-Biografico) (accessed February 27, 2021).

5   He is alluding to the *Formula* submitted to the pope in 1539, Sutto, 152n125.

6   "Their religious order would be one of clerics under a rule, but it would be constituted in such a way that they would be available to do the Pope's bidding, and they would direct their entire life by this norm that they had long previously thought about and established. At Tivoli, in 1539, on September 3, the Pope gladly heard and praised this proposal."

The Insolent Name of the Society of Jesus, Usurped by the Jesuits, and the Diverse Fashions They Expressed It, in Order to Get It Authorized

THE LAWYER. Our entire France was infinitely scandalized by the factious and proud name Jesuit, which they had taken for themselves: our Gallican church, first of all, and then the court of the *parlement*, had strictly forbidden them to use it. Du Mesnil, that great *avocat du roi* who pleaded the case, showed how odious this name was among Christians. He recited briefly the reasons why the bishop, the Faculty of Theology, and the University of Paris had rejected them as soon as they arrived. "The principal reasons were (said he), first of all, the insolent name or title: the Jesuits. And in truth, if it was unbearable to usurp that name among Jews, Turks, and pagans, it was all the more to be rejected by Christians, who have all professed to follow Jesus's rule. How blameworthy would the person be who, all on his own, attributed to himself and usurped the name and title Christian among Christians, or François among the French, or Paris among Parisians. In addition, the proper name of Jesus is so worthy and excellent, that his disciples and sectarians left it solely for their leader, and they took only the adjective Christian." On this same subject, Pasquier said in his plea: "I shall begin with the title they give themselves, and then I shall move on to their propositions. First, in the midst of Christians they call themselves Jesuits. Good Lord, doesn't that amount to suing the apostles? These great holy fathers[1] had the joy and honor of seeing Our Lord Jesus Christ face to face, and of participating daily in his holy exhortations; and after he had gone up to heaven, of receiving his Holy Spirit from him; and yet, knowing how humbly they should respect and honor this great and holy name of Jesus, in the city of Antioch they never dared call themselves Jesuits, but simply Christians, as they had decided to do. Ever since then, the affairs of our religion have gone along in such a way that, just as in Rome, the popes never took Saint Peter's name, owing to the honor and the reverence they bore for their leader; and in like manner, in all of Christendom, no Christian has been baptized with the name Jesus. Knowing full well that for all our good old church fathers, it would have

---

1 This is a subtle anti-papal dig. If the apostles were all Holy Fathers, current Holy Fathers would be all of their successors, that is, all bishops, not just the pope. [He just means the apostles, since the successors of Peter would not have seen Jesus face to face.]

© KONINKLIJKE BRILL NV, LEIDEN, 2021 | DOI:10.1163/9789004164062_009

been blasphemy to give a creature the name that applies to the sole Creator and Savior of mankind. You must therefore, Messieurs the Ignatians, acknowledge this blasphemy against God's honor, when you call yourselves Jesuits. You'll tell me that you aren't taking the name Jesus, but Jesuits, to show people that you are partisans of Jesus. What? The apostles, the other disciples of Our Lord, and the persons who succeeded them without interposition, in short, all the good old fathers of our first church, were less partisan than you are? And a special privilege was needed so that you, not they, can borrow that title? Besides, I don't know how one can willingly be cut off from the Society of Our Lord Jesus Christ, in order to bind oneself tightly to the vows of your arrogant superstition." Pasquier put it very well here, when he said that it amounted to suing the apostles: which has happened since then to Jesuit La Fon, who insisted that the word Christian was more arrogant than Jesuit.[2] But at this point, I want to show you the many different fashions in which they've diversified, in order to give power and authority to that title. Ignatius and the people who belong to him say that they want to reduce our church to what it was in the days of the apostles. They plan to administer the entire word of God, through the sacrament of penance and the sacrament of the Eucharist. And for this project, over a long time they gradually increased in number, without the authorization of the Holy See; and they wanted to be called the Society of Jesus. The apostles administered those two sacraments and they spread the word of God throughout the universe: these new entrepreneurs were therefore permitted to do likewise. I refute that. For they weren't the successors of the apostles, the bishops were; and beneath them were the curates. Jesuit devotion was founded on ignorance; and owing to that ignorance, they shouldn't be called the sectarians, but rather the deserters of Jesus who introduced a new schism into our church. Yet under that erroneous proposition, they called themselves the Society of Jesus, a title that wasn't given to them by Our Holy Father, but a title they gave to themselves. This can be seen at length in the bull of 1540: *Quicumque in Societate nostra, quam Jesu nomine insignari cupimus, vult sub Crucis vexillo militare.* "Whoever of our Society, that we desire to be referred to by the name of Jesus, wants to fight under the banner of the cross...." This clause was repeated word for word in Julius III's bull of 1550, which confirms their privileges. So, it would be absurd to suppose that Pope Paul III wanted to honor them with this lofty title, he who initially refused them and later accepted up to a certain number, with several timidities in his conscience.

---

2   La Fon was one of Father Richeome's pen names. That Pasquier was referring to La Fon, circa 1599, is strong evidence that he and Richeome had at least a nodding (or a reading) acquaintance.

Nonetheless, the Jesuits never lack new and untruthful inventions to get something authorized, so they circulated the rumor that they were taking this title in faith and homage to the Holy See. And indeed, the first chapter of their Constitutions begins: *Haec minima Congregatio, quae à sede Apostolica prima sui institutione, Societas Jesu nominata est.* "This little congregation, which at its earliest foundation was named the Society of Jesus by the Holy See."[3] And after that, Versoris, the lawyer, pleaded their cause, alleging that this passage showed that Pope Paul III had been their godfather, and that they had kept the name out of humility, and not out of ambition. Those are the words he used. I forgive the lawyer, who is an honorable person; for his plea was based on memoranda that had been given to him, and not on those prudent Jesuits whose dissembling is revealed by their bulls. Isn't that an impudent lie? But the authority of the Holy See didn't suffice to honor them with that lie; one must have recourse to miracles, that's to say, to their deceptions. Some years later, Maffei first, and then Ribadeneyra[4] invented the following: Ignatius, accompanied by Pierre Favre[5] and Diego Laínez,[6] passing by a church near Rome and praying to God, fell into an ecstasy during which he saw God the Father, who was recommending Ignatius and his companions to Jesus Christ his Son, who was carrying his cross and who bore the stigmata of his wounds. Jesus promised to take them into his protection; and that very hour, he said to Ignatius: *Ego vobis Romae propitius ero,* "I shall be propitious to you in Rome." And as soon as Ignatius came out of the church, he told his two companions about the apparition. I've not the least doubt that the account is a fable. Diego Laínez succeeded him as general and knew about this miracle. So why didn't he notify his agent, Ponce Cogordan, and Versoris, his lawyer, when the case was pleaded? Why did he conceal this great miracle, when it should have been revealed? The principal objection raised about them at the Colloquy of Poissy, and subsequently in the court of the Parlement of Paris, was the insolence of that arrogant title, the Society of Jesus. Why (I ask you) did Laínez and his companions not notice this, when the Gallican church and the Parlement forbade

---

3   *Constitutions*, "General Examen," ch. 1 (p. 23).

4   The story is found in Maffei, *De vita et moribus*, 100; and Pedro de Ribadeneyra, *Vita di Sant'Ignatio* (Naples: Caechium, 1572), 270. The episode is known as the vision of La Storta in a chapel at the gates of Rome.

5   Pierre Favre (1506–46) known in Latin as Petrus Faber or in French as Pierre Lefevre or Favre, was among Loyola's first recruits in Paris and co-founders of the Society. He played a significant role in the first years of the order but died prematurely. See *DHCJ*, 2:1369–70.

6   Laínez was a Spanish-born Jesuit. While studying in Paris, he met Ignatius of Loyola and was one of those who helped create the Society of Jesus. He was active in the Council of Trent during its second period; and he became the second superior general of the Society of Jesus. See *DHCJ*, 2:1601–5.

them to take that title? They didn't do it, particularly because neither the devil
nor the imposters had lodged in their quill pens, as they since have. And yet
this lie is of no profit to them, except that it's another lie that the eye can see.
For, having recounted this fable, Maffei adds this: *Atque id ipsum vel imprimis
fuit causae, cur Ignatius confirmatae postmodum Societati, salutare potissimum
Jesu nomen indiderit.* "That was why their Society having been confirmed,
Ignatius subsequently gave it this holy name of Jesus."[7] If what this liar says is
true, then Ignatius and his companions didn't use the title Society of Jesus until
after their order had been confirmed. And yet, by the request they presented
to Pope Paul III and inserted into the first bull of 1540, they had already taken
that very title for themselves.

And what needs especially to be weighed is that, four or five years ago, Jesuit
Montaignes[8] clearly recognized that what Maffei and Ribadeneyra wrote was
false, and he blamed the pope for inventing it. "I tell you," Montaignes said to
Arnauld, "it was the pope who named this holy Society, and the holy council
approved it, which suffices to shut your mouth." La Fon says the same thing:
the common people gave them the name Jesuit, at a time when the Holy See
was calling them the [Society of the] Holy Name of Jesus. And two pages later
one finds: "The Jesuits did not call themselves Jesuits; rather, it is the Holy See
that called them the Society of Jesus." I praise the conscientiousness of these
two honest Jesuits,[9] who remained silent about Ignatius's purported vision,
and who mocked the other two dissemblers in their souls; but I must point out
their ignorance, for if they had read Paul III's first bull, they would have found
that Ignatius and his nine companions called themselves the Society of Jesus
when they presented their request to the pope.

The Lawyer being in these vehement passions of the mind, A GUEST said
to him: It seems to me that you are laboring in vain. They didn't get the name
Jesuits from either God or the pope; they got it from the common people, that
great philosopher and accountant of our actions. Note that La Fon agrees.
But one must understand the way things went in that matter. Initially, they
called themselves the Company or Society of Jesus, but the people observed
their conduct and called them Jesuists, not Jesuits, pronouncing the *T* and the

---

7   Pasquier is not entirely straightforward with his translation here. "Subsequently" (*puis après*)
    is not in the original, and the Latin has "the name of Jesus, most powerful to save," rather than
    "this holy name of Jesus."

8   That is, Richeome, who went by the pen name Franciscus Montanus, or François Montaignes.

9   Montaignes and La Fon are, of course, not two persons: they are both Richeome as Pasquier
    clearly knew.

second *E* together.[10] For when the case was pleaded in 1564, the lawyers always called them Jesuists. See the advice given by Master Charles Dumoulin,[11] one of the leading jurisconsults of France, when they were admitted: *An jesuistae sint recipiendi in regno Franciae, et admittendi in Universitate Parisiensi.*[12] Throughout his speech, when he refers to them, he uses no other word than *jesuistae*. You'll find the same thing in Versoris's *Plaidoyer*, which they printed. They temper their name (he says), and they talk about the college of the Jesuists. And a bit later he says: "But they cannot discard it, since they must share a name that totally fits both their order and its colleges, which cannot be the Collège de Clermont, unless by chance it applies to the three colleges founded by the bishop of Clermont. They therefore must add: "called of the Jesuists." That very name was still being used among them at their college in Paris, when they were expelled from it. It's true that, as time passed, some of the people, to facilitate the pronunciation, removed the first *S* and called them Jesuits instead of Jesuists. And when Pasquier had his letters printed in 1586, and also his *Plaidoyer*, and in the *Plaidoyer* of du Mesnil, the lawyer, in 1594 as well, they were called Jesuits, which was the common usage of the time. This wasn't changed in Versoris's *Plaidoyer*. So, accept it as a fact that they were called Jesuists. One could dig deeper into papers of that day, which is a wise thing to consider: since there was none of the real Jesus in them, but only a hypocritical disguise: the common people gave them the name Jesuists. It's similar to what one sees in the Greek word σοφος, which means "sage," and which long ago gave rise to the word sophist, meaning a person who is muddled.[13] So, let's not envy the name Jesuists, taken by these new muddlers of Jesus and of our church. In like manner, in our day the word *Deus* has been

---

10   Throughout this long explanation, Pasquier talks about "Jésuistes." That word had four syllables: Zhay-zoo-ees-tuh, ending with a silent *S*. In an attempt to capture the pronunciation that he is discussing, the silent *E* and the final silent *S* have been dropped. The result in English is Jesuist as contrasted with Jesuit.

11   Charles Dumoulin (1500–66) was an *avocat* in the Parlement of Paris, a professor, and an eminent jurisconsult. He stood out for his Gallican intransigence. See Wim Decock, "Charles Dumoulin: (1500–1566)," in *Great Christian Jurists in French History*, ed. Olivier Descamps and Rafael Domingo (Cambridge: Cambridge University Press, 2019), 97–116.

12   Whether the Jesuits should be received in the kingdom of France and admitted to the University of Paris.

13   This is presumably a joke, since anyone with any knowledge of ancient rhetoric, which is to say any educated person of the time, would know that the connotations of "sophist" were originally positive.

turned into deists,[14] which is a new heresy. And as God shines in his sapience,[15] it won't be inappropriate to link the Jesuist and the sophist, for the Jesuist is nothing but the sophist of our Catholic religion.

THE LAWYER. You aren't unreasonable, and I not only subscribe to your opinion, I maintain in addition that anyone who doesn't want to recognize them as the Society of Jesus is a great beast. They really are that, but they're like Judas in the midst of the apostles, inasmuch as the Jesuits are all so many Judases ready to betray either their kings or their kingdoms, when they see that the moment has come to betray them. What will you give us if we deliver to you our sovereign lord or the persons who are troubling his state, so that you can be rid of him? (They'll say that to the prince who has the most men and the most money.) Haven't they tried to do that in France? And if our great King Henri IV had believed them, wouldn't they have done it? But, thank God, they encountered the obstacle that our affairs required.

14   The word appears in DAF (1564) and defines it as "celui, celle qui, reconnaissant un Dieu, rejette toute religion révélée" [Someone who recognizes a God but rejects all revealed religion.] The term is not included in Cotgrave.

15   Sapience is the quality of being wise. It is an old French word that comes from the Latin *sapientia*, good taste, good sense, wisdom.

The Jesuits Are Called Apostles in Portugal and in the Indies, and the Deceit They Used

THE LAWYER. It's really a great wrong and casts doubt on their Society of Jesus: for in their Society there must of necessity be a Jesus, since we find that there were apostles; and also, today, there are some in the kingdom of Portugal. An impiety, certainly, which shames our Catholic, Apostolic, Roman Church. Under the dark cover of an obedience that is plastered with makeup, and which they say they are going to take to the Holy See, we permitted these hypocrites to take the apostles' names, not only in Portugal but in several cities in the Indies as well, which are ruled by Portugal. Although this story is shameful, it merits being heard and known by all upright persons, so that they'll realize that the Jesuits used every trick to promote their reputation, at the expense of the true church of God.

I'll therefore tell you that when Ignatius was in Venice with his nine companions, Pierre Favre, whom they called *Faber* in Latin, Francis Xavier, Diego Laínes, Alfonso Salmerón,[1] Nicolás de Bobadilla,[2] Simão Rodrigues,[3] Paschase Broët,[4] Claude Jay,[5] and Jean Codure,[6] he also enrolled in their Society a

---

1   Alfonso Salmerón (1515–85), from Toledo was a close friend of Laínez; he became one of Loyola's first six companions. A theologian and exegete, he played an important role in drawing up the decrees on dogma at the Council of Trent. In various ways, he also was part of the Jesuit government. See *CEJ*, 709–10.

2   Nicolás de Bobadilla (1509–90) from Spain, was one of Loyola's first companions in Paris. He worked in German-speaking lands and became critical of the Jesuit governance after Ignatius's death. The last decades of his long life he spent doing ministries in the Italian Peninsula. See *CEJ*, 107.

3   Simão Rodrigues (1510–79), a Portuguese Jesuit, was one of Loyola's first six companions. He was the first provincial of Portugal and a controversial figure among the first Jesuits. See *CEJ*, 685.

4   Paschase Broët (c.1500–62), from French region of Picardy, was one of Loyola's Parisian companions. After the foundation of the Society, he was sent to Ireland with a papal mission. Afterwards, he carried out various administrative functions in the Italian Peninsula and France. He died of plague in Paris. See *CEJ*, 120.

5   Claude Jay, or Le Jay, or Jayus (1504–52), from French Savoy, met Loyola and his companions in Paris. After the approval of the Society, he was sent to German-speaking lands, where he spent most of his life doing ministries and founding colleges, including the one in Vienna, where he died. See *CEJ*, 417.

6   Jean Codure (1508–41), from a little town in the French Alps, joined the group of Ignatius's companions in Paris. He died less than a year after the foundation of the Society. See *CEJ*, 177–78.

© KONINKLIJKE BRILL NV, LEIDEN, 2021 | DOI:10.1163/9789004164062_010

certain Hosius Navarrein,[7] bachelor of theology, who, after several difficulties
of which Ignatius rid him, *Tandem Societatem cum Ignatio, animumque con-
junxit, et ad reliquos socios adnumeratus est*,[8] as Ribadeneyra put it. And indeed,
dividing Venice among them, after they had returned from Rome for the first
time, (according to the same author) *Ignatius, Favre, Laynez, Viceriam,
Franciscus Xavier et Salmeron, in montem Celesium; Johannes Codurius et Hosius
(quem nostris jam adnumeratum diximus) Tarnisium: Claudius Jaïus, et Simon
Rodericus, Bassanum; Paschasius et Bobadilla, Veronam concedunt.*[9] God willed
that, having assigned his companions to go to Rome, Ignatius saw, when saying
Mass at Monte Cassino, Hosius's soul in the sky, with a gay face. When he died,
their group was reduced to its first total of ten, the number, you'll tell me, for
whom they presented their request to Pope Paul III, and they only later added
others to make neither eleven, nor twelve companions, as they had done with
Hosius. Now, so the story goes, while they were in Rome, waiting until it pleased
the pope to approve their new project, John III, king of Portugal, wanted a few
of these devout pilgrims to send to the [East] Indies, most of which he possessed. By their long and daring navigation, the Portuguese had made a path in
these new lands (as our Jesuit fathers call them) and had turned themselves
into *seigneurs*, most of them *seigneurs* who had remained in their old idolatry;
and the other *seigneurs* were crude Christians, although they had been baptized. Considering which, they were advised by Master Diego de Gouvea,[10] the
former principal of the Collège de Sainte-Barbe in Paris, to take some of these
new pilgrims who were in Rome, in order to convert his subjects. The king
ordered Gouvea to write to Ignatius, who replied, in a letter, that he had no
power, and that everything depended on the Holy Father's wishes. After some
going back and forth, this duty was assigned to Francis Xavier of Navarre and
Simão Rodrigues of Portugal. They went before the king, who received them
with affability and courtesy. After their arrival, the pope admitted this new
group, up to a total of sixty. These two[11] were called apostles, a title they

---

7   Hoses or Hoces was not from Navarre but from Málaga, where he was born around the
     same time as Ignatius. He met Loyola in Alcalá and joined the group of Ignatius's com-
     panions in Venice but died soon after in 1538. See *DHCJ*, 2:1929.

8   "Later, however, he joined the Society wholeheartedly and he was counted with the rest of
     the companions."

9   "Ignatius, Favre, and Laínez were assigned to Vicenza; Francis Xavier and Salmerón to
     Monselice; John Codure and Hoces (whom we mentioned had joined our number) to
     Treviso; Claude Jay and Simão to Bassano; Paschase and Bobadilla to Verona."

10   Diego de Gouvea (1470–1557), a doctor of theology from the Sorbonne, later served the
     Portuguese crown in various capacities. See Agnès Pellerin, *Les Portugais à Paris: Au fil des
     siècles et des arrondissements* (Paris: Chandeigne, 2009), 46–48.

11   That is, Francis Xavier and Simão Rodrigues.

transmitted to their successors in that country. Orazio Torsellini,[12] a Jesuit, describes the situation in this way: *Ad extremum eximia illorum virtus* (he is referring to Xavier and Rodrigues) *rerumque humanarum despicientia cunctae civitati miraculo fuit. Jam in vulgus relatum erat duodecim Romae Sacerdotes (duo enim ad illos decem accesserunt) Societatem inter se coisse. Ex quo numero in duobus illis, quos apud se haberent, intueri sibi videbantur, nescio quod specimem vitae Apostolicae. Itaque eos populus, sive ex pari numero, sive ex quadam vitae similutidine, Apostolos, nimis amplo scilicet vocabulo, appellare coepit: et quamvis invitos et reclamantes vocitare perseverarit. Quippe natio Lusitana, non minus in coeptis constans, quàm in consiliis piis, nullis perpelli rebus potuit, ut revocaret quod semel dederat, ut credebat, veritati. Quin etiam eo progressa res est, ut ad caeteros quoque è Societate, tota fermè Lusitania, idem cognomen perveniret.* And this passage is truly of such merit that I'd be wronging these good folks if I didn't make it French, to show the piety with which they earned this sacred name. For all Jesuits honor him as their great saint.[13] "Finally, said Torsellini (speaking of Xavier and Rodrigues), their singular virtue and their scorn for human things, were considered a great miracle by the entire city. The people were then told that there were twelve priests in Rome (for they had added two more to the ten older ones) who had formed a society together, among whom were the two sent to the king. They seemed to see in them an indefinable air of the apostolic life. Therefore, the common people, either because the first number was the same, or because they were conforming to ways of doing things, called them apostles, a very daring name, even though that wasn't their intention. And the Portuguese nation, no less constant in its undertakings than in councils full of piety, can never forget that it believed it was true. These things went on in such a way that, until now, that same title has remained for all the others in that religious order or family." Was there ever a greater impiety and imposture than that? These two hypocrites, having been called apostles, finally started a rumor that two new members had been added to their sect, to make the twelve apostles. They didn't want to believe the bearer (says Torsellini). For even when Xavier reached the Indies, he was very careful not to lose that grand title. *Ergo ut antea in Lusitania, sic in India Apostolus vulgo coeptus est appellari: idemque postea cognomen à Francisco, quasi capite, ed ejus manavit socios*: "So, just as in Portugal, he was also called 'apostle to the

---

12   Orazio Torsellini (1545–99) was a Jesuit historian and professor at the Roman College. He was also rector of the Roman Seminary and of the colleges in Florence and Loreto. See DHCJ, 4:3827. The passage is from *De vita Francisci Xaverii* (Liège: Henricus Hovius, 1597), 35–36.

13   Francis Xavier was beatified in 1619 and canonized in 1622.

Indies': a nickname that subsequently was passed on to his companions, as from the leader." I pray you, tell me whether this isn't the heresy of Mani, whom the Manicheans followed. He had people call him Paraclete.[14] He had twelve disciples whom he called his apostles, and whom he distributed throughout the different provinces, in order to spread the venom of his heresy by their preaching. Ignatius, to tell the truth, didn't adopt the name Paraclete; but he wanted to be recognized as another Jesus Christ by those around him, as I'll show you when I discuss blind obedience. And not only did he take for himself this authority and power, he also gave it to all the generals of his order, his successors: they likewise embraced the title apostle, which their inferiors had adopted in Portugal. This can be seen in Rome, yet no one sees it. To the contrary, this religious group is respected with full honor, based on a false conviction about absolute obedience, which these *messieurs* pretend to be showing for popes. And so we let our jaws drop, because the Holy See has railed at several new opinions that contradict him? As for me, from now on I'll be very distressed if I don't find it strange. Oh, Holy See, pardon me, I pray you: for the ardent zeal that I vowed to show you, makes me proffer these words. God's judgments are great and inexpressible. To endure the fact that you can see, that you can know, that there is in Rome a Mani who continues, by diverse successors, from one person to another; and who doesn't have twelve apostles, but who has an infinity of apostles scattered here and there: sooner or later, God will avenge that, or his enemies will. THE LAWYER, appearing very upset at heart, was going to continue his angry words, when he was interrupted. THE JESUIT. Now, now, you are in danger of being dried up in the heat of the day. Hearing you talk like that, reminds me of those school-boy historiographers who once criticized the stupidity of King Alexander the Great, who tried to make people believe that he was Jupiter's son.[15] They attributed this to his excessive self-importance, yet no counsel was ever wiser than this one. Do you

---

14   Mani (216–74?), was a Persian [he was possibly born in modern Iraq] prophet. He founded the Manichaean religion, which advocated a dualistic doctrine that viewed the world as a fusion of spirit and matter, and of the contrary principles of good and evil. Paraclete means "consoler," which is an attribute of the Holy Spirit. See *Encyclopaedia Britannica*, https://www.britannica.com/biography/Mani-Iranian-religious-leader (accessed February 27, 2021).

15   By the time of his death, Alexander the Great was reportedly convinced he was the son of the Greek god Zeus (Jupiter). This impression came through his mother, Olympias, whose imperial family of Epirus traced their ancestry from Achilles. See, Donald L. Wasson, "Alexander the Great as a God," in *Ancient History Encyclopedia*, https://www.ancient.eu/article/925/ (accessed February 23, 2021).

know why? As long as he was aiming at the lands of King Darius,[16] he was very careful to use that title, for he wanted to increase his wealth in the usual way: war. But suddenly, he decided to go to the Indies, which were like a new world, separated from ours; and he wanted to convince the people that the Great Pontiff of Egypt had declared him the son of Jupiter; and from then on he made people worship him as such; but not the Macedonians, his natural subjects, who had been raised in the Grecian freedom of spirit: he wanted to be adored by all the barbarians, with such respect and trust that from then on they held that he was not a simple prince but a great god who was setting off to conquer the Indies. This advice fit him so well that he became the absolute master without having to fight. Kings, potentates, and the common people would say that their country was first conquered by Bacchus, and then by Hercules, both of whom were the children of Jupiter; and that when Alexander arrived, he was a third son, for whom dominance and total lordship were reserved. Do you think this same advice did not reach our religious family? You do not see that we have taken the title apostles anywhere but in Portugal: but seeing that we had to go to the same Indies to which Alexander had gone, we judged, as he did, that we have to be more authorized than everyone else, with a title that was ampler, holier, and more august: apostles. It would have been inappropriate to take that title in Portugal, if our Xavier had not passed it on, thanks to the intervention of those around him. Having reached the Indies, he would be considered another Saint Thomas,[17] who was sent there after the passion of Our Lord Jesus Christ. And it would be impossible to say how many souls we won thanks to that holy persuasion.

THE LAWYER. Ha, really! If you take it in this fashion, I'll withdraw it: for just as when you enter Italy, you borrow something indefinable from their charlatans, you wanted to do the same with Machiavelli in Portugal and the Indies. Yet you other *messieurs*, whom you were praising for having been nourished on theology for several years, you were negligent when you thumbed through the history of the kings in the Bible, from which you continually are gleaning things. Every time, and as often as the kings of Israel became idolaters, God frustrated their crowns, perhaps during their lifetime or perhaps by an event that doesn't permit the crowns to fall into their children's hands. So, think

---

16   Darius III, also called Codommanus (d.330 BCE) was the last king (r.336–330 BCE) of the Achaemenid dynasty. He was defeated by Alexander the Great at the battle of Gaugamela in 331. See *Encyclopaedia Britannica*, https://www.britannica.com/biography/Darius-III (accessed February 27, 2021).

17   Traditionally, Thomas the Apostle was believed to have travelled outside the Roman Empire and reached present-day India. See *Encyclopaedia Britannica*, https://www.britannica.com/biography/Saint-Thomas (accessed February 27, 2021).

about it, I pray you: God permitted the true kings of Portugal to remain heirless, and their kingdom served as flotsam and jetsam for the first prince to occupy. Think of it: Don António,[18] a bastard, and Catherine de Médicis, the queen mother of our kings, claimed a share; and finally, King Philip of Spain made himself the master, without a great dispute. I won't go into the details about his title: but as for me, I want to believe that the finest title he bore was God's Justice. In order to avenge the stubborn idolatry and blasphemy of the kings and of the people, he wanted the kingdom to pass from one family to another without full knowledge of the facts. And I'm assured that the king of Spain who is now reigning, will undergo similar mischief if he tolerates this impiety.

18   Don António, prior of Crato (1531–95) was the bastard cousin of Sebastian, king of Portugal, who reigned from 1557 to 1578. He protested in vain Philip II's annexation of Portugal. See *Encyclopaedia Britannica*, https://www.britannica.com/biography/Antonio-prior-of-Crato (accessed February 27, 2021).

CHAPTER 10

The Impieties of Guillaume Postel, Jesuit

THE LAWYER. But why would we find it strange that they are blasphemers, if several years after they took the title apostle, one of them was so abominable before God, and before men, as to put the power of Our Lord Jesus Christ in doubt, as far as our redemption is concerned? The person I'm talking about is Guillaume Postel, against whom Pasquier declaimed as follows, in his *Plaidoyer*:[1]

"But inasmuch as they sing solely about their piety into the ears of rather witless women, attaching that piety to the hem of their robes with a clasp or an *aiguillette*, let us see if they really are what they say they are. We have the Benedictines, the Bernardines, the Dominicans, the Franciscans, and other such orders. As soon as they professed their religious vows, they entered into such holy lives that, with the common consent of the church, they were registered on the calendar of saints. That is why several of the Jesuits, attracted by their good life, wanted to do the same. It also turns out that the first members of the Jesuit sect lived such holy and austere lives that not by a longshot did we close our door to them; on the contrary, we wanted to merge with them. About ten or twelve years ago,[2] one of your oldest disciples came through this city. The man surpasses you at knowing simple maneuvers: he was Master Guillaume Postel.[3] We saw him preach, read, and write. He wore a big cassock that came down to his knees, a long robe with a clasp, and a bonnet like a bishop's, accompanied by a pale and dried-up face that revealed merely a very great austerity; and he celebrated a Mass for us using several austere ceremonies not commonly seen in church. Well, what did he bring us? A Mother Janne,[4] an impiety, the most detestable heresy ever heard of, since the coming of Our

---

1 Étienne Pasquier, *Le Plaidoyé de M. Pasquier pour l'Université de Paris* (Paris: Abel l'Angelier, 1594).

2 That is, between 1551, when Postel returned from the Orient, and the spring of 1553, when he was prevented from teaching in public.

3 See William Bouwsma, Concordia mundi: *The Career and Thought of Guillaume Postel (1510–1581)* (Cambridge, MA: Harvard University Press, 1957).

4 Postel met an older woman named Joannna or Janne in Venice, 1547–49. He became convinced that she had supernatural powers, especially the ability to see Satan in the very center of the earth. He also admired her competence in explaining the most profound mysteries of the Zohar, a text of the Kabbalah (Sutto, 165n174). Her name, Janne, gave rise to a pun: she was a *Dame Janne*, that is, a "demijohn," a "half Janne," a large bottle made of glass or pottery, protected by woven straw or wicker, that was often used to transport alcohol.

Lord. The Donatists,[5] the Arians,[6] the Pelagians[7] never did such work. Where did Postel preach? Not in the mountains or the deserts, where one customarily plants a new religion: he did it in the very middle of France, in the city of Paris. What order did he belong to? To that venerable Society of Jesus.[8] Ha! If your Society really produces such monsters, if it gives rise to such damnable effects in us, please God we never enter that Society of Jesus!"

Today the Jesuits deny, loud and strong, that Postel was part of what they called their family. They not only deny it, they also deny that Pasquier ever raised that objection when he pleaded against them in the courts. They say that the objection is a new little lean-to shed that he added to his old plea, when he wanted to have it printed. Pasquier shows (says wise La Fon) "that he lost all the faculties of his soul, his understanding is full of shadows, his will is full of gall, his memory is full of forgetfulness: because when he pleaded that case in 1564, Postel was full of life, confined to the monastery of Saint-Martin-des-Champs in Paris, where he lived until 1580. Yet this good defense lawyer talks about him as if he'd died long ago. And we must note that Pasquier didn't say this when he pleaded. For he would have undergone the *amende*[9] for such an impudent lie and would have been whistled at by everyone who saw that Postel was present. But he posted twenty-one injurious placards about him afterward, wanting to shine the light on him; and he contradicted himself by forgetting to follow the advice in the proverb: *Oportet mendacem esse memorem*,[10] in order to baste these pieces of falsity together so effectively that no seam is visible."[11] And truly, it's not without cause that the Jesuits made this buffoon play at that set speech. For if Postel was a Jesuit, they are lost. So, I pray you, let's examine

---

5   The Donatists were heretics who denied the validity of sacraments that are not administered by a holy person. The sect was condemned in 314. See *Encyclopaedia Britannica*, https://www.britannica.com/topic/Donatists (accessed February 27, 2021).

6   The Arians denied the consubstantiality of the Son and the Father. Arianism was condemned in 325. See *Encyclopaedia Britannica*, https://www.britannica.com/topic/Arianism (accessed February 27, 2021).

7   The Pelagians denied the need for divine grace, the transmission of original sin, and the distinction between the natural order and the supernatural order. See *Encyclopaedia Britannica*, https://www.britannica.com/topic/Pelagianism (accessed February 27, 2021).

8   Guillaume Postel (1510–81) met Ignatius of Loyola in Paris and was a Jesuit for one year, 1544–45. Although he was expelled from the Society, allegedly for his strong support of Gallicanism, he continued to value it: Sutto, 164n178. Cf. Yvonne Petry, *Gender, Kabbalah, and the Reformation: The Mystical Theology of Guillaume Postel, 1510–1581* (Leiden: Brill, 2004), esp. 37.

9   *Amende* usually means a fine; but as the Glossary shows, an *amende* could also be a painful and humiliating physical punishment.

10   "A liar needs a good memory," Quintilian, *Institution oratoire*, IV, ii, 91.

11   *Response de René de la Fon*, 200–2; Sutto, 165n182.

three things. The first is Pasquier's objection. The second is whether Postel was in the Society. And lastly: what sort of impiety did he want to introduce into our religion, in the name of Mother Janne. For, as good companions say, the game is well worth the candle.[12]

Concerning the first point, Pasquier never talked about Postel as being a dead man. But be that as it may, this is how the passage begins: "About ten or twelve years ago one of your disciples passed through this city. He's a man who surpasses you, just as you surpass simple laborers." You can see that he spoke like a man who was full of life; but he soon added: "It was Master Guillaume Postel," referring back to ten or twelve years earlier, when Postel had built a heresy upon Mother Janne, as you can gather from that passage. Which shows that the Jesuits had neither understanding, nor judgment, nor memory, bragging in that manner about Pasquier. In 1594, they printed Versoris's *Plaidoyer*,[13] written back in 1564. It was a reply to Pasquier. Let's take out the book and read from it. On page 36, you'll find these words: "They raise the objection to us that Postel had also belonged to our Society, and that from bad fruits one can see how the tree is. I asked them what Judas's fruits were; should we condemn Our Lord and the apostles because of that?" And a bit later he says: "Postel was never a professed father in their house. He was a novice there, and he was sent away." Do you want a better eyewitness demonstration than that? In order to show that Pasquier was talking about Postel when he was alive, and that he raised that objection; for otherwise, when he wrote this objection, Versoris would have replied to what he was thinking. Next, let's see whether Postel was a member of their order: to verify this, I'll refer to what I just read to you. Versoris and Pasquier were two brave champions who were fighting with pointed weapons[14] in an enclosed camp, watched by the principal senate of France.[15] The blow that was directed at Postel offended the order, owing to his rank among them. If he hadn't been a Jesuit at the time, believe me, the great lawyer Versoris wouldn't have avoided the blow, as he did, but would have firmly denied it, as the Jesuits do now, judging that time would efface the memory of it. But knowing that the truth that was then present would have proved that he was lying; he wasn't so daring. By that means, tossed by the currents, he admitted that Postel had been a novice in the Jesuit order, but

---

12   That is, what you win by gambling is worth the cost of the candle. Candles were expensive.
13   *Plaidoyer de Pierre Versoris, Avocat en Parlement, pour les jésuites contre l'Université de Paris* (Paris, 1564).
14   In a joust, it was shocking if someone struck with pointed weapons, rather than with dull ones, as was usual.
15   That is, the Parlement of Paris contemporaries likened to the Senate of ancient Rome.

that the Society had thrown him out like trash. Now, you won't be able to give a precise date for when he was thrown out, because ever since the printing of his book about Mother Janne, which repelled everyone, it's been proved that he wasn't permitted to enter the novitiate; and a short time later the book was condemned, and the author was confined to the monastery of Saint-Martin. Previously he had been too great a personage in all sorts of learning and languages, and he couldn't be turned out: so, the public could see him in Paris, dressed like a Jesuit; he lived at the Collège des Lombards with Father Paschase Broët and the other Jesuits. That college was their first residence; and later, when they had the Hôtel de Langres, with its wide-open doors on the rue Saint-Jacques, he would eat and drink with them every day. At the time, he may have been confined to the monastery of Saint-Martin, so no one expressed a doubt that he was a Jesuit.

What impiety did he therefore base on Mother Janne? Pardon me, Messieurs, if I reveal that abomination to you. Having to fight against those so-called African navigators,[16] everyone understood that they produced as many new monsters as there were heads. Having spent several years as a royal professor of Greek at the University of Paris, he gave up his position and sailed off to Palestine, just as good Ignatius had done. From there, he headed for Venice, around the time of good Ignatius. Having set up housekeeping with an old bigot named Janne, he presented her as his stepmother. Somewhat later, he returned with his Jesuit companions to the Collège des Lombards in Paris, where he published a book entitled: On the Victory of Women,[17] in which he argued that, by his death and his passion, Our Lord Jesus Christ had merely redeemed the upper world, that is, man, and that his Mother Janne had been sent by God to save the lower world, that is, women. To this impiety he added his dreams about Pythagoras. Wanting to persuade people that the soul of Saint John the Evangelist had been infused into him, and that another madman, who had formerly been a goldsmith, had been infused with the soul of John the Baptist, he would go around town dressed like a Jew, in a coarse, leather-colored robe, bareheaded, longhaired, and barefooted. They did penance and preached that the world would soon end. This new Saint-John-the-Baptist-Postel subsequently was burned alive by a decree of the Parlement of Toulouse, which didn't want to take his feeble mind in payment. And in truth, they marveled that the same thing had not been done to Postel in Paris. For his book was sold

---

16   Pasquier is evoking some sort of sea monster that would grow from a chopped-off head. A
       possible candidate is Scylla, the six-headed monster who was believed to live in the straits
       of Messina, between Scylla and Charybdis.

17   *Les très merveilleuses victoires des femmes du nouveau monde* (Paris: Jehan Geullart, 1553).

openly by peddlers; and there's no excuse, except that the Jesuits, by I don't know what sort of exterior infatuations with which they charmed us, carry their safe-conduct certificate everywhere. I'm sure that Richeome will one day add this great miracle to his book of miracles.[18]

We today have other of Postel's budding flowers. For the same Pasquier, pleading the above case, said that Ignatius had been just as partial, and just as big a disturber of our church as Martin Luther was. That both were born roughly a century ago: Martin in 1483, Ignatius in 1491; that both had built their sects, saying that they would take all their principles from our primitive church, in order to lure more easily the simple people to their faction. But that Ignatius's sect was more to be feared than the Lutherans, going into detail about the reasons that invited him to say that: and especially that each of us should be on his guard against Luther, whom we judged to be a heretic. To the contrary, in Ignatius's sect it would be easy to be surprised by some tincture of counterfeited religious zeal in which it was draped. "This single conclusion (said the same La Fon) shows that Pasquier is full of shadows and malignity; and although he speaks earnestly, his soul is like the soul of that atheist whom I dare not name, who made a similar comparison between Moses[19] and his Law, and Mohammed and his sect, and who calls both of them impostors."[20] What? Someone who compares Ignatius and Luther is committing the same sort of impiety as the other person does, who compares Moses and Mohammed! Moses, specially chosen by God to deliver his children from captivity in Egypt, and from the tyranny of the pharaohs; Moses, to whom God appeared and spoke, and by whose prayers, with his hands raised to heaven, this same great God made the children of Israel victorious. I don't believe there was a man so wicked that he dared compare Moses and Mohammed; and if there were such a person, I think that our Jesuits are as wicked as he is, comparing Ignatius and Moses. This comparison was strange to me; but thumbing through other Jesuit

---

18   Richeome's *Trois discours pour la religion catholique, des miracles, des saints, et des images* (Bordeaux: Simon Millanges, 1597), was condemned by the Parlement of Paris in 1597.

19   The Treatise of the Three Impostors (*De tribus impostoribus*) was a mythical text arguing that the three main figures of the Abrahamic religions, namely Moses (Judaism), Jesus (Christianity), and Mohammed (Islam), were pretending to be someone else, for example a prophet or a son of God, in order to deceive others for fraudulent gain. The book was talked about from the eleventh to the eighteenth centuries, when hoaxes produced two actual books. See Jan W. Wojcik, Review of *The Treatise of the Three Impostors and the Problem of Enlightenment: A New Translation of the* Traité des trois Imposteurs, *Journal of the History of Philosophy* 37, no. 2 (1999): 368–70, doi:10.1353/hph.2008.0837.

20   *Response de René de la Fon*, 128 [Sutto 167n190].

books, I found that it was very familiar to them. For Father Annibale Codreto[21] had no doubts, when he wrote that their Society had taken his name; because God had given them to his dear son Jesus Christ, as companions, and Jesus had accepted them as such.[22] And in their annual letters of 1589, the Jesuits of the College of Our Lady of Loreto,[23] writing to their general, recount how a person influenced by a demon, having plotted with one of their religious by virtue of the name of Jesus, became somewhat angry; but when Ignatius's name was mentioned, the devil began to play the devil more than before, so frightened was he by that holy name. These blasphemies are the least peccadillos of our Jesuits: those religious have many others, of which I hope one day to draw up a good and faithful inventory. But because, moving from one statement to another without thinking about it, I'm following the progress and the flow of years, I want to return to our Ignatius and his companions, in order to show you their charlatanerie when they reached Rome, in order to be approved.

21   Hannibal du Coudret (1529–99) was part of the group to open in 1548 the first Jesuit school in Messina of which he later became a rector; he wrote for his superiors in Rome the *Ratio studiorum Collegii Messanensis*. See Aldo Scaglione, *The Liberal Arts and the Jesuit College System* (Amsterdam: John Benjamins Publishing, 1986), 135–36. See also Book III, ch. 3 below.

22   Antoine Arnauld had already written this in his *Plaidoyer de M.A.A. pour l'Université de Paris, demanderesse, contre les jésuites défendeurs* (Paris: Mamert Patisson, 1594), 832. La Fon denied this and asserted that du Coudret had never written about the Society (Sutto, 167n192).

23   On the Jesuits' presence in Loreto, see Vincenzo Lavenia, "Miracoli e memoria: I gesuiti a Loreto nelle storie della Compagnia (sec. XVI–XVII)," in *Figure della memoria culturale: Tipologie, identità, personaggi, testi e segni*, ed. Massimo Bonafin, special issue of *L'immagine riflessa: Testi, società, culture* 22 (2013): 331–48.

CHAPTER 11

The Studies of the Great Ignatius

THE LAWYER. Ignatius began his studies in 1524, at the age of thirty-three, in the city of Barcelona. Studies that he could not easily savor. For having (or so he boasted) a spirit totally raised to heaven, he couldn't stoop so low as to learn the declensions of Latin nouns. *Quam etiam rem* (wrote Maffei) *quasi futura praesagiens, etiam adjuvabat vafer humani generis inimicus, eo maxime tempore, creba, intelligentiae lumina eidem offerens, et recondita Scripturae sacrae mysteria patefaciens.*[1] I don't think a man ever spoke as truthfully as he did; for all of Ignatius's so-called celestial musings were true mummeries of the devil, who wanted to give us a man who, by his ignorance, would trouble the general state of our church. During this struggle he spent two years in Barcelona, at the end of which, wanting to get an early start on his studies, he went to the University of Alcalá, where he pretended to be studying logic, physics, and theology. *In Logicis* (wrote Maffei) *terminos quos appellant, in Phisicis Albertum, in theologia Magistrum sententiarum, qui maximè tum libri in Hispania tenebantur, evoluere, et plures quotidie coepit interpretes.*[2] I'll leave it to your imagination whether these books let themselves be handled by someone who had studied grammar for only two years, from necessity; or whether he employed the five senses that nature had given him, without flitting off to other plans; for even persons who are the most informed about letters, are not able to understand Albert,[3] and even less able to understand the Master of the Sentences,[4] the

---

1 "In this regard [wrote Maffei] the clever Enemy of the human race also helped, as if foretelling what was to come. At that time especially, the devil provided him frequent flashes of intelligence and opened up to him arcane mysteries of sacred scripture." Maffei, *De vita et moribus*, 51.

2 "To unfold the terminal Logics, as they are called [Aristotle's *Posterior Analytics*?], the Physics of Albert [the Great], the theology of the Master of the Sentences, books that were then held in Spain to be the greatest; and he started in on several commentators every day." Maffei, *De vita et moribus*, 54.

3 Albert the Great (*c.*1193–1280) was a Dominican friar. He taught in Paris and Cologne. His principal theological works are a commentary on the *Books of the Sentences* of Peter Lombard and on the *Summa theologiae* of Thomas Aquinas (1225–74). See *Encyclopaedia Britannica*, https://www.britannica.com/biography/Saint-Albertus-Magnus (accessed February 27, 2021).

4 Peter Lombard (*c.*1105–60) is known as the *Magister Sententiarum*, Master of the Sentences. His *Sentences* are a systematic compilation of theology, written around 1150; its name comes from the Latin word *sententiae*, that is, an assemblage of authoritative statements about

© KONINKLIJKE BRILL NV, LEIDEN, 2021 | DOI:10.1163/9789004164062_012

basic foundation of our Scholastic theology. In addition, the two years he spent, sometimes at Alcalá and sometimes at a different university, Salamanca, were nothing but imprisonments and extraordinary proceedings against him, that is to say, all so many interruptions of these imaginary studies; because the only study he had in his soul was to form lovely simulacres of a new sect. All of that was partly why, when he saw that his plans were not going to succeed in Spain, he wanted to go to France, and he arrived in Paris in February 1528. And then, according to Maffei and Ribadeneyra,[5] knowing the scant progress he had made during four years, because he had been hasty and had not organized his studies, he decided to take to the open road. Let's look at Maffei and see what he tells us:

> *Cumque experiendo jam cognovisset eam esse humanae mentis imbecilitatem, ut in plura uno eodemque tempore, vix atque aegrè sufficiat, damnata priore festinatione, posthac compendiis omissis, regia via procedere, et studiorum suorum novum initium ordiri coepit. Igitur ad Montis acuti Collegium, itare quotidie, atque inter procacium puerorum greges, matura jam aetate vir. Gramaticae Rudimenta repetere non dedignatus est. Simul etiam de stato precationis tempore, et vexatione corpusculi, quo plus otii et virium superesset, multum imminuit: Sic tamen ut illa praecipuè tria numquam, omiserit. Primum ut quotidie sacrificio Missae religiosè interesset: alterum, ut octavo quoque die, post Poenitentiae Sacramentum: coelesti pane sese reficeret: extremum, ut bis quotidie sua ejus diei dicta, facta, cogitata quam diligentissime recognosceret: conferensque hodiernum cum hesterno die hebdomadam cum hebdomada, mensemque cum mense, suos in spiritu vel progressus, vel regressus, per quam accurate exploraret, atque perpenderet.*[6]

---

a field of study. See *Encyclopaedia Britannica*, https://www.britannica.com/biography/Peter-Lombard (accessed February 27, 2021).

5   Maffei, *De vita et moribus*, 1, xviii; Ribadeneyra, *Vita Ignatii Loiolae*, 1, xvi.

6   "When he had learned by experience the weakness of the human mind, how it was only barely and with difficulty sufficient to do more than one thing at a time, he condemned his earlier haste and henceforth abandoned shortcuts and began to proceed along the royal road and commenced a new beginning of his studies. Therefore, he daily attended the college of Montagu, an already adult man with the flocks of cheeky boys. He did not disdain to relearn the rudiments of grammar. Also he cut back considerably on his routine of prayer and the mortification of his flesh, so as to have more leisure and strength, but in such a way that he never neglected the three most important things: first, that he participate in the ceremony of the mass every day without fail; secondly, that every eighth day he take the sacrament of penance and restore himself with heavenly bread; and finally, that twice a day he review the things that he had said, done, and thought on that day as diligently as possible, so that by

Let's follow the wafting breezes of the same Maffei. Ignatius having reached Paris, *tanta subitò rerum inopia oppressus est, ut ei cibum ostiatim quaeritare quotidie, et in hospitalem sancti Jacobi domum, infimis precibus, exorato ejus loci Praeside, demigrare necesse fuerit, gravi sanè incommode. Igitur in S. Jacobi hospitio, quo procul est in suburbano, extrema necessitate compulsus Ignatius, in tanto locorum intervallo, cum aliis afflictabatur commodis, tum vero quod cum ante lucem in Academia inciperent Scholae, nec nisi nocte desinerent, ipse, illius hospitii legibus, nec manè ante Solis ortum egredi poterat, et vespere ante occasum regredi cogebatur; sic ut inter eundum et redeundum, quamvis industrio ac diligendi discipulo, multum et de magistri dictatis, et de tota scholarum, exercitatione deperiret. Cui tanto detriment, cum in praesentia nullum aliud remedium occurreret, consilum coepit de more scholasticorum egentium, ea conditione locandi operam suam alicui ex Academiae primariis doctoribusque, ut quod sibi à rebus domesticis, otii superesset, id totum in scholastica disciplina, studiisque doctrinae consumeret.*[7] And soon after that, seeing that Ignatius was making little progress in his studies, *Rationem iniit multo commodiorem, ut initis vacationum feriis, in Belgium, atque interdum etiam in Angliam, sive Britanniam ad Hispanos negotiatores excurreret; quorum benigitate cùm facilè obtinuisset annuam pecuniae summam, Lutetiae toto studiorum tempore, certis pensionibus exigendam, commodius multo coepit in liberalium disciplinarumm cognitione versari: Cumque octodecim ferè menses Latinae linguae tribuisset in Montis acuti Collegio, in Collegium cui à Sancta Barbara nomen est, ad Philosophiae studia transiit: ibique trennio et mensibus sex (quod spatium temporis in curriculo Philosophiae, in*

---

comparing today with yesterday, week with week, and month with month, he might examine and assess as accurately as possible his own spiritual progress or regress." Maffei, *De vita et moribus*, 66–67.

7 "Suddenly he was afflicted with such great financial want that he found it necessary to go door to door, looking for food every day, and to enter the homeless shelter of Saint Jacques, after imploring the director of that institution with abject pleas. This led, of course, to serious inconveniences: the shelter of Saint Jacques lay quite far away in the suburbs, so Ignatius, compelled by his dire need, was afflicted with various inconveniences owing to the great distance between the places, especially because lessons at the academy began before dawn and only stopped at night; but according to the rules of the shelter, he was not allowed to leave before sunrise and was required to return in the evening, before dusk. Thus, between coming and going, no matter how diligent and energetic a pupil he was, he missed a great deal both of the teachers' lectures and the whole scholastic training. When he could find no other remedy for such a great loss, he adopted the plan of indigent scholars and hired himself out as a servant to one of the administrators or teachers of the academy, so that he could spend all of whatever leisure remained, after his domestic duties, on academic training, study, and learning."

Academia illa tribuitur) ita profecit, ut honorifico Magistri judicio (is erat Johannes Penna Philosophus) post consueta certamina, laurea caeterisque doctrinae insignibus decorates sit. Post haec in cenobiis dominicani gymnasio sacram Theologiam agressus est ingenti sane labore.[8] Ribadeneyra adds to Maffei's lies, saying: *Spatio Philosophae emenso, reliquum tempus, ad annum trigesimum quintum exeuntem; sacrae Theologiae tribuit, parque suscepto labori fructus, Dei benignate respondit.*[9] He means that Ignatius contributed as much honor to theology as to philosophy. He's telling the truth about that, there being no agreement about either profession.

Here, I've spread out for you the merchandise I took from Maffei's boutique: I don't want to win anything or lose anything. All history must contain either truth or some appearance of truth. This history has neither. For while Maffei was trying to present here the actions of a pious man, he turned him into a mediocre grammarian, a grammarian who never learned to speak Latin, or if he spoke it, he was like a magpie who spoke without understanding what he was saying. And yet, at the end of his studies, he's described as a great philosopher. It's not enough for a witness to give a deposition about something that's been done: if he wants people to believe him, he has to give a pertinent reason for what he's saying. Review everything I've read to you. First, Maffei agrees that all Ignatius's studies during his four years in Spain were of no use to him. So, he was obliged to enroll in the lowest classes of the Collège de Montaigu, along with the little school boys, in order to re-learn the first rudiments of Latin grammar. He did this for a mere eighteen months, then he enrolled in the philosophy classes. I'll show you that, during all that time, you won't find ten months of studying. During these eighteen months, he never

---

8   "He entered on a much more advantageous plan of traveling during school holidays to Belgium, and occasionally also to England or Britain, to visit Spanish merchants. Thanks to their generosity, he easily obtained an annual stipend during the entire time of his studies at Paris, charging certain fees, so that he began to be involved in the learning of the liberal arts in a much more effective way. When he had studied Latin for approximately 18 months at the college of Montague, he moved to the study of philosophy at the college named after St. Barbe. Having spent three and a half years there (this is the length of the course of study in philosophy required at that academy) he made such progress that, after the usual examinations, he was awarded the diploma and other marks of distinction in learning, earning a judgment of high honor from his master (this was John Penna the philosopher). After this he began his study of theology in the school of the Dominican monastery, and of course he worked very hard at it." Maffei, *De vita et moribus*, 69.

9   "Having completed philosophy, he gave the rest of his time up through 1535 to theology, and the result, undertaken with the same diligence, answered with the grace of God." Ribadeneyra, *Vita Ignatii Loiolae*, 208.

missed a Mass: every Sunday he would receive the Blessed Sacrament as if it were Easter: that wasn't supposed to be done without devotion. At a minimum, one must add Saturday, when he prepared himself; so, if he went to class on that day, and if he presented himself the next day at the communion table, he was wronging the Blessed Sacrament of the Altar. In addition, he entered his conscience daily in order to examine it; and if you're willing to let me say it, he entered his coffin. Fine studies, surely; and since they were spread over a long span of intervening time, they exceeded every other study; but while he was doing that, he was turning his back on his other studies, which we're talking about now. His first lodging was at Saint-Jacques-du-Haut-Pas, which was half of a quarter-league[10] from the Collège de Montaigu. How much time did he waste going back and forth? The door of that church, built by Hospitalers, was opened in the late morning and was closed in the early evening, which made him have to decipher a few lessons every day by himself. But he lost still more time, when one considers that he had to go from house to house and beg for alms in order to stay alive. He often had to wait for his food. To avoid that, he was obliged to serve at the college, a situation by which he could find food for his body more easily, but not food for his spirit. For, emerging from a hospital and from begging, in order to serve at table, he surely was given the most lowly and disagreeable tasks carried out by the servants in the college, such as making beds, sweeping the bedchambers, removing dirt from his master's clothes, dusting them off, setting the pot to boil, fetching wine, washing the porringers, and doing other small tasks related to that position. Judge how much time was left him for study. And lastly, in these eighteen months, he made several journeys during school holidays, to the Low Countries,[11] and to England to retrieve some money. I do wish that Maffei had told me how many days of vacation they gave the students, for this is a new thing for me. These journeys couldn't have been done in long segments, by a man on foot who was forced to beg his living; even crossing the water to reach England requires planning. When one combines all these circumstances, how much time, in those eighteen months, was left for studying grammar, at the end of which the person advances to philosophy? He couldn't write grammatically, yet without

10   A league was approximately three and one-half miles. Early modern people, who did a great deal of walking and who lived in towns where municipal clocks showed only hours or portions of hours, calculated time by the number of steps it took to cross a space that they knew, from experience or from hearsay, represented a half league or a quarter league. Or they estimated time by the distance they covered. We do roughly the same thing when we estimate the time it will take us to walk two, three, or six city blocks.

11   *Les Pays-Bas*, the Low Countries, more or less the northern part of today's Belgium, plus the Netherlands, and Luxembourg.

much hope they make him into a great philosopher, and then into a profound theologian. Schoolboys who have passed through the shoals of grammar and rhetoric, and who, in the process, have read the orators, historians, Greek and Latin poets for five or six years, are scarcely capable of being admitted to the philosophy class. And we think that this man, who never had the leisure time to study grammar for six months, was a great philosopher? Everything openly contradicts that tale. For even during the three and one-half years when he was a student, he was investigated by the Inquisition before Brother Matthew Ory,[12] inquisitor of the faith; and he barely was admitted to the hall at the Collège de Sainte-Barbe, under Master Jacques Govea, the principal, to attend the denunciation of Master Jean Penna, Ignatius's teacher.[13] He also coaxed his companions away from their usual studies, *et inani nescio qua simulatione sanctitatis, optimum illius Gymnasii statum ac disciplinam perverteret*,[14] says Ribadeneyra. Still more: during those three years of study he tangled in his nets Favre, Xavier, Laínez, Salmerón, Bobadilla, Rodrigues, his first companions or, to be more accurate, his first disciples, with whom he later wrote, at Montmartre, the first pencil outline of their Society. I learned all that from Maffei; yet that fine tale-teller is so ill-advised as to tell us that, in order to make himself competent in philosophy, Ignatius ignored all the devil's importunities, the better to tend to his studies. For Ignatius thoughtlessly called things that he considered to be devotions, the devil's importunities.

Let's set that philosopher aside and look at his theological studies. He became a master of arts in March 1532. Having sunk into a long and serious illness, he followed the physicians' advice and, in November 1535, returned to Spain for its air. Can you make a great theologian in three years out of someone who had no basic knowledge of grammar or philosophy? And to show you what a great ass he was, an ass at all sorts of letters, not an ass about things that involve worldly prudence, in which he surpassed, the Jesuits themselves tacitly avoid feeding us on fables. When painters want to represent Saint Jerome,[15] they put an open book in his hands, for he was reputed to be the most savant

12 For Ory, see William W. Meissner, *Ignatius of Loyola: The Psychology of a Saint* (New Haven: Yale University Press, 1992), 146, 178.

13 This refers to an old and dubious tales about encounters and disputes between the teachers of Ramus and Ignatius. See Jules-Étienne Joseph Quicherat, *Histoire de Sainte-Barbe* (Paris: Hachette, 1860) 1:224–36.

14 "Who was perverting the excellent standing and discipline of that school with some empty pretense of holiness." Ribadeneyra, *Vita Ignatii Loiolae*, 223.

15 Saint Jerome (347–420) completed and edited a Latin translation of the Bible into Latin. One of his attributes is indeed a book. See *Encyclopaedia Britannica*, https://www.britan nica.com/biography/Saint-Jerome (accessed February 27, 2021).

of all our doctors of the church. And when the Jesuits display a figure of their Ignatius, they put a rosary in his hands to show his ignorance. For rosaries are the prayers of simple women who can neither read nor write. That's how you'll find him depicted before the cross in an engraving for the frontispiece of Ribadeneyra's book that was printed in Lyon by Jacques Roussin in 1595.[16] And René de La Fon, with a sincere conscience that is very familiar to him, recognizes this frankly when he says: "No one ever reproached Saint Anthony,[17] or Saint Francis,[18] or the apostles, for placing the apostles after Saint Anthony and Saint Francis (those words are certainly worthy of a devout Jesuit). Had the apostles studied? They had collected the divine sciences from the Holy Spirit. Ignatius likewise had collected them from the same Holy Spirit; and although it was in a lesser quantity, the source was the same." And I truly think well of La Fon: he's a conscientious man who admits that his Ignatius is savant, like Saint Anthony, who prided himself on knowing nothing. I'm not attached to Ignatius for his ignorance, as those two ignorant Jesuits, Maffei and Ribadeneyra, are: they want us to believe that he was a great philosopher and theologian, not realizing that by making him known to the public wholesale, as they are doing, little by little they were disproving what they themselves had said about his studies. Nevertheless, I want each person to understand how the Holy Spirit was lodged in Ignatius and his companions, when they presented their request to Pope Paul III to have their sect approved.

16   See the available copies of this edition, http://www.worldcat.org/oclc/55122957 (accessed February 27, 2021).

17   Saint Anthony the Great (251–356), also known as Saint Anthony Abbot, was a "desert father," that is, a monk who lived in the wilderness (in this instance, the eastern desert of Egypt). See *Encyclopaedia Britannica*, https://www.britannica.com/biography/Saint-Anthony-of-Egypt (accessed February 27, 2021).

18   Saint Francis of Assisi (*c*.1181–1226) created the Franciscan order. *Encyclopaedia Britannica*, https://www.britannica.com/biography/Saint-Francis-of-Assisi (accessed February 27, 2021).

When Ignatius and His Companions Presented Themselves before Pope Paul III, They Were True Charlatans, and the Titles They Used Were False

THE LAWYER. No matter to which side I turn, I find only deceptive things among the Jesuits, even since the very beginning of their order. When Ignatius and his companions presented their request to Pope Paul III, to authorize their Holy Society of the Name of Jesus, they promised him that they would reduce the number of heretics in the bosom of the church, and convert to our faith the Turks and other unbelievers. For this, they weren't required to bring merely good will, they also had to have sufficient possessions and abilities. That's why they were very careful to call themselves simple scholars and not to use the title theologians, for they would have been mocked. Their spines were too weak to take on that quality. But following a middle path, they declared that they were masters of arts, not in Spain, not in Italy, but in the great and famous University of Paris; and they added that they had studied theology for several years. In order to be enlightened about the fruit that this new order might produce, the pope assigned three cardinals to report. Of these three, one came from Lucca: Bartolomeo Guidiccioni,[1] a person steeped in doctrine and piety (even the Jesuits attested to this), who had recently written a book against the new religious orders.[2] Being on home ground, he was a powerful adversary of the Society and had won the other two cardinals over to his opinion. But in the end, Ignatius won him over as much by prolonged importunities as by the thousands of Masses that he arranged to have celebrated for persons close to the cardinal. These three cardinals disputed only the general question about the novelty of the orders, without going deep into the details, to learn

---

1 Bartolomeo Guidiccioni (1470–1540), a native of Lucca, held a succession of powerful positions in the church, including cardinal and participant in the Council of Trent. As a householder of the Farnese family in his youth, he became the right-hand man of a Farnese pope, Paul III. As Pasquier says, he was a member of a congregation of three cardinals who approved the establishment of the Society of Jesus. Initially a dissenting voice, he became a strong supporter of the order. See *DBI*, https://www.treccani.it/enciclopedia/bartolomeo -guidiccioni_%28Dizionario-Biografico%29/ (accessed February 27, 2021).

2 In reality, he did not write works against religious orders. But in his writings about the reform, he opposed the creation of other "families" of religious. He even proposed that all male orders be eliminated, with the exception of the Benedictines, the Cistercians, the Franciscans, and the Dominicans, Sutto, 173n210.

whether these great promisers had issued from Horace's mountain, which gave birth to a mouse.[3] Let's now compensate for their shortcomings. Montaignes, speaking of their advent, puts it this way: "First, I reply that this Society of Jesus began at the University of Paris, and that it put down its first root there, in the form of ten masters of arts of the said university; one was from Biscay: Ignatius of Loyola; one was from Navarre: Francisco Xavier; two were Frenchmen: Paschase Broët and Jean Codury; three were Spaniards: Diego Laínez, Alfonso Salmerón, and Nicolas de Bobadila; two were from Savoy: Pierre Favre, and Claude Jaye; and one was a Portuguese: Simão Rodrigues." He gave them assurances that all of them had earned master's degrees in the University of Paris, for they had learned a lesson from Paul III's bull of 1540, the content of which went as follows: *Nuper si quidem accepimus quod dilecti filii Ignatius de Loyola et Petrus Faber, et Jacobus Laynez, necnon Claudius Jaius, Paschasius Broet, et Franciscus Xavier, necnon Alphonsus Salmeron, et Simon Rodericus, et Joannes Coduri, et Nicolaus de Bobadilla Presbyteri Pampilonen, Gebennen. Seguntin. Toletan. Visen. Ebredunen. et Palentin. civitatum et diocesium respectivè in artibus Magistri, in Universitate Paris. graduati, et in Theologicis studiis per plures annos exercitati, Spiritu S. afflati, jamdudum è diversis mundi regionibus decedentes in unum convenerunt.*[4] I'll leave you there, bearing the marvelous promise about these new wandering knights[5] and about what they obtained from the pope. All of them were full of life when Julius III became pope; from whom they received a confirmation in 1550, when they took those same titles. They can be found in Ribadeneyra, Book 3, chapter 21, where the complete bull is inserted. They all said they were masters of arts from the University of Paris, that they had all studied for several years at the Faculty of Theology, and that all of them were inspired by the Holy Spirit. I'd never heard that the Holy Spirit taught us to be liars, except for those pettifoggers. In order to call them that, before you, I'm going to have recourse to the Jesuits' two great

---

3 This alludes to Aesop's fable, "The Mountain in Labor." The fable itself is evoked in Horace's epistle on the art of poetry: "And don't start like the old writer of epic cycles: Of Priam's fate I'll sing, and the greatest of Wars. What could he produce to match his opening promise? Mountains will labour: what is born? A ridiculous mouse!" (*Ars poetica*, 136–39).

4 "Since we have learned that [our] beloved sons, Ignatius de Loyola, Pierre Favre, Diego Laínez, Claude Jay, Paschase Broët, Francisco Xavier, Alfonso Salmerón, Simão Rodrigues, Jean Codure, Nicolás de Bobadilla, Masters of Paris, from the dioceses respectively of Pamplona, Geneva, Siguenza, Toledo, Vizeu, Embrun, and Palencia respectively, masters in arts graduated from the University of Paris, engaged for many years in the study of theology, from various parts of the world have joined together into one body, inspired by the Holy Spirit."

5 *Chevaliers errants*, that is, knights who continually roam through the world, seeking new exploits to accomplish and wrongs to right, especially in the service of a lady or a good cause.

historiographers. For if you believe Maffei, neither Laínez, nor Salmerón, nor Bobadilla earned a master's degree at Paris; they earned them in a Spanish university that they call Complutensis Academia, which the Spaniards call Alcalá [de Henares]. Let's listen to what Ribadeneyra says: *Jacobus Lainez adolescens confecto Philosophiae cursu, Lutetiam ex Complutensi Academia cum Alphonsi Salmerone, item adulescentulo venerate, tum studendi, tum etiam Ignatium inquirendi, videndique gratia.*[6] In this passage I see that Diego Laínez was the only one to earn a master's degree at Alcalá; and as for Salmerón, he was a young chap who had come to Paris not only to study but to meet Ignatius. But here Maffei, who is more daring than his companion, declared that they had earned master-of-arts degrees in Spain: *Jacobus Lainez qui deinde Societati nostrae proximus ab Ignatio praefuit, et Alphonsus Salmeron Toletanus, Graecis et Latinis litteris admodum eruditus, uterque confecto Compluti, Philosophiae curriculo, Parisios, partim Theologiae caussa* [sic], *partim etiam noscendi Ignatii gratia profecti.*[7] Compare these two passages. Ribadeneyra depicts Salmerón as a young child who hasn't earned any degree; at any rate, he doesn't mention it, as he did for Diego Laínez. Maffei tells the public that he is accomplished in Greek and Latin literature, and that he had acquired a master's degree in Spain. Let's accept what Maffei says, for I don't take pleasure in showing that someone is wrong unless the wager is solid. The same Maffei adds two names: Nicolas de Bobadilla, et Simão Rodrigues: *Accessit ad hos Nicolaus Bobadilla Palentinus, doctus juvenis et Philosophiam publicè professus in oppido Hispaniae, Pintia, itemqué praestanti indole Simon Rodericus Lusitanus.*[8] I therefore place Bobadilla among the Spanish masters of arts, since he had taught philosophy before coming to France; but Rodrigues had not, because he's depicted as a very promising young man, and no longer, to borrow these words, *praestanti indole*, an outstanding young person. I know full well that Ribadeneyra, who was talking rather loosely about these seven men, says that after they had earned a master of arts, they made their first vow at Montmartre in 1534, on the feast of the Assumption of Our Lady; but he doesn't say that all of them had earned a

---

6   "The young Diego Laínez, when he had finished the philosophy course, had come to Paris from Alcalá with Alfonso Salmerón, likewise a very young man, to study and to search out and see Ignatius."

7   "Both Diego Laínez, who subsequently directed our Society after Ignatius, and Alfonse Salmerón of Toledo, who was quite learned in Greek and Latin literature, after completing their course in philosophy at Alcalá, went to Paris, partly to study theology and partly also to get to know Ignatius."

8   "These men were joined by Nicolas de Bobadilla of Palencia, a learned young man who taught philosophy in the Spanish City of Padilla de Duero, and also the very talented Portuguese Simão Rodrigues."

master's degree in Paris. The truth therefore is this: Let's say that you're willing to believe that, of the seven, four had earned a master of arts degree in Paris: Loyola, Favre, Xavier, Rodrigues; and that the other three had earned one in Spain: Laínez, Salmerón, and Bobadilla. A year later, Claude Jaye, Jean Codurie, and Paschase Broët joined the Society. Neither in Maffei, nor in Ribadeneyra, did any of them earn a license.[9] Therefore, if you are willing to believe that, of these ten companions, four had graduated in Paris, three in Spain, and the remaining three had not earned a master's degree, then you'll say in passing that, when all is said and done, Paschase Broët was a big ass. I say that because I not only met him, I also supervised him at the Clermont house on the rue de la Harpe in Paris. He was supervising the Jesuits. He was a great idol, and one can say what Ausonius said long ago about Rufus, a rhetorician:

> *Haec Ruffi tabula est? Nil verius: ipse ubi Ruffus?*
> *In cathedra: qui agit? Hoc quod et in tabula.*[10]

But I'm overdoing it, for he knew his inadequacies, and he never dared climb up into the pulpit to preach, or to give a lesson.

Now let's see how much study time these ten new champions devoted to theology: for they assured Pope Paul III that they had studied for several years. Maffei tells us that when they made their first vow at Montmartre, most of them had already finished their courses in theology, and that the others were devoting themselves to completing it, so that they could start off to conquer Turkish-style souls in Palestine, with the kind permission of Our Holy Father the Pope. This passage merits being read from start to finish: *Hosce igitur socios Dei beneficio nactus Ignatius* (he is talking about the first six companions) *quod jam diu moliebatur et agitabat animo, re ipsa aggredi primo quoque tempore statuit, ut Hierosolymas Pontificis maximi permissu repeteret, gentesque finitimas, Christiana quondam Religione praestantes, deinde Mahometis nepharia superstitione deceptas, vel à miserabili errore ad veritatem Evangelicam revocaret: vel certè (quod erat proximum) sanguinem ac vitam in caussa tam pia et*

---

9   *License*: "license." In the faculties of theology, law, and medicine, the license is the second degree one must earn. It permits one to read and teach publicly by virtue of the letters one has obtained, which are called "letters of license." (DAF, 1694).

10   Decimius Magnus Ausonius (*c.*310–*c.*395) was a Roman poet and teacher of rhetoric. See *Encyclopaedia Britannica*, https://www.britannica.com/biography/Decimus-Magnus -Ausonius (accessed February 28, 2021).
    Pasquier is quoting from his *Epigrams*, book 19 ("Epigrams on Various Matters"), epigram XIII: "This is a picture of Rufus, Nothing more lifelike. Where is Rufus himself? In his chair. What is he doing? The same thing as the picture."

gloriosa profunderet. Neque sanè difficile fuit, caeteros jam sponte currentes, et Dei amore incensos, in eandem sententiam et propositum adducer. Et quia ple-rique Theologiae studia nondum absoluverant, ne interim conceptus ardor animi refrigesceret, et simul ut ipsorum eo gratius divinae Majestati obsequium esset, quo majoroem sibimetipsi necessitatem servitutis ac Religionis imposuissent: implorato beatissimae Virginis patrocinio, ac S. Dionysii Areopagitae, cujus in tutela Parisii sunt, in aede suburbana, quae Mons Martyrum dicitur, sub con-fessionis et Eucharistiae mysteria sese obstrinxere singuli, emensis Theologiae spatiis, continuo nuntium rebus mortalibus remittendi, atque in paupertate perpetua serviendi gloriae divinae, salutique animorum ac nominatim ad consti-tuam diem, Hierosolymam eo consilio navigandi, ut in conversionem infidelium toto pectore incumberent, palmamque martyrii studiosè captarent. Id consilium si qua in re impediretur, anni circumacto spatio denique Roman adirent, suamque operam summo Pontifici Christi Vicario, ad spirituale proximorum auxilium sine ulla praemii pactione, vel temporum, aut locorum exceptione defferent. Id votum in eo templo vovere ingenti consensu et alacritate, anno post Christum natum 1534. decimo octavo Kal. Septembris, quo die Assumptionis Mariae Virginis anni-versaria gratulatio celebratur: idemque votum eodem loco dieque, pariter anno proximo ac tertio celebrarunt. Let's turn that passage into French, because it's important for my lecture that everyone understand.

"Ignatius having therefore acquired these six companions by the grace of God, resolved to do, as soon as possible, what he had planned within himself, which was to return to Jerusalem with the kind permission of Our Holy Father the Pope, and there to convert to our faith the adjacent nations, formerly brought up in the Christian religion and now infected with Mohammed's damnable superstition; or in any event, to shed his blood and his life for such a devout and glorious quarrel. And it was not difficult for him to win over his companions to his opinion, for they were vehemently stirred up by the love of God and were themselves dashing off to the Holy Land. But a few of them had not yet finished studying theology. Therefore, so that the great ardor that had begun in them would not cool down, and also so that their devotion would be all the more agreeable to God, and because they were taking fully upon themselves the heaviest yoke of servitude and religion, having implored the help of the Blessed Virgin Mary and Saint Denis the Areopagite,[11] the

---

11   Saint Denis, the third-century bishop of Paris, was martyred for his faith by decapitation.
      Some accounts placed this during Domitian's persecutions and identified Saint Denis of
      Paris with Denis the Areopagite, whom Saint Paul converted in Athens, on the prominent
      rock known as the Areopagus (Acts 17:34). According to a popular story, the decapitation
      took place on Montmartre Hill ("Mount of martyrs"), just north of Paris. Saint Denis of
      Paris then picked up his head and walked several miles northward. The abbey and basilica

patron saint of Paris, they gathered in the church of Montmartre, close to the city. Having made their confession and received the Blessed Sacrament of the Altar, they all made the following vow: that is to say, when they had completed their theology course, and had been awarded their doctorates, they would at once renounce all their possessions and would make a perpetual profession of poverty in honor of God and the salvation of souls. And they would fix a day when they would leave for Jerusalem, with the intention of, with all their hearts, setting about converting the infidels and sealing their faith with their own blood. If their plan was prevented by some new obstacle, when a year had rolled around, they would present themselves to the Holy Father, Vicar of Our Lord Jesus Christ, to whom they would promise total obedience, for the spiritual help of their neighbors and without hoping for money, and with no exception involving time and persons. Inside that church they made this vow unanimously, to the great contentment and joy of everyone, in the year of the Incarnation of Our Savior Jesus Christ 1534, August 15, day of the Assumption of Our Lady, and renewable two years later on the same day and in the same place."

I translated the words *emenso Theologiae cursu*[12] as: When they had completed their theology course, and had been awarded their doctorate in theology. For I see that the same Maffei, who wanted to demonstrate that Laínez and Salmerón had received the master of arts degree in Spain, used similar wording: *Uterque confecto Compluti Philosophiae curriculo* (after having completed both courses in philosophy in Alcalá;[13] and Ribadeneyra wanted to say that Ignatius and his first six companions had acquired a similar degree in 1534. *Confecto* (says he) *Philosophiae cursu* (finishing the philosophy course).

From this passage you learn that, as early as 1534, the majority of these seven companions were doctors of theology, and that the others wanted to finish their course. Now, since none of them had a doctorate, that's a bold-faced lie: for if it were true, when they presented themselves to Pope Paul III, they certainly wouldn't have hidden the title doctor, in favor of the titles they'd already acquired, and they would have been very careful not to call themselves merely

---

of Saint-Denis (now in a northern suburb of Paris) was erected on his burial site. Over time, Denis came to be revered as a patron saint of Paris. As late as the mid-sixteenth century, some scholars argued that Saint Denis of Paris and Denis the Areopagite were one and the same person. Both were also traditionally identified with the anonymous fifth-century author of the revered Neoplatonic Christian treatises *On the Divine Names* and *On the Celestial Hierarchy*.

12   He does not specify the text where these words appear: is he thinking of the phrase "spatio philosophiae emenso," which appears in a passage of Ribadeneyra quoted in ch. 10.

13   "Each having completed the course of philosophy at Alcalá."

masters of arts. I'll go even farther: for I'll show you clearly that none of the seven, nor the three others who subsequently became their companions, had ever studied theology. For if they had started the course, as Maffei assures us they did, they would have studied for several years: but the word several doesn't denote merely two or three years, but at least four or five years. One doesn't say that a man is between several persons when he is accompanied by only three persons. The rule followed in the Faculty of Theology of Paris is that when one has begun a course, once the first two years have expired, the student is obliged to participate in a public disputation in the theology colleges that were created for that purpose, presided over by a doctor who acts as his godfather and who helps him reply to the objections that are raised. This first attempt having been completed (among themselves they call it the Attempt), the student is declared a formed Bachelor, and henceforth is permitted to wear the shoulder-hood when he goes about town, and the red garment of the bachelor when he is in a school. When our two Jesuits presented themselves to Pope Paul III, they didn't call themselves bachelors in theology; they therefore hadn't yet begun the course, nor had they studied theology for merely two years. So where do we find, in them, those several years during which they said they had studied?

There's only one solution to this objection: one must freely recognize that Maffei lied when he asserted that some were doctors of theology and others were studying for the course. But (someone will tell me) it was possible to do this without registering for the philosophy course given at the Collège de la Sorbonne. Each of them would have to study in different ways, some more, some very much more, once they had earned a master of arts. As for me, who isn't fighting in order to win, but only fighting for the truth, I've no doubt that Maffei was a liar on that point, just as he's been a liar on several other points, and just as Ribadeneyra lies. So, let's look at how much time Ignatius and his disciples had for studying theology, without signing up for a class. Maffei and Ribadeneyra, the Jesuits, have discussed this, as if they were colorblind: so I'll talk with you about the historical truth. I went to thumb through the old registers of the University of Paris, about master of arts degrees, starting back in 1520 and up until 1536, when Ignatius's ten companions left France and started off for Venice. I thumbed through them in the company of Du Val, the university scribe, and with Violette, the beadle of the French nation, who has the registers. And this is what I found, in the alphabetical order they had created for the registers. According to the register, Pierre Favre and Francisco Xavier became masters of arts in 1529: *Petrus Faber Geben. Franciscus Xavier Pampil. Ignatius in 1532: Ignatius Loyola Pampil.* Claude Jay and Simão Rodrigues in 1534: *Claudius Jaius Geben ... Simon Rodericus Visensis.* Alfonso Salmerón and Jean Codury in 1535, in these words: *Alphonsus Salmeron Tolet., Joannes Codure Ebrun*. I've been very careful about extracting everything that the above register has about the French nation, under which heading the licenses and master's degrees for Spain, Savoy, Provence, Italy are included. For according to what Maffei and Ribadeneyra say, Paschase Broët came from the diocese of Amiens, and this would therefore have been stated in the request presented to Pope Paul III, which makes no mention of that diocese.

Here, then, is the truth: there were three of them, two of whom indubitably had not earned a degree in Paris, but had earned one in Spain: Laínez, and Bobadilla, and the last one, Paschase Broët, didn't earn one, either in Spain or in France. Moreover, as for the study of theology, where do we find the several years we're missing for Jaye and Rodrigues, who became masters in March 1534? And for Salmerón and Codury, who earned their master's in 1535. Because our two historiographers[14] agree that in November 1536, they left the city of Paris in order to go to Italy with their master, Ignatius. And as for Ignatius, you won't be able to provide him with study time in that spot for more than three years, especially because he was afflicted with a long illness. The physicians advised a change of air, so he returned to Spain in November 1535. And yet these grand personages promised, thanks to their knowledge, to convert to our religion heretics as well as unbelievers and infidels. Believe me, if the three cardinals assigned by the pope to learn the facts about them, had sounded them out to the quick, they would have found that when they entered Italy, they breathed in some of the mores and humors of the charlatans who go through the city streets, distributing treacle. These charlatans are accustomed to parking themselves in the main square, where they give a long harangue, promising to heal all sorts of ailments by their unguents, powders, oils, and waters; and they make several other promises that unusually turn out to be nothing.

14   Maffei and Ribadeneyra.

It Very Much Appears That the Approval Granted by Paul III to the Jesuit Sect Is Null and Void

THE LAWYER. After the Lawyer had finished the above speech, the Jesuit began talking to him. THE JESUIT. To what end did you talk to us at such length about this subject that, to me, seems totally frivolous? I wish that our first fathers and the teachers of our order had not all been masters of arts of the university of Paris: I wish some of them had not graduated; I wish that none of them had a bachelor's degree, and even more a doctorate in theology; I wish that none of them had studied at that faculty; in short, to please you, I wish everything that you wish. I beg you, what does all that matter, since Pope Paul III authorized us, and ten years later Julius, his successor, confirmed what we were newly professing? Popes who could make themselves believed over all the rules of law, by the absolute power that is attributed to this great dignity. I would willingly tell you that if these good fathers had merely been simple scholars, I can scarcely recognize you as one. You (I say), who now want to put their titles in doubt by searching through old papers: you must know that the pope, in the decorative little box where he keeps his thoughts, compensates for all the defects of law and fact.[1]

THE LAWYER. That would be a good thing to say if, in Pope Paul III's bull, the copyists of the Roman Curia had, by a special declaration, added some derogatory clause to the truth of the facts. Yet not everyone approves that proposition. As for me, I'll be very careful not to put in doubt the power of the Holy See, which is either confirmed by an infinity of passages in the Holy Scripture, or is authorized by the antique doctors of our church. However, things being as they are above, there's every reason and subject to maintain that the approval of your sect by Paul III is void, not because of the power that was in him, but because a manifest deceit was used. Listen, please, to what I want to tell you. Just as soon as Ignatius had laid down his weapons, to espouse another life, he seriously weighed becoming a leader in the Church Militant. His first demonstration of this took place around 1536,[2] at the university of Alcalá, where he

---

1 Lawyer that he is, Pasquier focuses briefly on "the defects of law and of fact" (*les defauts de droit et de fait*). See the Glossary.
2 The correct date is 1526 (Sutto, 180n225).

attracted three Spanish students: Arteaga,[3] Calixto,[4] and Cáceres.[5] From then on, he imprinted in his spirit some opinion of Jesuitery.[6] He had heard tell that Saint John the Baptist, showing Our Lord Jesus Christ to the Jews, called him the Lamb of God who had come down from heaven to expiate our sins. This savant man mistook the bean for the bean-pod, and he thought that one couldn't imitate Jesus better than by wearing a garment of undyed wool, of the color that came directly from the ewe: to the point that he and his three companions wore long-skirted garments made of that material. Or, as Ribadeneyra put it, *Quos propterea a panni similtudine, Ensayalados, vulgo, Hispanio vocabulo appellabant*, that is to say, in vulgar Spanish, all of the same material, covered in sackcloth.[7] And prior to him, Maffei had said: *Nativi coloris lanea cuncti utebantur*, the whole thing made of natural-colored wool. The merchants in their usual jargon call it broadcloth, serge, or wool the color of the animal. These four men were usually together, and among other things they acted as if they were studying theology, without wearing a long robe or a mantel, but simply one of these long-skirted coats. They were joined by a Frenchman[8] who wasn't granted the leisure time to dress like the other four. For these novel garments attracted the attention of the Inquisition, and they were called before Master Juan Rodrigues de Figueroa,[9] grand vicar of the archbishop of Toledo, who ordered them to change their garments. He ordered Ignatius and Arteaga to wear black, Calixto and Cáceres to wear clothes the color of tanned leather; and as for the Frenchman, he should make no change in his garments. A few months later, having realized that Ignatius was an unlettered man with no knowledge of doctrine, he forbade him to catechize the common people for four whole years, during which time he could make himself capable of

---

3   Juan de Arteaga y Avendaño (?–1540) bishop-elect of Ciudad Real and Chiapas, Mexico. He had planned to join Loyola in Paris. See https://sites.google.com/site/amdg1540/bio/arteaga (accessed February 28, 2021).

4   Calixto de Sà may have been born in Segovia. Before joining Loyola, he made a pilgrimage to the Holy Land. He had planned to go to Paris with Loyola but changed his mind. He journeyed twice to Mexico and became very rich, then he returned to Spain and settled in Salamanca. See https://sites.google.com/site/amdg1540/bio/sa_calixto (accessed February 28, 2021).

5   Lope de Cáceres was a native of Segovia and had been in the service of the viceroy of Catalonia. After Ignatius went to Paris, Cáseres returned to Segovia. See https://sites.google.com/site/amdg1540/bio/caceres_lope (accessed February 28, 2021).

6   *Jésuiterie*, "Jesuitery": Hypocritical reasoning or action.

7   "Which they used to call *ensayalados* in Spanish because of their similarity to rags."

8   His name was Juan Raynal. He became a monk at Salamanca.

9   Juan Rodríguez de Figueroa (1490–1565) was the vicar of Archbishop Alonso de Fonseca, president of the royal council. See https://sites.google.com/site/amdg1540/bio/rodriguez_j (accessed February 28, 2021).

conducting catechisms. His disciples, no longer wanting to be the targets of special searches by the courts, abandoned him. He saw that his undertakings weren't going to succeed, because a sect of some sort of hypocrites had quite recently been suppressed in Spain: they called themselves the Illuminated Ones.[10] He debated going to France, hoping that he would be more successful there; and he saw that no matter what the subject, if one wanted to be victorious, one had to be stubborn. In 1532 he, Favre, Xavier, Laínez, Salmerón, Bobadilla, and Rodrigues finally made that vow in the church of Montmartre, on the feast of the Assumption. Once they all were doctors of theology, they would set off for Palestine, at the pope's good pleasure, to convert infidels, as I've already told you. If, after a year, there was some hindrance that prevented them from doing so, they would turn their projects over to the Pope, to order them as he saw fit. It took a long while to do what was necessary to accomplish this vow, for the proposal made at the Faculty of Theology of Paris was that, having received the master of arts, they would pause for five full years (which later were reduced to four) before anyone could register for the theology course. Of the seven first companions, and the three last companions, only two obeyed this wise order and could have enrolled in that class: they were Pierre Favre and Francis Xavier, who both passed their master's degree in 1529 and therefore could be admitted in 1535. As for all the others, only one of them completed the desired five years, after earning his master's. And likewise, there was one, Paschase Broët, who didn't have a master of arts; and two others, Laínez and Bobadilla, had earned their master of arts in Spain, but hadn't been adopted into the university of Paris, and were therefore not admissible. However, although they'd made the vow, to the detriment of that vow they all left France in late 1536 and in 1537, and were in Venice where, having rested up for several months, all of them went to Rome for the third Thursday of Lent, not only in order to get the pope's permission but also to put themselves forward for the holy orders of the priesthood, and also to go to Jerusalem to preach the Gospel, feigning that they not only were masters of arts, but that they had studied theology for several years. The pope approved their request, without full knowledge of the facts (because they had confined themselves to Palestine); and they received a little money from His Holiness, but some Spaniards even shared with them the contents of their purse. Thus these new pilgrims carried

---

10   He is referring here to the *alumbrados*, "the enlightened ones." Ignatius is considered by some scholars as a sympathizer of this movement and reflecting some of their ideas in his *Spiritual Exercises*. See Stefania Pastore, "Unwise Paths: Ignatius of Loyola and the Years of Alcalá de Henares," in Robert A. Maryks, ed. *A Companion to Ignatius of Loyola: Life, Writings, Spirituality, Influence* (Leiden: Brill, 2014), 25–44.

off two hundred and ten ducats that they had kept in a Venetian bank, to pay for their new pilgrimage. I swear to you that Ignatius was one of the finest worldly-wise persons of our day. Having been received like this, they began to forget their first vow and to act the clown and be fed by several cities of the Venetian state. There they resolved to turn back to Rome, in order to warn Pope Paul III that a new war had broken out between the Venetians and the Turks, and that it was a great barrier to their plan to journey over the water. In the city of Rome, they planned a new and very different Formula[11] for their Society, and they spent two whole years working it out. During that time, Pope Paul III wouldn't yield to their supplications, for he was besieged by some importune persons, even by Cardinal Contarini,[12] because almost every novelty soon finds a patron.

Let me tell you now about God's special miracle that occurred around the same time, to demonstrate that these ten new adventurers were real tricksters. They said that the sea lanes were closed to them, owing to the war we were fighting with the Turks, and that they therefore couldn't carry out their first plan. But a new way suddenly opened for them, to convert the infidels to our religion with no danger. Everything I'm going to tell you here comes from their two evangelists, and this tale certainly merits being trumpeted throughout the entire universe. I've mentioned that John III, king of Portugal, owned a large part of the East Indies, sown with an infinite number of unbelievers whom he wanted to convert to our Christian religion. In several nations, a rumor was circulating about the devotion of these new companions, who said that they had centered all their vows on such conversions. The king sent letters summoning them to come before him, so that he could put the path to the Indies under his protection. But Ignatius, subtle and crafty, turned a deaf ear to this coup, and forgot both his first vow made at Montmartre and his second, renewed vow made in Rome, by means of which they had procured money: so he sent only Xavier and Rodrigues to the king, and he kept the remaining seven close to him. Doesn't that show you that Ignatius was a statesman, not a religious, and that in his soul he was laughing at the first vow he had made at Montmartre?

---

11   For these Formulas, see *Constitutions*, "Formulas of the Institutes," 3–16.

12   Gasparo Contarini (1483–1542), a secular Venetian nobleman, was made a cardinal by Paul III in order to bind an able man of evangelical disposition to the Roman interests. When Ignatius was in Rome, Contarini was a new cardinal. He eventually figured among the most prominent spiritual leaders of the reform movement within the Roman church. See, for example, Andrea Vanni, "Cardinal Gasparo Contarini," in *Oxford Bibliographies Online: Renaissance and Reformation*, https://www.oxfordbibliographies.com/view/document/obo-9780195399301/obo-9780195399301-0310.xml (accessed April 18, 2020).

From what I've said above, you've understood the sort of vow they made at Montmartre: they wouldn't set off to conquer souls until they had earned doctorates; and, moreover, they were informing the public that all of them had masters of arts degrees from Paris and had spent several years studying theology. All of which was false. Paul III raised difficulties about approving them, although he believed them to be what they claimed, and although he was infinitely importuned by Cardinal Contarini, their protector. So, what would the pope have done if he'd received confirmed news about the truth of their story? It seems to me that, with an admirable majesty and a venerable antiquity that was in him, I can see the pope saying this to these new associates:

POPE PAUL III. "All these new religious orders are to be feared, and for this reason they were forbidden by two general councils, one held in this city of Rome, the other at Lyon.[13] You present us with a new religious order, bearing the name the Society of Jesus, as true imitators of him and his apostles. Your intention derogates from your profession, or to be more exact, the profession that you promise is contrary to your request and implies, in itself, a contradiction. For if you are children of the apostles, one of the first lessons they taught us, was what was ordered at the general assembly, for some just occasion it was ordered differently, like everything coming from the depth and the trunk onto which the branches are grafted[14] *Placuit Spiritui sancto, et nobis*, "it pleased the Holy Spirit and us," they would say about such matters, not dividing the Holy Spirit's cause from that of the church, nor the cause of the church from that of the Holy Spirit. If you stay especially close to the apostles' way, as you claim to be doing, does it follow that, by means of a new religious order, you want to contravene the old constitutional canons? I know full well that, as the vicar of Jesus Christ, I can dispense you from that and can greatly praise the obedience you bring to our Holy See.

"But putting aside everything that has to do with the general *ordonnance*, and casting my eye solely on you in particular, everything that you are proposing now degenerates. I find that, in the beginning, there was a little bit of God's work in you; as you progressed, there was a great deal of the man; and at the end, there were three or four times more devil. Wanting to espouse a dangerous devotion, you intentionally chose the church of Montmartre, near Paris, to show that you would be ready to seal with your blood that testimony to your faith, as often as necessary. A beautiful and holy resolution that cannot

---

13   The putative Pope Paul III is referring to two councils, one held in 1215 (Fourth Lateran Council) and the other in 1274 (Second Council of Lyon).

14   This sentence seems to be corrupted. The translation is a literal rendering of the sentence and its punctuation.

be praised enough. Taking that same step, you entered into the sacrament of penance; with a devout heart you heard Mass; and afterward you received Communion on the feast of the Assumption of Our Lady, the most solemn feast day of all her feast days, desiring that this holy Virgin be a witness to the vow you were making to God. You continued this for two years, after a Mass said on that day and in that place: these are many holy circumstances that obligated you to carry out the vow you made at that time. Shall we therefore see what that vow was? You promised God that once each of you had completed the course in theology, you would renounce all your possessions and inheritances, would go to Palestine to convert the enemies of our faith; and if, after a year, you had not been able to go there, you would come and appease me and receive my orders. As the first step in carrying out this fine plan, you chose Venice, which is the general meeting place of pilgrims to Jerusalem. Before going any farther, you, Ignatius (for I am talking to you especially, as head of this undertaking), wisely went to Spain to put your companions' affairs in order, and yours as well. And then, with great zeal, you boarded ship at Valencia and headed for Venice, trampling all the fears that people were stirring up in you about that great pirate, Redbeard the Turk.[15] You reached Venice and came here shortly afterward, to receive my blessing and my permission for your journey, and for your residence in Palestine. You obtained everything you wanted from me, and more gold and silver, which you got from various alms, as a down-payment for your journey: and having received that blessing, you returned to Venice, debating whether you would keep your promise. I should like to know what turned you away from doing so. The war (you say), which has again burst out between the Venetians and the Turks. What war? Where are the preparations? The galleys? The ships? What arms do you see being stirred up to that end? We are the perpetual enemies of the Turks, and they of us: but for all that, they continue to give passports and to assure the pilgrims' personal safety, in return for paying specific tribute established long ago. Does this purported war prevent our religious who dwell at the Holy Sepulcher from continuing to live there?[16] In addition, what is making you hasten to change your vow?

---

15   Barbarossa (in Italian, "Redbeard") was the name given to Khayr al-Din, also named Khiḍr (?–1546). He led naval raids as ruler of Algiers and, later, admiral of the Ottoman fleet.

16   He is alluding to the Church of the Holy Sepulcher in Jerusalem, about which Louis Moréri's *Grand dictionnaire historique*, 19th ed. (Paris: Pitteri, 1744), 3:34 says: "Most of that mountain has been surrounded by a great enclosure that includes the Church of the Holy Sepulcher, surrounded by several chapels and little private churches, with lodgings for Catholics, Greeks, Armenians, Syrians, Copts and Abyssinians. [...]. Near the portal of the Church of the Holy Sepulcher is a resting-place for the Turks" (s.v. "Calvaire"). Franciscan monks represented the Roman Catholic church there.

For something delayed from one year to another is not lost. Especially because the Venetians and the Turks are now on the verge of declaring peace, a peace that is either already settled, or on the point of being settled. Moreover, if the passages are closed to you on that side, they are open toward the Indies. Your bargain does not include fear: the king is leading you by the hand: why flee from the arena? You once made a journey that exposed your lives to a thousand dangers. Therefore, go with God to that new world, and do not come to us in order to plant a new world in our ancient church.

"It is not the war between Venice and the Turks that is making you turn away from your vows: it is the war you are waging with your consciences. In this there is a tincture of man, much more than I wanted. When you first arrived at my court, from Venice, you did not know the countenance with which I would receive you, and the countenance of the persons around me. By good fortune, or misfortune (I cannot say which of the two), you found more favors than you hoped for: kind faces, favorable greetings, gold and silver for your journey. That is why, having returned to Venice, you thought that your shortest and surest route was to start off for Rome immediately, with several promises to submit to the Holy See and to forget what was in your original vow. But let us give something to your humanity and let us accept your new excuse about wars as payment. What connivance can I contribute to the lies in which you now want to circumscribe me and trap me? You all call yourselves masters of arts of the great and famous University of Paris. I see three of you who have never graduated. You state publicly that you studied theology there for several years: where shall I find that several in the two of your brethren who did not receive their master's until 1534, and in the two others who did it in 1535 and set off for Venice in 1536? Where shall I find it (I say) in Ignatius, who left the city of Paris three years after getting his master's? Where shall I find another person who never earned any degree? In short, I only find two of your brethren, Favre and Xavier, who had the free time to tend to those studies. I know very well what you will say to me: you will say that if this involves some lying on your part, it is excusable, because it was done to a good end. That it is a pious fraud; and I shall reply, in one brief sentence: Our religion cannot endure a fraudulent piety. Let us leave these two particularities, and let us go to the great, knotted heart of the matter: How will I dissimulate about the breaking of your vows, in which the devil is involved? You promised and swore before God that you would not go any farther in your undertaking, until you had finished your course in theology: where is that finish, or rather, where is the beginning? Calculate for me the length of time during which each of you enrolled, at one time or another. If you began, what is preventing your from completing, for there is more for you to fear in Paris. Thanks be to God, the war between the emperor and the king of France has calmed down.[17] Nothing was pressing you to carry out so feverishly the vow you made at Montmartre. It came from a holy devotion that had previously not obliged you to do anything; but now that this vow has been made, it is necessary.

"If this exercise is not carried out, is it not necessary for the conquest of souls, as you promise? You approve of making an auricular confession to the ministry of our church. It is a very sacred thing: the transubstantiation of the body of Our Lord Jesus Christ in the communion of the faithful. A thing that is very sacred, if the word Very did not convey something more. These are instruments for maintaining Catholics in our ancient religion, but they do not always suffice to convert those who have been raised over a long time either in their idolatry or in their Mohammedanism. Each has its impious superstitions, and its maxims that contradict our Christian faith. In addition, do you not know that this devil, Martin Luther (I want to call him a devil because he issues from Saint Martin's devil)[18] expressly armed himself against these two sacraments by means of an infinity of sophistries, gleaned from the Holy Scriptures out of context? If you undertake to stand up to him, as you promise, it is not the doing of a scholar or a mere master of arts, it is the doing of the wisest and most learned of theologians. For otherwise, if you imagine that you are defending our cause, you will be prevaricators. What weapons must you use against all these unbelievers? Our four evangelists, along with the commentaries of our good, believing doctors: for example, Saint Jerome, Saint Augustine,[19]

---

17   Charles V (1500–58) was king of Spain and Holy Roman emperor. He abdicated these and other positions in 1554–56. As the pope's discourse suggests, the on-and-off wars between France and the Habsburgs (they are known as the Habsburg–Valois Wars) did in fact calm for a brief time in 1534–36, but they were rekindled in 1536, when French troops invaded northern Italian Peninsula, and Spanish troops invaded France. Another truce was signed in 1538. See *Encyclopaedia Britannica*, https://www.britannica.com/biogra phy/Charles-V-Holy-Roman-emperor (accessed February 28, 2021).

18   Saint Martin (316–397), third bishop of Tours, met the devil along the road. The devil asked him where he was going. Martin replied that he would go wherever the Lord called him. The devil having vowed to resist that, Martin said: The Lord is my helper. The devil immediately disappeared, and Martin went on his way, freeing people from the errors of heathenism. In this allusion to the saint and the devil, Pasquier is equating the heretic Martin Luther with the devil chased away by Saint Martin. See *Encyclopaedia Britannica*, https://www.britannica.com/biography/Saint-Martin-of-Tours (accessed February 28, 2021).

19   Augustine of Hippo (354–430) was an early Christian theologian whose writings influenced the development of Western Christianity. Among his most important works are *The City of God, On Christian Doctrine*, and *Confessions*. See *Encyclopaedia Britannica*, https://www.britannica.com/biography/Saint-Augustine (accessed February 28, 2021).

Saint Ambrose,[20] Saint Gregory of Nazianzen,[21] the other Saint Gregory[22] (the first pope to bear that name), Saint John Chrysostom,[23] Saint Bernard,[24] and several others whom our church lists on the calendar of beatified souls? All of whom turn toward moral theology, and use it as a great sword to combat those who are misled about our faith. But I shall soon tell you about a greater one, in order to enter an enclosed field of combat, weapons in hand: Peter Lombard the Master of Sentences, or Saint Thomas Aquinas,[25] inimitable persons in what is called Scholastic doctrine. They are the two champions with whom we can fight our enemies to the bitter end. This is not something one studies for only two or three years. The old discipline required at least six years for public exercises, and for private ones, the totality of our lives. Since you have made a vow to God to be distilled in that alembic, why should I dispense you from doing so? Given that you are devoting yourself to the conversion of as many infidels as heretics, if you have not yet done it, you must do it: unless you want to act out the fable of Phaeton,[26] and teach new wagon-masters how to drive the sun's horses, in order to set fire to and burn up the whole earth. If you have

20   Ambrose (c.340–397), bishop of Milan, became one of the most influential ecclesiastical figures of the fourth century. He ranks with Augustine, Jerome, and Gregory the Great as one of the Latin doctors of the church. See *Encyclopaedia Britannica*, https://www.britan nica.com/biography/Saint-Ambrose (accessed February 28, 2021).

21   Gregory of Nazianzen (c.329–390), also known as Gregory the Theologian, was arch-bishop of Constantinople. He was widely considered the most accomplished rhetorical stylist of his day. See *Encyclopaedia Britannica*, https://www.britannica.com/biography/ Saint-Gregory-of-Nazianzus (accessed February 28, 2021).

22   Pope Saint Gregory I (c.540–604), also called Gregory the Great, is known for his prolific writings. Among them are his *Dialogues*, which are translations of Eastern Christian texts. See *Encyclopaedia Britannica*, https://www.britannica.com/biography/ St-Gregory-the-Great (accessed February 28, 2021).

23   Saint John Chrysostom (c.349–407) was one of the prolific authors in the early Christian church, exceeded only by Augustine of Hippo. See *Encyclopaedia Britannica*, https:// www.britannica.com/biography/Saint-John-Chrysostom (accessed February 28, 2021).

24   Bernard of Clairvaux (1090–1153), a French abbot, was a major figure in the reform of Benedictine monasticism. This reform led to the creation of the Cistercian order. See *Encyclopaedia Britannica*, https://www.britannica.com/biography/Saint-Bernard-of -Clairvaux (accessed February 28, 2021).

25   Thomas Aquinas (1225–74) was a philosopher, theologian (*Summa theologiae*), and jurist in the tradition of Scholasticism. He is also known as the Doctor Angelicus, or the Doctor Communis. See *Encyclopaedia Britannica*, https://www.britannica.com/biography/ Saint-Thomas-Aquinas (accessed February 28, 2021).

26   According to ancient Greek myths, the sun was put into a chariot, and every day the god Helios would drive the chariot along the sky, causing the sun to rise and set. One day, Phaeton, Helios's son, secretly took the chariot for a drive; but he lost control of the horses and was killed. See *Encyclopaedia Britannica*, https://www.britannica.com/topic/ Helios-Greek-god (accessed February 28, 2021).

some spark of religion in your souls, it is not up to you to revoke the vow you made to God. The place, the day, the mysteries of the church (repeated two and three times) that you bring there: they obligate you, with no hope of a dispensation; and as for me, I do not want, nor am I able to grant a dispensation. Divine and evangelical law, our canonical constitutions, my faith, my religion, and the Universal Church of which I am the head, forbid me to do so."

THE LAWYER. Do you think that Pope Paul III would have flatly refused, if he'd learned about the false titles they'd taken, and about their lies about studying theology, and about the vow they'd made at Montmartre. As a result of not having been informed, did they have such trouble winning him over before getting him to yield? I've no doubts when I say that, since their religious order was received and approved thanks to a manifest trick and deception, the authorization is null and void. Consequently, nothing built upon that foundation is in effect and valid. Let the Jesuit fortify himself as much as he wishes, with all the other bulls he has obtained, as a consequence of the first bulls issued in 1540. The root is maggoty, so the tree couldn't produce fruit. Until now, I've shown you what a dolt Ignatius was, and I've pointed out how he and his companions lied, and how ignorant they were of theology. Next, I want to show you that their sect, which they call the Society of Jesus, is built upon an ignorance of the antiquity of our church.

First, the Management of Our Church by the Bishops; Second, the Ancient Religious Orders; Third, the Universities; and How the Jesuit Sect Is Built on the Ignorance of All This Antiquity

THE LAWYER. Not only do the religious orders approved by our church, but also all faithful Christians of whatever rank one wants to view them, not belong to the Society (Christian humility forbids us to speak so arrogantly), but they follow Our Savior and Redeemer Jesus Christ, on whose model, and on the model of his apostles, we ought to shape our actions, with the least possible ill that we can. In this, his great and inexhaustible mercy consists of usually taking our good will for the effect. Ignatius, a new apprentice in sacred letters, chose nine companions who were just as new to this matter as he was. When introducing their sect, they believed that, in everything and by everything, they were conforming to the principles of our primitive church; and for that reason, they said that they belonged to the Society of Jesus. Let's therefore see what the first, second, and third plans were for our church, and what the Jesuits' Institutes are, so that by encountering and confronting the one and the other, we may make a judgment about the title they took: that arrogant and factious name, the Society of Jesus, which they, above all other Christians, took.

When Our Lord wanted to go up to heaven, he ordered all his apostles to care for his flock, and he especially said it three times to Saint Peter, the apostle on whom he had previously promised to build his church. Having subsequently spread the sparks of his Holy Spirit over them, their understanding and devotion consisted of sowing the seeds of his Gospel throughout the universe. Their usual dwelling place was the city of Jerusalem, which they initially assigned to one companion, and they assigned other members to the different provinces of the Levant. Having completed their embassies, they met together in a full assembly to recount what they had done. Saint James, known as the Just, was elected by common suffrage, to preside over the church of Jerusalem in particular: that's why Saint Peter's supervision and his general primacy among the apostles weren't taken from him. For you can see that, at the first council of Jerusalem, it was he who took the first step, he who made the proposals, he who resolved to do things, and he who was followed by Saint James and all the apostles.[1] And in the entire history of their acts, written down by Saint Luke, the principal miracles were done by Saint Peter, and the general administration of this holy group was put into his hands. With them were several persons who had converted to the Christian religion: sometimes they were called bishops, and sometimes priests, from the Greek word that means elder. We learn this from Saint Luke, in chapters 15 and 16 of Acts, and in chapter 20, when Saint Paul was taking leave of the Ephesians. At the end of the harangue, he addressed them, calling them bishops, although earlier he had called them priests. True, this policy didn't last very long among them, especially since, for the convenience of so many shepherds in the church, and so many sheep, the provinces were turned over to the more capable persons, who were called bishops; and the lesser administrative units (cities, market towns, and small towns) were turned over to priests named by the church, who exercised their ministry under the authority of the bishops. We have since come to call them curates. You'll find a very fine remark about all this antiquity in Venerable Bede: *Sicut duodecim Apostolos, formam Episcoporum praemonstrare nemo est qui dubitet, sic et hos septuaginta discipulos, figuram Presbyterorum, id est, secundi Ordinis Sacerdotes, gessisse sciendum est. Tametsi primis Ecclesiae temporibus, ut Apostolica scriptura testis est, utrique Presbyteri, utrique vocabantur Episcopi. Quorum unum sapientiae maturitatem, alterum industriam curae pastoralis significat.*[2] I cited these passages for you on purpose, to counter the ignorance of a new Jesuit, who says that those who maintain that bishops and priests were the same positions in the beginning, are rekindling Aerius's heresy.[3] Our general church spent fifteen or sixteen years in Jerusalem, which was the common fountain from which all their envoys came; and after that, the apostles chose various provinces and distributed the others to bishops. Egypt was given to Saint Mark, Peter's disciple; he established his See in the city of Alexandria in year 48 after the birth of Our Lord, that is, fourteen years or thereabouts after his Ascension. That's the first plan of our Christian Church, in which

---

1 Acts 15:4–21.

2 The citation come from Book III of Bede's commentary to Luke: "There is no one who doubts that just like twelve apostles prefigure the office of bishops, so it is known that those seventy disciples represent the office of presbyters, that is priests of the second order, although in the early days of the church, as the apostolic Scripture testifies, both were called presbyters, and both were called bishops. Of these two, one stands for maturity of wisdom, the other for zeal of pastoral care."

3 Aerius of Pontus was a fourth-century *presbyter* (priest). The doctrines he taught ran counter to the beliefs of the Roman Catholic Church. He failed to make his teachings widely popular, and his sect died out soon after his death. See "Aerius," in *Oxford Reference*, https://www.oxfordreference.com/view/10.1093/oi/authority.20110803095353733 (accessed February 27, 2021).

you'll note, according to the diverse times, the primacy and authority of the Holy See of Rome, the patriarchates of Constantinople, Alexandria, Antioch, and Jerusalem, the archbishoprics and bishoprics, the priesthoods and the specific curates of cities, market towns, and villages.

That state of affairs persisted for a long time in the true church. The exceptional persecutions of our people by several emperors caused some to withdraw to deserted areas, in order to avoid these cruelties. Others, from devotion, exceeded the common sense of all the people. The latter had as protectors two great prophets: Elijah in the Old Testament and Saint John the Baptist in the New Testament. But John was quickly martyred by order of Herod the Tyrant,[4] and that great devotion ended with his life. Philo the Jew[5] seems to have attributed to him the renewal of the See of Saint Mark in Egypt: for he says that some of the people of his nation had abandoned their possessions, and had sworn to live in a reclusive society, saying prayers and *oraisons*: these were prefiguarations, not the real monasteries that later became a part of our religion. Those about whom Philo was speaking were Jews who, having become Christians, went to lodge at Lake Maryot in Egypt, or who were not yet very steeped in our religion, and who mingled Christianity and Judaism. We learn this from Sozomen,[6] Nicephorus,[7] and even from Eusebius,[8] who doesn't stray very far from the subject.

---

4   Herod Antipater (*c.*20 BCE–39 CE) is also named Antipas. He was not really a king: he was a "tetrarch," that is, someone who ruled over a "quarter." He is remembered for the roles he played in the executions of John the Baptist and Jesus of Nazareth. See *Encyclopaedia Britannica*, https://www.britannica.com/biography/Herod-Antipas (accessed February 28, 2021).

5   Philo of Alexandria (*c.*20 BCE–50 CE) also called Philo Judaeus, was a Hellenistic Jewish philosopher. He used philosophical allegory to harmonize Greek philosophy with sacred Jewish texts. See *Encyclopaedia Britannica*, https://www.britannica.com/biography/Philo-Judaeus (accessed February 28, 2021).

6   Sozomen (*c.*400–*c.*450), that is, Salminius Hermias Sozomenus, was born into a Christian family near Gaza. He is known for his history of the Christian church, *The Ecclesiastical History*. See *Encyclopaedia Britannica*, https://www.britannica.com/biography/Sozomen (accessed February 28, 2021).

7   Nicephorus (*c.*1256–1335) was a Greek historian of the Byzantine church and a priest at the Church of Hagia Sophia, Constantinople. See *Encyclopaedia Britannica*, https://www.britannica.com/biography/Nicephorus-Callistus-Xanthopoulos (accessed February 28, 2021).

8   Eusebius of Caesarea (*c.*260–340), also known as Eusebius Pamphili, was the major historian of early Christianity. He contributed to making Caesarea a center of Christian learning and gave his personal library to the city. See *Encyclopaedia Britannica*, https://www.britannica.com/biography/Eusebius-of-Caesarea (accessed February 28, 2021).

The first Christian religious who, from devotion, embraced the solitary life that had hitherto been unknown, was Paul the Elder.[9] We learn this from Saint Jerome, who learned it from Macarius[10] and Aniathas,[11] Saint Anthony's disciples. And his successor was Saint Anthony, who spent a long interval in a holy and devout life. *Hujus vitae* (says the same Saint Jerome) *author Paulus, illustrator Antonius, et ut ad superiora veniam, Princeps Joannes Baptista*. "This life (he says) began with Paul, advanced to Saint Anthony, and if we must climb higher still, Saint John the Baptist was the first standard bearer." Certainly a fine thing, and worthy of being commented upon here: how God wanted to establish in his church two great and holy families, one consisting of bishops and priests, and the other of abbots, monks, and religious. In the first flock he wanted Saint Paul to be his chosen vessel; and in the other family, it would be that other Saint Paul who took the first step and overture to our monasteries. This man, as I've said, had as a successor Saint Anthony, from whom, as from a great fountain, several streams issued: Macarius, Aniathas, Julian,[12] Paul the Young Man,[13] and others, to whom God made himself manifest through several miracles. This extraordinary solitude couldn't easily be lodged in every devout soul, but it could be lodged in those that were (if you'll permit me to say it) paradoxes. By means of this, the others vowed themselves to solitude, but they took a moderate path. Staying far from ordinary people, they formed a community among them that was reclusive, and that was separated from where people lived. This being easier to endure, it was visited more often than the former community. Writing to Rusticus,[14] who wanted to adopt the solitary way, Saint Jerome said: *Primum tractandum est, utrum solus, an cum aliis in*

---

9   Paul of Thebes, also known as Paul the Anchorite, Paul Simplex, or Paul the First Hermit, was a disciple of Saint Anthony. He is regarded as the first Christian hermit and was said to have lived alone in the desert from the age of sixteen to the age of 113. See *Encyclopaedia Britannica*, https://www.britannica.com/biography/Saint-Paul-of-Thebes (accessed February 28, 2021).

10   Macarius of Egypt (c.300–c.391) was a monk who lived in the desert. He is credited with writing fifty *Spiritual Homilies*. See *Encyclopaedia Britannica*, https://www.britannica .com/biography/Macarius-the-Egyptian (accessed February 28, 2021).

11   Saint Jerome mentions him in passing, but gives no further particulars (Sutto, 190n261).

12   Julian (c.300–377), a Syrian hermit, Sutto, 190n260. See *Encyclopaedia Britannica*, https:// www.britannica.com/biography/Macarius-the-Egyptian (accessed February 28, 2021).

13   Pasquier wrote: *Paul le jeune*, "Paul the Younger." He may be referring to Paul the Hermit, who became a hermit at a young age and spent the rest of his long life in a cave. See *Encyclopaedia Britannica*, https://www.britannica.com/biography/Saint-Paul-of-Thebes (accessed February 28, 2021).

14   Saint Rusticus (?–461) wanted to embrace the contemplative life, but as Pasquier's quote from Saint Jerome's letter reveals, Jerome advised him to pursue his studies. Named bishop of Narbonne circa 430, he was unable to stop the spread of Arianism throughout

Monasterio vivere debeas. Mihi quidem placet ut habeas contubernium, nec ipse te doceas. "It is necessary (he said) first to consider whether you want to live all alone, or with others in a monastery. As for me, it seems that it is better to live in company than it is to want be your only preceptor." During the time when Saint Anthony was living in Egypt, Saint Hilarion[15] was practicing the same sort of life in Syria and Palestine. Moved by the great renown about him that Saint Anthony had scattered throughout Christendom, he went to visit Anthony and came out marvelously edified: yet, by a new devotion, he wanted to make it more communicable than it had been before; so that, following his example, an infinity of monasteries rose in Palestine such as had hitherto been unknown. He would visit them on certain days, as generals and superiors of religious orders do; sometimes he was followed by many of his monks. Saint Jerome goes into detail about this in his life: and all of that makes me almost believe that the first monasteries, as we see them today, began under him. Well, I can say that the anchorites[16] of Egypt emerged at the same time under Saint Anthony, as the coenobites[17] did under Saint Hilarion, which I'll discuss later. *Ante Hilarionem nulla Monasteria erant in Palestina, nec quisquam Monachum ante S. Hilarionem noverat in Syria: ille fundator hujus conversationis et studii, in hac provincia fuit: Habebat Dominus Jesus in Aegypto senem Antonium, habebat in Palestina, Hilarionem juniorem.* "Before the coming of Hilarion, there were no monasteries in Palestine, and no monks in Syria. He was the first author and master of conversation and study in that province. Our Lord Jesus Christ had, in Egypt, Anthony, who was very old, and in Palestine he had Hilarion, who was younger than he." Saint Anthony was ninety when he died, and Saint Hilarion was eighty.

Gaul. See *The Catholic Encyclopedia*, https://www.newadvent.org/cathen/13275a.htm (accessed February 27, 2021).

15   Hilarion (291–371) was an anchorite who spent most of his life in the desert, following the example of Anthony the Great. He is credited with being the founder of Palestinian monasticism. See *Encyclopaedia Britannica*, https://www.britannica.com/biography/Saint-Hilarion (accessed February 28, 2021).

16   An anchorite is someone who withdraws from secular society in order to lead a life centered on prayer, asceticism, the Eucharist. An anchorite differs from a hermit in that the former were required to take a vow of stability of place and therefore generally opted for permanent enclosure in a cell attached to a church. And, again unlike hermits, anchorites were subject to a rite of consecration that closely resembled a funeral, after which they were considered dead to the world, a sort of living saint. Anchorites had a certain degree of autonomy, for the only ecclesiastical authority to which they answered was the bishop.

17   Cenobitic monasticism stresses community life. In the West, the community often belongs to a religious order, and the monk's life is regulated by a religious rule. An older style of monasticism in which the monk lives like a hermit, is called "eremitic."

Now, all these people (I mean those who were living alone in the desert, and the others who lived in monasteries) wore clothing that distinguished them and set them apart from the rest of the people. For this reason (said Saint Cyprian, talking about false monks), neither the desert, nor the monk's cowl instead of the robe, nor fasts, served these monks as a guarantee: beneath this sort of halter a very worldly soul is often hidden. And Saint Jerome, in his life of Hilarion, says: *Igitur Hilarion 80. aetatis suae anno, cùm absens esset Hesechius, quasi testamenti vice, brevem manu sua scripsit epistolam, omnes divitias suas ei derelinquens, Evangelium scilicet et tunicam facceam, cucullam et palliolum.* "Whereupon Hilarion, age eighty (Hesychius[18] being absent), wrote a note as if it had been his last will, in which he left him all his wealth, that is to say, the Gospels, his monk's cowl, his scapulary, and his cape." Clothes that are still worn today in monasteries, where their exercises consisted of fasting, prayer, and the hours, not so much in order to earn their livelihood as to avoid the obstacles and temptations of the devil. No one could even be admitted to a monastery in Egypt unless he knew how to make something. A lesson they had learned from the great patron, Saint Anthony, who professed to know nothing, judging that the amusement of literature disturbed spiritual meditations and, as such, had nothing in common with the priesthood. That's why Saint John Chrysostom, a priest as well as a true monk, said that it was like a king, with a simple man who merely led a private life; and yet their office was neither to preach nor to teach the common people. Saint Jerome, wrote to Paulin the Monk,[19] saying: "If you want to exercise the duties of a priest, if you want to be called to the lofty position of bishop, then live in cities and castles, and act in such a way that the gain for other souls will be the salvation of your own soul. But if you want to be what people say you are, a monk, that is, alone, what are you doing in the cities that are not the residence of single persons, but of various persons? Bishops and priests have the apostles as a mirror; and having succeeded them, they make themselves the successors of their merits.

---

18 Hesychius, a hermit, was Saint Hilarion's follower in Palestine. He followed the saint to Egypt and Sicily. Learning of the saint's death on Cyprus, he sailed there and brought Hilarion's remains to Majuma, near Gaza. See Robert Wiśniewski, *Cult of Saints*, E00694, http://csla.history.ox.ac.uk/record.php?recid=E00694 (accessed February 28, 2021).

19 Paulinus of Nola (353–431) was born not far from Bordeaux. He abandoned a promising career in the Roman administration and was baptized as a Christian. After his wife's death, he became bishop of Nola in Campania. There, he began a correspondence with Christian leaders throughout the empire. His renunciation of wealth and position led to his being held up as an example by many of his contemporaries, including Augustine, Jerome, Martin, and Ambrose. He was also known for his poetry. See *Encyclopaedia Britannica*, https://www.britannica.com/biography/Saint-Paulinus-of-Nola (accessed February 27, 2021).

As for us, let's place before our eyes Saint Paul, Julian, Hilarion, Macarius, the banner-bearers of our profession; and in order not to forget the Holy Scripture, let us remember Elijah and Elias. Let us only begin eating in the evening, and for our meal let us have herbs, and from time to time small fish that we think appropriate for great banquets." The same Saint Jerome, having been begged to preach to a mother by a good son, in order to have a reconciliation with one of her daughters, said: "You take me for a man who can sit in an episcopal chair and who does not know that I am shut up in a cell, far from the troops, and that I have vowed only to grieve with you over past troubles, or to avoid the present ones."

Time (as I've said) gave us two sorts of monk. One sort lived alone in the desert: they were the anchorites. The others, who lived in monasteries, were called *cenobia* by the Greeks: cenobites. Saint Jerome described their manner of living and their disciplines, in his lovely Epistle that begins: *Audia filia*. And inasmuch as the monks were neither priests nor clerics, over time their superiors were permitted to be priests and to administer the sacraments to them. That was the case for Saint Jerome, who was simultaneously an abbot and a priest. That was the case for John, bishop of Constantinople, who corrected Epiphanius,[20] bishop of Cyprus, his inferior, for having turned some monks at the monastery of Saint Jerome into priests. He apologized for having so many monks who did not have enough priests to minister to them. And Saint Ambrose, in his funeral oration for Eusebius,[21] bishop of Vercelli, among other distinctive things, praised him for having admitted to the priesthood all the monks of his diocese, religious who had mingled the orders of the clergy with their devotion, and who served as a great nursery for our church, in order to turn them into archbishops and bishops who, owing to their holy lives and the profundity of their knowledge, made great advances in our Christian religion. That was what Gregory of Nazianzen and Basil[22] did: both were monks, and both were bishops, and in diverse ways they established an infinity of

---

20   Epiphanius of Salamis (315–402) was bishop of Salamis, Cyprus, in the late fourth century. A strong defender of orthodoxy, he is best known for the *Panarion*, a large compendium of the heresies of his own time that often contains the only surviving fragments of suppressed texts. See *Encyclopaedia Britannica*, https://www.britannica.com/biography/Saint-Epiphanius-of-Constantia (accessed February 27, 2021).

21   Eusebius of Vercelli (*c.*283–371) was an Italian bishop. He supported the dogma of the divinity of the Son against Arianism. See *Encyclopaedia Britannica*, https://www.britannica.com/biography/Eusebius-of-Vercelli (accessed February 27, 2021).

22   Basil of Caesarea (*c.*329–379), also called St. Basil the Great, was bishop of Caesarea Mazaca in central Anatolia. He opposed the heresies of the early Christian church. His ability to balance his theological convictions with his political connections made him a powerful advocate for the Nicene Creed; along with his mother and sister he was also a major figure

monasteries and religious orders, part of which have been transmitted to us. Here I leave you some deliberate words that were introduced over the years, being satisfied with informing you about the first plan. There remains for me to say a few words about our universities organized for teaching theology as well as humane letters and the sciences. Neither during the days of the apostles, nor long after, was our church especially weighed down by readings. The activities of the apostles, and after them the bishops, consisted of preaching the Gospel of God and administering the holy sacraments. We owe that first institution to the church of Alexandria where, in the days of Emperor Commodus,[23] and by the authority of Bishop Julian,[24] Pantaenus,[25] a person of exceptional erudition, opened the first of the schools for holy writing; and that (says Eusebius)[26] planted in the church of Alexandria the custom that has continued to our day: there would be masters and doctors to teach the Holy Scripture, persons who excel in every science and all erudition. He was succeeded by Clement of Alexandria,[27] who was very renowned among the learned persons of his day; and Clement was succeeded by Origen,[28] who took under his wing Heraclas,[29] the first of his students. The other bishops adopted this praiseworthy custom of teaching young people, and the custom spread in

---

in the development of Eastern monasticism. See *Encyclopaedia Britannica*, https://www.britannica.com/biography/Saint-Basil-the-Great (accessed February 27, 2021).

23 Commodus (161–192), born Lucius Aurelius Commodus, was a Roman emperor. He reigned jointly with his father, Marcus Aurelius, from 177 to 180; he then reigned alone from 180 to his assassination in 192. See *Encyclopaedia Britannica*, https://www.britannica.com/biography/Commodus (accessed February 27, 2021).

24 Julian (Yulianus) of Alexandria, eleventh pope of Alexandria (178–189) and patriarch of the Holy See of Saint Mark.

25 Pantaenus the Philosopher (?–c.200), a Greek, was a significant figure in the Catechetical School of Alexandria. He was instrumental in developing Christian theology. See *Encyclopaedia Britannica*, https://www.britannica.com/biography/Pantaenus (accessed February 27, 2021).

26 Pasquier is referring to Eusebius of Caesarea.

27 Titus Flavius Clemens (150–c.215), also known as Clement of Alexandria, taught at the Catechetical School of Alexandria. A convert to Christianity, he was familiar with classical Greek philosophy and literature. His major works demonstrate that Clement was influenced by Hellenistic philosophy to a greater extent than any other Christian thinker of his day. See *Encyclopaedia Britannica*, https://www.britannica.com/biography/Saint-Clement-of-Alexandria (accessed February 27, 2021).

28 Origen of Alexandria (c.184–c.253), also known as Origen Adamantius, spent half his career in Alexandria. He was a prolific writer. See *Encyclopaedia Britannica*, https://www.britannica.com/biography/Origen (accessed February 27, 2021).

29 Heraclas (or Herakles) of Alexandria was the thirteenth bishop of Alexandria, serving 232–48. He was the first bishop of Alexandria to be called pope. One of Origen's first pupils, he succeeded him as head of the school in 231. See Richard Patrick Crosland

such a way that universities were introduced among us, to teach letters. The bishops are the first and last judges, and to this end they have a chancellor beneath them who knows each discipline and subject matter. As for monks and religious, they lack the power to give lessons, other than to the persons who belong to their orders.

I summarized for you, above, the origins of the first organization of our church: bishops, abbots, and universities, upon which, like three great and strong pillars, our religion was built. Now let's see what the Jesuits' organization is. They are able folks who, like our priests, don't wear any external mark of being monks, yet they make three substantial vows: chastity, poverty, and obedience, which are shared by other religious; and they add begging, both general and particular, for those taking their final vow, when they become fathers. These are persons who, in addition, say that they are dedicated to preaching and administering the holy sacraments of penance and communion, and they give public lessons in all sorts of disciplines to all sorts of students, without being subject to the old rules of the university. In all the above, they don't even want to recognize, as their superiors, the bishops who have their separate workrooms. It's true that, for enclosure and for accomplishing their holy devotion, they offer to go to every part of the world where it pleases the pope to order them, to convert infidels and unbelievers, thereby bringing back into use the old discipline of the apostles. Let's, therefore, see if, when the antiquity of our church is compared with their novelty, we can worthily give them a place in our midst, and whether they can say that the Society of Jesus at least anticipates all our other Christians.

Hanson, *The Search for the Christian Doctrine of God: The Arian Controversy 318–381 AD* (New York: Bloomsbury, 1988), 72–74.

One Cannot Give a Place to the Jesuits in All the Three Ancient Orders of Our Church, and That Is Why They Do Not Dare Attend Processions

THE LAWYER. They say that most dreams come from a long meditation that the day has imprinted in our heads, concerning some subject that returned at night to our fantasies while we are sleeping. That happened to me a few days ago. For as one of the principal conversations that I nourish in my spirit deals with Jesuits, one night, among others, I happened to dream about what I've been telling you. And I beg you, Messieurs, not to think that I'm telling you this in order to make you laugh, or as a joke: I'm doing it as wisely as I can. The subject is so dignified that if I behaved otherwise, I'd deserve to be censured by the magistrate. If you aren't willing to accept it as a dream, take it as a celestial vision like the one Ignatius saw, when God the Father appeared to him and recommended him to Jesus Christ his Son; or when he showed him all the tools he had used to make that round machine, or when Durus,[1] Xavier's first disciple, saw a deserted chapel and Our Lord Jesus Christ as a child, who put himself between them in order to be reconciled with the Virgin his mother, who was angry with him.

THE LAWYER-DREAMER. It therefore seemed to me that I was watching, while sleeping, a general review of his church that God was conducting, from the passion of Our Savior and Redeemer Jesus Christ all the way to now. As in a great and solemn procession, the apostles went first, followed by the popes, patriarchs, archbishops, bishops, curates, priests, and all the ecclesiastics who, not being monks, are called secular. In second position marched those good old hermit fathers, the first authors and founders of the monasteries; and after them came several great abbots and religious of the orders of Saint Augustine and Saint Benedict: from whom, like two great fountains, emerged all the other religious orders, the ones called regular. In third position came the universities, with their rectors and four faculties: theology, decrees, medicine, and the arts, with all their henchmen and a large group of students, some big and some little. Saint Peter carried the banner for the first group, Saint Anthony for the second. Some persons in the third group wanted to give the banner to Peter

---

1   Probably Francisco Durão (b.1528), one of Francis Xavier's early disciples, who accompanied him to Malacca.

© KONINKLIJKE BRILL NV, LEIDEN, 2021 | DOI:10.1163/9789004164062_016

Lombard, former bishop of Paris and Master of Sentences; and this idea had been opposed; so this time the banner ended up being carried by Master Jean Gerson,[2] doctor of theology and, in his day, chancellor of the university of Paris.

There I saw good FATHER IGNATIUS; and next to him were Favre, Xavier, Salmerón, Bobadilla, Rodrigues, Broët, Jaye, and Codury, his first companions. After them came Diego Laínez, Francisco Borgia,[3] Everard Mercurian,[4] Claudio Acquaviva, all of them successively generals of the order. Lower down were their provincials, rectors, fathers, principals, regents, presidents, spiritual and temporal coadjutors, and approved scholars. All of them, led by Captain Ignatius, wanted to be beneath the banner, first the banner of Saint Peter, then the banner of Saint Anthony, and finally the banners of the universities.

At first, IGNATIUS didn't doubt that he'd be received by the apostles: for preaching and administering the holy sacraments of penance and the altar, and then that great Mission vow that the fathers promised to the Holy See, seemed to be within easy reach. That's why, with a brash expression on his face, he presented himself to Saint Peter. I'm going to tell you about everything they said to each other, and I beg you not to find fault with me, because my dream took advantage of the privilege that dreams have: some persons are pleased to fall into these fantasies, without observing the rules about time or good behavior that one reserves for other exchanges. SAINT PETER. Good folks, you are most welcome, for the principal concern of our vocation was to convert to our faith the greatest number of souls possible. IGNATIUS. We have the very same thing in mind, through the special Mission vow taken by those who were your successors in Rome. SAINT PETER. That's good, but what are your names? IGNATIUS. What our vocation wants: the Society of Jesus. In consideration of which the common people, inspired by the blessed Holy Spirit, called us Jesuits. A name

2   Jean Charlier de Gerson (1363–1429) was a French scholar and educator. A theologian and mystic, he was one of the leaders of the conciliar movement for church reform that ended the Great Schism between the popes of Rome and the popes of Avignon, which makes him a distinctly provocative choice. He was elected chancellor of the University of Paris in 1395. The *Imitatio Christi*, Ignatius's favorite devotional work, was ascribed to him at that time. See *Encyclopaedia Britannica*, https://www.britannica.com/biography/Jean-de-Gerson (accessed February 28, 2021).

3   Francisco de Borja (1510–72), or Borgia, duke of Gandía, entered the newly founded Society of Jesus in 1546. In 1565, he was elected the third superior general after the death of Diego Laínez. See *DHCJ*, 2:1601–5.

4   Everard Mercurian (1514–80) was the fourth superior general of the Society. During his tenure (1573–80), he compiled the "Summary of the Constitutions" from the manuscripts of St. Ignatius, and he drew up the "Common Rules" of the Society, and the particular rules of each office. On his generalate, see Thomas M. McCoog, ed., *The Mercurian Project: Forming Jesuit Culture (1573–1580)* (Rome: IHSI, 2004).

that today seems to have miraculously spread throughout the whole universe, so agreeable was it to God. SAINT PETER. Rather, it was agreeable to the devil, who wanted to encircle everyone in the skirts of your habit. That's not the first time your tricks have been tried, and it won't be the last. Every day the devil lies in wait to surprise God's church. What? We who were truly nurtured in the society of Jesus,[5] to whom he communicates all his secrets, as much as, and for as long as he was garbed in human flesh, as a lowly being; and having risen into the heavens, he made us participants along the way of his Holy Spirit. We didn't dare take that title, but we called ourselves Christians, first in the church at Antioch where our holy brethren, Paul and Barnabas presided.[6] This title was approved in the church of God, from our time all the way to today: and you, who want to be one of us, you use a new and arrogant word, and call yourselves Jesuits? IGNATIUS. Please pardon us, for it was not done from arrogance; it was done from humility. Our Lord had two names, one is his proper name: Jesus, which at the time was an ordinary name that various Jews had borne and still bear, as is the case among persons of lowly and base condition. The other name was Christ, far nobler and honorable, for it belonged only to kings, pontiffs, and prophets who called themselves the Christs of God. You chose that name for that reason, and we, on the contrary, chose Jesus, because the Jews didn't hold it in esteem, since it was far lesser and humbler than the other name. So, there is arrogance in choosing the one or the other, and it is very easy to judge where it comes from. In addition, we do not think that the name Christian was imposed by the church within the walls of Antioch, but that it came casually by the voice of the people, with no deliberations, and that it was a silent inspiration from God.

THE THRONG. Hearing this, an infinity of holy and devout persons who belonged to the first rank began to grumble, and the others mutinied loftily, saying that no further attention should be paid to Ignatius. He must be driven from our church, along with all his followers. And they said that, owing to that proposition (the founding of their order) there was, in Jesuitry, a great amount of Jewery: just as the ancient Jews tried Our Lord Jesus Christ, so today the new Jews are doing it to the apostles. That our primitive church hadn't taken the name of Jesus when it seemed to be a widespread name among the Jews, they took it because the apostles, and other true and faithful disciples of Jesus

---

5   Saint Peter is being witty: he indeed lived in the "society" (or "company") of Jesus, long before the creation of the Society of Jesus, *La Compagnie de Jésus*.

6   Barnabas was a Cypriot Jew who was made an apostle in Acts 14:14. He and Paul the Apostle undertook missionary journeys for the prominent Christian disciples in Jerusalem, and they successfully evangelized the Gentiles in various Hellenized cities of Anatolia. Barnabas himself was entrusted with the community in Antioch.

Christ, were acquainted with the virtue, energy, and superlative splendor of
that holy name, something unknown to all Jews. And so, Saint Matthew and
Saint Luke, taking one position, maintained that God the Father had been the
godfather,[7] through the mouth of the angel Gabriel, his ambassador, whom
he had specifically sent to tell the Virgin Mary that the child who would be
born of her virginal womb would be called Jesus (a name that means Savior),
inasmuch as he would be the Savior of the world. At this, Eusebius, bishop of
Caesarea, began writing a fine commentary on the difference between the two
words. And the great Saint Augustine, bishop of Hippo in Africa, demonstrated
that if God the Father had been the godfather, then the name Jesus would have
been a hidden mystery, a prophecy of the great prophet Moses, to whom God
had announced that he hadn't called him to lead his children out of Israel,
to the Promised Land, and that, for this reason, he must find a surrogate to
replace him, before leaving this world. Moses chose Auses, but when choosing
him, with the same gesture Moses changed his name to Jesus: "So that in the
future (said this great African bishop), he would no longer be called Moses but
Jesus.[8] That is to say, the people of God would enter the promised land not
by the Law but by grace; and just as this first Jesus was not the real one,
but only the prefiguration, that promised land was not the real one but the
prefigured one."

No notable bishop, no antique doctors of the church, who were part of
this first squadron, were of that opinion. They all made a gentle nip at the
Ignatians. At that point, Saint Peter (who maintained primacy over the entire
church) spoke with admirable majesty. SAINT PETER. It is not for you, nor for
me, to give a reason for what was done in Antioch: when God's church gave
us the name Christians, it was the Holy Spirit's work. And just as it is not the
servant's task to learn the reasons why his master orders him to do something,
but simply to obey, just so, by the inspiration of his Holy Spirit, God commands
us to be called Christians, and no one is permitted to know why. There is no
quicker way to create heretics than to be too curious about such reasons. And

7   In the France of Pasquier's day, the godfather chose the newborn infant's baptismal name.
    Having announced Jesus's name through prophecies, he was therefore considered to be a
    godfather.
8   In reality, it was Joshua who was selected to lead the Jews to the Promised Land, Deut. 3:28.
    The Vulgate printed at Lyon in 1676 calls him "Joshua," but Pasquier calls him "Auses," which
    would be pronounced: "O-sé." Was Pasquier referring to the name "Oshea," (O-shé-a), a vari-
    ant of Hosea (which is derived from Yeshua and "Yahweh")? If so, he was in contact with
    etymologists, because the proper name "Jesus," as used in English, comes from the Latinized
    Greek name (*Iēsous*), which in Hebrew is Yeshua or Jeshua. Which brings readers back, full
    circle, to "Joshua."

yet, do not think that it was simply by the people's suffrage that this name was imposed upon us. Just as God the Father was the godfather for the name Jesus, I can say something very true: by the faith and by the homage that I first gave to Our Lord by this word Christ, he established his church upon me, and he gave me the keys to it, in the midst of his own people. For we all asked who the people were saying he was, and some of his disciples replied: Some say you are Saint John the Baptist, others say Elijah, others say one of the ancient prophets. "But you (he said to us, his apostles), who do you think I am?" I immediately replied: You are the Christ, the living son of God. And he immediately told me that these words did not come from me, but from the revelation of God his Father; and without pausing he said that I was Peter, and that he would build his church on that stone, and everything I would bind on Earth would also be bound in heaven.[9] Since Christ admitted that he would build his church on me, it was a tacit lesson that he was telling us what he willed: that after he had risen to heaven he wanted his church to be called Christian; and as far as that plan was concerned, none of our brethren feared taking that title in Antioch. Since then, I personally have ordained Evodius[10] as bishop of Antioch, and by the same means I confirmed the name Christian in my church. I am amazed (he turns to Ignatius) that you embrace, as you say you do, the seat of Rome, where my successors preside. Yet from the very moment you entered the city, you have been contemptuous of my decrees. For that consideration alone, you cannot be enrolled in this first rank. IGNATIUS. You do not want to receive us, yet from an abundance of piety we make the three vows: chastity, obedience, poverty! And in addition, general and particular begging is done by the religious in our order who have attained the rank of father! SAINT PETER. That is yet another reason for us not to accept you: for although our usual deportment includes chastity, obedience, and scorn for temporal possessions, it is never in the form of a vow that has later been introduced into the church by those whom you see in this second rank. In like manner, it is certain that we never attach our devotions to begging. IGNATIUS. But we administer the holy sacraments of penance and communion, as you do: and in addition, we are ready to go anywhere your successors order us to go, for the advancement of the Christian faith. SAINT PETER. That very thing is done today when mendicant religious administer those two sacraments; and there are some who are in

---

9   This doubtless is Pasquier's own translation of the Vulgate, chiefly Matt. 16:13–20 and
      Luke 9:18–20.

10   Evodius (?–c.69), or Euodias, was bishop of Antioch. He is said to have succeeded Saint
      Peter when Peter left for Rome and is regarded as one of the first identifiable Christians.
      He may have been converted by Peter himself. See *Encyclopaedia Britannica*, https://
      www.newadvent.org/cathen/05653a.htm (accessed February 28, 2021).

the Indies, in Palestine, at Pera, a district near Constantinople, to convert the infidels; and yet, they haven't arranged things with us, before whom you should withdraw, and realize that there are too many disagreements between us and you, for you to fit in.

Ignatius, seeing himself dismissed in that way from the first rank in the procession, was not at all surprised: he deemed that his affairs would succeed better in the second rank, especially because he had been dealing with Saint Anthony, who was honored by all the first hermits. IGNATIUS.[11] I know that, in the midst of his holy and devout meditations, Saint Anthony gloried in igno-rance; and I am sure that if he were to sniff me out, he would find that I have nothing to cede to him on this point. THE LAWYER-DREAMER. However, hav-ing made his proposition in a way that pleased him, or that can please him, and in order to insinuate himself into his good graces, he remonstrated to him that, like him, he had spent his whole life in celestial contemplations, and not on books. It was very true that several literary persons, some of them preach-ers, the others teachers, and all of them priests, had grafted themselves to him, administering the sacraments. The holy and venerable antiquity of this good hermit replied to Ignatius in this way. SAINT ANTHONY. Brethren, I laud your intention, but it has nothing in common with ours. Our devotion, and the devotion of these good fathers, the first teachers of the religious orders, has been solitude without priesthood and without learning. Our learning consists of weighing things at great length with God, deeming all the human sciences to be pure vanity. And as for ecclesiastical functions, they aren't our duty, they are the duty of our bishops, who distribute them to us as their manna, through the innocence of their lower churchmen. Your rules do not mutually agree with ours. Brethren, for God, go in peace, and let us live sweetly, resting our con-sciences in our cells. Yet you shall be able to find, below us, some young shoot that can take root, like those that, with the permission of the Holy See, are called to the orders of priesthood, and that can, like you, preach and adminis-ter the holy sacraments of penance and communion.

At this point, IGNATIUS addressed them; and when he had finished talking about his reasons for coming, SAINT BENEDICT spoke for them all. If (he said to them), you belong to our order, you necessarily must be anchorites and her-mits, or else coenobites and conventuals. If you are anchorites, your profession derogates; so, you will have no difficulty excusing us, for the burden is too pain-ful. But if you are coenobites and conventuals, as we are, then where is your cowl, where is your scapulary, which Latin-speakers called the *cuculla*? And your cape? Because in the past, Elijah, the first prefiguration of our Institute,

---

11   The transition from St. Peter to St. Anthony, in this paragraph, is somewhat unclear.

and after him Saint John the Baptist, wore garments that were distinctly different from those worn by the common people. Where is that great crown on your
shaven heads, about which Saint Jerome commented, to the effect that, in our
poverty, we depict kings and monarchs? Where among you are the extraordinary young men whom you can observe, not only above the common people,
but also above the bishops and curates? Where, in your houses, are the cloisters
we have in our monasteries? To this, IGNATIUS, and those who were accompanying him, curtly and emphatically replied that the members of the Society
were not monks, but merely religious. SAINT BENEDICT. If that is the case, you
are therefore a quintessence of monks. And just as the Faculty of medicine
does not want to admit to its schools those Paracelsites,[12] those abstractors of
quintessences, in like manner we cannot admit Jesuits to our schools. By refusing the Paracelsite and the Jesuit, there will be rhyme and reason together. So,
establish your retreat elsewhere: for just as you disdain the holy title of monk,
you are disdained by monks. Masters of arts, coming from the university of
Paris: at least that's how you present yourselves to Pope Paul III. I'm of the
opinion that, as masters of arts, you were returning to the very same university
where several others will find you fit: there are only a few of them who won't
welcome you.

Ignatius, seeing that his affairs were going from bad to worse, judged that
misfortune was in fact present. He therefore addressed all his brethren. IGNA-
TIUS. Now that it is a question of universities, I know my limits, and how easy
it would be to best me, if I don't present myself to those lofty doctors. Just as,
in the beginning, I only taught young children, and just as you others have
taught all manner of scholars, contrary to our first Institute, I beg you (he
turned to Father Claudio Acquaviva), since today all the superiority[13] of our
Society resides in you, to be willing, as general of that Society, to take over the
administrative duties of Master Jean Gerson. Perhaps you'll be shown more
favor than I showed all the others. ACQUAVIVA not only didn't refuse him, he
considered that command to be very agreeable. All the more so, since he and
his brethren were boasting about teaching literature free of charge. On those

---

12   Theophrastus Bombastus von Hohenheim, called Paracelsus (1493/94–1541), was a Swiss
      physician and alchemist. A medical pioneer, he emphasized the value of observation
      combined with received wisdom. An early modern movement known as Paracelsianism,
      based on his theories and therapies, developed in the second half of the sixteenth cen-
      tury. It represented one of the most comprehensive alternatives to the learned medicine
      based on Galen's physiology. See *Encyclopaedia Britannica*, https://www.britannica.com/
      biography/Paracelsus (accessed February 28, 2021).
13   This is an ironical statement: if Acquaviva embodies "superiority," it is because he is the
      superior general of the Society.

grounds, he believed that his religious have a great advantage over all the other teachers; but he found that the shoe pinched: for he was treated more roughly by the teachers; and that's where the bulk of the squabble was, because both sides having been nourished on the nit-picking of Scholasticism, it was good kick, good catch. Let's therefore listen to their arguments. After Acquaviva had made his proposition and his demand, Gerson, who is one of the leading doctors of theology ever known in France, turned to him. GERSON. You want to join our Society, so you are willing to recognize our bishop as your superior, and as our superior, especially as far as teaching youths is concerned: for here the superior is our first judge. And indeed, since he is vice-director, having the title chancellor and canon of the Paris Church, I am carrying the banner of the University of Paris, which leads all the others. ACQUAVIVA. I do not understand your jargon. We belong to a far greater master. Our Holy Father the Pope gave us authority over the bishops. GERSON. With your very first step, you stumble; and that point alone should send you back to Rome to go through your lessons and should banish you from all French universities.[14] But let us move on. Our universities are composed to two sorts of men: seculars and regulars, and we follow the same policies for both sorts. The seculars can become masters of arts, and earn doctorates in theology, in canon law, in medicine: once they have acquired their degrees, they can give lessons to students who approach them, be it inside the colleges or outside them. Regulars can only be doctors of theology and teach the young men who belong to their order, and nothing more. Which of the two sorts are you? Do not give the answer, I pray you, that the rectors and disciples of our university of Paris got in 1564 when, wanting to be incorporated into them, and having asked you a similar question, you replied three and four times that you were *tales quales vos Curia declaraverat*.[15] For, guided by that, the lawyer who pleaded against you thought it meant that you were just as you were, and not worthy of being listed on the university inventory. ACQUAVIVA. Do not make us marvel at that. At the time, we resembled the bear who has given birth to a cub: at first, it seems to be a heavy mass of flesh, but after the mother has licked it continually, it finally takes the true shape of a bear. So it was with us. For to tell the truth, our Ignatius and his companions didn't specifically designate what we were. But after having exercised our spirits in diverse ways on that obscure matter, they

---

14   In asserting the pope's general and delegable authority over bishops Acquaviva has contradicted the conciliarist doctrines defended by Gerson and, traditionally, the University of Paris. See Jacques Grès-Gayer, *Le gallicanisme de Sorbonne: Chroniques de la Faculté de théologie de Paris (1657–1688)* (Paris: Honoré Champion, 2002).

15   "Exactly as the Curia had defined you." This was part of an interrogation to which the Jesuits were subjected in February 1565 (Sutto, 201n305).

called us, not monks, but regular clerics, which is what our great Ribadeneyra called us; and if I am not mistaken, the same title was given to us by the Council of Trent, and was made public a few months after we had pleaded our case, which would go into force on the following May 1. GERSON. That doesn't answer my question. You must give a categorical answer, so that you will be in one of those predicaments experienced by seculars or regulars. ACQUAVIVA. Was my answer not complete enough, when I told you that we were regular clerics? For, being that, we are not obligated to enslave ourselves to the ancient rules of the universities, being neither pure seculars nor pure regulars. And we can, with all our vows, be graduated from all your faculties, and can give public lessons to youths in all fields of knowledge, without imploring or recognizing the authority of your bishops. GERSON. You are therefore a hermaphrodite, just as Pasquier presents you in his *Recherches de la France*. Just as you are, at one and the same time, seculars and regulars combined, you are neither one nor the other. And so, just as you are not obligated to be slaves to our statutes, we are not obligated to let you be registered in our universities. ACQUAVIVA. And why would you refuse us, since we teach children free of charge? GERSON. You are real beguilers. The first persons who came to Paris to teach literature were Alcuin,[16] Rabban,[17] Eanbald,[18] Claude,[19] and disciples of the Venerable Bede[20] who cried out publicly that they had knowledge for sale. You, on the other hand, want to teach free of charge. And yet the truth is that, in sixty years, your order has acquired two or three times more possessions than all the

---

16   Alcuin of York (*c.*732–804) was an English scholar and teacher at the court of Charlemagne. A contemporary called him the most learned man to be found anywhere. Among his pupils were many of the leading intellectuals of the Carolingian era. There is no reason to believe he, or any of the others in this list, taught at Paris specifically. See *Encyclopaedia Britannica*, https://www.britannica.com/biography/Alcuin (accessed February 28, 2021).

17   [The reference is certainly to …] Rabanus Maurus (*c.*789–856), a Benedictine monk originally from Mainz who studied under Alcuin and spent most of his career at the abbey of Fulda. See *Encyclopaedia Britannica*, https://www.britannica.com/biography/Rabanus-Maurus (accessed February 28, 2021).

18   Eanbald was a student at York with Alcuin, who called him a "brother and most faithful friend." Eanbald was elected archbishop of York in 780. See David Rollason, "Eanbald (II) (*fl.* 796–803), archbishop of York," *Oxford Dictionary of National Biography*, https://www.oxforddnb.com/view/10.1093/ref:odnb/9780198614128.001.0001/odnb-9780198614128-e-8391 (accessed February 28, 2021).

19   Claude Clement Scot (?–*c.*826), professor at the palatine school, under Charlemagne and Louis the Pious.

20   Bede (672/3–735), known as the Venerable Bede, was an English Benedictine monk and teacher. He visited numerous monasteries and abbeys across the British Isles. One of his students was Alcuin. See *Encyclopaedia Britannica*, https://www.britannica.com/biography/Saint-Bede-the-Venerable (accessed February 28, 2021).

universities of France, from the time of their foundation. Moreover, were you not censured by our university of Paris in 1554? ACQUAVIVA. You can say what you please, my memory is fresh: the very same Faculty of Theology approved us, despite that antique censure. For in 1594, concerning some individuals who were deceptively taking the name of the University of Paris, the Sorbonne issued a decree in our favor in the court of the Parlement of Paris, by which it withdrew the case.

Upon hearing this, the entire SORBONNE cried out: You are sophist liars and very bad grammarians. We know very well that, first, the lawyer who was pleading for you wanted to do some target-shooting; and after him came your des Montaignes, followed by La Fon. But that was in order for you to keep enjoying your usual privilege. You know very well which beadle brought our decree here and read it aloud, for it all too impudently imposes on Christian people: *Die nona Julii, anno Domini 1594. Viso et audito à facultate Theologiae Parisiensi legitimè congregata in majore aula Sorbonae, libello supplici, à venerabilibus Patribus Societatis Jesu, ipsi facultati proposito, quo quidem exposuerunt superioribus mensibus, D. Rectorem, tam suo, quàm omnium facultatum nomine, libellum supplicem supremae Parlamenti Curiae obtulisse, quo petierit ut ipsi, eorumque Societas universa, ex toto Galliae regno pelleretur, ac credibile non esse sacratissimam facultatem huic petitioni consensum praebuisse. Ac propterea supplicarunt quatenus placeret dictae facultati, declaratione testificari, hujus petitionis et litis intentae, nullo modo participes esse. Ipsa facultas, matura deliberatione super hoc habita, in hunc modum censuit, SE QUIDEM censere praedictos Patres redigendos et recensendos esse in ordinem et disciplinam Universitatis. Regno autem Gallico esse nullo modo expellendos. Signé Panet dictae facultatis Bidellus.*

The full-length decree was inserted into your *Plaidoyé* of 1594, and also into chapter 44 of La Fon's book. Everyone must understand what it says:

> On June 9, in the year of grace 1594, seen and heard by the Faculty of Theology of Paris, well and duly assembled in the great hall of the Collège de la Sorbonne, the petition presented by the venerable fathers of the Society of Jesus, by which they have given to understand that several months ago Monsieur the Rector of the university, both in his own name, and in the name of all the faculties, presented a request to the court of the Parlement, tending by this to think that they, the remainder of their group, must leave France, and that it was not credible that the sacred faculty could have consented to this petition. Therefore, they beg that it may please the court to declare that they never consented to this. About which our faculty, after mature deliberation, gave its opinion, which is this: It was necessary to reduce the said fathers of the Society of Jesus to

the measure and discipline of the university, but it would not be appropriate to drive them out of the kingdom.

The Latin word *redigere* is much stronger than the French word *réduire*[21] that I used for lack of a better word. Indeed, Latin dictionaries teach that *Redigere est vi quadam vel industria ducere ad aliquid, vel aliquo.*[22] Do you call it approving of your Society when, in the event that you are not chased from the kingdom by any means, we want you to be reduced in number, in accordance with the policies of our university? Put behind you all the dice you cast over your new vows; submit yourself to the discipline of our university; recognize that the bishop is your superior, as we do; receive only licenses in theology; and do not read to persons other than the ones who belong to your religious order, as all other religious do, each in his own place. We shall agree with you, and we shall daringly maintain, before the highest court of France, that you should remain with us. However, by your writings, you impudently and falsely turn this decree into a trophy, as if we had given you full reign, while a mere reading of it would prove you wrong; so, return to your former ways, because in everything, and everywhere, your maxims do not measure up to those we have inherited from a long, holy, and venerable antiquity.

Gerson having finished this decree, IGNATIUS and all his first companions disappeared. But suddenly, ACQUAVIVA, having seen that these means had left him and his brethren in the lurch, cried out: You don't want to make room near you on earth; but despite everything, as long as you are there, we will find room in the heavens for our Ignatius and our Xavier. For we would rather use the money we have in various banks, than not have them canonized. STUDENTS. Then all the little students began whistling, and the older ones shouted: A fox, a fox, who wants to give money to have our Ignatius canonized? ACQUAVIVA was not in the least troubled, thinking that they had said Hosanna, Hosanna, in his honor. He took the chair on which he was sitting and put out his hands to be kissed by everyone who entered his bedchamber, just as he had done on the day he was elected general. But he suddenly realized that he had been mistaken: for that bevy of young frolickers was baying even more than before. In order to calm them down, Gerson spoke. GERSON. Children, do not believe that, in Rome, they are ever so unwise as to make God a present of those two

---

21   *Redigere* means to bring back, to reduce in number. *Réduire* means constrain, force, require. It can also mean reduce to a piteous state, submit to laws, make someone do his duty (DAF 1694).

22   This definition of Latin "redigere" can be found in Ambrogio Calepino, *Ambrosii Calepini dictionarium* (Lyons: Gryphium, 1550), which (with preposition "ad" means to reduce to something).

souls. The Jesuits have been hoping for it for a long time; and to succeed, they have employed, not money (for I do not think that sort of trade goes on in Rome, in order to sanctify souls); but all sorts of lies, foul play, and hypocrisies, in order to surprise the Holy See. For do you think that Maffei's, Ribadeneyra's, and Torsellini's pens have not given birth in recent years to fabulous visions of Ignatius, and miraculous fables about Xavier, if only to serve as false witnesses to that canonization? But the finest I see is that, like actors who think that their play is handsomer if they perform in daylight with torches, and with the windows closed, in the same way the Jesuits of Rome do not spare all sorts of burning candles around Ignatius's tomb, in order to show the sanctity of the place. And even Torsellini says that Xavier's body was brought to the city of Goa, where he rests. There was a candle as big as your lower arm, lighted for twenty-two days, and as many nights, without being consumed. But until now, all these lights could not illuminate the hearts of the holy consistory of Rome, to make these two new saints, and I do not think they will ever do it. A YOUNG BOY in the troop cried out: Monsieur, our master, remove that opinion from your head. Since lies and importunities are natural to Jesuits, in the end they will win out. Do you remember reading in Boccaccio about how Capellet du Prat, superlative at all sorts of wickedness, was canonized by the idiot souls at the Cordeliers' monastery in Dijon?[23] Why could not something like that happen to Loyola, the founder of the Jesuit order, of which Messire Guillaume Duprat, bishop of Clermont, was the first benefactor in France? At that point, a still louder noise arose about this proposition, so that you wouldn't have heard God making thunder. And since the noises were in that stirrup in the ear, some of THE WISER STUDENTS began to clap their hands, as one does during public debates, when, having argued for a long while, one or the other side wants to end it.

THE LAWYER. That woke me up. I was wondrously astonished by that dream, in which I heard the words of our very-veritable Guillaume de Lorris when, at the beginning of his *Romance of the Rose*, said that every dream is not a lie.[24]

---

23   This tale is told on the "First Day" of the *Decameron* of Giovanni Boccaccio (1313–75). In a train-of-thought moment, Pasquier has his character's mind leap from Capellet Du Prat to Guillaume Duprat.

24   Guillaume de Lorris (*c.*1200–40) wrote the first section of the Romance of the Rose (*Roman de la* Rose). The long poem was completed forty years later by Jean de Meun, or Meung (*c.*1240–*c.*1305). These are the lines in question, translated from the French by Harry W. Robbins. See Guillaume de Lorris and Jean de Meun, *The Romance of the Rose* (New York: Dutton, 1962): "Many a man holds dreams to be but lies, / All fabulous; but there have been some dreams / No whit deceptive, as was later found. / One might well cite Macrobius, who wrote / The story of the Dream of Scipio, / And was assured that dreams are often true." 1:1–6.

Which seemed to me to be verified by my dream. I know how highly the Jesuits recommend the Council of Trent, on which they base part of the approval of their Society. Now, this council very specifically orders all ecclesiastics, be they secular or be they regular, to attend processions, the exception being reclusive monks such as the Carthusians and the Celestines. However, the Jesuits have never attended, not only before the cloture of the Council but after it as well. True, under Gregory XIII they observed a bull that forbade them to attend; but prior to that, their Constitutions included the same prohibitions. I shall move on to another point: Élisabeth Rossel,[25] one of Ignatius's favorites, went about Rome trying to create an order of female Jesuits. Ignatius never agreed to this, knowing that he'd be preparing material for everyone to joke about. For, in what clothing or posture would they have put women in their houses? The nuns of the order of Saint Benedict, of Saint Bernard, of Saint Domenic, of Saint Francis wear the habits of their orders; the Jesuits dress like priests. The women would have been called *prestresses*, priestresses. But let's return to our processions, which all good and bold Catholics religiously embrace. Ignatius boasted of being the same everywhere. Why, then, did he forbid his brethren to participate in processions? He did it because he knew that his men, encountering other religious groups there, wouldn't know what rank to occupy. For their sect was a new, bastard religion, a bit of this and a bit of that from all the different orders, with nothing clear and pure from our ancient church. Why call them the Society of Jesus? To do so is to err, but at this point I'll give them a more suitable name. Here before you, I recall having read in the *Romance of the Rose* that when Saint Louis[26] brought the Carmelite friars to France from Mount Carmel, they were called the barred ones, because they wore mantles with different black and white bands. Since the Jesuit sect is a multi-colored religious group with various pieces of our ancient church, pieces that don't fit together very well, it should be called the Mottled Ones. And their disciples should be the Motleys.[27]

---

25   Isabel [Ferrer] Roser (?–1554); Ignatius called her *la Rossel*. She was a Catalan noblewoman, married to Pere Joan Roser, a merchant, who helped Loyola after he returned from the Holy Land to Barcelona, sponsoring his studies. She later requested membership in the Society for herself and two female companions. The request was granted but was later rescinded. See *DHCJ*, 4:3413.

26   Louis IX (1214–70), king of France, is commonly known as Saint Louis. When he left the Holy Land in 1254, at the end of the first crusade, he took with him six discalced Carmelites from the monastery on Mount Carmel. For the allusion to the monks, see *Romance of the Rose*, par. 56, verses 48–92. See *Encyclopaedia Britannica*, https://www.britannica.com/biography/Louis-IX (accessed February 28, 2021).

27   The French words are *bigarrées* and *bigarrez*. These words are derogatory and describe eyes that are part green and part brown, fabrics that mingle two not very attractive colors,

Here the Lawyer fell silent, giving the Gentleman a chance to get a word in. THE GENTLEMAN. I don't know if it's true that you had the dream you recounted, but I can say that it's full of truth. And in addition, you couldn't say anything that better expresses your dream than an image does. But so that you may take our *Romance of the Rose* into account, it seems to me that we should use it as a model, and should call the Jesuits the *Papelards*[28] and their Society the *Papelardie*. THE LAWYER. I beg you not to mingle the authority of the Holy See with the quarrel of these hypocrites. THE GENTLEMAN. And if you'll be so kind as to hear me to the end.

---

or statements that mingle two languages. ("Mottled" and "motley" is the present translator's attempt to mimic Pasquier's word-play.)

28   *Papelard* is a derogatory term. It denotes a hypocrite or a falsely devout person and is
applied to papists.

Without Wounding the Authority of the Holy See, One Can Truly Call the Jesuits *Papelards*, and Their Sect the *Papelardie*

THE GENTLEMAN. Never, in France, have we not embraced the papacy with full honor, respect, and devotion; never, both here in France and elsewhere, have some people not abusively used that holy name in subterfuges. If we see an out-right usurer, an adulterer, a thief, mutter each day a few *Our Father*'s at Mass, that won't change his wretched life. Or we may see a monk in his cloister, under a cowl, his face ashen, his countenance hypocritical, nourishing rancor, greed, envy, lechery in his heart. Both are *Papelards*, and their actions are *Papelardies*. What, then is the papacy? It's the real source and fountain from which we draw the union of our Christian faith. What is a *Papalardie*? It's the mark of the papacy on those who appear to want to be considered upright persons, superior to oth-ers, and who, in their souls, are worse. Here's a lesson I learned from that same *Romance of the Rose*: Guillaume de Lorris shows us an orchard surrounded by high walls hung with portraits of Hate, Envy, Felony, Greed, Sadness, Poverty. And among these portraits was the wall of *Papalardie*, described as follows. I'm pro-viding it here in the antique language of the poet Lorris, and in the new language of Clément Marot.[1] The first for its authenticity, the second for its grace.[2]

> The image standing next was well portrayed
> To be a hypocrite, but she was named

---

1 Clément Marot (1496–1544) learned as a boy the art of the *rhétoriqueur*, a poet who com-bined stilted language with the allegorical manner of the late Middle Ages. He then studied law. Making his way into upper-class circles during these heady years of the Renaissance, he began writing the style of verse that was favored at the royal court. An on-and-off Protestant, Marot wrote verse versions of the *Psalms* that Protestant congregations continued to sing for centuries. At the end of his life, he moved to Geneva and to Savoy, regions that tended to be sympathetic to Protestants. The modernized translation of the *Romance of the Rose* is gener-ally described as "attributed to Clément Marot." See *Encyclopaedia Britannica*, https://www .britannica.com/biography/Clement-Marot (accessed February 28, 2021).
2 The two French versions quoted by Pasquier have been omitted from this translation, but they are reproduced by Sutto, 207–8. These two versions reflect two aesthetics: authenticity-antiquity versus innovation-modernity. As such, they shed light on Pasquier's Gallicanism and his search for the pristine church of the Merovingians and the Carolingians. In the place of the two French versions, readers will find here an English translation of verses 186–209. See Robbins, *Romance of the Rose*, 10–11.

© KONINKLIJKE BRILL NV, LEIDEN, 2021 | DOI:10.1163/9789004164062_017

Papelardie. She it is who secretly
Contrives to take us unaware, and then
She does not hesitate at any ill.
Outwardly she appears a saint demure,
With simple, humble, pious person's face;
But under heaven there's no evil scheme
That she has never pondered in her heart.
The figure well her character did show,
Though she was of a candid countenance.
Well shod and clothed like good convent nun,
She held a psalter in her hand, and took
Much pains to make her feigned prayers to God
And call all male and female saints.
She was not gay or jolly, but she seemed
Attentive always to perform good works.
She wore a haircloth shirt, and she was lean,
As though with fasting weary, half dead.
To her and to her like will be refused
Entrance to Paradise. The Gospel says
Such folk emaciate their cheeks for praise
Among mankind, and for vainglory lose
Their chance to enter Heaven and see God.[3]

When the *Romance* was written, Wycliffe,[4] Jan Hus,[5] Jerome of Prague,[6] Martin
Luther, and John Calvin had not yet come into this world, to wage war on the

---

3   This English translation is that of Harry W. Robbins, *Romance of the Rose*, 10–11. One word of
    Robbins's translation has been changed, to conform to a crucial point that Pasquier is mak-
    ing: "Pope Holy" has been replaced by Lorris's *Papelardie,* italicized. Italics have been used
    for all occurrences of *Papelardie* and *Papelard.* This entire chapter is based on similarities in
    the sound of a few words: *pape* and *papauté,* and *papelard* and *papalardie*: that is, "pope" and
    "papacy." This permits Pasquier to equate the pope and the Jesuit hypocrite.
4   John Wycliffe (1330–84) was a theologian at Oxford University. For him, scripture was the pri-
    mary authority. Believing that any literate person should have access to Scripture, he started
    a movement to translate the Bible into English. In 1415, his writings were banned, and he was
    declared a heretic. See *Encyclopaedia Britannica,* https://www.britannica.com/biography/
    John-Wycliffe (accessed February 28, 2021).
5   Jan Hus (1369–1415), rector at the university of Prague, was attracted to Wycliffe's writings. He
    and his followers wanted the Scripture to be translated into Czech. He was accused of her-
    esy and was burned at the stake at the Council of Constance. See *Encyclopaedia Britannica,*
    https://www.britannica.com/biography/Jan-Hus (accessed February 28, 2021).
6   Jerome of Prague (1379–1416) was one of the chief followers of Jan Hus. He too was burned at
    the stake for heresy. See *Encyclopaedia Britannica,* https://www.britannica.com/biography/
    Jerome-of-Prague (accessed February 28, 2021).

Holy See. Guillaume de Lorris lived during the reign of Saint Louis, yet the word *Papelardie* was being used. Do you want to see if all the particularities that he lists are encountered in our Jesuits? To tell the truth, I confess that none of them wears a hair shirt, and that, in a parallel manner, they don't recognize the extraordinary fasts that other religious groups observe. They are cunningly dispensed from such fasts by their statutes. But in order to brush up the other points to be made, they only go to bed if the Holy See grants permission. As if they were the elder sons of the papacy. And if you should happen to see them kneeling before a crucifix or an image of Our Lady, explain their prayers by counting their rosaries; and you should look closely at their frequent confessions and communions, in the presence of the populace, with indescribable leaden faces accompanied by their hypocrisies. Yet they don't stop contriving, under cover, the ruin of the countries where they live, and the assassinations of kings and princes who displease them. Even their Masses, confessions, and communions are guides to their Machiavelisms. What name could we give them that's more appropriate than *Papelards*? For as to their Society of Jesus, that insolent name can't be granted to them by upright persons, except to further authorize their *Papelardie*. Their sect, so they say, was first planned in Paris, sworn and confirmed at Montmartre, in the heart of France. The words *Papelard* and *Papelardie* are French. I think we'll do a great deal for them, by surrendering those words to them, as suitable in every way for their profession. By not having taken in vain, until today, the name of Jesus, the merit of his cross is not lessened; nor was it lessened because they played the wretch (as I shall say with Guillaume de Lorris), taking the papacy as a false pretext. The ancient authority of the Holy See will neither increase it nor diminish it. It is strong enough to sustain itself without the help of this new state as a vassal, or rather without the help of the devil's new artifice. And so, under the name of Jesus, it will have greater means to catch us unawares in the ruin and intervention of all the orders of Christianity, and even of the Holy See.

THE LAWYER. You won't be contradicted by me, or by another member of our group, or so I believe. For according to your proposition, the *Papelard* is a person who nourishes us on fine illusions, and who keeps a back-shop in his soul that is totaliy different. You are a past master of the art of *Papelardie*, having up to now given us to understand that you don't know anything about Jesuism, about which you can teach a lesson. Now, since I see you are disposed to help me, permit me to finish what I started; and, having told you about the Jesuit sect in general, I'll tell you two or three lawyerly tidbits about good Ignatius, which is the goal at which I'm aiming.

On Ignatius of Loyola's Fabulous Visions, and on the Miraculous Fables of Francisco Xavier

THE LAWYER. After his death in 1556, no one dared write a life of Ignatius: it was too great a task. The first to attempt it was Pietro Maffei, a priest of the Society: three books that he dedicated to Father Claudio Acquaviva, their general. Ten years later, that prompted Pedro Ribadeneyra, another priest of the Society, to try to outdo his companion: five books in which, as a first step, he tried to show that his history is beyond reproach; because before the Society was established, he began to follow Ignatius around Rome, although he was not yet fourteen. He was totally devoted to him, to the point that he boasts of having seen some things, and he recounts other things based on the faithful memory of Luis Gonçalves,[1] to whom Ignatius had talked a great deal during the year before his death. Both authors were contradicted in Latin texts, the first by Christofle Severe, and the second by Chrestien Simon Liton, both of whom belonged to a different religion than ours.[2] But I won't spend time on them, nor on the two Jesuits, who naturally are liars, because they think they are helping to advance their sects, believing that they aren't deceiving God when they deceive others about some lie that's advantageous to them. I'll point out here the most noteworthy visions they claim to have encountered in their great Sophi.

According to their account, Ignatius, this scion of the noble family of Loyola, was sent at a young age by his mother and father to the court of King Ferdinand the Catholic.[3] In 1522, having been commissioned to defend the city of Pamplona, which was being besieged by the French, his leg was broken by a cannon ball and the other leg was seriously injured. The city surrendered

---

1   Luis Gonçalves da Câmara (c.1519–75) was a Portuguese Jesuit. A confidant of Ignatius of Loyola, he wrote a sort of a biography of him based on his "interviews" with him, incorrectly called Loyola's autobiography. He was the preceptor and confessor of Prince Sebastian of Portugal (1554–78; r.1557–58). See Book III, ch. 16 below.

2   For these authors, see Sutto, 210nn329–30.

3   Ferdinand II of Aragon (1452–1516) was king from 1479 to his death. His marriage to Isabella, the future queen of Castile, laid the cornerstone for the united Spanish monarchy. Ferdinand and his wife played a role in the discovery of the New World: in 1492 they sponsored Christopher Columbus's first voyage to the Americas. See *Encyclopaedia Britannica*, https://www.britannica.com/biography/Ferdinand-II-king-of-Spain (accessed February 28, 2021).

in 1522, and he was captured. We, the French, politely sent him back to his family, gravely ill and almost despaired of by his physicians and surgeons. On the night when he went through his great crisis,[4] Saint Peter, in whom he had always put his trust, appeared to him with a sure promise to heal him, which he did. For he immediately began to feel better, and he began his convalescence. He wanted to spend the time reading love stories, but none was to be had; so they loaned him the life of Our Lord Jesus Christ and the legend of the saints, which he read. He was seized by an admirable devotion to change his old life, and the Blessed Virgin came to him at night with a smiling face, holding her child in her arms. After that vision, he immediately gave up all sorts of worldly things. But Ribadeneyra stretches things still more and says that Loyola was kneeling before the image of Our Lady, in prayer and *oraison*, when a great earthquake shook the house where he was praying. And while he was considering all these devotions, the devil appeared to him, sometimes hideous and wanting to catch his attention, sometimes with fine promises, and other times with fears and terror that the devil would place before Ignatius's eyes. Entering the Dominican church, he became so ecstatic that he rose up into the firmament and saw the Holy Trinity as three persons, and as an essence. This made him write a book about the Trinity, *quoquo modo potuit stylo*.[5] This wasn't the end of these miraculous visions (says Maffei), inasmuch as God subsequently showed him how he'd guarded this great universe that he was building. Moreover, having heard Mass in the Dominican church, "just as the priest was raising the host, in the church Ignatius saw Jesus Christ in body and flesh, as when he was on earth." Maffei expresses it better in Latin: *Dum a Sacerdote de more salutaris hostia attolitur, vidit Ignatius illa specie Christum, Deum eundem, et hominem verissime continere*.[6] Ribadeneyra says that while Ignatius was listening to a sermon in Barcelona, Isabelle Rosell, lady of honor, saw his head surrounded with rays, like the sun; and elsewhere he says that Ignatius spent seven whole days without eating, and every day spent seven hours kneeling in continual prayer. He scourged himself three times a day, an activity he wanted to continue even if it cost him his life. The next Sunday, his confessor ordered him to eat: otherwise he would not give him absolution, since he was trying to kill himself. He did this while keeping watch at night. But there is a still more admirable story than that one. One Saturday, at vespers, he fell into such an ecstasy that, for seven full days, he did not move his hands or his feet, so

---

4   That is, when the fever broke, and he began to recover.
5   "In whatever style he was able."
6   "While the salvation-giving host was being lifted up by the priest as usual, Ignatius saw that Christ, both God and man, was truly contained in that image."

everyone thought he was dead. Only a few persons noticed a little palpitation of his heart. They debated whether they should bury him; and on the following Saturday, as vespers neared, it was as if he had been awakened from a deep sleep. He began to open his eyes and invoked God's holy name. Each of the two historiographers recounts the apparition of God the Father and of Jesus Christ his Son, with the stigmata and carrying his cross; and they tell how God the Father recommended that his Son take the Jesuit cause under his protection in Rome, which he promised to do. Moreover, Ignatius having withdrawn to the monastery of Monte Cassino, Hosius, one of his companions who had died in Padua, appeared to him, rising to heaven with several others, *splendidiore, quam reliqui, habitu, gloriasque, multo illustriore*.[7] Notified that one of his companions, Simão Rodrigues, was ill, he went to visit him, and heaven notified him that he would be cured. He wasn't mistaken about that, and he reassured Pierre Favre, his close confidant. Indeed, those are visions and miracles involving Ignatius that aren't second to the miracles we read about in the Gospels and the Acts of the Apostles, and some of these encounters surpass them.

To move along the way in paradise, we enter it by the sacrament of baptism; and Our Lord, baptized by Saint John the Baptist, coming out of the water saw the heavens open, and the Holy Spirit in the form of a sort of dove came down and remained on his head, and a voice from heaven was heard, saying: "This is my beloved Son, with whom I am well pleased."[8] When Ignatius thought he was opening the door to let his companions enter, he saw God the Father and Jesus Christ his Son, who said to him: "Go safely: for I doubtlessly shall help you in the city of Rome."[9] It takes a stretch of the imagination to see the Holy Spirit depicted as a sort of bird, and it was even more of a stretch, I think, when Ignatius saw God the Father, and likewise God the Son, as complete bodies. Jesus was tempted by the devil only once;[10] Ignatius was tempted twice, wearing different sorts of garments and saying very persuasive words. Jesus fasted in the desert for forty days, neither eating nor drinking; Ignatius did so for only seven days; but to compensate for the other fasting, he scourged himself three times each day, and he would remain kneeling for seven hours, praying to God. The one whom Our Lord chose as his preferred vessel was Saint Paul: when he wanted to convert him, he didn't appear to him, he merely assailed him

---

7   "With a robe more splendid than the rest, and a much brighter glow" (quoting probably Ribadeneyra).

8   Matt. 3:17.

9   This is a paraphrase of Ribadeneyra: "I will be favorable to you in Rome"—a famous vision of Ignatius at La Storta, at the gates of Rome. See Chapter 8 above.

10   Matt. 4:1–11; Mark 1:12–13; Luke 4:1–13.

with bitter words: "Saul, Saul, why are you persecuting me?"[11] And he added that he was Jesus Christ. At this, Saul, trembling, immediately joined his companions. He was blind for three days and didn't eat or drink. This miracle is nothing compared to what Ignatius experienced when his spirit was lifted to the firmament, where he saw the Trinity in three persons and one essence. And afterwards he was in ecstasy for seven whole days without seeing, drinking, or eating. In addition, there was a specific declaration (beyond what is recorded in the Old Testament) about the means that God used to construct and build this great universe. That blessing was never communicated to anyone but the great Ignatius. In the sacrament of the altar, we all recognize the transubstantiation of Jesus Christ's body and blood. We recognize this not by our bodily eyes, but simply by our faith: Ignatius granted a special favor to us all, for in the elevation of the host, he saw Jesus Christ as God and as man. I leave for you the trembling of his house, which matches the trembling of Saint Paul and Silas.[12] And I leave you a few other visions that I recounted earlier. When I read Ribadeneyra from start to finish, I found his surname and his entire book to be banter;[13] and as for Maffei, I think he was changed into Morpheus, who introduces various phantoms into the spirits of sleepers.

I don't doubt that God was able to work all those miracles in the person of Ignatius, and of greater persons than he, if he had wanted to. He was our God at the time of the apostles. God, without beginning and without end: but God who made them, that I don't deny; and I maintain that they are blasphemous impostors whom the devil caused to fall from the quill pens of two Jesuits, so as to confuse the simple people, with the help of their unfortunate superstition. I'll let you verify this by a demonstration involving your eyes. The most urgent proofs are the ones we call presumptions of right and of fact, which result from several individual things that come together, but which we are not willing to accept because it goes against everyone's common sense. The greatest judgment ever rendered is Solomon's: the true mother and the woman who claims to be the mother. This led him to be called the Wise, although it

---

11   Acts 9:4.

12   Pasquier wrote "Sylla." Although it cannot be ruled out that he was thinking of the sea monster Scylla from the *Odyssey*, it seems more likely that he was thinking of Silas, with whom St. Paul experienced an earthquake (Acts 16:25–29). Silas is first mentioned in Acts 15:22, where he and Judas Barsabbas are selected by the community elders to go to Antioch with Paul and Barnabas. (The names Scylla and Silas sound almost the same in French: "see-lá," "see-lás.")

13   That is to say, Pasquier sees a similarity between Ribadeneyra and the French word *ribauld*, which means rogue, ruffian, rascal, scoundrel, and so forth. In reality, his name comes from a Spanish town located on the banks of the River Neyra: Riva de Neyra; "v" and "b" are interchangeable in Spanish as they are phonetically very close in this language.

was only based on this presumption. As for me, I think that having presumptions that are more violent than Solomon's, shows that the visions put forth by these hypocrites are illusions and phantoms.

I'll make this matter very clear and I'll leave aside the scruple that I've already touched upon: two Jesuits wrote it. No, that's not where I want to stop. I tell you, I can't make sense of Maffei. He wrote it, therefore it's true: I deny that, and I want to know who taught him that. I'll tell you later. As far as history is concerned, that's why I paused more when reading Ribadeneyra, who says that ever since he was a boy, he'd been in Rome with Ignatius, and that everything he recounts was told to him by Luis Gonçalves, who heard it from Ignatius a year before his death. Starting with the date when he was elected general, that honest Jesuit was therefore able to talk about everything that Ignatius did in Rome; but he couldn't talk about things that happened before he went to Rome. And everything he recounts, he heard from Luis Gonçalves. If I were a scrupulous contradictor, I'd say that Ribadeneyra shouldn't be believed when he says that Gonçalves told him something: in like manner, Gonçalves shouldn't be believed, if he were still alive. He's a saint whose feast day isn't celebrated, and he maintains that he heard all these tales from Loyola. I'm going to trample these considerations underfoot. I believe that Ribadeneyra heard about all these marvelous effects from Gonçalves, and Gonçalves heard them from Ignatius. Shall we believe Ignatius's own facts? He alone could say that, early on, Saint Peter appeared to him, and that the Virgin Mary later appeared; that he spent two separate days visibly tempted by the devil; that he saw the Trinity in the firmament, Jesus Christ in his whole body and in the flesh, inside the host; the soul of Hoces[14] his companion rise up to heaven; that God promised him every help in Rome; that all of this was done by Ignatius alone; that he is the only witness. This makes me say that lending the least bit of credence to it would mean that we're all slow-witted.

If I were to stop at this point, I'd have enough to show you that one must neither accept all these miracles nor bet on them; but I can go farther than that. When Pasquier pleaded his case, one of the finest parts of his plea was where he firmly told the Jesuits to name some miracle that their Ignatius had wrought, and that all the great and holy fathers, such as Saint Benedict, Saint Dominic, Saint Francis, and others, got their religious orders authorized by working a miracle. We learn this from their legends; but Ignatius didn't work a single miracle. Earlier I went, word by word, through the passage that talked of Postel's impiety. Ignatius died eight years before that plea. By his death, every desire had been dissipated; even if someone had recounted what had miraculously

---

14   See Chapter 9 above.

happened to him, one doesn't talk about a living man so frankly. For over seven months this case had been bandied back and forth, at the University of Paris and in the court of the Parlement, where the universal fact of their order was at play. Diego Laínez, Ignatius's companion and his successor as general, knew that, or should have known it; and they had too much time and leisure to send off the memoranda. Yet in Versoris's plea, there's no mention of visions or miracles. This shows that they were new lies, invented by these *Papelards* after the case had been pleaded.

And let's add that all the visions recounted by Maffei and Ribadeneyra reached Spain before Ignatius had received the blessing of the Holy See, and before his order was approved. After he was elected general, you won't find, in the writings of those two Jesuit priests, any apparition that could have come from heaven, nor any miracle worked during his lifetime, or after his death. And yet if a miracle was to surge from him, that's the time, or a bit later, when the Holy See would have gotten its hands on it. In Rome, you view Ignatius as a great manager, the better to introduce a new tyranny into our antique religion, but there isn't a word about miracles. And why? Because all the visions attributed to him happened in Spain, with the exception of two, which were in rarely visited places in Italy. But neither he nor his disciples dared to feed Rome all these fibs. I specifically mention Rome, where *Juvenesque, senesque, et pueri nasum Rhinocerôtis habent.*[15]

Do you also want me to show you, through your own eyes, another person's imposture based on the same idea? Among Ignatius's companions or disciples was a certain Francisco Xavier, who was assigned to go to the Indies by order of King John of Portugal. Ribadeneyra had begun his history simply by mentioning the country; but the deeper the Jesuits go into a subject, the richer they are in lies. Indeed, Orazio Torsellini has recently taken a position in the ranks and has outbid his companion like a usurer. For never, while Our Lord Jesus Christ was on earth, or after his Ascension, did Saint Peter and Saint Paul work as many miracles as Xavier worked in the Indies. He was a prophet who predicted the future, who read men's thoughts, made the lame walk steadily, made the mute speak and the deaf hear, cured lepers of their leprosy, made sick folks who had been abandoned by their physicians get out of bed and stand up. He did all of this. By saying the *Credo*, and by laying a Gospel on these people, he resuscitated dead men. In the seventh chapter of Torsellini's second book, he resuscitated six; moreover, on the return journey from Japan, finding one of his companions on a bier, about to be buried, he brought him

---

15   Martial's *Epigrams*, III, iii, 5–6, "Young men and old men and even boys have the nose of the rhinoceros."

back to life, as he did with a pagan girl. But the beauty of the tale lies in the fact that, having gotten up, she recognized Xavier, and she told her father that he was the one who had pulled her soul out of hell. This is something that had never before happened in our religion: he converted several people through translators and interpreters, and he also worked several miracles by procuration, even involving persons who scarcely knew anything about our church. For, having converted small children to Christianity and catechizing them, he would give them his rosary; and having touched the sick with it, he would heal them. At Meliopore, he met a rich bourgeois possessed by several devils. Xavier was asked to come to him; but he couldn't leave, so he sent one of these little children, along with the cross. Having positioned the cross, the child recited the Gospel over this possessed person, as Xavier had ordered him to do, and he immediately chased all the devils away, who were mainly angry at having been chased away by a child who was still an apprentice in our Christian faith (*Hoc magis indignantes* [says the author] *quod per puerum pellebantur et eum Neophytum*).[16] Another time, it so happened that, having again been begged to heal a demoniac, and being unable to go in person, Xavier passed this task on to a few little children, instructing them in detail about what they had to do, and putting a cross in their hands. The children who went to see the possessed person had been told to kiss the cross and say a few good words over him. They knew by heart those statements on that subject; and the faith of these little folks, and the faith of Xavier, made the devil come out of the body. But he soon got his revenge; for while Xavier was kneeling before the Virgin Mary, he rubbed the man on his chest and back, in such a way that this poor man could only have recourse to the Virgin and would cry out to her; *Domina opitulare, Domina non opitulaberis*?[17] And from then on, he had to remain in bed in order to heal his wounds. I'll leave a few other peculiarities with you, in order to move through the other miracles worked by Xavier at the time of his death, or since his death. Having died at Sives,[18] his body was wrapped in quicklime, so that it would be consumed quickly and wouldn't rot, but sixteen months later, the body having been taken to Goa, where it lies at rest, it was found to be as fresh and as whole as if he were alive. As soon as he had been brought to that city, at the foot of his tomb they placed a candle that was only a foot and one-half long. It remained lighted for twenty-two days and as

---

16   "All the more indignant that they were expelled by a boy, and him a new convert." Torsellini, *De vita S. Francisci Xaverii*, lib. 2.

17   "Lady, assist me; Lady, won't you assist me?"

18   Xavier died on Shangchuan Island, off the Chinese coast. Pasquier's text is either corrupted or the place name is phonetic.

many nights, but it was not consumed. A man who could only see to the tip of his nose got the priests to open the coffin: he took the dead man's hand and rubbed his eyes, and by so doing he recovered his sight. This dead body worked several other miracles; but I find none as noteworthy as these two: one of his disciples carried off the scourge with which he used to strike himself, and a woman named Marie Sarra cut off a little end of his cincture, which she encased in silver and wore hanging from her neck. By touching these two gems, these two devout souls healed an infinity of persons with all sorts of ailments.

All these miracles took place in the Indies. If you believe Torsellini, several others took place after the Jesuit order had been approved; but Xavier's holiness didn't compare with the holiness of Ignatius, his superior and the first person to draw up the Institutes of the Society, in whose person the Holy Spirit had been inspired, albeit less abundantly than in the apostles, as the wise La Fon says. All his visions ceased the day the order was approved, and he settled in Rome. But, by contrast, they proliferated in Xavier. Whence came that diversity? I'll tell you: if the good Ignatius had set up housekeeping in the Indies, and Xavier in Rome, Ignatius would have worked an infinity of miracles, and Xavier would have remained fallow; because in such matters, it's less costly to believe than to go searching to see if they're true. All these speeches are truly what we say in the proverb: tales told by women as they spin, that is to say, they are good to pass on to simple women when they are spinning with their distaff near the hearth. A Jesuit in Rome, Father Giustiniani,[19] created some fake lepers, so that he could later declare their healing to be miraculous. Then he started a rumor that a pistol shot had pierced his clothing and had nestled against his flesh without hurting him, so that, by the miraculous grace of God, he had not been wounded. At first the populace believed these things, but they finally viewed them as impostures. This silenced all the impostures of our Roman Jesuits: for when someone wanted to talk about a great public deceiver, they'd call him a second Jesuit Justinian.

You may find that what I'm saying is strange. Let's not go searching for their fibs in Spain or the Indies. For several years now, a book has been circulating in France that recounts the death of Theodore Beza and how, when he was dying, one of their religious converted him to our Catholic, Apostolic, and Roman Catholic religion. Following his example, several citizens did likewise, all of it thanks to the ministry of their Jesuit brethren. We believed it for a while; but

---

19   Benedetto Giustiniani (1550–1622), native of Genoa, was professor of rhetoric and theology at the Roman College and theologian of the Apostolic Penitentiary in Rome. He is known for his published commentaries on the letters of the New Testament. See *DHCJ*, 2:3613.

then, by a new miracle, Beza was resuscitated and wrote some letters in Latin and French, by which he refuted them for their impudence. How, then, can they manage to find fables in foreign countries, when they feel assured that they'll make us feast on those sorts of tales?

Finally, in order to demonstrate what great liars Maffei and Ribadeneyra are (since I began with them, I'll finish with them), I'll say that in Spain Ribadeneyra depicts an Ignatius who suddenly left the opinion of the world behind him, *Caesariem quam elegantem habebat, solutam et impexam reliquit, ungues et barbam excrescere sivit.*[20] Look at Ribadeneyra's portrait at the beginning of his book. There's nothing as dainty as he is, and in addition he has neither hair, nor beard, nor long nails. This causes me to say that, just as one recognizes *ab unguibus leonem,* "from the claws of the lion," this single passage speaks falsely about Ignatius's hair, beard, and nails: you can judge what the rest of their books amount to. And to tell you the truth, when I find Maffei, Ribadeneyra, and Torsellini using a rather exquisite Latin language, for a subject so full of lies, they make me recall our old novels about Perceforest, Lancelot of the Lake, Tristan of Lyonnois, and other knights of the Round Table who have all joined hands and sworn reciprocal friendship, in favor of which some fine quill pens gave us stories that follow one another to the horizon, in the finest French of their day.[21] In like manner, these three Jesuits have given us, not a history, but a romance full of fables about the life of Ignatius and his companions, all of them wandering knights of the long robe, who had promised themselves a link to an indissoluble society. Each thing in its turn.

---

20   This abridged citation comes from a longer paragraph in Ribadeneyra's *Life of Ignatius*: "Because in his worldly career he had been too interested in grooming and preening himself, he wanted to make up for this excessive attention with a thoroughgoing neglect. So, he left his hair, which he had worn in the fashionable style of that day, loose and uncombed. He always kept his head uncovered, night and day. He neglected his nails and his beard so that they grew long."

21   He is alluding to medieval Arthurian romances (Sutto, 218n369).

CHAPTER 18

On Ignatius's Machiavellisms, to Make His Sect Stylish

THE LAWYER having finished his speech, the Gentleman spoke to him. THE GENTLEMAN. You shall judge as you please the two who wrote lives of Ignatius, unless I can manage to convince you that our century has had a greater man, a man who is worthier of creating a new sect than he is. I'll not even make an exception for Ismael, Sophi of Persia[1] When I say sect, Messieurs, I beg you not to be scandalized. I use the word in its naïve sense, that is, a formulary for life and discipline, just as, in the past, one talked about sects of philosophers. I see three men who are enmeshed in that craft of our time: Martin Luther, a German; John Calvin, a Frenchman; Ignatius of Loyola, a Spaniard. All three of them are very great persons, each in himself. I won't touch upon the teachings of the first two, which I condemn; but neither Luther nor Calvin were as great as Loyola. Luther stirred up all of Germany, Calvin stirred up all our France, even though he was not living there, but in Geneva; and Loyola not only stirred up Spain and countries under Spanish domination, he also stirred up several other nations. And here's a marvelous thing: the first two increased their reputation and their renown by their pens; and the third never wrote anything. For, as you yourself have accurately said, he was over thirty when he began studying Latin grammar. Before that, he had written three books in Spanish: he called them the *Spiritual Exercises*, the *Trinity*, and the lives of Jesus Christ, the Virgin, and a few saints.[2] However, like basket-work, they didn't have a long life; for he realized that his style was minimal and that little depth lay in him. Luther was formed in a monastery, and Calvin in colleges. They wanted to oppose the principles of our Roman Church, and as students they spent their time in contentious debates and writings. Loyola came from an old noble family and had grown up in the court of a great king. He wielded his facts as a

---

1   Ismail I (1487–1524), Shah of Persia, ruled 1501–24. He founded the Safavid dynasty and forcibly converted Iran to Shi'ism, thereby separating his growing Safavid state from its strong Suni neighbors. Ismail was a prolific poet. See *Encyclopaedia Britannica*, https://www.britannica.com/biography/Ismail-I-shah-of-Iran (accessed February 28, 2021).
2   *The Spiritual Exercises* were first printed in 1548. The booklet on the Trinity has been lost, if indeed Ignatius ever wrote it. The third book takes the form of notes begun in the castle of Loyola and inspired by reading the *Vita Christi* of Ludolf of Saxony (1295–1378), and the *Flos sanctorum* of Jacobo de Vorágine (1239–98).

gentleman does. For, desiring to perpetuate the new tyranny that he was developing, he foresaw that instead of the pen, which could be contradicted, he should simply have recourse to heaven, which one could not retract. Don't you remember how Minos, king of Crete,[3] wanted to give his subjects new laws, and he made them believe that he had been in communication with Jupiter about it. Lycurgus[4] in Sparta, with Apollo; Numa Pompilius[5] in Rome, with Egerie[6] the nymph; and Sertorius,[7] in order to have more authority over his soldiers, tamed them like a doe, as if he were saying that one of their imaginary Gods had transformed himself in her? These are Machiavelisms from Antiquity that were produced before Machiavelli came into this world. And an infinity of persons who have never read his books machiavellize today, in our midst. Believe that the same conversations were going through the great Ignatius's thoughts, and assure me that before dying, he recounted to Luis Gonçalves (as we learn from Ribadeneyra) all the appearances of God, the Virgin Mary, Saint Peter, and even of Our Lord Jesus Christ, when he promised to help Ignatius with everything in Rome, where he hoped that he and the generals who would succeed him would be the first despots. And what I'm going to tell you right now makes me admire him even more. We read that, after Augustus had been certain of Rome's tyranny, ten years later, in order to chase away every desire, he acted in the Senate as if he nonetheless wanted to live a private life, and

---

3 In Greek mythology, Minos, the son of Zeus and Europa, was the first king of Crete. He reigned over Crete and the islands of the Aegean Sea. At his residence at Knossos, he would receive instructions from Zeus about the legislation he gave to the island. He was the author of the Cretan constitution. See *Encyclopaedia Britannica*, https://www.britannica.com/topic/Minos (accessed February 28, 2021).

4 Lycurgus (*fl.* 7th cent. BCE) was the quasi-legendary lawgiver of Sparta. He established the military-oriented reform of Spartan society in accordance with the oracle of Apollo at Delphi. See *Encyclopaedia Britannica*, https://www.britannica.com/topic/Lycurgus-Spartan-lawgiver (accessed February 28, 2021).

5 Numa Pompilius (753–673 BCE) was the legendary second king of Rome, succeeding Romulus. Many of Rome's most important religious and political institutions are attributed to him, and Machiavelli famously praised him for inventing supernatural sanction for them in order to convince the common people. See *Encyclopaedia Britannica*, https://www.britannica.com/biography/Numa-Pompilius (accessed February 28, 2021).

6 Egeria, a nymph, was said to have played a role in the early history of Rome. She was the divine consort and counselor of Numa Pompilius, to whom she imparted laws and rituals pertaining to the ancient Roman religion. See *Encyclopaedia Britannica*, https://www.britannica.com/topic/Egeria (accessed February 28, 2021).

7 Quintus Sertorius (*c.*123–72 BCE) was a Roman statesman and general. Although he was strict and severe with his soldiers, he made the burdens of the people as light as possible. The natives gave him a snow-white fawn that followed him about and that was believed to communicate to him the advice of the goddess Diana. See *Encyclopaedia Britannica*, https://www.britannica.com/biography/Quintus-Sertorius (accessed February 28, 2021).

to strip himself of all the majesty of empire that he had brought together in his person, which he was prevented from doing by the very humble supplications of all the senators, his slaves. And in this way, with the consent of all the principal lords of the city, he continued, without jealousy, the extraordinary power he had taken from the state. The same can be seen with Ignatius and his general: for having exercised absolute power for ten years or so, he summoned most of the Jesuit fathers to Rome; and in full congregation he begged them to please dispense him from that charge from that time on, for it was a burden too heavy for his shoulders. But with all modesty, and praising his modesty, they strongly resisted him: doing that would be prejudicial to their order. On the other hand, the fathers begged him to work on their Constitutions, to expand them, reduce them, modify them as he saw fit. From that time on, he set his hand to it; so it's what you see today. But he didn't want them published until they had been confirmed by a general congregation. However, he left in writing, in a little chest, a sort of paper journal about all the things that had gone on between him and the Holy Spirit, and the visions that had inspired him while drawing up these Constitutions. Memoranda that were found and displayed after his death to everyone's great astonishment, during the general congregation held in Rome in 1558, where everything he had ordered was approved and, at that point, was put into the hands of the printers and booksellers. You say things that blame Ignatius for all these apparitions; and you say that they were impostures forged by him, whose people had come up with miraculous fables. Excuse me, I beg you, for I'd wittingly tell you to judge them as if you had a master of arts, and not as if you were a statesman. I don't doubt, I repeat, that Ignatius talked about all these visions and miracles that he alone had witnessed. But when? Not in the flower of his life, which he was using for action; not when he was fighting long illness and advancing old age, when he saw himself as if on the edge of the grave. Thinking that there was no better way of assuring the future of his order after his death, and of having its statutes approved, than to nourish his people, but not with those holy illuminations, to which he was opposed; but he did not become involved in all the vain disputes and quibbling of Martin Luther and John Calvin. Were there ever finer, wiser, more daring traits than these?

CHAPTER 19

Closing Book I

THE GENTLEMAN had scarcely finished these remarks when the Lawyer made his reply. THE LAWYER. You and I won't enter that enclosed field where this quarrel is going on, so that we can fight. Everything that Maffei and Ribadeneyra wrote about Ignatius is false, and everything you've said is true. What I said to you earlier is a sort of pre-game. Now I'm deliberating how to talk to you about their wishes, which, as I can show you, is an erroneous and heretical doctrine, combined with an infinity of Machiavelisms and Anabaptisms that were annexed to them over time. Meanwhile, the Lawyer was ready to move ahead, not realizing that it was already very late. THE GENTLEMAN. If you are participating in this debate, the best thing is to postpone the game until tomorrow morning. It's quite late. You, Messieurs my new guests, are exhausted from the road, and you especially, my dear friend (he was speaking to the Lawyer). It's too late for you to go on talking, and for us to go on listening. Moreover, I'm treating you today as my prisoners; but don't imagine that I'll release you tomorrow. Let's hang the white flags of a truce before our eyes, our ears, and our thoughts. In addition, all this talk seems more appropriate for the morning than for the evening. It even merits not being resumed unexpectedly: indeed, if your sleepiness permits, you should review what you want to say. Never has a good lawyer who has carefully prepared an important trial, been disappointed at having a long delay in order to prepare some more; and I don't think that any case more weighty than this one has ever been pleaded.

The Gentleman's opinion won, and each man retired to his bedchamber until seven the next morning. Everyone had gone to church, not in order to give God what we owe him, but to give him the fewest troubles that we could. Everyone went into the large reception room and shut the door. The Gentleman specifically instructed his domestics that none of them should be so brash as to interrupt us, no matter what business might come up. THE GENTLEMAN. Now, hush, let's continue our tale, for there is no more meritorious work than the one we've undertaken. But we must banish every bit of calumny from our discourse. We mustn't thoughtlessly afflict a group of innocent people, since several of us maintain that there are Jesuits here. The Lawyer promised to do this in a very polite fashion, protesting at first that he hadn't sown this quarrel owing to his personal ill will toward the Jesuits, but rather for the public good. THE LAWYER. And to demonstrate it to you, I'm setting aside all the subtleties

and flowery nosegays with which persons of my profession are accustomed to
decorate their speeches. Instead, I'll read accurately the passages on which my
argument is based. If, after me, someone wants to contribute a prettier house-
robe, he may do so without my envying him in the least. For the finest artifice
that I plan to use, is to use no artifice. But inasmuch as the Jesuits are currently
working on their reestablishment in France, I'll begin by what touches us most.
Now, in one of his trunks the Lawyer had all the bulls and Constitutions concerning the Jesuits, and several other books on the same subject, both for and
against them, which he laid out for display, just as he had done for everything
he had said the previous evening to confirm what he said. So, let's watch him
come on stage and act his character.

Book II

Our Gallican Church and the Jesuit Sect Are Incompatible

THE LAWYER. Let's sweep all our anger under the rug, for although it's appropriate to feel angry about heresy, anger sometimes makes one go to sleep angry: and anger sometimes makes us drunk and makes our spirits stagger off. The Jesuits want to be reestablished in Paris they initially entered like foxes: and ever since then, they've been devouring the blood of Frenchmen like hungry beasts. And yet, if their religious order is at all compatible with our Gallican church, let's forget all the woes and calamities they procured for us during our recent Troubles, and let's not envy them for residing in the capital city of France. Being lodged in the principal city of the realm, by the authority of the sovereign magistrate, is no small advantage for those who want to plant a new religious group and make it expand.

1.   They are setting two big words before us, in order to shut our mouths. The word Jesus, before which every knee must bend. And the word pope, whom we ought to revere with all honor and submission. But to whom are they peddling their wares? Aren't we followers of Jesus too? Aren't we true children of the Holy See? We all recognize, by a common and general faith, that we belong to and share the church of Jesus, by the merit of his passion, having been regenerated by the holy sacrament of baptism.[1]

The Jesuits, taking an arrogantly factious name, describe themselves as alone belonging to the Society of Jesus. A title they were forbidden to use, not only by our Gallican church but also by the court of the Parlement of Paris, in 1561.[2]

2.   In this France, we admit, with all humility and earnestness, that Our Holy Father the Pope is the primate, but not the prince of all churches. In that

---

1   In this chapter, and especially in articles 1–6, Pasquier lays out the principal tenets of the Gallican church and compares each tenet with the position taken by the Society of Jesus concerning papal authority, the temporal, and the spiritual. See also the Glossary, "Church," "Gallican," and "Gallicanism." Sutto, 222–32, cites the various sources (bulls, decretals, decrees of one or another church council, and so forth) upon which each numbered article in this chapter is based.

2   The French prelates meeting at the Colloquy of Poissy passed a resolution in August of 1561 approving the Jesuits but requiring them to use a name other than "Society of Jesus"; the Parlement of Paris ratified this decision in February of 1562.

faith, we live and die under him, renewing our oath of fidelity, from the day of our baptism to the day of our death.

A Jesuit, as a special vassal above all others, recognizes him as his prince, in whose hands his oath of fidelity is renewed, every time the pope changes.

3.   Our Gallican church holds that the pope is lower than the general and ecumenical council. We learned that from Gerson, our great theologian, and from the Council of Constance.[3] Thus, when, in the long-gone past, a decree emanated from the pope, to the prejudice of our kings or their kingdom, our ancestors appealed to the future ecumenical council.

A Jesuit holds the very opposite opinion, and he does it the way a Roman courtier does it.

4.   Whatever the dissimulation in which the Jesuit garbs the new things he writes, he recognizes the pope as the prince of all kingdoms, for both the temporal and the spiritual. The popes are recognized as such in their decretals, and even more recently in the bull of the great jubilee, issued for the year 1600.[4] Saint Peter and Saint Paul, who are their successors, are called princes of the earth. If the Jesuit has doubts about this article, he is a heretic within his sect.

Our Gallican church has never believed that the pope has any power over the temporal of our kings.

5.   The Jesuits obey the pope by what they describe as blind obedience: a proposition that has ferocious consequences for the king and all his subjects. And a proposition that we do not observe and of which we strongly disapprove in our Gallican church.

6.   By an ancient tradition that has passed down, hand to hand, by the apostles, each diocese has its bishop, against whom it is prohibited to undertake anything.

The entire Jesuit sect is nothing other than a general infraction of the authorities of the archbishops and bishops, and it even holds that the bishop has no jurisdiction or power beyond what he receives from the pope.

7.   Administering the Word of God and the holy sacraments belongs, first, to the archbishops and bishops, then to the curates in their parishes, and to no one else, unless they have permission from each of them in their jurisdictions.

---

3   See Book I, ch. 15 above.
4   The bull *Annus Domini placabilis* issued by Pope Clement VIII (r.1592–1605) in 1599.

> The Jesuit takes for himself full power to announce the Word of God, and to administer the holy sacraments of penance and the Eucharist, wherever he pleases, to the disadvantage of the *ordinaires*.

8. Only the bishop in his diocese can give a dispensation to eat forbidden dishes, as necessity requires. On this, the Jesuit recognizes only the superiors of his order.

9. We do not admit to the priesthood children born of adultery or incest. The Jesuit admits them without any distinction.

10. According to our ancient canonical constitutions, the clergy can only celebrate Mass before noon. The Jesuit can sing after noon, if he so desires.

11. Priests are forbidden to celebrate Mass elsewhere than in our churches, except when it is a question of replacing someone who is ill; and this requires the curate's permission.

> The Jesuit can make a private oratory in his house, and everywhere he passes, and he can say Mass there and have a portable altar.

12. One of the most ancient devotions in our church is processions, for even Tertullian refers to them:[5] and we find that Mamertus,[6] bishop of Vienne, introduced the rogations that we observe every year during the week of Our Lord's Ascension.

> The Jesuit not only does not approve of processions, he maintains that they are forbidden.

13. In our churches we celebrate anniversaries in memory of those who have given us some possessions as alms. The Jesuit is very willing to accept the alms that are given to him, but he does not allow anniversaries or obituaries.

14. In our churches, we have a certain place near the high altar: we call it the choir. The priests celebrate the divine service there, in order to be separate from the common people.

> The Jesuit does not have a choir.

15. We usually celebrate our canonical hours in the church, aloud, so that everyone can share in them. The Jesuit is not compelled to do so, but he can say them very softly.

16. Since our France has always abounded in devotion, above all other nations, it has a special privilege from God: all the heads of religious

---

5 Pasquier refers here probably to Tertulian's (155–220) *De praescriptio*, xliii.

6 Saint Mamertus (?–*c.*475), bishop of Vienne in France, was instrumental in the establishment of Rogation days, that is, days devoted to prayer, fasting, processions, and litanies to the saints. The aim was to appease God's wrath, especially in the form of calamities such as earthquakes. See *Encyclopaedia Britannica*, https://www.britannica.com/biography/Saint -Mamertus-of-Vienne (accessed February 28, 2021).

orders have used the ancient rules of Saint Augustine and Saint Benedict,[7] and have sworn that their perpetual domiciles will be in Gaul: Cluny, Cîteau, Prémontré, Grandmont. That is not the case with the Carthusians, whose general resides in the Dauphiné.[8] And if there are a few who do not reside there, from time to time they at least recognize that their flock is in France. In addition to the fact that the generals of the Jesuits have vowed to reside in Rome, one never sees them come to France to see their religious,[9] so minimally French are they.

17. We do not have provincials in France, for any religious order whatsoever, unless they are French. The general of the Jesuits distributes the provincials as he pleases;[10] they are a merchandise that was sold to us dearly during our recent Troubles.

18. In our Gallican church, we do not recognize any religious who devote themselves to the divine service in churches, if they do not wear the cowl and the other monastic garb that venerable antiquity has bequeathed to all of them. There is no difference between the garb of a secular priest and a member of the Jesuit order.[11]

7　On the Rule of Saint Augustine, see https://www.newadvent.org/cathen/02079b.htm and on the Rule of Saint Benedict, see https://www.newadvent.org/cathen/02436a.htm (accessed June 4, 2020).

8　The province of Dauphiné, extending from the Rhone River into the Alps, was part of the Holy Roman Empire until it was merged into the French crown in 1349, though it was not fully integrated into the kingdom until the end of the fifteenth century. Pasquier seems to be alluding to its ecclesiastical independence in the Middle Ages, under the authority of the archbishop of Vienne. See *Encyclopaedia Britannica*, https://www.britannica.com/place/Dauphine (accessed February 28, 2021).

9　Ignatius of Loyola, the first superior general, left Rome to visit a Jesuit community as superior general only once (in Loreto); his successor Diego Laínez traveled to France in 1564 for political reasons but he did visit some Jesuit communities there. France was also visited by the third superior general, Francisco de Borja, in 1571. Both Laínez and Borja returned from their trips ill and died as a result. Mercurian and Acquaviva did not travel outside Rome as superiors general and used their envoys known as visitors to deal with the issues of Jesuit local communities.

10　The first superior provincial for the entire territory of France was Pasqual de Broët, one of the first companions of Ignatius and of French origins, who was appointed in 1552. Due to the growth of the Society, separate provinces of Aquitaine (1564), Lyons (1582), Toulouse (1608), and Champagne (1616) were established subsequently. All superiors provincial are appointed by superiors general.

11　See *Const.* [577]: "The clothing too should have three characteristics: first, it should be proper; second, conformed to the usage of the country of residence and third, not contradictory to the poverty we profess, as would happen through the wearing of silk or expensive cloths. These ought not to be used, in order that in everything fitting humility and lowliness may be preserved for greater divine glory."

19.   From time immemorial, we have confined our religious to cloisters, so that they can live a solitary life and can walk about and be refreshed from their studies. A Jesuit would be wronging his splendor if he conformed to the others.

20.   Once our religious have made the three ordinary and substantial vows of poverty, chastity, and obedience, they cannot return to the world in order to resume their previous life, other than with the consent of their abbot. In addition to the simple vow of the Jesuits, after two years of novitiate, they make the three vows common to all other religious orders; yet they can be sent away by their general, whenever and as often as it pleases him.[12]

21.   Our religious, having made their three vows, are incapable of receiving any inheritance.

As long as he has taken only his simple vow, the Jesuit can receive possessions, as if he had not left the world.[13]

22.   Other religious enter the order solely with the intention to study, so that, in time, they can be admitted to the priesthood. The Jesuit receives religious who are called temporal coadjutors, and who profess to be ignorant and are never admitted to holy orders.[14]

23.   All other religious have certain days when they fast and abstain from special dishes that are not common among the people. Ever since the time when they began to call themselves religious, the Jesuits have not observed any of these fasts.[15]

24.   According to the ancient *ordonnances* of Kings Charles v, Charles vi, and Charles vii,[16] the principals of colleges who are alien and born outside the kingdom, are not received, unless they are naturalized. The general of the Jesuits establishes in the colleges of his order the rectors and principals whom he chooses, without taking into account whether or not they belong to the French nation.

25.   In our religious orders, no religious are allowed to teach the humanities except to members of their own order. The Jesuit gives lessons to all comers.

---

12   On the authority to dismiss, see *Const.* [208], [736].

13   Cfr. *Const.* [572].

14   Cfr. *Const.* [150].

15   Cfr. *Const.* [8], [582].

16   There were three successive French kings named Charles: Charles v reigned from 1364 to 1380, at the peak of the Hundred Years' War (1337–1453); Charles vi, who became mad, reigned from 1380 to 1422; and Charles vii reigned from 1422 to 1461.

26. The degree known as the master of arts is not awarded to our religious, only the doctorate in theology, if they are capable. The Jesuit is awarded not only the master of arts but also the degree in theology.

27. The order we observe in our universities is that the bishop is the first judge; and for that reason, in every cathedral church where there is a university there is also a chancellor of the university with income from a prebend. That chancellor distributes the bachelor's degrees, licetiates, master's degrees, and doctorates after the public disputations and appropations held in the long-established locations. The Jesuit knows nothing of this: he needs a stable all to himself. In the beginning, the general created masters and doctors with absolute power; and ever since then, these degrees have been earned under the provincial's authority, after having been examined by two or three persons selected for that purpose.

28. In stronger terms, in France one only receives the master's degree and the doctorate from renowned universities. The Jesuit, inverting our entire antique discipline, can give masters of arts and doctorates in theology wherever they have colleges, even if they are not in universities.

29. Concerning the alienation of the property of the church that depends on bishoprics or abbeys, the communities must assemble with the approval of their heads, in order to come to an agreement; and after the superior intervenes, a proctor such as the *procureur* for the possessions of the church is chosen; all of this in order to discuss and examine whether the alienation should be carried out. As for the alienation of Jesuit possessions, it requires only the will and the absolute power of their general, and no other ceremony.[17]

30. Our kings receive a charitable subsidy from the churches of their kingdom: we call it the *décimes*.[18] If you believe in the Jesuits' privileges, they are exempted from the *décimes*.[19]

31. Our kings cannot be excommunicated by popes, as I shall demonstrate when the time comes. The Jesuits swear that there is no such rule.[20]

---

17   Cfr. *Const.* [402 §2].

18   Initially, the clergy gave these subsidies to the king, for exceptional needs, but after the Colloquy of Poissy (1561), these subsidies were paid every ten years.

19   Created to finance the crusades, the *décime* was a tax paid to the king: one tenth of the income on church property. In Pasquier's day, the *décime* helped the monarchy pay for the wars against the Huguenots.

20   On the Jesuit support of the doctrine of papal *potestas indirecta*, see Harro Höpfl, *Jesuit Political Thought: The Society of Jesus and the State, c. 1540–1640* (Cambridge: Cambridge University Press, 2008), 345–65.

32. It is not within the pope's power to transfer our kingdom to whomever he pleases, for failure to obey him, as I also hope to demonstrate. The Jesuit firmly maintains that the pope, responding to events, can transfer not only kingdoms but also the Holy Roman Empire.

And from one long list I pass on to you the other propositions about which they contradict us.

33. *Non possunt Clerici à Judice seculari, etiamsi leges civiles non servent.*

34. *Bona tam Ecclesiastica, quam secularia Clerici, libera sunt à tributis Principum secularium.*

35. *Exemptio Clericorum in rebus politicis, tum quoad personas, tum quoad bona, introducta est humano jure pariter et divino.*[21] I'll tell you later about the doctrine of Emmanuel Sà,[22] doctor of theology of the Society of Jesus at Antwerp, who in the introductory Epistle of his *Aphorismes de Confession*, declares that he worked on it for forty full years. He puts his indubitable propositions in alphabetical order.

36. *Clerici familia ejusdem est cum ipso fori.*

37. *Clerici bona possunt per judicem Ecclesiasticum confiscari, in casibus laici sic per leges puniuntur.*

38. *Clericus ob falsum testimonium coram judice seculari non potest per eum puniri.*

39. *Clericus percussus a laico potest agere coram judice Ecclesiastico.*

40. *Clericus potest uti consuetudine et statuto laicorum ad suam utilitatem,* which means that the custom is not binding, if it displeases him.

41. *Episcopus potest sub poena excommunicationis cogere exhiberi sibi testamenta defunctorum, eaque exequenda curare.*

42. *Episcopus potest imponere beneficio quo confert, pensionem ad alendum pauperem clericum.*

43. *Non solet succedere faemina in feudo.*

44. *Intestato Clerico, non habenti cognatos, succedere debet Ecclesia cui serviebat, sed forte iam succedit Camera Apostolica.*

---

21 33. Clergy cannot be judged by a secular judge, although they do observe civil laws. 34. Both the ecclesiastical goods as well the secular goods of a cleric, are free from tribute to secular princes. 35. Exemption of clergy in political matters, both in regard of their persons and their goods, has been introduced equally by human and divine law.

22 Manuel Sà (1528–96), a Portuguese Jesuit and professor of theology and exegesis at the Roman College, wrote a popular *Aphorismi confessariorum* (Venice, 1592). Its French translation, *Les aphorismes des confesseurs,* was published in Paris (Chevalier, 1600, and Chaudière, 1601). See *DHCJ*, 4:3454; Sutto, 229–31nn67–81; Maryks, *Saint Cicero*, 41, 112–14. For various editions of the *Aphorismi* available online, see https://play.google.com/store/search?c=books&q=%22aphorismi+confessariorum%22 (accessed March 4, 2021).

45. *Ad supplicium ductus reus non tenetur fateri quod male negavit nisi alioqui grave damnum sequeretur.*

46. *Reus non est cogendus à Confessore fateri crimen.*[23] These are all propositions that firmly derogate from those that we observe by the common law of France. And what is still more wicked and intolerable is that, by two other articles, it states the following:

47. CLERICI REBELLIO IN REGEM, NON EST CRIMEN LAESAE MAJESTATIS QUIA NON EST SUBDITUS REGI.

48. COGNITO MAGNO REIPUBLICAE PERICULO PER CONFESSIONEM, SUFFICIT GENERALITER MONERE UT CAVEATUR. POTEST ET IS CUI PARATUM EST MALUM MONERI UT CAVEAT, TALI LOCO ET TEMPORE, MODO NON SIT PERICULUM UT PRODATUR POENITENS. These last two articles merit being made French, so that everyone will know how dangerous those Jesuit vermin[24] are in a state: "THE TONSURED CLERIC WHO REBELS AGAINST HIS KING, DOES NOT COMMIT THE CRIME OF LÈSE MAJESTY, FOR HE IS NOT A SUBJECT OF THE KING." "WHEN, IN CONFESSION, THE PRIEST HAS LEARNED ABOUT A GREAT PERIL THAT A PERSON WHO IS CONFESSING WANTS TO PURSUE AGAINST THE REPUBLIC, IT SUFFICES TO WARN THE MAGISTRATE IN GENERAL TERMS, SO THAT HE WILL BE ON GUARD. AND ONE CAN LIKEWISE NOTIFY THE PERSON AT WHOM THE PERIL IS DIRECTED, TO BEWARE IN A SPECIFIC PLACE AND TIME, IN SUCH A MANNER THAT, WHILE WARNING HIM, ONE DOES NOT REVEAL THE IDENTITY OF THE PENITENT."

---

23   36. A cleric's household is subject to the same [ecclesiastical] jurisdiction as himself. 37. A cleric's goods can be confiscated by an ecclesiastical judge, in the cases of laymen thus they are punished by the laws. 38. A clergyman cannot be punished by a secular judge for giving false witness before him. 39. A clergyman beaten by a layman can bring a case before an ecclesiastical judge. 40. A cleric can use the customs and statutes of the laity for his own profit. 41. A bishop can, under penalty of excommunication, compel the will and testaments of the deceased to be exhibited and see to it that they are performed. 42. A bishop can give a pension from a benefice which he bestowed to maintain a poor cleric. 43. A woman is not accustomed to succeed to an estate. 44. When a clergyman dies intestate, and without relatives, the church served by him ought to be his heir, but sometimes the Camera Apostolica succeeds him. 45. A condemned man led to the gallows is not to be compelled to confess the evil he denied unless some evil may ensue. 46. A condemned man must not be compelled to confess his crime by his confessor.

24   It is interesting to note that the image of Jesuit vermin appeared later, among others, in the Nazi anti-Jesuit propaganda, in which the Jesuits were described as "public vermin" (*Volksschädlinge*). See "The Jesuit: The Obscurantist without a Homeland," A Propaganda Pamphlet by Hubert Hermanns (1933), http://germanhistorydocs.ghi-dc.org/sub_image .cfm?image_id=2068 (accessed March 4, 2021).

Good God, can we bear that garbage in our France? I know that, thanks to God, our kings have never been tyrants; but the Jesuits propose two maxims that, should they take place, will expose every sovereign prince to the mercy of his people.

49.   *REX POTEST PER REMPUB. PRIVARI OB TYRANNIDEM, ET SI NON FACIT OFFICIUM SUUM, CUM EST CAUSSA ALIQUA JUSTA, ELIGI POTEST ALIUS A MAJORI PARTE POPULI. QUIDAM TAMEN SOLAM TYRANNIDEM CAUSSAM PUTANT.*

50.   *TYRANNICE GUBERNANS, LATA SENTENTIA, POTEST DEPONI A POPULO, ETIAM QUI JURAVIT EI PERPETUAM OBEDIENTIAM, SI MONITUS NON VULT CORRIGI.*[25]

Should these two articles take place, no prince, no matter who he may be, can feel sure in his state. And I beg you to note that this confessionary was printed in 1589,[26] that is to say, it confirms and authorizes what had been cooked up against the late king[27] at the beginning of that year, when several ill-advised persons wanted to declare him a tyrant.

51.   In France we have what is known as the *appel comme d'abus,* against the fulmination of apostolic bulls when they usurp either the majesty of our kings or the majesty of the ancient church councils, received and approved in our Gallican church, or when they usurp the Gallican liberties,[28] or the royal jurisdiction or decrees of the sovereign courts. I repeat: *appel comme d'abus,* one of the principal sinews of the conservation of our state. The Jesuit does not want to recognize this, for several reasons that touch him closely, and that I don't want to discuss here.

52.   The Jesuits recognize, as their judge, only the pope or their general; so, we want to refer back to that antique Roman labyrinth, about which our good Saint Bernard complained to Pope Eugenius,[29] in his *De consideratione.*

---

25   49. The king can be deprived by the state for tyranny, and if he does not do his duty, when there is some just cause, another can be chosen from the greater part of the populace. However, some people think the only cause is tyranny. 50. The king ruling tyrannically can be deposed implicitly by the people, even those who swore perpetual obedience to him, if having been warned he does not want to be corrected.

26   The oldest edition that we know of is the Venetian one from 1592. See Robert A. Maryks, "Census of the Books Written by Jesuits on Sacramental Confession (1554–1650)," *Annali di storia moderna e contemporanea* 10 (2004): [415]–519, here 418.

27   That is Henri III.

28   See the Glossary, "Gallican," and see Parsons, *Church in the Republic,* especially 3–5, 9–13, 97–99, 126–31.

29   Eugenius III was pope from 1145 to 1153. He proclaimed the second crusade, which was the first of many failures by the Christians to recapture and hold the lands won in the first crusade. Although he cites "La Consolation," Pasquier had rather in mind Eugenius's

And we saw a noble example of this in Bordeaux, when Sager,[30] rector of the Jesuit college, declared that he would not obey the mayor and the city council, who had sent for him to quell an uprising. He said that he recognized them as political magistrates acting upon the bourgeois of the city, and that they and the other judges, irrespective of their nation, title, dignity, and authority, had no power over them. Only the pope or the general of their order had that power. And we have allowed that religious order to live in our midst! That truly amounts to letting vermin come in, vermin who over time will gnaw at both the spiritual and the temporal of our state.

THE JESUIT. It won't take me long to reply to your curious research.[31] For contrary to what you have said, with one word I am giving you a seat on the General Council of Trent, which approved us and authorized us.

THE LAWYER. I agree that you have thirty[32] in the match, but we have forty-five more than you.[33] As far as doctrine is concerned, this council is an abbreviation of all the other antique councils. It therefore should be embraced[34] by every devout soul; but it should be totally rejected as far as both secular and

---

De consideratione. See Migne, ed., *Patrologia Latina*, vol. 182, col. 727–808 (cited by Sutto, 231n84). As for the allusion to a labyrinth, ceremonial books from the time of Eugenius reveal that the antechamber of the sacristy at Santa Maria in Trastevere once had a pavement labyrinth of the Chartres type; it remained in place into the nineteenth century. See Randall Rosenfield, *Music and Medieval Manuscripts: Paleography and Performance* (Abingdon-on-Thames: Routledge, 2017), 340.

30   Charles Sager (1538–96) was rector of the college of Bordeaux and preacher at Dijon in Burgundy at the end of the League. See Henri Fouqueray, s.j., *Histoire de la Compagnie de Jésus en France des origines à la suppression*, 5 vols. (Paris: Picard, 1910–25), passim.

31   Remember that, in 1565, Pasquier published the first volume of his *Recherches de la France*, in which he quoted from a variety of historical sources. That sort of research was described as curious (*curieuse*), that is, information that Cotgrave describes as quaint, and that DAF 1694 defines as new, rare, excellent things. Are we listening to the Jesuit (Richeome?) converse with the Lawyer (Pasquier was a lawyer) about the intriguing primary sources that Pasquier has been quoting in his *Recherches*?

32   This is a witticism: *trente*, with a lower-case *t*, means "thirty." The (Council of) Trent is spelled in French and pronounced the same way, but is written with a capital *T*. In short, the witticism involves a pun: *trente-Trente*, that is, thirty-Trent.

33   The witticism continues with an evocation of the rules for playing a medieval ancestor of tennis (*le jeu de paume*): 15–30–40 (Sutto, 232n87).

34   This word, *embrassé*, "embraced" sets Pasquier off on yet another elaborate pun: *embrasé*, turned to blazing embers. In short, Gallican that he was, Pasquier is contrasting the embrace of the Council of Trent and the burning of the kingdom of France as he knew and loved it. Although it is not part of a pun, the next sentence ends with *police*, that is, order in the state; the rules that are observed in a city or a state. The breach in the wall

ecclesiastical discipline are concerned. And as for whether our entire kingdom would be burned up, who would entertain that idea? The persons who have a good nose can sniff out that everything that was ordered at the time, came from Jesuit souls; and I assert that this involves everything that concerns policing the realm. When naught but that consideration remains, you must banish it from France, because we can't recognize you without approving that council: and approving it creates too great a breach, not only for the majesty of our kings but also for the liberties of our Gallican church.

(*bresche*) that he sees as a threat to France would, of course, result from the absence of *police*, and therefore the absence of a strong wall that would ensure order.

The Popes Who Authorized the Jesuits When They First Arrived, Never Believed That They Could or Should Reside in France

Thus did THE LAWYER finish his speech. The Jesuit, thinking that he had a great advantage over the Lawyer, began talking. THE JESUIT. Let us set the Council of Trent to one side, although it is a strong piece that establishes our order. At the very least, you cannot say that we are not helped by an infinite number of bulls issued by Popes Paul III and Julius III, Pius IV[1] and Pius V,[2] and Gregory XIII, all of whom have not only approved us but have rewarded us with several great privileges that had never before been granted to another religious order, as I told you last night. Consequently, you and the others who are devoting yourselves to waging war against us, should be declared heretics.

THE LAWYER. Certainly, a great objection: for you couldn't use more powerful weapons against me; and I'm very relieved that my whole speech is beginning, continuing, and ending by the authority of the Holy See. *Abs Jove principium, Jovis omnia plena.*[3] The Holy See has approved you (you say). I agree, but only to please you. So those who disapprove of your Society are heretics: I deny that. The Faculty of Theology and the University of Paris, our entire Gallican church, so many communities, so many upright and honorable people who formed parties opposed to you in 1564: they disapproved of you. Not for that did you ever hear tell that they would have been declared heretics in Rome. All the more so since the popes, when they authorized you, never thought you'd reside in France. They knew that their loftiness is the mother of the union of the Universal Church. They were unaware of the liberties of our Gallican church, which are the exact opposite of what the Jesuits profess; and lodging them

---

1 Pius IV (1499–1565), born Giovanni Angelo Medici, was pope from late December 1559 until his death. He presided over the final session of the Council of Trent (1545–63). See *Encyclopaedia Britannica*, https://www.britannica.com/biography/Pius-IV (accessed February 28, 2021).

2 Pius V (1504–72), born Antonio Ghislieri, succeeded Pope Pius IV in 1565 and ruled until his death. Aware of the need to restore discipline and morality in Rome, he reduced the cost of litigation and fees before the curia, while at the same time asserting the importance of ceremonial in general and the liturgy of the Mass in particular. See *Encyclopaedia Britannica*, https://www.britannica.com/biography/Saint-Pius-V (accessed February 28, 2021).

3 Virgil, *Eclogues*, III, 60. The actual text differs somewhat from Pasquier's recollection of it: *Ab Jove principium musae, Jovis omnia plena*; that is, "From Jove the Muse began; Jove filleth all."

in France would have been like planting an infinity of schisms and divisions. That's why they aren't displeased with the judgments against these messieurs, by the assembly of our entire clergy at Poissy, and by the Parlement of Paris. For, by a good inspiration from God and from his Holy Spirit, let's follow in the footsteps of Paul III, to whom the Jesuits, when they met him the first time, feigned wanting to go to Palestine and establish their residence there, in order to convert the Turks. Not only were they favorably received by the pope, but he also ordered that, in addition, they be given money to cover the cost of their journey. But when they came back a second time, so that he could approve of their new plan, Paul delayed for two whole years before agreeing. And why? Because, in their first plan, he saw no danger for Christianity, other than for those who were going to carry out the plan. The second time, there was reassurance about their persons, but there was a great danger and risk for all of Christianity. And after several refusals and dismissals, he let himself be carried away by the importunities of Cardinal Contarini: he not only believed that they shouldn't dwell in France, he also believed that they shouldn't dwell in the various parts of Christendom, other than very soberly.[4]

What, then? Should we conclude that this great pope wanted this new order he had approved, to lie fallow? Certainly not. And if you examine the real point being made in this bit of history, you'll be satisfied. If, in 1539, the Jesuits had only promised to make the three substantial vows of the other religious orders, he'd never have admitted them, considering the fashion in which they presented themselves. Monks who called themselves by a biased name: the Society of Jesus.[5] Who didn't want to live in cloisters in order to lead a solitary life, and who didn't want to reduce themselves to the extraordinary abstinence from meats and the fasting of other religious orders. Monks who wanted to preach and administer the holy sacraments of penance and the Eucharist, without getting permission from the bishops. All these circumstances, combined, promised I don't know what sort of great disorder, rather than edification.[6]

Who, then, invited him to receive them? First there was the vow of absolute obedience to the Holy See; and after that came the mission vow,[7] by which

---

4 See the discussion on Pope Paul III and Cardinal Contarini in Book 1, Chapter 13.

5 The term monks (*moines*) is an inaccurate description of the Jesuits. Canonically, they were clerics regular, hence different from mendicant friars.

6 On the Jesuit distinctiveness, see John W. O'Malley, "The Distinctiveness of the Society of Jesus," *Journal of Jesuit Studies* 3, no. 1 (2016): 1–16, doi: https://doi.org/10.1163/22141332-00301001 (accessed March 4, 2021).

7 On the meaning of this vow known as "the fourth vow," see John W. O'Malley, "The Fourth Vow in Its Ignatian Context: A Historical Study," *Studies in the Spirituality of the Jesuits* 15 (1983).

Ignatius and his companions promised that, if ordered by the pope, they would go to every pagan land in order to remove them from their idolatry and plant Christianity there. It was a brigade of Argonauts[8] who were promising to set sail, not for the Golden Fleece, as Jason did, but in order to transport the fleece of the Pascal Lamb under the banner of Jesus Christ. A truly fine profession, in favor of which Pope Paul permitted these new pilgrims, who were increasing in number in order to make illustrious the name Jesus, to call themselves the Society of Jesus, to wear the garments of priests rather than those of monks, not to shut themselves up in cloisters, and to administer both the word of God and the holy sacraments simultaneously; for they were vowing to conquer lands where there were no bishops or curates: a conquest to be done not by actual weapons but by spiritual ones alone. Send them to these new lands to which they've promised to go: never was a religious order asked to do more than this one was, if only they fulfilled their promises, not by words but by effect. Transplant them into the midst of the Christian churches, and especially our Gallican church: instead of a religious order, you create a disorder whose consequences are as dangerous as the Lutheran sect. And, so that no one will think I'm talking to the air, in the bull of 1540, repeated in full in the bull of 1550,[9] they promised to go, without tergiversation or delay, wherever the pope ordered, *ad profectum animarum et fidei propagationem, sive* (says the text) *miserit nos ad Turcas, sive ad quoscunque alios infideles, etiam in partibus quas Indias vocant, existentes, sive ad quoscumque haereticos, seu schismaticos, seu etiam ad quosvis fideles*: that is to say, "to go everywhere that the pope shall order without tergiversation or delay, for the salvation of souls and the advancement or our faith, either to the Turks or to the other unbelievers, or to the countries that are called the Indies, or to all those who are faithful." If they had understood that there would be new seminaries throughout Christendom, it would have been ridiculous to list, in last place, the countries with faithful Christians, even if it seems that these words (*seu etiam ad quoscumque fideles*) had been added from the contrary side, as a sort of necessity. Now, these great promisers and travelers, forgetting what their first Institute was, created only a dozen colleges here and there, in countries that we don't know (if we're supposed to believe them);[10] and they've built an infinite number of colleges in our midst,

---

8   In Greek mythology, a winged ram with golden fleece (a symbol of authority and kingship) was captured by Jason and his crew of Argonauts, thereby placing Jason rightfully on the throne. See *Encyclopaedia Britannica*, https://www.britannica.com/topic/Golden-Fleece (accessed February 28, 2021).

9   That is the bull *Exposcit debitum* by Pope Julius III. This was discussed in Book 1, Chapter 3.

10   The Jesuits established a handful overseas colleges in the sixteenth century: Angola, Brazil, Mexico, Peru, India, Macau, and the Philippines. Most Jesuit schools beyond Europe were

in order to plant a new papacy there, and to trample underfoot the ancient one under which the church militant triumphed. We aren't outside the church of Saint Peter, when we condemn these new brethren in France; we are conforming without sophistry to the original and primitive wills of Pope Paul III and Pope Julius III. And even if, at the time, they'd willed something different, our Gallican church, in its antiquity, can make humble remonstrances to popes, when they allow themselves to be carried away by the unwarranted pleading of individuals, to the prejudice of the church. That's what Saint Irenaeus,[11] bishop of Lyon, did; so did Saint Martin,[12] bishop of Tours, the titular apostle of our France. And so did our good Saint Louis.[13] That didn't cause them to be deemed heretics, any more than Saint Paul was so judged, when he stood up to Saint Peter, who was condemning him.[14]

set up in the seventeenth century, including New France. Before the suppression of the Society in 1773, the Jesuits ran about 845 schools: seminaries, universities, and colleges. See *DHCJ*, 2:1206–7. By 1599, thirty schools were founded in France. For the complete list of Jesuit schools in France, see Paul Grendler, "Jesuit Schools and Universities in Europe 1548–1773," *Brill Research Perspectives in Jesuit Studies* 1, no. 1 (2019): 54–59.

11   Irenaeus (*c.*140–*c.*202) was a Greek cleric noted for developing Christian theology by combating heresy and defining orthodoxy. To counter the doctrines of the gnostic sects, he offered three pillars of orthodoxy: the Scriptures, Tradition handed down from the apostles, and the teachings of the apostles' successors. See *Encyclopaedia Britannica*, https://www.britannica.com/biography/Saint-Irenaeus (accessed February 28, 2021).

12   Saint Martin of Tours (?–397) was converted to Christianity at a young age. He embraced Trinitarianism and, after his consecration as a bishop in 371, he was active in suppressing the Gallo-Roman religion. He opposed the violent persecution of the Priscillianist sect of ascetics. Sutto, 234n91, comments: "This is an allusion to the independence of the church from political power in the face of Maximus's usurpation." Emperor Maximus (335–388) was Roman emperor in the western portion of the empire. In 383, he usurped the throne from Emperor Gratian (r.367–383), and a year later was made emperor in Britannia and Gaul. See *Encyclopaedia Britannica*, https://www.britannica.com/biography/Saint-Martin-of-Tours (accessed February 28, 2021).

13   "This is an allusion to the Pragmatic Sanction of Saint Louis (1260), an apocryphal text that probably was written circa 1450 to justify the sanction of 1438." See Sutto, 235n92.

14   See Gal. 2:11–21. See Sutto, 235n93.

The Jesuits' Teaching of Humane Letters, Philosophy, and Theology to All Sorts of Scholars Is Contrary to Their First Institute; and Concerning the Progress and the Surprises They Used to Promote This New Tyranny, to the Detriment of the Ancient Discipline of the Universities

THE LAWYER. Don't think, Messieurs, that when Ignatius and his companions presented themselves before Pope Paul III, they offered to teach young people, as the Jesuits have done ever since. I've told you about Ignatius, and how much he knew about the different branches of learning. It was he who drew up the first plan for the Society; and being aware of his strengths, he simply promised to teach little children their *Credo*,[1] just as our curates do, or as their vicars do in elementary schools. This is something that I'll prove to you as I spin out this story. When they arrived in Rome for the first time, to receive the papal blessing for their imaginary journey to Palestine, Maffei says that during their stay, *veteri Ecclesia instituto plebem puerosque Christiana catechesi, vicatim erudire institerunt*.[2] And then, having assembled to draw up the articles for their future society, *Ac simul concepta verborum formula sese obstringerent, puerili aetati per Catechesim, erudiendae*.[3] Ribadeneyra repeats this, saying that this article was drawn up by them at this time, *Pueros rudimenta fidei doceant*.[4]

Now, let's look at their bulls again, starting with the one dated 1540, by which wise Paul III, fearing everything about these new associates, ratified their request after several entreaties: but he did it on condition that there couldn't be more than sixty of them. Here's the beginning of the request, and the promise that they made: *Quicumque in Societate, quam Jesu nomine insigniri cupimus,*

---

1 The document that is being referred to is the *Formula Instituti* that Ignatius, and his companions, drew as a result of their discernment in Rome 1539–40. It had been already discussed in Book I, Chapter 13.

2 According to the ancient custom of the church, they decided to educate in the Christian catechism the people and the children from street to street.

3 And at the same time the words are so formulated that they are obliged to be educated in the catechism at a young age.

4 So that they might teach children the rudiments of faith.

© KONINKLIJKE BRILL NV, LEIDEN, 2021 | DOI:10.1163/9789004164062_023

vult sub crucis vexillo, Deo militare, et soli Domino, ac Ecclesiae ipsius sponsae, sub Romano Pontifice, Christi in terris Vicario, servire, post solemne Castitatis, Paupertatis, et Obedientiae votum, proponat sibi in animo, se partem esse Societatis, ad hoc potissimum institutae, ut ad fidei defensionem, et propagationem, et profectum, in vita et doctrina Christiana, per publicas praedicationes, et verbi Dei ministerium, spiritualia exercitia, et charitatis opera, et nominatim per PUERORUM ET RUDIUM IN CHRISTIANISMO INSTITUTIONEM. And since this final clause was somewhat vague, it is explained briefly, later in the same bull: ET NOMINATIM COMMENDATAM HABEANT INSTITUTIONEM PUERORUM ET RUDIUM IN DOCTRINA CHRISTIANA, DECEM PRAECEPTORUM ET ALIORUM SIMILITER RUDIMENTORUM. That's clear, and yet they could have colleges, not everywhere, but at approved universities, and not in order to receive pupils who come and go, but only those who would be in their seminary. *Possint* (reads that same bull) *in Universitatibus habere Collegium, seu Collegia habentia reditus, census, seu possessiones, usibus et necessitatibus studentium applicandas, retenta penes Praepositum et Societatem, omnimoda gubernatione, seu superintendentia super dicta Collegia.*[5] Since the possessions of the colleges were destined for those who would be studying there, this couldn't apply to non-boarders, but only to those who vowed to enter their order, and who have come to be called approved scholars; but as for the others, it was only to teach the *Credo* to young children, as we see schoolmasters and priests do. That can be seen in the word *puer*, an age group that is a bit older, but not as much as what Romans call *infans*. And in fact, if we want to mention an old man whose feebleness brings him back to the rank of a child, we say: *repuerascit.*[6] *Infans* is a person who can neither walk nor talk. *Puer* is a child who is beginning to walk and to talk, just as Horace depicts him in his book on the art of poetry:

---

5 "Whoever wishes to serve as a soldier for God beneath the banner of the cross in the Society, which we desire to be designated by the name of Jesus, and to serve the Lord alone and the Church his bride, under the Roman pontiff, his vicar on earth, after his solemn vow of chastity, poverty and obedience he should keep in mind that he is a member of a Society founded chiefly for this lofty purpose: namely for the defence of the faith, and its propagation and success, in life and Christian doctrine, by public preaching, and the ministry of the word of God, spiritual exercises, and works of charity, and expressly by the education of children ignorant in Christianity. [...] AND EXPRESSLY LET THEM HOLD IN ESTEEM THE EDUCATION OF CHILDREN AND THOSE IGNORANT OF CHRISTIAN DOCTRINE, OF THE TEN COMMANDMENTS AND SIMILAR RUDIMENTS. [...] They could have a college or colleges in universities having revenues, annuities, or possessions which are to be applied for the use and needs of students, retained in the power of the general and Society, in every direction, or superintendency of the aforementioned college."

6 "He has become a boy again."

Reddere qui voces jam scit puer, et pede certo
Signat humum.[7]

In 1543, the Jesuits were permitted to receive, with no limits in the number, all those who wanted to join the order.[8] And just as Pope Paul III opened the door to them on that side, he closed it to them on the other. For by the bull of 1545,[9] they repeated word for word the privileges that had been granted them by the first bull of 1540; but as for teaching little children their *Credo*, it wasn't mentioned. And will you please weigh that? In 1545 and 1546, their privileges were expanded,[10] and especially in 1549.[11] Although none of these bulls talk about teaching little children, in the latter bulls, colleges were specifically mentioned for the members of their order. If you want to know why, and where, this diversity came from, I'll tell you. They were restricted to sixty persons by the first establishment of their Society, and Pope Paul didn't take much trouble to open the elementary schools to them, so that they could teach the *Credo* to young children; but when he opened the door fully to persons who wanted to belong to their Society, he wanted them to have rules like the other religious orders and monasteries, who can't teach young persons unless those young people are members of their order.

Things went on in this way until 1549, when Pope Paul died and was succeeded by Julius III.[12] In the beginning, they had dealt with a pope who, although overwhelmed by the entreaties of one person or another, had yielded over time: so they were more restrained under him. But soon after his death, they learned the lesson that Lysander the Lacedemonian[13] had learned. He used to say that a good captain should be dressed in the skins of foxes and lions, a lesson made famous by Machiavelli in *The Prince*.[14] And so, don't

---

7   "The boy who just knows how to talk and treads the ground with firm foot," Horace, *The Art of Poetry*, verse 158.

8   See Pope Paul III's bull *Iniunctum nobis*.

9   The bull referred here is Paul III's *Cum inter*.

10   In Paul III's *Exponi nobis* (1546).

11   In Paul III's *Licet debitum*.

12   In 1555.

13   Lysander Lacedemonius (?–395 BCE) was a Spartan admiral. In 404 BCE, he forced the Athenians to capitulate, thereby bringing the Peloponnesian War to an end. He played a key role in Sparta's domination for the next decade. See *Encyclopaedia Britannica*, https://www.britannica.com/biography/Lysander-Greek-military-leader (accessed February 28, 2021).

14   "The lion cannot protect himself from traps, and the fox cannot defend himself from wolves. One must therefore be a fox to recognize traps, and a lion to frighten wolves," Machiavelli, *The Prince*, ch. 18.

expect more from this tale of the history of our Jesuits than you'll get from that tale about the fox and the lion; and in the process you'll find that they were gallant disciples of Machiavelli. Ignatius was a worldly-wise man who knew that the Society he invented had many novelties introduced to the detriment of the ancient order and discipline of our church, and that it would be difficult to approve of them. He decided that he needed a new confirmation by Julius, but he wanted to get something from the agreement. I told you that, by Paul's first bull, they were permitted to teach little children the first statements in the *Credo*, to preach, and to have colleges founded to raise and teach young persons: a nursery that would supply their Society, and nothing more. And after that, although all their initial privileges were confirmed by all the subsequent bulls, no mention was made of this teaching. They presented their request to Julius in a narration about the bull of 1540; and sly as foxes, they inserted the word *lectiones*, which isn't mentioned in the first bull; and they hid everything that had been mentioned in the other bulls. And as for their colleges, they came with a new right. The best thing to do is to read the entire document. By this new request, Ignatius returned to his *Quicumque in Societate nostra, etc. proponat sibi in animo se partem esse Societatis ad hoc potissimum institutae, ut ad fidei defensionem et profectum animarum, in vita et doctrina Christiana per publicas praedicationes, LECTIONES, et aliud Dei quodcumque ministerium, ac spiritualia exercitia, PUERORUM AC RUDIUM IN CHRISTIANISMO INSTITU-TIONEM.*[15] That's the first surprise, and it involves two points. The first point is the word *lectiones*, which was newly added after *praedicationes*. The other point involved catechizing little children, a right that had been taken away from them in 1543. But nonetheless, all of that doesn't address establishing colleges and routinely teaching youths, as they've been doing ever since. By those bulls, they were occasionally permitted to give public lessons about theology, which we saw their Maldonado[16] do on two feast days. On the first day, he explained the Canon of the Mass; and on the second day, he explained the Psalm, *Dixit Dominus Domino meo*. Otherwise, the latter restriction would have

---

15   "Whoever in our Society, etc. should keep in mind that he is a member of a Society founded chiefly for this lofty purpose: namely for the defence of the faith and the perfection of souls, in life and Christian doctrine, by public preaching, LECTURES and any other ministry of the word of God, and spiritual exercises, THE EDUCATION OF CHILDREN IGNORANT IN CHRISTIANITY."

16   Juan Maldonado (1533–83) joined the Society in Rome in 1562. In 1563, he was sent to Paris to lecture in theology at the newly opened Collège de Clermont. He also gave lectures at the royal court and brought about the conversion of various Protestant nobles. In 1574, the Sorbonne accused him of opposing the doctrine of immaculate conception, which resulted in the conflict that involved the nuncio, the bishop of Paris, Jesuit superior general, and the pope. Consequently, Maldonado had to leave Paris. See *DHCJ*, 3:2484.

been frustrating for small children, if the word *lectiones* had been expanded to include the public exercise of all sorts of learning, as is done in the other colleges. And in these public lessons on theology, which should be done like preaching and sermons, for the advancement of our faith, there was nothing innovative for our antique discipline. For although religious can only teach humane letters and philosophy to members of their order, they aren't forbidden to read theology aloud publicly. Our fathers therefore saw a Jacobin friar who was a *Cenomani*,[17] and a Franciscan of the Friars Minor who was called *Cornibus*;[18] and we ourselves can recall having recently heard a Panigarola[19] give public lessons on theology in Paris.

The only change I find in this bull of 1550 is that, while the bull of 1540 ordered them not to have colleges elsewhere than in approved universities, Julius III's bull permits them to have them anywhere. Let's read the text of that bull: *Quia tamen domus, quas Dominus dederit ad operandum in vinea ipsius et non ad scholastica studia, destinanda erunt, cum valdè opportunum fore alioqui videatur ut ex juvenibus ad pietatem propensis, et ad litterarum studia tractanda, idoneis, operarii eidem vinea Domini parentur, qui Societatis nostrae, etiam professae, velut quoddam Seminarium existant, possit professa Societas, ad studiorum commoditatem, Scholarium habere Collegia, ubicumque ad ea construenda et dotata, aliqui ex devotione movebuntur. Quae simulac constructa et dotata fuerint (non tamen ex bonis quorum collatio ad sedem Apostolicam pertinet) ex nunc authoritate Apostolica erigi supplicamus, ac pro erectis haberi. Quae Collegia habere possint reditus, census, seu possessiones, usibus et necessiatibus studentium applicandas, retenta, penes Praepositum, vel Societatem omnimoda gubernatione, seu superintendentia super dicta Collegia, et praedictos studentes, quoad Rectorum seu Gubernatorum ac studentium electionem, et eorundem admissionem, emissionem, receptionem, exclusionem, statutorum ordinationem, et circa studentium instructionem, eruditionem, aedificationem,*

---

17   Nicolas de Gorron (?–c.1295), a Dominican, wrote a commentary on the *Sentences* of Peter Lombard. He was described as *Cenomanensis*, that is, from Cisalpine Gaul (northern Italy). See http://beauchesne.immanens.com/appli/article.php?id=7195 (accessed February 28, 2021).

18   Richard Rufus of Cornwall (?–c.1260), that is, was a Franciscan whose commentaries are among the earliest that are known. See Rega Wood, "Richard Rufus of Cornwall and Aristotle's Physics," *Franciscan Studies* 52 (1992): 247–81.

19   Francesco Panigarola (1548–94) was an Italian Franciscan preacher. His sermons attracted much attention in Rome. In 1587, he was made bishop of Asti, and shortly after that he was sent to France as an assistant to the papal legate. Pasquier doubtlessly heard him speak during this sojourn in Paris. See Fabio Giunta, "Il predicatore di Francesco Panigarola: Un nuovo modello di eloquenza sacra per il Seicento," *Acta neophilologica* 45, nos. 1–2 (2012): 109–18, https://doi.org/10.4312/an.45.1-2.109-118.

ac correctionem victus, vestitusque et aliarum rerum necessariarum eis minis-
trandrum modum, atque aliam omnimodo gubernationem, regimen ac curam,
ut neque studentes dictis bonis abuti, neque Societas professa in proprios usus
convertere possit, sed studentium necessitate subvenire.[20] That was the request
they presented and which Julius III validated. In it you'll find some confusion
about the words *Societas professa*, professed Society, and other terms that I'll
decipher for you when the opportunity presents itself. It's enough right now to
note that, in this passage, there's another novelty: according to their first bull,
they couldn't have colleges elsewhere than in approved universities; but by the
second bull, they were permitted to have colleges wherever they had founded
some churches of their Society, which they call, in their jargon, houses. The
words churches or *moutiers*[21] offended their delicate ears. And in addition, you
see that the colleges about which they are talking, which are annexed to their
houses, are only destined for scholars from their order. As a result of this new
change, nothing changed the antique way of policing the universities. For
all the other religious orders teach in their monasteries, which are scattered
here and there throughout the provinces, and then they send them to the
universities to complete their studies and earn a degree in theology, if they're
capable of doing so. Hence, in the great and famous University of Paris, every

---

20   "However, the houses which the Lord will provide are to be dedicated to labor in his vine-
      yard and not to the pursuit of scholastic studies; since it appears altogether proper that
      workers should be provided for that same vineyard from among the young men who are
      inclined to piety and capable of applying themselves to learning, in order that they may
      be a kind of seminary for the Society, including the professed Society. Consequently, to
      provide facilities for studies, the professed Society should be capable of having colleges
      of scholastics wherever benefactors will be moved by their devotion to build and endow
      them. We now petition that as soon as these colleges will have been built and endowed
      (but not from resources that it pertains to the Holy See to apply), they may be established
      through authorization of the Holy See or considered to be so established. These colleges
      should be capable of possessing fixed revenues, rights to rentals, or possessions that are
      to be applied to the uses and needs of the students. The general of the Society retains the
      full government or superintendency over the aforementioned colleges and students; and
      this pertains to the choice of rectors or governors and of the scholastics; the admission,
      dismissal, reception, and exclusion of the same; the enactment of statutes; the arrange-
      ment, instruction, edification, and correction of the scholastics; the manner of supplying
      them with food, clothing, and all other necessary materials; and every other kind of gov-
      ernment, control, and care. All this should be managed in such a way that neither may
      the students be able to abuse the aforementioned goods, nor may the professed Society
      be able to convert them to its own uses but may use them to provide for the needs of the
      scholastics."
21   *Moutier* or *monstier* was an archaic word meaning "church" or "monastery." [Cf. Furetière
      s.v.]

noteworthy monastery has a house to lodge the religious to whom they want to teach theology.

Now, this is how a disorder and a general mutation of the antiquity of our universities began. We didn't know what it was to create religious with master of arts degrees, and we knew even less about having them do their theology degree elsewhere than at a university, which administers all sorts of rigorous public examinations. Julius III inverted this wise system in favor of the Jesuits. For he wanted a Jesuit, no matter where he studied, be it an university or elsewhere, to receive free of charge the degrees of bachelor, master, license, doctor, in any faculty whatsoever; and if one wanted to obligate the Jesuit to observe the honest and praiseworthy custom of times gone by, he can still become a master or a doctor, simply on the basis of a statement from the general, and his authorization; and as a result he enjoys the same privileges, freedoms, and liberties as the others. This pope's judgment was very bizarre: you know the story about his big monkey, a barbary ape who'd only obey a little beggar boy. The master became Cardinal del Monte;[22] and then, having been made pope, he gave the beggar boy all his benefits[23] and created a new cardinal whom upright and honest Italians call Cardinal Monkey. I therefore don't find it strange that this pope, propelled by a similar desire, wanted to move ahead by extraordinarily big steps, having never before seen these new monkeys of our Catholic religion at a university. And just so you won't think that I want to usurp the Jesuits' privilege, and stuff you, as they are stuffed, with some impudent lie, let's read the text of the bull *Necnon Scholaribus* (he wrote, referring to the approved scholars at their colleges) *Collegiorum, Societatis hujusmodi, in Universitatibus alicujus studii generalis existentium, quod ipsi (si praevio rigoroso et publico examine eisdem Universitatibus idonei reperti fuerint, Rectores Universitatum hujusmodi, et eos gratis et amore Dei, absque aliqua pecuniarum solutione promovere recusaverint) in Collegiis predictis a Praeposito Generali pro tempore, existente, vel de eius licentia a quovis ex inferioribus Praepositis, vel Rectoribus hujusmodi Collegiorum, cum duobus etiam, vel tribus Doctoribus, vel Magistris, per eosdem eligendis: Scholaribus vero Collegiorum eorundem, extra Universitates existentium, studiorum suorum cursu absoluto, ac rigoroso examine praecedente, à dicto Praeposito Generali, vel de eius licentia à quovis ex Praepositis, vel Rectoribus hujusmodi Collegiorum cum duobus etiam vel tribus Doctoribus, vel Magistris, per eosdem eligendis, quoscumque Baccalaureatus, et Magisterii, Licentiaturae, ac Doctoratus gradus accipere,*

---

22   See Book I, ch. 3 above.

23   A *bénéfice*, "*benefit*," is an ecclesiastical title or dignity accompanied by an income.

Praepositis, vel Rectoribus, cum Doctoribus hujusmodi, ut eosdem Scholares ad gradus ipsos promovere, eisdemque Scholaribus, ut postquam promoti fuerint, in eis legere, disputare, ac quoscumque alios actus ad haec necessarios, facere, exequi, omnibus et singulis privilegiis praerogativis, immunitatibus, exemptionibus, libertatibus, antelationibus, favoribus, gratiis, indultis, ac omnibus et singulis aliis, quibus alii in quibusvis Universitatibus studiorum hujusmodi, rigoroso examine praevio, ac alias justa inibi observari solitos et requisitos usus, ordinationes, ritus ac mores, pro tempore promoti, de jure vel consuetudine, aut alias quomodo libet utuntur, potiuntur, et gaudent, ac uti, potiri et gaudere poterunt, quomodolibet in futurum, non solum ad ipsorum instar, sed pariformiter, et aequè principaliter absque ulla penitus differentia, uti, potiri, gaudere in omnibus et per omnia, perinde ac si gradus hujusmodi in eisdem Universitatibus, et non eorum Collegiis accepissent.[24]

Those who have been raised in the Latin language will find that Julius III is speaking solely about Jesuit scholars. It's a clause related to all the previous bulls in which their colleges were discussed; and in this one in particular, he ordered that the scholars of this order should study in the universities, or outside them; and having been well and duly examined, if they were found

---

24 *Necnon scholaribus* is the title of a cited paragraph of Julius III's bull, *Sacrae religionis* (1552): "[We also grant permission] to the students of the colleges of the Society that are among the student bodies of any university to receive any bachelor's, master's, licentiate, and doctor's degrees in the said colleges from the superior general in office at the time, or by his permission from any of the lower superiors or rectors of such colleges, with two or three doctors or masters as well to be chosen by them (if [the students], upon a rigorous public examination in these universities, have been found suitable, and the rectors of the universities have refused to promote them free of charge and from the love of God, without the payment of money). The students of these colleges outside the universities, upon completing their course of studies and a rigorous examination, may receive [the above degrees] from the said superior general, or by his permission from any of the superiors or rectors of these colleges, with two or three doctors or masters to be chosen by them. The superiors and rectors, with the doctors, may promote these students to these degrees, and the students, after they have been promoted, may lecture and dispute therewith, and carry out and perform the other acts connected with them, and may use, possess, and enjoy in any way for the future each and all of the privileges, prerogatives, immunities, exemptions, liberties, preferences, favors, graces, and indults, and each and all of the other things which the others in any of the universities use, possess, and enjoy by law or custom, or otherwise, on the occasion of their promotion, after a rigorous examination and otherwise according to the usages, ordinances, rites, and customs usually observed therein and required. And they are to use, possess, and enjoy them in everything and in every way, not only in imitation of the others, but in like manner and as equally of first rank, with no difference whatever, just as if they had received these degrees in those universities and not in their colleges."

capable, they would be received free of charge into the ranks of licenses and doctorates (a statement that can't be extended to outsiders). And if someone wants to take money from them, their general has the power to declare them graduates, or to have them graduate; and after they've received the degrees, they can read, dispute, and do all the other required acts: in a word, enjoy the same prerogatives as the others. What? Are you extending the word read to include everyone who comes and goes, just as in other colleges there are masters who are laypersons? Not really: for whatever power was granted them here, it was like granting it to persons who were regular clergy (for that's what they call themselves); and it therefore was like granting permission to those new masters and doctors to give lessons to their approved scholastics, just as if they had graduated from the universities. A Jesuit, adhering to his good customs, brings all the sophistry that he wants: when read from the beginning to the end, this passage can't be understood in any other way. If Julius III had understood that the Jesuit who has graduated could present a lesson to all comers and goers, just as a layperson can, do you believe that he'd have forgotten to mention it specifically? You see (someone will say to me), the many ways he employed to authorize the Jesuits to do such readings. Do you find that strange? For he couldn't do much more, since by a novelty never before seen, in return for the simple avowal of the general of that order, he wanted the Jesuits to give lessons to their religious? Corrupting all the ancient sinews of the universities, this policy couldn't be sufficiently expressed in order to authorize it.

Until now, I've discussed what their bulls were saying about their colleges. So now, let's see what their history shows on that score. Since neither the antiquity of the universities nor the novelty of their bulls permitted them to open their schools to all sorts of scholars, or to have in their colleges others than their seminarians, with the support of Messire Guillaume du Prat, bishop of Clermont, who lodged them in Billom, one of the cities in his bishopric,[25] they nonetheless opened a college there, not only for the members of their order but for all other students. Oh, what rare obedience on the part of the French toward the Roman church! They boasted about having bulls from Julius III that gave them permission to do this. Hearing that, we judged that merely mentioning the title meant that it should be deemed a good and valid one. And yet (I commented to a gentleman from Gascony) they had no title beyond their *villonnerie*, their villonnery, their knavery. He brusquely replied that he thought they had chosen to put their first French college in the city of Billon, confusing Villon with Billon, as Gascons customarily do, for they pronounce *V* where

25   This had been already discussed in Book I, Chapter 4.

there should be a *B*, and *B* where there should be a *V*. I replied that no letter should be changed, all the more so since our laws order us to mix all coins in the *billon*, that is, base metal, and that the Jesuit colleges bore that hallmark.[26]

In the city of Billom, their villonnery began and soon expanded, first in Toulouse and then in Paris, thanks to the huge legacy from du Prat. And none of us dared stand up against all their unwarranted undertakings, for our France honored the Holy See, beneath which they falsely took cover. Obedience that we ought religiously to embrace. But cheaters shouldn't be permitted to take advantage of it, and no one is more self-interested than Our Holy Father the pope, if he wants to preserve his authority toward everyone and against everyone. True God, where are our eyes? Run your eyes over all their bulls for 1540, 1543, 1545, 1546, 1549, to see whether you find permission for them to open and administer their colleges, as the other universities do. I'm opening myself up to any condemnation that may be ordered against me. All their noteworthy acts are mere impostures; and if you talk to them secretly, they'll tell you that these are miracles that God wrought through Saint Ignatius. When they first came before Paul III, to be accepted, they all said they were masters of arts from the University of Paris; and today Maffei, mocking the entire consistory of Rome, agrees that three master's degrees were awarded in Spain; and he and Ribadeneira don't say where Broët, Jaye, and Codury were awarded master's degrees. And when they opened their colleges in France, they referred only to the authority of the Holy See, an authority that they were falsely alleging. Where did these illusions come from? From the miracles of the great Ignatius, who blinded everyone.

I'll now pick up the thread of their bulls, in order to determine when they were granted this power to give lessons to every scholar. The Troubles of 1561 burst forth in France, owing to the diversity of religious groups. At first, the Jesuits deemed this a most propitious time to grow, not owing to favor toward

---

26 Billom is situated some thirty kilometers from du Prat's cathedral city of Clermont (today known as Clermont-Ferrand). Villon is far to the north, in Burgundy. Today the Gascons, who live in the foothills of the Pyrenees Mountains, are still mocked for their *B*'s and *V*'s. Pasquier is playing with sounds, but above all he is playing with meanings. And he is doing it to the detriment of the Jesuits. Billom was a Jesuit house; *villonnerie* (pronounced in Gascony as "billonnery") was synonymous with knavery; and *billonage* refers to debasing coinage. All three words begin with the same sound, as a Gascon would pronounce it: Bee-yuh, Bee-yuh, and Bee-yuh. Together they suggest that the Jesuits of Billom (not Villon) are knaves who threaten to debase the value of whatever they touch.

their sect, but owing to the disfavor encountered during a civil war. By a note-worthy surprise they obtained new bulls from Pope Pius IV,[27] which state:

> *Insuper tibi moderno et pro tempore existenti Praeposito Generali dictae Societatis, ut per te, vel illum, vel aliquem ex Praepositis, vel Rectoribus Collegiorum vestrorum, tam in Universitatibus studiorum generalium, quam extra illas ubilibet consistentium, in quibus ordinariae studiorum, artium liberalium, et Theologiae lectiones habentur, cursusque ordinarii peragentur, ut dictae Societatis Scholares et pauperes externos, qui dictas lectiones frequentaverint, et etiam divites (si officiales Universitatum eos promovere recusaverint) eum per examinatores vestrae Societatis idonei inventi sint (solutis tamen per divites, suis juribus, Universitatibus) in ves-tris Collegiis Universitatum quarumcumque, et aliis extra Universitates, consistentibus Collegiis vestris, alios quoslibet Scholares, qui inibi sub eorum obedientia, directione, vel disciplina studuerint, ad quoscumque Baccalaureatus, Licentiariae, Magisterii, doctoratus, gradus, JUXTA JULII PRAEDECESSORIS NOSTRI TENOREM, promovere, ipsique sic promoti, privilegiis, aliisque IN EISDEM LITERIS contentis ple-nariè uti, potiri, gaudere liberè ac licitè valeant, authoritate praefata concedimus, et ampliamus: necnon praesantes literas, et in eis contenta, de subreptionis vel obreptionis, aut nullitatis vitio, seu intensionis defectu, quovis praetextu quaesitove colore, nullo unquam tempore notari, vel impugnari possint.[28]*

---

27   *Etsi ex debito* and *Exponi nobis* (both from 1561). "Surprise" was a legal concept suggesting the invalidity of a document due to misinformation provided to the issuing authority.

28   "Moreover, we grant the following to you, the current superior general of the said Society. that through you, or him [the general], or any of the superiors or rectors of your schools, whether they be universities of general studies [*studia generalia*] or schools anywhere outside of them as long as they hold classes in theology and the liberal arts and pursue them in a regular program: that the Scholastics of the said Society, needy extern students, even wealthy students (if the officials of the universities had refused to admit them), and any other students whomsoever if they study under your care and discipline in any of your colleges attached to a university or those colleges not so attached who are found worthy by your examiners to promote to the degrees of bachelor, licentiate, and magiste-rial doctorate according to the provisions of Julius [II], Our predecessor. We confirm and insist that those thus promoted legitimately and fully enjoy the privileges contained in the decree of Pope Julius. We further decree that this document and its contents can by no means at any time ever be marked or challenged for a flaw of concealment, misrepre-sentation, nullity, or any other defect of Our intention., and it cannot at all be included in any way under revocations of similar or dissimilar favors and other contrary dispositions."

This decretal marks the first opening of their colleges to all manner of scholars: but on what is it founded? On the bull of Julius III, a fact that it repeats
twice. Was there ever a greater surprise and obreption than this? For Pope
Julius never thought about it. And that's why these sophists added, at the end
of this bull of Pius IV, that no one can argue obreption, subreption, or lack
of will, wanting each of us to close his eyes and tie up his judgment, in order
not to know that a clear dishonor was being introduced anew, against the
ancient honor of the universities, by which our church has always remained
strong. But some Jesuit who has reached the final stage will tell me that the
pope added the word *ampliamus*. Was there ever a coup, be it a coup d'état
or a more important coup involving religion, of more perilous consequence
than that one? I grant that these new sirs should be permitted to be graduates of all the faculties, as stated in Julius's bull. I grant that, by Pius's last bull,
their colleges were open to all comers and goers. Yet the one and the other
were new schisms in our universities. But who can tolerate the statement that
their scholars, be they Jesuits or be they non-boarders, that is outsiders, should
receive licenses, having obtained attestations from two or three persons of
their order, and having paid the money due the chancellors, rectors, and deputies of the universities. Isn't that like turning the superiors of the universities
into mere notaries for the Jesuits and their scholars? Doesn't that shame the
rectors of the universities who have done nothing? Isn't this submitting them
to the conscience of their general, or to the consciences of two or three of his
men, introducing chaos, a mixture and a confusion of everything in our universities? To be accurate, there's no better way to create a whole nursery for
heretics than to create a seminary for Jesuits and leave the doctories and the
masteries of the scholars up to the opinions of these new Templars. Yet from
the very word, *ampliamus*, which was industriously slipped into the bull by
these master workers, with supple twists of the wrist, we shall accept this new
disorder, at the end of which the pope will plug his ears and stop our mouths,
in order not to hear the surprises, the obreptions and the subreptions of these
Reverend Fathers in God, who allowed this final clause to be added by a copy-
ist at the Roman Curia. Read all seven of the bulls that preceded it, and you'll
find nothing like it. Why did they especially want this to be added? Because
they knew in their consciences that, contrary to all reason, they had obtained
this last bull by obreptionment. If I try to call out their consciences, they'll
make fun of me. For, the very year when they obtained these bulls in Rome (it
was in 1561), they promised the Gallican church that they would renounce all
the special privileges that had been granted them in Rome. An abjuration that
they confirmed by a public oath in the assembled court of the parlement, and

that they've never observed. And what makes a person really think about this, is that they're very careful not to show Pius v's bulls to our clergy, nor to the parlement. For if they were to show them, they'd not only have been ridiculed, they'd have been abandoned, as folk who had no souls.

Up until now, you've seen a great deal of the fox in them. Now you'll see the lion, because in 1571 they obtained other bulls from Pope Pius v,[29] in this form and substance:

Decernimus et declaramus quod praeceptores hujusmodi Societatis, tam litterarum humanarum quàm liberalium artium, Philosophiae, Theologiae, vel cujusvis earum facultatum, in suis Collegiis, etiam in locis ubi Universitates extiterint, suas lectiones, etiam publicas legere (dummodo per duas horas de mane, et per unam de sero, cum lectoribus Universitatum non concurrant) liberè et licitè possint: quodque quibuscumque scholasticis liceat in hujusmodi Collegiis, lectiones et alias scholasticas exercitationes frequentare, ac quicumque in eis, Philosophiae vel Theologiae fuerint auditores, in quavis Universitate, ad gradus admitti possint, et cursuum quos in eis Collegiis fecerint, ratio habeatur. Ita ut si ipsi in examine sufficientes inventi fuerint, non minus, sed pariformiter, et absque ulla penitus differentia, quam si in Universitatibus praefatis studuissent, ad gradus quoscumque, tam Baccalaureatus, quàm Licentiariae et Doctoratus, admitti possint et debeant, eisque super praemissis licentiam et facultatem concedimus. Districtius inhibentes, Universitatum quarumcumque Rectoribus et aliis

---

29   The following quotation is from *Cum litterarum*. See *Institutum*, 40: "We decree and declare that professors of this Society who in their colleges teach the humanities, the liberal arts, philosophy, theology, or any other discipline can even in localities where there is a university freely and legitimately hold classes and public lectures for two hours in the morning and one in the afternoon as long as they do not conflict with those of the universities. We also decree and declare that all students are free to attend lectures and other academic exercises in these colleges. Moreover, any student of philosophy or theology in any university can be admitted to the program in these colleges. Those who complete the program and do sufficiently well in the examination can and must be granted a bachelor, licentiate, or doctoral degree. They can do this not with less but with the same legitimacy, without any difference, than if they had studied at the universities, and to them We grant the same faculties and authority. We strictly forbid the rectors of Universities and anybody else from under any excuse daring or presuming to disturb or hinder the rectors and students in the aforementioned colleges. We also decree under pain of major excommunication and all other penalties We might determine, inflict, or impose that this document can never be weakened or called into question for defect in legal form or unclarity about Our intention. Even less can it be included in any way under revocations of similar or dissimilar favors and other contrary dispositions."

quibuscumque, sub excommunicationis majoris, aliisque arbitrio nostro, moderandis, infligendis, et imponendis poenis, ne Collegiorum hujusmodi Rectores et Scholares in praemissis, quovis quaesito colore, molestare audeant, vel praesumant. Decernentes quoque praesentes litteras, ullo unquam tempore, de subreptionis, vel obreptionis vitio, aut intentionis nostrae, vel alio quopiam defectu notari, vel impugnari nullatenus posse minusque sub quibusvis similium, vel dissimilium gratiarum revocationibus, et aliis contrariis dispositionibus comprehendi posse.

Oh, admirable not-philosophers, not-theologians, but wrangling lawyers in the Roman Curia! Whoever wants a formulary for wrangling, must have recourse to their bulls; where, however, with infinite daring they encounter the fury of a lion. With an indefinable sophistry they added that word *ampliamus*; but in the recent bulls one finds only lightning from heaven, censures, and excommunications in the superlative, against anyone who raises an eyebrow in order to oppose their tyranny. It's true that in order not to encounter them at an inopportune moment, I'd have liked some Jesuit Oedipus[30] to break the code and explain that final clause, which shouldn't have been added, if they considered that bull to be among those with which one couldn't be discontented. In that bull, Pius v had made an exception for two morning hours, but he only mentions one hour. Among our Jesuits there's always been an increase in what they undertake, to the prejudice of antiquity.

Indeed, that's the complete history of the instruction of young people as the Jesuits claim it to be; and they've gained ground, foot by foot, against the ancient orders of the universities. They've used all sorts of surprises and unwarranted artifices, which aren't familiar to learned persons, but which are familiar to that riff-raff, the common people, who take advantage of the absolute power of the Holy See. If I dare say so, it puts the papacy and the rest of the people on alms. Thanks to those clauses written by the Roman chancellery, they think they can fight us with sharp weapons. Yet a *procureur général* can bravely beat them down by an *appel comme d'abus*. These bulls were not only extorted by surprise, they were also undertaken directly against the liberties of our Gallican church, against the rights of the *ordinaires*, and against the antique privileges of our universities. For why wouldn't one receive that *appel*, seeing that the Signoria of Venice, thanks to the wisdom that accompanies its

---

30   The Sphinx gave Oedipus a riddle: What animal goes on four feet in the morning, two at noon, and three in the evening? Oedipus guessed correctly: man creeps on hands and knees in childhood, walks upright in adulthood, and in old age uses a cane.

every action, and knowing the disorder that these new people have brought, by their decree of December 23, 1591, expressly forbade them to give public or private lessons to anyone but a member of their Society?[31] A decree that can't be sufficiently solemnized, a decree that shows us that we're truly faint-hearted if we don't follow in its traces. It's a ship's light that should serve all nations, so that they can reach a safe harbor.

31   Pasquier refers here to what historian of Jesuit education Paul Grendler called "the best-known episode of university–Jesuit friction." It occurred in Padua (under the Venetian rule), where Jesuits had a flourishing upper school, which was considered a rival to the local university. In lieu of the senate's ruling, the Jesuits eventually closed the school. See Paul Grendler, *The University of Mantua, the Gonzaga & the Jesuits, 1584–1630* (Baltimore: Johns Hopkins University Press, 2009), 21.

The Foundation of Jesuit Cheating Comes from the Instruction of Young People, and Why Our Ancients Did Not Want Young People to Be Taught Learning in Religious Orders

THE JESUIT. Everything should be deemed good that is done for a good end. What does it matter if there is surprise and obreption in our bulls? The pope has granted us a dispensation. And was not our intention based solely on Christian charity? Charity in the form of instructing young persons, which is the real plan for our religious order, and where we henceforth want to be the first workers. THE LAWYER. That's a fine thing to say. And as for me, I think the only charity that you've brought to this work is true cheating. If they take that charity away from you, they will, at the same time, take away your cheating. Excuse me, I beg you, for letting that word escape from my mouth: and excuse me if, in the process, it becomes familiar to me; for it's my misfortune to conclude that your entire profession is full of cheating. Having no ability to diversify my language, as several of your brethren do, I'm among those who call bread bread and wine wine. And I also call cheating cheating, unless you prefer that I sometimes call it cheating and sometimes idle chat. And because this point weighs more heavily on my chest, I want to get to the very bottom of it.

If the discipline that is tolerated among your brethren is good, why isn't it general in all the other religious orders, which are just as much in favor of charity as you are? Why aren't they permitted to admit all sorts of outside scholars routinely, as you do? Is it possible that our good old fathers lacked judgment, and that we're now obliged to have recourse to these new fathers? A wiser discipline than that one has never existed. Besides, they think that every new object is beautiful to a child, and that their spirits, like wax, easily receive all sorts of impressions. They thought that one should not seduce them, but should let them enter religious orders with an honest freedom of conscience; and that by attending the ordinary lessons given by monks, they could be fervently converted: for which they would later repent, at a time when the time for doing so had passed. And that's why the Jesuits very easily surprise children born into good families: they have no trap more certain for catching them than that one. If they see some of their disciples who are supervising them, they attract them with the bait on their little twisted string; and having caught them, they make them vanish from their parents' presence, so that they can't return. A fine deception (you'll be telling me), this freeing of a child from the vain servitude of the world. But, on the other hand, once you know the procedures, it's a deception worthy of an exemplary animadversion. The rectors inform the classroom teachers about the abilities of the children in their classes, their spirit, their manners; and they make a detailed presentation like the one I could show you, for I have a printed example that goes as follows:

Below the first item they put, in each cell of the chart, the name of the child, his class, his age, according to the virtues they think he possesses. Every year, each college sends letters to the general, which they call annual letters, and by which they notify him of the great number of souls they have gained, and how much their confessions helped on this matter; and they accompany their letters with this catalog. When the general has thought about this carefully, he orders the provincials or the rectors to make it difficult for this bird to escape from his cage. From then on, the Jesuits do this fine and fruitful labor: some hear confessions, some flatter, some give exhortations in their bedchambers. And it's very difficult for a poor child to free himself from the net, when he's being watched in this way.

I'll tell you a tale about a young man of great promise who was almost surprised. The Jesuits saw that he was gifted in several good ways, and that his spirit was inclined to devotion. They thought this youth would be just right for them. He was a boarding pupil in the Parisian college. One of the fathers began to spy on him, and among other things he asked him what would afflict him most about dying, if it should happen that God wanted to dispose of him. The fear of the other world (said the child) and the sins I've committed. And who would deliver you from that fear (continued the Jesuit)? What would you say? I would be very obligated (replied the child). Now, you can rest assured (concluded the Jesuit), if you want to be one of us: for our Society of Jesus frees one from all sins. The young fellow, being manipulated like this, was ready to believe him and had prepared his bundle for going off, in accordance with what he recalled he was supposed to do, which was to not take leave of his father and mother, but to go at once to one of the Jesuit houses that they named. There he'd be given some money, which would help him reach the next house: in short, at each house he'd find money to pay the costs of his journey, and he'd reach Rome and receive the general's orders there. He was on the brink of departing when, by good fortune, his father came to visit him and found him totally changed. He wanted to know why, but the child was hesitant: the father pressed him, urged him fervently, with paternal severity, to conceal nothing from him. Finally, he learned everything that had gone on. Thanks to which, without a moment's delay, he retrieved the child: and after all the smoke had dissipated from his head, the child was sent to a different college, where things went so well for him that I'm certain he'll gather much fruit in the place where he is today. Praising God and thanking him daily for having rescued him from so perilous a journey, thanks to his holy grace.

The Artifice by Which the Jesuits Enrich Themselves from the Castoff Possessions of Their Novices

THE LAWYER. In this manner, the Jesuits win over the young persons in their colleges, be they boarders or be they non-boarders; so, it's no surprise that they also become rich on their castoff property. It's a general and most accepted rule that *"whoever confiscates the body, confiscates the possessions."* I don't intend to take an inventory here of the great wealth they've acquired, for I haven't counted the money in their purses. But I'll say that people often object to this practice. The person who made a very humble request to the king[1] says that, of the three or four hundred who have vowed themselves to their Society, only three or four offer their possessions as a gift; and François des Montaignes, who wrote the book called *De la Vérité défendue* (The truth defended), says that out of two thousand, only two hundred have done so. The art of being wise liars consists of not varying; and yet both of these lessons are faulty, and it must be said that, of three or four hundred, there aren't four; and of two thousand, there aren't two hundred who have given them their possessions. And it would be impossible for a novice to keep this from happening, for the Jesuits have a marvelous and infallible skill at achieving this. They have two books containing statutes. The first is titled *Constitutio Societatis Jesu*; it is divided into ten parts. The second is called *Constitutiones et declarationes examinis generalis*. These books are in my baggage, along with the book that contains all their bulls.[2]

In their Examen you'll find, in chapter 4, articles 1, 2, and 3, the following texts about the distribution of the possessions of those who are entering the Society:

---

1 He is referring to Louis Richeome, the Jesuit, and his *Très humble remonstrance et requeste des religieux de la Compagnie de Jésus* (Bordeaux: S. Millanges, 1598 and 1602).

2 The sources to which he is referring are available in English in the one-volume edition of *The Constitutions* published by the Institute of Jesuit Sources (IJS). The three documents are: *Formulas of the Institute of the Society of Jesus, Approved and Confirmed by Popes Paul III and Julius III*, 3–16; *The General Examen with its Declarations*, 23–54; and the *Constitutions* themselves, 56–406. The IJS version has not been quoted here; instead, Pasquier's own rendering in French has been translated into English, the better to remain close to his reading of these Constitutions.

© KONINKLIJKE BRILL NV, LEIDEN, 2021 | DOI:10.1163/9789004164062_025

1. *Quicumque Societatem ingredi volunt, antequam in domo aliqua vel Collegio ejus vivere sub obedientia incipiant, debent omnia bona sua temporalia quae habuerint distribuere et renunciare, ac disponere de his quae ipsis obvenire possent: eaque distributio primum in res debitas et obligatoria, si quae fuerint, et tunc quàm citissimè fieri potuerit, providere oportebit. Si verò tales nullae fuerint, in pia et sancta opera fiet, juxta illud: Dispersit, dedit pauperibus: et illud Christi; si vis perfectus esse, vade et vende omnia quae habes, et da pauperibus, et sequere me. Dispensando tamen haec bona propriam devotionem, et à se omnem fiduciam submovendo, eadem ullo tempore recuperandi.*

2. *Quod si statim propter aliquas honestas caussas non relinquet, promittat se promptè relicturum omnia post unum ab ingressu, absolutum annum, quandocumque per Superiorem et injunctum fuerit, in reliquo tempore probationis, quo completo, post professionem professi, et ante tria vota publica, Coadjutores re ipsa relinquere debent, ac pauperibus, ut dictum est, dispensare, ut consilium Evangelicum, quod non dicit, de Consanguineis, sed pauperibus, perfectiùs sequantur; et ut melius exemplum omnibus exhibeant, inordinatum erga parentes affectum exuendi et incommoda inordinatae distributionis, quae à dicto amore procedit declinandi atque ut ad parentes et consanguineos recurrendi, et ad inutilem ipsorum memoriam, aditu praecluso, firmius et stabilius in sua vocatione perseverent.*

THE LAWYER. I didn't want to translate into French [*read:* English] all the passages concerning the education of youths, because only the regents of the universities are interested, and they know Latin. But for the other passages that concern the rest of the people, I put both the French and the Latin.[3]

---

3 Here begins, therefore, an English rendering of Pasquier's version of the French text. In other words, the above translation reveals Pasquier's understanding of what the Latin text is saying. At times it veers from a close translation to a paraphrase. Here is the official rendering of these same three paragraphs: "1. All those who seek admission into the Society ought, before they begin to live under obedience in any house or college belonging to it, to distribute all the temporal goods they might have and renounce and dispose of those they might expect to receive. This should be done first of all in regard to matters of debt and obligation if there are any (and in that case provision should be made as soon as possible); if there are none, they should make the distribution in favor of pious and holy causes, according to the words, 'He scatters abroad, he gives to the poor' [Ps. 111:9; 2 Cor. 9:9], and according to those of Christ, 'If you wish to be perfect, go, sell what you have, and give to the poor; then come, follow me' [Matt. 19:21], thus making the distribution according to their own devotion and removing from themselves all hope of ever possessing those goods at any time. 2. If for some good reasons a candidate does not abandon those goods immediately, he will promise to give them all up, as was stated, with promptitude after one year from his entrance has

All those (say the articles cited above) who are preparing to enter our Society, before they begin to live in one of the houses or colleges, observing obedience, must renounce all the temporal goods they have and must distribute them; and in like manner must dispose of the goods they might have in the future; and this distribution involves paying their debts first, as soon as possible. If they have no debts, this property should be given to pious and holy works, in conformity with what is said: *Dispersit, dedit pauperibus*, He has scattered and given to the poor, and to the poverty of Jesus Christ. *Si vis perfectus esse, vade et vende omnia quae habes, et da pauperibus, et sequere me*: If you want to remain fulfilled, go and sell everything you possess and give it to the paupers, and follow me. Disposing nonetheless of his goods, according to and in conformity with the devotion that is in him and banishing from himself all hope and notion of ever being able to return.

And if, for good reasons, he does not abandon those possessions promptly, he must at least promise to give them up at once, after a year has elapsed and ended, as ordered by his superior for the remainder of his probation, for whatever time remains of his probation; and when this period has passed, having professed his profession, and before having made the three public vows, the coadjutors should, in reality and in fact, abandon and distribute these possessions to the poor (as said above), in order to follow the most perfect advice of the Gospel: Which does not say give to your relatives, but give to the poor. And in order to demonstrate to everyone a greater example of stripping oneself of a disorderly affection for one's father and mother, and in the same manner to demonstrate the dangers of a badly arranged distribution, which stems from

---

elapsed at whatsoever time during the remainder of the period of probation the superior will give him the order. When this period has passed, the professed before their profession, and the coadjutors before their three public vows, must relinquish them in fact and distribute them to the poor, as was stated. This is done to follow more perfectly the evangelical counsel, which does not say give to your relatives, but to the poor; and also to give to all a better example of divesting oneself of disordered love of relatives, to avoid the disadvantage of a disordered distribution which proceeds from the aforementioned love, and, by closing the door on recourse to parents and relatives and profitless remembrance of them, to help them persevere in their vocation with greater firmness and stability. 3. However, if there should be doubt whether it would be more perfect to make the gift or renunciation of these goods in favor of the relatives rather than others, because of their equal or greater need and other just considerations, even so, since there is danger that flesh and blood may draw candidates to err in such a judgment, they must be content to leave this matter in the hands of one, two, or three persons of exemplary life and learning (such as each one may choose with the superior's approval), and to acquiesce in what these persons decide to be more perfect and conducive to the greater glory of Christ our Lord." See *Constitutions*, General Examen, ch. 4, [53]–[55], pp. 34–35.

this friendship; and so that, banishing one's every thought of returning to one's father, mother, and relatives, and to the useless memory of them, he perseveres in his vocation more firmly and more stably.

THE LAWYER. Oh, holy Christian lesson of the Jesuits, who want a young man who is going to devote himself to their Society, not only to dispose of the possessions that have come to him but also, before entering the Society, dispose of the possessions that may come to him, And even holier, and more to be marveled at, they teach him to forget all the affection that God orders the child to show to his father and his mother: and after that, to his closest relatives; and they call this "inordinate affection."[4] And the Jesuits also order that, during the two years of his probation, he'll give all his possessions to the poor as alms: and that he won't leave them to the persons who are his closest relations, and who should inherit from him. All of this, so that our new religious won't want to return to his father's house. But I beg our Jesuits to remember this holy lesson: for I hope that their remembrance will later be appropriate in its place. However, I expect it will be the catastrophe of this devout comedy.

> 3. *Si tamen dubtaretur num majoris foret perfectionis, dare vel renuntiare consanguineis, hujusmodi bona, quàm aliis propter pacem, vel majorem ipsorum penuriam, et justas alias ob caussas, nihilominus ad declinandum errandi in hujusmodi judicio periculum, quod ab affectu sanguinis solet proficisci, contenti esse debebunt hoc, arbitrio unius, duorum aut trium, qui vita et doctrina commendatur (quos unusquisque cum Superioris authoritate elegerit) reliniquere, et in eo conquiescere quod illi perfectius, et ad majorem Christi Domini nostri glorium esse censebunt.*

However, if there be some uncertainty (says the Latin), whether it would be more meritorious to give alms to one's relatives rather than to others whom we do not know, owing to the equal or greater poverty of those relatives compared to strangers. In that case, in order to avoid the mishaps that can stem from a special affection for one's bloodline, they must leave the decision to one, two, or three persons whose way of life and doctrine are praiseworthy and who will be selected with the approval of their superior.

THE LAWYER, continuing: That's where I was waiting for them, having followed step by step their approach. They finally reached the wall, and all that

---

4   "Inordinate affections" [*afecciones desordenadas*] is one of the key terms in Loyola's *Spiritual Exercises* that he borrowed from the late-medieval tradition of the Devotio Moderna. It appears also a few times in the Jesuit Constitutions. See *Constitutions*, 421.

remained was to climb the ladder, or to make a breach in the wall in order to capture the city. What can we hope for from the decision of an arbiter, if not what we read about Quintus Fabius Labeo, who was named arbiter by the Roman Senate, to decide a disagreement over the boundary between Nola and the Neapolitans?[5] He went to that place and, speaking separately with each side, admonished them to give up their individual wishes and to choose peace instead of continuing their discord. Having agreed to this, out of the respect they bore him, they placed the boundary markers where he thought they should be, and he gave the Roman people all the country between the markers about which they were arguing. They couldn't complain about this, Valerius tells us, because they had consulted their prudent counselor; and therefore (that author continued), owing to a dishonest illusion, a new tribute was added for the city. I know very well that my judgment about this will be the subject of calumny, and that some persons will say that the gloze is finding its way into the text, for I bear them a particular animosity. I call upon God as my witness: I've done them no ill, beyond my concern for the public good. I don't envy the other religious orders, except when those who enter them make a present of their possessions: because I don't see them as entering by suborna-tion, but by devotions conducted by the Holy Spirit. But as for the Jesuits, that's a totally different story. Man's hand alone artistically operates there, through a long trema.[6] First, it instructs young children. Be the boys boarding students or be they day students, the Jesuits cast their eyes upon those who behave well; and irrespective of whether the record book shows their inadequacies or their abilities, which (as I have said) is sent to their general, they win them over by appealing bait; and when the students have been won over, the Jesuits make the owners remove their clothes and send the clothes to other countries, to make the boys forget about them. Then, having been caught in the Jesuits' nets, and just when they are on the verge of becoming desperate, the Jesuits pre-vent them from leaving anything for their father, their mother, their relatives, and they give them instead to the poor. But to what poor? They don't offer an explanation. And really, a person's understanding would be very crippled if he didn't grasp that beneath this general situation lies a personal one; and that, by making that choice, this young man will all the sooner collide with the Society to which he is about to devote himself, and which he views as the

---

5   Quinttus Fabius Labeo was a Roman general, consul in 183 BCE, and poet. The anecdote is
    from Valerius Maximus, *Facta et dicta*, bk. 7 ch. 3.
6   A *tresme* (or *tréma*) is a diacritical mark (two dots) that is placed over two consecutive vow-
    els, to show that the vowels are sounded separately. In Pasquier's day the combined vowels
    were perceived as adding length to the syllable.

supporting wall of our Catholic Church. In the end, if this timid conscience writes something about his parents' poverty, they don't want to permit him to be generous toward them; his perplexity is referred to the judgment of two or three of their Jesuits. Isn't all that done by dragging matters out, or by dragging words, in order to tyrannize the poor young man and force him to take the final step, and give his property to this poor Society that is overflowing with so many possessions? Otherwise, if he wanted to disagree and take a contrary position, from the very first he would think that he was a disobedient child, who would bring no devotion to the order. But (since thoughts are free) let's presuppose that these two or three so-called prudent counselors favor the Society. What guarantee would this new Jesuit have, if he contradicted them? He (I say) whom they order about from his very first lesson, and whom they order to forget the holy things that God has given, I mean the love of his father and his mother, in order to obey his superiors. Would he dare raise an eyebrow to show his disagreement? And yet, why would they accuse us of faulty judgment? For, without bargaining so much, they can say that they are the apostles of our day (that's what they called themselves in Portugal), and that just as, in the primitive church of Jerusalem, those who wanted to be Christians were supposed to bring all their possessions and money to the apostles' feet, so do pious and devout souls give away all their possessions. And then, are you telling me that I'm not their humble and very affectionate servant? Besides, in all of Ribadeneyra, I find nothing as fine as what he teaches us about Ignatius and his companions. For some time, they had asserted that they had been living off the Venetians: they would go twice each day, throughout the day, begging for alms, and one of them usually remained at home, to prepare a meal with the small amount they had been given as alms. It was Ignatius who took on that duty, demonstrating in that way that no matter how devout he showed himself to be, his heart was in the kitchen.[7] A lesson that his successors learned very well.

---

7 Cf. Ribadeneyra, *Vita* [131], which describes the stay of Ignatius, Favre, and Laínez just outside the town of Vicenza, in a chapel called San Pietro in Vivarolo: "Twice a day, they went into town to look for food, of which they brought back precious little. For they hardly had enough bread on which to get by. If they came by a little oil or butter (which was extremely rare), they thought it was a great treat. Of the three, one would stay at home, to soften with water the hard and mouldy bread and boil it. This was usually Ignatius."

The University of Paris Was Ruined by the Jesuit's Crafty Liberality When Teaching the Young

THE LAWYER. I want to be more charitable toward them than they've been toward us. Let's not envy them the possessions they earn from their new guests, if they do indeed earn money by reading.[1] They've produced several good men for us, to direct our kingdom. I beg you to tell me, Messieurs, have your children, whom you gave to the Jesuits to be taught, gained some advantage over their companions as far as learning is concerned, or public responsibilities? Have you found in the sovereign courts some presidents or councilors whom the Jesuits have marked, and who are ahead of the others? Not only have I seen none but, to the contrary, either none of them have been admitted, or else, if there are any, their number is very small. In whom you will have observed only somber, gloomy humors that aren't suited for the public. In the other colleges, where they aren't being filled with fantastic monkey-like grimaces, but with the lively spirit of our ancient religion, they are shaped to every duty, be those duties political or be they ecclesiastical. The Jesuits have no aim, other than increasing their republic: that's why (I don't want to lie) their school produces certain outstanding persons: they select their elite scholars. Those are the ones who, during their youth, when they're being seduced by their elders, were caught up by their beguiling and can't extinguish, with age, the natural fire that's in them. Moreover, they are null for the convenience of the public.

And truly, God really did dazzle our eyes, when we first permitted the Jesuits not only to read but to read free of charge; and when we didn't realize that the offering they were making to the University of Paris was like the artificial horse that the Greeks claimed to have made in order to offer it to Palladium, who was inside Troy.[2] A horse, moreover, that carried within it the ruin and destruction of the city. And we stole it from our Jesuits, who were feigning to present it to the Pallas of our France, in Paris, that is, their college. They ruined

---

1 *Lectures*: today we would say teaching. Reading aloud was a serious activity in Pasquier's day. Costly books were read aloud; lectures ("reading") were read aloud. And as the next paragraph shows, in their "republic" (of letters) the Jesuits "read free of charge."

2 In Greek and Roman mythology, the "palladium" (or *palladion*) was a figure of great antiquity on which the well-being of Troy was said to depend. It was a hollow wooden statue of Pallas Athena that Odysseus and Diomedes stole from Troy, before taking the city by the ruse of the Trojan horse.

our great university. A generation of vipers who, as soon as they hatched, killed their mother. For Ignatius and his nine companions had no titles when they presented themselves to Pope Paul III as masters of arts in the University of Paris, as I said earlier. But were we blind when we supposed that those who, by their vows, were professing poverty, both in general and in particular, wanted to, or could, show a generosity worthy of a monarch: that is, teach letters without taking any money? Before their arrival, the university was flourishing: it offered general access to most of the nations of Europe. This can be noted not only by the ancient four great schools that are in the rue du Fouarre,[3] but also by the *procureurs* of the different nationalities who were close to the rector; for there is a school and a *procureur* for the Germanic nation, which included the English, the Scottish, and others. Did people talk about that university? They said that good literature had come from Athens to Rome, to merge, and that Rome merged with Paris. From the very beginning, the children of good French families were taken there to learn; or else they did their next level of study in other cities. And finally, their general meeting place was Paris, where they completed their education. In their colleges, the principals lodged the scholars whom they called boarders and who received modest stipends; and the non-boarders paid at most one or two pennies for the right to enter. The regents received some tips from their auditors: these tips were called *Lendits*,[4] more for some, less for others, as their parents wished; for no one was obligated other than by the shame they felt at the honest generosity of their companions; and acting to that effect, the regent felt no generosity toward them. And yet this was done with such modesty that the regents, having sweated and labored beside these children, would send them off one day to celebrate in a garden, where they once again observed the ancient liberty that the masters had exercised in Rome toward their servants on days when Saturnalia was celebrated.[5] One can't say that, during all these proceedings, there was a single bit of avarice. So, you never saw either principals or regents whose possessions increased greatly. Each one studied as best he could, with no other intention other than to become rich in reputation, and to be surrounded in his studies by a great number of scholars. Just as honor is the only great hope of being spurred on to do well, the principals would strive to outdo one another at seeing who had

---

3   The rue du Fouarre is situated on the Left Bank near the Seine, opposite Notre-Dame. The schools of the Four Nations were located there: France, Normandy, Picardy, and England.

4   Cotgrave defines thusly the *Lendit*: "gate-money, [...] or yearelie presents bestowed by the schollers of Universities (especially those of Paris) on their Tutors."

5   A feast day that the ancient Romans celebrated in honor of the god Saturn, and during which slaves had the right to speak freely to their masters. Saturnalia was celebrated for several days each December. See *Encyclopaedia Britannica*, https://www.britannica.com/topic/Saturnalia-Roman-festival (accessed July 4, 2021).

the best regents, in order to win. In this way, the University of Paris glittered, but then all that noble ambition went up in smoke. They described themselves as protectors of the Catholic religion. By means of which fathers, who could only see the ends of their noses, sent their children there to stay; un-confirmed scholars were happy to save their access to the entrance doors, to save their *lendits*, their candles; and thus did their college swell; and for the pensions of their scholars, these generous Jesuits began to take two or three times more than was taken in the other colleges: a thing that these infatuated fathers didn't deny them. In this manner, the desire of the other regents and readers at the university to show off as they had before gradually slowed down. This was like a spleen within us that can't grow, but that can only diminish the other parts of our body. Thus, the Jesuit's growth, by means of his unwarranted artifice, was the ruination of the University of Paris, which, thanks be to God, is becoming stronger today, ever since the decree of 1594 by the court of the parlement. But what emerged from all that? The principals and the regents, in the midst of their noble avarice, have remained poor; and the Jesuits, in the midst of their intoxicating generosity, became very rich. And that's what Monseigneur du Mesnil, the *avocat général du roi*, wisely told Versoris and Pasquier, communicating the cause of the Jesuits and the university to the *parquet*, that is, to the magistrates known as the *gens du roi*,[6] *Timeo Danaos et dona ferentes.*[7] I see that the curious Jesuit, in his request presented to the king, says that, in Rome, Our Holy Father the Pope assigned to them the instruction of all the nobility and youth of Rome, for a total of two thousand scholars and five seminaries of young Romans, Greeks, English, Germans, Hungarians. We're not jealous of their great happiness, either in Rome or in Italy; and still less will we send it to the Jesuits, who find themselves in a good position. They are permitted to be totally Italian, as long as they skedaddle from our France and let us live in repose: and to this end, I'm giving them these two lines of poetry, to serve as *lettres de dimissoire*:

> *Vos qui cuncta datis (rapitis tamen) ITE ALIO, ite*
> *Coeslestes immò procul abs JESU ITE scelesti.*[8]

---

6   The *gens du roi*, "the king's men" of the parlement, consisted of a *procureur général* (solicitor general), under whom were usually two *avocats du roi* (attorneys general). They were also known as the *parquet*. Together, the king's men represented the monarch's interests before the court.

7   Virgil, *Aeneid*, II, 49, written between 29 and 19 BCE. "I fear the Danaans [Greeks], even when they bear gifts," that is, the Trojan horse mentioned above.

8   *You who give everything (yet you plunder) go to another place, go*
    Rather, go far from Jesus, wicked divines.

Or, by the form known as amplification,[9] let them also take these:

Discere qui gratis soliti, gratisque docere,
Aedificare domos, fucorum alvearia gratis,
Justitiae sanctam gratis corrumpere dextram,
Edicta, intrepidi, contemnere Regia gratis
Testamenta senum captare, et praedia gratis,
Qui populi mores turbatis et otia gratis
Cum tactae nares, hieiri majoris odore,
Cantatis gratis, gratis plorare jubentes,
Sedibus antiquis, mira quos pellitis arte,
Vos ego adoro lubens: O Servatoris Jesu,
Foelices socii, et fatui nova numina secli,
Omnia qui facitis gratis, discedite gratis.[10]

THE NARRATOR-PASQUIER. To while away the time while crossing the mountains, with a very warm heart I give them a poem in Latin that Adrianus Turnebus[11] wrote for them, a few months after their case was tried. It was then translated, verse by verse, by Étienne Pasquier:

---

9   Amplification was a rhetorical device used to embellish a sentence by adding additional information. It was often used when a simple sentence was too abrupt. These structural additions conveyed further meanings by describing and repeating a statement or an idea. The goal was to call the listener's or reader's attention to an idea they might otherwise miss. The Jesuits were often accused of being prolix and over-elaborate in their rhetoric, so this is probably a subtle dig at them.

10   *You that doe brag you freely learne and teach,*
Houses and hives for drones you freely reach.
The course of iustice freely you corrupt,
And Kings Edicts you freely interrupt.
Mens wills and farmes, by you are freely caught,
By you the people freely are made naught.
And when your noses greater gaine doe wind,
You sing your selves, others to mourne you bind
Whom you have coosend of their ancient seates,
Your craft, the Father of his child defeates.
Most willingly (loe here) I honour you,
O, of our Saviour IESVS holy crue:
New Idols, of a new and foolish age,
Freely depart, with all your equipage.

11   Adrianus Turnebus (1512–65) was Pasquier's relative. A classical scholar, he became a professor at the Collège Royal in 1547. His works consist chiefly of philological dissertations; commentaries on various Greek and Latin authors of antiquity, plus translations of Greek authors into Latin and French. Kurt Sier, "Turnebus, Adrianus," in *Brill's New*

On the generosity of the Jesuits, a poem by Adrianus Turnebus

Among the leading and most recommendable persons of our century, for his good life, his morals, and his Catholic religion, and in all sorts of literature, in the University of Paris we had the great Adrianus Turnebus, king's professor, praised and honored by all the writers who have written about him since his death: among others, Génébrard,[12] archbishop of Aix, in his *Chronographie: Adrianus Turnebus, in Graecis Praeceptor meus, Professor Regium, natus annos 53, obit Lutetiae prid. Id. Jun. 1565.*[13]

Catholicus, etsi haeretici contrarium spargere conati sunt.[14] This learned religious glories at having had him as a preceptor, and bears witness to his Catholic faith, a testimonial that, all alone, is worth one hundred others. I believe that the Jesuits would not be distressed at receiving honest praise for them, written in Latin verse, shortly before his death, and then made French, line by line, and printed in Paris.

In Sotericum gratos docentem

Te gratis narras, Soterice, velle docere,
Ut gratis agat ergo tuo suadeto patrono
Qui vocem multo vaenalem venditat auro,
Procurator item facito tuus improbet aurum,
Summittatque genu, nulla mercede redemptus,
Quinetiam santum te quaeso doceto Senatum,
Ne petat à nostro statui sibi commoda Rege,

Pauly Supplements I – Volume 6: History of Classical Scholarship: A Biographical Dictionary, ed. Chad M. Schroeder, http://dx.doi.org/10.1163/2214-8647_bnps6_COM_00711 (accessed March 1, 2021).

Note: Pasquier's allusion to Turnebus adds that he was "my preceptor in Greek, Royal professor, born 53, died in Paris on the ides of June 1565." The numbers appear to be related to Génébrard's birth year, but they may have been inverted. At any rate, Turnebus was not born in 1553. For a letter to Turnebus from Pasquier on the art of translating, see Étienne Pasquier, *Choix de lettres sur la littérature, la langue et la traduction*, ed. Dorothy Thickett (Geneva: Droz, 1956), 131–38.

12   Gilbert Génébrard (1535–97), a Benedictine monk, was professor of Hebrew and exegesis at the Collège Royal. His four-volume *Chronographiae libri IV* was published in Paris. He was one of the most learned professors at the University of Paris, and he became famous throughout Europe for his writings. See https://www.jewishvirtuallibrary.org/g-x00e9-n-x 00e9-brard-gilbert-x00b0 (accessed March 1, 2021).

13   "Adrien Turnèbe, my preceptor in Greek, Royal Professor, born in 1553, died in Paris on the Ides of June 1565."

14   A Catholic, even if heretics have tried to spread the opposite.

Sportellasque dari. Sed Procurator opellam
Si vendit, si Caussidicus sua verba locare
Consuevit, si legitima mercede Senator
Donatur, decus ut queat ordinis inde tueri,
Stoica quae dicis credent paradoxa forenses?
Lucra aspernanti nemo tibi credet eorum.
Illa fori quaecumque vides subsellia, quaestus
Implet, et augustum magna emolumenta tribunal,
Quae si quis tollat, fuerit mox Curia sola.

Te simulatorem, comoedumque esse putabunt,
Nec stipe contentum censebunt esse minuta,
Sed testamentis inhiare, lucrisque beatis,
Insidiatorem captatoremque loquentur,
Atque eleemosinas avertere pauperis, atque
Amplas sectari praedas, contemnere parvas.
Mallem equidem tibi grata foret mercedula parva.
Quam congesta simul Claromontana talenta,
Judicio quae ferre rapax conaris iniquo.
Debita pauperibus, non nexae ad guttura vesti.
Sed pietas jam nota tua est, animusque benignus,
Magna petis, qui parva fugis, pietatis avarae
Hujus amore tuum pectus fervescit et ardet,
Nemo velit quisquam caussa stipis esse latronum
In numero, majora cupit, spoliare paratus.
Et jugulare homines, queis sit dare praemia promptus,
Ut trahat in fraudem, spoliisque exinde fruatur;
Exiguum sic tu pretium contemnere suetus,
Illicis ut jugules, fortunisque omnibus orbes,
Evertasque bonis, exhaeredesque propinquos.
Et testatoris censu potiaris opimo,
Cui curatorem Praetor dare debuit olim.
Eia age nobiscum sic quaeso paciscere, triplex
Accipias pretium, legataque cuncta relinquas.
Abstineasque manus alieno, et munera temnas:
Verum hoc Harpyiam certò nolle pacisci,
Gratuitum jactare igitur nolito laborem,
Quando in fortunas praedo grassaris opimas.

Quid quod cum soleas quartus, quintusve docere,
Fucorum ignavas pecudes praesepe saginat
Mille, quibus nec discendi, nec cura docendi?
At nemo nostrum sese tolerare potis sit
Mercede, ignavos nedum nutrire queamus:
Praeterea quare affectas in ea urbe Professor
Esse, Professores aliis quae mittere suevit?
Discipulos quae vix, tot habet, quot docta Magistros
Ostendunt festis ut compita pieta Calendis.
Unum assem quoniam discentibus ipse remittis,
Iccirco-ne urbeis rodent pecuaria mandrae
Ignavae, phariaeque examina saeva locustae?
Questiculum justum qui negligit, imputat idque
Civibus, et regno, et prorsus se pernegat esse
Cuiquam oneri, nec habet fundatas censibus ullis
Queis sese tueatur opes, censore Catone,
Exuviis hominum et praeda pascatur oportet.
Mercedem cur quae debetur, negligis illam
Quae non debetur tamen exigis? ede quid illi
Sint abs te docti, quorum bona predo tulisti,
Quorum Legatis nunc fortunatus abundas.
Hoc tibi propositum est, haec mens, cumulare bonorum
Congeriem, villas et praedia quaerere multa,
Atque potestatem vitaeque necisque parare
In stupidum vulgus, quod tu cum feceris, hortos
Mox Epicuraeos, segnisque, saturque petesses.
Grammaticosque omneis, Doctores, atque Magistros.
Discipulorum inter cathedras plorare jubebis.

Against the Jesuit who teaches free of charge

You tell us, Blockhead, that you read free of charge,
See to it, then, that your Lawyer pleads free of charge,
In the Palais he sells his tongue for its weight in gold,
See to it that your procureur is still working for you
And is bending his knee with no hope of wages.
See to it that this holy Senate with which you are dealing,
Gets wages from the king with scorn and with horror,
With no living bribes: but if the procureur
Sells himself, if the lawyer likewise praises his language,

If the Senate cannot live without fair wages,
In order to uphold its rank by making a gain,
And if it really believes in your frivolous tomorrow,
It will believe that you are avoiding the profit that plagues you.
This royal tribunal, this magnificent seat.
While waiting for profit, swells up these men's pleas,
And without him this great Palais would be deserted.

For this they'll think you a joker or a hypocrite,
Who won't take a little piece of paper into account,
While you bay at the last wills of old women,
They'll call you a deceiver who, seeing things obliquely,
Gathers up what should have gone to alms for the poor,
Leaving the least in order to be better rewarded,
Of course, I'd be happier if you were content
With little, rather than amass Clermont's possessions,
Stolen by you, and which you turn into a trophy,
Possessions for the poor, not for a clasp for your robe.
But piety is already too manifest for us,
You flee low things, to make a conquest in a higher place,
With miserly piety, your heart boils and burns:
If one does not want to share in a theft,
The clever assassin aspires to still greater gain,
By fine semblances of the self he attracts the passer-by,
Whom he robs when he can, then gropes in his blood;
Thus do you spy on the spoils of the world,
Which you want to strangle, and pay little in return,
So that the maker of the last will, surprised by you,
Will frustrate his heir with a fine inheritance,
That will-maker who shouldn't have a guardian.
Draw up that bargain with us, I beg you,
See that you are paid three times: but forget
These presents, stay distant from these legacies:
But, Oh, Harpy, don't make this agreement;
Don't make your generosity public knowledge,
You who, like a brigand, overrun our faculties.

What? You let one plus one, and no more, stir in their seats?
And you let a thousand silly molting goslings live beneath you,
Who don't want to teach or see a single book,

While we can barely live on what we earn,
To the point that we can't nourish so many beasts?
Moreover, why must you loan the regents
This place that bestows thousands upon others?
A place that is almost more full of regents than of scholars,
As month after month, the painted crossroads sign teaches you;
And because your hand doesn't grab a single little coin
From the listener, must such vermin
Lodge in our bosom, gnaw at us, undermine us?
Who, when gaining a little, says it should be ignored
And who wants to list it as an item in a financial register,
To unburden the common people, and yet there is nothing
To live on: there is no eye that doesn't very clearly see
That this person is nourished by theft and larceny.

Verily, how is it that the gain that's due you, doesn't please you,
And the person who does, will you take him? Show me
A learned sample that came from you,
From those who, by their legacies, have taken you as their object.
But this is your real aim, your plan, your project,
To acquire lands, possessions, to amass a little heap
Of silver, and to give you everything as spoils:
Then, when you have done that, like Epicurus,
You'll live with your belly full, far from cares, far from worries,
Oh, Bacon Fat, stuffed and at ease, you are making fun
Of a poor master of arts who weeps at his desk.

CHAPTER 7

The Jesuit Sect Has Encountered Peter Abelard's Heresy on Several Occasions

THE NARRATOR. In his plea, having remonstrated about the impiety and blasphemy of Postel, the Jesuit, Pasquier attacked their metaphysician, Maldonado.[1] Approximately six weeks or two months earlier, before a large audience made up of young children who were teasing his spirit, Maldonado gave two contradictory lessons at the Deity's expense. In the first lesson, by natural reasons he attempted to prove that there is a God; and by the second, to prove that there is no God. Today the Jesuits, by the pen of René de La Fon,[2] maintain that the Diety should be proved by natural reasons, or that the for and the against should be argued: and that a person who takes a contrary position and who simply stops at faith, is impious. This proposition, along with what I've seen them practicing since they came to Paris and lodged here, makes me think of Peter Abelard,[3] who was fiercely set upon by Saint Bernard: and I think that I won't be doing anything inappropriate, if I tell you the tale, and then compare him to the Jesuits. Ignatius even had, as his first schoolmaster in Barcelona, a man named Ardebal.[4] You will note that Abelard is an anagram, without a single letter being dropped.

Peter Abelard was born into a very old and very noble Breton family. As the eldest son, he was privileged over his four younger brothers. (In that region,

---

1   See Chapter 3 above.

2   See Book 1, Chapter 5.

3   Peter Abelard (1079–1142) was a Scholastic philosopher as well as a theologian and logician. His teaching career ended circa 1136, when he was accused of heresy. He challenged Bernard of Clairvaux (1090–1153) to withdraw his accusations or else to accuse Abelard publicly. Bernard avoided this trap, however, and called a private meeting of the assembled bishops, persuading them to condemn, one by one, each of the heretical propositions he attributed to Abelard. Refusing to answer to these propositions, Abelard left the assembly, appealed to the pope, and set off for Rome, hoping that the pope would be more supportive. But the pope excommunicated him. Not long before Abelard's death, he and Bernard were reconciled. Abelard's love affair with Héloïse scarcely needs recounting here, beyond the sketch that Pasquier provides for his readers. See *Encyclopaedia Britannica*, https://www.britannica.com/biography/Peter-Abelard (accessed March 1, 2021).

4   Jerónimo Ardévol (?–1551), who taught Latin in Barcelona, promised to teach Ignatius free of charge. See George E. Ganss, ed. *Ignatius of Loyola: The Spiritual Exercises and Selected Works* (New York: Paulist Press, 199), 35.

this right was no small thing.) He left them all his possessions, in order to devote himself totally to letters, in which he had already made great progress before leaving Brittany. But in order to be more accomplished, he wanted to be at the fountainhead of letters. There, he met two great masters: Guillaume de Champeaux in philosophy,[5] and Anselm in theology,[6] who taught a variety of subjects at the bishopric, where the university was housed. Abelard hadn't studied much philosophy, but since his spirit was great, albeit extravagant, he had a great advantage over his companions, and he even equaled Champeaux, his teacher; and without earning a license, and owing to his reputation, he occupied a chair. Having defended, he went to teach at Corbeil, near Melun; he then returned to Paris, where he read aloud outside the city walls. For a while after that, he studied theology under Anselm, making good progress. And by more extraordinary self-assurance, he began to teach without having been approved by the university, thereby making all the older teachers discontented, but not the young people, who usually enjoy such novelties. Since he believed in all these things beyond measure, an unmeasurable misfortune happened to him: for he impregnated a well-brought-up girl named Héloïse and was forced to marry her secretly in order to satisfy her uncle, a canon in Paris. Then, wanting to have this marriage annulled, he sent his wife to a convent for women at Argenteuil. The uncle was offended, and shortly after that, had someone cut off Abelard's privy parts, which had led him to err. Finally, overwhelmed with shame, and his wounds having healed, he became a monk at the abbey of Saint-Denis-en-France, and Héloïse became a veiled nun at the priory of Argenteuil. Yet that restless spirit could not be contained in the ancient discipline of our church. For he began to teach in his monastery, teaching both philosophy and theology, and he attracted to him an infinite number of scholars. The University of Paris began grumbling about him to the prelates. He himself didn't hide this in a long letter (a general collection of texts about his life) from which I copied this passage: *Cum autem in divina Scriptura non minorem gratiam, quam in seculari, mihi Dominus contulisse videretur, coeperunt admodum ex utraque lectione scholae nostrae multiplicari, et caeterae vehementer omneis attenuari. Unde maximè Magistrorum invidiam*

---

5   Guillaume de Champeaux (*c.*1070–1121), latinized as Gulielmus de Campellis. He taught at the school of Notre-Dame of Paris; among his pupils was Abelard. When Abelard replaced Champeaux, Abelard called him the "supreme master" of dialectic. See *Encyclopaedia Britannica*, https://www.britannica.com/biography/William-of-Champeaux (accessed March 1, 2021).

6   Anselm of Laon (?–1117) taught Abelard in and later expelled him from the cathedral school of Laon (not, as Pasquier implies, Paris). He oversaw the compilation of the "glossa ordinaria," the standard medieval scriptural commentary. See *Encyclopaedia Britannica*, https://www.britannica.com/biography/Anselm-of-Laon (accessed March 1, 2021).

atque odium adversum me concitavi. Qui in omnibus quae poterant, mihi derogantes, duo praecipuè absenti semper objiciebant: quod scilicet proposito Monachi valdè sit contrarium, secularium librorum studio detinexi, et quod sine Magistro ad Magisterium divinae lectionis accedere praesumpsissem, ut sic inde omne mihi doctrinae scholaris exercitium interdiceretur. Ad quod incessanter, Episcopos, Archiepiscopos, Abbates, et quascumque poterant Religiosi nominis personas incitabant.[7] A passage, about which I'll point out in passing, that it serves infinitely the point I'm making: just as this was deemed credible when read, it was likewise credible when written: for he wrote a book called *De unitate et trinitate divina,* in favor of his disciples (so he said) *qui humanas et Philosophicas rationes requiebant, et plus quàm intelligi, quàm quae dici possint, efflagitabant. Dicentes quidam verborum superfluam esse prolationem, quam intelligentia non sequeretur: nec credi posse aliquid nisi prius intellectum, et ridiculosum esse aliquem aliis praedicare, quod ne ipse, nec illi quos doceret, intellectu capere possent: Domino ipso arguente, quod caeci essent ductores caecorum.*[8] This book offended the entire French clergy. The church council met in the city of Soissons, presided over by Cuno, bishop of Praeneste, legate for the Holy See in France.[9] From the bishop's mouth, Abelard heard his book read aloud. It was finally declared heretical, and it was ordered burned in the market square. And the author of the book should be confined forever to the monastery of Saint-Médard, and he was specifically forbidden to go outside. He had several student scholars, some of whom had been made

---

7 "Since the Lord had apparently blessed me with no less persuasiveness in expounding the Scriptures than in lecturing on secular subjects, the numbers of my students in these two courses began to increase greatly and the attendance at all the other schools was correspondingly diminished. Thus, I aroused the envy and hatred of the other teachers. They always sought to belittle me in everything that they could, taking advantage of my absence, they brought two principal charges against me: namely, that it was contrary to the monastic profession to be concerned with the study of secular books; and second, that I had presumed to teach theology without ever having been taught therein myself. This they did in order that my teaching of every kind might be prohibited, and to this end they continually stirred up bishops, archbishops, abbots and whatever other dignitaries of the church they could reach."

8 "They kept asking about rational and philosophical expositions and were insisting more upon what could be understood than mere declarations; saying that a flow of words is useless if reason does not follow them, that nothing could be believed unless it was first understood and that it is ridiculous for a man to proclaim to others what neither he nor his pupils can grasp by their intelligence: the Lord himself had argued that they were the blind leaders of the blind."

9 Cuno, or Conon (?–1122), bishop of Praeneste, cardinal, and papal legate, was an influential figure in diplomacy. See Rainer Berndt, *Schrift, Schreiber, Schenker: Studien zur Pariser Abtei Sankt Viktor in Paris und den Viktorinern* (Berlin: Akademie-Verlag, 2005), 111.

cardinals and who brought him near to Pope Innocent II.[10] To the point that, by their intercession, he found a way to be rehabilitated at the monastery of Saint-Denis, where he again did something crazy and was almost scourged. Finally, he received permission from the king to withdraw to Champagne, and there he built an oratory that he dedicated to the Trinity, more out of vengeance than devotion, in order to wager everything upon it and against those who had condemned his book. But, seeing that this displeased the prelates, and that he risked being censured once again, he changed the name to Paraclete (which means Consoler), especially dedicated to the Holy Spirit: it meant that this place had been the harbor of his consolation, after he had encountered tempests and storms. This too displeased our church, as he himself tells us. For all the churches (that's what I understand him to be saying) were consecrated to the name of God the Father, God the Son, or the blessed Holy Spirit. To that objection he, who was a great Sophist, replied that if Paul, talking to the Corinthians,[11] had ordered each person to build in himself a spiritual temple of the Holy Spirit, one ought not to think it wrong to make a material one. In that place, and interested in new things, he opened philosophy and theology schools to the public. This made several curious scholars, hearing of it, leave the cities in order to come and find him, and to remain near him, constructing little lodgings and cells, where they slept on straw: *et pro delicatis cibis* (said he), *herbis agrestibus, et pane pro cibario utebantur*.[12] This really amounted to the creation of a new sect by a person who had been condemned by the church and the university. Preachers declaimed against him, as an arch-heretic, displeasing in this way as many secular seigneurs as ecclesiastics: but above all, Saint Bernard took this quarrel into his own hands, as we learn from his letters. For despite condemnation by the church council, Abelard was stubbornly continuing to teach his error. Protected by favor and by his friends in the Roman Curia, he wrote to Cardinal Yves:[13]

> *Damnatus est Suessione, cum opera suo, coram Legato Romanae Ecclesiae,*
> *sed quasi non sufficeret illi, illa condemnatio interum facit, unde iterum*

---

10   Innocent II was pope from 1130 to 1143. His election was controversial, and he struggled for recognition against the supporters of Antipope Anacletus II (1090–1138). He went on to preside over the Second Lateran Council (1139). See *Encyclopaedia Britannica*, https://www.britannica.com/biography/Innocent-II (accessed March 1, 2021).

11   1 Cor. 3:9–17.

12   For fine food they used bitter herbs and bread for rations.

13   Ivo of Chartres (*c*.1040–1115) was bishop of Chartres from 1090 to his death. He played a very important role in the development of canon law. See *Encyclopaedia Britannica*, https://www.britannica.com/biography/Saint-Ivo-of-Chartres (accessed March 1, 2021).

damnetur, et jam novissimus error pejor est priore. Sequutus est tamen, quoniam Cardinales et Clericos Curiae se discipulos habuisse gloriatur, et eos in defensione praeteriti et praesentis erroris adsumit, à quibus judicari timere debuit, et damnari. And a bit earlier: *Magister Petrus Abelardus, sine regula Monachus, sine sollicitudine Praelatus, nec ordinem tenet, nec ab ordine tenetur. Homo sui dissimilis est, intus Herodes, foris Joannes, totus ambiguus, nihil habens de Monacho, praeter nomen et habitum.*[14] And he wrote to Pope Innocent II: *Habemus in Francia novum, de vetere Magistro, Theologum, qui ab ineunte aetate sua, in arte Dialectica lusit, et nunc in Scripturis sanctis insanit. Olim damnata et sopita dogmata, tam sua videlicet, quàm aliena suscitare conatur, insuper et nova addit. Qui dum omnium quae sunt in coelo sursum, et quae sunt in terra deorsum nihil praeter nescio quid nescire dignatur, ponit in coelo os suum, et scrutatur alta Dei, rediensque ad nos refert verba ineffabilia, quae non licet homini loqui. ET DUM PARATUS EST DE OMNIBUS REDDERE RATIONEM, et contra rationem praesumit et contra fidem. Quid enim magis contra rationem, quam rationem transcendere? Et quid magis contra fidem, quam credere nolle quicquid non possis ratione attingere? Denique exponere volens illus Sapientis: Qui credit citò levis est corde. Citò credere (inquit) est adhibere fidem ante rationem. Cùm hoc Salomon non de fide in Deum, sed de muta inter nos dixerit credulitate. Nam illam quae in Deum est fidem. B. Papa Gregorius plane negat habere meritum, si ei humana ratio praebeat experimentum. Laudat autem Apostolos quod ad unius jussionis vocem, sequuti sint Redemptorem. Scit nimirum pro laude dictum: in auditu auris obediunt mihi: Increpatos è regione discipulos quod tardius credidissent. Denique laudatur Maria quod rationem fide praevenit: et punitur Zacharias, quod fidem ratione tentavit. Et rursum commendatur Abraam qui contra se in spem credidit. At contra Theologus noster: Quid (inquit) ad doctrinam loqui proficit, si quod docere voluimus et exponi, exponi non potest ut intelligatur.*[15]

---

14 "He had been condemned at the Council of Soissons, together with his works, before a legate of the Roman Church, but as though it did not have sufficient weight, the condemnation was repeated, whence he was again condemned, and the most recent error was worse than the former. It happened, however, since he boasted that the cardinals and the curial clergy had been his students, and he included them in the defence of his past and present error, by whom he ought to be afraid to be judged and condemned. [...] Master Peter Abelard, a monk without rule, a priest without a flock, does not belong to an order, and is not protected by an order. He is a man unlike himself, Herod within, outside John, completely ambiguous, having nothing of the monk, beside the name and habit."

15 "We have in France a new theologian, an ex teacher, who from his earliest youth has dabbled in the art of dialectic and now raves about the Holy Scriptures. He tries to raise

Here, wasn't Saint Bernard putting on trial our new Jesuits, when they make it so easy to prove, by their natural reasons, the for and the against the Deity? Saint Bernard (I say), who in this was followed by the archbishop of Reims, the bishops of Soissons, Châlons, and Arras who, at the end of their letter wrote to the same pope: *Quia ergo homo ille multitudinem trahit post se, et populum qui sibi credat, habet, necesse est ut huic contagio, celeri remodio occurratis.*[16] Finally, Pope Innocent interposed his decretal sentence, bearing these words:

> *Communicato fratrum nostrorum Episcoporum et Cardinalium consilio, destinata nobis à vestra discretione, capitula, et universa ipsius Petri dogmata, sanctorum Canonum authoritate, cum suo authore damnavimus, eique tanquam haeretico perpetuum silentium imposuimus. Universos autem erroris sui sectatores et defensores, a fidelium consortio sequestrandos, excommunicationisque vinculo innodandos esse censemus.*[17]

The Jesuits say that Pasquier impiously accused of impiety the Jesuit Maldonado (those are the words they used) because in one of his lessons he had proved to

---

teachings, once condemned and silenced, both his own and others, and has added new ones besides. He who deems to know everything in heaven above and on earth below apart from 'I do not know' lefts his face to heaven and gazes on the depths of God, bringing back to us words that cannot be spoken, which it is not lawful for a man to speak. HE IS EVEN PREPARED TO SUPPLY A REASON FOR EVERYTHING, yet he presumes against reason and against faith. For what is more contrary to reason than to try to transcend reason by means of reason? And what is more contrary to faith than not to want to believe whatever cannot be arrived at by means of reason? And finally wanting to explain those lines of the wise man: He who believes quickly, is light of heart. To believe quickly, he said, to put faith before reason. Since Solomon said this not about faith in God, but mutual belief among us. For Blessed Pope Gregory clearly said that the faith that is in God, had merit, if human reason presents experience of it. However, he praises the Apostles because at the voice of one command, they followed Our Saviour. He evidently knows the saying for faith: 'They obey me in the hearing of their ears'. The disciples from the local area protested because they had believed too late. And finally, Mary is praised because she anticipated reason with faith; and Zacharias, because he tested faith with reason. And again, Abraham is commended, who believed against himself in hope. But on the contrary our Theologian said: 'What does it profit to speak about doctrine, if that which we wanted to teach and explain, cannot be explained so that it is understood.'"

16   "And so, because that man draws a crowd behind him and has people who believe in him, it is necessary you encounter this contagion with a swift cure."

17   "On the advice received by our brother bishops and cardinals, and chapters sent to us at your discretion, we have condemned the universal dogma of this Peter, on the authority of the holy canons, together with their author, and we have imposed perpetual silence on him as tough a heretic. We have decreed that all sectarians and defenders of his error be kept from consort with the faithful and be bound by the chain of excommunication."

his scholars, by natural reasons, that there is a God, and in the other lesson had proved that there is none. And they themselves are all heretics by the proposition they support when, wanting to lift the wings of their spirits higher than heaven, they fall into the depths of the abysses of hell; or else Pope Innocent II, Saint Bernard, and our entire Gallican church were wrong. But because this isn't the goal at which I'm aiming, but only examines the deformities and the conformities between Ignatius and his circle on the one hand, and Abelard, that great heretic and disrupter of our University of Paris, on the other, I'll tell you, first, that both of them were born into lofty and noble families. The difference between them was that Abelard was older than his brothers; Ignatius was younger. Abelard was learned, with a great mind; Ignatius had not studied literature. That's why Abelard wanted to build a lion-like sect and, by that means, succumb beneath the burden of his hopes; and Ignatius built a fox-like sect that, by that means, made root cuttings for it. But if one ignores these differences, they concur on several other things. Abelard wrote a book about the Trinity that was condemned by the church; Ignatius wrote a book on the same subject, a book that he himself condemned, showing by this that he was wiser and more astute than Abelard. Although Abelard didn't earn a license degree, from the beginning he wanted a chair, so that he could read at the University of Paris.[18] The same thing was done, not by Ignatius, who was ignorant, but by his Jesuit disciples. For you won't find him saying that none of the very first regents who read at the University of Paris had graduated.

Abelard, a religious of Saint-Denis, taught not only philosophy but also theology: that's what our Jesuit religious do. Back then, didn't the university disapprove of a monk's teaching philosophy to foreign scholars and outlanders? That's one of the university's principal complaints about the Jesuits. Abelard taught theology without having earned a license, something about which the prelates of France complained. He was doing nothing that the Jesuits haven't done since and are continuing to do today. It's one of the university's principal complaints about the Jesuits. Abelard was condemned by our Gallican church: Ignatius and his disciples were first condemned by the Faculty of Theology of Paris, and then by our clergy, assembled at Poissy. Abelard introduced the heresy of wanting to prove, by natural reasons, something that depends on our Christian faith. The Jesuits not only agree with that damnable opinion, they also maintain that it is impious and atheistic to believe in God with all humility, and not to approve that for natural reasons, one can prove to children that there is a God, and that there is no God.

---

18   Neither academic degrees nor the University of Paris existed in Abelard's lifetime, something Pasquier himself had shown.

Abelard received great support from the cardinals in the Roman Curia; and that's what is dooming us today. For not only are the Jesuits in great favor there, but they also go too far and call everyone a heretic who doesn't acquiesce to their heresies. Abelard was a religious who was not religious, who only wore the garb of a religious. This provoked Saint Bernard to say that he was *sine ratione Monachus, qui nec ordinem tenebat, nec tenebatur ab ordine*.[19] I beg you to tell me what order the Jesuits keep, and in what order they are kept. True, on his exterior, Abelard looked like a Saint John the Baptist, but inside he was a Herod. As for our Jesuits, I've never identified a Saint John the Baptist in their preaching, but I've overly much recognized a Herod as far as cruelty goes, having princes assassinated and chasing them from their kingdoms and their principalities. There's also a disproportion: for the latter persons feast on bacon fat, and by their Constitutions they aren't obligated to observe unusual fasts, as other religious orders are. On the contrary, the disciples and partisans of Abelard slept on straw in little huts; and to live, they were satisfied with bread and herbs from the fields. Lastly, from a sort of partiality, Abelard took that great and holy name Paraclete, for which we condemned him; and with the same zeal, the Jesuits have taken the name Jesus, which they've been forbidden to do.

Conclusion: despite the discontent of our prelates, the name Paraclete survived for Abelard's oratory, which today is called by a corrupted name, Paraclit, which is a religious order of nuns whose first abbess was Abelard's wife. Likewise, the name Jesus has remained with our Jesuits, in order to enjoy Abelard's privileges in everything, and everywhere. And as far as I can judge, I haven't found a sole one who was more pleasant to encounter than the Jesuit in 1594, who defended the Collège de Clermont when Arnauld, having anew, and in the full parlement, objected to the name and the title Jesuit.[20] He replied mockingly: Monsieur Pasquier objected to that in the past, and that was years ago. There's one more thing to say about the general comparison between Abelard and our Jesuits: Saint Bernard, that great person, talked to the Holy See about those new disrupters of our church and our universities. When I get to him, I'll show that God had spread, in his soul, the rays and sparks of his Holy Spirit, as much as, and more than, any man who is still alive.

19   A monk without reason, who neither belonged to an order nor was acknowledged by any
      order.
20   See Book I, Chapter 5.

Jesuits Claim the Right to Remove from Their College Children Who Are in the Guardianship of Their Fathers and Their Mothers, without Their Permission

Since Jesuits put every bit of the Holy Scripture to work, not in order to sustain our church but merely to sustain their sect, they maintain that they can attract any child to them, despite their fathers and mothers, as something unnecessary, for the love and honor of God. A rule they observe very religiously for children from good families, against whom they can commit some aggression. They caused the disappearance of a young fifteen-year-old child, the older son of Ayrault,[1] the *lieutenant criminel* for the court of the *présidial* of Angers, a person who is unusually praise-worthy, and who asked if he could petition the court of the Parlement of Paris to have him reunited with his son. Both sides having been amply heard, that court, by its decree of May 20, 1586, ordered that he be instructed to provide further information about the Jesuits' inducements toward his son. Meanwhile, it is prohibited and forbidden for the provincial, rector, and principal of the Collège de Clermont to attempt anything against the requests presented by Ayrault, nor to receive his son into the Society under penalty of a fine: and by the same means, they were enjoined to communicate that decree to the other colleges of their Society. This, despite the fact that these beatific fathers didn't want to return the child, which was why this poor father was forced to resort to tears, then to his pen, and to print a book about paternal power. In it he demonstrates that the Jesuits are impudently taking advantage of passages from the Holy Scripture: indeed, they are taking them crudely and

---

1   This incident involved Pierre Ayrault (1536–1601) and his son René Ayrault (1567–1644), who later was a professor of rhetoric and rector at several Jesuit colleges. The son was calling himself a Jesuit. For more on *De la Puissance paternelle* (Tours: Jamet Mettayer, 1593), see Simon Goulart, *Mémoires de la Ligue* (Amsterdam: Arkstée and Merkus, 1758), 6:156. This is not the first time the Society was accused of this sort of kidnapping. Take Octavian César, the fifteen-year-old son of the secretary to the duke of Monteleone: Cardinal Caraffa upheld the parents' right, but the pope intervened in Ignatius's favor. In the end, the boy decided not to remain with the Jesuits (Sutto, 267n159). On the context of this issue, see Barbara Diefendorf, "Give us Back our Children: Patriarchal Authority and Parental Consent to Religious Vocation in Early Counter-Reformation France," *Journal of Modern History* 68 (1996): 265–307.

© KONINKLIJKE BRILL NV, LEIDEN, 2021 | DOI:10.1163/9789004164062_028

literally, as the Jesuits did to the father's disadvantage. He presents himself as an upright and honorable man would, a man who felt pain at having his son stolen from him. I'll speak about it dispassionately, and I'll say that it's hard to see a child become a religious against his father and mother's wishes, even if the child wants it. And yet I deem the boy not only excusable but praiseworthy, when, having reached a competent age, he goes to a monastery, although his father and mother aren't happy about it: but when subornation by monks is involved, it merits an unusual punishment.

For several years they've been trying to blame the Carthusians of Paris for having deceived the father, and for having received a young man into their religious order. The prior was therefore summoned by the court of the Parlement; and with admirable self-assurance he maintained that he'd been instructed to smooth things over. "We do not go to seek them out (said he). We live a solitary life, far from the city, but still in the city. We do not attract them to us by lessons or by the spoken word. To the contrary, we make a very free profession of silence, and our monks talk to no one without the superior's permission. If some mature person, impelled by the grace of the Holy Spirit, wants to become one of us, why would we tamper with his wishes when the young person is disposed to such devotions? That would mean being envious of God over a beautiful communion host that is going to be sacrificed, and we would be traitors to the general good of the church if we behaved otherwise." Having heard the arguments, the court sent the case to a higher court, which it hadn't done for the Jesuits in the Ayrault case. You'll understand later why there were such diverse reasons. If a wish could be made about these matters, before all the children became monks, I'd want all of them to follow in the footsteps of Elisha,[2] who didn't want to give himself to Elijah until he had first taken leave of his father. And if they happen not to do so, having simply won themselves over through God's inspiration, I don't believe (and I'll repeat it) they can be blamed, nor can the monastery that received them. But as for the Jesuits, it's a totally different conversation; and I recall that one day I happened to be with a poor, deranged father whose child had been stolen and taken away. Yielding passionately to his anger, he spoke as follows to the rector of the Parisian Jesuits:

> I did not give you my child to make a Jesuit of him, but to instruct him in humane letters, and not to make a mistake and stray from our Catholic religion, with the intention of making him the successor of my wishes, my property, and my rank, deeming that you had some religion in your

2   1 Kings 19:20.

soul. But where, wretched man, did you find that, by auricular confession and a false devotion, by hypocritical words, by a filthy-faced clown, you were permitted to induce my poor child to be stolen away from his father, in order to steal him away from God? That's why I will not call it robbing God, when, for his first devotional step, you are teaching him to hide from his father? Innocent, I say, when, in the weakness of his age and his spirit, you gave him the leisure to recognize, over time, what he was promising to God, by making the vow of a monastic order. An acrobat of our Christian religion, who does slight of hand in order to make a child pass, by *invisibilium* (he's there, he isn't there), in order to turn him away from his father's presence and from the magistrate's presence. And then, as a general refrain, we hear that it is the work of the Holy Spirit, who is continually in your mouth, just as prostitutes only sing about their chastity. Do you deem yourself unfortunate that my first project was to prepare him to wear my robe?[3] If, however, having left the family house and having reached the age of discretion, he wanted to leave the world, would I envy his happiness? Not to make a gypsy of him, who flits as you do, in front of everyone, feigning to tell a favorable fortune for everyone, yet unable to tell it to himself; but in order to fit him into the mold of our antique religions, and with one hand enclose him in a cloister, to lead a solitary life, to see to one's fasting, prayers, and *oraisons*, to wear that hairshirt, and to see to it that his cloister was a *palais* to him,[4] that fish were like manna from heaven, that a hairshirt was as soft as a linen shirt. And after the solitude passed in long night watches and devotions, he left his monastery like a strong and valiant warrior, not in order to assassinate kings, not in order to conquer kingdoms and turn them over to the princes who will pay the most, but in order to assassinate sin and to conquer lost souls, preaching in the midst of churches what should have belonged to eternal beatitude. I don't ask the judges of the world to seek revenge for what it cost you (detestable deceiver). The great Judge of Judges will avenge me: but that will not happen until the magistrate has been chastised, either by fear or by his long connivance in abetting a crime. Later, he will toss you into the fire, as the father tosses the willow switch with which he has chastised his children.

---

3 That is, to wear the long or the short robe that identified someone as holding a specific position in the legal profession.

4 Robe and *Palais*: the son may be a religious, but his father continues to see him as a lawyer who wears a distinctive robe to indicate that he has purchased an office in the Parlement, which was housed in the *Palais* (Palace) on the Île de la Cité.

In the Jesuit college of Paris, I saw a poor father playing in this way with his documents: and to tell the truth, I would have liked that upright man to dilute his anger a bit more, for it seemed to be exceeding the limits of modesty. But what modesty would you desire in a father whose child has been stolen? He must, of necessity, lose patience. Indeed, here's the just anguish of a poor, weeping father who wasn't lamenting that his son had become a religious, but who was lamenting that the Jesuits had done it by seductions, subornations, and impostures. Have you ever heard tell that it's a great weight on one's conscience, when we marry our children while they are quite young, because we teach them to hate their wives before they've learned to love them? It's the same way with young children who are tricked into this spiritual marriage. For although everything smiles on them when they first enter, thanks to the charms and sweet attractions of their confessors, and although they later have imprinted in their souls a long repentance for their flightiness: they curse the year, the month, the week, the day, the hour, and the moment when they were thus deceived. And although a few of them get dispensations, their number is small. Besides, as much, and as long as we mingle the instruction of the young with this so-called monkery, we'll never be able to escape this wretched confusion. From which, thanks be to God, the city of Paris is today preserved. But I'm addressing those who deceive, and who cover this new monster with their authority.

CHAPTER 9

Concerning the First Vow Made by the Jesuits, Which They Call the Simple Vow

THE LAWYER. Having proposed to discuss eventually the vows made by our Jesuits, I'm vowing not to combat them with anything but their own weapons. In the past, they've been so wary that very few people knew about their affairs. Today, printed copies of their bulls and their statutes are in their colleges; but the name of the printer is omitted, and they don't easily pass from one outsider's hands to another's. That's why, in the past, one didn't talk about them so brashly: but the force of truth is such that, with time, the truth is uncovered; and so, the cabal of these old teaching savants couldn't be kept so secret, and in the course of time, their books made their way out of their colleges. On those books I've modeled the present speech. I'll begin with their simple vow, a vow I can assert is new, prodigious, and which cannot be tolerated in our church without that church toppling, at least as far as religious orders and monasteries are concerned. Judging from the lesson that the Jesuit taught us yesterday, you'll understand that the first vow of their order is the one they call simple. By it, the person who vows to be a member of the religious family first makes three vows that are common to other religious orders: chastity, poverty, and obedience. And after that time, as far as vows are concerned, he can't terminate the agreement; but it is in the general's power to do so whenever he wishes, and to send him home, even if he's been a Jesuit for ten or twenty years, and even longer. And if he's established in that simple vow, he's capable of inheriting anything, be it direct or collateral, despite the vow of poverty that he's made. Let's not rob them of the honor due the one and the other, and let's see the Jesuit Montaignes's comments about this.

By these speeches (said Montaignes, addressing Arnauld), two lies that you told will be refuted. One lie is that the vow of poverty is never administered until every hope of inheriting is lost; for it is administered at the end of the novitiate, as was mentioned. If, despite that vow of poverty, they retain some hope of having control over their possessions for several years, with the approval of their superiors, AND ARE CAPABLE OF INHERITING, don't be scandalized, and don't, for that reason, call the Jesuits avaricious. This waiting period is not for them: they have renounced their right, as I have already said. It is for the convenience and utility of the persons involved. For, it being lawful that, for just causes, they be dismissed from the Society, according to its privileges they do not undergo any prejudice, and they can live on their means; or, on the other hand, having been stripped of possessions, they will be needy, or will beg, or will remain in the Society, which not only will find it inconvenient and prejudicial but will also be concerned about their bodies, and still more about their souls. This is a new right (say you), it is my right. It is new and marvelous, says Navarrus, the great canonist. It is a new right, as well as the simple vow of chastity that those of this Society take, and that prevents marriage, and annuls it when it has been contracted. But still it is a right, although a new one, being made by the prince and head of the church, who created the right of the other religious orders, and the rest of canon law. This novelty does not prevent the nature of a thing. Are new grapes just as much grapes as those on the vine planted by Noah? Every right is new when it begins, yet it did not cease being a right. Sixteen hundred years from now, that right will be older than the canons of the apostles are today. The second lie to be refuted by this same speech is that the Jesuits send people away, once they have exhausted themselves by laboring. For, since they are not retained because of the hope of acquiring their possessions, they are not sent away because they are poor, but for another just reason. Otherwise, in the end they would have to dismiss everyone who makes a profession, that is, those who are stripped of every possession; and they would not receive anyone who isn't rich, which they don't do. If there is some difficult person who wants to correct himself, after having been bandaged and purged for a long while, he bears the burden of the troubles that result from his duress, and the Society invokes its right. Which it however does only rarely, and with the authorization of the general alone, and almost always with the approval of those who are sent away, who were not employed, but rather endured; and sometimes one waited ten or twenty years for them to become agreeable. To such a point do they love even those who give them trouble. And thus, you are iniquitous to the Jesuits in everything and everywhere, calumniating them for seducing men and receiving them into their Society, and for sending them away.

"Someone who is more scrupulous and more knowledgeable than you, will ask with what good conscience those who formerly took a religious vow can be sent away and absolved; for this vow is a divine obligation that God alone can fulfill, as a proper right of his domain. To that I reply that the vow obligates the person who makes it, in accordance with his intention. If someone vows to fast in the Carthusian fashion, he obligates himself to fast like the Carthusians, and not like someone in a different order that doesn't observe such fasts. Those who make vows in this Society do it according to the intention and ways of the Society. The intention is that they feel obligated to remain in the order in such a way that if there were a just cause, they can be dismissed and absolved of their obligation. The person who has bound himself in this way is not viewed as being at fault for being constrained to keep his promise or to be dismissed, being either unable or unwilling to do his duty, and correct himself, and carry out the vow. For there was a condition to his vow: *volenti non fit injuria*,[1] and the person who leaves without permission is an apostate and bears the ignominy and the mark of his sin. But if a person can leave by a command of the general, or by or at his good pleasure, JUDGING THAT, FOR SOME NECESSITY OF SPIRIT OR OF BODY, OR OF HIS PARENTS OR OF THE PUBLIC, OR ANOTHER EQUITABLE REASON, HE MUST BE DISMISSED, AND THEN HE REMAINS ABSOLVED OF HIS VOWS."

---

1   *Volenti non fit injuria* (To a willing person, injury is not done). This common-law doctrine states that if someone willingly places himself in a position where harm might result, he cannot bring a claim against the other person.

One Cannot Excuse the Presence of Heresy and Machiavellism in the Jesuits' Simple Vow

THE LAWYER. So much for the Jesuit Montaignes. Here, with clasped hands, I beg Our Holy Father the Pope, and I solemnly request that all the kings, princes, potentates, and lords who fight beneath his standard in our Church Militant, should please unseal their eyes and place each individual's hand on his conscience, for the universal salvation of our Christendom. With whom am I dealing here? With the Jesuits who, replying to Arnauld's plea, thought they would harm their sanctity if, with the simplicity so typical of other people, they had given their speech this title: *Defences au Plaidoyé d'Arnauld*, Legal Defense to Arnauld's Plea. But along with a luxurious title on the front of their book, they put: *La Vérité défendue pour la religion catholique en la cause des jésuites contre le Plaidoyer d'Antoine Arnauld*.[1] I'm citing it in full, and I want to labor with them over the word Catholic. Nothing has been so recommended, and so commanded by God and his church, as maintaining the vows we make to it. I'd be extremely inept with both my time and my pen, if I wanted to prove this by citing passages from the Old and the New Testaments, as well as from the authoritative statements of our ancient doctors of the church. Now, ever since devotion sneaked religious orders and monastic orders into our church, we have introduced, when entering, the three substantial vows: poverty, chastity, and obedience. That rule was so narrowly observed that the pope himself, although he had the plenitude of power over our consciences, nonetheless never opened the door in order to dispense a religious totally, unless it involved favoring a sovereign prince who must meet the very urgent needs of his state. And Our Lord, wanting to show that such dispensations didn't please him, would sometimes interpose the rigor of his justice in good earnest. This was observed long ago in the kingdom of Naples, where the entire royal line ended

---

1 The final quotation in ch. 9 comes from "François des Montaignes," and this paragraph continues the citation. "Montaignes" was, of course, Louis Richeome. The full title was: *La Verité défendue pour la religion catholique en la cause des jésuites contre le Plaidoyer d'Antoine Arnaud par François des Montaignes* (Frankfurt: Vilhem des Sclaffer, 1595), 135–37. Translated, the title reads: "The Truth forbidden for the Catholic religion in the case of the Jesuits against Antoine Arnauld's *Plaidoyer*." (Note: Sutto's bibliography [464] omits *catholique*, the very word that was causing Pasquier problems.)

with Constance,[2] a professed nun. Public necessity seemed to require her to quit the veil in order to renew the royal blood that flowed in her veins. She was absolved from her vow by the Holy See, and she immediately wed Emperor Frederick II. From that union sprang Manfred, and from him came Conradin.[3] But no wedding ever brought more ruin to Italy than this one: because for an infinite amount of time, the pope and the emperor were perpetually divided into Guelphs and Ghibellines. As for their children, they went through many misfortunes: Manfred was killed in battle; and later, his son Conradin was captured by Charles of Anjou,[4] king of Naples, who ordered him beheaded on a scaffold. I have selected this specific example in order to show how much God dislikes these de-monkings, and the authority he gave to Our Holy Father the Pope, who is also accustomed to collecting an infinity of considerations before taking a step forward. But above all, it's a general rule in Rome that, in all families that aren't sovereign, the pope doesn't turn a religious into a layman, but simply commutes the rigor of the first vow into something easier to bear. This took place in France recently. For it so happened that the seigneur of Bouchage, born into a most noble house, became a Capuchin; and after the deaths of all his brothers, the necessities of the time seemed to be calling him back into the world. All that his relatives could obtain from Rome was the commutation of his vow into a vow to the Order of Saint John of Jerusalem.[5] In our Christian church, religious who have vowed poverty are never permitted

---

2   Constance d'Hauteville (1154–98), the daughter of Roger II king of Sicily (1095–1154; r.1130–54), and wife of Henry VI of Hohenstaufen (1165–97; r.1191–97), was the mother of Emperor Frederick II (1194–1250; r.1220–50). In 1198, she had three-year-old Frederick crowned king of Sicily with herself as regent, and in his name, she dissolved the ties her late husband had created between the government of Sicily and the empire. She was not betrothed until she was thirty; this fact later gave rise to stories that she had become a nun and required papal dispensation to marry. See Sutto, 274n164. Cf. "Constance of Hauteville," *Oxford Reference*, https://www.oxfordreference.com/view/10.1093/oi/authority.20110803095633627 (accessed March 1, 2021).

3   Manfred (c.1232–66) was king of Sicily, 1258–66. An illegitimate son of Emperor Frederick II of Hohenstaufen, he was regent for Conradin (1252–68), who lost his father when he was only two. See *Encyclopaedia Britannica*, https://www.britannica.com/biography/Manfred-king-of-Sicily (accessed March 1, 2021).

4   Charles II (c.1254–1309), commonly called Charles of Anjou. See *Encyclopaedia Britannica*, https://www.britannica.com/biography/Charles-II-king-of-Naples (accessed March 1, 2021).

5   Henri de Joyeuse, duc de Bouchage and later duc de Joyeuse (1567–1608), was a member of the Catholic League. After his wife's death, he became a Capuchin friar under the name of Père Ange (Father Angel). In 1592, he removed his Capuchin habit in favor of military garb and served his king as a lieutenant general and marshal of France. His brothers having died, the title duc de Joyeuse was passed to him; but because he had taken the vow of poverty, he was not permitted to succeed a relative. Still less was he permitted to leave his monastery in order to resume a secular life. Peace having returned, he went back to his monastery and his

to succeed a relative, and still less to be released from a monastery in order to resume a secular life. The pope himself never grants such permission. And in our church, we permit Jesuit religious to inherit, and we permit the general to dismiss whomever he pleases? *Dii talem terris avertite pestem*.[6] It's not a privilege, it's a new monster that has been introduced into our Christianity. In the end, the Jesuit thinks he is getting even with God for this heresy, when he says that the thing that enters the vow is what one puts into it. It would be better if he said that he is entering the game, all the more so because, by giving this reason for the simple vow, he is playing a game with God. And he is one of those scoffers whom David criticized in his first psalm.[7] In sum, the Jesuits want to say that their simple vow is a vow that seems small, and they think they can fool God by the very same sophistry that the pagan of Antiquity applied when he said *Juravi lingua, mentem injuratam habeo*.[8] That protestation was condemned by all the ancient pagans, but not by the Christians. And so, the typical Jesuit says that his tongue has taken a vow of poverty; but that he had a back room in his soul that was chanting a totally different lesson. And by this escape-hole, in order to approve of his new doctrine, he plays three roles at once: the Jesuit, the Heretic, and the Machaivellist. And there are those who say that the great canonist, Navarrus, used to call their simple vow "*novum et mirabile*," "new and wonderful." Saint Bernard, repeating Abelard's heresy, did not say less, for he said: *Ambulabat in magnis et in mirabilibus*.[9]

---

wealth went to his daughter and her husband. See *Encyclopaedia Britannica*, https://www.britannica.com/biography/Henri-de-Joyeuse (accessed March 1, 2021).

6   "May God avert from the earth such a scourge," Virgil, *Aeneid*, III, 620.

7   "Blessed is the man who does not ... sit in company with scoffers," Ps. 1:1.

8   "I have sworn with my tongue, but I have a mind unsworn," Cicero, *De officiis*, III, xxix.

9   St. Bernard, "In Cantica," Sermon VIII, 5.

How the Jesuits Engage the Authority of the Holy See in Order to Excuse the Heresy of Their Simple Vow

THE LAWYER. "But these two privileges (says Montaignes) are granted to us by the head and prince of the church." See how these upright persons wrong the authority of the Holy See; and see the disarray in which they place the Holy See, making it the defender of this heresy. I'll never permit this to reach the ears of the enemies of our church, who by the same means do not understand how all these things happened. The truth is that, prior to Gregory XIII, no pope had ever gotten the idea of granting it to them; yet as early as the arrival of Ignatius, they were observing this simple vow, as one can see by the bull of the same Gregory, dated 1584. On this point, every good Catholic will maintain that it was a new heresy, introduced by them against the holy and ancient decrees. Tell me, you upright folks, what has become of the souls of your holy Ignatius of Loyola, Diego Laynez, Francisco de Borja, Everard Mercurian, the first four generals of your sect? Where is the soul of Francis Xavier, canonized among the savages, or the souls of Peter Faber, Nicolas de Bobadilla, Paschase Broët: in short, all your disciples who, since 1540, have lived and died in this heresy, up until 1584? In that year, you obtained permission for the future, not absolution for the past, as happened later for those who had died. However, we had these masters and preceptors of our young people in their colleges, these holy fathers and theologians in our churches who preached to us. And yet it was as professed heretics: instead of reestablishing our afflicted religion, by establishing the splendor of theirs, they totally subverted ours, and had no other grounds for their heresy than their detestable avarice.

In the past (that Jesuit adds), one could object to that about us, but not today, owing to this new bull. In truth, this reply would seem, *prima facie*, to be very strong, and therefore to impose silence upon us; yet when you've heard how, and when, and by what artifice it was obtained, you'll find nothing that isn't Jesuit in all of this. They diversified their vows, but I don't find a vow as solemn as the one I'm going tell you about now: it consists of carrying out their good or their bad opinions on their private authority, without showing the Holy See any respect; and after having misbehaved for a long time, they spied out opportunities during the Troubles, in order to obtain authorization as persons who are very necessary for maintaining our religion. In doing this, they give the law to those from whom they feign to be getting it. The fisherman preaches in troubled waters, and the Jesuit does it in our Troubles.[1] Their Society began in that fashion; and after several refusals, it was accepted by Pope Paul III in 1540 and 1543, in consideration of the Troubles that were going on in Germany at the time, between the Catholics and the Lutherans. In this fashion, in 1561, that is to say, when the Troubles were beginning to sprout in France between Catholics and Huguenots, they obtained from Pope Pius IV their great privilege to trouble the antique discipline of all the universities. They did the same thing in 1584, when Father Claude Matthieu,[2] their provincial for France, stirred up the humors of Rome, not only against the Huguenots but also against the late Most Catholic King,[3] as if they had favored them. And filling Pope Gregory with an infinity of vain hopes, they thought that they could, without danger, lift their mask and get him to approve something they had never dared unveil to the other popes: the turpitude of their simple vow. To such an extent that, in June 1584, they obtained the confirmation of this vow; and five months later, at the opening of the parlement, the late King Henri III of France, who didn't lack spies, published an order against the persons who were negotiating a League in foreign countries. On its own, this encounter was sufficient to efface the memory of Pope Gregory's bull, as well as some powerful decretals of Boniface VIII,[4] for the unfriendly things he had vowed against France.

---

1   Although it may be a simple mistake, Pasquier seems to be consciously playing with an old saying: *Le pecheur pêche en eau trouble* (The fisherman fishes in troubled waters). The saying refers to how easily fish are caught in nets that are made invisible by murky and turbulent water. By extension, and metaphorically, the saying suggests that someone is profiting from confusion or is using unscrupulous means to attain his goal. But wittingly or unwittingly, Pasquier skews the saying, to paint a witty picture. That is, French has three words with similar pronunciation: *pêcher* (to fish), *precher* (to preach) and *pécher* (to sin). To this should be added the confusion created by Pasquier's archaic, accent-less spelling: *pescher, prescher*, which facilitates misreadings. Whatever the explanation for his mis-formulation of the saying, he is telling his readers that the sinner (or perhaps the fisherman) is preaching (but not fishing or sinning?) in troubled waters. Then, carrying the joke-mistake a bit farther, he says that the Jesuit is preaching (or fishing, or sinning) and meddling in the Troubles that France has been going through during the Wars of Religion (1562–98).

2   Claude Matthieu (1537–87) was the provincial for Aquitaine, 1571–74; for France, 1574–82; and superior of the professed house in Paris, 1582–84. He was also a confessor to Henry III for a few months and supported the Catholic League. See Sutto, 177n175; *DHCJ*, 3:2579.

3   The Latin title *Rex Catholicissimus* was granted to the monarchs of Spain by Pope Alexander VI (r.1492–1503) who came from the Spanish (Valencian) family of Borja. Francisco de Borja, Alexander VI's grandson, became the third superior general of the Society.

4   Boniface VIII (1230–1303) reigned from 1294 to 1303. Today, he is probably best remembered for his feuds with King Philip IV of France (r.1285–1314). See *Encyclopaedia Britannica*, https://www.britannica.com/biography/Boniface-VIII (accessed March 1, 2021).

But I'm on even stronger terms, for I don't want people to think that Gregory gave some valid consent to it. Be that as it may, having summarily spoken about the novitiate, he said that the religious were making the following simple vow: *In Societatem cooptantur, ac quantum est ex parte ipsorum perpetuò, ex parte verò Societatis JUXTA APOSTOLICA INDULTA, ET CONSTITUTIONES PRAEDICTAS, tandiu obligati sunt, quandiu Praepositus Generalis eos retinendos censuerit. Quod ad Societatis conservationem maxime est necessarium, IDQUE AB ILLIUS EXORDIO PROVISUM, et post, experimento comprobatum est. Idque inito ingressus, illis explicitè manifestatur, atque ipsi conditionem hanc amplectuntur: quae eis si quos dimittere oporteat, multò est commodior, ut liberi potius, quàm votis obligati dimittantur, aliisque justis et rationalibus de caussis.* Which means: "When the time at the novitiate has been completed, and the vows of poverty, chastity, and obedience have been sworn, they are incorporated into the Society for the rest of their lives, ACCORDING TO THE APOSTOLIC INDULTS AND AFORESAID CONSTITUTIONS, for as long as it pleases their general to retain them. A thing greatly necessary for the conservation of the Society, AND AS SOON AS THE SOCIETY ANNOUNCES HIS ARRIVAL and he has been found to be very useful thanks to his experience, and he is given to understand this upon entering. A condition that they embrace as being more expedient for them, that (if some of them should have to be sent away) they may go free and clear, than if they remain obligated by their vow, and for other just and reasonable considerations." In this article you don't learn that the religious who makes the simple vow can succeed someone, but that's supplied by an article that comes later and that reads as follows: *Et licet qui ad gradus professorum et Coadjutorum formatorum nondum pervenerunt, bonorum suorum jus atque dominum, tum alias ob justus caussas, tum etiam ut majorem habeat Societas libertatem, illos si opus fuerit remittendi et cum minori offensione dimittendi.* "And although (says the Latin) those who have not yet reached the degrees of professed and formed coadjutors can possess their belongings and domains, for several good reasons, and especially so that the Society shall have more liberty to send them away if necessary, and with less doubt on its conscience, etc." From these two articles you see, first of all, that the general is permitted to cancel a simple vow, whenever and as often as he wishes; he can send his religious away as many times as he pleases; and he can send him back home free and clear of his vow. Second, this religious can possess temporal things: a clause that they have expanded to include inheritances, as you see in Montaignes. Third, from the very beginning of their order they behaved this way; and finally, that Gregory confirmed these two privileges for them, according to the indults that had been granted to them, and according to their Constitutions. I'll make this dispute very clear. Let's go back through all the bulls that they had previously obtained. There's only one where you find that their general is permitted to dismiss religious when he wishes, or that they can receive an inheritance during their simple vow. There are twenty-three bulls, the bulls of Pope Paul III: 1540, 1543, 1545, 1546, 1549. Those of Julius, his successor: 1550, 1552; of Pius IV, 1561; of Pius V, 1565, 1568, 1571, in March and July; of Gregory XIII, 1572, 1573, 1575, January and May 1576, February, July, October, December 1578; January and May. None of these bulls mention either a dismissal, or a succession, or possessing things. All these bulls were printed by the pope in one volume. The one published in 1584 is inserted throughout the summary of the bulls drawn up by Matteus Toscanus,[5] and also in Ribadeneyra, in Book 3 of his life of Ignatius. If they claim to have several other bulls, let them display them; because when it is a matter of things that are not, and that do not appear, one makes the same judgment. If I see (and I do see), that all the previous bulls did not mention these two privileges, the truth is, therefore, that the bulls circumvent the religion of the Holy See: just as in 1561, when they wanted to trouble the entire ancient order of the universities, they gave Pope Pius V to understand that what he was granting to them was nothing but a confirmation of Julius III's grant to them. And so, it is a surprise, an obreption, and a subreption; consequently, the bull of 1584 should not be heeded.

I remain in agreement with them (please God that I don't rob them of the truth in the case that's being presented, or in any other one): their Constitutions say that their general can grant leave when he wishes. But Pope Gregory doesn't interpose his permission in consideration of these Constitutions alone, but by the preceding apostolic indults, which, however, are not to be found: for a simple Constitution of their order wouldn't have sufficed to make Pope Gregory consent to the infraction of all the antique constitutions of the church, in favor of these new people.

I also recognize that, as far as this first point is concerned, when the novices[6] entered Jesuism, they were aware of it. Indeed, four or five days after a novice enters the novitiate house, to spend his two years of probation there, the examiners are told to give them all their apostolic letters, their statutes and Constitutions, even the General Examen that the novice must undergo, so that he can be informed of the facts that it is appropriate for him to know, once he has entered that order; and he can no longer, ex post facto, repent over it.

---

5   Pasquier confused two authors whose names include "Matthaeus" or a variant of that name. The summary of bulls to which he refers here, *Summa Constitutionum* (1587–96), was actually compiled by "Petrus Matthaeus," that is, Pierre Matthieu (see Book III, ch. 9).

6   For life in the Paris novitiate, see Patricia M. Ranum, ed. and trans., *Beginning to Be a Jesuit: Instructions for the Paris Novitiate circa 1685* (St. Louis, MO: Institute of Jesuit Sources, 2011).

Now, by their Constitutions, one learns that the general is permitted to absolve a religious of his simple vow, any time, and as many times as he pleases; and these Constitutions having been communicated to them, one can't say that one isn't informed about this privilege that's given to the general; and one can say of them on this point, what the Jesuit Montaignes said: *volenti non fit injuria*, if it so happens that this permission is admissible in our Christian church, and if Gregory hadn't been circumvented and hadn't granted it to the Jesuit church.

But regarding the second privilege, which permits a religious, while under the simple vow, to receive an inheritance and to possess temporal things, not only is there nothing in all those specific ancient bulls, there is also nothing in the totality of their ancient bulls, and nothing in the totality of their Constitutions: indeed, everything contradicts that intention. When they enter the order, they are supposed to make both a particular and a general vow of poverty, according to the bulls of Paul III of 1540, and likewise the bulls of Julius from 1550 on; and because it so happened that a more precise explanation was needed, they made it fully understood in chapter 4 of their General Examen, where, as I said earlier, they expressly ordered them not only to dispose of the possessions they had acquired, but also dispose of the possessions from which they expect nothing. *Debent omnia bona sua temporalia quae habuerint distribuere et renuntiare, ac disponere de his quae ipsis obvenire possent*, "they should" (says the Latin) "distribute all the temporal possessions they might have and renounce and dispose of those they might expect to receive."[7] Note in passing the Jesuit's wise resolution: whoever wants to enter the order disposes of the possessions he doesn't have. They are ordered to give their possessions to the poor as alms, and not to leave them to their relatives, to renounce all the love they bear for them, or to renounce the love of their fathers and mothers: all this, in order to take from them every thought of returning to their father's house. *Ut ad parentes et consanguineos recurrendi, et ad inutilem ipsorum memoriam, firmius et stabilius in sua vocatione perseverent.*[8] At the end of all that, no sooner have they abandoned all their possessions during the first years of their novitiate, than they are permitted, after having made the vow of poverty, to inherit from the persons they were ordered to forget, and the love and the memory of them. I conclude that this privilege to inherit that is granted to someone who has made the vow of poverty, is, first, contrary to the holy decrees of God and his church; second, it is contrary to common sense; and third, it is founded on

---

7 *Constitutions*, General Examen, ch. 4, 1 (p. 34).

8 "And by closing the door on recourse to parents and relative and profitless remembrance of them, to help them persevere in their vocation with greater firmness and stability." *Constitutions*, General Examen, ch. 4, 2 (p. 34).

two inexcusable and very intentional lies. The first lie is that one presupposes, on the basis of the bull, that their Constitutions permitted them to inherit during the time of their simple vow; the second lie is that the novices were given to understand that, having made the simple vow, they can now inherit. But on the contrary, all their Constitutions resist this in very clear words. Give, therefore, all the shapes you want to this bull of Gregory's: there's nothing that commits the authority of the Holy See in their favor.

I confess frankly that when Jesuit Montaignes proposed that the prince and head of the church had permitted them to make this unfortunate vow, I began to tremble, weighing my position against the consequences of this for all of Christendom. But when I'd been enlightened by reading the bull, Oh, you impudent impostors (said I), who want a protector for your impiety toward the Holy See! Has the papacy ever been a finer target than this one, confronting our adversaries? I don't want this single piece of paper in their hands, so that they can triumph, if it's true. It's a charity that you upright persons who preach only about charity, attribute to the desolation of the Holy See, whose unique protectors you claim to be. And yet, if Pope Gregory took some other opportunity to behave otherwise, in order to gratify you at a time when you were promising nothing less than to lay down the law for sovereign princes, and for the pope himself, I don't want to prevail over his bull, nor over the antique liberties of our Gallican church, which can't tolerate such special permission in France, nor prevail over the majesty of our kings who protect our liberties, nor over the authority of our parlements beneath those kings. Wherein lies the maintenance of ecclesiastical discipline: the less I'm willing to advise the calling of the ecumenical council in the future, as our ancient Frenchmen used to do on such matters, the less I stir up the duty of all the *procureurs généraux* in the parlements, to make an *appel comme d'abus*, for the fulmination of that bull. Which would be the shortest way. God forbid that I furnish memoranda that can be prejudicial to the Holy See; but if that great pope were alive, I'd throw myself at his feet and make an appeal to him; and I'd beg him in all humility to please consider whether, with his absolute power, he could put two incompatible things in a single subject. Whether, contrary to God's law, one lodges wealth in poverty. Whether this article seems to forget divine law and lacks common sense. I would abundantly beg him to look and see whether he had heard someone grant a permission that he didn't grant to himself, and to grant, indifferently, to the general of the Jesuits, a thing that the popes themselves had never granted; and that, without thinking about the vow of poverty, chastity, and obedience, which religious are obligated to observe, the general of their order can absolve them when he pleases. I'd further remonstrate that the monastic vows that one makes to God should be simple: but they aren't simple for the new Jesuism, nor for the antique Christianism. And just as, long ago in Rome, when one passed from one family to another via new affiliations (which they called adoptions), vows had to be pure, simple, and unconditional. And all the more so, when we left our carnal fathers in order to be adopted, like a poor beggar, into the family of our spiritual father, the Father of Fathers, it was necessary to enter it purely and simply, and not bring along the sly foxiness of the Jesuits' simple vow. Several other peculiarities could also be pointed out, which make me return to our discussion and the examination of our theology, be it Scholastic or be it moral. I'll be content simply to say, for the present, that all these remonstrances are superfluous, since Pope Gregory never gave his consent to this vow, having been deceived and surprised by what the Jesuits falsely gave people to understand, and that nothing is as contrary to consent as error is.

In Addition to the Heresy in the Simple Vow of the Jesuits, There Is Also Manifest Cheating

THE LAWYER. I still can't make things watertight, seeing these hypocritical heretics reigning in our churches and wanting to bestow the law on every faithful Christian: and yet, not a general change but a reform from good to better is needed. That's why someone in the past, having been borne toward the oracle, wanted to know which religion was best. The antique religion replied to the oracle. And then, having asked which religion was the most antique, it replied: The best one. The oracle wanted to teach us that no novelty should be rejected, when it is accompanied by good and valuable reasons. Jesuit Montaignes, in order to show that one must not fear the novelty of their simple vow, says that sixteen hundred years from now, it will be more antique than the canons of the apostles are today. In this, he is mocking God and the world: for that very thing can be alleged in favor of Luther's erroneous doctrine, which is older than Ignatius's doctrine by twenty-three or twenty-four years. And it can be said about all the others who, in our time, have strayed from the antique path of the church. I don't take its novelty away from the simple vow; and it is greatly to be feared, on religious issues, and especially for the Catholic, Apostolic, Roman Church, of which one can truly say: *Moribus antiquis res stat Romana, virisque.*[1]

I'm simply picking up again the heresy that is in that novelty, which couldn't be amended by a great length of time. *Veritati* (said Tertullian) *praescribere nemo potest, non patrocinia personarum, non privilegium regionum.*[2] A heresy that cannot be annulled by a lapse of time, however long it may be. Let's therefore consider the reasons why the Jesuits want to give a passport to the novelty of their simple vow. Montaignes, giving a reason for permitting a Jesuit religious to inherit and to own things, irrespective of the vow of poverty he has made, says this: "Because it can happen that, after ten or twenty years, the Jesuit who proves incorrigible will be dismissed by the general of our order, and will be sent away from his Jesuit house. From Christian charity, we want

---

1   "The Roman state stands on its ancient customs and men," Ennius, in Cicero, *De republica*, V, 1.
2   The quotation is inaccurate. It should read: *hoc exigere veritatem, cui nemo praescribere potest, non spatium temporum, non patrocina personarum, non privilegium regionum* (This observance is exacted by truth, on which no one can impose prescription—no space of times, no influence of persons, no privilege of regions). Tertullian, *De virginibus velandis*, 1.

to see to it that he does not have to beg or be a vagabond. And to that, add that we rarely apply that chastisement, and we almost always do it in the manner that pleases the persons being dismissed." This is a truly charitable revenge. In other religious orders, if a religious turns out to be unruly, they sometimes present him with a scourge right in the meeting of the chapter; sometimes they make him fast on bread and water, locked up in a dark room, depending on the number of demerits, to serve as an example for his brethren. And thus, without acting against the antique vow of our Catholic religion, and without turning things into a scandal, the monk is pulled along by rigor, which couldn't be done by gentleness. But in the holy order of the Jesuits, instead of chastising their badly behaved religious, they are invited to do wrong honestly, and to make themselves incorrigible, when they are weary of being there. So that their general has the opportunity to send them back to their old houses, in order to end their days there, fat on bacon and stuffed with wealth. What new idea of the Republic or of religion is this? Moreover, since they rarely set into motion this punishment, which I call repressiation and eating-nasty-little-fishes, was it necessary to invert the ancient constitutions of our church and damn an infinity of souls who were infected by this new faith, in order to put three or four corrupted Jesuits at their ease?

Let's talk French. It's not that: for at the end of the chapter, Montaignes himself admits that their general can send them back to an earlier house, not only when they've been delinquent but for every other occurrence as well. "But (says he) the one who leaves because of a notification from the general, or at the general's good pleasure, judging that for some necessity of spirit or body, or something involving his parents, or public, or for some other equitable reason, he must be dismissed: he remains absolved of his vows." You can see that it isn't under a false pretext for chastisement that they are permitted to collect an inheritance (a chastisement that is moreover ridiculous and impious). It favors the general's power, which is greater and more absolute than the power of the popes over our Universal Church. Good God, why don't you practice what the other religious orders do, without making any innovations in our Catholic, Apostolic, Roman Church? You'd be very unhappy about it: it's not the Christian charity that summons you, it's Jesuit charity. Your entire profession is nothing but deceit that's particular to our families in religion; and that's a widespread knavery in all the kingdoms you inhabit. And I'll show that the one and the other are indubitably to be found in this simple vow. You aspire only to have possessions, riches, lands, feigning to have no other goal but heaven. If you understand that once your novice's two years of probation have expired, he'll be capable of inheriting, why, with so much beating-around-the-bush and artifices, do you urge him, during his novitiate, to get rid of his possessions before making the simple vow? Certainly, anyone would be lacking in understanding if he didn't make a judgment after this first attempt and didn't strip himself of his possessions before becoming one of your brethren. You then keep him on a leash for ten, twenty, thirty years, that is to say, for as much and as long as he can collect inheritances; for then, his hope of success growing weak, he makes his second vow, which is your first solemn vow: and this having been done, he can no longer possess any temporal things, nor can he be dismissed by the general, even if he is incorrigible; and you henceforth use on him the same means that are used at other monasteries, against delinquent religious.

But before he enters the order, these possessions either remain flotsam and jetsam for the first occupant, or else the Jesuit promptly disposes of them in order to help the poor. I let you imagine, Messieurs, who these poor might be: for, caught so deeply in their nets, he has developed very little without gratifying them with his property; so what can they hope for from him, all tangled-up as he is, if not the same generosity. As if he assumed that, being nourished for a long time in their midst, and wanting to make the second solemn vow, he dared, or he wanted, or he could distribute his possessions elsewhere than to the profit of those under whose power he expects to end his days, with no hope of respite. But to tell the truth, that's an idle question: for Montaignes has replied without artifice, saying that "this expectation of possessions is not for them, for they have renounced that right, but it is to provide for them later, in the event that they are sent away." If, then, they can't be sent away, this good belongs to their order. Was there ever a deceit more extraordinary than this one? Hey, really, I'm not astonished that these messieurs rarely send their school Jesuit back to his house: for if they did so, that tasty morsel would escape their palate.

But why, during the time of this simple vow, is the Jesuit kept at a distance from his relatives? Why is he sent from one area to another, if not to draw closer to some new inheritance? No one is assured of its quality, and the right that he claims can't be revoked. At the most, he's finally freed from his vow, in order to be preserved from all encumbrances and obstacles. In so doing, he'll say that he's the real heir, and he'll use a pre-arranged code-word. After this, he'll return to the Jesuits and give them his abilities, as alms. Add to this, and this is a point that strikes out at the state, the fact that by this means it is easy for the Jesuit eventually to make himself the master and lord of several cities, market towns, villages, and chateaux, according to the titles of the persons he has attracted to him. Let's presuppose that there are a dozen gentlemen from good families who have become Jesuits, and that a foreign or civil war has carried off all their brothers. The Jesuits of the simple vow will be their successors; and by making that first solemn vow, they'll enrich their order by that amount. In the end, they'll become monarchs.

But let's put the subject of possessions aside: I want their general to be permitted to send them home, and not become rich from plundering a great family. Just see what the consequence is, of sending into our midst a man who has been nourished for ten or twenty years on hypocrisy and on the Jesuits' doctrine. Or, to be more accurate, who has been nourished on their barbarous impieties, such as the ones I'll relate to you in detail when the time comes. Isn't it in order to infect our France in indirect ways, as we indeed see that it has been infected? For how many are there in this kingdom who, having been merely their scholars and disciples, thrive on the brutal opinions of murderers, assassins, ambushers, rebels against their prince? What can you expect from those who, having been nourished for ten or twenty years in Jesuit houses, return to us? I want to point out, in addition, that in these simple vows a certain breed of men is lodged: they specifically profess their ignorance. They are called temporal coadjutors; and by means of them, a village can be populated by and filled with Jesuits. I therefore conclude that this simple vow contains an underlying heresy, Machiavelism, deceit, and, above all, imposture in its dealings with the Holy See. Everything is in ruins, not only families but also the republics where Jesuits dwell.

The Jesuit Provincials Authorize Themselves to Dismiss Their Inferiors of the Simple Vow, Just as Their General Does

THE LAWYER. In everything I told you above, I don't see how the Jesuits can make any excuse about their simple vow. And yet, so that no one will think that I feel a particular spirit of animosity against them, I'll be very relieved to excuse them, unless the only one who can dismiss someone is the general of their Society, even when he's induced to do it for some great and urgent necessity. Let's grant him this omnipotence over his people, which Our Holy Father the Pope doesn't attribute to himself over all the other religious of our Catholic church. But permitting a provincial to do it, and do it within his province, not for a necessity that isn't based on a law, but in order to gratify the person who asks to be absolved of his vow, makes me believe that whatever conniving we want to do in dealing with them, no good Catholic can in any manner tolerate it. This was done in 1594, at the Jesuit college of Paris. In that college dwelled a Jesuit of the simple vow, who had been promoted to the holy priesthood. He had taught for several years at Bourges, Nevers, Pont-à-Mousson, and at the time he was teaching the oldest students in Paris. This person was troubled by the hypocrisy, and by other irregularities that he observed to be reigning in all these people. No longer able to endure this rank spot in his heart, he presented himself to Father Clément Dupuy,[1] provincial at Paris, and begged him to send him away, for he didn't intend to stay with them any longer. Father Dupuy insisted just the opposite, remonstrating that since he wasn't a professed father of the great vow, but had made the simple vow of poverty, chastity, and obedience, he was obligated to observe that vow for the rest of his life, just as all the religious of other monastic orders do; and he couldn't have his vows dissolved without the superior's permission. The Jesuit opposed this, saying that he didn't want to leave on his own, nor did he intend to do so; but that the superior couldn't refuse his request. He maintained that there had to be something reciprocal here, when it came to the will and to power; and that just as the superior couldn't dismiss his inferior against the latter's will, the inferior could force his superior to send him away, even if he wasn't actually disposed

---

1   Clément Dupuy (1552–98) was provincial for Aquitaine from 1588 to 1598 and provincial for France from 1592 to 1597. See Fouqueray, *Histoire de la Compagnie de Jésus en France*, passim.

to be sent away. And he maintained that there was as much irregularity in the first proposition, as in the second; and that if one of them was just, the other was also just. This question certainly was one of the most acute for the Society, and if the obedience that they all were vowing toward their general is like the obedience that I'll set forth in its place, this obscurity fully merited being clarified by him and his assistants. Yet Father Dupuy, who was well-nurtured on, and informed about the statutes of his order, didn't send a letter to Rome but, on the basis of his personal authority, issued the following letters-patent:

> *Clemens Puteanus Praepositus Societatis Jesu in Provincia Franciae, omnibus quorum interest et in quorum manus hae literae venerint. S. in Domino nostro Jesu Christo. Fidem facio N. quamvis in Societate nostra alinqundiu vixerit, professionem tamen in ea non emisisse, quin potiùs ex caussis rationi consonis, ipso petente, liberum ab omni, erga ipsam, obligatione esse dimissum. Testamur etiam eum ad omnes sacros ordines in eadem fuisse legitimè promotum, nec ullum scimus impedimentum quò minus eis Domino ministrare possit. In cujus rei testimonium, eidem N. has litteras manu nostra scriptas, sigilllo societatis nostrae obsignatas dedimus. Parisiis vigesimo quarto Augusti, 1594.*

That is to say:

> Clément Dupuy, provost of the Society of Jesus, in the province of France: to all those who are interested, and who see the present letters, Greetings in Our Lord Jesus Christ. I certify that (person's name), while he lived for some time in our Society, was however never professed, rather for other good causes requiring this, we have sent him away free and clear of every obligation he had to our Society. In like manner, we bear witness that he was promoted in the Society to all the holy orders, and that there is nothing that prevents him from being able to celebrate Mass. For assurance of which we have given him these papers written with our hand and sealed with the seal of our Society. Done at Paris, this August 24, 1594.

I'm not naming the person in whose favor these letters were written. He's a very erudite person and is recognized as such at the University of Paris.[2] A person

---

2   This individual is Jules César Bulenger (1558–1626) who, after twelve years of religious life, requested, in 1594, to reenter the secular world, in order to help his family. He taught for twenty years at the universities of Paris, Toulouse, and Pisa. He reentered the Society of Jesus in 1620. See Sutto, 288n197.

(I say) who had spent not only a few years with the Jesuits, but several years, and who had received holy orders, and who had taught in various colleges of their Society. True, not being a professed father, but merely having made the simple vow, he was given *lettres dimissoires* like the above letter, in which, although it is done for just reason, if you talk with him, he'll say that there was no other letter, just the one to the effect that he didn't want to stay longer. This I learned from him personally: and so, you see that it is he who requests to leave, it is not the superior's request. And admittedly, since Father Clément Dupuy behaved in this fashion, I'm assured that he could do it by some hidden cabal between the two of them, without polishing his authority as general; and if he could, I don't doubt that similar authority would be attributed to all the other provincials. Good God, what sort of discipline is this? What respect and obedience does it show for the Holy See? Today the general can clean up the Gregorian of 1594,[3] but will the provincials find that this power has been granted to them in these bulls? Moreover, as a result of an inferior's mere importuning, can they send him back to his house, to the prejudice of the three substantial and ordinary vows made by all religious orders: poverty, chastity, and obedience? What sort of religious order is this one, where everything is permitted against our religion? Aren't all these messieurs deceivers who live in our midst? But you'll hear many other things about the vows of the rest of the entire Society, if you'll please lend me your ears, as you have done up until now.

---

3   This is an allusion to the bull *Ascendente Domino* issued in 1584 by Pope Gregory XIII (r.1572–85). See Sutto, 288n198.

How the Jesuit Fathers of the Great and Third Vow Mock God When They Vow to Be Beggars

THE LAWYER. From the Jesuit father who is present among us right now, you've heard how, after the simple vow, they make a solemn vow by which they add nothing to the first vow; except that, having taken this second one, they can no longer inherit or be sent away by their general. The third vow remains: it's the three-story one that, in addition to vowing poverty, chastity, and obedience, makes a special mission vow to Our Holy Father the Pope, and that, moreover, involves going to the Indies and to Turkey, to conquer souls, should His Holiness so order. But above all, I'm making a great deal of the precise sort of poverty that is ordered by their Constitutions. Let's run through all the religious orders: there isn't a single one where poverty is so highly recommended, with the exception of the Capuchins, who live from hand to mouth and whose tomorrow depends solely on God's goodness. The founding principle of the professed, that is, the Jesuits of the great vow, is to make a vow of poverty, both in general and in particular, just as all the mendicant orders do. But because that poverty needed explaining, let's see the commentaries they make about it in their Constitutions. They have three sorts of residences: one for their novices, the other is for the religious who are solely obligated to take solemn vows and who live in what they call a house, which is where their church is; and a third house is called a college, and that is for the religious who are obligated only to take the simple vow, which includes the approved scholars and the coadjutors, be they spiritual or be they temporal.

In domibus vel Ecclesiis quae à Societate, ad auxilium animarum admittentur, reditus nulli, ne Sacristae quidem, aut fabricae applicati, haberi possunt, sed nec ulla alia ratione, ita ut penes Societatem, eorum sit ulla dispensatio, sed in solo Deo, cui per ipsius gratiam, ea inservit, fiducia constituatur, sine reditibus ullis, ipsum nobis profecturum de rebus omnibus convenientibus, ad ipsius majorem laudem et gloriam.

Professi vivant ex eleemosynis, in domibus, cum aliquò non mittuntur, nec officium Rectorum, ordinarium, in Collegii, vel Universitatibus Societatis habeant, nisi ipsarum necessitas, vel magna utilitas exigeret, nec reditibus eorum in Domibus utantur.

> *Parati sint ad mendicandum ostiatim, quando vel obedientia, vel neces-*
> *sitas id exiget. Et sit unus, vel plures, ad eleemosinas petendas, quibus*
> *personae societatis sustententur, destinati, quas eleemosinas simpliciter,*
> *amore Domini nostri petent.*
>
> *Non solum reditus, sed nec possessiones habeant in particulari, nec in*
> *communi, Domus vel Ecclesiae.*[1]

That is to say:

> In the houses or churches which the Society accepts for the salvation of
> souls, one cannot appropriate any income, not even for the sacristy, or for
> maintenance, or even for any reason whatsoever, so that the Society will
> have the care of distributing it. But the Society must rely on God alone,
> whom it serves by his divine grace, and it trusts that, with no income,
> God will provide for everything we need, for the exaltation of his honor
> and glory.
>
> The professed (that is to say, religious who have taken the great final
> vow) live from alms in houses, and do not usually accept the ordinary
> duties of rectors in the colleges or universities, unless necessity or urgent
> utility requires it, and they do not use the revenues of these colleges in
> their houses.
>
> They must be ready to go and beg from door to door, if obedience or
> necessity so requires: and to this end there is one of them, or several of
> them, who seek the alms by which the upright persons of the Society are
> fed, which they request simply, for the honor of Our Lord.
>
> The houses and the churches of the Society not only have no invested
> income, but they have no inheritances, either in particular or in general.

When all these details are assembled, was there ever a more obstinate vow
of poverty than this one? And that's why Pius v, first, and then Gregory xiii,
ordered that this Society be listed among the mendicant orders. If they observed
what they were ordered to do, I'd excuse them with a warm heart for the heresy
in their first vow. All the more so since, having possessed things for a long time
during their simple vow, finally, in order to satisfy God, and having reached
the period when they make their great vow, they henceforth don't merely take
the title Father, but they also vow that they themselves will beg alms. I'd honor

---

1   The excerpts that Pasquier supplies come from a Latin version of the *Constitutions*, part
    VI, ch. II, 2, 3, 10, and 5. The English version closely reflects Pasquier's own translation into
    French, rather than the English translation published by the Institute of Jesuit Sources.

them as true imitators of Saint Peter's penance, after he had denied his Master, and I'd place them above all the other mendicant orders; but when have you ever seen them carrying a beggar's bag through the city streets? Yet they live at ease and in opulence, not on God's manna (for they aren't children of Israel) but on a remarkable sophistiquery. And here's how. The houses in which these blissful fathers live cannot possess anything, but only the colleges. Under the authority of their general, they all keep an eye on the management of the colleges: they are the Cincinnatuses[2] of ancient Rome, proud that they owned no gold, although they gave orders to those who had it. In like manner, these messieurs give orders to those who possess things, although they aren't supposed to possess any real estate except their begging purse. If you presuppose this foundation, you'll easily judge the result: for that explains why, being fathers, they are cared for and fed by their children, and it's more honest for them to beg for alms at their colleges, when ordering people about, than it is to go through the whole city begging. That's how they industriously offer God bundles of straw, just as Cain did.[3] Nevertheless, in this they are the true and legitimate children of their good Father Ignatius, who in all his actions reserved taking care of the kitchen for himself. Ribadeneyra teaches us that when Ignatius, Diego Laynes, and Peter Faber were living in Venetian territory, while the latter two were begging alms to stay alive, Ignatius would stay at home and prepare dinner with the small amount of their alms. And having later been made general of his order, he began to carry out this charge. *Atque ut quò altius ascenderat, eò se gereret submissius, exemploque suo omnes ad pietatis stadium provocaret, culinam statim est ingressus, in eaque per multos dies, et coquum agens, et alia vilia ministeria obire coepit.* "And to show (says Ribadeneyra) that the higher Ignatius rose, the more he wanted to lower himself, in order to invite all his men to piety by his example, he entered the kitchen at once and became the cook, and there he did other lowly tasks." Now, among these crafts, you see that the kitchen is listed first. That was in order to teach his disciples that, in the house of piety that they wanted to build, everything had to begin with the kitchen, a lesson they learned very well and retained. Nothing was more familiar to them, through their bulls and their Constitutions, than begging; and nevertheless, men never understood so well the art of trapping coins as they

---

2   Lucius Quinctius Cincinnatus (*c.*519–*c.*430 BCE) was a patrician who opposed the rights of common citizens (plebians). Impoverished during his old age, he worked a small farm. During a time of trouble, his fellow citizens begged him to lead them. He left his plow and took control of the state; but as soon as this crisis had ended, he immediately resigned his near-absolute authority and returned to his plow. See *Encyclopaedia Britannica*, https://www .britannica.com/biography/Lucius-Quinctius-Cincinnatus (accessed March 1, 2021).

3   Cain offered God dried-up plants, Gen. 4:1–16.

did, in order to live at their ease. Exercising this craft, they play more rounds of catch-the-coins, than either Master Peter Patelin,[4] François de Villon,[5] or Rabelais's Panurge.[6] For what those three venerable doctors did was mere trickery, but what our Jesuit reverend fathers in God do, is for catching whales, not tiny gudgeon-fishes. They have the instruction of the young as their first fishhook, and they have the tricks they use to catch them: the auricular confessions they know how to use profitably in a household, the visits to the sick, the help they give until the last breath in order not to lose them from sight, the extraordinary absolutions they say they can give and with which they stuff these persons in order to draw out some rich legacies, the artifice behind their simple vow, and a thousand other hypocrisies that they call charities. But under those conditions, their charities begin with themselves, because the *ad aliquid* predicament is no accident for them but is totally the substance of their sect.[7] To the point that one can justifiably call them not Jesuit Order but Ordure Jesite,[8] simply by moving a letter from one word to another. For although they pretend to buy nothing at retail, they sell, at wholesale, the administration of the holy sacraments, at a higher price than Elisha's servant Gehazi was willing to sell spiritual gifts to Naaman.[9] And I've never read anything as beautiful as this noteworthy sentence by Jesuit Montaignes: "If God (he said) wants to be importuned by those who are begging him, rich persons who want to do good and to imitate such a fine patron, should be patient when the poor do to them

---

4   "La Farce de maître Pierre Pathelin" is an anonymous fifteenth-century play that was extraor-
     dinarily popular for over a century and is echoed in the works of François Rabelais (?–1553).
     All but one of the five characters is dishonest in some way.

5   François Villon (1431–*c.*1463) was a ne'er-do-well poet who had multiple encounters with the
     law. He wrote about some of these experiences in his poems. Like Pasquier, he sprinkled his
     poems with hidden jokes and peppered them with slang. (Does this translator dare suggest
     that Pasquier was thinking of Villon when he wove "villonery" and the city of Villon into his
     word-play about the college of Billom?). See *Encyclopaedia Britannica*, https://www.britan-
     nica.com/biography/Francois-Villon (accessed March 1, 2021).

6   Panurge is one of the chief characters in *Gargantua et Pantagruel*, a novel by Rabelais.
     Especially important in the third and fourth books of *Gargantua*, Panurge is an exceedingly
     crafty knight, libertine, and coward. He can speak many languages, including some early
     examples of a constructed language. An expression associated with Panurge is "Panurge's
     sheep," which alludes to a person who blindly follows others, regardless of the consequences.

7   Just a bit of word play: the vocabulary in this sentence (*ad aliquid*, accident, substance, pre-
     dicament) is borrowed from a discussion of metaphysics by Aquinas.

8   The word play is: Or-dre Jé-su-ite (Jesuit order) versus Or-du-re Jé-site (Garbage) plus,
     perhaps, J'hé-zite (I hesitate). Hesitation is, of course, the opposite of following an order
     promptly.

9   2 Kings 5:19–27.

what the patron who gives away riches wants done to him." God bless you, Jesuit soul. Past-master at the art of asking, whose words, falling onto the ear of a poor patient, can produce marvelous effects in favor of this holy order. For sixty years they've been finding more treasures in their sophistic begging than all the other monasteries in France have found in two or three hundred years.

The Jesuits' Vow of Chastity Contains Yet Another Heresy, and a Brief Discussion of the Title Fathers, That the Jesuits of the Great Vow Call Themselves

I, THE LAWYER. Looking over all the vows made by our Jesuits, I found something with which to find fault, as I told you earlier, and as I will tell you here and there, when the subject comes up: but I didn't see anything innovative on chastity. At any rate, neither in their bulls nor in their Constitutions did I find anything about it. Still, when I read chapter 50 of Montaignes's *La Vérité défendue*, I saw that they have a cabal that hasn't yet come to the attention of the Holy See, nor to the attention of the church as a whole, no more than the simple vow came to their attention during the forty years when it was being made without permission. For when Montaignes wanted to brush aside the novelty of this simple vow, this is what he said: "It is a new right, just as the vow of chastity is, taken by those in the Society who prevent marriage from taking place, and who annul it when it does take place." Since Montaignes states it, I deem it to be very true; for even if his name is a pseudonym, the author of the book, a provincial in Paris, was an inexhaustible well of Jesuit doctrine. At first, I thought he meant that after they had taken that vow of chastity, they couldn't marry, under penalty of annulment of the marriage, and that the children born of that union would be declared incestuous. But when I thought it over later, I realized that this law wasn't new, it was very old; and that although this Jesuit says that their vow of chastity is new, and although it causes existing marriages to be broken and annulled, I felt sure that, by this new vow, a married man who becomes a Jesuit breaks the sacred bonds of marriage, which can only be dissolved by a natural death. Was there ever a heresy more prejudicial to all of Christendom than this one? God wants those who are married by him, that is to say, by his church, not to be separated or sundered by man, except in cases of adultery. An *ordonnance* so closely observed across time and antiquity, that when a woman who commits a misdeed is confined to a convent, her husband isn't to blame, except that he isn't permitted to remarry in our Catholic, Apostolic, and Roman Church, but must bear his share of the penance for the sin committed by his wife. To the point that our church has viewed these two bodies as indivisible. I know full well that some persons think that if a woman

© KONINKLIJKE BRILL NV, LEIDEN, 2021 | DOI:10.1163/9789004164062_035

is found guilty of adultery, her husband can marry another woman.[1] But which of the two errs the most: those persons or the Jesuit? Those persons merely interpret literally, deeming that God has permitted a remarriage, since in every other case, except for adultery, God forbade the man and the woman to separate; and yet, the church has never believed that those words referred to the rupture of the marriage, which was an unerasable sacrament, if not unerasable by death, at least unerasable owing to the mere separation of the bodies. A few people in olden times were so caught up with this, that some judged by command, as Tertullian did, while others judged by counsel, as Saint Jerome did: the surviving member of the couple should not remarry, as if their marriage had not been dissolved by the first husband's death. That's what I say, not in order to approve of their opinions, for Tertullian's opinion was condemned by the church, and Saint Jerome's was restricted by several lofty persons. I say this in order to show you that, for at least as much and as long as we live, we can't break or dissolve the sacrament of marriage, not even for adultery. And so, what new monster are the Jesuits introducing into our church, to the effect that the person who becomes one of their brethren, can break his marriage without its being a transgression for the wife? Not even if a husband simply becomes discontented, because the laws of Christianity forbid it. I've heard tell that other religious groups and orders sometimes had a few ill-advised scatterbrains who became monks, not from devotion but from despair at not having obtained from their sweethearts the trinkets they were seeking. But breaking marriages, when there's no adultery, but simply a husband's discontent, disguised as a foolish devotion, only the a-Christly[2] Jesuits have cleared the way for that, ever since our Christian religion was constructed.

If they hold marriage in such horror, why, having progressed to their final vow, do they call themselves fathers? The title isn't really as arrogant as the title Jesuits, although it's full of ambition and pride. At the very least, I know that Saint Jerome would not have approved of it: writing about chapter 4 of Saint Paul's epistle to the Galatians, he said that the word *abbé* signified father[3] in Hebrew and in Syriac; and Our Lord declared that the name father belonged only to God his Father.[4] So they must not have approved the fact that, in a few

---

1   This was the Protestant position.

2   Here Pasquier coins an adjective: *Achriste*, that is, "a + Christe," (without Christ). His model probably was *athéiste*, "a + theos" (without god). Cotgrave's dictionary of 1611, which usually meshes very closely with Pasquier's vocabulary, shows that allusions to atheism were in use: *Athéisme, Athée, Athéiste*, which meant "atheisme, infidelitie, denying of, or not believing, in God."

3   Gal. 4:6 does not say "abbot"; it says "Abba, Father."

4   Matt. 23:9, "Call no one on earth your father: you have but one Father in heaven."

monasteries, some persons called themselves abbots or fathers. I think he had heard tell of the leaders of monks whom we call abbots. What would they say today, if they saw the Jesuits of the great vow take the title fathers? For in other religious orders, their superior is called abbot, he being the person whom the religious should recognize as their father. And as for these religious, they are called brothers or brethren, as if all of them were his children. The title father belongs only to the leading dignities of the church: pope, patriarch, abbot; and each Jesuit of the great vow, taking it as his portion, shows that the feigned simplicity of his robe covers a marvelous arrogance. I know full well that they'll tell me that the Capuchins, who seem to have created an irreproachable order, do the same; and I'll reply that, in this instance, the fault lies with the Capuchin and shouldn't serve the Jesuits as a guarantor. Diogenes the Cynic,[5] who pretended to scorn worldly things, was no less prideful than Plato when, in his mendicancy, he boasted of crushing Plato's pride under his feet; and I don't mean to say that there is no ambition under the patched grey habit of the Capuchin: although it may be concealing an excuse. For the first Capuchin who wanted to reform the Franciscan order, thought he'd make monks of them, along the lines of those good hermits whom Antiquity called fathers. And indeed, we call their lives, the Lives of the Fathers. And if I should see the mendicancy of the Jesuits reduced to that of the Capuchins, I'll easily excuse their use of fathers. But there, one can see a manifest ambition: because the Jesuits aren't content to call themselves that; so, they add the word *Révérend*, Reverend, which is used for cardinals and bishops. See the works of Bellarmine, printed before he was a cardinal.[6] They read: *R.P. Roberti Bellarmini, etc.* which is, as I've said, the abbreviation for *Révérend Père*, Reverend Father. See the life of Francisco de Borja, third general of the order, translated from Spanish into Latin by Andreas Scottus, Jesuit, the privilege granted to Troguese printer at Antwerp, which states that he has permission to print *Vita Francisci Borgiae, tertii Societ. Jesu Generalis, à Reverendo Patre Andrea Scotto Latinè scripta.*

For the friendship I bear them, I truly grieve that they have so ambitiously wanted the name father. All the more so, since it has caused a few lovers of

---

5   Diogenes (*c.*410–323 BCE), known as Diogenes the Cynic, was a Greek philosopher. He used his simple lifestyle and behavior to criticize the social values and institutions of what he saw as a corrupt, confused society. See *Encyclopaedia Britannica*, https://www.britannica.com/biography/Diogenes-Greek-philosopher (accessed March 1, 2021).

6   Robert Bellarmine (1542–1621) was one of the most prominent Jesuit writers of the period. He was professor of theology and rector of the Roman College. He was involved in the negotiations with the Catholic League and was created cardinal in 1599. See *DHCJ*, 1:387–89.

curiosities to make anagrams[7] from these two words (*SECTA JESUITARUM*), where they found a great deal of shame and modesty. And indeed, having recently found myself among some persons who were talking about the title fathers, and who seemed to be well-informed, another member of the group maintained the contrary, saying that the anagram in those words, *SECTA JESU-ITARUM*, was contrary to that proposition. Which he firmly believed: for (said he), if prognostication about our fortunes or habits depends on names, and on not dropping a single letter, as we saw in the anagram of King Francis I, based on the name François de Valois, *De Façon Suis Royal*, I'm royally fashioned. And in the name of the great poet Étienne Jodelle:[8] *Jo le Delien est né*. Jo of the Delian League is born. If the anagram that one finds in those two words, *SECTA JESUITARUM*, is right, then it is an impossibility of all impossibilities to be fathers:

> *TUTE MARES VICIAS, non scortum,*
> *Non tibi conjunx,*
> *Dic Jesita mihi qui Pater esse potes?*[9]

To which I replied that trusting in names or in anagrams is true madness: that was Julius Scaliger's[10] very elegant reply to Cardano.[11] And in addition, I'm sure that your anagram is lying, as I shall demonstrate by another totally contrary one.

---

7   An anagram is a word or phrase formed by rearranging the letters of a different word or phrase, typically using all the original letters exactly once. The original word or phrase (in this instance *Secta jesuitarum*), is known as the "subject" of the anagram. The goal is to produce anagrams that reflect or comment on their subject.

8   Etienne Jodelle (1532–73), a dramatist and poet, was close to the poetic circle known as the *Plé̈ade* (as was Pasquier). He applied their principles to the theater, in order to create a classical drama that would differ in every respect from the morality plays and farces being performed on the French stage. See *Encyclopaedia Britannica*, https://www.britan nica.com/biography/Etienne-Jodelle (accessed March 1, 2021).

9   The contemporary English renders wittily thus:
With women you lie not, but with males rather,
Speak Jesuit, how canst thou be a father?

10   Julius Caesar Scaliger (1484–1558) was an Italian scholar most of whose career was in France. One of the leading humanists of his day, he was sympathetic to Protestantism. See *Encyclopaedia Britannica*, https://www.britannica.com/biography/Julius-Caesar-Scaliger (accessed March 1, 2021).

11   Gerolamo Cardano (1501–76) was an Italian polymath whose interests ran the gamut from mathematics, physics, and chemistry, to astronomy, astrology, and philosophy. His autobiography, *De vita propria*, was published in 1576. See http://www.treccani.it/enciclopedia/gerolamo-cardano_%28Dizionario-Biografico%29 (accessed March 1, 2021).

TU MATRES VICIAS, thorosque sacros,
Antistes pie, virginesque sanctas;
Hoc qui martyrio fidem propagat,
Hoc qui consilio propagat orbem,
Is verè est pater, et pater beatus:
O tuam veneror beatitatem,
Ampletorque piam paternitatem,
Jesuita Patrum Pater supreme.[12]

The difference between these two anagrams that state the done and the undone, show that you mustn't believe them. Also, I believe it to be a very certain thing; and if you'll permit me to state it, as an article of faith, the Jesuits observe their vow of chastity with as much strictness, holiness, and religion as they observe their vow about mendicancy. So, let's banish this garbage from our utterances. ANOTHER MAN. You are very eager to favor them for no reason; so, don't argue that your anagram lacks an *E*, and that mine uses the entire name. What I've told you about them is an inseparable accident, what dialecticians call *Proprium quarto modo.*[13] Remember the Templars who, beneath the mantle of an order that formerly was approved, wandered across the world in order to amplify our faith with their swords, which was one of the things for which they were condemned. See whether the Jesuits of today are following in their footsteps: I'm infinitely suspicious of the actions of a man who wanders across the world, as the Jesuits do. I don't believe any of it (I replied), and everything you say is pure calumnies and lies.

12   Thou stainest Mothers, and the marriage bed,
       Prelate, by thee are holy Virgins sped.
       Who by this martyrdome graceth the steeple,
       Who by this still begets faith in the people:
       He is a father, and a father blest,
       Thy happiness I honour with the rest:
       Iesuit, I bow to thy paternitee,
       Father of Fathers in the highest degree.
13   *Proprium quarto modo*: "proper according to the fourth mode." The word *proprium* (proper) denotes something that naturally and essentially belongs to any being. There are four kinds or "modes" of "proper," the fourth one (*proprium quarto* modo) being the highest and most exclusive. That is, it applies to only one kind and to all that belong to that kind. So, one says that laughing is proper to man, and only to man; while neighing is proper to the horse, and only to the horse.

About the Mission Vow, and How They Use It to Make Fun of Us All, Especially Our Holy Father the Pope

THE LAWYER. In all the other religious orders, those who enter make three vows. In the case of the Jesuit order, to win the good graces of Pope Paul III, Ignatius added the mission vow, not for all the religious, but only for those who would make the great final vow. Here are the terms of their bull: they promise, without haggling, to go wherever it pleases the popes to order them, *Ad profectum animarum et fidei propagationem, sive ad quoscumque alios infideles, etiam in partibus quas Indias vocant, existentes, etc.*[1] The person who, in 1594, published the defense of the Collège de Clermont against the University of Paris,[2] says this about the grandeur and excellence of this new vow: "The defenders have a special vow to obey the pope, but *circa Missiones tantum*,[3] which is based on their being called by God to help the church, and to defend it against its enemies, that is, the infidels or heretics, they must necessarily be sent." And a bit later the text says "And could not be more properly sent than by the one who is seated in Saint Peter's chair and who governs the entire church. And like the pilot on the poop deck, attached to the rudder, he dispatches some to the prow and the anchors, others to the sails and the ropes and the other tasks on the ship." Let's pause and look at this fine passage, before we go further. The first promise in this vow rested on the conversion of the Turks, who follow Mohammedanism; and next come all the other infidels, or all those who inhabited certain countries unknown to us that were called the Indies. I beg you, tell me whether you've ever heard that they went there, or to the country of the Grand Turk, emperor at Constantinople, or to the country of the Sophy, emperor of the Persians, to fulfill their promise. Some of you will point out that they weren't ordered to go there by the Holy Father. I agree, because the weather was too hot for them. To what countries, then, did they go? To the countries that are farthest from us, *quas Indias vocant*, which are

---

1   "To the perfection of the souls and the propagation of the faith, or to any other infidels, even in the parts of the Indies, which they call, existentes, etc."

2   That person is none other than Pasquier, who in 1594 published the *plaidoyer* he had written back in 1565.

3   *Circa missiones* (*or Misiones*) *tantum*: on several occasions Pasquier uses this expression to denote the so-called mission vow.

© KONINKLIJKE BRILL NV, LEIDEN, 2021 | DOI:10.1163/9789004164062_036

called the Indies, which Ignatius had artfully added, as something more difficult to carry out than Turkey; and yet he knew, being a Spaniard, that nothing
is as easy as to undertake as that task, as I told you when I recounted the apos-
tolate of the Jesuits in Portugal and in the Indies, who were ruled by Jean III,
king of Portugal. Do you think, Messieurs, that if it had pleased the pope to
send some religious from the four mendicant orders, they would have baulked
at this undertaking, and would have been permitted to go about in secular
clothes, like our Jesuit here?[4] Instead of a Xavier sent by Ignatius, they would
have found five hundred Jesuits, folks full of devotion and doctrine, to be the
crew on this holy voyage. And why? Because it was a harmless devotion, going
along beneath the banner of a Christian king who had power over the lives and
the deaths of those whom he wanted to bring gently to our Christian religion,
a voyage without fear. But as for all of Turkey, which lives beneath princes who
are the enemies of our Christianity, I don't see that the pope ordered them, nor
that these worldly-wise Jesuits were in a hurry to go there. And yet, read the
first bull. It seems that Ignatius proposed the journey to Turkey as an easier
undertaking. It seems that it pleased God that one of the successors of Paul III
got it into his head to order our Jesuits to go to Constantinople and convert the
Mohammedans, in order to see, in good earnest, what sort of obedience they
would have shown for this holy mission vow. We would have seen what miracles they might have worked there. And now, listen, not to a new courser but to
a discourser, in his Very Humble Remonstrance and Request Presented to the
King:[5] "We live not only beneath Christian princes, we also live beneath Gentile
potentates who are not acquainted with the law and the fear of God. We also
have colleges in Japan, far to the east of our hemisphere; we have some to the
west, in Brazil, which is the beginning of America; in Lima and in Cuzco, which
is at the end of Peru and at the extremity of the Ponent. We have them in
Mexico, which is in the middle of these two regions. Toward the north of Goa,
a city that is two-thirds of the distance between Lisbon and Japan, a route that
covers six thousand leagues. We have colleges in several places, in both the
East Indies and the West Indies. Not counting our colleges in Europe, which
are far more numerous than our enemies would like, and far fewer than the
upright folks and the zeal-stirrers of the faith desire. Without having built colleges, the workers for this Society, who strive to preserve Christians or to
convert pagans, are frequently in the mountains of Lebanon, Egypt, Africa, and

---

4   Remember: the Jesuit who is travelling with them is disguised as a layman.
5   The "discourser" is Montaignes, that is, Richeome.

China." I read this passage with one of my friends, as Apollonius of Tyana,[6] the impostor, had done, claiming in the presence of the Greeks that the Gymnosophists,[7] who were in the Indies, had witnessed his miracles. On this subject, Aeneas of Gaza,[8] in his *Theophrastus*, says that it was inappropriate for this impudent fellow to cite, as proof of these impostures, persons who were so far from our habitable land, and who remained in a sort of separate world. I was saying that our Theatine-like[9] Jesuits were doing the same things today; and, in order to stuff us with vain hopes and fibs, they were sending us to those same Indies and to other countries whose names we barely recognize. But when he heard this, my friend, smiling, told me that there was some Picrochole[10] in their facts. What Picrochole? (I replied to him). I think it's the name of a devil, like Macrobius.[11] I see clearly (the other replied to me) that you haven't studied your Rabelais, who talked about a great war that King Picrochole had undertaken against Grandgosier, in order to get some cakes. After that crazyhead had counted all the regions of France that he imagined had already been conquered, his trained bowmen, who were following him, added: And will also batter the kingdoms of Tunis, Hippo, Algiers, Bône, Cyrene, and all of Barbary.

---

6   Apollonius of Tyana (*c.*15–*c.*100 AD), called "the Impostor," was a charismatic teacher and miracle worker. He may have belonged to a branch of ancient philosophy called neo-Pythagoreanism. Accounts of his life frequently compare him to the Jewish sage and miracle worker Jesus of Nazareth. See *Encyclopaedia Britannica*, https://www.britannica .com/biography/Apollonius-of-Tyana (accessed March 1, 2021).

7   "Gymnosophists" was a generic Greek term for Indian sages, conceived of as members of an ancient Indian sect that wore very little clothing and that was given to asceticism and contemplation.

8   Aeneas of Gaza (?–*c.*518) was a neo-Platonic philosopher and a convert to Christianity. Like many Christian neo-Platonists, he held Plato in higher esteem than Aristotle. His *Theophrastus* is a dialogue. See Sebastian Gertz, John Dillon, Donald Russell, trans., *Aeneas of Gaza, Theophrastus, with Zacharias of Mytilene, Ammonius: Ancient Commentators on Aristotle* (London: Bristol Classical Press, 2012).

9   The Theatines, a religious order created in the 1520s by Gaetano dei Conti di Thiene (1480–1547), had as its chief object the recall of the clergy to an edifying life and the laity to the practice of virtue. The future St. Cajetan and his companions founded oratories and preached the Gospel. They did not come to France until 1644. Their constitutions were written by Cardinal Gian Pietro Carafa (1476–1559), the future Pope Paul IV (r.1555–59). Loyola expressed his reservations about them. The Jesuits were often confused with the Theatines. See *Encyclopaedia Britannica*, https://www.britannica.com/topic/Theatines (accessed March 1, 2021).

10   Picrochole is a fictional character created by François Rabelais for his novel *Gargantua and Pantagruel*, where Picrochole attacks the kingdom of Grandgousier. The war is named for him: *la guerre picrocholine*, "the Picrocholine War."

11   Macrobius refers to imaginary people to whom the ancients attributed a longevity of a thousand years and eternal youth. See Sutto, 299n238.

In addition, you will hold in your hands Majorca, Minorca, Sardinia, Corsica, and other islands in the Ligurian Sea, and the Balearic Islands. Moving along the coast to the left, you will dominate all of Narbonic Gaul, Provence, Allobroges, Siena, Florence, Lucca; you will capture Italy; and there is Naples, Calabria, Apulia, and Sicily, all of them sacked, and Malta. From there, we shall capture Candia, Cyprus, Rhodes, and the Cyclade Islands, and we'll have a view on the Morea.[12] It seems that, through Picrochole, that wise fool Rabelais wanted to list the imaginary victories of our Jesuits, whose knapsacks were lying there but not yet open. You're gloating (I replied). Let's leave this clowning to Jesuit La Fon: for on this subject I can't do anything but laugh. If the Jesuits had chosen one of Munster's cosmographers,[13] he could add several other savage countries, and it would have been hard for us to contradict him. I recall that, one day, the wise Tulenus[14] saw Jurisconsult Baudouin[15] strolling with André Thevet,[16] the traveler, who said that they shouldn't retract anything, because one of them had always been in his bedchamber, glued to his books, and the other had employed all his study time in travelling without seeing a book. Without being rebuked, one of them could, under a false title, claim that he had made several journeys; and the other, that he had visited several countries without being supervised. You'll even find him offering himself to our Jesuits. For over forty years they've boasted of making these great conquests, in most of those countries. Their *status* records show that when their general dies, all the fathers from the other Jesuit provinces mark out states and dignities and must go to Rome in order to proceed to elect a successor. After Ignatius's death in 1565, Francisco de Borja was elected: in both elections, they had carefully stated the good qualities of the provincial fathers, but I don't see a single one from those distant countries who participated in the aforesaid election. Every year each college is obligated to send letters to the general, to

12   The journey from one shore of the Mediterranean to the others, set forth by the bowmen, is borrowed directly from Rabelais, *Gargantua*, book 1, ch. xxxiii.

13   That is, an associate of Sebastian Munster, whose *Cosmographia universalis* was printed at Basel in 1544.

14   "Tulenus," that is, Pierre Chastel (?–1582), bishop of Tulle in 1539, grand almoner in 1548, and bishop of Orléans in 1551. He traveled in the Near East, 1533–36. See Sutto, 300n241.

15   François Baudouin (1520–73), jurist, theologian, historian, and professor of law. He was respected by his contemporaries as a statesman and jurist, even as they frowned upon his perceived inconstancy in matters of faith: for he was a Calvinist who converted to Catholicism. See *Encyclopaedia Britannica*, https://www.britannica.com/biography/Francois-Baudouin (accessed March 1, 2021).

16   André Thevet (1516–90) was a French Franciscan, explorer, and cosmographer who left an account of his journey to Brazil in the 1550s. See *Dictionary of Canadian Biography*, http://www.biographi.ca/en/bio/thevet_andre_1E.html (accessed March 1, 2021).

certify their deportment. I've looked at all the letters written to General Aquaviva in 1583, but there's no mention of all these colleges. As far as I can see, their conquest of souls has been marvelously great ever since.

Let's stick to the facts, and let's not talk about imaginings, but about common sense. If the Jesuits are spread out over so many barbarous countries, and if they've converted as many souls to our faith as they boast that they have, they would have needed the gift of tongues, in order to convert them. Our Holy Father has the power to send them into these unknown lands, but not to let them stray from the benefits of knowing tongues. It was a grace of the Holy Spirit that was especially reserved for the apostles, in order to multiply our Christian faith. Consider whether there's some appearance of this in what I'm saying. Even more, where are the kings, princes, and savage lords who, since their conversions, have come to kiss the feet of Our Holy Father in order to receive his blessing. I mean that they've been participating in a masquerade in Rome for sixty years, with three beggars disguised as kings, and that's all. I therefore put their mission vow under the heading of coins counted but never received: for, what these upright persons have been saying to us is a true imposture.

Still, it's an imposture that is nothing, compared with what they're doing to the Holy Father. Everyone must agree that he alone, and privately, can send religious to the infidel countries, to convert them, and that he can't be given a companion for this task. Yet there's nothing for which the Jesuits scorn his authority more than that this small part of the Mission depends on the Holy See, and all the rest resides in the general.

> *Possit tamen ipsemet Praepositus pro tempore existens, suos quocumque locorum, etiam inter Infideles, cùm expedire in Domino judicabit, mittere ac revocare: et per nos ac successors nostros, ad locum aliquem missos sine temporis certi limitatione, cùm id expedire ad Dei gloriam, et animarum auxilium visum fuerit (super quo conscientiam dicti Praepositi oneramus) ad alia loca transmittere liberè et licitè valeat.*

That is to say:

> And yet the general can, as often as he deems it expedient for the honor of Our Lord, freely and lawfully send his religious everywhere, even to the Infidels, and can revoke them when he pleases. And in like manner, he can send back to other places those who we sent without limitation of time. For this turns to the honor of God and the salvation of our souls, something with which we burden his conscience.

From that, you can see that the general not only can assign the Missions, as the pope does: but in addition, as he pleases, he cuts, carves, and gnaws at the missions that have been assigned by the pope. Moreover, only the fathers of the final vow are obligated toward the pope to do Missions, and in doing this, they find that the Holy See is incredibly obligated to them. Their general can do still more. For, by the Constitutions, he is permitted to send, wherever he wants, those who are in either the grand vow or the other vows, without *acception* or *exception*[17] of persons.

> *Idem Generalis in Missionibus omnem habebit potestatem, eis tamen nulla ratione repugnando, quae à sede Apostolica (ut in septima parte dicitur) profiscuntur. Mittere ergo poterit omnes sibi subditos, sive professionem emiserint, sive non emiserint, quos mittendos indicaverit, ad quaslibet mundi partes, ad quodvis tempus, vel definitum, vel indefinitum, prout ei videbitur ad quamvis actionem, ex his quibus ad proximorum auxilium, Societas solet, exercendam. Poterit etiam missos revocare, et in omnibus denique, ut ad majorem Dei gloriam fore senserit, procedere.*

The same general (reads the Latin) has all power over the action of the Mission, without however derogating from those of the Holy See (as was stated in part seven of the Constitutions), yet he will be able to send all those who are beneath him, whether they have taken the great vow of profession, or not (if he deems them worthy of it), to all the climates of the earth, for whatever time he deems good, assigned in advance or not assigned, in order to exercise there everything the Society is accustomed to doing for the good of its neighbors. He will also recall those who have been sent; and as he finds it, it should turn to the greater glory of God.

I don't find it strange that their general can give orders to those who have been sent by the pope, since he has permission to do this by the bull of 1549. But as for what depends on their Constitutions alone, and as for whom the general can send wherever he wishes, it's not only the professed fathers but all the other inferiors in his order; so, I can only be infinitely scandalized. Doing this involves giving the general too much and giving too little to Our Holy Father the Pope. Yet no matter how often they trumpet the mission vow to us, by which

---

17   *Acception* means to show preference for one person over another; but *exception* means that a rule or order does not include someone or something that normally would be included.

their fathers of the great vow are obligated to the Holy See, they make fun of him and of us. Because that vow is superfluous: their Constitutions being such, concerning their general, as I have just now reminded you. Constitutions, however, for which they have no pope as a godfather, and which are extraordinarily punishable, because they have usurped this right from the Holy See on their own private authority.

On the Blind Obedience That the Jesuits Have for the Pope, and That They Are Disavowing Today in Their New Books

THE LAWYER. Pasquier, pleading the cause of the University of Paris against the Jesuits, objected that they were making a special submission to the pope, which countervened the liberties of our Gallican Church, in everything and everywhere. This submission brought, first, a schism to the church between the papist Jesuit and the true Catholic Frenchman. Moreover, it was a submission of such consequence that if some bad disagreement were to arise between the popes and our kings, the Jesuits would be even more the sworn enemies of the crown whom we were nurturing in France. When they heard this objection, Versoris, their lawyer, made the reply that one can read in his plea. But since time has soothed their spirits, they have since decided to parry this blow with a new sophistry, saying that they have no other special vow for the pope beyond the mission vow, and that in all the rest they conform to us. Thus, they wanted to save themselves in 1594, when their cause was pleaded for the second time in the Parlement of Paris, as you've seen in the passages about the things that they are forbidden to do, which I touched upon earlier. And Montaignes, in his book called *La Vérité défendue*, wrote: "Their vow is contained in these words about their profession, after the three religious vows. *Insuper promitto specialem obedientiam summo Pontifici circa missiones.* This means nothing other than that the professed religious promise to obey the pope in a special way, without tergiversation or excuses, in any part of the world, be it the Indies, the Turks, among the infidels and the heretics, in order to convert them, or to go elsewhere among the faithful, to help them." But what pleases me is the person who wrote *The Most Humble Remonstrance and Request to the King for the Society of Jesus*.[1] Having caulked the leaks in his case with several hypocritical reasons, when he came to this high point of obedience toward the pope, he closed his book, as if inadvertently, and as if he had forgotten to reply. Then he added, as a sort of tool-shed annex that's about twenty lines long, and that's called Addition to page 56: "This same author has taught our enemies to view as calumny a vow that the professed fathers of our Society make to the Holy See, about which they have made a note stating that we promise to obey him

---

1 The author is Richeome, under the pseudonym Montaignes.

in everything and everywhere, whatever he commands, and that if the pope is a Spaniard, we will be Spaniards if he wishes. Not only is this note contrary to the truth, it is inappropriate and does not fit into the text. This vow contains nothing but a promise to employ ourselves promptly when it pleases the Holy See, among the infidels, pagans, and heretics, in order to convert them to the faith. The words of the vow are: I promise in addition a special obedience to Our Holy Father about Missions. This vow doesn't contain any particular obligation and can only be praiseworthy at a time when there's such a great need for good workers, to help the church that is harried; and it doesn't weaken or prevent in any way the submission, obedience, and fidelity that all subjects owe their princes: the French to the king of France, the Poles to the king of Poland, and so on with the others. Why, then, are they crying out that we make a vow to obey anything, anywhere, whatever we are ordered? And that this vow will turn us into Spaniards, if the pope so wishes? What is the connection between such an antecedent and such a consequence?" Let's set that word Spain aside. I won't take advantage of it. Neither for nor against the Jesuit. Each prince plays his character on this great world-stage, as he can, for the advancement of his affairs. This isn't unseemly according to the rules of statesmanship, which permit princes to love treason and to hate traitors. That's how, during our recent Troubles, the ministry of the Jesuits was helped. One day they'll find that there are very dangerous officers in its countries, and this will be based on what went on in France. Let's speak only about our current dispute: but let's do it without sophistry, if I manage to obtain that from our Jesuits. I don't want to combat them, other than by what they write. In chapter 1 of the third part of their Constitutions, where their vow of obedience to the pope and to their superiors is discussed in detail. Here are the exact words; and by them, each person will know what impudent liars the Jesuits are, even when they present their humblest request to the king.

> *Et quoniam quae ad votum castitatis pertinent, interpretatione non indigent, cùm constet quàm sit perfectè observanda: nempe enitendo Angelicam puritatem imitari, et mentis et corporis munditia. His supositis, de sancta obedientia dicetur, quam quidem omnes plurimum observare, et in ea excellere studeant, NEC SOLUM IN REBUS OBLIGATORIIS SED ETIAM in aliis, licet nihil aliud quàm signum voluntatis Superioris, siné ullo praecepto videretur. Versari autem debet ob oculos, Deus creator, et Dominus noster, propter quem homini obedientia praestatur, et ut in spiritu amoris, et non cum perturbatione timoris, procedatur, curandum est. Ita ut omnes constanti animo incumbamus, ut nihil perfectionis cum divina gratia consequi possimus, in absoluta omnium constitutionum observatione, nostrique*

instituti peculiari ratione adimplenda, praetermittamus, et exactissimè omnes nervos virium nostrarum ad hanc virtutem obedientiae, imprimis SUMMO PONTIFICI DEINDE SUPERIORIBUS SOCIETATIS exhibendam intendamus. Ita ut omnibus in rebus ad quas potest se cum charitate obedientia extendere, ad ejus vocem, perinde ac si à Christo Domino egrederetur (quando quidem ipsius loco est, ac pro ipsius amore ac reverentia, obedientiam praestamus) quàm promptissimi simus, re quavis, atque adeo litera à nobis inchoata, nedum perfecta, studio obediendi, relicta, ad eum scopum vires omnes ac intentionem, in Domino convertendo: ut facta obedientia, tum in exequutione, tum in voluntate, tum in intellectu, sit nobis semper ex omni parte perfecta, cum magna celeritate, spirituali gaudio et perseverantia, quicquid nobis injunctum fuerit, obeundo, omnia justa esse nobis persuadendo, omnem sententiam, ac judicium nostrum contrarium CAECA QUADAM OBEDIENTIA, abnegando: Et id qiuden in omnibus quae à Superiore disponuntur, ubi definiri non possit aliquod peccati genus intercedere. Et sibi quisque persuadeat quod qui sub obedientia vivunt, se ferri ac regi à divina providentia per Superiores suos, sinere debent, perinde ac si cadavre essent, quod quoquo versus se ferri, et quacumque ratione tractari se sinit. Vel similiter atque senis baculus, qui ubicumque et quacunque in re velit, eo uti, qui eum mani tenet, ei inseruit. Sic enim obediens rem quamcunque cui eum Superior, ad auxilium totius Religionis velit impendere, cum animi hilaritate debet exequi. Pro certo habens quod ea ratione potius, quàm re alia quavis, quam praestare possit, propriam voluntatem, ac judicium diversum sectando, divinae voluntati respondebit.

For this passage the note reads:

Obedientia quod ad exequutionem attinet, tunc praestatur, cum res jussa completur: quod ad voluntatem, cùm ille qui obedit, idipsum vult quod ille qui jubet: Quod ad intellectum, cum id ipsum sentit quod ille, et quod jubetur, benè juberi existimat: Et est imperfecta ea obedientia, in qua praeter exequutionem non est haec ejusdem voluntatis et sententiae, inter eum qui jubet, et cui jubetur, consensio.

I'll put these passages into the least bad French that I can, for we all have an interest in their being understood:

And inasmuch as what concerns chastity needs no explanation, there being no doubt about how strictly it should be observed, that is to say, by trying to conform to angelic purity through bodily and spiritual cleanliness. This presupposes that we'll speak of the holy obedience we ought to observe and excel at, through very careful study. AND NOT ONLY IN OBLIGATORY THINGS BUT in others as well, but at this time it seems that there is only an indication of the superior's will, not his express order. This is appropriate for us to put before the eyes of God our Creator and Lord, wanting to obey man and give orders to proceed with a gay spirit that's not greatly troubled by fear. So that we all will move ahead with a firm heart, in order not to forget any of the perfection that we, by the grace of God, can acquire by strictly following the Constitutions and the special Institute of our order: and let's strongly tighten all the sinews of our strength for that virtue of obedience, in order to make the vow FIRST OF ALL TO OUR HOLY FATHER THE POPE, THEN TO ALL THE SUPERIORS OF OUR SOCIETY. To the point that, in everything to which obedience can charitably reach out to, we ought to drop everything we are doing, even if it be a missive just begun and not completed, we should desire to obey quickly, and should respond quickly to their voices, just as if they had emanated from Our Lord Jesus Christ. It's also true that, in his place, and for his honor and reverence, we should obey them. Turning all our strength and intentions toward God, may this obedience be in everything, and in everything may it be accomplished, in execution, will, and judgment, doing what we are told with all speed, spiritual joy, and perseverance; and may we, by BLIND OBEDIENCE TO HIM, strip ourselves of contrary opinions and judgments. And do this, in all the things ordered by our superior, where one cannot discern (as it has been said) that there is some sort of sin. And may each person be convinced that those who live under obedience should allow themselves to be carried away and be governed by divine providence, through his superiors, as if he were a dead body that allows itself to be carried and moved in any fashion one wants. Or else, like the staff in the old man's hand that he uses everywhere, and in everything where he needs help. The person who is obeying should do what is ordered of him for the help of all religion, and should be assured that, by following this way, he will satisfy God's will better than if, acting differently, he followed his own way and his contrary judgment.

The note explains:

> Obedience, as far as it involves execution, is practiced when one accomplishes what is ordered; and as far as the will is concerned, when one desires the same thing as the person who is giving the order. And as for

judgment or intelligence, when one agrees with the other person and believes that what one has been ordered to do has been justly ordered. And obedience is imperfect when there is neither the execution nor the confirming of wills and judgments, all together, between the one who commands and the one who receives the command.

Don't you see that the Jesuits were impudent liars, when they said that their special vow to the pope was only related to the Mission, and when they said that those who said something different were calumniators. For this extract that I've shown you, shows that they are obligated to obey, not only ABOUT THE OBLIGATORY THINGS of their order, but about all the other things as well; and with a command so strict and absolute that it's impossible to be more so. But to whom are they lying? To the majesty of their king: because the above humble supplication and remonstrance is addressed to him alone. To lie boldly, in the face of one's king: the Jesuit doesn't think he's transgressing, nor does he think that, when he confirms his lie by breaking his word, while touching the holy Gospels. And why, then? Because when he receives the order to lie to his general, his vow of obedience is so precise that he thinks he's been freed of all sin, and that he would fail more if, in telling the truth, he hadn't obeyed him. I can't hold back my anger. For if this vow of blind obedience to the pope is bad, why do these good folks observe it? If it's good, why do they disavow it, even on so lofty a subject? And of what stuff is it made? As for me, who wants to live and die in the faith that my godparents and the guarantors of my inheritance promised for me to God, on the day of my baptism, I'll never doubt that I can recognize myself in the midst of my Catholic, Apostolic, and Roman adversaries, as my predecessors did. Behind this disavowal, they must understand something that I must say to you: don't think that the Jesuits are men like us other men. They have two souls in their bodies. One is Roman, and it is inside Rome; the other is French, and it is in France. In order to be welcome in Rome, they talk only of this absolute obedience, involving everything the pope might order them to do. In France they disavow it totally, in order not to be banished. For, so that you'll understand, our France lives under obedience to the Roman church, but with certain liberties[2] by means of which it preserves itself against both the temporal and the spiritual undertakings of the Roman Curia. Popes are men, made of the same pieces as all other men: to the point that there sometimes is humanity in their holiness. If a pope falls prey to the surprises and the false information coming from those around him, he would undertake a war against our kings, would believe that the Jesuits are

---

2   A reminder: he is alluding to the so-called Gallican liberties.

just so many strict enemies against them. The pope strikes with his principal sword, that is, his censures. A declaration of heresy soon follows, then a crusade is announced. So, mingle together the factions and the preaching of the Jesuits, and the vow of blind obedience, unknown in all Antiquity. Believe that it would mean putting our kingdom into an amazing disarray. Remember how Pope Sixtus IV failed to catch unawares the Florentine state about the House of Medicis, when Giulio was killed in church hearing Mass.[3] Think that it would have been quite possible for those lords to protect themselves from this unexpected conspiracy, if there had been a band of Jesuits in their city. Remember, too, something that was going on in France under Pope Sixtus V, not all that long ago, and which hasn't yet been forgotten: at first, we were afflicted by his connivance and his contributions to our Troubles. Both Sixtus IV and Sixtus V had been Franciscan monks; both subsequently were popes. The former made a vow against the Republic of Florence, but there were not yet any Jesuits in the world. The Jesuits led the Republic of Florence by the hand, against the flourishing kingdom of France. You'll find that they had a big reason to disavow their special vow of blind obedience to the papacy: they know in their consciences that no state will be safe against the anger of a pope, while they remain, and as long as they remain.

---

3   On April 26, 1477, the so-called Pazzi Conspiracy took place. Hoping to overthrow the Medicis, the Pazzi family killed Giuliano de' Medici (1453–78) and seriously injured his brother Lorenzo (r.1469–92). See *Encyclopaedia Britannica*, https://www.britannica.com/event/Pazzi-conspiracy (accessed March 1, 2021).

CHAPTER 18

The Jesuits' Solution for Concealing the Impiety of Their Blind Obedience

THE LAWYER was finishing this speech, when the Jesuit, thinking that there was a new impediment hanging over him, interrupted him. THE JESUIT. You are making our hair curl in such a marvelous way, and you are doing it so blindly, that you don't see that the passage you pointed out bears within it the solution for everything for which you are reproaching us. No matter what obedience is ordered of us, it is always on this condition: *ubi definiri non possit aliquod peccati genus*, there, and in case no species of sin is noticed.[1] And that is what Montaignes, one of our brethren, as you previously argued, wisely said. THE LAWYER: You aren't teaching me anything new, and I wouldn't have failed to pluck on that cord if you hadn't interrupted me. True, you took some pity on me; and by this brief intermission, you wanted me to grab a bit of breath. For to tell you the truth, I'm getting weary. Still, before finishing, I'll admit that the clause you cited is twisted up in it. For you other messieurs never fail to find a loophole to conceal your modesty. Grant me four or five words, along with the rest of this point, and I'll declare that you've won this case. Your vow obligates you, and binds you, to believe that when either Our Holy Father the Pope or your superiors order you to do something, even if it isn't obligatory for the order, you should think that God is speaking from their mouths. And as soon as you receive an order, even an unspoken one that takes the form of a wink, you must stop whatever you're working on, even a letter just begun, and you must obey. In obeying, your hand, your heart, and your judgment, all combined, should participate. On this matter, you should be like a cadaver or a staff, which doesn't move unless pushed by the person touching it. And finally, the obedience that you show must be blind. That, in sum, is your vow, which you say you're going to limit by these words: *moyennant que l'on ne trouve appercevance de péché*, "as long as there is no appearance of sin." What if I think I've been ordered to commit a sin by the person who, you think, recognizes that God is present in the command? Moreover, are you giving me the leisure to think about it, if I could do so, seeing that I must obey in the time of a single wink? In addition to issuing a command, you order that it be carried out with the help of my will and my judgment. By this you take all knowledge

---

1 "And in which no species of sin can be judged to be present," *Constitutions*, VI, ch. 1, 1 (p. 220).

from me, even wanting me to be like a staff in an old man's hand. And as a conclusion, this obedience, which you want to be blind, has eyes, if I'm permitted
to base my judgment on the good or the evil in the command. And really, one
shouldn't have eyes or judgment, any more than you do in your blind obedience; nor should one say that the four or five words that Ignatius slipped into
this clause, are useless and frustrating. If I had only that, it would be too much
to make your sophistry visible; but I don't want to remain on such a lovely path.
The person who wrote that constitution is Ignatius: for Ribadeneyra admits
that all your Constitutions come from him. Ignatius is, therefore, the most
faithful translator of his intention. Pedro Maffei, a priest of your Society, wrote
Ignatius's life, and it was approved by your General Aquaviva, because he's the
one to whom the book is dedicated. I don't think he would have permitted it
to be printed, much less dedicated to him, if he hadn't deemed this story to be
greatly to the advantage of your order. Now, pay attention to the commentary
we can draw from this book, in order to show how Ignatius wanted the obedience of his followers to be blind:

> *Obedientiae studium, quibuscumque rebus potuit semper ostendit: Romano*
> *quidem Pontifici, cujus in verba praecipuo quodam sacramento juraverat,*
> *ita era praesto, ut adipsius nutum sese paratum exhiberet. Confecta jam*
> *aetate, unius baculi adminiculo, pedibus, quocunque opus esset, peregre*
> *proficisci, vel etiam navigium ascendere plané exarmatum, seque eodem*
> *pontifice jubente mari ventisque, sine ulla dubitatione committere. Quem*
> *ipsius animum vir quidam primarius cum haud satis probaret, et in ejus-*
> *modi re, consilium prudentiamque requireret, Prudentiam quidem non*
> *obedientis, verùm imperantis esse respondit Ignatius. Et sane cum in soci-*
> *etate nostra, virtutem hanc, caeteris virtutibus anteferret, tum nihil huic*
> *laudi tam contrarium dicebat esse, quàm in Superiorum jussis et consi-*
> *lio examinando, moram, vel potius arrogantiam, negabatque obedientis*
> *nomine dignum haberi oportere, qui legitimo Superiori, non, cum voluntate,*
> *judicium quoque submitteret. Id enim gratissimum esse Deo holocaustum,*
> *cum omnes animi vires, ac praesertim intelligentia et mens, quae summum*
> *in homine obtinent locum in obsequium Christi coguntur. Qui verò inviti ac*
> *dissentientes, actu exteriore dumtaxat, jussa praepositorum exequerentur,*
> *hos inter vilissima mancipia, vel pecudes potius numerandos aiebat.* And
> a bit later: *Quinetiam in sermone quotidiano usurpare saepe consueverat,*
> *qui ad Superioris nutum, voluntatis propensionem solummodo, non etiam*

judicii consensionem accomodarent, eos altero tantum pede intra Religionis
septa versari.[2]

That's the obedience that Ignatius wanted to be shown, first to the pope and
then to the superiors of his order. Let's gather together all the above papers.
Here's a man who clamps death between his teeth: he must walk. Here's a ship
crushed in a storm: this honest man must enter it, if the pope orders him to
enter it. God very specifically forbids me to kill myself, under pain of eternal
damnation. In these two commands, I see my very pressing death: was there
ever more reason to say that a person wasn't forced to obey? And every time, by
Ignatius's obedience, not only do we have to obey, but if we don't do so, we're
committing a great and enormous sin. Was there ever a greater reason to say
that one didn't have to obey? Obey, and you sin against Ignatius's orders, which
the Jesuits deem to be greater than God's orders. If Tertullian was criticized by
our ancestors for having forbidden a Christian to flee from one city to another:
that is, if he was criticized for wanting to make them murderers of themselves,
what should we say today about Ignatius's cruel proposition? Be that as it may,
you see that our Jesuits were mockers when, in order to excuse the impiety of
their blind obedience, they added: WHERE THEY DO NOT DISCERN whether
there is sin. Not only did Ignatius not permit his religious to discern it, but he
also did the contrary: he deemed them worse than slaves or brutish beasts,
if they disobeyed an order. And to make you increasingly see the will of that
great legislator, this is what Maffei adds: *Atque ad sapientem hanc sanctamque*

---

2   "He always showed enthusiasm for obedience by all the means he could: indeed, he was so
    ready that he would show that he was prepared to obey the command of the Roman pontiff,
    to whom he was sworn by special oath. When the time was right, he set off on foot on a pil-
    grimage, wherever there was need, with only a staff to rest upon; nor even to board a ship,
    clearly not sea-worthy, nor to commit himself to sea and wind whenever the same Pontiff
    commanded, without any hesitation. When a certain principal did not sufficiently approve
    his decision, as lacking wisdom and discretion, Ignatius replied that wisdom was not for the
    one obeying, but for the one commanding. And clearly in our Society he would place this vir-
    tue above all virtues, so he used to say that nothing was so contrary to the recommendation
    of obedience, as delay, or rather arrogance in questioning the reason of our Superiors' orders
    and he said that he was worthy to be called obedient who did not submit both his will and
    his judgement to his lawful superior. It was a most acceptable sacrifice to God, when all the
    powers of a man's mind, especially judgement and understanding, which hold the highest
    position in humankind, are compelled to obey Christ. Indeed, he used to say that those who
    unwillingly and with dissent only in outward show performed their superiors' orders should
    be numbered among the lowest slaves or rather sheep. [...] Indeed, he was accustomed to
    say in his everyday speech that those who brought only a ready will, and not the consent
    of their judgement to fulfilling their Superior's will, had only one foot within the cloister of
    their order."

stultitiam caecae (ut ipse aiebat) Obedientiae, suos ut essent ad subita et seria promptiores, interdum etiam fictis in rebus erudiebat.[3] And about this proposition, he recounts how, one day, a priest of the Society, garbed in his chasuble and emerging from the robing room, and holding the chalice in his hands, to go celebrate Mass, received a message from Ignatius to come to him promptly. The Jesuit obeyed and left his chasuble and the chalice. Ignatius asked him if he had disapproved of this order: It was very just (replied the priest), since it came from you. Well, (replied Ignatius) be informed that I didn't give the order because I wanted you to do something: I did it in order to test your obedience. By quitting the sacrifice of the Mass that you were supposed to be celebrating, you did a far more meritorious act than if you'd completed it. Moreover, since the mystery of God's altar has so much merit, it is written that the obedience is preferable to the sacrifice. Another time, a Jesuit priest was hearing the confession of a young gentleman, and Ignatius sent for him. The priest replied that he couldn't come to see him until he had given absolution to his penitent. Unhappy about this reply, Ignatius sent for him a second time. Seeing this, the priest, who was hearing confession, begged the gentleman to be patient; and the priest went to find Ignatius, who at once said: What! I had to send for you twice? And with sharp words, he treated the man very roughly, not because he wanted the man to do something, but because he wanted to see the sort of obedience, he would bring to things that he was ordered to do in all seriousness. He wanted to see whether there was some way to begin an examen and to make him think about sin, honor, dignity, decorum, and duty in the church: they forbade two Jesuit priests to obey the general. Yet he didn't want to be rewarded in that way, for an inferior should not be made aware of whether he has sinned, or not; and prudence was not required of the person who was ordered, but of the person who gave the order. These are, then, real tricks, these are mockeries, these are illusions and phantoms with which the Jesuit wants to deceive us, when he claims that one isn't obliged to obey if the order has some appearance of sin. For, to the contrary, all sins are covered and erased when one obeys.

That, Messieurs, is what I wanted to talk with you about this morning. And because we've satisfied our talkative spirits, it seems to me that it's well past the time for nourishing our bodies; so please excuse me if I stop here. But if you protest, after the noontime meal I'll go into detail about the remaining things to be said on this subject.

---

3   And so that his followers would be readier all of a sudden for this wise and holy foolishness of blind obedience (as he used to call it) he was sometimes even educating them in fictive situations.

About Ignatius's Wisdom and the New Jesuits' Silliness. A Conversation between the Jesuit and the Author of the Present Discourses

The group not only agreed with the Lawyer's proposal, it also thanked him for the trouble he'd taken and that he was promising to take, resolved as we all were to be as favorable an audience in the afternoon as in the morning. But the Gentleman began talking. THE GENTLEMAN. If I'm king in my house, as the charcoal-maker is in his house, then I order that the afternoon will be spent going for a promenade; and you, Monsieur, my great friend (said he, addressing the Lawyer), you're permitted to promenade your thoughts until tomorrow morning when, God willing, we'll finish our talking. THE NARRATOR. It was done just as he ordered. The meal was brought to us; and when the table was cleared, each rose from his seat in order to take whatever paths pleased him: gardens, flowerbeds, neat rows of trees, fields, meadows, shrubbery. For our host's place was quite varied. And as for me, I approached the Jesuit, whom I found in good humor; and having circled the house with him a few times, I began talking to him. THE NARRATOR. What do you think of our Lawyer? It seems to me that he said some very pertinent things and talked very freely about your brethren. THE JESUIT. It is not for me to judge, all the more so since, if I said that he talked very well, I would be wronging our Society. If I said that he talked badly, you would think that I was flattering my brethren. Consequently, no matter what my answer might be, I should recuse myself. Let us put all those rhetorical skills aside. THE NARRATOR. You and I are here in a place of truth, so we must not dissimulate. Don't you recall having read, in Herodotus,[1] that a woman, having removed her nightshirt in bed, near her husband, showed her privy places. Since you've removed the clothing of your order, I think it very easy for you to remove the hypocrisy that your critics say

---

1 Herodotus (c.484–c.425 BCE), was an ancient Greek whose *Histories* was a detailed record of his inquiry into the origins of the Greco-Persian Wars (498–448 BCE). He is widely considered to be the first to treat a historical subject by collecting historical materials and then arranging them into a historiographic narrative. He also recorded local customs in foreign countries. See *Encyclopaedia Britannica*, https://www.britannica.com/biography/Herodotus-Greek-historian (accessed March 1, 2021).

© KONINKLIJKE BRILL NV, LEIDEN, 2021 | DOI:10.1163/9789004164062_039

you are sheltering in your houses. You are a traveler: Homer[2] can never better represent men's wisdom than by a Ulysses who had seen several countries. Since you've been chosen by your general to go across the country, sounding out the diversity of your manners and opinions, and to give him a report, it's not by being alone in the fields at times, that you'll get the leisure time to philosophize about your brethren. Therefore, I affectionately beg you to tell me, sincerely, how you judge them; and at the same time, to tell me what you think of the Lawyer's remarks. For although you're very enthralled by your Constitutions, your thoughts are free. That's something about which the legislator of your order hasn't been able to give an order. THE JESUIT. Since you are entreating me so honestly, I would be marvelously discourteous if I did not obey you. The Lawyer is wrong, but not as wrong as some would like to say. If he spoke ill of our Society, we are the cause. No one is wounded other than by himself. The greatest secret that I can find in the matter of religious orders is that their secrets not be divulged, and that each religious, according to his profession, should live with a conscience at rest. Among the ancient priests of pagan law, I note that the Druids were very respected, and nothing contributed more to their reputations than old prudence about not writing down their doctrine, but keeping it and carrying it out strictly from person to person, as part of a long ancestral tradition that they transmitted to their successors. If we had followed in the footsteps of our great and wise Ignatius, we would not have fallen into that error. Because it was his opinion that we should remain closed off and discreet, so that people would not know our rules. So, our ceremonies, or to be more accurate, our devotions, can be viewed by the common people, but not read. If I dare use this expression, our enemies were groping around when they talked about us. Now that our bulls and Constitutions can be gone through by one person or another, I suspect that we shall be lost, and that while some held us in honor, in the future they will hold us in horror. That is why I cannot sufficiently praise our Ignatius's prudence. For as long as he lived, he not only planned but actually applied the Constitutions that he had drawn up, for the maintenance of our order; but he did not want them published during his lifetime, and they were only applied after his death and after the Congregation we held in Rome in 1558. We thought at the time that we were creating great men, and never was there such a silly notion as that, as events

---

2   Homer is the legendary author of the *Iliad* and the *Odyssey*, epic poems that are the central works of ancient Greek literature. It is generally accepted that these poems about Ulysses and his roaming were composed at some point around the late eighth or early seventh century BCE. See *Encyclopaedia Britannica*, https://www.britannica.com/biography/Homer-Greek-poet (accessed March 1, 2021).

have demonstrated to us. Did he have a latticework grill that impeded his religious from taking up pen and paper in order to defend us, or to justify us when we were assailed? Perhaps he did it from Christian charity, and perhaps from worldly wisdom as well. *Spreta* (said wise Tacitus) *exolescunt: Si irascare, agnita videntur.*[3] Never was there an act that seemed to bring greater prejudice to our Society than the censure by the Faculty of theology of Paris in 1554. Some persons with itchy hands wanted to reply: they were either the foremost or the smuggest ones, and they made people believe that they would gain the upper hand. Yet Ignatius, subtler and more judicious than they, very specifically forbade them to do so. And there is no doubt that, thanks to this advice, he gained a greater advantage by remaining silent than all the paper-patchers and menders have done since then by writing. For it is certain that, after many years, this censure would have been buried in the coffin of forgetfulness, if we had not given them the material for renewing it by scuffling, sometimes with the general and sometimes with a number of persons in France. During Ignatius's lifetime, as I mentioned, we were not permitted to shine a light on our concepts publicly, no matter how assured we were. Today, even the least of our brethren shamelessly uses his pen and his wits, without considering the good or the evil that he can create for the order by his writings. Their spirits are especially contented by a written cacozelia[4] that later can be seen to have cost dearly, making a number of false and erroneous propositions modeled after their silliness. And God knows how many ill-willed persons know how to profit from it. I see a Giovanni Pietro Maffei first, circa 1587, followed by a Pedro Ribadeneyra in 1592, who shed light on the life of our good Ignatius; and Orazio Torcellini wrote the life of Francisco Xavier, along with much hypocrisy (I greatly regret letting that word escape me), absurdity, and contrariety that, I am sure, must provide us very soon with a man who is full of leisure and spite, and who will provide us with a verbal dissection that will shame the memory of these two holy fathers, and the memory of the confusions in our order. Just imagine, what a savant priest he is, our Emmanuel Sà.[5] When he had his *Confessional Aphorisms* printed, he said that he is a doctor of theology of our Society; and in that book he boasts of having worked on it for forty full years. How many articles did you find in that book that do not bewail the desolation of kings and kingdoms? If he had been as wise as our first fathers, these would

---

3   "If you show contempt for abuse, it will gradually die away; if you show irritation, it will be seen as deserved." Tacitus, *Annals*, IV, xxxiv.

4   *Cacozélie*, "cacozelia," refers to a stylistic affectation in diction, such as tossing in foreign words to make a text learned or selecting metaphors that will make bad things seem worse.

5   Emmanuel Sà, *Aphorismi confessariorum ex doctorum sententiis collecti* (Venice, 1592).

be good lessons to whisper in the ears of those idiots who think we are the great penitentiary of the Holy See; and, as such, usually seek us out to hear them confess their huge sin. But by trumpeting all these sinful circumstances in his book, he is teaching us what an Emmanuel Sà is, who worked forty whole years in order to finally have himself declared barely wise. As far as our Reverend Father Robert Bellarmine is concerned, I recognize him to be a very able man, a man who, by his writings, has found his way to the red hat: but I can say, as something that is very true, that in seeing to his affairs, he spoils ours, as you can see by his books on the translation of the Empire and the indulgences of Rome. By the latter book, he even touched upon several peculiarities that do not involve pardons and for which pardons must be begged from king and bishops. I do not propose to offend him here, but if I ever find myself in his presence, I shall whisper a few words in his ear, and I shall beg him to henceforth give his pen a bit more modesty, which I am sure he will do, having reached the position that made him write that way. Perhaps he was merely hoping to be pope one day. But I think he is so sagacious that he does not attach his opinions to that impossibility. For an infinity of reasons that I prefer to think about rather than talk about, the wise Consistory of Rome will never permit a Jesuit to rise to the lofty level of the papacy.

Ever since the decree issued against us in 1594, in Paris, I have seen five books that our brethren have had printed. The titles are: *Le Plaidoyé de Maître Pierre Versoris avocat en Parlement, pour les prêtres et écoliers du Collège de Clermont, fondé en l'Université de Paris, demandeurs contre ladite université défenderesse. Défenses du Collège de Clermont contre les requêtes des religieux de la Compagnie de Jésus, au très-Chrétien Roy de France et de Navarre Henri quatrième de ce nom. La Vérité défendue pour la Religion Catholique en la cause des Jésuites, contre le Plaidoyé d'Antoine Arnauld, par François des Montaignes. Réponse de René de La Fon pour les religieux de la Compagnie de Jésus, au Plaidoié de Simon Marion contre iceux le 16 d'octobre 1597. Avec autres notes sur le Plaidoyé et autres sujets des Recherches d'Étienne Pasquier.*[6] Believe me: there is not a single one of these nice authors who, in defending us, does not accuse us. And from time to time,

---

6   "The Plea of Master Pierre Versoris, lawyer in the parlement, for the priests and scholars of the Collège de Clermont, founded in the University of Paris, plaintiffs against the said university, plaintiff. – Interdictions of the Collège de Clermont against the requests and pleas against them, previously printed. – Most humble remonstrance and request of the religious of the Society of Jesus, to the Most Christian King of France and of Navarre, Henri fourth of the name. – Truth defended for the Catholic religion in the case of the Jesuits against the Plea of Antoine Arnaud, by François des Montaignes. – Reply of René de La Fon for the religious of the Society of Jesus in the plea of Simon Marion against the said persons, October 16, 1597. – With other notes about the Plea and other subjects in the *Recherches* of Etienne Pasquier."

you would find a few daring points that have a bit of the flavor of the scholar. Having said that, I have said everything. Our Society does not please everyone. Not even a number of frank Catholics. It is a misfortune that accompanies us in the midst of the blessings we receive from God. A misfortune, however, that we aggravate by another one. For if we find someone who does not applaud us, we promptly declare him a heretic. That is a new privilege we have given ourselves: we turn nasty statements into religion, and we think we are rid of it if, under a disguised name, we let our insults ring forth. Benito Arias Montanus,[7] a person who never made a mistake about our Catholic religion, had a Bible printed at Antwerp in 1584 with some brief remarks where he complains about the outrage that our brethren had done to him. *Qui cùm, sibi soli sapere* (said he, referring to us) *soli benè vivere, Jesumque proprius insequi et comitari videantur, atque id palam professi jactitent, me qui minimum atque adeo inutilem Jesu Christi discipulum ago, odio habuerunt gratis. Atque hi quod neminem qui alias benè audiat, imiprobare audent, aliorum quos ad eam rem occulté inducere possint, ingeniis et nominibus abutuntur.*[8] We were making too much of what others were writing against him, and we were not daring to attack him with our pens. We were doing this at the time; but since then, we have worked out a new formula: we write books under pseudonyms. That is the case for the two books that are circulating under the names of François des Montaignes and René de La Fon, which I have not been able to read without getting very angry. And in the book supposedly written by Montaignes, I find that the author chose a name that matched his book: *Parturient montes, nascetur ridiculus mus.*[9] Think of the masterpiece he wrote, revealing not only the secrets of our simple vow but also those of chastity; think of the disarray in which he puts us near kings, when we place their crowns at the full and unadorned disposition of the Holy See. And I shall add that because our hands were shaking, this book was translated into Latin by one of our brethren named des Montaignes, *Montanus*, the

---

7 Benito Arias Montano (c.1527–98), also known as Montanus, was an orientalist and Spanish humanist. Philip II put him in charge of editing a polyglot Bible, which was printed at Antwerp, 1569–72, by Plantin. See "Benito Arias Montano," in *OBO: Renaissance and Reformation*, https://www.oxfordbibliographies.com/view/document/obo-9780195399301/obo-9780195399301-0459.xml (accessed March 1, 2021).

8 Those who, since they think they alone are wise and live well, and closely follow and accompany Jesus and, having confessed this openly, boast of it; they freely hated me who is a small and virtually useless follower of Jesus Christ. And these men, because they dare not disapprove of anyone who listens well to others, abuse the name and skills of others whom they could secretly persuade to such a course.

9 "Mountains will labor, to birth will come a laughter-rousing mouse" (Horace, *Poetic Art*, verse 139).

name of a remarkable antique heretic;[10] so that our enemies would always have something bad to say about us. As for La Fon, the person who dreamed up that name should have said Le Fou instead,[11] because I have found a lot of craziness and a great deal of buffoonery in him. Étienne Pasquier wrote several books that were well-received in France and in other nations. Even in his book about *La Vérité défendue*, Montaignes mentioned him favorably. That little fool La Fon, in order to compensate for his companion's defect, drowned him in curses, more than a prostitute from a brothel would do. And I wager that Pasquier, whose hand is far from asleep, does not stand there speechless. In this way, it will be one good turn for another. THE NARRATOR. Don't believe it, for when I spoke to him about it, this was his reply: Monsieur my friend, this disguised Jesuit resembles a mardi-gras mask that got a dispensation for the day and that carries around some blacking that he smears on those who are in the way, and who, if they want to suffer the consequences, will serve as a foot-wiper rug for ordinary people My *Recherches* on France, which includes my *Plaidoyer*, have their safe-conduct glued on their forehead: let people read my research, it will speak for me. And let anyone who doesn't want to read it, come to me, and they'll answer for that research. If some learned man finds abstruseness in it, I'll be very highly honored if he'll let me enlighten him. For, in sum, I'm making myself believe that this charlatan, who was thinking of suing me, was sometimes suing Saint Paul, sometimes Saint Luke, sometimes Lactance,[12] and sometimes Saint Bernard and the venerable Bede; and even more, their Bellarmine, whose authority has far greater merit for them than the authority of Saint Paul. It's a remarkable virtue of the Jesuits: the more they advance, the less wise they become. Do you want to know why? The first lesson they are given when they enter the novitiate is to recognize Jesus Christ absolutely, not only in the person of their general but also in the person of their other superiors. And as soon as one of them advances to a different grade, he thinks that he is, to the others, what his superiors were to him. To the point that he believes that his fantastic imaginings are the articles of our faith. And in this vain belief,

---

10   Montanus (*fl.* 2nd century), founded Montanism, a schismatic movement of Christianity from the second to ninth centuries. The prophetic movement initially expected an imminent transformation of the world but later evolved into a sectarianism that claimed a new revelation. See *Encyclopaedia Britannica*, https://www.britannica .com/biography/Montanus-religious-leader (accessed March 1, 2021).

11   *Le fou*, means "the crazy man."

12   Lucius Caecilius Firmianus (*c.*250–325), known as Lactantius, was called the Christian Cicero, owing to his elegant Latin prose. He guided the developing religious policy of Emperor Constantine I. His apologetic works explained Christianity in terms that would be acceptable to non-Christians. See *Encyclopedia Britannica*, https://www.britannica .com/biography/Lactantius (accessed March 1, 2021).

he overflows with a thousand foolishnesses. It suffices for you that I don't want that miscarriage of a book to be born alive, as a result of my reply. When the Jesuits' library in Paris was sold,[13] they had my Latin Epigrams. In book 6 they will find this quatrain, which I offer them as my sole reply to that fool:

Carmine nescio quis nos corrodente lacessit,
Respondere sibi me cupit, haud faciam.
Rursus at ecce magis, magis insectatur et urget,
Respondere sciat me sibi, dum taceo.[14]

THE NARRATOR. That's what I can tell you about Pasquier's reply, by which you can see that he neglects your La Fon. THE JESUIT. He may have been going too far. For don't think that our religious family had nothing to do with all the books I classified. The rules we follow when publishing our books demonstrate that. The author resembles the choirboys in cathedrals or collegials, who carry the books ahead of the others; and after one of them has sung a verse, he is followed by all the musicians. It is like that for us. The person who carries his book sings first, communicates it to the provincial, the rector, the fathers, the regent, both at the house and at the college where they reside. All of them, by common accord, make their contribution: so that the general management of household affairs comes from the author, but most of the individual pieces come from several other persons. That is the first way in which we use this fabric. After that, comes another way: by our Constitutions we are expressly forbidden to expose a book to the light without our general's permission. He looks at the book, or his four assistants look at it, or the others he has delegated look at it. In short, take it as a very certain proposition that if all the books written by me were named above[15] and are described as available, it is because

---

13   That is, sold after the Jesuits' expulsion from Paris in 1595.
14   I do not know who provokes us in biting verse,
       he desires that I reply to him, I will not do it.
       But see, again and more! he presses on and is more critical,
       let him know that I reply to him, while I stay silent.
       The contemporary English translation renders:
       With biting verse I know not who provokes
       Me to make aunswere, but I meane to cease
       Yet more and more, he follows me with strokes
       I make him aunswere, when I hold my peace.
       The poem was published in Pasquier's *Oeuvres* (Amsterdam [Trévoux]: Compagnie des libraires associés, 1723), 1, col. 1212.
15   Two books by Jesuits appear on the above list: Montaignes, author of *La Vérité défendue*, and La Fon, who published a reply. One can presume that the disguised Jesuit is none other than Richeome.

our entire order approves. THE NARRATOR. If that's how it works, your order is marvelously ignorant, permitting all these ferocious books to go about the streets. And one wouldn't need a lot of them to return your sect to the begging purse where your historiographers say that it was born. THE JESUIT. That is what matters most: to see our superiors, with an appetite for blind vengeance, go crazy alongside the crazy people. But meanwhile, what did Pasquier say when he saw this noble Epitaph that our La Fon wrote about him, which reads:

> Now, he still lives joyously, and he still writes and dreams, if he wishes, against the Jesuits. He will dream in season about his old age, until some-one in the Society, or if they disdain him, someone speaking for the public, makes a general review of what he has shed light on, and a col-lection of his ignorances, dreams, asinine remarks, malicious remarks, heresies, Machiavelisms, in order to construct for him a tomb of macabre memory, where he will be locked away alive, where crows and vultures are attracted by the odor for one hundred leagues around, and where men do not dare come closer than a hundred paces without holding their noses for the stink, where the brambles and the nettles grow, where the vipers and basilisks, the barn owls and the birds wading in a marsh sing, so that by such a monument, those who are alive at present, and those who will live in future centuries, may know that, as a distinctive persecu-tor and calumniator, the Jesuits had a distinctive liar and a capital enemy of virtue and of virtuous folk, and that, at the expense of a proud, igno-rant person, all the calumniators may learn to think more carefully about what they say and write against religious orders, and not be impudently scandalized by their defamatory and blasphemous writings about God's holy church.

THE NARRATOR. You ask me what Pasquier said about it. I'll tell you. In a few words he told me that this placard with the Epitaph was worthy only of a Jesuit soul. Therefore, he wanted it engraved on the portals of all their col-leges, as a true image of their piety. So that everyone will know that it wasn't without good reason that they called themselves the Society of Jesus, who, on the tree of the cross, prayed to God his Father for those who had crucified him. THE JESUIT and I, THE NARRATOR, spent the afternoon talking about this, and about other things that were not praises, by which I recognized that this upright man had several good features that were unusual in the other Jesuits. And I found that there is a great difference between the person who shuts him-self up in a bedchamber and becomes wise solely by reading books, and the other sort of person who, in addition to reading books, communicates with others by speaking. The study of the former person smells musty, and the study of the latter person, who studies without studying, has great advantages over the study of the former. As for me, I didn't tire of being in the Jesuit's company, and I believe I would have spent the rest of the day with him, if a misfortune that tried to rob me of my contentment hadn't deprived me. It took the form of the arrival of two or three silly persons who began to jeer at me, saying that they saw clearly that it was my intention to become a Jesuit. I replied to them: No doubt about it, if all the others were like him. And so, we let our words stroll where they wished until supper. During that time, there were only stupid remarks and joking words. Serious statements were postponed until the next morning. When we returned to the hall, everyone looked at the Lawyer, whom the Gentleman begged to finish the narrative of his career. Which THE LAWYER did in the following manner.

Book III

∴

On the Anabaptism in the Jesuits' Blind Obedience toward Their Superiors. And How, Owing to That, No King or Prince Can Protect Himself from Being Ambushed

THE LAWYER. I've told you about the Jesuits' doctrine, their deceptions, and how, when obtaining their privileges, they maliciously circumvented the Holy See. I'm reserving this morning for the affairs of state that they annexed to their doctrine, where, by an abundance of piety that rules within them, they mingled with it the lesson we learn from Machiavelli, in his treatise *The Prince*, in the chapter called *Della sceleratezza*.[1] In their deliberations, the murders and the parricides of kings and princes are as familiar to them as the most heinous assassins in the world. In addition, they've permitted themselves to perturb the kingdoms where they've set foot. All of us are astonished at it: but if you dispassionately examine the blind obedience that they vow to their superiors, it will be very easy to enlighten you. I specify superiors, because Jesuits likewise vow blind obedience to the popes, even if the declaration isn't as precise. In the clause I read to you yesterday, they refer only once to the pope, but they refer several times to their superiors, so eager was Lawgiver Ignatius to teach how this obedience to superiors should be done.[2]

On this, I'll say frankly that although we in France don't accept the Jesuits' special obedience to the popes, it's incomparably more tolerable than the other obedience. For as far as I'm concerned, I believe that the opinions of those lofty prelates are so well-regulated that, if one vowed a stricter obedience to them, they wouldn't want to overdo it. They are persons who, in the main, come from lowly places and who, by their virtues, merits, and self-sufficiency, were first made bishops, then cardinals, and finally they mounted onto that high throne of the papacy. This was done in such a manner that their prudent counsels, their holiness, their long experience, and their seniority, have in all likelihood worn down in them all those foolish passions that ordinarily carry us away. But to make that sort of judgment about the superiors of the Jesuit order: I can't

---

1 Chapter 8 is titled: "Di quelli che per sceleratezza sono pervenuti al principato." Cf. Pasquier's earlier discussion of Jesuit Machiavellism in Book 11, chapter 10.
2 Cf. Book 11, chapter 2.

© KONINKLIJKE BRILL NV, LEIDEN, 2021 | DOI:10.1163/9789004164062_040

do it, I don't dare do it, I don't want to do it. The honor, the reverence, and the respect I bear for the Holy See prevent me from doing so. But nonetheless, having mentioned the pope once in their chapter on obedience (as I've said), they talk only about their superiors, that is, their general, their provincials, their rectors. For those are the ones who, each in respect to his own rank, are described as a superior by the others. Now, owing to the obedience that their inferiority owes them, you've learned that they are ordered to believe that the command has emanated from Jesus Christ, through them as an instrument; and that for this reason they should obey, and do it in a single wink of the eye, not only for things that are obligatory in the order, but also for everything else.[3] Without haggling, one obeys, and the will is bound to the execution of an order, and the judgment is bound to the will. So, the inferior believes that this order is very just, since it was given to him. He believes that one resembles a dead body, or a staff, which only moves by someone's hand: in short, that this obedience has no eyes.[4] To accept this absolute command in a pedant, and in the process to mask it by God's presumed presence, amounts to putting a specific law suit into the hands of someone who is a rabid man.

And when I think about that vow, I seem to see the Anabaptists[5] who claimed to have been sent by God to make everything go from good to better. They circulated a book of *rétablissement*, reestablishment. Their king was Jan van Leiden;[6] and beneath him were certain false prophets who were their superiors, and who made the populace believe that they were communicating

---

3   For the role that obedience played in the life of one Jesuit, Jean-Joseph Surin, see Moshe Sluhovsky, ed., and Patricia M. Ranum, trans., *Into the Dark Night and Back: The Mystical Writings of Jean-Joseph Surin* (Leiden: Brill, 2018), passim.

4   This is an allusion to Ignatius's letter (composed by Polanco) "To the Members of the Society in Portugal, Rome, March 26, 1553," in Ignatius of Loyola: *Letters and Instructions*, ed. John W. Padberg et al. (St. Louis, MO: Institute of Jesuit Sources, 1996), 412–21, https://jesuit portal.bc.edu/research/documents/1553_ignatiusonobedience/ (accessed February 1, 2021).

5   Anabaptism: a Protestant radical movement that arose in the sixteenth century and that advocated baptism and church membership of adult believers only. See Martin Rothkegel, "Anabaptists," in *Encyclopedia of Early Modern History Online*, ed. Graeme Dunphy and Andrew Gow, http://dx.doi.org/10.1163/2352-0272_emho_COM_028674 (accessed February 1, 2021).

6   Jan van Leiden (Jan Beukelszoon, 1509–36), was an Anabaptist leader. In 1533, he moved from Leiden to Münster, where he became an influential prophet. He turned that city into a millenarian Anabaptist theocracy, and proclaimed himself king of Münster. In 1535, the insurrection was suppressed after a siege of the fortified city, and Jan was captured, tortured, and executed. See C. S. Mackay, "General Introduction," in *Narrative of the Anabaptist Madness: The Overthrow of Münster, the Famous Metropolis of Westphalia* (Leiden: Brill, 2007), https://doi.org/10.1163/ej.9789004157217.i-776.7 (accessed February 1, 2021).

with God, sometimes by dreams, sometimes by lies,[7] and that nothing was undertaken except by God's revelation, when their Holy Spirit would blow into the mouths of those who were most disposed to their raging-mad opinions. They distributed them throughout the Dutch provinces, as their apostles, in order to attract and seduce the feeblest believers. By this means, they turned all of Germany into a gargoyle, having established their monstrous domination in the city of Münster,[8] sometimes ordering murders and assassinations, and sometimes carrying them out with their own hands, attributing them solely to God's inspiration. And having as their prey all the kings, princes, and potentates, they made it public knowledge that they'd been expressly sent by God to chase those rulers away. This proposition led to their plan to assassinate them, if no one was forewarned of their plans. Tell me, I pray you, what is covered by this great vow of the Jesuits to their superiors, if not the obedience of the Anabaptists. Let's imagine a painting of a general of their order who, by some uncontrolled passion or by some precise bit of ignorance, inappropriately wants to become a reformer, not only of our religion but of all political states, and who, when he's in the midst of his states, harangues them in this manner:

THE GENERAL. "My children, you know that I am here to give you an order. Our Lord Jesus Christ is in my mouth: therefore, you must obey me everywhere, and in everything. God sends out his Holy Spirit in our good Father Ignatius, in order to sustain his church, which was on the brink of collapse owing to the errors of the Lutherans, errors that have spread across Europe, to the regret of good Catholics. Since it pleases God that we be the successors of that holy man, we must, like him, be the first workers, in order to uproot it. We see heresies reigning in several kingdoms; here a subject takes up arms against his king, and there the prince tyrannizes his subjects; here a princess is a heretic, and not far from her a king makes the same religious profession, while others stuff us with things that appear to be good, and with bait that deceives us.[9] It is up to us: it is up to us, my children, to defend God's cause, and the cause of his poor subjects, not as something that seems small, as our predecessors have done, but from the heart. Those who have done so in the past have stroked the wound, and consequently have irritated it. We shall do meritorious work by freeing the countryside of it. We must carry out the lofty justice of God, who will never be

---

7 This is an allusion to the opening two lines of *The Romance of the Rose* that Pasquier cited in Book I: "Many a man holds dreams to be but lies, all fabulous." Sutto, 320n5.

8 Pasquier wrote *Monstre*, that is, "monster." *Monstrueux*, "monstrous," follows this apparent lapsus. But is it a lapsus? Or is it yet another word-game: Münster, Monster, Monstrous, and as a closing surprise, Gargoyle.

9 Pasquier seems to be referring to the Netherlands (taking up arms against the king); France (tyranny); England (princess); and Scotland (king).

aggrieved; we must be arbiters of his will. To the detriment of badly reigning kings, let us make their kingdoms fall before those whom, in our consciences, we know to be worthy. If you don't feel strong enough in yourselves, to carry out my orders, may it at least be a lesson that you will teach in the middle of God's church. The iron and the fire must be employed, for fear that gangrene will settle there. Eventually we'll find good workers and surgeons. But above all, you must place there the holy tools of confession, the Mass, Communion, so that with the greatest assurance in their consciences, they will wend their way toward this holy work. The needs of Christian affairs command us to do this, and the duty of our tasks obligates us. Those are the messages I receive from Our Savior and Redeemer, Jesus Christ, who suffered and died on the cross for us, and for whom, in exchange, we should die rather than make a speedy end of these wicked princes. These are (I say) the messages I receive from God whose vicar I am (I, so unworthy) over you."

The LAWYER. I'll leave here for you the badly interpreted passages, examples, and authorities of the Holy Scripture that this monsieur can cite. For atheologians[10] never fail, any more than necromancers do, to invoke their spirits and demons, or their healing of illnesses. And yet, all of that is part of Anabaptism, or else it is the commands of that old man of the Mountain (recited by our Annalists), that prince of assassins who charmed his subjects in order to get them to ambush and kill our princes, who were traveling to the Levant to deliver the Holy Land.[11] From this comes a word that remains current to this day: assassins, that is, murderous traitors. Isn't all this found in our Jesuits? Wasn't this doctrine scattered in the midst of this holy religious order? Haven't we seen the splinters? The first assassination attempt in Antwerp that the late Prince of Orange survived, wasn't it at the Jesuits' instigation?[12] And when he

---

10   *Athéologien* (atheologian): one who is not a theologian; one who has no knowledge of theology; an ignorant theologian. The word is not in Cotgrave (1611), Nicot (1606), or DAF 1694.

11   "The Assassins" was the name of a Muslim sect that formed in Persia during the late eleventh century. It held travelers for ransom. The leader was the mysterious Hassan ibn al-Sabbah (*c.*1050–1124), known as the "Old Man of the Mountain." See "Assassins (Hashishin), sect of," in *The Oxford Dictionary of the Middle Ages* (Oxford: Oxford University Press, 2010), https://www.oxfordreference.com/view/10.1093/acref/9780198662624.001.0001/acref -9780198662624-e-0586 (accessed February 1, 2021).

12   William I, prince of Orange (1533–84), also known as William the Silent or William the Taciturn, was the principal leader of the Dutch revolt against the Spanish Hapsburgs. The revolt resulted in the formal independence of the United Provinces in 1581. On March 18, 1582, Juan de Jáuregui (1562–82), a Spaniard, attempted to assassinate William. The prince survived his serious injuries; Jáuregui was immediately killed by one of William's guards. Philippe de l'Estoile believed that the Spaniard had been urged on by a Jesuit (Sutto,

was murdered in 1584, during a second attempt by Balthasar Gérard,[13] a native of the county of Burgundy, and again when Pierre Panne Tonnelier,[14] residing at Ypres, was sent to kill Prince Maurice of Orange, count of Nassau, the son of the other prince of Orange, from whom did they seek advice? Before being executed, Gérard admitted that he had withdrawn to the lodging of a Jesuit whose name he didn't know, but that he was a redhead and a regent at the college of Trier. This regent assured him that he'd been in communication about this undertaking with three of his companions, who had found that he belonged totally to God, and who, before leaving, had given him his blessing, assuring him that if he died in this quarrel, he'd be listed on the calendar of martyrs. And the second man confessed that the Jesuits of Douai having promised him that an emolument would be given to one of his sons, the Jesuit provincial gave him his blessing and said: Go in peace, my friend. For you go like an angel, guarded by God. And after that confession, he was executed in the city of Leiden by a sentence issued on June 22, 1598. I know full well that the Jesuits will say that they advised the assassination of two princes who had taken up arms against their king. And I told them that all of them, such as they are, must therefore be put to death for having been the first to undertake something in our recent Troubles, not only against the late king but also against the king who is currently reigning.[15] But these murders go much farther: for he wanted to incite Robert Bruce, a Scottish gentleman, to kill the late Sir John Maitland,[16] out of hatred for his being a very faithful subject who had committed the fault of wanting to agree with Bruce. His trial took place in Brussels. Weren't they

---

322n9). Cf. Yolanda Rodríguez Pérez, *The Dutch Revolt through Spanish Eyes: Self and Other in Historical and Literary Texts of Golden Age Spain (c. 1548–1673)* (Bern: Peter Lang, 2008), esp. 81.

13   Balthasar Gérard, or Gerardts (*c.*1557–84), a Catholic and native of Dôle (Franche-Comté), was a subject and supporter of Philip 11 of Spain. One source says that he was incited by a Jesuit from Trier; another says that the instigators were a Jesuit in Rome and the duke of Parma. Gérard was tried and brutally executed. Cf. Sabina Pavone, "Banishment, Exile and Opposition: Jesuit Crises before the 1760s," *Lusitania sacra* 32 (July–December 2015): 105–19, here 110.

14   See Book 1, ch. 1 above.

15   The two kings are Henri 111, assassinated in 1589 (and therefore the "late" king), and his successor, Henri 1v, assassinated in 1610 and therefore the "king currently reigning" when Pasquier's book was published in 1602.

16   John Maitland of Thirlestane (*c.*1545–95) was lord chancellor of Scotland. The alleged assassination attempt has been subject of no scholarly study. On Jesuits in early modern Scotland, see a special issue of the *Journal of Jesuit Studies* on the subject, https://brill .com/view/journals/jjs/7/1/jjs.7.issue-1.xml (accessed February 1, 2021).

complicitous with a Jacobin[17] in the assassination of the late king?[18] Didn't they make several attempts on the life of Elizabeth, queen of England?[19] And lastly, didn't they make an attempt on our king's life, first by Pierre Barrière,[20] and then by Jean Châtel?[21]

17   In France, the Dominican friars were known as "Jacobins," because the chapel of the order's main convent was situated on the rue Saint-Jacques and was dedicated to Saint James the Great (that is, Saint Jacobus).

18   Jacques Clément (*c.*1566–89), a Dominican lay-brother, became a fanatical partisan of the Catholic League. In August 1589, he stabbed Henri III and was himself killed by a guard. See Orest Ranum, *Tyranny from Ancient Greece to Renaissance France* (Cham: Palgrave Pivot, 2020), 143–45.

19   Cf. Francis Edwards, S.J., *Plots & Plotters in the Reign of Elizabeth I* (Dublin: Four Courts Press, 2002).

20   Pierre Barrière (?–1593) was a would-be assassin of Henri IV of France. He was denounced by a Dominican priest to whom he had confessed and was broken on the wheel and dismembered. Cf. Cuttica, "Tyrannicide and Political Authority," 273.

21   Jean Châtel (1575–94), the son of a cloth merchant, attempted to assassinate Henri IV in 1594. Under questioning, Châtel revealed that he had been educated by the Jesuits of that college. His former teachers, Fathers Hay and Guéret, were fortunate to be exiled; a third teacher, Father Guignard, was hanged and burned at the stake for his presumed part in the affair. The Collège de Clermont was closed, and the building was confiscated. The Jesuit order was banned from France, but the ban was quickly lifted. Indeed, the imminent return of the Society forms a background for Pasquier's *Catéchisme des jésuites*. Cf. Ranum, *Tyranny from Ancient Greece to Renaissance France*.

On the Extraordinary Trial Conducted in the Low Countries against Robert Bruce, a Scottish Gentleman Who Had Been Denounced by Father William Crichton, Jesuit, for Being Unwilling to Carry Out the Assassination of the Chancellor of Scotland

THE LAWYER. Special trials are held for those who assassinate, or who want to assassinate, but this is the first time that someone has been tried for being unwilling to do it. That trial is the subject of this chapter. Shortly after the death of Mary, Queen of Scots,[1] the late king of Spain[2] ordered the duke of Parma, governor of his Netherlands,[3] to send Robert Bruce,[4] a Scottish gentleman, to James VI, king of Scotland,[5] bearing letters by which he promised men and money, in order to avenge the death of the queen, James's mother, for whom Bruce claimed a special affection, she having vowed to be a Roman Catholic until her very last breath. He wanted the king, her son, to continue that affection as a sort of succession. He also promised that he would be an heir to the

---

1 Mary Stuart (Stewart) (1542–87), queen of Scotland (1542–67) and queen consort of France (1559–60). She was executed by order of Elizabeth I on February 8, 1587. See *Encyclopaedia Britannica*, https://www.britannica.com/biography/Mary-queen-of-Scotland (accessed February 1, 2021).

2 Philip II (1527–98), king of Spain (1554–98) and Portugal (1580–98). He failed to suppress the revolt of the Netherlands (1566) and to invade England (1588). See *Encyclopaedia Britannica*, https://www.britannica.com/biography/Philip-II-king-of-Spain-and-Portugal (accessed February 1, 2021).

3 Alessandro Farnese (1545–92), son of Ottavio and Margaret, duke of Parma and Piacenza, was the regent of the Spanish Netherlands (1578–92) for Philip II, the Habsburg king of Spain. See *Encyclopaedia Britannica*, https://www.britannica.com/biography/Alessandro-Farnese-duke-of-Parma-and-Piacenza (accessed February 1, 2021).

4 Robert Bruce (*c.*1554–1631), son of Sir Alexander Bruce, one of the foremost barons of the kingdom. He studied at St. Andrew's and Paris. Through his mother he was related to King James VI. For his relationship with the Jesuits, see McCoog, *Society of Jesus in Ireland, Scotland, and England*, 121, 245, 342.

5 In 1587, when Mary, Queen of Scots, was executed, her son, James Charles Stuart, was reigning as James VI king of Scotland; in 1603, he began ruling as James I of England. He was the "king of Scotland" to whom Pasquier alludes.

virtues and the religion of that fine princess. I've debated how to treat this affair at length, and in detail, although I have good and faithful memories about it. I'll simply say that this gentleman had, at that time, been entrusted with some large sums of money, so that he could load sixty ships in order to, first of all, transport food and munitions to the Low Countries, and then to transport the soldiers whom the Spanish had resolved to send to England. It was hoped that Queen Elizabeth of England[6] would be assailed on both sides. Shortly after Bruce's arrival in Scotland, (he'd been nurtured by the Jesuits since his youth), Father William Crichton,[7] a Scot who had once been rector at the Jesuit college of Lyon, was travelling with the bishop of Dumblane,[8] whom Sixtus v[9] had sent to King James VI of Scotland, to negotiate a marriage with the Infanta of Spain,[10] on condition that he be willing to become a Catholic and to join them against the English. Sir John Maitland,[11] the chancellor, opposed these negotiations for several reasons, and he advised his master to have none of it. So, the bishop returned home without having accomplished a thing, leaving Crichton in Scotland, where he joined Bruce. And thinking that Chancellor Maitland, all on his own, had turned the king away from the things he was being offered, he debated playing a real Jesuit trick on him. A Catholic lord had invited the king and his chancellor to a banquet. Crichton asked Bruce to go see him and supply some money that this lord could use, and order him to

---

6   Elizabeth I (1533–1603), queen of England from 1558 to 1603, during a period often called the Elizabethan Age. See *Encyclopaedia Britannica*, https://www.britannica.com/biography/Elizabeth-I (accessed February 1, 2021).

7   William Crichton (Creiton, 1534–1617) was a Scottish Jesuit trained in Paris, Rome, Leipzig, and Leuven. He was instrumental in the attempts to convert King James VI to Catholicism. In 1584, he set off for Scotland with a plan of invasion. Captured by the Dutch in the sea, he was delivered to the English authorities, imprisoned, and liberated in 1587. He continued to plan the invasion until the failure of the Armada in 1588. See Thomas M. McCoog, "Converting a King: The Jesuit William Crichton and King James VI and I," *Journal of Jesuit Studies* 7, no. 1 (2020): 11–33, https://brill.com/view/journals/jjs/7/1/article-p11_11.xml (accessed February 1, 2021).

8   Crichton and the Scottish William Chisholm (III) (1551–1629), bishop of Vaison and not Dunblane (whose bishop had been his uncle by the same name). See *Oxford Dictionary of National Biography*, https://doi.org/10.1093/odnb/9780192683120.013.5327 (accessed February 1, 2021). See also McCoog, "Converting a King," 21.

9   Pope Sixtus V (r.1585–90) commissioned Bishop Chisholm to convert James VI during his mission to Scotland in 1584.

10   Infanta Isabella Clara Eugenia of Spain (1566–1633; r.1598–1621). See McCoog, "Converting a King," 19–20.

11   John Maitland (1543–95), 1st Lord Maitland of Thirlestane, lord chancellor of Scotland from 1587 to 1595 and chief adviser to King James VI. See *Encyclopaedia Britannica*, https://www.britannica.com/biography/John-Maitland-1st-Lord-Maitland (accessed February 1, 2021). See also McCoog, *Society of Jesus in Ireland, Scotland, and England, 1589–1597*, 55 ff.

have the chancellor killed, being convinced that he'd get him to do whatever he wanted for money. Bruce refused outright, not only because he'd been sent to do something else, as he showed by the instructions and memoranda he had received from the duke of Parma; but above all because he'd be ashamed to carry out that undertaking, after having first acted as if he were the chancellor's friend. Besides, this murder would never be viewed favorably, taking place in the midst of a feast and in the presence of the king, who would be the principal person to receive the insult, as much for the scant importance that would be shown to his majesty, as for the homicide that would be committed on the person he valued so highly for his fidelity and his wisdom. Doing this would give him a reason to become irritated with the Catholics, for being murderers, infamous persons, and traitors to God and the world, and who until then had received all possible graces and courtesies from their king. Crichton realized that this coup had failed, but he wanted to gamble on someone else, and to induce Bruce to give fifteen hundred crowns to three gentlemen who were offering to kill the chancellor in another less scandalous manner. But Bruce replied that killing a man with one's own hands, or paying money to have it done, amounted to the same thing. As for him, he was a private man who had no authority over anyone's life, and still less over the life of a chancellor who was the head of justice. Besides, in addition to not having an order from the duke of Parma to use his money to that end, Maitland was beloved by the king, his master, and held two positions: the office of chancellor and the office of first secretary of state. After his death, there would be two lords who were worse than he was toward the Catholics; favored by the king, they would divide the castoff things of the other man. In short, for the uncertain possessions being promised there, one must not commit a sure evil, even if one has been assured that it would be good. And since it was a question of the advancement of our Catholic religion, it would totally ruin that religion if one tried to promote it by murders and assassinations, to everyone's great scandal, and to the perpetual dishonor of the holy order of the Jesuits. That's what Bruce was saying in his conscience, as a person who, having spent his entire youth in the Jesuits' colleges, felt great reverence for them. But for all that, Father Crichton didn't want to give up, because he and his companions have their old, poorly reasoned commonplace sayings, to prove that assassinations are permitted. By means of which Bruce, the target of still more entreaties than before, asked whether, in good conscience, he could consent to this undertaking, or whether he could be excused. To which the Jesuit replied: No. But once the murder had been committed, and Bruce came to confess to the Jesuit, the latter would absolve him. Then Bruce replied as follows: Since Your Reverence recognizes that I'll have to confess what I did, you'll also recognize that I'll be committing a sin; and I don't know whether, once I've committed it, God will give me the grace to be able to confess it. In addition, I believe that confessing wrongdoing with deliberation, with the intention of confessing it and being absolved, is scarcely valid. So, the surest way is not to get myself into such a hazardous position.

Thus, was my Jesuit de-horned; but later he knew full well how to get his revenge. The duke of Parma died; and finding his position occupied by the duke of Fuentes,[12] a Spaniard who was the nephew of the duke d'Alba,[13] Crichton accused Bruce to his face, for two faults: first, he had mismanaged the king's finances; and second, he was a traitor, because he'd been unwilling to supply the money to pay for Maitland's murder, Maitland being the accuser's principal target. A truly great crime in the Jesuit republic, a crime for which he was kept in prison in Brussels for fourteen whole months. As for the first accusation, Crichton didn't make much of a fuss about it. But he endlessly insisted on the second accusation, to the point that the prisoner didn't deny the crime. The trial moved ahead. Finally, after Bruce had suffered for a long while, the prison doors opened for him, but there was no condemnation of this saintly Jesuit father, no reparations, no dispensations, no damages and interest. Because (and it's credible) having brought suit over this devout accusation, he'd done nothing that wasn't related to the holy propositions of his order.

---

12   Pedro Enríquez de Acevedo (1525–1610) was governor general of the Spanish Netherlands from 1595 to 1600, and governor of Milan and its vicinity from 1600 to his death. Pasquier is therefore recounting recent events. See *Treccani*, https://www.treccani.it/enciclopedia/fuentes-pedro-enriquez-de-acevedo-conte-di_%28Enciclopedia-Italiana%29/ (accessed February 1, 2021).

13   Fernando Álvarez de Toledo y Pimentel, third duke of Alba (1507–82), governor of Milan (1555–56) and viceroy of Naples (1556–58). See *Encyclopaedia Britannica*, https://www.britannica.com/biography/Fernando-Alvarez-de-Toledo-y-Pimentel-3er-duque-de-Alba (accessed February 1, 2021).

On the Assassination That William Parry, Englishman, Urged On by the Jesuits, Wanted to Commit against Elizabeth, Queen of England, in 1584

THE LAWYER. The person who wrote the Very Humble Remonstrance and Request to the King,[1] wanting to demonstrate that, calumniously, the Jesuits are being accused of not attacking the queen of England, says this: "As for the English, those who have written the truth bear testimony to our fidelity, and have not dared accuse us of attempting anything against the queen in her state; and those who would like to calumniate us are incapable of attaching their lies to our behavior, by any realistic reason of truth." I shall now demonstrate that this Jesuit is a second Herodotus. I'm doing him quite a bit of honor when I compare him with that great person, who was said to have been the father of misleading history.

William Parry,[2] a doctor of law and a man of great understanding, but full of self-will, had consumed all his possessions and most of his wife's. He was even accused of having fiercely quarreled with Hugh Hare,[3] a gentleman of the Temple. In 1582, he debated whether he should flee his country and sail off to France. Having reached Paris, he wanted to become acquainted with some English gentlemen, who had fled their country because of their religion. They were uncertain about approaching him, thinking that he'd come on purpose, in order to spy on their activities. For that reason, he set off for Lyon, and then for Venice where, because he was English, he was immediately turned over to the Inquisition; but he gave such a good account of his Catholic religion

---

1   Louis Richeome, *Très-humble Remonstrance et Requeste des religieux de la Compagnie de Jesus* (Bordeaux: S. Millanges, 1598).

2   William Parry (?–1585), a courtier and spy, considered assassinating Queen Elizabeth of England. Parry has a special place in the parliamentary history of this period—he was the only serving member of the House of Commons to be arrested for high treason and executed. He was hanged, drawn, and quartered. See ODNB, https://doi.org/10.1093/ref:odnb/21437 (accessed February 1, 2021).

3   Hugh Hare was a barrister at one of the four Inns of Court of London. Two of those inns are called "temples." Parry assaulted Hare, for which he was sentenced to death but pardoned by the queen. See ODNB, https://doi.org/10.1093/ref:odnb/21437 (accessed February 1, 2021).

that the judges decided he should return home. Beloved by all the Catholics, and by Father Benedetto Palmio,[4] a Jesuit of great reputation among his brethren, who was of the opinion that he should do what the person did who long ago burned the temple of Ephesus, so that people would talk about him.[5] He planned to kill the queen, his natural lady,[6] and in that way to set fire to the four corners of England, basing his undertaking on delivering his country from tyranny, and enabling the Scottish queen, who was a Catholic princess, to advance to the crown. He has since recognized, while in prison, that this opinion came to him by his own instinct, without his having told the Queen of Scots about it before leaving England. But because this was a lofty undertaking, and because it involved giving a great blow to his conscience about God, he conferred with Palmio, who was following the usual maxim of his sect: he not only turned him from it, but he also thoroughly agreed with him; and here the only thing that could cause him trouble was the amount of time it would take. He then turned back to Lyon, where he revealed his identity to the Jesuits, and was praised and honored by them. Shortly afterward, he returned to Paris, where some English gentlemen had sought refuge. Having heard his plan, they began to embrace it, even Thomas Morgan,[7] who assured him that he would soon be in England, and his undertaking would be finished; and he would give an order to have a powerful army come from Scotland, to ensure the kingdom for the Scottish queen. Now, although Parry seemed totally resolved, he fell prey to remorse. Indeed, he informed some persons from the English Church, who all made him change his mind, even a learned priest named Watts,[8] who wisely remonstrated that all the rules of God and of the world made him reluctant to decide. Irresolute, he debated about finding out what the Jesuits in Paris

---

4   Benedetto Palmio (1525–98) was a famous Jesuit preacher. In 1557, he was named rector of the college of Padua, and—between 1565 and 1580—he was the provincial for Milan and the assistant for Italy. See *DHCJ*, 3:2962–63.

5   Herostratus was a Greek arsonist who sought notoriety by destroying the temple of Artemis (the event occurred in 356 BCE), one of the seven wonders of the ancient world. This led to a law forbidding anyone to mention his name. The law proved ineffective, and Herostratus came to personify someone who commits a criminal act in order to gain attention.

6   *Sa Dame naturelle*, that is, "his natural lady." "Natural" in the sense that, since Perry was a natural-born subject of the queen, his allegiance to her is "absolute, pure and indefinite [...] and this originally is due by nature and birthright." See *The Reports of Sir Edward Coke* (Clark, NJ: The Lawbook Exchange Ltd, n.d.), 1:9, par. 2. That text dates from 1572–1616.

7   Thomas Morgan of Llantarnam (1546–1606) was the Parisian agent of Mary, Queen of Scots. He was imprisoned for five years after the Parry affair, but that did not keep him from participating in the Babington plot to kill Queen Elizabeth of England. See McCoog, *Society of Jesus in Ireland, Scotland, and England, 1598–1606*, 10–11.

8   William Watts (?–1583) was a secular priest at the seminary in Douai. He was sent to England in 1578 and to Scotland in 1581 as agent of Robert Parsons. See McCoog, "Converting a King," 13.

were thinking. He got in contact with Father Hannibal du Coudret,[9] to whom he recounted, in confession, his first thoughts about it, and the uncertainty Watts had induced in him. But the Jesuit, who had no shortage of persuasive arguments, told him that Watts and all the others who were putting these scruples in his soul, were Huguenots. Having set him straight on his first path, the priest gave him Communion with a few other lords, employing the commonly used formula. The Englishman, convinced, took leave of them and returned to England, determined to make the effects of his treachery felt. To do that, he sought every means to kiss the queen's hands, saying that he had some very important things to tell her. This was around February 1583. Finally introduced into her presence, he recounted to her at length the story of his journey, and how, pretending to be a refugee, he had revealed all the practices and plots that the English Catholics were cooking up against her majesty. He had even promised to be the first person to undertake to kill her. All this had led to his being very much believed among them. But he nonetheless would rather die a thousand deaths than sully his soul with such a damnable thought. He was a very well-spoken man, had a fine presence, and had prepared himself; and he wasn't improvising the part he would play. The queen, who didn't lack spies, saw that a part of what he had told her was true. This added some credence; and finding this honest liberty agreeable, she ordered him not to leave her court: and meanwhile, he should write some letters that would sound out what her enemies wanted. He promised to do so, and with this promise, stuffing this princess with tricks, he was often at her ear. Indeed, one day, when she was hunting for deer, she was distant from her householders, and she dismounted in a wood, in order to rest at the foot of a tree. Parry, who was near her, twice wanted to kill her, but he was held back by the private upright moments she had spent with him. Another time, walking with her after supper in the garden of the palace called Whitehall, which looks out on the Thames,[10] and where he had a small boat in order to escape after the attack, while he was searching for an opportunity, the queen escaped him as follows: he thought he could wait until twilight and kill her near the garden exit. But she went back to the palace and said that it was time to return to her chamber, for the dew was falling, and she was going to be bled the next day by order of her physicians. And smiling, she added that they wouldn't draw as much blood as many persons desired. Having said that, she withdrew, leaving Parry astonished at having failed in such a fine undertaking.

---

9   See Book I, ch. II.

10   Whitehall Palace was Elizabeth's home in Westminster, which became the setting of pageantry, courtship, and marriage negotiations.

Now, as this was going on near the queen, Parry was thinking that he needed a confidant to help him. He turned to Edmund Neville,[11] his friend, a gentleman who was experiencing afflictions in England as a result of his religion. He visited Neville several times; and having sworn an oath on the Gospels, not to reveal what would be said to him, he told him all the details of his plan and asked him to join them. For he was a person who had every reason to feel the wrongs that had been done to him; and it was the true and unique way to reestablish the Catholic religion in England and establish the Queen of Scots there. By doing this, both of them would have a big piece of the cake. Since Neville couldn't honestly savor this new advice, Parry asked him if he had Father Allen's book,[12] which was continually spurring him on in this undertaking, although he himself was quite disposed to it. According to this book, it was permitted to excommunicate kings, depose them, contradict them; and civil wars over religion were honorable. "I have very easy access to the queen (he said), which you too will have when you're known at court. After we've done our coup, we'll get into a boat that's all ready to take us downriver and, from there, to the sea. On my honor, you and I can do this without any trouble." Neville promised him many great things but didn't give him either an absolute Yes or a No; so, in the end he decided to delay no longer in notifying the queen, to whom he recounted everything on February 8, 1584. He told her everything that had gone on between him and Parry, who at the time was supping with the earl of Leicester.[13] The queen surprised everyone by ordering Walsingham,[14] her principal secretary of state, to arrest both Parry and Leicester, but

11   Edmund Neville (before 1555–c.1620), a distant cousin of Parry, was an English courtier and possible conspirator. He was allegedly involved in the Parry plot and was imprisoned in the Tower of London after the affair. He probably was a Spanish agent. See Victor H. Matthews, "Edmund Neville: A Catholic in Elizabethan England," *Historical Magazine of the Protestant Episcopal Church* 54, no. 2 (1985): 115–23; and *ODNB*, https://doi.org/10.1093/ref:odnb/19927 (accessed February 1, 2021).

12   William Allen (1532–94) was a professor at Oxford and author of *A true, sincere and modest defence of English catholics that suffer for their faith* (Ingolstadt, 1584). He was exiled to Leuven in 1561. In 1568, he founded the seminary of Douai and another one in Rome (1579) to prepare priests of the English mission. He was made a cardinal in 1587 at King Philip II's request. After the failure of the Armada, he continued to stay in Rome until his death. See *ODNB*, https://doi.org/10.1093/ref:odnb/391 (accessed February 1, 2021).

13   Robert Dudley, count of Leicester (1532/33–88), became a member of the queen's council in 1558 and was her longtime favorite. In 1585, he led an English expeditionary force to the Low Countries and in 1588, lieutenant general of the army against the Armada. See *ODNB*, https://www.britannica.com/biography/Robert-Dudley-earl-of-Leicester-Baron-Denbigh (accessed February 1, 2021).

14   Francis Walsingham (c.1532–90) was Elizabeth's principal secretary, 1573–90. In the early 1570s, he was sent to Paris as an ambassador for foreign affairs. He had long been in charge

nonetheless to treat Parry gently, in order to draw the truth from him. This he did, remonstrating that the queen had some new information about a plot against her; and because the malcontents placed some trust in him, begged him to say whether he'd learned anything about it. Questioned two or three times on this matter, he said he had never heard anything. He'd confessed to the story about him and Neville, and as an excuse had added that what he had done was a feint, and that he was doing it to sound out the opinions of those who were hatching some discontent in their souls. Walsingham later told several persons that he'd been sent away, fully absolved. But when he strongly denied this, he was shown Neville's deposition, which greatly astonished him, and he invited him to spend the night. The next morning Parry went to his bedchamber and told him that he recalled having said something to Neville about a detail of religious doctrine, as a reply to the book called *The Execution of Justice in England*,[15] which proved that, in order to advance the Catholic religion, it was legal to take a prince's life; but that, as for him, he'd never mentioned any undertaking against the queen. Parry and Neville were sent to different prisons, Neville for having concealed this plot for more than six months, and Parry for the treason of which he was accused. Both of them were questioned, and their interrogation having subsequently been carried out, they produced written confessions, Neville on February 10 and Parry on February 11 and 13. Neville's confession contained the subornations and prosecutions involving Parry: Parry's confession about how treason was first planned in Venice, was helped by the supporting exhortations of Palmio the Jesuit. This was later confirmed by the Jesuits of Lyon and was finally totally ended by Hannibal du Coudret and some other Jesuits in Paris, where, as part of their devotions, he confessed and received Communion. And it seems to me that the matter shouldn't be kept silent; for when interrogated by his judges, he admitted that when he first talked to the queen about the plots that the fugitive Catholics were cooking up against her, in order to be reintegrated into their houses, she had replied to him that her opinion had never involved mistreating anyone over religion, except when, under cover of religion, they had wanted to attack her and her state; and that in the future no one would be troubled about the primacy of the pope, as long as they behaved as good and loyal subjects should. Neville, reexamined, and confronted by Parry, persisted

---

of the queen's secret service. See *ODNB*, https://doi.org/10.1093/ref:odnb/28624 (accessed December 26, 2020).

15   The exact title is: *The execution of Justice in England for maintenance of public and Christian peace against certeine stirrers of sedition* (London: C. Barker, 1583). The book was translated into Latin, French, Dutch, and Italian. Allen replied to it in his *True, sincere and modest defence of English catholics*. See Sutto, 328n34, 329n38.

in his deposition. Nonetheless, it was something very frustrating, for Parry had confessed enough, even saying that in his house there were several missives, instructions, and memoranda that would condemn him. And so, while he was in prison, he wrote letters to the queen in which he most humbly begged her to be willing to absolve him of guilt, but not of the punishment he merited. For judges, he was assigned Christopher Wray,[16] a knight, the principal head of England's courts, and several other lords of mark, who had him imprisoned in Westminster and promptly interrogated in the presence of all the people; and he confessed to his treason. His previous confessions were read to him, missives were sent to him for that effect, and other pieces pertaining to the verification of the crime, all of which he recognized as containing the truth; and he added that he'd done no plotting that involved religion since the first year of the queen's reign, and had only participated in [the devotion to] the *agnus dei*;[17] and in addition he had written down his opinion about the heir to the crown, in order to induce the people to rebel. This criminal case went on from February 8, 1584, to February 25, when Parry was sentenced to be hanged by the neck, and the rope would immediately be cut and he would be eviscerated and his entrails thrown into the fire and burned before his eyes, then his head would be cut off and his body quartered. And from the prison he would be dragged on a rack throughout the entire city of London, to the place of execution. This decree was read aloud, but not immediately carried out. On March 2, Parry was turned over to the executioner of high justice. He was notified of this by the sheriffs of London and Middlesex. As if he were going to a wedding, he dressed in a long house-robe of black damask, and around the collar of his shirt there was a large starched ruff like the ones worn in that country. And taking leave of the other prisoners, with a gay face he gave the concierge a ring set with a valuable diamond, saying that he was very sorry that he couldn't gratify him better. From there he was dragged on a rack; and having climbed to the ladder, they say that he begged the executioner not to disarrange his ruff when putting the rope around his neck. Thus died this great martyr of the Jesuits, promising

---

16   Christopher Wray (c.1522–92) was judge and speaker of the House of Commons in 1571. In 1574, he became chief justice of the queen's bench. See ODNB, https://doi.org/10.1093/ref:odnb/30014 (accessed February 1, 2021).

17   He is alluding to the plot of John Somerville (1560–83), who publicly proclaimed his desire and intention to assassinate Elizabeth. It is likely that Somerville was of unsound mind and had neither the inclination nor the capacity to carry out his threat. Still, he was imprisoned in the Tower and tortured. He was alleged to have hanged himself in jail before he could be executed. See ODNB, https://doi.org/10.1093/ref:odnb/26022 (accessed February 1, 2021). *Agnus dei* was a pendant blessed by the pope that was used by Catholics in England. See Aislinn Muller, "The Agnus Dei, Catholic Devotion, and Confessional Politics in Early Modern England," *British Catholic History* 34, no. 1 (2018): 1–28.

himself nothing less than paradise in payment for his detestable undertaking. I've told you a story that covers fourteen or fifteen months, for he returned to England in January 1583 and was executed in March 1585. In his plea, Master Antoine Arnauld[18] reproached them for this attempt. Montaignes,[19] who wrote against him, did not answer, thereby showing by his silence that the objection was truthful: for in objections of lesser consequence, he spared nothing in his replies. The person who defended the Collège de Clermont admitted that Parry was executed to death for this purported treason, but that it was a charity given him by the great enemies of the Jesuits. Which is to cover oneself neatly with a wet sack. His trial is in the law registers. And a special animosity would not have easily caused that man to be condemned to death, a man who by his dissimulation and his hypocrisy didn't win the least bit of the queen's favor. Next, I'll tell you about another tragedy carried out against that same princess.

18   See Book I, ch. 10.
19   See Book I, ch. 5.

About Another Assassination Pursued in 1597 against the Queen of England by the Jesuits

THE LAWYER. The miracle wrought by the Jesuits played a great role in Parry's conversion, but not so great nor of such stuff as the one I'm going to recount for you now. For in his final confessions, Parry admitted that he'd played a part in all the conspiracies mounted against the queen for religion, except one. But the person I'm going to speak about now had always involved the English religion;[1] and yet it was the work of an English Jesuit, who not only had blessedly converted to our religion, but who had also been induced to kill his queen. If his undertaking had succeeded, it would have merited being added to the book of miracles written by Louis Richeome of the Society of Jesus.[2]

In 1595, Edward Squire,[3] an Englishman who frequently went to the queen's stables, joined Drake's fleet that was setting off for the New World.[4] Owing to a sudden tempest at sea, the ship on which Squire was sailing was captured at Guadeloupe, and Squire was taken to Spain as a prisoner of war. Having been noticed by Father Richard Walpole,[5] a man of great authority, he was freed by the intercession of this Jesuit, who began to spy on him. Finding him firm in his English religion, he obtained another prison for him that involved his conscience. Questioned by intermediaries of the Inquisition, he knew so well how to manage things that, in the end, he became a Catholic, perhaps less because

---

1 Pasquier repeatedly wrote: *de la Religion Anglesche*. In other words, here he is phonetically reproducing "English." That he knew better is proved by his occasional lapses into the more usual *Anglois*. That this phonetic spelling recurs in his text, suggests that it results from a witticism, not ignorance.

2 In 1597, Richeome published *Trois discours pour la religion catholique*. Book 1 is titled "Les Miracles," the miracles. See Book 1, ch. 5.

3 Edward Squire (?–1598) was an English scrivener and sailor, and an alleged conspirator against the life of Queen Elizabeth. A long controversy about the truth of the matter followed his execution. See *ODNB*, https://doi.org/10.1093/ref:odnb/26190 (accessed December 27, 2020).

4 Francis Drake (1540–96), an English sea captain, pirate, and explorer; he carried out the second circumnavigation of the globe in a single expedition, 1577–80. He was second-in-command of the English fleet in the victorious battle against the Spanish Armada in 1588. He died of dysentery after unsuccessfully attacking the Spaniards at San Juan, Puerto Rico. See *ODNB*, https://doi.org/10.1093/ref:odnb/8022 (accessed February 1, 2021).

5 Richard Walpole (1564–1607) was ordained a priest in 1589 and entered the Society of Jesus in 1593. Over the years, he taught in the English colleges at Rome (where he was a secretary to Parsons), Seville, and Valladolid. Three brothers of his were also Jesuits. See *DHCJ* 4:4010–11.

he wanted to change his religion, than to get out of prison. Be that as it may, the Jesuit finds all of that praiseworthy. So, having won this first advantage over Squire, the Jesuit didn't give him a moment to catch his breath, but sought all sorts of artifices that will make him fall into his nets: he remonstrated to him about the afflictions of the English Catholics who were in the area, and still more about those who had abandoned their country and all their possessions, in order to live with free consciences. That the Earl of Essex,[6] who at the time was grand marshal and later was made viceroy of Ireland was the greatest author of these misfortunes; one had to rid the country of him by poison, giving him the means to succeed at this without a risk. Not the least bit convinced, he carried on regardless; and he recounted the queen's life, which he was just as happy to see end, as the earl was. What a fine offering to God this would be. Squire shouldn't fear for his person, owing to the means he had given him. And if his undertaking didn't succeed quite as they hoped, he should rest assured that he would exchange his present state for the state of a glorious saint and martyr in paradise. He pursued him in such a fashion that he finally got him to agree to what he wanted. And seeing his mind waver from time to time, he heard his confession frequently, in order to confirm these thoughts. He would show him that he should no longer withdraw into himself to deliberate; that the bargain had been made between him and his conscience; and that it was no longer a question of good or evil, but simply of maintaining his vow. If he failed to maintain it, he would commit an irreconcilable fault toward God and would be precipitated into the depths of hell. As an example, he pointed out Jepthe,[7] who preferred to kill his daughter rather than break a vow he had made. This poor wretch, manipulated like that, finally gave the Jesuit a very determined resolution. The Jesuit once again led him to a confession that acted as the cloture of their holy plot, gave him his blessing, and told him to rise and put his left hand near his collar and, with the other, make the sign of the cross. Having first muttered some Latin words, he then said, in English: My Son, God wants to bless and fortify you. Have courage, I'm engaging my soul for your soul; and dead or alive, you'll have a place in my prayers. After this accolade, Squire took leave of Walpole and started back to England. Now, the instructions that the Jesuit had given him involved a poison hidden between two pig-bladders, which the Jesuit had given him as a present, having ordered him to touch it only with gloves on, so that he himself would not

---

6   Robert Devereux, second earl of Essex (1565–1601), soldier, and politician was Elizabeth's favorite. He was lord lieutenant (rather than viceroy) of Ireland during the Nine Years' War (1595–1603). He died on the scaffold for having plotted against her in the so-called Essex rebellion. See *ODNB*, https://doi.org/10.1093/ref:odnb/7565 (February 1, 2021).

7   See Judg. 11:29–40.

be poisoned. When the queen wanted to mount one of her hackneys, he was supposed to make several small holes in the first bladder and rub the pommel of the saddle with it, making sure that the queen, unavoidably passing her hand over it and bringing it to her face, would die from this strong poison. The same thing should be done to the earl of Essex, who was preparing to sail to the Island of Terceira in the Azores,[8] and who was raising some troops when Squire arrived. Squire presented himself to a councilor of state; and since he had been quite favorably received upon his arrival, he deliberated whether to carry out his plan against the queen before the embarkation of the earl, in whose suite he wanted to be. He thought that if the poison could only do its work slowly, and would do that work during his absence, he'd be totally beyond suspicion. Having concluded this, he looked around for various ways to carry out his plan. He heard that she wanted to mount her horse, so he entered the stable, where he found the saddled horse. So, pretending to help her, he rubbed the pommel with the pig-bladder, hidden in his hand and covered with a glove. The whole thing was done according to the lesson that his father confessor had taught him. And as he worked, he sang: God owes good life to the queen, repeating that verse several times. God didn't want the poison to work. But this wicked man didn't give up hope that, in the end, he would carry out his operation. Believing this, he embarked six days later; and when the earl was sailing between Faial and São Miguel Island, as the noonday meal was being served, Squire rubbed the arms of his chair with the same poison. And since the earl had no appetite, Squire assumed that the wager was won; but he was mistaken, just as he had been about the first attempt. Several months passed, and Walpole received no news about the queen's death; so, believing that Squire had played a prank on him, he deliberated about getting revenge, and to this end he sent an Englishman, who said he had escaped from the Spanish Inquisition. Squire recounted in detail the plans for the conspiracy, and he set off specifically to notify the queen. From the beginning, they thought that he was a scoundrel hired by some enemy of Squire's; yet for a thing of such importance, one mustn't make light of anything. A report was drawn up; and when he returned, he was arrested, so that the truth could be discovered. Seeing that he was deemed guilty of the real causes and consequences, forced by his conscience, he admitted everything. He finally was sentenced to death and was executed in 1598. A vengeance truly worthy of a Jesuit, yet very miraculous. The queen of England only learned of this treason from the person who had given the first advice; and if Richeome believes me, he'll add this miracle to his book.

---

8   Devereux participated in the English expedition to the Azores in 1597 with Walter Raleigh
    (1552–1618) as his second-in-command.

The Jesuits Today Pretend to Disapprove of Their Heinous Doctrine Concerning the Murders of Princes and Rebellions against the State

THE LAWYER. Before the arrival of the Jesuits, in our church we did not know what it was to kill kings and sovereign princes by ambush. That merchandise comes from their own shops, through that impious vow of blind obedience that they make to their superiors. So, the lives of princes depend today on those upright men. And their profession is such that they disavow it today in their books and their fine words, which are never lacking. And because, among their parricides, there is none more noteworthy than the parricides that Barrière, and then Châtel, wanted to commit upon our king, I'll first touch upon Barrière's, which Montaignes calls an imposture, and of which the Jesuits must be totally absolved.[1]

> The truth is (said he, replying to Arnauld) that Barrière testifies that he'd asked a Jesuit to advise him about his plan. That's the truth. He went to see Varade,[2] a Parisian Jesuit, who promptly sent him away, showing by his manner and his words that he was distraught, and didn't want to hear his confession. What you weren't careful about saying is also true: Barrière was asking everyone what they thought of his undertaking; and at Lyon, quite a bit earlier, near the Saone River, he had called together some theologians to give him advice; but no Jesuit was present. *Item*, on August 2, he had his funeral celebrated solemnly in the church of Saint-Paul of that city, leaving there his black sash and his weapons as a trophy for the victory he would one day win. *Item*, he testified that a Jesuit of Lyon dissuaded him from this undertaking. In this action, all these things show this man's vanity, and show the innocence of those whom you are turning into criminals, owing to such cruel exaggerations and to the bloody flux of your lying tongue. And even if that testimony were (but it wasn't) the most urgent in the world against the Jesuits, being constructed from instruments of torture, it wouldn't suffice as the basis of full proof.

---

1 See Chapter 1 above.

2 Ambroise Varade (?–1610) was the rector of the Paris Jesuits' boarding house, 1587–93. He was burned in effigy by the Parlement. Varade reappears in the next chapter. See Nelson, *Jesuits and Monarchy*, 13, 24.

Montaignes, the Jesuit, denies this fact: every nasty case can be denied. He argues that Arnauld is lying, since there isn't a single true word in everything, I set down above. Let's move on to the condemnation decree that the second Jesuit issues against his order, in the very humble request that he presented to the king.

> The second crime (says he), which concerns Your Majesty personally, is more vexing and has greater need of being refuted. For, saying that we are the enemies of kings and of the state, without being specific, amounts to creating an excessively broad thesis that cannot easily be defended: but saying it specifically gets a bit closer. And yet our enemies have tried to enclose us in the finery of a hypothesis: let us say that we are your personal enemies, and the enemies of your state. The general thesis served as the hue and cry that began the hunt; but the hypothesis sounded the capture, and the end of the hunt. Sire, before demonstrating our innocence here, we beg Your Majesty: things went on while you were of an opinion that you have since abandoned, should create no presumption that is prejudicial to our justification. You will recall, if you please, the very magnanimous response of one of your ancestors. It is on everyone's lips, because it is worthy of being repeated: It is not up to the king of France to continue the quarrels of a duke of Orléans.[3] Sire, you are no less magnanimous than that king, and you will be no less praised. Indeed, the praise will be greater, saying: It is not up to the king of France to avenge the quarrels of the king of Navarre, nor should the eldest son of the church be upset because someone has opposed an opinion that is contrary to the church.
>
> May it please Your Majesty to do us the favor that he does for all his subjects, and to bury everything that occurred at that time, in an eternal forgetfulness. You nonetheless recall that we have never advised anything against your person in particular, as our enemies have often tried to prove, and have never been able to do. And in the other things that ecclesiastics, preachers, and others said or did, we have said and done a great deal less than these persons have done for you. They always carried around with them bad summary notes instead of good texts. For if they now dare, in broad daylight and during the

---

3   This is said to have been King Louis XII's (1462–1515) reply to courtiers who were pressuring him to take revenge on the duke de la Trémoïlle. Note how Pasquier repeats the saying, but with a slight variation: "It's worthy of being repeated: It's not up to the king of France to continue the quarrels of a duke of Orléans. [...] It's not up to the king of France to avenge the quarrels of the king of Navarre."

serenity of peace, to load down the truth with a thousand inventions that run counter to the truth, what could they do, then, amid the noises and fogs of war, where lies are circulating and are in season, and where Truth does not dare to show her face? Time of war, time of lies, goes the old saying.

If we obtain this amnesty from Your Majesty, we will have the upper hand, and this second accusation will lose its strength. For nothing can keep that accusation from falling to the ground at the least little bump. By what argument can they prove that we are your majesty's personal enemies? What do they claim is the source of this hatred? And with what speeches do they encircle that conclusion? Is it because you are king? Our Society honors kings: that is proved by testimonies, by experience, and by reason. Is it as much, and more than the first accusation? Is it because you are king of France? France is our country, and you, its king, are our father. What will we love, if we do not love our father and our mother? Is it because you are a great warrior, captain of kings, and king of captains? This virtue makes us love our friends and our enemies at all times. And is it because you are mild in your conversation, subtle in your maxims, free in your ways of doing things, firm in your promises, quick in your actions, tireless in the face of pain, daring in the face of danger, formidable in combat, moderate in victory, and royal everywhere? These qualities cannot engender hatred, they engender the opposite: they are loving in everything and admirable in the person of a king.[4]

This text especially concerns the person of the king; and a bit before this passage, there is another passage by which this upright Jesuit maintained that it was wrong to accuse them of having been obstinate toward the state:

To these testimonies, Sire, we add a second argument based on reason. How likely is it that our profession states that we are enemies of kings and of their states? Are we so ignorant of God's law, that we do not know that it is God who gives them? That by him kings reign, and by him legislators make good laws? That naming and making kings is a right of patronage proper to the divine and supreme majesty? That in their royalty, kings bear the image of God; and that in that quality, God orders us to obey them, to honor them, and to serve their salvation and their state? And if we know these things, if we have preached about them, have written about them, and if we preach and write about them now, how can it be

4   The quoted passages in the final pages of this chapter are excerpts from Richeome's *La Vérité defendue* (Truth defended).

that we have so little conscience as to hate what we believe God loves, to scorn what he values, to destroy what he maintains? So little judgment when it comes to making something public, but doing something else?

Just because we are religious, are we more barbaric than the barbarians themselves? Than the cannibals and the Mamluks, who only know how to hate, yet nonetheless love their princes?

I praise these two passages (Jesuit, whoever you may be),[5] and I wish your soul were as clean as your spirit is handsome, and I wish I could see your words neatly threaded. I cannot not love you, although I see you painting naïve images of the singular and admirable virtues of the soul, the spirit, and the body, which glow in our king. I must also honor you, seeing that you portray the idea of the obedience that a subject owes his king. If your spirit concurs with your pen, I'm certain you will condemn all those who have wanted to attack either the person of this great prince, who is incomparable, or our kingdom, which surpasses all others. Your soul is too generous (despite your being a Jesuit) to judge differently. Or what if I show you that everything your companion has said in his *Verité défendue*, is nothing but a lie, as far as Barrière is concerned, and that he came to assassinate the king whom you exalt so highly, on the express advice of the members of your Society and your brethren. Not when he was merely king of Navarre, but now that he has been called to the crown of France, and is nestled in the bosom of our Catholic, Apostolic, and Roman Church. If, in addition, I show you that the general rebellion in France, undertaken in the name of the Holy League, was begun, then guided by your holy religious against Henri III, king of France, one of the most Catholic kings that France has ever had, what will be your judgement against your brethren? I surrender to my conscience, but it's the conscience of a good and virtuous Catholic, not the conscience of a hypocritical Jesuit. For these two passages are the two decrees of your condemnation: and I claim a right to them, to show that if you are reestablished now, it will be from lack of judgment, from faulty judgment. I'll discuss these two points in their order: I'll begin with Barrière, then Châtel, and after that I'll turn to the Troubles and the general revolt of which you others were the principal instigators in the kingdom.

---

5   Throughout this entire paragraph, Pasquier addresses this Jesuit (whoever he may be) with the pronoun *tu*. Scorn or irony? Or a moment of intimacy toward someone he hates in principle? He appears to be speaking to the disguised Jesuit who is the Gentleman's guest.

The Prodigious History of the Detestable Parricide Attempted against King Henri IV, Most Christian King of France and Navarre, Incited by Jesuits

THE LAWYER. I'll faithfully recount for you the story of Barrière, and you can believe me, at the risk of my possessions, my body, and my honor. For I got it from a friend of mine, who is another myself[1] and who was in the city of Melun when the event took place. He spoke to Barrière twice in the presence of Lugoli, his judge,[2] who witnessed the execution and heard everything he said on the wheel, down to his final sigh. He held in his hands the knife that I'll talk about later, and he later drew up excerpts from the trial by order of the king, in order to create a manifesto[3] that circulated in this kingdom and which he shared with me, and which I have before me.

Having made his peace with God and having made his truce with those who were his enemies at the time, the king wanted to move from the city of Saint-Denis to Fontainebleau. As he entered Melun, he received word from Ludovico Brancaleone,[4] an Italian gentleman whom he didn't know: a soldier who spoke very deliberately had left Lyon in order to kill him. He believed it, because he had not only seen him, he had also drunk with him twice at the monastery of the Jacobins.[5] This man was tall in stature and had strong, powerful limbs; his beard was the color of hazelnuts. He was wearing a morocco-leather collar and orange-tinted shoe-covers. The king isn't easily astonished, yet he's very prudent. Without making much of a fuss, he summoned Lugoli, who at the time was the *lieutenant général* of the long robe in the *prévôté* of the Hôtel. Having recounted what he'd heard, Brancaleone was ordered to search the city quietly for the man who had been described. The same day, the informer spied the man in the king's house. But since he was surrounded by several persons, he lost sight of him and gave it no more thought. God wanted to delay the

---

1　This doubtlessly is the person he mentioned in the first paragraph of Book I, ch. 1.

2　Pierre de Lugoli (?–1600), the provost of the king's household, was an official in the court that policed and judged incidents taking place in royal houses and gardens.

3　*Manifeste* (manifesto): a public text by which a prince, a state, a party, or a high-ranking person explains his conduct in some affair of great importance.

4　Ludovico Brancaleone (dates unknown), an Italian nobleman who was in the service of Queen Consort Louise of Lorraine (1553–1601), widow of Henry III.

5　That is, the Dominicans.

entertainment until the next day, when the traitor was lodged in a hamlet near the ruins of the village of Saint-Liesne.[6] He wanted to enter the city by Saint John's gate. He was deemed suspicious because of the above-mentioned remarks. It was August 27, 1593. Lugoli ordered him brought to the prison, where he interrogated him. And having noted that the prisoner didn't vary his words, he bound his arms and feet with irons, for it was an important affair. As soon as he had left, Anne Rousse, the jailer's wife, asked the prisoner what he wanted for his main meal; he replied that he didn't want to eat or drink, they should simply bring him some poison. This reply made the persons who were listening give more thought to his actions. Among others, there was a priest who was a prisoner: his name was Messire Pierre Lhermite,[7] and in accordance with the debauchery of the time, he had progressed from priest to being a determined soldier for the League. Having learned from him that both men had belonged to that party, Barrière accosted him; and after a bit of negotiating, the priest asked him if he had a knife on him. The other man, thinking that they'd found just what he needed, replied Yes. And he immediately pulled from his britches a knife that was shaped like this: the blade was well-fashioned until two inches from the handle; the back was like usual knives, and the other five inches were sharp on both sides, like a sword, and the point had gilded stippling, as on a dagger. Truly a murderer's knife, one that wouldn't fail when put to use. With a smile, the priest said that this knife would be good for paring one's fingernails, but that if someone saw it, he'd be dead. Barrière begged him to help him hide it, which he promised to do, and he grabbed it. But he immediately sent a message to Lugoli, informing him about what had gone on between them, and he gave him the knife. Lugoli questioned and examined the jailer about the poison, questioned the priest about the knife, questioned the Italian gentleman about what had gone on at Lyon. On August 28, the prisoner was questioned three times. And from these interrogations you will see that his name was Pierre Barrière, nicknamed La Barre, a native of the city of Orléans, a bargeman by his first calling. Having then been debauched by a captain at the tower, he had entered the service of a highborn lady, whom he left; and for an entire year he was an armed man in the company of Sieur d'Albigny,[8] at whose

---

6   Today the hamlet of Saint-Liesne, which in Pasquier's day centered around an eleventh-
    century church, is a part of the city of Melun.
7   The name is spelled out in other sources as L'Hermite. See, for example, Louis Joseph de
    Condé, *Mémoires de Condé, servant d'éclaircissement et de preuves à l'histoire de M. de Thou*
    [...]: *Mémoires pour servir à l'histoire de Charles IX, et de Henri IV, Rois de France* (Paris, 1745),
    174.
8   Charles de Simiane, lord of Albigny (1570–1609), was a captain for the League and gover-
    nor of Savoy since 1602. See Robert Oresko, "Bastards as Clients: The House of Savoy and

side he fought for the League until he was captured by Seigneur de la Guesle,[9] governor of Issoire, where he had stayed for a few days. Back when he was living with that highborn lady, he got the idea of killing the king with either a knife or a pistol aimed through his guards: and he therefore believed that he'd be making a great sacrifice to God, by killing a prince of a different religion than his own. Having been dismissed by Monsieur de la Guesle, he went to Lyon, where he inquired from a religious, whether it would be just for him to kill the king, who had converted to our religion. The reply was No. He had sold his mantle there, and a silk stocking too, in order to survive. From Lyon, he passed through Burgundy, then on to Paris. Finally, he reached Melun, where he slept in a barn near the church of Saint-Liesne; and a few days previously he had made his Easter-time confession at Brie-Comte-Robert, on a day when the shops were open; and he then went to the royal court in search of a master. If he was killed, his party would be angry. He had bought the knife in Paris for fifteen sous and had bought it with the sole intention of using it at table. The next day, August 29, he was heard for the fourth time on several subjects, and he said that, at Lyon, he could have been the lieutenant of the Marquis of Saint-Sorlin;[10] or, under him, he could have commanded a company of light-horse cavalry, if he wished. Lugoli then pressured him, asking why, since he had held that rank in the League, he had given it up in order to come and search for a master at the royal court. When he heard that, he fell silent and replied that he'd said what needed to be said. Four witnesses against him were questioned: Brancaleone, who told about Barrière's advice at Lyon about killing the king, and that he didn't hide this from him; the jailer's wife, about poison; Messire Pierre Lhermite, about the knife. Monsieur Thomas Boucher, priest at Brie-Comte-Robert,[11] summoned, declared that he'd heard Barrière's confession a week earlier, and had given him communion the next morning, and that the man had told him that he'd also made his confession four days earlier, in the city of Saint-Denis; but he didn't tell him that he wanted to attempt to assassinate the king. All these witnesses having been listed and confronted, not

---

Its Illegitimate Children," in Roger Mettam and Charles Giry-Deloison, *Patronages et clientélismes 1550–1750 (France, Angleterre, Espagne, Italie)* (Lille: Publications de l'Institut de recherches historiques du Septentrion, 1995), 39–67, esp. 49.

9   Jacques de la Guesle (1557–1612), a *procureur général* in the Parlement of Paris. See Robert J. Knecht, *Hero or Tyrant?: Henry III, King of France, 1574–89* (n.p.: Taylor & Francis, 2016), 299 ff.

10   Henri de Savoie, duc de Nemours, marquis of Saint-Sorlin (1572–1632), the brother and the successor of the former duke, Charles-Emmanuel. See *Encyclopaedia Britannica*, https://www.britannica.com/biography/Henri-I-de-Savoie-duc-de-Nemours (accessed February 1, 2021).

11   See Condé, *Mémoires de Condé*, 174–75.

only were they not reproached, but they stated that their depositions contained the truth, except the deposition of Brancaleone, in which, he said, he'd been told about the undertaking that Barrière was cooking up against the king. He admitted that he'd eaten and drunk twice with him at the Jacobins. The case having been investigated by Lugoli in this manner, by letters-patent the king delegated six councilors of state to be judges, among them two presidents from the sovereign courts. Not a single soul would doubt that there was sufficient evidence, or even too much evidence to declare him guilty of the crime for which he was being prosecuted. He confessed to having wanted to kill the king in the past, before the king's conversion; but since that time, he had debated with four monks about whether he could justly kill him. A witness of some standing said that he'd drunk with him while he was proposing to go to the court for that very purpose. He had described to the king all the particularities by which Barrière could be recognized: he was a man who, judged by his conscience, ever since the first intervention at the prison had asked for poison as his main dish; and who was found to be carrying a knife of the above size: he was a man, I say, who admitted having held a rank in the League, which he had voluntarily left in order simply to find a master at court. And so, by a decree of August 31, he was sentenced to be dragged through the streets on a cart and pinched with hot irons. This done, he would be led to the great marketplace of the city, then have his right fist burned while holding the knife; and having been placed on a scaffold, he would have his arms, legs, and thighs broken by the executioner of high justice; and after his death, his body would be converted to ashes and thrown into the river; and his house would be razed, and all his possessions seized and confiscated by the king; and before the execution he would be given both ordinary and extraordinary questioning, in order to learn, from his own mouth, the identity of those who had induced him to attempt this unfortunate undertaking.

Up to that point, you see nothing about this prisoner that involves the Parisian Jesuits, and in like manner nothing had made him distraught, as Montaignes wanted to portray him; but one sees a shrewd man who fended off blows in every way he could, a man whose judges extracted the truth from him during four different interrogations. The decree having been pronounced that same day, two of his judges, plus Lugoli, were appointed to see him undergo the questioning and interrogation. The wretch, feeling them at work, begged them not to stretch him with a cord, and he would tell the whole truth. So he confessed to all the details about Lyon, as Brancaleone had listed them for the king. And he admitted that, while in that city, he had spoken with four monks: a Carmelite, a Jacobin, a Capuchin, and a Jesuit, with whom he had plotted to commit this murder; and he had gone off, the day after the Assumption of Our Lady, as follows: having reached Paris, he'd lodged on the rue de la Huchette, where he inquired who were the most zealous churchmen for the League: they named the curate of Saint-André-des-Arts.[12] He promptly went to see him, and he told him what he was debating about; the curate approved highly and gave him a drink, saying that he would win great glory in paradise; but that the best thing, before going any farther, would be to see the rector of the Jesuits,[13] who might help him make a firmer resolution. He went to see him: the Jesuit told him that he had been rector for only three weeks, and he said some lovely words to the effect that the resolution that Barrière had made was very holy, and he must show great courage and steadfastness, confess his sins, and receive communion on Easter. From there, the Jesuit led him to his bedchamber and blessed him. The next day, when he arrived at the lodging, his confession was heard by another Jesuit, to whom he didn't reveal who he was, and after that, he received the Body of Our Lord at the Jesuit college. He also spoke with another Jesuit who preached in Paris, and who often said bad things about the king, who found his advice to be very holy and very meritorious. After that, he bought the knife that was described for the court, on which that sharp point had been made: and he then left Paris and went to Saint-Denis, where the king was, firmly resolved to kill him in the church; but seeing him at Mass, devoutly, he couldn't do it, as if his arms were crippled and his limbs paralyzed. From there, he followed the king to the fort of Gournay, then to Brie-Comte-Robert where, having been confessed and been given communion, he missed the king while he was pulling his knife from his britches. Finally, he reached Melun, where he was arrested. And because his judges were emphasizing that it was a very bad deed to have received the Blessed Sacrament of the Altar twice, when he had that unfortunate intention in his soul and realized that it could only lead to his damnation, he shouted that he was, then, very unfortunate, and he thanked God for having turned him away from such an evil deed. They read his confessions to him, in which he persisted: confessions, I tell you, that he made without receiving more than one pull on the rope. From there, he was dragged to the place of execution; and while he was on the scaffold, Lugoli ordered him to tell the truth, and to be very careful not to accuse anyone who was innocent. To which he replied that everything he had said in the questioning room

---

12   Christophe Aubry (?–1601), curate of Saint-André-des-Arts, was famous for the verbal violence in his sermons. He was executed in effigy in January 1595. See Vanessa Harding, *The Dead and the Living in Paris and London* (Cambridge: Cambridge University Press, 2002), 152.

13   Ambroise Varade. See ch. 5 above.

was true, and he asked God, the king, and the court to pardon him. This done, and his fist having been scorched and burned, and after that his arms, thighs, and legs broken, he was put on the wheel. The judges intended to let him lie there, languishing, until he had pointed out his accomplices. There, he was once again asked whether he wanted to say something in order to unburden his conscience; and he replied that everything he had confessed to was true, and that there were two swarthy priests who had left Lyon for that same purpose, but that he'd wanted to get ahead of them in order to carry off the honor, humbly begging his judges not to permit his soul to be lost owing to the despair of his body. Hearing this, Lugoli had him strangled by order of the other judges, and the next day his body was turned to ashes, and the ashes were thrown into the river. Later, the execution having been carried out on Tuesday, August 31, the news was brought by some citizens of Melun (for the roads were free on both sides thanks to the truce): on the previous Sunday, they had heard, in Paris, a sermon by Commolet,[14] the Jesuit, who, at the end of his sermon, had begged all listeners to be patient; for (he said) in a few days you shall see a very specific miracle of Our Lord, or even will find that it has already happened. These words, uttered loudly and clearly in the presence of an infinite number of witnesses, made the judges very certain that everything that Barrière had said was true.

14   See Book 1, ch. 4 above.

How Very Prejudicial to Our Church the Barbaric Impiety of the Jesuits Would Have Been, If Their Execrable Advice Had Had Its Effect

THE LAWYER. I've very faithfully told you about Barrière's trial, and you can pull together everything that's written in the plea of the Collège de Clermont, and also in Montaignes's mythical truth. They are fairy tales full of ridiculous wishes, like the ones we can read in most of the Jesuits' annual letters.[1] And in addition, you'll see that Barrière wasn't a simple and innocent man: he was very resolved, was on his guard as much as possible when facing the magistrate; and after having been found guilty, he didn't permit himself to wail, as Montaignes gives us to understand. For he was never stretched by ropes. Before his arrest, the judges weren't thinking about the Jesuits; but having found sufficient reason to sentence him to death, and owing to the gravity of the crime, they immediately ordered that the questioning be done, so that he would reveal his accomplices. Without waiting to be tortured, and seeing that he was done for, he declared in detail how everything had gone; and he accused four religious of Lyon, and among others a Jesuit who isn't named; but that gentleman, in his deposition, told us that it was Petrus Majorius.[2] Later he recounted what was done to him at the Jesuit college in Paris by the top person there. He didn't know his name, but Montaignes tells us: he says it was Varade. Also, it was well known, at the time, that he was in charge of the college. In addition, the king having since that time returned to Paris, Varade quickly went away, having no sure witness against him other than his conscience. As for Commolet, he needed no other witnesses than the people who attended his sermon. The roads were open at the time, for there was a truce. Several upright persons who had sought refuge in Melun, and who then came to Paris, heard about the great miracle he was predicting. When it comes down to it, before facing his punishment, and while he was on the scaffold, the criminal didn't change everything he had said and admitted, first, in the questioning room, and then

---

1 "Annual letters": each Jesuit house sent a yearly letter to Rome describing the achievements of that year. Pasquier suggests that they are full of exaggerations.

2 Pierre Majorius (1542–1604), rector of the colleges at Avignon, Lyon, and Kolozsvar (modern Romania), and vice-provincial of Austria. Henri Fouqueray, s.j., *Histoire de la Compagnie de Jésus en France des origines à la suppression*, 5 vols. (Paris: Picard, 1910–25), 33, 239, 263–64.

© KONINKLIJKE BRILL NV, LEIDEN, 2021 | DOI:10.1163/9789004164062_046

on the wheel. He was full of understanding, for on his body they simply broke his arms, thighs, and legs. And when they let him loose after he had persevered, he begged Lugoli not to reduce him to despair at losing his soul after losing his body. When he said that, they strangled him, but first he reported to all his judges, and obtained their permission to do so. It is therefore an impudent lie to propose that Varade, having found his brain altered, didn't want to stop at him. It is, I tell you, a valiant lie, to say that Barrière's confessions were extorted from him during the questioning. He wasn't made to undergo the questioning; moreover, on the scaffold he persisted in saying his confession twice, as I've just shown. As for the rest, and as for the assembly of theologians, and the scarf lost at Saint Paul's church,[3] if there'd been something, he would have said so, with the same frankness as for everything he confessed to having seen, first in Lyon and then in Paris. Now I'll return to the cajoling words that the second Jesuit fed to the king, so that the Jesuits would be reestablished. Where are those fine words now? "It's not up to the king of France to avenge the quarrels of the king of Navarre,[4] nor is it up to the eldest son of the church to suffer the effects of what has been done contrary to the opposing opinion of the church."[5] Isn't that an impudent trickster, who once again wants to catch our king unawares, to the sound of his flute? All along, I've been stating the Jesuit's fine words, so that everyone will know that it's impossible to say things better. All along, I've written down Barrière's story, so that everyone may know that it's impossible to do worse, and that there's no animal in the world more cruel, sly, and savage than the Jesuit, and therefore it's necessary to ward off all his types of treason.

But I beg you, look at the thread that was used for those stretched-out nets! As much as, and as long as the king belonged to the other religion, and not to ours,[6] the Jesuits never proposed that he be assassinated, not even at the height of our Troubles. And when he reconciled with our church, they feigned to fear that he had become a Catholic by deceit, and they waged a terrible war against him. But when? In the midst of the sworn truce, at a time when each person was assured of his physical safety, owing to the public oath that both

---

3   Sutto, 343n72 points out that a white scarf was the sign that one belonged to the League. True, but the scarf that Barrière left in the church was black (Book III, ch. 5).

4   That is, Henri de Bourbon, king of Navarre, the future King Henri IV of France.

5   Here, Pasquier is quoting from Richeome's *Très humble remonstrance*, 41. See Sutto, 343n73.

6   While still an infant, Henri IV was baptized as a Catholic, but he was raised by his mother, who belonged to the "Reformed" or Protestant religion. He embraced Catholicism under duress in the wake of the 1572 St. Bartholomew's Day massacres, but soon renounced it again. His official conversion to Catholicism in 1593 was controversial and his motives have been subject of dispute among historians. See Michael Wolfe, *The Conversion of Henri IV: Politics, Power, and Religious Belief in Early Modern France* (Cambridge, MA: Harvard University Press, 1993).

sides had taken reciprocally. Where did this new advice come from? Until he was a Catholic, those Judases never seriously weighed having the king assassinated; because they thought that as long as he was plunged into his error, the people whom the Jesuits were supporting in the rebellion would never stoop to obeying him. But as soon as he had converted, seeing that they were spinning on the wheel of fortune, and thinking that diminishing him would return his subjects to their ancient duty, they pushed on, thinking that he had to be killed, whatever the cost, so that they could turn the kingdom over to the one who turned out to be the strongest and who shared their devotions.

I want this subject not only to be treated before Our Holy Father and his Consistory, but also before the lowest person in this world, as long as he has ever so little religion and judgment. Was there ever a more abominable impiety than that? Our Jesuits charmed a weak spirit by the holy sacraments of the church, and they suborned that spirit to kill the king? Not because he was a heretic, but because they suspected that his conversion involved dissimulation. They were suspicious of him? I don't believe it. But even if they were suspicious of him, did the life of a great king have to depend on their vain imaginings; and on this claim, they were advising such a detestable parricide? Even traded paradise with the person who would undertake that parricide? Moreover, in order to give more gloss to their wickedness, they took advantage of the holy sacrament of Communion? Oh, God! Since the creation of the world, was there ever a more wretched atheism? They weren't aiming at a simple king of Navarre; they were aiming at the greatest king that France has ever had. This wasn't a prince whose faith was the opposite of ours, it was one who was totally submitting to being brought back into the bosom of the church. And we're going to lend an ear to that Jesuit toady! I'm fooling myself: for we must listen to that Jesuit toady, so that his conclusions will serve as condemnations of him and of all who are associated with him.

But see the fruit that our Catholic, Apostolic, Roman Church would have produced if this execrable advice had succeeded. Don't doubt that when the king converted, the Huguenots felt great heartbreak in their souls. Let's suppose that his life went poorly, owing to the intervention of the clergy: True God, what trophies would they have displayed in their assemblies! How many reasons would their ministers have had to thunder, to lightning-strike, to mingle heaven and earth in their pulpits, in order to maintain that it was a great blow from heaven? All the more so because, since the king had left their true church (those are the very words they used), God would have permitted him to be promptly removed from this world; and this would be done through the ministry of those to whom he had surrendered. Wouldn't they have found a very great pretext for saying that to them? In their pulpits, our preachers manage a thousand encounters that are less appropriate than that one. Wouldn't that have been the means of maintaining them in their errors, under a great and specious title, instead of discouraging them from doing so? Didn't all of that turn on the ruin and desolation of the Holy See, whose protectors our Jesuits boast of being? Their proposition isn't Catholic, it's Anabaptist, and it makes them live again, makes them want to take the lives of kings.

On the Assassination That Jean Châtel, Nurtured at the School of the Parisian Jesuits, Wanted to Attempt against the King in 1594

THE LAWYER. On the Feast of Saint John the Evangelist, December 27, 1594, having reconquered Paris, the king entered his chamber, followed by several princes and lords. His mouth was unexpectedly struck by a knife, which neither he nor the persons present had noticed. As soon as Jean Châtel, only nineteen years old, struck that blow, he dropped the knife and stood still in the midst of the crowd. He was young, and no one could imagine that this furious undertaking could have been done by this very young person. Everyone looked amazed, and this young wolf could almost have escaped. But God didn't want that detestable crime to go unpunished: someone cast eyes on him, and he was captured by chance. But since he'd been promised the Jesuits' paradise, if he were to die for this crime as one of their martyrs, he confessed more rapidly than expected; and he was sentenced to death by a decree of the court of the Parlement of Paris. Here, the Jesuits treat their innocence as a great trophy, saying that neither during the questioning, nor at any other time did he place the responsibility on any of them, but that everything he'd done came from his own instinct; and by that confession, he preserved it until his last breath. As for me, I've no greater argument than that one, to show that the craft of assassination was lodged in the Jesuits' Collège de Clermont. For, among the other colleges that they administered, and in which they taught literature, how does it happen that no scholar undertook a plan as damnable as the one being nurtured in their house? Because we all agree that Châtel had studied there and had even completed his philosophy classes. True, they say that he hadn't been there for eight months, and that he no longer resided there. The reason for this discrepancy is quick to grasp: at the other colleges, they didn't know that teaching the murder of kings was special to our college. But then, in Jesuit colleges they preached the opposite of what they taught. Also, they were all too generous with their sermons. Although this young boy, whose soul had been infected by their poison, had left their schools, he wasn't cured. *Quae semel est imbuta recens, servabit odorem testa diu.*[1] That's why, relying on the

---

[1] "A jar will long retain the odor of what it was dipped in when new." Horace, *Epistles*, I, ii, 69–70.

old instructions and memoranda of the Jesuits, he thought he should make a sacrifice to God by committing that sort of parricide. The same thing happened in the past in Italy. There was a Cola Mantouan[2] who taught humane letters to the youths of Milan and who, in the principal discourses of his lectures, said little beyond: Blessed is the person who, with his blood, redeemed a republic from a tyrant's servitude. In this manner, three gentlemen, of the houses and families of Lampugnani, Visconti, and Olgiati, having reached the age of maturity, conspired privately to carry out their preceptor's teachings. And during the Christmas festivities, on the feast of Saint Stephen, just as Gian Galeazzo,[3] duke of Milan, was entering the great church in order to hear Mass, they knew in their hearts that they would actually massacre him right before everyone's eyes. At the time, they felt quite sure that it would be very difficult to escape the fury of the duke's guards, and that's just what happened. Two persons were killed on the spot, and the third person, who had escaped, was captured a few days later, taken to the gibbet, and never accused anyone but himself and his companions, no more than Châtel did.[4] Nonetheless, the historiographers of Italy note that the teachings of Cola, their master, were the first instigations.[5] For that reason, our Jesuits are mockers, when they think they can excuse Châtel's replies. I don't know if his replies were what they say they were. I know full well that all their lessons and sermons tended toward this parricide: they offered themselves as the sole surety for the person who would carry out this great masterpiece, in return for all their paradise.

2   Nicola Capponi, known as Cola Montano (?–1482) was an Italian humanist from Bologna. He inculcated his pupils with a hatred for tyranny. See Sutto, 345n75.

3   Gian Andrea Lampugnani (?–1476), Carlo Visconti (?–1476), and Gerolamo Olgiati (?–1476), were students of Capponi who organized a plot that led to the assassination of Galeazzo Maria Sforza (1444–76), duke of Milan, on December 26, 1476. See *Treccani*, https://www.treccani.it/enciclopedia/capponi-nicola-detto-cola-montano_(Dizionario-Biografico) (accessed February 1, 2021) for the critical analysis of the episode.

4   Apparently, all three assassins were arrested, tried, and sentenced to death.

5   See, for example, Machiavelli, *Istorie fiorentine*, VII, 33.

It Is a Heresy to Approve of the Assassins of Princes, Even Though the Princes Were Tyrants

THE LAWYER. If hypocrisy isn't currently being disguised in the Jesuits' latest writings, one mustn't doubt that they not only have professed it, but that they glory in the parricides of kings and sovereign princes. In addition to an infinity of examples that I've collected, there is a Petrus Matheus,[1] a doctor in one sort of law, and in the other sort too. In 1587, he made a collection of several Latin poems by Italian poets; and, the following year, he produced a mingle-mangle of several decretals from the time of Pope Gregory IX to the time of Sixtus V. Now, between the two most beautiful poems, one finds the most shameful ones: Bembo's "Priapus," where he shows his wit when talking about the herb that we call *la menthe*, "mint": that word comes close to the Latin word *mentula*.[2] And there's also Fracastoro's[3] "Syphilis," which describes the origin and progress of syphilis; and in this second collection, of all the religious orders that rely on pontifical constitutions, there isn't one that he celebrates as much as the Jesuit order. They make a great fuss over that man's judgment of them, and they often put him on show. Now, just look at the speech he gave

---

1 Pasquier confused the poet Johannes Matthaeus Toscanus (1526–88) with "Petrus Matheus," that is, Pierre Matthieu, the compiler of *Summa constitutionum summorum pontificum* (Lyon: Landry, 1588). See above, Book II, ch. II. Toscanus was a student and friend of the poet Jean Dorat (1508–88), who was a member of the Pleiade and a protegé of Queen Catherine de' Medicis. See Toscanus's *Carmina illustrium poetarum Italorum* (Paris: Gorbinus, 1577). For Pierre Matthieu, the compiler of bulls, see above, Book II, ch. II.

2 Pietro Bembo (1470–1547) was an Italian humanist, poet, and cardinal. His poem "Priapus" (included in his *Libellus carminum* of 1553) is a lighthearted ode to the joys of sexuality. The play on words involves similar words: *menta* (mint) and *mentula* (little [*pusilla*] mint or penis):

> Nomine si cupias cognoscere, Menta pusilla est.
> Rides? Sic illam Roma diserta vocat.
> Sed quae, docti homines cum dicunt, Menta pusilla est,
> Haec mihi non docto maxima vel nimia.
> Parcite Romulidae, verbo sum lapsus in uno:
> An cuiquam nimium tale quid esse potest?

3 Girolamo Fracastoro (c.1476–1553) was an Italian physician and poet. He is best known for his *Syphilis sive morbus Gallicus* (1530), that is, "Syphilis or the French Disease," a rhymed work that gives an account of the disease that he named. See *DBI*, https://www.treccani.it/enciclopedia/girolamo-fracastoro_(Dizionario-Biografico) (accessed February 1, 2021).

after the Pauline Index of 1559.[4] *Dum superseminat inimicus homo Zizaniam adsunt divino Pneumate acciti Patres societatis Jesu, qui Petri sedem illustrant, in Lutherum arma divini eloquii parant, TYRANNOS AGREDIUNTUR, lollium ab agro dominico evellunt, et fidei christianae praeclarissimi buccinatores, verbo et exempo cunctis praelucent.* This passage was copied out word for word by Montaignes, and was completely translated in this fashion: "While the enemy sows tares, here are the fathers of the Society of Jesus called by the divine Spirit, and who make illustrious the throne of Saint Peter, who take up the weapons of God's Word against Luther, WHO ASSAIL THE TYRANTS, rip the tares from the Master's field, and like excellent trumpets of the faith of God, they are the very first ones, by their words and by the example of their lives." Montaignes said that a Jesuit didn't write that. I agree: but Petrus Matheus was a man (I don't know if he's still alive), whose soul was totally Jesuit, and to whom the entire sect has great obligations. For, in addition to the panegyric in their honor that he placed below Paul III's bull, he added, above Gregory's bull of 1584, all the Jesuit houses and colleges, although his catalogue shows several imaginary ones. And he doesn't understand their affairs any more than the person who, using the disguised name Montaignes,[5] has falsified Truth. If he is still as natural and as familiar with the Jesuits as he is when assailing tyrants or Lutherans, I'm convinced that anyone who wanted to remove murders from their religious order, would resemble a foolish physician who, seeing that half the members of a body are paralyzed and crippled, wants to cut away that half in order to save the other half: for by doing so, he would lose both parts at the same time. Here Montaignes, in the same chapter, uses a quibbling sophistry and says that the word tyrant has nothing in common with the word king. That's a good way to have a prince killed, and then to dispute whether he should be called king or tyrant; for why draw this distinction if that isn't one's aim?

This question has been resolved for a long time, and I'm displeased that it is necessary to put it in doubt. John, duke of Burgundy, having assassinated, at the Barbette gate,[6] Louis duke of Orléans, the son and brother of kings, put forward a young doctor of theology named Master Jean Petit,[7] with whom he

---

4 He is referring to the Pauline Index of Prohibited Books. This translation corrects Pasquier's and Sutto's chronology, which was 1540 and 1545, respectively.

5 This is yet another allusion to Louis Richeome, the Jesuit. See Book II, ch. 5.

6 On November 23, 1411. See Sutto, 347n89.

7 Jean Petit (1360?–1411) was a professor of theology at the University of Paris. He was a spokesman for the university in the quarrel known as the "Great Schism." He is primarily known for his apology for the assassination perpetrated by Jean the Fearless, duke of Burgundy (1371–1419). See Sutto, 347n90. Cf. Claude Gauvard, "Jean Petit," in *Encyclopedia of the Middle*

had talked while still a student. This man went to the open area in front of Notre Dame of Paris to preach to an infinity of persons, saying that this murder was just, for it involved a tyrant. And he presented several heady reasons and expert evidence to the effect that he was permitted to do this. The duke of Burgundy won his lawsuit in popular opinion: and he immediately let this same error creep into the hearts of young theologians, insisting that it was lawful to kill a tyrant. Until Master Jean Gerson, chancellor of the University of Paris (one of the church's greatest theologians),[8] unable to bear the continued circulation of this damnable opinion, went to the city of Constance where the general council was being held,[9] and had this proposition declared heretical, as we learn by session 15:

> *Praecipua sollicitudine volens haec sacro-sancta Synodus ad extirpationem*
> *errorum et haeresum in diversis mundi partibus invalescentium providere,*
> *sicut tenetur, et ad hoc collecta est, nuper accepit quod nonnullae erroneae*

Ages, https://www.oxfordreference.com/view/10.1093/acref/9780227679319.001.0001/acref-9780227679319-e-1472 (accessed February 1, 2021). A member of the French royal house, John the Fearless played an important role in French politics during the Hundred Years' War. His rash and unscrupulous politics culminated in his assassination in 1419. See *Encyclopaedia Britannica*, https://www.britannica.com/biography/John-duke-of-Burgundy (accessed February 1, 2021).

8   See Book II, ch. 1.

9   Council of Constance (1414–18) was the sixteenth ecumenical council of the Roman Catholic Church. In its fifteenth session on July 6, 1415, it dealt with the teaching of John Wyclif (*c.*1320–84), Jan Hus (1369–1415), and Jean Petit. Pasquier's citation is the condemnation of Petit's proposition regarding tyrants. Here is the English translation of the Latin original of this paragraph: "This most holy synod wishes to proceed with special care to the eradication of errors and heresies which are growing in various parts of the world, as is its duty and the purpose for which it has assembled. It has recently learnt that various propositions have been taught that are erroneous both in the faith and as regards good morals, are scandalous in many ways and threaten to subvert the constitution and order of every state. Among these propositions this one has been reported: Any tyrant can and ought to be killed, licitly and meritoriously, by any of his vassals or subjects, even by means of plots and blandishments or flattery, notwithstanding any oath taken, or treaty made with the tyrant, and without waiting for a sentence or a command from any judge. This holy synod, wishing to oppose this error and to eradicate it completely, declares, decrees and defines, after mature deliberation, that this doctrine is erroneous in the faith and with regard to morals, and it rejects and condemns the doctrine as heretical, scandalous and seditious and as leading the way through perjury to frauds, deceptions, lies and betrayals. It declares, decrees and defines, moreover, that those who stubbornly assert this very pernicious doctrine are heretics and are to be punished as such according to canonical and legitimate sanctions." See https://www.papalencyclicals.net/councils/ecum16.htm (accessed February 1, 2021).

assertiones infide et bonis moribus, ac multipliciter scandalosae, totius Reipublicae statum et ordinem subvertere molientes, dogmatizatae sunt: Inter quas haec assertio delata est. QUILIBET TYRANNUS potest et debet licite et meritorie occidi per quemcumque Vasalum suum et subditum, etiam per insidias, vel blanditias, vel adulationes, nonobstante quocunque juramento, seu confoederatione, factis cum eo, non expectata sententia, vel mandato judicis cujuscunque. Adversus hunc errorem fatagens haec sancta Synodus insurgere, et ipsum funditus tollere, decernit, et definit hujusmodi doctrinam erroneam esse in fide, et in moribus, ipsamque tanquam scandalosam, et ad fraudes, deceptiones, mendacia, proditiones, perjuria vias dantem, reprobat et condemnat.

Which means:

This holy Council, as it is being held and has to that end been assembled, in order to provide for the extirpation of errors and heresies, which are beginning to spread in several parts of this world, has of late been warned that they are dogmatizing and teaching some doctrines that are counter to the faith and to good morals, and that are variously scandalous, to the subversion of the order and state of the republic, among them the following: *Every tyrant can, and should, be legally and deservedly killed by one of his vassals and subjects: either by ambush, by gentle attractions, or by flattery, despite any oath of fidelity or alliance made with him, without awaiting a sentence or order from any judge* [Pasquier's emphasis]. Against which error this holy Council, desiring to stiffen itself and to totally uproot it, declares, orders, and judges this doctrine to be erroneous in faith and in morals, and reproves it and condemns it as scandalous, and as creating an opening for deceits, frauds, lies, treasons, and perjuries.

This is an article that I respect and revere, not only because it was decreed at that great Council of Constance, by which both the church's abuse and its heresy were extirpated, but also because it came from the boutique of our France, which was Gerson's first and principal promotor against the new theologians who, at the time, had embraced this opinion, which the Jesuits have since revived in the death of good King Henri III, whom they called the Tyrant. And they would have done the same thing against our present king, if God, by his holy grace, hadn't preserved him.[10] But because the Jesuits pretend to disavow their Petrus Matheus, saying that he wasn't part of their sect, what will they say about Father Emmanuel Sà,[11] who claims to be a doctor of theology from their Society, and who, in two articles of his, maintained that it was lawful to kill a tyrant and let a king's subjects chase him from his kingdom, should his opinions become disordered. As if the people can, or should, tell the king what is legal, the king whom God has given to him, to be his sovereign magistrate.

I'm ashamed at having to prove that no subject should attack his prince, no matter what character he is playing. But having undertaken to combat the Jesuits' heresy, which they've indeed practiced, and which they now want to turn into a verbal excuse, I'll give them so much that they'll vomit it up. Oh, Jesuit: Learn, therefore, this lesson from me. For I owe that charity to every Christian. We should obey our kings, regardless of who they are, I mean whether they are good or bad. That's what the Sage teaches us in his Proverbs; Saint Peter, in his Epistles; Saint Paul, to the Romans, to Titus, to Timothy. The prophet Baruch, referring to Nebuchadnezzar, whom God, among all the princes, had caused to fall into an outcast state. And finally, David's fine example of being persecuted by Saul, his king. Just as God gives us kings, we must receive them without knowing, as you do, whether they are kings or tyrants. The hearts of kings are in God's hands. Kings carry out his justice, so it can please him to chastise us more or less. We should only show our opposition to this by offering him our humble prayers. If we don't behave that way, we represent those impertinent giants depicted by the antique poets: they wanted to climb a ladder to heaven in order to be similar to the gods; and, in less than a wink, they were thrown from the top to the bottom by their god Jupin.[12] A king must not, however, overdo his power; he must know that he is a father; and consequently, he must never become easily irritated with his subjects, who are his children. Otherwise, when he is thinking about it the least, God, the Father of fathers and the King of kings, will wreak his vengeance upon him, with his terrible and horrible arm. In sum, since you,[13] Jesuit, pay blind

---

10   The "good king" is Henri III, assassinated in 1589; and the "present king" is Henri IV, who was the target of at least twelve assassination attempts. The final, and fatal, attempt would take place in 1610. See Roland Mousnier, *The Assassination of Henry IV* (New York: Scribner, 1973).

11   See Book II, ch. 1.

12   This is an evocation of book 1 of Ovid's *Metamorphoses*. The Jupins were the sons of Earth and Sky. They were half men and half serpents. Zeus vanquished them with the help of Athena and Heracles. See Sutto, 349n99.

13   Here, and for the remainder of this paragraph, the Jesuit is scornfully addressed as *tu*.

obedience to your superiors, who are merely your adopted seigneurs, you owed a hundred times more obedience to your king, who is your true, legitimate, natural lord and father. Therefore, you are a very dangerous lad, putting into your writings the distinction between king and tyrant. Not that I don't know that there's a great difference between the one and the other; but he blindfolds us concerning their obedience. Otherwise, it's a rebellious little lean-to shack that pits the subject against his prince: a rebellion (I say) that produces more ills than the tyranny one obeys.

A Memorable Act by Ignatius, Where the Jesuits Learned to Kill, or to Have Killed, Those Who Do Not Adhere to Their Opinions

THE LAWYER. There were, inside the borders of Spain, I don't know how many *marranos*[1] who had been chased out by King Ferdinand, who for that reason was called the Catholic.[2] An epithet that his successors have since accepted. Among this riffraff, one of them mounted a mule and accosted Ignatius along the road, not very long after he had changed his first way of living. And having told one another where they were headed, they talked of various things, until they finally came to the Blessed Virgin Mary. The Moor recognized her as having really been a virgin before her conception, but not after it, basing his opinion on natural reasons that have nothing in common with our faith. Ignatius insisted that the opposite was true, and he did so in a holy way: this holy Lady had been a virgin, before, and at the time, and after giving birth, and he set out to prove it. But being at the time a mere apprentice, or if you want me to tell the truth, he was learning the A-B-C's of our religion, he was not up to maneuvering such a lofty subject. So, of all his arguments, a justified anger was all that remained to him. The Moor, making fun of Ignatius in his soul, spurred his mule, and let him run for a long while, leaving Ignatius alone. Indignant at not having bested the other man by flattering him, Ignatius thought about his sword, and wondered whether he should pursue him at full speed, in order to kill him. However, since he was a conscientious man, he was extremely perplexed: for on the one hand, it displeased him to see a monster full of impiety and blasphemy walking about on the earth, and on the other hand he was

---

1   *Marranos* is a pejorative term (referring to pig) applied to Iberian converts from Judaism who were believed to practice secretly Judaism or their descendants, known also as *conversos*. On the Jesuits and *conversos*, see Robert A. Maryks, *The Jesuit Order as a Synagogue of Jews: Purity-of-Blood Laws in the Early Society of Jesus* (Brill: Leiden, 2009) and the special issue of the *Journal of Jesuit Studies* 8, no. 2 (2021), https://brill.com/view/journals/jjs/8/2/jjs.8.issue-2.xml (accessed March 21, 2021) on that topic. The protagonist of the mule episode below is a *marisco*, a convert or a descendant of a converted Muslim. See Emanuele Colombo, "Defeating the Infidels, Helping Their Souls: Ignatius Loyola and Islam," in *A Companion to Ignatius of Loyola*, ed. Maryks, 179–97.

2   Ferdinand II and V (1452–1516) was king of Aragon and Castile. In 1492, he and his spouse Isabella I of Castile (1451–1504), known as "Catholic monarchs," expelled all unconverted Jews from their domains.

thinking of his fear of offending the Virgin Mary while defending her cause. During this debate, balancing between Yes and No, he finally decided to seek his mule's advice. Thanks to a fork in the road, he had seen his man go by, and he knew the choice he would make. Thanks to admirable wisdom, he resolved not to let loose the reins of his anger, but to rest the reins on his beast's neck; so that if, on this forked road, the mule followed its instincts, it would unfailingly take the Moor's path, which would be the end of him; but God willed the mule to choose the other path. This made Ignatius quickly calm down, guessing that this was what had happened to his mule, by divine inspiration. God sometimes gives false prophets advice through their beasts, as we read about Balaam's ass[3] and about Ignatius's mule, without which he would have furiously carried out his plan. I therefore don't find it strange that he passed this same fury to his successors, with whom I don't want to argue about whether it is done well, or not. I refer them to the mule to make their decision, which he did.

Hearing this, the Jesuit wanted to express his thoughts. THE JESUIT. You'll excuse me, but I seem to be reciting all this at length. For Ribadeneyra, who is one of those who have borrowed this tale, says that Ignatius was surprised by remembering his Old Adam.[4] *Homo quippe militaris fallaci veri honoris imitatione olim elusus.*[5] He had entered into that mad idea of vengeance. But having since then reached the church of Our Lady of Montserrat, he placed all his weapons before her altar, having first, for three days, made a written confession of all his sins. *Ibi optimo confessario, totius vitae suae crimina per triduum ex scripto confessus est, illique homini omnium primo, animi sui propositum aperuit, jumentum reliquit, gladiuim pugionemque, quibus Mundo meruerat, ante aram beatissimae Matris Dei apendi jussit.* This happened in 1522. THE LAWYER. Really, I didn't notice those four or five lines when I read Ribadeneyra, and I affectionately thank you for having called attention to them, for I'm lacking only that point in order to declare your sect to be very unfortunate and very wicked. Seeing that you have before your eyes this lovely mirror of your father and author, you haven't had other things in your heads since then, beyond troubling the kingdoms where you live, and even our France, as I'll presently tell you.

---

3 Num. 22: 21–35.

4 *Son viel Adam* (his old Adam): the evil supposedly inherent in human nature.

5 Ribadeneyra, *Vita*, ch. 3: "Ignatius was still too much of a soldier and held on to fallacious ideals of honor."

On the Holy League That the Jesuits Introduced into France in 1585, and How They Are the Cause of the Huguenots' Resurgence

THE LAWYER. Up to now, I've told you about the murders, parricides, and assassinations aimed at kings and princes. Now I'm going to talk about the ruins and desolations of kingdoms that they have brought about, and I'll begin with ours. "It is not up to the king of France (says the Jesuit[1] in his Very Humble Request) to avenge the quarrel involving the king of Navarre, nor is it up to the oldest son of the church to feel that he's taking a position contrary to that of the church." Fine words, which I often repeat to myself, so greatly do they please me. As if the Jesuits had merely collided with the king now reigning, and hadn't collided with the late Henri III, who is not only dressed up in the title Most Christian that's been given to our kings over many long years, but who, among the most Christian kings was in particular the most Catholic king. At the beginning of his reign, we saw him follow the Jesuits, having been charmed by them and thinking them to be the most Catholic. Then came the Minim brothers of Nigeon, near Paris,[2] where he had his bedchamber in order to do his devotions at nightfall, on feast days, and on certain days when he attended their matins; then came the Capuchins and the Feuillants; and in order to have one combined devotion, he founded the Confraternity of the Penitents and Beaten.[3] And after that, the congregation of the Hieronymites, at Our Lady of Vincennes, where he and his brethren dressed like the monks on feast days and

---

1 Pasquier is alluding to Richeome's *Très humble remonstrance*, 41. Note how carefully he avoids mentioning Richeome, citing here instead "the Jesuit," which of course is synonymous with "the religious of the Society of Jesus" who, according to the title, requested this otherwise anonymous book.

2 See P. J. S. Whitmore, *The Order of Minims in Seventeenth-Century France* (Nijhoff: The Hague, 1967).

3 In 1583, Henri III created a new nocturnal procession for Holy Week and an arch-congregation called the White Penitents of Paris, or more familiarly, the *Penitents blancs-battus* (the white and beaten penitents). In a country torn by religious wars, he hoped to convert Protestants and bring peace by prayers and penance. See http://www.penitents.fr/Histoire.html (accessed January 31, 2021).

© KONINKLIJKE BRILL NV, LEIDEN, 2021 | DOI:10.1163/9789004164062_050

high holidays, when they shut themselves up there.[4] I know full well that his enemies wanted to credit that to hypocrisy. To his misfortune, or to be more accurate, owing to the unfortunate artifice of his enemies, everything he did was considered evil. If you said that the great majority of those who joined that party did so from hypocrisy, simply to please him, I believe you'd be telling the truth. But as for him, I don't doubt that it was to please God. One is lacking in common sense, if one says that a king, raised in the midst of delights and abundant pleasures, would have wanted to choose that painful life, if he hadn't been impelled by true zeal and devotion. He who, moreover, had ten thousand ways of making himself believed. Such hypocrisy can find its way into the hearts of little companions who, by mimicking the religious, take for themselves a new splendor, but not the splendor of those who have already acquired it from their antique stock.

The hypocritical Jesuit must therefore scratch out, on his paper, the statement to the effect that the war I'll be talking about later was undertaken against a king who had a different opinion than usual. We need only think about this: who undertook to do it? For it's been attributed to princes and great seigneurs who are taking total advantage of it. I'll talk about this later. After the decree of 1564, we in France lived in calm until 1567. During that time, we were doomed by the interview with the Spanish conducted at Bayonne,[5] because it put umbrage (and perhaps not inappropriately) into the spirits of those who weren't too assured, umbrage that caused ten thousand ills in France, the memory of which makes my hair stand on end. Let's now look at the deportment of the Jesuits during this general debauchery. Having obtained a truce by the suspension of their lawsuit with the University in 1564, they thought they'd also have sufficient leisure to unleash their ambition. When the case was tried, they simply stuck to their irregular protests. The most circumspect foresaw dimly that, in the end, this boil could produce only malignant and smelly pus, but no one could, or dared, state it specifically, because this exterior simplicity with which they veiled the interior of their thoughts was surprising, even for those who wished them the most ill. All the more so since they believed that the Jesuits wanted to advance our religion by good examples, prayers, good morals, holy exhortations, but not by arms. But did they remain in those terms?[6] Not in the least. Into their houses they introduced knowledge of the affairs of state, made themselves judges of the actions of

---

4   Henry III founded a confraternity of Hieronymites at Vincennes in December 1583. See
     Knecht, *Hero or Tyrant?*, 217.

5   June 1564. See Sutto, 352n109.

6   In the 1602 edition, Pasquier's text (p. 235ᵛ) reads *terimes*: "mais demeurerent-ils en ces
     terimes?" But that must be the typesetter's error. It should read *termes* (terms), as other editions (1677, 1717) have.

kings, managed them to their liking, waged wars in order to fulfill their plans; and in the pulpits from which they preached, they used only little drums, fifes, and trumpets in order to stir the princes to combat with one another. And peculiarly, one should have no doubt that they were the authors, promoters, and trouble-makers of our recent Troubles. This is something they not only don't deny, but their books are transformed into trophies, as you'll note in the book by Jesuit La Fon.[7]

Here, I haven't undertaken to narrate for you the whole long history of these Troubles. But I'll tell you that until 1576, we never used the term League. It was only used in Italy, the Jesuits' principal sanctuary. When an assembly of the three estates[8] was called at Blois,[9] a seigneur of rank in Paris (I don't want to name him), whose soul was totally Jesuit and who usually would leave the parish Mass in favor of a Jesuit one, sent the deputies for Paris some memoranda that I'll tell you about. At that assembly, they raised objections with a view to waging an immortal war against the Huguenots, without respite, and yet they were asking to have the *tailles*[10] reduced or removed. A thing incompatible with the first proposition, for the *tailles* were created in order to pay for wars. As a result, the person to whom I'm referring, having deliberated with the Jesuits, laid out a third way: form a league against the Huguenots; and those who voluntarily enrolled in the League would be obliged to contribute to the costs of this new war. These memoranda having been received and presented, the deputies named a certain prince and great noble as their leader.[11] The late king knew how consequential this overture was, and that the result would be the creation of three parties in France: his (which strictly speaking was not a party), the party of the League, and the party of the Huguenots. In order to break up this coup wisely, he said that he would view the League as good, but that he wanted to be the head of it. He said this so that the League wouldn't fly higher than permitted by the wings he was giving it. In that way, the first stone of our ruin was thrown. The *prévôt des marchands* and the *échevins*[12] of

---

7   René de La Fon's *Réponse* (see below).

8   The expression "three estates" refers to the three divisions of society: the nobility (first estate), the clergy (second), and the commoners (third).

9   Where the court resided in 1588.

10 *Tailles*: a tax levied by the king on his subjects or on lands held under him. Nobles and clergy were exempt.

11 This person may be Henri I de Lorraine, duke of Guise (1550–88). A powerful opponent of the queen mother, Catherine de' Medici, Guise was assassinated at Blois by order of Henri III, and the next day his brother, the cardinal, was murdered. In the next sentence, "the late king" is Henri III. See Knecht, *Hero or Tyrant?*, 259 ff.

12 *Échevins* (aldermen) were municipal officers who, along with the *prévôt des marchands* (akin to a mayor), formed the city council of Paris. Paris had four *échevins* selected from among the leading merchants.

Paris, having returned, didn't want this opinion of the League to abort, for they judged it to be very holy; and they awarded their commissions by blocks of ten, so that those who wanted to contribute could subscribe. The *dizainiers*[13] took them to houses. Some of the more daring *dizainiers* were opposed, and the others, in greater number, and fearing for the worst, subscribed. The commission was carried to Messire Christophle de Thou,[14] whose memory can't be sufficiently honored. Not only was this good man unwilling to sign it, but he kept it; and the next day, in the full Parlement, he expressed his detestation for this unfortunate novelty, a very certain desolation of our state. His authority, his prudence, his reasons were so persuasive that everyone espoused his opinion. And from then on, opinion in favor of the League began to fade, whatever it was, and it was postponed until a time that was more appropriate for the organizers.

No sooner had the meeting of the estates been closed than Father Émond Auger, Jesuit,[15] thanks to some beautiful hypocrisy, won the king's ear; and after him came Father Claude Mathieu[16] from Lorraine. Both received such a share of the king's good graces that Montaignes informs us that the king made them enter his coach and ride with him. In the end, this good king knew that these charlatans, especially Auger, wanted to take from him the management of affairs of state. By this means, he gave the order, through his ambassador in Rome, to have Auger removed from France by letters of obedience from his general.[17] By the time the assembly of the estates ended, the king had pacified his subjects, thanks to an edict dated 1577, which he said was all his. And yet, owing to his prudence, he would have driven out the Reformed Protestant Religion without bloodshed, if the Jesuits had given him the leisure to complete the work he'd begun. All the more so since, in the midst of the peace, he was waging a gentle war with the Huguenots; but in the opinion of the nobles, he was stronger than material weapons were. For the edict of 1577 didn't in the least serve as a liberty for the Huguenots, unless the king summoned them, either to the estates of the jurisdiction, or to the governments of provinces

---

13   *Dizainiers*: officials responsible for the smallest unit of the municipal administration.

14   Christophe de Thou (1508–82) was an eminent lawyer and first president of the Parlement of Paris. He had been an advisor to Henri III of France. See Édouard Mougis, *Histoire du Parlement de Paris* (Paris: Picard, 1916), 216.

15   See Book I, ch. 3 above.

16   Claude Mathieu (1537–87), provincial of Aquitaine, 1571–74, provincial of France, 1574–82, and, since 1578, visitor of the houses in Aquitaine. See Fouqueray, *Histoire de la Compagnie de Jésus en France*, 2:ch. 5.

17   "It seems more likely that Henri III did everything possible to keep Auger near him. Pasquier would therefore seem to be commenting on Mathieu." See Sutto, 354n116.

or cities. In addition, he had introduced the military order of the Holy Spirit, to which only princes and Catholic noblemen can be admitted, and also the order of the Hieronymites of Our Lady of Vincennes, who were all Catholic, Apostolic, and Roman, and of whom, removing all traces of his princely dignities, he was a brother in devotion. The increasing nearness to these persons made the others more distant from him. Believe me, this was no small spur to bringing them back to the good path. For there's nothing that the great seigneurs of France desire more than to draw near their king. Nor is there anything that afflicts the common people more than a desire to be eligible to participate in the estates general. It's a mental illness for the French. As soon as a man of the long robe,[18] or a merchant, has acquired a store of silver by his industry, they find nothing more recommendable for their children than for them to be part of the estates whose members are judges or financiers. To the point that the new religion was coming undone all on its own. And the ashamed elders who remained in their religion, in order not to be accused of frivolity, weren't upset that their children were being taught in our schools and consequently in the discipline of our religion. In this manner, everything was progressing from bad to good and from good to better. The peasant was guiding his plow, the artisan was plying his craft, the merchant was selling, the lawyer and the procureurs were doing their practices. The citizen was enjoying his income, the magistrate his wages, the Catholic was practicing his religion throughout all of France, with no obstacles. Those who were Huguenots were living hidden in a back-corner of France, when our Jesuits, seeing them distanced from the favor of their prince, began to prepare this ambush.

Since the Society of the Jesuits is composed of all sorts of people, fit for all sorts of employments, among them was a Father Henry Sammier[19] from Luxembourg, a man who was inclined towards and resolute in all sorts of adventures. In 1581, they sent him to several Catholic princes, to sound out them out; and to tell the truth, they couldn't have chosen better. For he could transform himself into a variety of forms, sometimes dressed like a soldier, sometimes a priest, sometimes a simple local inhabitant. A game of dice, or cards, or wenches were as familiar to him as his book of hours. And he would

---

18 The most important civilian judges, for example the presidents of a parlement, wore long robes, as contrasted with the shorter robes worn by their lesser colleagues.

19 The Jesuit whom Pasquier calls "Sammier" was in reality Henri Samerie (1540–1610) who was a Jesuit from Luxembourg indeed, where he also died. He entered the Society in 1561 in Cologne. Disguised as a physician, he visited in England the imprisoned Mary Queen of Scots two or three times in the early 1580s. See Thomas M. McCoog, *English and Welsh Jesuits 1555–1560: Part 2* (London: Catholic Record Society, 1994), 288 and John H. Pollen, "Mary Stuart's Jesuit Chaplain," *The Month* 117 (1911).

say that, by doing this, he didn't feel as if he were sinning, because he was doing it in order to do a good work and to exalt the glory of God. To avoid being discovered, he would change his name as often as he changed clothes, according to the regions where he wanted to conduct his negotiations. He left Lorraine and from there went to Germany, Italy, and Spain. Now, the general point of his instructions was the great danger to our Catholic religion: the king's connivance was quietly favoring the Huguenot party, of which his brother, the duke,[20] was openly the protector in the Low Countries. Their holy Society of Jesus resolved to take that quarrel in hand, under the authority of a great prince, making sure that it would be helped by God: for this was being done for the advancement of God's name and his church. Thus did Sammier gather intelligence on all sides, and make himself sure of the one side and the other; but the season was not good for displaying all their plans, as long as Monsieur the Duke was alive, and the united forces of the two brothers were sufficient to injure everyone who might want to stand up to them. All of this was a prelude to our Troubles. He died in 1583.[21] With this obstacle removed, the Jesuits admitted to their quarrel the seigneurs who pleased them. At that time, Father Claude Mathieu, the provincial of Paris, became more active in the party than before. He sat in on all the deliberations and council meetings, and he took it upon himself to go to Rome, while Father Henri Sammier would go to Spain. Each made the most of his ambassadorial mission. Pope Gregory XIII[22] and the king of Spain[23] each promised to furnish a large sum of money in order to pay for the war. These ambassadors having returned, we saw banners waving and all of France covered with soldiers. Several cities experienced surprise attacks, where previously no one had ever practiced the new religion. In this way, three parties had been formed: the party of the king, which was quite encumbered; the party of the Holy League (that's what the Jesuit war was called); and the party of the Religion, as the Huguenots called their faction. Then came the death of Pope Gregory;[24] and at that point the Jesuits thought that the number of those who shared their opinion should be reduced by half. For this,

---

20   Hercule-François, duke of Alençon, and then duke of Anjou (1554–84), was the fourth and youngest son of Henri II and Catherine de' Medici. In other words, Hercule-François was Francis II, Charles IX, and Henri III's youngest brother. As the youngest son, Hercule-François was called "Monsieur the Duke," or simply "Monsieur." See *Encyclopaedia Britannica*, https://www.britannica.com/biography/Francois-duc-dAnjou (accessed January 31, 2021).

21   Pasquier is inaccurate here. Hercule-François died on June 10, 1584.

22   See Book 11, ch. 14.

23   Philip II.

24   Gregory XIII died on April 10, 1585. He was succeeded by Sixtus V (r.1585–90).

Father Mathieu retraced the road to Rome, where he found Sixtus, the newly elected pope from whom, to his very great contentment, he got the same promise as the one offered by his predecessor. Mathieu died in 1588 at Ancona, on the return journey.[25] As a result, a new Jesuit was sent: Father Odon Pigenat,[26] from Burgundy. He was the new provincial of France, owing to the death of Mathieu, whom Sixtus had refused. This permitted several Catholic men to avoid proposing a peace, but to wish for it in their souls. But they still wanted to curb our thoughts, for this proposition didn't please our Jesuits. They make two sorts of Catholics: some are called the Politic Ones, and the others are the Zealous Catholics, or Leaguers, beloved by the populace because the Leaguers wanted an endless war. A distinction that planted a little hot-house of wars between Catholic and Catholic, and that together made peace with our enemy. Did I say peace? By that means we put the sword in our enemies' hands, we opened the way for him to prowl, to advance, to add to, and to grow without resistance on our part, weakened as we were by this new division. Arms came from all sides, and yet it wasn't so much a civil war as a general throat-cutting that spread across France. To remedy this, our two kings successively needed all their chess pieces. The Huguenots favored their quarrel, in order to manage and sustain the state; and by their notoriety, the Jesuit colleges were the general wellspring of the opposing party. Here, their coded Gospels were forged and sent to foreign lands; there, their apostles were distributed in various provinces, some to maintain the Troubles by their preaching, as Father Jacques Commolet did in Paris,[27] and as Father Bernard Rouillet[28] did in Bourges. The others saw to the murders and the assassinations, as Varade did,[29] and even Commolet. Only in Paris, in the midst of the Sixteen,[30] that is, the dregs of the populace who were nurturing the sedition, did Father Odon Pigenat tread on

---

25   Mathieu died in 1587.

26   Odon Pigenat (1534–1607), rector of the Collège de Clermont, 1573–82, vice-provincial of France 1578–82, and provincial of France, 1582–92. See Fouqueray, *Histoire de la Compagnie de Jésus en France*, 2:142 ff.

27   See ch. 7 above.

28   For Bernard Roillet (1548–99), a Jesuit preacher, see Fouqueray, *Histoire de la Compagnie de Jésus en France*, 2:passim.

29   See ch. 5 above.

30   In Paris, the most committed element of the League (it seized power in 1589) was known as the Sixteen (*Seize*), after the number of quarters in the city from which members were elected. The Sixteen remained a powerful force for more than three years. See J. H. M. Salmon, "The Paris Sixteen, 1584–94: The Social Analysis of a Revolutionary Movement," *The Journal of Modern History* 44, no. 4 (1972): 540–76; Knecht, *Hero or Tyrant?*, 227.

every credibility, prerogative, and authority. That's something about which all Jesuits agree, in the books they've had printed since 1594.

I've said, and it's true, that Jesuism[31] concurred with Anabaptism on two propositions, that is: getting involved in affairs of state, and being able to have kings and princes assassinated, as their affairs dictate. I'll add that, in leading this new Jesuit war inside France, there's some conformity with the names that the Anabaptists assumed in Germany in 1535. For as their first prophet they had a Jan Matthys,[32] under Jan of Leiden their king, and Bernard Rotman[33] and Bernard Knipperdolling,[34] the most superlative persons of their faction when it came to seducing the poor folk, just as our Jesuits had their Father Claude Mathieu, and their Bernard Rouillet. I won't enumerate for you all the other particularities of our Troubles, being satisfied to point out that our Jesuits were their first seminary; and I'll simply discuss the fruit we gathered from it. Withdrawing his ire from us, God wanted everything to be calm at last. In this new reestablishment, the Huguenots, during our Troubles, thought themselves one of the instruments and tools that would conserve the crown for the king, just as several Catholic subjects thought that, once peace had come, they wouldn't be pieces of trash in our midst. They therefore importuned the king with diverse requests to get back their ancient privileges stated in the Edicts of pacification,[35] from which they had been almost totally barred since the peace of 1577. "We have," they would say, "followed the late king's fortune, and your fortune too, during your adversities; we have exposed our lives and our possessions in order to sustain your majesties against the Jesuit

---

31   Did Pasquier invent this term: *Jésuisme*, "Jesuism"?

32   Jan Matthys (Matthias, Mathyszoon, Mattijs, Matthijszoon; *c.*1500–34) was a baker in Haarlem and one of the driving forces of the Anabaptist rebellion in Münster (ch. 1 above). See https://gameo.org/index.php?title=Jan_Matthijsz_van_Haarlem_(d._1534) (accessed January 31, 2021).

33   Bernard Rotman (1495–1536), a theologian and minister, was one of the leaders of the movement in Münster.

34   Bernard Knipperdolling (?–1536) was a merchant draper of Münster, known as the tailor-king during the Münster rebellion. See *Narrative of the Anabaptist Madness*, https://doi.org/10.1163/ej.9789004157217.i-776.7 (accessed January 31, 2021).

35   The so-called edict of pacification signed at Amboise in 1563 officially ended the first phase of the French Wars of Religion. An edict signed at Saint-Germain in 1562, had permitted Protestant services in the private homes of nobles. The edict of 1563 restored peace to France by guaranteeing religious privileges and freedoms for Huguenots. However, the Parlement of Paris, which had expelled its Huguenot members, resisted registering the edict until the distant day when Charles IX would reach his majority and a council could be created to decide the religious question. See "Treaty of Amboise," https://www.oxfordreference.com/view/10.1093/oi/authority.20110803095407346 (accessed January 31, 2021).

faction that was calling upon foreigners, in order to make them the master and seigneur of your kingdom. Having served you well, may we not be part of your republic? And must the Jesuits, who have served in everything and everywhere, reign and triumph in your France?" What could a wise king do when besieged by as just an entreaty as that? It would amount to approving their request, in order to avoid the lesser of two evils, and not returning to the Chaos from which we had recently emerged. Tell me, Messieurs, I beg you, to whom do we owe France's new wake-up alarm,[36] if not to our Jesuits, the firebrands of our recent Troubles? Troubles without which the Huguenots would lose all credit. It's a chain, and a link of obligations, that we have with that holy Society of Jesus.

---

36 This is an allusion to a printed sheet called *Le Réveille-matin des François et de leurs voisins* (The wake-up call of the French and of their neighbors), printed in Edinburgh by J. James in 1574. A Protestant reaction to the St. Bartholemew's Day massacres, it called for resistance to the French monarchy. An anonymous 1589 League pamphlet advanced resistance theories from the opposite perspective: "Le reveille-matin des Catholiques unis contenant les raisons par lesquelles ils ne doivent se soubmettre à l'heretique, ny subir jugement devant les Politiques ses fauteurs & adherans." Pasquier may be implying that this was a Jesuit work.

The Auricular Confession of the Jesuits Has Been the Strongest Sword of the Rebellion, and How They Fence with It

THE LAWYER. In vain do we trudge along the road to pious works, if we don't begin with confession, followed by an appropriate repentance. The Jesuit has permission to do this to all those who present themselves to him, to the prejudice of the *ordinaires*. But they have a marvelous privilege, a privilege that was never given to a monk, or even to curates, who are the ecclesiastical persons with the most authority after bishops. Paul III's bull of 1545 says that, having given them permission to preach wherever they please:

> *Nec non* (it reads) *illis ex vobis qui presbiteri fuerint, quorumcunque utriusque sexus Christi fidelium, ad vos undecunque accedentium confessiones audiendi, et confessionibus eorum diligenter auditis, ipsos et eorum singulos, ab omnibus et singulis eorum peccatis, criminibus, excessibus et delictis quantumcunque gravibus et enormibus, etiam sedi Apostolicae reservatis, et à quibusvis ex ipsis casibus resultantibus, sententiis, censuris et poenis Ecclesiasticis (exceptis contentis in Bulla quae in die Coenae Domini solita est legi) ac eis pro commissis, poenitentiam salutarem injungendi [...].*

That is to say:

> We give permission to our priests to be able to hear the confessions of the faithful of one and the other sex, irrespective of where they come from, and having diligently heard these confessions, to be able to absolve, for each and every person, their sins, crimes, excesses, and misdemeanors, even if they are grave and enormous, even if reserved for the Holy See and the circumstances that result from it, by sentences, censures or ecclesiastical sanctions (other than those contained in the bull, which is customarily read on Holy Thursday) and to order a salutary penance for the faults committed by those who are confessing.[1]

---

1 Paul III's brief (not bull) of June 3, 1545, *Cum inter cunctas*. See the translation of the entire brief in *Studies in Jesuit Spirituality* 52, no. 2 (2020): 28–30.

Just as the privileges that they believe have been given them for teaching the young, have inverted the entire ancient order of famous universities, so this great and extraordinary special favor that was granted to them for confessions, is the reason why the great majority of the common people, owing to atrocious sins, has left the old penitentiary's way at cathedral churches, in order to have recourse to the Jesuits, who, as you can see, are all penitentiaries, by means of this bull. And God knows how these holy and blissful fathers have taken advantage of it. The first outbreak of our Troubles took place in 1585; and from then on, those who went to the Jesuits to confess, and who claimed to be good subjects and faithful servants of the king (for they were questioned on that matter), were sent back by the Jesuits without having received absolution. Arnauld objected to this; here is the cold reply to his plea: *Seventeenth point* (said Arnauld): after 1585, the aforesaid defenders often denied absolution to the late king's followers.[2] The aforesaid defenders replied that this wasn't true, although they know that several persons have often accused them of it or have made a deposition before the late king in his study. And who could be the witnesses, if not those to whom absolution had been refused? There's no fire without some smoke. Read the Jesuits' annual letters for 1589, when the great fury of the Troubles was beginning. You'll find that the number of confessions had increased infinitely, especially at the Jesuit college in Paris. *Totius vitae confessiones audita trecenta*, "We have heard three hundred general confessions of entire life," the henchmen of this college wrote to General Acquaviva. If you ask me where the common peoples' new devotion for the Jesuits comes from, I have an answer. Our kings represent the true image of God. Now, that year there were three extraordinary events that were against them: the rebellion against the late king Henri III, under the pretext of the title Tyranny, for the finest title they gave him at that time was Tyrant. In addition, there was the parricide committed on his person by a monk. And finally, there was the continuation of the rebellion against King Henri IV, now reigning, owing to his religion. Have no doubt: those whose consciences could be bought cheaply, as could the consciences of several preachers, were not seriously prevented by these accessories. And that's why, during our Troubles, they would go to these new penitentiaries and confess, some doing it in order to be enlightened about whether it was a sin not to obey their king, and some seeking absolution. But

---

2   Pasquier is apparently referring to the plea of Antoine Arnauld in the 1594 suit between the university and the Jesuits that briefly revived the 1574 dispute. This phrase does not appear in the published version, *Plaidoyé de M. Antoine Arnauld ... pour l'Université de Paris demanderesse, contre les Jesuites defendeurs, des 12. & 13. juillet 1594* (Lyons: Guichard Juillieron and Thibaud Ancelin, 1594), though a close paraphrase may be found on p. 15.

that amounted to asking the wolf to watch over the lamb, because their confessions were just so many instructions, or to be more accurate, destructions, in order to teach rebellion: denying absolution to them, who in their consciences were not confirmed in the disobedience toward the two kings, or to the others who were preparing to recognize them. And it's a most horrible thing: before absolving them, the usual formula made them swear on the holy Gospels, which were part of their breviaries, never to recognize these two kings as their legitimate seigneurs. What I'm telling you, I learned from several persons who were put through that strainer; and I know one, among others, who touches me deeply and who, because he didn't want to believe them, walked off, right in front of his confessor, without receiving absolution. So much for the realm in general. But as far as individual families are concerned, the Jesuits have two goals in helping themselves by hearing confessions: first, to be informed about the penitent, not only about his sins but also whether those who live with him, or with whom he is living, or even all the people who live nearby, are following the rules: as if it were a sin not to reveal the sins of other people in confession, whether one knows the sins, or whether one thinks one knows them. Doing this is like having as many informers in a city, as there are Jesuit confessors. Second, and this concerns them more closely, is that by sucking out the soul of a timid conscience through the ear, one sucks, or to be more accurate one drowns his good in the same way, by promising a great deal of spiritual possessions in the other world after his death, to the person who, during his life, gives alms from his temporal possessions. A thing about which they have described infinite conveniences, if you believe those who wanted to make them legendary: for otherwise, I can't call upon the lives of those holy fathers. I'll add this (and it's a point on which I'd like to be enlightened by our ancient doctors of theology): one must not only accuse oneself, one must also accuse all one's accomplices; and from the viewpoint of the magistrate, the criminal having been sentenced to death, and having first admitted his infraction to his confessor, he isn't obligated to reveal it to his judge, or he can firmly deny it before being executed, saying he is even before God, although he henceforth lies after having revealed the depth of his conscience to the priest. This stirs great scruples in the soul of the judge, who remains marvelously consoled when, after the condemned criminal's denials, he sees him admit the truth, as he is dying.

On the General Congregation of the Jesuits, Held in Rome in 1593, Where They Were Forbidden to Become Involved in Affairs of State

THE LAWYER. I earlier recounted how the Jesuits were the first flames, followed by the general brazier of our last Troubles. As proof, I don't need any surer testimony than this one: Acquaviva, their general, saw that, by the Troubles, he couldn't win what he'd promised at the beginning; so he appointed the oldest provincials, rectors, and fathers of the order, to attend a general congregation that he wanted to hold in Rome. Things dragged on for some ten months, while the king settled down into the bosom of the church, in July 1593.[1] From that time on, each person studied how to bring about a good peace for France, and how to smooth the way for it. One, two, three truces were worked out, the usual prognostics of a future peace. During these truces, everyone had safe access from one party to the other. The Jesuits were spying during this time, having been sent by God to have the king assassinated: Barrière presented himself at just the right time, to do this, but in vain. These upright persons, seeing that everything, both in general and in particular, was degenerating and was contrary to their plans, acted as if they wanted to end the war with the princes, by means of their congregation. In the month of November 1593, this decree was issued:

> *Ut ab omni specie mali abstineatur, et querelis etiam ex falsis suspicionibus, provenientibus, praecipitur nostris omnibus, in virtute sanctae obedientiae, et sub poena inhabilitatis ad quaevis officia et dignitates, seu praelationes, vocisque tam activae quam passivae privationes, ne quispiam publicis et secularium Principum negotiis, ulla ratione se immiscere, nec etiam quantumvis, perquoscumque, requisitus, aut rogatus, ejusmodi res tractandi curam suscipere audeat, vel presumat. Idque serio commendatur superioribus ne permittant nostros iis rebus ullo modo implicari, et siquos ad ea propensos animadverterent, eos loco mutandos quam primum commutent, si alicubi sit occasio, vel periculum se ejusmodi implicationibus irretiendi.*[2]

---

1   Henri IV converted to Catholicism on July 25, 1593.
2   Cf. *Canones trium congregationum Soc. Jesu auctoritate tertiae congregat. confecti* (Rome, 1606), 147–48.

So that (he said), one will abstain from everything that can seem bad, and so that one will avoid as much as possible all laments, from this time forth, if they come from false suspicions; and our brethren are enjoined, by virtue of holy obedience, and on penalty of being declared incompetent for all offices, dignities, or superiorities, and to lose the voice-vote and suffrage, both active and passive, in any fashion whatsoever (henceforth begged and required by the one and the other), not to be so brash as to become involved in the public and secular negotiations of princes; and it is very strictly ordered that superiors not permit our brethren to become wrapped up in those matters, in any fashion whatsoever; and if they find some who are inclined, they ought immediately make them go to another country, if they see that they are subject to it, or are in danger of becoming tangled up in such perplexities.

The Jesuits profit greatly from that article, and they say that, owing to this decree, they will no longer become involved. But, Oh, holy, blind Obedience, where are you dwelling now? If you are the first and principal substance of their vows, then all the principal Jesuit fathers are heretics in their sect. For after that great and holy decree, Father Jacques Commolet did not, for all that, stop his meddling; for in a sermon he took the theme from the third chapter of Judges, where there is talk of a certain Aod, who had killed Moab and who ran away.[3] Having scandal-mongered for a long while about the death of King Henri III, and having placed that unfortunate Judas-Jacobin in the arms of the blessed, he finally exclaimed, with his mouth wide open: "We need (he said) an Ehud, be he a monk, be he a soldier, be he a soldier's boy, be he a shepherd: no matter, but we need an Ehud. We need only that coup in order to put our affairs into a desirable state." Arnauld strongly objected to this, but neither the person who had forbidden his plea, nor Montaignes, gave a reply: this makes me think that they were in agreement.[4] In 1597, Walpole, the Jesuit,[5] gave some poison to Squire in order to poison the queen of England, his sovereign lady. The Jesuits of Douai, in 1598, sent the barrel-maker of Ypres to kill Count Maurice of Nassau.[6] Were all those people obeying this synodal order? Oh, God, poor Jesuit religion (I said to a friend of this Society), your Obedience is fleeing headlong down the road: for not only do you not obey your own individual superiors, but you also do what has been ordered by chapters throughout the entire order. To this he

---

3   Judg. 3:15–30.
4   See *Plaidoyé de M. Antoine Arnauld*, 19–20.
5   See ch. 4 above.
6   See ch. 1 above.

wisely replied that I hadn't understood the article very well; it didn't purely and simply forbid getting involved, but, right there, it said: "in case the superiors found some danger in getting involved in such matters," *Si alicubi sit occasio vel periculum se ejusmodi implicationibs irretiendi.* And so, this decree is truly a thing at which princes can wonder, so that they will be less on their guard than formerly. And to tell the truth, getting mixed up in the affairs of state, and causing princes to die, all of that is as essential to their order as confessions are.

Do Jesuits Have Spanish Souls, as Their Enemies Say They Do, or Do They Belong to the Highest Bidder?

THE LAWYER. I see several people send lightning bolts at them, saying that they have Spanish souls. They, on the other hand, fear nothing in their books more than they fear acquiring that reputation in France. I'd like to rid them of that fear; and since they are in need, I'd like to be their lawyer in this specific instance, not so much for the friendship I bear them, as because the truth orders me to do so. Indeed, they held Spaniards in great favor in the middle and at the end of our Troubles; and that's why they fear that the memory will revive. But I deny that their souls were Spanish. It wasn't owing to a special devotion for the late king of Spain, more than for another king; it was because, if one studies Jesuits, who measure justice by the convenience of their affairs, they usually devote themselves to the one whom they think is the strongest, and from whom they expect to extract the most: which, for those who imprint a neutrality in their souls, is no small secret for things involving the state. And that lesson was practiced during our last Troubles by Pope Sixtus V, a wise and shrewd person, as he had been in Rome in the past. The ills of the time were so great, after the two brothers' deaths at Blois,[1] that some young theologians, infected by the Jesuits' poison, let loose the subjects' reins against their king in 1589. But from that time on, they themselves admitted that their advice shouldn't have an effect, unless the Holy See first approved of it. This, despite the Jesuit Commolet and his supporters, who the next day trumpeted war from their pulpits, against the late king, saying that this had been decreed. This led to the overflowing debauchery that we henceforth saw throughout France. To take up arms against one's king is a heresy, but a still greater heresy is to wait for the approval or the disapproval of the Holy See. Thus, all of a sudden two sovereign powers were assassinated: the spiritual power of the Holy See and the temporal power of the king. If he'd wanted to, Pope Sixtus could have attenuated all our Troubles with a single stroke of the pen, by excommunicating

---

1   On December 23, 1588, in the Château de Blois, Henry I, duke of Guise, was murdered by order of King Henry III. His brother, Louis de Lorraine, cardinal of Guise (1555–88) was also slain. The leadership of the League therefore fell to their brother, Charles de Lorraine, duke of Mayenne. See Alexander Wilkinson, "'Homicides Royaux': The Assassination of the Duc and Cardinal de Guise and the Radicalization of French Public Opinion," *French History* 18, no. 2 (2004): 129–53.

those who, to his disappointment, and under his authority, had taken up arms against their king, whom he knew to be very Catholic. He was very careful not to do that, all the more so since he would have been censuring those who, at the time, had all the force on their side, and favoring a poor king against whom heaven and earth seemed to be conspiring. To the contrary, he had him reprimanded and said that he should come and explain his actions in Rome, against all the laws, customs, freedoms, and privileges of our France. When he assumed the crown, the king presently reigning belonged to the opposing religion, and as such the pope initially wanted to censure him; but when he realized the value of that king, and when his enemies stuffed His Holiness with false rumors, feigning to have won imaginary victories against him, he began to withdraw from the game, not wanting to be personally involved. From there he moved ahead, underhandedly treating the king with all the courtesy one could have wanted. Don't think that Sixtus wanted more trouble for the late king, or more good for our king who reigns today; but in doing this, he favored his affairs more by being prudent. Still, shortly before he died, a few silly scholars reproached him for favoring the king's party; and during that quarrel, some overly brash spirits were saying that he had been poisoned. Which I'm unwilling to believe, even if it was true.

The same thing applies to our Jesuits, who like nothing so well as to advance their republic, which they call the Society of Jesus; and because it only began and progressed during the Troubles, they didn't aim at troubling the kingdoms where they resided; and during this agitation, they always favored those who could lay down the law to the weakest: something I'll verify for you by an eyewitness. Having set fire to the four corners and the center of France, and the late king having been reduced to taking baby steps, they devoted themselves above all to the person who was captain general of the League,[2] because everything was smiling on him. And as long as Fortune wore an agreeable face, all their sermons were about nothing but his splendor and his merits. But when they saw that he was going downhill, and when he was forced to call for help from the king of Spain, then they began to turn their faces toward a duke, in order to espouse the party of a king whom they deemed very powerful. Today there's a new Spanish king.[3] Whether he'll be fortunate or unfortunate, only God knows. I'll never be unhappy if he wears as many crowns on his head

---

2   The duke of Mayenne.

3   King Philip II died in September 1598 and was succeeded by his son Philip III. The duke to whom Pasquier alludes is probably Alessandro Farnese, duke of Parma and regent of the Spanish Netherlands. Parma ended the siege of Paris in 1590 and the siege of Rouen in 1592, thereby saving the League's actions against a Protestant monarch. See ch. 2 above.

as the late king, his father. Imagine that, thanks to a new opinion about war, which easily finds a nesting place in the head of a young prince, he wanted to break with us; and imagine that one thing after another was going well for us in his lands. Do you think you'd see messieurs the Jesuits totally French, although they were Spanish-born? They are true birds of prey, who let themselves be lifted by the wind. It's very appropriate for a sovereign prince to play the role that Sixtus played; but it's a very bad example for a subject, and the consequences are more perilous. So, I'm telling you that, in whatever direction you turn your thoughts, you won't find out why one must nourish Jesuits in a kingdom. They're all so many, I won't say spies, I'll say enemies of their prince, when he's at his weakest. And during a time when a new impartiality is needed in Rome, if the pope were afflicted, he'd feel the effects, despite the personal vassalage that they swear to each new pope.

The Lawyer had scarcely finished this speech when he was addressed by his host. THE GENTLEMAN. Be careful not to deceive yourself, and don't let your proposition imply an intrinsic contrariness. For if the Jesuit is naturally concerned with whoever gives him the most, as you argue, one must conclude that he is naturally Spanish, not French. Do we know why? He knows that, no matter how much he stirs up the conscience of one individual or another by his new confessions, in all of France he will never gain a footing like the one he has in Spain, where the sovereign magistrate went from one extreme to the other. For in the past, the Spaniards were accused of being marranos,[4] whose religion was mongrel and not totally Christian; but today, in order to purge themselves of that calumnious accusation (that's what I'm calling it) they especially embrace, without exception or reserve, the Jesuits, whom they consider to be the vassals of the papacy. And relying on this opinion, they grant them an infinity of prerogatives over all the common people, and even over magistrates, to whom they lay down the law. Now, in this France, where antiquity has given us the title of elder son of the Roman Church, it is nonetheless done with certain modifications that the Jesuits will never uproot from our heads, no matter how continuously they make assertions to the contrary. And that's why, assuming that they would have a greater advantage than they actually do, since the Spaniard commands in France, they always lean toward that party, rather than toward ours, as if they were natural Frenchmen. They are persons of state who are attached to certainty, rather than uncertainty. After this little parenthetical remark, don't feel that I'm interrupting you; and please pick up the main thread of your speech. THE LAWYER. I'll do that, and I'll recount a strange thing that I observed about all their undertakings.

4   See ch. 10 above.

The Jesuits Caused the Death of Mary, Queen of Scots: A Brief Discourse on the Ruin They Created for England

THE LAWYER. Having discussed our France, it won't be inappropriate to set sail for England, where Mary, Queen of Scots,[1] had been detained for nineteen years as a prisoner of state. This princess was infinitely Catholic, and she was earnestly preparing to think about the English Puritans; for Elizabeth, their queen, had no closer relative to succeed her than the queen of Scotland. Now, since the Jesuits were stirring up the opinions of the potentates in 1582, and were inciting them to take up arms, Father Henri Sammier, their ambassador in England, came to stir up some trouble in the state. At the time, he was dressed as a soldier, wearing a slashed orange satin doublet and, in the slashed openings, green silk; a pair of good pistols at the saddletree, a sword at his side, a scarf at his neck. I learned this from people who were rather close to him. Wearing this costume, with one or another Catholic lord he was carrying on a muffled revolt against their queen, Elizabeth, who was afterwards sold to them dearly through the prudence of Milord Cecil.[2] From there, he went to talk with the queen of Scots, whom he gave to understand that he and the brethren of his order were negotiating with all the Catholic princes, not only to reestablish the Catholic religion in England, but also to liberate that desolate princess. Making all sorts of pleas, he beseeched her to please understand and to prepare all her servants and subjects to carry out so great a masterwork. He assured her that, by what he would be doing, he would conserve the kingdom of England for her. That was what he was planning with her; but since the Jesuit naturally has two souls, he was negotiating in one way with the lords of England in favor of a more powerful prince, in order to dispossess that poor lady of her future rights; and he and his brethren were turning the principal Catholics away from the service they had promised this princess. He

---

1 See ch. 3 above. John Hungerford Pollen, ed., *Mary Queen of Scots and the Babington Plot …* (Edinburgh: Scottish History Society, 1922).

2 William Cecil, lord Burghley (1520–98), lord treasurer in 1572 and principal advisor to Queen Elizabeth. See *Encyclopaedia Britannica*, https://www.britannica.com/biography/William-Cecil-1st-Baron-Burghley (accessed January 31, 2021).

© KONINKLIJKE BRILL NV, LEIDEN, 2021 | DOI:10.1163/9789004164062_054

remonstrated to them that their means were too weak to hope for any material help. And indeed, around that time the Jesuits printed the rights of that other prince who was laying claim to the English crown.[3] They hoped that this book would find its way to several places in Christendom. And this was their principal plan: Sammier would continue to pursue the queen by hue and cry. She baulked at first, foreseeing the misfortune that could befall her. And the impudent Jesuit told her that if she wanted to be lukewarm, he knew the ways by which she and the king of Scotland, her son,[4] would be forever deprived of their hope for England, and that his memoranda said: *quod si molesta fuisset, nec illa, nec filius ejus regnarent.*[5] So she was forced to acquiesce. And from then on, Monsieur de Guise, not knowing the ploys and factions that these gentlemen were cooking up under the table, promised to join the party of the queen, his cousin.[6] And in truth, valiant and generous prince that he was, I'm sure he would have succeeded if the Jesuits hadn't involved him in another new quarrel. But having embraced that quarrel on the one hand and having quit his cousin's quarrel on the other hand, in the end he was left in the lurch. As soon as the Queen of Scots was informed of this new advice, she began shedding great tears; and kneeling, she cried out: "My God, have pity on me. For both my cousin and I are indubitably doomed." Meanwhile, confusion became lodged in England, thanks to the Jesuit's intrigues. The queen's plots in Scotland, where she lacked a leader, having been discovered, justice was done to the Jesuits and to the intrigues. The poor Catholics, who had previously lived with restful consciences, were forced to abandon wives, children, and houses, in order to avoid the magistrates' severity. Even William Parry, executed in 1584, confessed that the goal of murdering the queen of England, which he had planned, was to establish the Queen of Scots, if she would consent. This confession led to a dispute in the hearts of Queen Elizabeth of England, and her council. Finally, the trial of that poor Scottish princess was held and completed. By a decree of Parliament, she was sentenced to be beheaded; and with incredible constancy, she died a Catholic. From this, you can deduce that the Jesuits weren't the only blacksmiths working for her death. And that they hadn't made the Catholic religion secure in England: to the contrary, they are

---

3   Probably Philip II of Spain: see below, ch. 13.

4   James VI of Scotland, who later reigned as James I of England, was the son of Mary, Queen of Scots.

5   "If she were troublesome, neither she, nor her son would reign."

6   François II de Lorraine, duke of Guise (1519–63) was the brother of Marie de Guise, the mother of Mary, Queen of Scots. See *Encyclopaedia Britannica*, https://www.britannica.com/biography/Francois-de-Lorraine-2e-duc-de-Guise (accessed February 1, 2021).

the reason why it was totally banished from England, and why an infinity of honest and highborn families were ruined. By this means, they made secure the erroneous doctrine of the Puritans, and they removed every hope that our religious could return, short of a great miracle from God.[7]

---

7 Cf. Francis Edwards, s.j., *Plots and Plotters in the Reign of Elizabeth I* (Dublin: Four Courts Press, 2002).

The Jesuits Get Involved in the Affairs of State, and after They Have Troubled Kingdoms, Everything Turns Out the Opposite of What They Hope

THE LAWYER. When Jesus Christ taught us that we must give back to God what belonged to him, and give back to the emperor in Rome the things to which he had a right,[1] he meant that when we pay the emperor the tribute due him, we ought also return to God his tribute, and not go beyond the bounds of our calling. That's why a good and true religious should simply tend to fasting, prayers, and sermons. I know that our kings sometimes summon prelates to advise them, as they please, or as they find them capable of doing this: but they don't create a rule that applies to everyone. If the spirit of division known as the devil weren't lodged with the Jesuits, I'd say that never was there a wiser decree than the one issued by their congregation of 1593, by which they were forbidden to become involved in affairs of state. Not only because God forbids it, for that's the least of their worries, but also because, when discussing this as a statesman would, I don't see that they've ever dealt with such outcomes for their undertakings, as they hoped. They resemble the sun in March, which stirs up our humors but isn't strong enough to dissipate and resolve them. I'll say even more: for their misfortune is such that, by favoring one party, when they've shuffled the cards in order to end the game, it's always a misadventure for the person whose partisans they've been. So that, although, as we humans say, the Jesuit is no small enemy, by a hidden judgment of God it is more expedient for us to have the Jesuits against us, than to have them for us. I'll demonstrate this for you by five or six noteworthy examples.

They wanted to stir up the state of England, and they used every means at their disposal. What fruit did this advice bear for them? The ruin of an infinity of poor Catholics whom they abused, and who previously lived comfortably in their houses; the death of the queen of Scots; the assurance they gave to the queen of England over a long period; and the ruin of her religion and her state.

---

1   "Then repay to Caesar what belongs to Caesar and to God what belongs to God" (Luke 20:25).

I'll talk about the part of Scotland that borders on England, where dwelled Father William Crichton[2] and Father James Gordon,[3] Scots. Discontented about something, Crichton got the idea of leaving Scotland. He went straight to Spain with the permission of his general. Once there, he tried to insinuate himself into the king's good graces.[4] And he made a family tree showing the genealogy of the Infanta, the king's daughter,[5] to show that the two crowns, England and Scotland, belonged to him. To invite the same king to take up arms against the king of Scotland, he circulated a defamatory booklet against him. The king of Spain refused to listen, so Crichton got the idea of sending letters that would suborn the Scottish Catholic nobility. To this end, he wrote letters in 1592 to Gordon and to other Jesuits who were in Scotland, by which he gave them to understand the favor he enjoyed with the king, who at his instigation had resolved not only to invade England but also to reestablish the ancient religion in Scotland. But first of all, this great prince wanted to make sure of the affection of the Catholic lords, who would sign blank forms to be filled later with procurations bearing their names. Having done this, he obtained the king's word that they would be given 250,000 crowns to distribute. When the Scots Jesuits were notified, they took back several blank forms and gave them to George Ker[6] to carry. Ker having been discovered, owing to the indiscretion of Father Robert Abercromby,[7] Jesuit, he was captured with the letters and the blank forms. And the king of Scotland, deeming that the notice he had given to Crichton was true, ordered the decapitation of Lord Fintry,[8] a gifted lord with some good qualities. The same thing would have happened to Lord Angus, the loftiest person in the country, if he hadn't subtly opened the prisons. Later, owing to the continuation of the Troubles, his

---

2 On Crichton, see ch. 2 above. He participated in numerous intrigues involving the Jesuits, including his mission with James Gordon Huntley, 1584.

3 James Gordon Huntl[e]y (1541–1620) was a professor of theology, philosophy, and Hebrew at Pont-à-Mousson, Paris, and Bordeaux. He was sent to Ireland as apostolic nuncio. For documents about this plot, see Sutto, 368–69nn145–57. Cf. *ODNB* https://www.oxforddnb .com/view/10.1093/ref:odnb/9780198614128.001.0001/odnb-9780198614128-e-11048 (accessed January 31, 2021).

4 King Philip II, who died in September 1598.

5 See ch. 3 above.

6 He was the younger brother of Mark Ker, Lord Newbattle.

7 Robert Abercromby (c.1536–1613) was a Scottish Jesuit. He was a spiritual director of Queen Anne of Denmark (1574–1619), the spouse of James VI. Before travelling back to Scotland, he worked in Poland, where he also died. See *DHCJ* 1:4–5.

8 David Graham of Fintry (?–1593) was executed for having participated in the affair of the Spanish Blanks. See Francis Shearman, "The Spanish Blanks," *The Innes Review* 3 (1952): 101–3.

castles were razed, along with those of the earl of Huntley,[9] the most powerful of them all, and of the earl of Erroll,[10] constable of Scotland. All of them have since converted to the Reformed religion, not only in order to return to grace, but also to live in their country in safety for their bodies and their possessions. To the point that, when everything is added up, Scotland lost the little that remained of our Catholic religion in 1596.

The same thing happened in the kingdoms of Portugal and Aragon. First, I'll tell you about Portugal. It's difficult to believe that the Jesuits sought the death of King Sebastian,[11] as several writers have implied. For, as Montaignes has very well demonstrated, he favored them too much. But this is what happened. Of all the nations that speak Spanish [*sic*], none is as bigoted as Portugal: and among all the kings of Portugal, none was as great a bigot as Sebastian. The subtle and circumspect Jesuits judged that this territory was totally suitable for cultivating their vine. And in order to be more credible, from the moment they arrived, they had people call them apostles, rather than Jesuits, connecting themselves in this way to the persons who were Our Lord's followers. The title has stuck with them, and on that they are in agreement. The kingdom could fall into the hands of their Jesuit family, and several times they requested that no one in the future could be king of Portugal if he wasn't a Jesuit, and elected by their order, just as the pope in Rome is elected by the College of Cardinals. And because this king (although superstitious, or although Superstition itself) could not or, to be more accurate, would not dare to yield, they replied to him that God had ordained it, as he would be informed by a voice from heaven, near the sea. And so, this poor king, ill-used in this way, went there two or three times, but they couldn't play-act their parts about this voice being heard. In their group they still had their Justinian-the-Imposter, who in Rome counterfeited lepers. These messieurs, having realized that they couldn't attain their goal, did not, however, want to quit the match. This king, a Jesuit in his soul,

---

9   George Gordon, first marquis and sixth earl of Huntly (c.1563–1636), was the nephew of James Gordon Huntly. See *Encyclopaedia Britannica*, https://www.britannica.com/biogra phy/George-Gordon-1st-Marquess-and-6th-Earl-of-Huntly (accessed January 31, 2021).

10   Francis Hay, ninth earl of Erroll (1564–1631), a leader of the Catholic party in Scotland. See *Encyclopaedia Britannica*, https://www.britannica.com/biography/Francis-Hay-9th -earl-of-Erroll (accessed January 31, 2021).

11   Sebastian I of Portugal (1554–78) became king in 1557. He was killed at the battle of Alcazar-Quivir in 1578. See *Encyclopaedia Britannica*, https://www.britannica.com/ biography/Sebastian-king-of-Portugal (accessed January 31, 2021). As a prince he had as exclusive tutors and confessors the Jesuits Amador Rebelo (1539–1622) and Luís Gonçalves da Câmara (c.1515–75). See Dauril Alden, *The Making of an Enterprise: The Society of Jesus in Portugal, Its Empire, and Beyond: 1540–1750* (Stanford, CA: Stanford University Press, 1996), 81–82.

hadn't wanted to marry. Now, in order to make themselves more necessary to him, they counseled him to set out to conquer the kingdom of Fez, where he was killed in battle, losing both his life and his kingdom. So that's the fruit that King Sebastian gathered from believing the Jesuits.[12] What I've just told you, I learned from the late and very Catholic marquis de Pisani, who at the time was the French ambassador to the court of Spain.[13]

I'll skip over everything that has happened since then in that kingdom, for it isn't related to my tale. I've now reached what happened to the kingdom of Aragon, where you'll see similar luck brought about by the Jesuits' folly. The Aragonese were very old and had great privileges against the absolute power of their kings. And indeed, at the coronations of their kings, they took this oath of fidelity: *Nos, que valemos tanto como vos, y potemos mas que vos, vos elegemos Rey, con estas y estas conditiones intra vos y nos, que el que manda mas que vos.* That is to say: "We who are worth as much as you, and who can do more than you, we make you our king, with this and this condition between you and us: that there is one who commands you."[14] And beneath that, they listed all their privileges, which the kings promised and swore to observe very strictly. Now, their privileges had been transgressed upon, in the person of Dom Antonio Pérez,[15] their compatriot, secretary of state to the late king of Spain. He had escaped from a long imprisonment in Castille, and he fled to Aragon, where he recounted all the wrongs that had been done to him, to the prejudice of the antique freedoms and liberties of the kingdom. Everyone applauded his lament, especially the Jesuits, who celebrate every opportunity for Troubles. And they began with confessions (one of their principal tools), in

---

12   Cf. Alden, *Making of an Enterprise*, 83–85.

13   Jean de Vivonne, seigneur de Saint-Gouard and marquis de Pisani (1530–99), whose Paris residence, the Hôtel de Pisani, later became the Hôtel de Rambouillet, where his Roman-born daughter, Julie d'Angennes, held her *salon* in the 1620s. See Alain Tallon, "Henri IV and Papacy after the League," in Forrestal and Nelson, eds., *Politics and Religion*, 21–41, here 37n6.

14   The exact oath formula of the Aragonese kings that set their relation to nobility was: "Nos, que somos y valemos tanto como vos, pero juntos más que vos, os hacemos Principal, Rey y Señor entre los iguales, con tal que guardéis nuestros fueros y libertades; y si no, no." See Clizia Magoni, *Fueros y libertades: El mito de la constitución aragonesa en la Europa moderna* (Zaragoza: El Justicia de Aragón, 2012), 418; and the classic study of Ralph Giesey, *If Not, Not: The Oathe of the Aragonese and the Legendary Laws of Sobrarbe* (Princeton: Princeton University Press, 1968), 21–24.

15   Antonio Pérez (1534–1611), was secretary to Philip II. He was imprisoned after the affair of the succession to the Portuguese throne. He lived in exile in France after the failure of the Aragonese revolt. See *Encyclopaedia Britannica*, https://www.britannica.com/biography/Antonio-Perez (accessed January 31, 2021). Cf. François Mignet, *Antonio Pérez et Philippe II*, 3rd ed. (Paris: Charpentier, 1854).

order to win the will of the ones and the others, against their king in Saragossa, the capital city of the realm. They advised them to arrange an uprising. And with their blood boiling, everyone ran to get weapons. On his side, the king of Spain likewise armed himself. Now, when the Jesuits saw the Aragonese armed and standing there, ready to leap into battle, in order to oppose the royal army, they turned their coats and, by preaching and confessions, they began to play a very different game. It no longer was a question of talking about their privileges, which concerned only worldly folks. Instead, they thought about their consciences before God, which were specifically ordering them to obey their king: they should throw themselves at his feet and he would show them mercy. They were certain of this, for they had letters to that effect, bearing his seal. Relying on this promise, some individuals withdrew near to the king's lieutenant general, who pardoned them. Following their example, several others did the same. By this means, the Aragonese army collapsed, all on its own. The king of Spain's chief magistrates entered Saragossa without striking a blow, and they began to put their weapons in play, demolishing several houses in both the city and the surrounding countryside, killing the loftiest nobles, and building a citadel in the city, where they established a garrison. And ever since then, the king of Spain has been in absolute command, as he is in all his other lands. Those who think ill of the Jesuits, maintain that from the very beginning, they stirred up this rebellion by a double game that usually was their companion. If that's true, they were all the more wicked. As for me, I don't presume anything evil: I impute it to their innocence, and to their becoming involved in affairs of state, in which they are schoolboys; and they doom the persons who foolishly lend them an ear.

THE GENTLEMAN. I don't know how many people wish them ill, for they've never given me trouble; but I don't doubt that when they suborned the Aragonese to revolt, it was a concealed game meant to favor the affairs of the king of Spain. For as you know all too well, kings are sometimes very much at ease about such rebellions, the better to have reasons to suppress the ancient privileges of their subjects, and to lay them at others' feet. And therefore, persisting in my first opinion, I increasingly realize that the Jesuit has a Spanish soul, I mean, a soul that is naturally devoted to the king of Spain. Moreover, if one viewed Aragonese history from that angle, your proposition would leave people speechless, for their undertaking was very successful.

THE LAWYER (speaking to the Gentleman): It's all one and the same. You shall judge it as you please; and as for how I judge it, I see it differently, and I think my lesson is truer. But in order not to make me stray from my road, you'll find nothing more admirable on the subject I've proposed here, which happened not so long ago to the king of Poland, Sigismond Báthory, who is also king of Sweden.[16] That prince is totally Jesuit. Incessantly solicited by the Jesuits to lodge them in his kingdom of Sweden, he ponders how to please them. His usual place of residence is Poland; and as for Sweden, Duke Charles,[17] his uncle, is his lieutenant general. Therefore, wanting the king to see that the Jesuits' request would be answered, he promptly told his uncle what he wanted. Charles pointed out that the common people will never consider that family acceptable, and he begged the king, his nephew, not to be stubborn toward his subjects, to whom, at the time of his coronation, he had promised never to receive Jesuits in his kingdom: and the estates of that country had signed. But he, who only saw things through their eyes, and only heard through their ears, debated taking the big step, despite these humble remonstrances; and he debated whether he should enter his kingdom with weapons, in order to be believed. His subjects wanted to prepare for this, so they too took up arms: and things were managed in such a fashion that this prince was beaten, first by sea, and then along a land route; and he was taken prisoner and rather promptly released; and he has been returned to his kingdom with the promise that he can order the estates to assemble and to maintain their conclusions, whatever they were. The estates were called: he escaped during the convocation, leaving garrisons in a few fortified places that were loyal to him. Back in Poland, and spurred on by the Jesuits who control him, he pulls together the main-mast of his shipwreck and implores the estates of Poland to avenge the insult that he claims has been done to him. While he's busy with these preparations (he's still busy), the Poles don't want to listen, so his uncle takes from him the forts that had remained to him in Sweden, and he's on the point of losing his kingdom, acquired thanks to the valor of Gustave,[18] his grandfather, and conserved by

---

16   Pasquier is confused here: Stephen Báthory (1533–86) ruled Transylvania in the 1570s and was elected king of Poland in 1576. He protected Jesuit houses in Poland and helped them grow. He was never king of Sweden. See *Encyclopaedia Britannica*, https://www .britannica.com/biography/Stephen-Bathory (accessed January 31, 2021). The king of Sweden was Sigismund III Vasa (1566–1632), who reigned from 1592 until 1599, when he was deposed. See *Encyclopaedia Britannica*, https://www.britannica.com/biography/ Sigismund-III-Vasa (accessed January 31, 2021). Sigismund was educated by the Jesuits as a prince, and as a king of Poland 1587–1632 promoted the mission of the Society of Jesus in Poland-Lithuania. Indeed, he appointed the Jesuit Piotr Skarga (1536–1612) as a royal chaplain and a court preacher. See Robert A. Maryks, "Skarga, Piotr, SJ (1536–1612)," in *Cambridge Encyclopedia of the Jesuits*, 741–42.

17   Charles, duke of Sudermania (1550–1611), regent of Sweden (1599–1604) who became king of Sweden in 1604, as Charles IX. See *Encyclopaedia Britannica*, https://www.britannica .com/biography/Charles-IX-king-of-Sweden (accessed January 31, 2021).

18   Gustav I Vasa (1485–1560), who became king of Sweden in 1523. See *Encyclopaedia Britannica*, https://www.britannica.com/biography/Gustav-I-Vasa (accessed January 31, 2021).

the prudence of his father.[19] Poland isn't very secure for him. And from all this ruination, his only obligation is to the Jesuits, whose protector he wants to be.

Having travelled in all those far-off lands, I'm now returning to mine. The Jesuits troubled the state of France, feigning to be doing it in order to extirpate Huguenotery. In this quarrel, there's a cry for help to the Spanish, who didn't espouse such little hopes, and who saw themselves commanding in Paris openly armed, and who above all others were favored by the Jesuits, who were totally managing the anarchy of the Sixteen Tyrants of the Populace.[20] I won't say anything about the results for the Spanish. Well, I'll say that the entry of our king into Paris[21] was so glorious that the Spaniards were very happy to hold their lives in fealty and homage to him. And in addition, the Jesuits' traitorous plan turned to smoke, and these traitors were the reason why, by a decree of the Parlement, they were not only driven from the fair city of Paris but also from the jurisdiction of the Parlement. In short, I don't see how, having made a troublesome scramble of all the kingdoms, their undertakings have succeeded.

---

19   John III Vasa (1537–92), the son of Gustav I Vasa, who became king of Sweden in 1568. See *Encyclopaedia Britannica*, https://www.britannica.com/biography/John-III-king-of -Sweden (accessed January 31, 2021).

20   That is, the *Seize*, the representatives of the sixteen quarters of Paris, who were the dominant force in the capital, 1585–91. See ch. 11 above.

21   March 22, 1594.

The Pope Does Not Have the Power to Transfer the Kingdom of France from One Person to Another, to Counter the Dangerous Proposition of Jesuism, and Other Discussions on the Same Subject

THE LAWYER. Not content with trying to assassinate our king during the Troubles, the Jesuits today are trying to assassinate our royalty by their pens, during the peace. Some persons maintain that, in Rome, the pope can transfer empires and kingdoms from one hand to another, when he deems it good to do so. It merits a cardinal's hat, like the hat of Father Bellarmine,[1] Jesuit. And whoever takes up the same proposition in France, is worthy of a red hat, but not the sort worn by cardinals. Kings die when it pleases God to summon them; royalty never dies. That's why the court of the Parlement of Paris, when accompanying the bodies of our kings for their funerals, never wears mourning, but wears scarlet: a true observance of the perpetual splendor of the royalty. Now, one of the chief ornaments of our crown is that our kings can't be censured by Rome; nor can their kingdom be banned, or as a result transferred. It's a law: not a dictated law, but a born law, a law we haven't studied, adopted, or been taught over a long time-span, but a law that is pulled out from our France, is inspired by it, and nurses its own breasts to the point of exhaustion. We aren't taught by it, we are suckled by it: and if someone brought from Rome some fulminations against the majesty of our kings, and if, as a consequence, someone wanted to forbid the kingdom to do something, we aren't obliged to obey. Nor, for that matter, do our kings ever lose the title Most Christian, nor the title of eldest children of the church. The Jesuit was condemned by decree: he's still dragging his halter, but he'll always be a Jesuit, that is to say, a place where divisions, partialities, and discords are sowed within our France. Let's, then, listen to the person who, taking the name Montaignes, has written for us the

---

1 The Jesuit cardinal Robert Bellarmine. See Book II, ch. 15 above. Pasquier is probably referring here to Robert Bellarmine, *Disputationes Roberti Bellarmini Politiani, Societatis Jesu, de controversiis Christianae fidei, adversus hujus temporis haereticos, tribus tomis comprehensae: Ad S.D.N. Sixtum V pont. max.* (Ingolstadt, 1586–93). See Robert Bellarmine, *On Temporal and Spiritual Authority: On Laymen or Secular People; On the Temporal Power of the Pope; Against William Barclay On the Primary Duty of the Supreme Pontiff*, ed. and transl. Stefania Tutino (Indianapolis: Liberty Fund, 2012).

book of lying Truth.[2] Having said that the temporal belonged exclusively to kings, and the spiritual to the Holy Father, who was making no claim to their sovereignties, he maintains that if kings have to commit a fault, God has put into the pope's hand the rods with which to chastise them and deprive them of their kingdoms.

"That is useful for princes (says Montaignes) who usually are brought back to their duty by fear about their temporal, which they prefer, even though they are bad, rather than by their fears about the spiritual, which they don't use unless their conscience is good, which wasn't always the case. But the pope isn't God. Neither was Samuel, who carried out that order against Saul. Yet he had anointed King Saul through the prophet, and that same person stripped him of it. And that same person had the kingdom transferred, and David was made king.[3] In the time of Uzziah, king of Judah, the high priest, who was no more a king than Samuel was, transferred the kingdom from the father to the son, the former having become a leper, owing to his pride. Now, this separation was done by the will of the high priest, as he was ordered by the Law; and consequently, he was deposed.[4] Jehoiada wasn't God, he was the pontiff and the lieutenant of God when he ordered the death of Queen Athaliah, who governed tyrannically, and put the kingdom into the hands of Joash, a prince of the blood and a legitimate successor to the crown.[5] All of these persons carried out God's commands, just as the pope does. And God can transfer a kingdom in ten thousand ways, by the weapons of pagans, Moors, Turks, and other foreign nations, causing the Assyrians to conquer the Greeks, the Greeks the Assyrians, the one and the other the Jews, and the Romans all of them. Among Christians, there can't be a gentler way, a more reasonable and more assured way, than the intervention and authority of the head of the church and common father of the Christians who, especially helped by God, and by persons of science and conscience, will probably do nothing against the rights of the legitimate successors, and who will dispassionately proceed in all modesty and gentleness, in a case so important, always striving toward the honor of God, the public good, and the good of the individual."

In sum, according to this fine proposition of our Spoil-Everything Jesuit, the pope has the power to transfer kingdoms from one hand to another, when he thinks he should; and in so doing he can't be checked, all the more so since

---

2   Pasquier seems to be referring to Richeome's own *La Vérité défendue* (The truth defended). See Book 11, ch. 10 above.

3   1 Sam. 10:15–16.

4   2 Chron. 26:16–23.

5   2 Kings 11.

if God can do it, then his vicar can do the same thing, although the pope is less privileged in our Christianity when it comes to kings, than the prophets were in the days of the Mosaic Law. Your folly reduces me to being a marvelous accessory, making me now fight the authority of the Holy See. First of all, if you want to discuss this proposition in a human sense, where will you find that a king who establishes his lieutenants general according to provinces, grants them, in everything, an authority that is similar to his authority over his subjects? And to say that God has transmitted his omnipotence to any man whomsoever: there you are committing a blasphemy against God's majesty. Moreover, where, Sophist, do you find that one must beg for such examples in the Old Testament, in order to transplant them to the New Testament? That's how you and your brethren capture unawares the conscience of a poor, blinded populace. If your reasoning has some merit and effect, we today must go back to doing circumcision, as it was done under the Mosaic Law. And under that same heading, a subject will be permitted to kill his king: because Ehud killed Eglon,[6] king of Moab, with impunity. Since you call yourself a Jesuit, let's follow in the steps of Jesus Christ. For, all our thoughts should turn to that. And directing my thoughts to this goal, I want to show you that I'm a true Catholic of the pope, and that you are a true Catholic deceiver.

We think about the power of Our Lord Jesus Christ as having two periods. The first, when, in order to redeem us, he came down to earth from heaven; the other, when, having suffered death and the passion, he rose from earth to heaven. In the first case, it's the time of his humility, in consideration of which he declared that he hadn't come to arbitrate a division, by which they wanted to tell him that he separated the power of God and the power that was due a Roman emperor.[7] When Pilate asked him whether he was a king, he replied that his kingdom was not of this earth.[8] In the second phase, it's the time of his glory, to which one must link all these fine verses by the prophet David, when he said that the entire earth belonged to the Lord: Ask me, and I shall give you people and inheritances, and they will be your possessions until the end of the earth. And in addition, he was Lord of lords and King of kings.[9]

Let's not play the Sophist about the Holy Scriptures. For the more you ambitious Jesuits give to the pope, in order to authorize, not his splendor but your splendor, the more you take from him. When did Jesus Christ give his vicariate to Saint Peter? He gave it while he was still on earth, and was on the verge of

---

6 Judg. 2:15–30.
7 "Repay to Caesar what belongs to Caesar and to God what belongs to God" (Matt. 22:21).
8 "My kingdom does not belong to this world" (John 18:36).
9 1 Chron. 29:1–17; and then Ps. 136:2–3.

finishing his pilgrimage, so that he would be depicted, here below, in his state of humility. Also, he gave the key to heaven, not the key to earth, in order to teach us that he was putting Saint Peter in charge of the spiritual, without mingling any of the temporal with it. And indeed, our ancient popes were extremely ignorant and called themselves the serfs of the serfs, if they heard Jesus Christ depicted as he is in the plenitude of his glory, and after he rose to heaven in order to sit at the right hand of God his Father. Therefore, it was a heresy for Luther to have taught his followers that the pope wasn't the head of the church and the grand vicar of Jesus Christ. It was another heresy for Ignatius to stand up to Luther and maintain that not only was the pope the vicar of Jesus Christ in his state of humility, but he was also his vicar in his state of glory. Now, that state of the pope is really Catholic, that recognizes and avows him, according to its original Institution, without adding any of the men.

I'm back to you, Jesuit: let's see how dangerous your proposition is. Our kings know what is helpful to them for the conservation of their state; and like mariners, they are sometimes forced to lower sails during a storm. That won't please a pope who has other considerations in his head. He'll summon our kings to form opinions modeled on his. If they don't obey after two or three warnings, he'll act against them by censures, and all at once he'll cause a divorce between them and their subjects; or if that doesn't succeed, he'll place an interdict on their kingdom and make it the prey of the first prince who has the strength to get involved. True God! Into what disarray are you putting all our affairs?

Now, Jesuit, learn this doctrine from me. For I don't want the French people to be infected with your poison; nor do I want foreigners to read your book, deeming the majesty of our kings to be shrunk by your coming. First, we maintain, and we hold as an article that is inviolable in France, that it isn't within the pope's power to exercise liberality in our kingdom, to the profit of anyone whomsoever. No matter what fault we may encounter in our kings, I won't make an exception for a single one of them. The pope has no power beyond the power that God has given him; he is neither the Samuel, nor the Judas whom God ordered to do this, under the ancient Law. For under the new law, which we call the New Testament, that isn't at all the case: the pope cannot, by means of his spiritual sword, give the law to the temporal. I don't say that a king of France must therefore forget himself, either in the Catholic religion or in the governing of his subjects, toward whom he should be a second father. For if he forgets himself, he should consider it very certain that God will sooner or later forget him and will take revenge on him in some unhoped-for way. But that he must go and seek that remedy in Rome, I deny it.

As for this first maxim, I'll raise no doubts about it. What I say after that will be more obscure. All the more so because we hold that there is another very certain article in this France, to the effect that the pope can't excommunicate our kings. Something we learned over a very long time, a time that can't be longer. I recall having read that Lothair, king of Austrasia, dying, abandoned his brother and heir, Louis, emperor and king of Italy. King Charles the Bald, their uncle, took it over by a so-called right of politeness.[10] Louis turned to Pope Adrian, who took up the cause for him and admonished Charles the Bald to respect his nephew's rights, under penalty of excommunication.[11] But Charles the Bald didn't obey. The pope therefore hoped to mingle censures with bitter denunciations. Although he knew the great authority wielded by Hincmar,[12] archbishop of Reims, he ordered him not to give communion to Charles, on penalty of being excommunicated himself. Never was a papal order more just and more holy than that one. For, what pretext was there for an uncle to defraud his nephew from inheriting from late brother? Nonetheless, never was an *ordonnance* more unfavorably received than that one. Because Hincmar had given apostolic letters to several prelates and barons of France, to know how he was supposed to govern in this matter. He passed on to Pope Adrian the opinions that he had collected, and especially the opinion that everyone was scandalized by his decree, saying that they had never seen such orders, even where the kings were heretics, schismatics, or tyrants, and maintaining that kingdoms were acquired at sword point, not by excommunications by the Holy See or by prelates. And when I set down in writing (said Hincmar) the power that Our Lord granted Saint Peter, and which is transmitted to the popes in Rome, they reply to me:

> *Petite Dominum Apostolicum ut quia Rex et Episcopus simul esse non potest: Et sui antecessores Ecclesiasticum ordinem (quod suum est) et non Rempublicam (quod regum est) disposuerunt, non praecipiat nobis habere regem, qui nos in sic longinquis partibus adjuvare non possit, contra subitaneos et frequentes Paganorum impetus: et nos Francos jubeat servire, cui*

---

10 *Bienséance* (politeness): when a prince or lord seized for himself a region, a land, an inheritance, people jokingly said that the property was his by the right of *bienséance*, the right of "politeness." That is, he had no real right to take it.

11 [H]Adrian III (d.885) was pope from 884 to 885. Adrian's main political challenge was keeping the peace among Charlemagne's heirs, who were competing for power and who, generation after generation, kept subdividing the empire. These repeated subdivisions made it difficult to defend Rome. See *Encyclopaedia Britannica*, https://www.britannica.com/biography/Saint-Adrian-III (accessed January 31, 2021).

12 Hincmar of Reims (*c.*806–82), archbishop, canon lawyer, and theologian, was the most influential political counselor and churchman of the Carolingian era. See *Encyclopaedia Britannica*, https://www.britannica.com/biography/Hincmar-of-Reims (accessed February 1).

nolumus servire. Quia istud jugum sui antecessores, nostris antecessoribus non imposerunt. Quia Scriptum in Sanctis libris audimus, ut pro libertate et haeridate nostra usque ad mortem certare debeamus.

And a bit later: *Propterea si Dominus Apostolicus vult pacem quaerere, sic quaerat pacem, ut rixam non moveat.* And finally, Hincmar closed his letter with these words: *Et ut mihi experimento videtur, propter meam interdictionem, vel propter linguae humanae gladium, nisi alius eis obstiterit, Rex vester, vel Regni ejus primores non dimittent, ut quod coeperint quantum poterunt, non exsequantur.*[13] From this missive you can see that the pope not only wanted to censure King Charles the Bald, for failure to obey him about so just a matter, but he also declared himself to be the judge of empires and kingdoms. Which neither the king nor his subjects wanted to grant, maintaining that the pope couldn't mingle religion and the state, and that they were resolved to stand up to him, whatever the cost and whatever the condition. As being a new law that he wanted to introduce into France to the prejudice of our kings.

I know full well that some honest man will say to me: "What? You give total primacy and superiority to the pope for the spiritual, yet you limit his general power in your king, if from this time forth he strays from the true path? In regard to the temporal, I am most willing; but for this high point of the spiritual, everything degenerates in opposition to that proposition." To which I give this answer: My dear friend, in France we recognize the pope as the head of our Catholic and universal church; but on that point, it isn't inappropriate for our kings to be freed from their censures. And so, we view all the old

---

13   "Tell the Apostolic Lord: since the king cannot also be at the same time the bishop, and the pope's predecessors regulated the ecclesiastical order, which pertains to them, not the *respublica*, which pertains to kings, let the pope not order us to have a king who, in our faraway lands, cannot help us against the sudden and frequent attacks of the pagans; and let him not command us, who are Franks, to be slaves. For his predecessors did not impose such a yoke on our predecessors; and we cannot bear it, we who have heard it written in the Sacred Books that we should fight until death for our freedom and our patrimony. [...] Therefore, when the pope wants to seek peace, he should seek peace without creating occasion for war. [...]. And as I find by proof, our king or the peers of his realm are not minded either for my excommunication or the sword of man's tongue (unless some other matter comes to stop them) to desist from prosecuting what they have begun." Letter from Hincmar to Hadrian from 870. See *Recueil des historiens des Gaules et de la France*, ed. Martin Bouquet et al., 24 vols. (Paris, 1738–1833), 7:540B. See also George Tavard, "Episcopacy and Apostolic Succession according to Hincmar of Reims," *Theological Studies* 34 (1973): 594–623, here 600; P. R. McKeon, "Toward a Reestablishment of the Correspondence of Pope Hadrian II: The Letters Exchanged between Rome and the Kingdom of Charles the Bald regarding Hincmar of Laon," *Revue bénédictine* 81 (1971): 169–85, here 172–73.

monasteries as naturally subject to the jurisdiction of their bishops. Several of them are exempted from it, owing to special privileges. Our ancient kings were the first protectors of the Holy See, both against the tyranny of the emperors at Constantinople, and against incursions and invasions by the Lombards, who daily were at the gates of Rome. King Pepin won the entire exarchate of Ravenna, which he gave to the popes as a gift; he delivered their city from the long siege that Aistulf,[14] king of the Lombards, had laid. And Charlemagne, Pepin's son, chased from Lombardy Didier,[15] their king, and all his tribe, proclaiming himself king not only of the entire city of Rome but also of all Italy, where he subsequently was recognized and crowned emperor of the West by Pope Leo,[16] to whom he returned his former freedom against the petulant Roman people, who were insulting him. And after that, it was decreed that the elected popes couldn't assume their offices until they'd been confirmed by him and his successors. I'm also sure that, from that time on, he and his posterity were freed of all censures and excommunications by the Holy See. And although we don't have a specific constitution, one can grasp what it was, from an *ordonnance* of that same emperor, summarized by Ivo, bishop of Chartres:[17] *Si quos culpatores Regia potestas, aut in gratiam benignitatis receperit, aut mensae suae participes fecerit, hos et sacerdotum, et populorum conventus suscipere Ecclesiastica communione debebit, ut quod principalis pietas recepit, nec à Sacerdotibus Dei extraneum habeatur.*[18] If the domain or the benevolence of our kings made the excommunicated person free and absolved of ecclesiastical censures, one must say that our kings couldn't be excommunicated. Our kings had the right

---

14 Aistulf, king of Lombards (?–756) carried on a policy of expansion against the papacy. In 751, he captured Ravenna and threatened Rome. The popes, despairing, turned to the Franks (including King Pepin the Short [Pippin, *c.*714–768], who crossed the Alps, defeated Aistulf, and gave the pope the lands he had conquered). See *Encyclopaedia Britannica*, https://www.britannica.com/biography/Aistulf; and https://www.britannica.com/biography/Pippin-III (accessed January 31, 2021).

15 Desiderius, also known as Desiderio or Didier (d.774), was king of Lombards in 756. He is chiefly known for his connection to Charlemagne, who married his daughter and conquered his realm. See David S. Sefton, "Pope Hadrian I and the Fall of the Kingdom of the Lombards," *The Catholic Historical Review* 65 (1979): 206–20.

16 Leo III (759–816) was elected pope in 795. Charlemagne protected him from his enemies in Rome. See *Encyclopaedia Britannica*, https://www.britannica.com/biography/Saint-Leo-III (accessed January 31, 2021).

17 Ivo (*c.*1040–1116), became bishop of Chartres in 1090. See *Encyclopaedia Britannica*, https://www.britannica.com/biography/Saint-Ivo-of-Chartres (accessed January 31, 2021).

18 "If the king shall receive any culprit into the favor of his clemency or make him partaker of his own table. the whole company of the priests and people, shall likewise receive him into the communion of the church; that which the prince's piety has admitted, be not by the priests, held as rejected."

to confirm popes after their elections, a right that the popes claimed had been returned to them: therefore, one shouldn't envy us either, because the antiquity of Rome relieved our kings of all excommunications and censures. Be that as it may, Pope Gregory IV,[19] wanting to contravene this, in order to please the children of King Louis the Debonair,[20] a son of Charlemagne, the good bishops and prelates of France notified him that if he had come to excommunicate their king, he would return to Rome excommunicated. An abrupt remark (I admit it), but so effective that the pope, in order to conceal the game, he was playing, said that he had merely come to France to work out a peace between father and children, which he did. And if he'd acted differently, he would have returned home discontented. In France, we embrace so tightly this privilege for our kings that I can say that it either was born with our Crown, when Clovis became a Christian, or else it was born during the second lineage, shortly after our kings took into their hands the defense and protection of the Roman church. We see this successively observed in Charlemagne, in his son Louis the Debonair, and in his grandson Charles the Bald. Likewise, during the third lineage: when our kings were somewhat misguided and it was deemed appropriate to make use of the authority of the church, either the pope or his legate had to meet with the assembled Gallican Church. And when all the affairs of France were calm between the king and his subjects, no censures of our kings ever came from Rome. In our archives there is a bull of Pope Boniface VIII that states: *Ut nec Rex Franciae, nec Regina, nec liberi eorum excommunicari possint*; the king of France, the queen, and their children can't be excommunicated.[21]

---

19   Gregory IV (?–844) was pope from 827 to 844. During his pontificate, the papacy attempted to intervene in the quarrels between Emperor Louis I the Pious (778–840) and his sons. This pontificate also saw the breakup of the Carolingian empire in 843. See *Encyclopaedia Britannica*, https://www.britannica.com/biography/Gregory-IV (accessed January 31, 2021).

20   Louis the Pious also called the Fair or the Debonair, was king of the Franks and co-emperor (as Louis I) with his father, Charlemagne, from 813. As Charlemagne's only surviving adult son, he became the sole ruler of the Franks after his father's death in 814, a throne he occupied until his death, save for 833–34, when he was deposed. See *Encyclopaedia Britannica*, https://www.britannica.com/biography/Louis-I-Holy-Roman-emperor (accessed February 1, 2021).

21   Sutto, 379n194, comments: "It obviously cannot be a passage from a bull of Boniface VIII. Perhaps Pasquier was using an anonymous gloss of the bull *Unam sanctam*, where the excommunication of a king is strictly limited." It is possible, however, Pasquier refers here to Pope Clement VI's (r.1342–52) letter from 1351 to Joanna I, countess of Auvergne and Boulogne (1326–60), queen consort of France since 1350. Part XIII of that letter bears the title: "Quod rex and regina, et eorum liberi, sub patria potestate existentes non possunt excomunicari, aut interdici ab aliquo." See *Constitutiones Innocentii XI., Alexandri VIII., & Innocentii XII.* (N.p.: n.p., 1730), 188.

Since then, it has happened that this pope, having become the enemy of King Philip the Fair,[22] wanted to excommunicate him; but never did censures cost a pope as dearly as those did. His nuncios were taken prisoner, bulls were burned, and Boniface, who was captured by Nogaret,[23] the chancellor of France, died from chagrin at having been disgraced by his enemy. In this, Philip did nothing without informing the entire clergy of France and obtaining its approval. And this excommunication just missed provoking a coup that would have been prejudicial to the king and his kingdom; but on the other hand, it brought shame and confusion to the person who had ordered it. Benedict XIII,[24] otherwise known as Peter of the Moon, was dwelling in Avignon: an interdict was issued against Charles VI[25] and his kingdom, the king seated in his *lit de justice* in the Parlement of Paris, May 21, 1408, ordered that the bull must be lacerated, and that Gonsalve and Conseloux, its bearers, should be presented on scaffolds and be publicly scolded, which means that the people were being told that the king couldn't be excommunicated. This was carried out in August as ignominiously as possible. On the miters of the two nuncios were these words: These persons were disloyal to the church and to the king. Julius II[26] subsequently did something similar to King Louis XII;[27] and by the general assembly of the Gallican Church, held at Tours in 1510, his censures were censured. Without straying from our own day, similar censures came from Rome in

---

22   Philip IV, king of France (1268–1314), also called Philip the Fair, relied on skilled civil servants such as Guillaume de Nogaret to govern the kingdom. He and his advisors were instrumental in transforming France from a feudal country to a centralized state. See *Encyclopaedia Britannica*, https://www.britannica.com/biography/Philip-IV-king-of-France (accessed January 31, 2021).

23   Guillaume de Nogaret (*c.*1265–1313) was a professor of law at Montpellier. In 1302, while chancellor to Philip the Fair, he arrested Boniface VIII. See *Encyclopaedia Britannica*, https://www.britannica.com/biography/Guillaume-de-Nogaret (accessed January 31, 2021).

24   Benedict XIII (*c.*1328–1423), the anti-pope, was born Pedro de Luna (his detractors called him *el Papa Luna*, Pope Moon). He ruled from Avignon during the Western Schism that split the Catholic church into two segments. Benedict was elected in 1394 to succeed Clement VII. He was deposed in 1417. See *Encyclopaedia Britannica*, https://www.britannica.com/biography/Benedict-XIII-antipope (accessed January 31, 2021).

25   Charles VI, king of France (1368–1422), came to be known as Charles the Mad. See *Encyclopaedia Britannica*, https://www.britannica.com/biography/Charles-VI-king-of-France (accessed January 31, 2021).

26   Julius II (1443–1513), born Giuliano della Rovere, ruled the Papal States, 1503–13. His pontificate was marked by an active foreign policy, ambitious building projects, and patronage of the arts. See *Encyclopaedia Britannica*, https://www.britannica.com/biography/Julius-II (accessed January 31, 2021).

27   Louis XII, king of France (1462–1515), ruled from 1498 to his death. See *Encyclopaedia Britannica*, https://www.britannica.com/biography/Louis-XII (accessed January 31, 2021).

1591, during the recent Troubles. And by a decree of the court of the Parlement of Paris, at the time transferred to Tours, and of the Sovereign Chamber, meeting in Châlons in Champagne, it was ordered that the bulls be burned by the executioner of high justice; and they were. In this France, a proposition decreed that, in the peace treaty of Arras of 1481,[28] between King Louis XI, Archduke Maximilian of Austria, and the estates of the Low Countries, the deputies of Maximilian and those of the estates stipulated that, for our estates, the king promised to maintain the treaty; and to this end he and his son would submit to all ecclesiastical censures, *Nonobstant le privilège des rois de France, par lequel ni lui ni son royaume ne pouvoient être contraints par censures ecclésiastiques.*[29] A treaty confirmed later in the same year by King Louis, at Plessis-lèz-Tours, states thusly this confirmation: We and our aforesaid son, and our kingdom, have given our submission, for the maintenance of the said treaty, despite the privilege that we, our successors, and our kingdom not be submissive nor constrained by censures. This was subsequently also confirmed by the decree issued in 1549. In order to immortalize his memory by a very noble act, Charles, cardinal of Lorraine,[30] archbishop of Reims, founded a university at Reims that had several great privileges. For spiritual matters, he was first given permission by King Henri II,[31] and then by Pope Paul III, who issued very ample bulls that, among other clauses, included this one:

> *Nos igitur pium et laudabile* [*ipsorum*] *Henrici Regis, et Caroli Cardinalis desiderium* [*in Domino*] *plurimum commendantes, praefatum Henricum regem à quibusvis excommunicationis, suspensionis et interdicti, aliisque Ecclesiasticis sententiis et censuris,* [*et*] *poenis à jure vel ab homine, quavis ocasione vel causa latis, si quibus quomodolibet innodatus existit, ad effectum praesentium duntaxat consequendum, harum serie absolventes* [...].[32]

---

28 The peace Treaty of Arras was signed in 1482 (not 1481) between Louis XI of France (r.1461–83) and Archduke Maximilian I of Austria (1459–1519) who was the heir of the Burgundian Netherlands.

29 "Despite the privilege of the kings of France, by which neither he nor his kingdom could be constrained by ecclesiastical censures."

30 See Book I, ch. 4 above.

31 See Book I, ch. 4.

32 "Thus, highly praising the pious and laudable desires of King Henri and Cardinal Charles, and absolving the aforesaid King Henri by these presents from the effects and consequences of whatever excommunications, suspensions, or interdictions and other ecclesiastical sentences and punishments imposed automatically or by individuals for whatever cause or occasion, if such exist that are binding in whatever way...." See Guillaume Marlot, *Histoire de la ville, cité et université de Reims métropolitaine de la Gaule*

We could not ask for greater courtesy or favor than that: our king, with no supplications of his own, would be absolved of every excommunication that he might encounter by law and by fact. Yet the same liberality that the university was offered was refused by the court of the Parlement of Paris, because when the bulls and the king's letters-patent were verified, the decree of the penultimate day of January 1549 stated that: "On condition that, despite this claimed absolution, one could not infer that the king has been, or in the future can be at all, for any cause whatsoever, subject to apostolic excommunications and censures, nor prejudice the rights, privileges, and preeminences of the king and his kingdom." It's not as if the decree issued against Jean Châtel on December 29, 1594, did not include this particular topic. Among other things, he was found guilty of having maintained that "our king Henry IV, now reigning, was not in the church until he had received papal approval, for which he repented and begged the pardon of God, the king, and the courts."

I've talked about all this, not from the ill-will I bear for the Holy See: I'd rather have God send me death. I've talked about it in order to show you that, along with their crown, our kings bear their assurance of safe-conduct for everything, and are not subject to being ambushed by their enemies in the papal circle. And yet, you see these unfortunate Jesuits, enemies of our tranquility, give us just the opposite instructions: that is to say, explosives and preparations for a rebellion, there, in case our kings aren't getting along with the popes. This shows that it's not without reason that the Jesuits have been driven out of France by decree of the Parlement of Paris.

Belgique: Divisée en douze livres; Contenant l'estat ecclésiastique et civil du païs, 4 vols. (Reims: Jacquet, 1846), 4:679.

Decree of the Parlement of Paris against the Jesuits in 1594, and a Chapter Excerpted from Book 3 of the *Recherches de la France* by Étienne Pasquier

PASQUIER, speaking through the Lawyer, says: Having dedicated this book to the liberties of our Gallican Church, I do not think I am straying far from my intention to talk about the Jesuit sect, which has propositions that are the total opposite of ours, to subvert our state. After the Jesuits had collected the big legacy that they had received from Messire Guillaume du Prat, bishop of Clermont, they bought the Hôtel de Langres on the rue Saint-Jacques in the city of Paris.[1] There, according to their liking, they created a sort of college and monastery in a variety of domiciles; and having taken the liberty of teaching youths without the permission of the rectors, they asked the university several times to be incorporated into it. Not having succeeded, for the same purpose they presented a request to the court of the Parlement in 1564. The university, everyone assembled, did me the honor of choosing me to be its lawyer. When I prepared for the trial (armed with the holy decree that the Faculty of Theology had issued against the Jesuits in 1554, attended by those two great buttresses of our Catholic religion, our Master Picard and our Master Maillart), I thought I could, in total freedom of conscience, fight this monster in an enclosed field.[2] This monster was neither secular nor regular. It was both at the same time, and it therefore introduced a hermaphrodite order into our church. For two mornings, Master Pierre de Versoris and I presented our arguments before an infinity of persons who were waiting for the results, he representing the Jesuits, and I the university. Master Baptiste du Menil, *avocat du roi*, a highly respected person, was on my side. In my plea, I showed the irregular profession practices they followed, the judgment by the Faculty of Theology ten years earlier, the opposition expressed by Monsieur Brûlart, the *procureur du roi*,[3] when they were received, to the effect that their vow ran counter to ours; that nurturing the Jesuits in our midst meant introducing a schism, and just as many Spanish spies and sworn enemies of France whose results would be felt at the first stirrings that the misfortune of the times would bring to us. Despite all that,

---

1   See Book I, ch. 4 and Book II, ch. 3 above.
2   See Book I, ch. 6 above.
3   See Book I, ch. 4 above.

© KONINKLIJKE BRILL NV, LEIDEN, 2021 | DOI:10.1163/9789004164062_057

we were appointed to the council. Each person won and lost his case. For the Jesuits would not be incorporated into the corps of the university, but neither were they forbidden to continue their accustomed lectures.[4] When God wants to afflict a state, he plants the roots well in advance. These new arrivals won the hearts of the common people by hypocritical behavior and fine promises. For it was as if they had the gift of tongues that the Holy Spirit cast over the apostles: they boasted of going to preach the Gospel in the midst of savages, yet they scarcely knew how to speak their mother tongue. Amid these fair charms, everyone let himself be captivated, as if by a bird-caller's whistle. But since they had introduced a mingled religion of seculars and regulars, troubling in this way the entire hierarchical order of our church, they debated how to trouble in the future all the politic states of Christianity. All the more so since, by a new rule, they began to mingle the state and their religion. And since it is very easy to fall from freedom into unbridled license, upon this irregularity they planted a heresy that was more detestable than one can state: they maintained that it is permissible to kill a prince who did not conform to their principles. They trampled not only upon the reprimand that Our Lord gave Saint Peter, when he pulled out his sword to defend him, but they also trampled upon the article of the Council of Constance, which anathematized those who were putting forward that proposition.[5] When I pleaded that case, I didn't use these two propositions against them. For they were hatching things in their souls and had perhaps already hatched them. Well, said I, one shouldn't hope that anything good will come of this monster. But if they had wanted some results, I would never have thought of the maxim of the Old Man of the Mountain who, at the time of our overseas wars, distributed his subjects, known as assassins, throughout the provinces, to kill Christian princes, nor the abominable Anabaptism that came into Germany when we were youths. Still, they practiced both propositions, in the sight and knowledge of all Christianity. For, as for the former proposition, all of us know that having gained a foothold in Portugal, not under the name Jesuits but under the name apostles, they used all manner of impostures to make King Sebastian willing to issue a general law to the effect that no one can be called to the crown if he does not belong to their Society, and also that he must be elected by the voice-votes and suffrage of the Society. They could not achieve this, although they were dealing with the most bigoted and superstitious prince possible.

---

4 *Lectures* can refer to "lectures"; but it can also refer to "readings," that is, reading aloud before assembled listeners.
5 See Book II, ch. 1 above.

I was doing my best to stick to the subject of our France; they were the first firebrands of that wretched League that ruined our kingdom from rooftop to cellar. The League was first planned among the Jesuits; and having finished their plans, they delegated their Father Claude Mathieu, from Lorraine, and Father Henri Sammier, from Luxembourg (that's how they address their oldest priests), to serve as trumpeters throughout all the foreign nations; and since then, they have declared themselves openly Spaniards, as much by their preaching as by their public lessons. In favor of this they wanted to launch their second proposition, not because our king was distanced from our religion at the time (for they knew that this was an obstacle that would prevent him from reigning). As soon as they saw him drawn into the bosom of the church, they suborned Pierre Barrière, a man whose hand was determined but whose soul and conscience were weak. They had him go to confession at their Parisian college, and then receive communion; and having strengthened him with a sure promise of paradise, like a true martyr, if he died during this quarrel, they let the valiant fighter go. Three times God stayed his hand. Finally, having been captured at Melun, he was punished in 1593, just as he deserved. I am not telling you anything that I have not seen, for I spoke with him when he was a prisoner. Search for all the impieties you please, you will not find one as barbarous as this one. To advise something impious, and to give it a mask of piety, like this one; and to talk about losing a soul, a king, a paradise, and our church, all together, in order to make their Moorish plans possible. All these new productions were the reason why, the city of Paris having been reduced to obeying the king, the University of Paris again wanted to bring up against the Jesuits the old paths taken by their appointee to the council. The case was pleaded powerfully and dignifiedly by Master Antoine Arnauld; but just as the verdict was being decided, another matter made them judge it anew. In the royal house of the Louvre, surrounded by the nobility, Jean Châtel, a Parisian, nineteen years of age, the offspring of that wretched seminary, strikes our king, Henri IV, with a knife. Châtel is captured; his trial is conducted and completed, and a decree is issued on December 29, 1594, to this effect:

> *Veu par la Cour les grand Chambre et Tournelle assemblées, le proces criminel commencé à faire par le Prevost de l'Hostel du Roy, et depuis parachevé d'instruire à la requeste du Procureur general du Roy, demandeur et accusateur à l'encontre de Jean Chastel natif de Paris, escolier, ayant fait le cours de ses estudes au College de Clermont, prisonnier és prisons de la Conciergerie du Palais, pour raison du tres-execrable et abominable parricide attenté sur la personne du Roy. Interrogatoires et confessions dudict Jean Chastel ouy et interrogé en ladite Cour, ledit Chastel sur le fait dudit*

*parricide: Ouy aussi en icelle Jean Gueret Prestre, soit disant de la congre-
gation et Societé du nom de Jesus, demeurant audit College, et cy devant
precepteur dudit Jean Chastel, Pierre Chastel et Denise Hazard, pere et mere
dudit Jean: Conclusions du Procureur general du Roy, et tout consideré IL
SERA DIT que la ditte Cour à declaré et declare ledit Jean Chastel attaint et
convaincu du crime de leze majesté divine et humaine au premier chef, par
le tresmeschant et tres-detestable parricide attenté sur la personne du Roy.
Pour reparation duquel crime a condamné et condamne le dit Jean Chastel
a faire amande honorable devant la principale porte de l'Eglise de Paris,
nud en chemise, tenant une torche de cire ardente du poids de deux livres,
et illec à genoux dire et declarer que malheureusement et proditoirement il
a attenté ledit tres-inhumain et tresabominable parricide, et blessé le Roy
d'un cousteau en la face: et par fausses et damnables instructions il a dit au
process estre permis de tuer les Rois, et que le Roy Henry 4 à presant regnant,
n'est en l'Eglise, jusqu'a ce qu'il ait l'approbation du Pape dont il se repend
et demande pardon à Dieu, au Roy et à Justice. Ce fait estre mené et conduit
dans un tombereau en la Place de Greve: Illec tenaillé aux bras et cuisses, et
sa main dextre, tenant en icelle le cousteau, duquel il s'est efforcé commettre
ledit Parricide, couppee: et apres son corps tiré et demembré avec quattre
chevaux, et ses membres et corps jettez au feu, et consommez en cendre,
et les cendres jettees au vent; a declare tous et chacuns ses biens acquis et
confisquez au Roy. Avant laquelle execution sera ledit Jean Chastel appliqué
à la question, tant ordinaire, qu'extraordinaire, pour sçavoir la verité de ses
complices, et d'aucuns cas resultans du process. A fait et fait inhibitions et
defences à quelques personnes, de quelque qualité et condition quelles soi-
ent, sur peine de crime de leze majesté, de dire n'y proferer en aucun lieu
public lesdits propos, lesquels laditte Cour à déclaré et declare scandaleux,
seditieux et contraires a la parolle de Dieu, et condamnez comme here-
tiques, par les S. decretz. Ordonne que les Prestres et escoliers du College de
Clairmont, et tous autres soy disans de ladite Societé, comme corrupteurs
de la jeunesse, perturbateurs du repos public, ennemis du Roy et de l'Estat,
vuideront dedans trois jours apres la signification du present arrest, hors de
Paris, et autres villes et lieux où sont leurs Colleges, et quinzaine apres hors
de Royaume, sur peine où ils y seront trouvez ledit temps passé, d'estre punis
comme criminels et coupables dudit crime de leze majesté. Seront les biens,
tant meubles qu'immeubles à eux appartenans employez en oeuvres pita-
bles, et distribution d'iceux faite ainsi que par la Cour sera ordonné. Outre
fait defenses à tous subjects du Roy d'envoier des escoliers aux Colleges de la
ditte Societé qui sont hors du Royaume, pour y estre instruits sur la mesme
peine de crime de leze Majesté. Ordonne la Cour que les extraicts du present*

arrest seront envoyez aux bailliages et senechaucees de ce resort, pour estre
executé selon sa forme et teneur. Enjoint aux Baillifs et Seneschaus, leurs
Lieutenans generaux et particuliers, proceder à l'Execution dedans le delay
contenu en icelui, et aux substituts du Procureur general tenir la main à
ladite execution, faire informer des contraventions, et certifier la cour de
leurs diligences au mois, surpeine de privation de leurs Estats. Signé Du
Tillet. Prononcé audit Jean Chastel, executé le 19 de Decembre 1594.[6]

6   In this group of French documents, the original spelling, absence of accent marks, and punc-
    tuation have been maintained; the translations into English are very close to the original
    French: "Seen by the court of the Great Chamber and the Tournelle, assembled, the criminal
    trial begun by the *prévôt* of the king's hôtel, and since then completed at the request of the
    procureur général of the king, plaintiff and accuser of Jean Châtel, native of Paris, student,
    having taken classes for his studies at the Collège de Clermont, a prisoner in the prisons of
    the Conciergerie of the *Palais*, as a result of the very execrable and abominable parricide
    attempted on the king's person. Interrogations and confessions of the said Jean Châtel heard,
    and the said Châtel questioned in the said court, on the facts of the said parricide. Also heard
    was Jean Gueret, priest, said to belong to the congregation and Society of the name of Jesus,
    dwelling at the said college, formerly the preceptor of the said Jean Châtel; Pierre Châtel and
    Denise Hazard, the father and mother of the said Jean: Conclusions of the procureur general
    of the king, and everything considered, IT SHALL BE SAID that the said court has declared
    and declares the said Jean Châtel attainted and convicted of the crime of divine and human
    lèse-majesté primarily, by the very wicked and very detestable parricide attempted on the
    king's person. In reparation for which crime the said Jean Châtel has been sentenced and is
    sentenced to make honorable amends before the principal door of the cathedral church of
    Paris, naked and in a nightshirt, holding a torch of burning wax weighing two pounds, and
    then, kneeling, to say and declare that unfortunately and treacherously he attempted the
    said very inhumane and very abominable parricide, and wounded the king with a knife to
    the face: and by false and damnable instruction, during the trial he said that it is permissible
    to kill kings, and that King Henri IV, presently reigning, does not belong to the church until
    he has the pope's approbation, for which he repents and begs pardon from God, the king,
    and the courts. This having been done, he shall be led and conducted in a cart to the Place
    de Grève: and then his arms and thighs shall be pinched with a pincher, and his right hand,
    holding the knife with which he attempted to commit the said parricide, shall be cut off; and
    after that his body shall be pulled and dismembered by four horses, and his limbs and body
    thrown into the fire, and consumed to ashes, and the ashes thrown to the winds; the court
    has declared all and each of his possessions to have been acquired by and confiscated by the
    king. Before which execution the said Jean Châtel, will have the question [i.e. torture] applied
    to him, both ordinary and extraordinary, in order to know the truth about his accomplices,
    and other cases resulting from the trial. Has made and makes inhibitions and interdictions to
    whatever persons, whatever their rank and condition, on pain of the crime of lèse-majesté, to
    say or offer in any public place the said words, which the said court has declared and declares
    scandalous, seditious, and contrary to the Word of God, and found guilty as heretical, by the
    holy decrees. Orders that the priests and scholars of the Collège de Clermont, and all other
    persons belonging to the said Society, as corrupters of youth, troublers of the public peace,
    enemies of the king and the state, shall within three days after the signing of this decree, be
    outside Paris and other cities and places where they have their colleges, and two weeks after

During the procedure of which this decree is a part, some judges in the Parlement were chosen to go to the Collège de Clermont. Some papers were ordered seized, among them some manuscript books in the hand of Master Jean Guignard,[7] a Jesuit priest, containing several false and seditious ways of proving that it had been lawful to assassinate the late King Henri III, and some instructions for killing King Henri IV, his successor. Indeed, this is the end of both the master-Jesuits and their unfortunate schoolboy.

Another decree against Jean Guignard, priest, regent in the Jesuit college of the city of Paris:

> *Veu. Par la Cour, les grand Chambre et Tournelle assemblees le procets criminal fait par l'un des Conseillers dicelle, à la requeste du Procureur general du Roy, à l'encontre de Jean Guignard Prestre, regent au College de Clairmont de cette ville de Paris, prisonniers es prisons de la Conciergerie du Palais, pour avoir esté trouvé saisi de plusieurs livres, contenan entr'autres choses, approbation du trescruel et tresinhumain parricide dui feu Roy, que Dieu absolve, et inductions pour faire tuer le Roy à present regnant: interrogatoires et confessions dudit Guignard, lesdits livres representez, reconnus composez par lui, et escrits de sa main: conclusions du Procureur general du Roy: ouy et interrogé ledit Guignard sur les cas à luy imposez et contenus esdits livres: et tout consideré.*
>
> *Il sera dit que laditte Cour a declaré et declare ledit Guignard attaint et convaincu du crime de leze Majesté, et d'avoir compose et escrit lesdits livres contenans plusieurs faux et seditieux moyens, pour prouver qu'il avoit esté loisible de commettre ledit parricide, et estoit permis de tuer le Roy Henry 4 à present regnant. Pour reparation de ce a condamné et condamne ledit Guignard à faire amande honorable nud en chemise, la corde au col, devant la principalle porte de l'Eglise de Paris: et illec estant à genoux, tenant en ces mains une torche de cire ardente du poids de deux livres dire et declarer: Que meschamment, mal-heureusement et contre verité il a escrit le feu Roy*

that, shall be outside the realm, on penalty of being punished as criminals and being found guilty of the crime of lèse-majesté, wherever they may be after that time. The possessions that belong to them, both moveable and in real estate, shall be used for charitable works and shall be distributed as the court shall order. In addition, all the king's subjects are forbidden to send scholars to the colleges of the said Society that are outside the realm, under penalty of being tried for the same punishment for the crime of lèse-majesté. The court orders that excerpts from the present decree shall be sent to the *bailliages* and *sénéchaussées* of this jurisdiction, to be carried out according to their form and tenor. Enjoined to the bailiffs and *sénéchaux*, and their general and particular lieutenants."

7   Jean Guignard (1563–95) was the librarian at the Collège de Clermont, and also professor of theology and prefect of the older students. See *DHCJ*, 2:1840–41.

*avoir esté justement tué par Jaques Clement, et que si le Roy à present
regnant ne mourroit à la guerre, il le falloit faire mourir, dont il se repent, et
demande pardon à Dieu, au Roy et à Justice, Ce fait mené et conduit en la
place de Greve pendu et estranglé a une potence, qui y sera pour cet effect
plantée: Et apres le corps mort, reduit et consume en cendre en un feu qui
sera fait au pied de laditte potence. A declaré et declare tous et uns chacuns ses biens acquis et confisquez au Roy. Prononcé audit Jean Guignard,
et executé le septiieme jour de Janvier 1595.*[8]

Another decree, against Pierre Châtel, Jean Châtel's father, and Jean Gueret, a
so-called priest of the congregation and Society of the name of Jesus:

*Veu par la Cour les grand Chambre et Tournelle assemblees, le process crimi-
nal commencé à faire par le Prevost de l'Hostel du Roy, et depuis parachevé
d'instruire en icelle, à la requeste du Procureur general du Roy demandeur et
accusateur à l'encontre le Jean Gueret Prestre, soy disant de la Congregation
et Societé du nom de Jesus, demeurant au College de Clairmont, et cy devant*

---

8 "Seen by the court of the Parlement, the great chamber and the Tournelle assembled, the
criminal trial presided over by one of the councilors of that court, at the request of the *procureur général* of the king, against Jean Guignard, priest, regent at the Collège de Clermont
in this city of Paris, prisoner in the prisons of the Conciergerie of the *Palais*, because several
books were found and confiscated, containing among other things an approval of the very
cruel and very inhumane parricide of the late king, may God absolve him, and inductions to
have the king now reigning killed: interrogations and confessions of the said Guignard, the
said book shown, recognized as being written by him and written in his hand: conclusions of
the procureur general of the king: the said Guignard heard and questioned about the cases
imposed upon him and contained in the said books, and everything considered.
   It shall be stated that the said court has declared and declares that the said Guignard is
guilty and convicted of the crime of lèse-majesté, and of having composed and written the
said books containing several false and seditious means of proving that it had been legal
to commit the said parricide, and it was permitted to kill King Henri IV now reigning. As a
reparation for this, the court has sentenced and sentences the said Guignard to make honorable amends, naked and in a shirt, the rope around his neck, before the principal door of the
cathedral church of Paris: and kneeling there, holding in his hands a torch of burning wax
weighing two pounds, he will say and declare: That wickedly, unfortunately, and counter to
the truth, he wrote that the late king had been justly killed by Jacques Clément, and that
if the king presently reigning does not die in battle, he will have to be killed, for which he
repents and begs God, the king, and the courts to pardon him. This done, he will be led to and
conducted around the Place de Grève, hanged and strangled on gallows that will be planted
there to this end: and when the body is dead, reduced and consumed to ashes in a fire that is
burning at the foot of the said gallows. The court has declared and declares to all and sundry
that his possessions have been acquired and confiscated by the king. Read aloud to the said
Jean Guignard and carried out on the seventh day of January 1595."

precepteur de Jean Chastel nagueres execute à mort, par arrest de laditte Cour, Pierre Chastel marchant drapier, bourgeois de Paris, Denise Hazard sa femme, pere et mere dudit Jean Chastel, Jean le Comte et Catherine Chastel sa femme, Magdelaine Chastel, filles desdits Pierre Chastel et Denise Hazard, Antoine de Villiers, Pierre Roussel, Simonne Turin et Louise Camus leur serviteur et servants, Maistre Claude l'Allemant prestre, Curé de S. Pierre des Arcis, Maistre Jaques Bernard prestre, clerc de laditte Eglise, et Maistre Lucs Morin, prestre habitué en icelle, prisonniers es prisons de la Conciergerie du Palais, Interrogatoires, confessions et denegatiens desdits prisonniers, confrontation faite dudit Jean Chastel audit Pierre Chastel son pere, information faite contre ledit Pierre Chastel, confrontation à lui faite des tesmoins ouis en icelle, le procets criminal fait audit Jean Chastel pour raison du tresexecrable et abominable parricide attenté sur la personne du Roy: le procets verbal de l'execution de l'arrest de mort donné contre ledit Jean Chastel, le vingt-neusvieme de Decembre derner passé, conclusions du Procureur general du Roy, ouis et interrogez en ladite Cour, ledit Gueret, Pierre Chastel et Hazard sur les cas a eux imposés et contenus audit process: Autres interrogatoires et denegations[9] *faites par lesdits Gueret et Pierre Chastel, en la question a eux baillee par ordonnance de ladite Cour, et tout consideré.*

Il sera dit que ladite Cour pour les cas contenus audit process, a banni et bannit lesdits Gueret et Pierre Chastel du Royaume de France, assavoir ledit Gueret à perpetuité, et ledit Chastel pour le temps et espace de noeuf-ans, et a perpetuité de la ville et faux-bours de Paris: A eux enjoint de garder leur ban a peine d'estre pendus et estranglez, sans autre forme ny figure de process: a declare et declare tous et chacuns les biens dudit Gueret acquis et confisquez au Roy: et a condamné et condamne ledit Pierre Chastel en deux mille ecus d'amande envers le Roy, applicable à l'acquit et pour la fourniture du pain des prisonniers de la Conciergerie, et a tenir prison jusques a plein payement de ladite somme: Et ne courra le jour du banissement sinon du jour qu'il aura icelle payee. Ordonne ladite Cour que la maison en laquelle estoit demeurant ledit Chastel sera abbatue, demolie et rasee, et la place appliquee au public, sans qu'a l'avenir on y puisse bastir. En laquelle place pour memoire perpetulle du tres-meschant et tresdetestable parricide attenté sur la personne du Roy, sera mis et erigé un pilier eminent de pierre de taille, avec un tableau, auquel seront inscrits les causes de ladite demolition, et erection dudit pilier, lequel sera fait des deniers provenans des

---

9　*Dénégation* (denegation): a term used in jurisprudence. The action by which one denies something before a court. A disavowal.

demolitions de ladite maison. Et pour le regard desdits Hazard, le Comte,
Catherine et Madelaine Chastel, de Villiers, Roussel, Turin, Camus
l'Allemant, Bernard et Morin le septieme de Janvier, et ausdits Gueret et
Pierre Chastel le dixieme dudit mois mil cinque cens quattre vings quinze.[10]

---

10   "Seen by the court, the Great Chamber and Tonnelle assembled, the criminal trial begun
      by the prévôt of the king's Hôtel, and since that time completed in this court, at the request
      of the king's procureur general, plaintiff and accuser of Jean Gueret, priest, claiming to
      belong to the congregation and Society of the name of Jesus, residing in the College de
      Clermont and formerly preceptor of Jean Châtel, previously executed to death, by decree
      of the said court, Pierre Châtel, merchant draper, bourgeois of Paris, Denise Hazard his
      wife, father and mother of the said Jean Châtel, Jean Le Comte and Catherine Châtel his
      wife, Magdelaine Châtel, daughters of the said Pierre Châtel and Denise Hazard, Antoine
      de Villiers, Pierre Roussel, Simonne Turin and Louise Camus, their serving men and serv-
      ing women, Master Claude L'Allemant, priest and curate of Saint-Pierre-des-Arcis, Master
      Jacques Bernard, priest and clergyman of the said church, and Master Lucas Morin, priest
      who helps with the Mass at that church, prisoners in the Conciergerie of the *Palais*, inqui-
      ries, confessions, and disavowals of the said prisoners, confrontation carried out between
      the said Jean Châtel and the said Pierre Châtel his father, inquiry made about the said
      Pierre Châtel, confrontation of him and the witnesses heard during that inquiry, criminal
      trial conducted for the said Jean Châtel on the subject of the very execrable and abomi-
      nable parricide attempted on the king's person: the official report of the execution of the
      death decree issued against the said Jean Châtel, on the twenty-ninth of December just
      past, conclusions of the king's procureur general, heard and questioned in the said court
      the said Gueret, Pierre Châtel and Hazard on the cases imposed upon them and con-
      tained in the said trial: other interrogations and disavowals done by the said Gueret and
      Pierre Chatel, during the torture given them by order of the said court, and everything
      considered:
          It will be stated that the said court, for the cases contained in the said trial, has ban-
      ished and banishes the said Gueret and Pierre Châtel from the kingdom of France, that
      is to say, the said Gueret in perpetuity, and the said Châtel for the time and space of nine
      years, and in perpetuity from the city and suburbs of Paris: they are enjoined to observe
      their banishment or be hanged and strangled, with no other form or figure of a trial: have
      declared and declare to all and sundry that the possessions of the said Gueret have been
      acquired and confiscated for the king: and the said Pierre Châtel has been sentenced and
      is sentenced to a fine of two thousand crowns to the king, applicable to the purchase price
      and supply of bread to the prisoners of the Conciergerie, and to remain in prison until the
      said sum has been fully paid: and the time of the banishment will begin to be counted
      on the day when he has paid this. The said court orders that the house in which the said
      Châtel lived will be torn down, demolished, and razed, and the spot will become public,
      and no one will be able to build on it in the future. In that place, as a perpetual memorial
      to the very wicked and very detestable parricide attempted on the person of the king, a
      tall pillar of dressed stone will be placed and erected, with a plaque, on which will be
      inscribed the causes of this demolition and the erection of the said pillar, which will be
      done with the money coming from the demolition of the said house. And as for the said
      Hazard, Le Comte, Catherine and Magdelaine Châtel, de Villiers, Roussel, Turin, Camus,
      L'Allemant, Bernard, and Morin, the said court orders that their prison cells be opened.

Those are the three decrees of the court of the Parlement of Paris, in which you can see the diligence, religiosity, and justice with which the court acted; how the accused persons were punished to a greater or a lesser degree; and how the suspects were freed with full authority, in an affair of great conse-quence for the general state of France. Let us see now, please, the comments that our Jesuits made and are making about these decrees: because for some time now, their ability to speak has returned.

> Read aloud to the said Hazard, Le Comte, Catherine and Magdelaine Châtel, de Villiers, Roussel, Turin, Camus, L'Allemant, Bernard, and Morin on the seventh of January, and to the said Gueret and Pierre Chastel, on the tenth of the said month, one thousand five hundred ninety-five."

By Covert Words, the Jesuits Claim That the Decree against Jean Châtel Was Unjust, and How God Permitted Him to Be Punished in Order to Make the Jesuits' Punishment More Exemplary for Posterity

THE JESUIT. Here our Jesuits are railing about the decree involving Jean Châtel; and they feign to be excusing the Parlement, accusing it of having committed an injustice by finding him guilty. "We are (said the Jesuit Counterfeiter-of-Holiness, in the humble request he presented to the king)[1] the enemies of kings, of the state, and of your person, and we are the seducers of the young. We oppose these block accusations: we oppose, first, the testimony in your court of the Parlement of Paris. The court had heard the lawyers who were carrying and emptying their sacks full of such consequential accusations.[2] It had very diligently been urged to find our side guilty. It had spent some nine months of leisure weighing rights, that is, from April 30 until Christmas. It had not found us guilty, and it left us in total peace and possession of our rights, reserving for itself a more opportune season for reasoning and for doing justice to those who had so wretchedly calumniated us. This judicial corps was composed of the greatest legal lights in the world, and of the strongest and most solid members of your state. If it had viewed the least of these crimes as being as well-proved as they were importunely objected to, would it have failed to find us immediately guilty? And not having found us guilty, did it not, by its silence, find our accusers guilty, and give very sure testimony of our innocence? If it found us guilty after that, is it not by virtue of the lawyers' preliminary condemnations, without however, losing the case?"[3] And several pages lower: "In July 1594, at the time of the great lawsuit stirred up by two pleading lawyers, they threw Barrière in our faces, and they committed several similar violations in order to carve this crime on our reputation. But these were blunt words, not arguments with a knife-like point, bits of a tongue,

---

1   This is an allusion to Richeome-Montaignes and his *Tres humble remonstrance et requeste*.

2   Legal and notarial documents were tied into small and stored in rather small, easy to carry burlap sacks that could be hung from rafters. In short, these sacks served simultaneously as briefcases and filing drawers.

3   In this quote and the next, Pasquier is quoting Richeome, *Très humble remontrance et requeste*, and he also cites René de La Fon's *Réponse*.

not truth. The Parlement paid no attention, and it absolved us by its silence."
René de La Fon takes the same down-payment and also wants to show that
Châtel's conviction absolves the entire Society, because when torture was
applied, he did not accuse one single person. And they certainly had some very
bad eavesdroppers at that event: for although the wretch, by his replies to the
questions he was being asked, pardoned individuals who were named, he
accused the entire order, as I shall show more amply later. In addition, both
Jesuits are very ignorant when it comes to decrees of the sovereign courts. The
court (says the first Jesuit) did not judge that case quickly, despite our poignant
accusations to which people objected: so, by their silence, they declared us
innocent. Moreover, they objected to the facts about Barrière; and without
pausing on that subject, the court did not want to find us guilty. However, it
was tacitly willing to absolve us. I beg you, Messieurs the Dialecticians, whom
you praise for being superior to everyone else in Scholastic theology, what rules
will you find that will make these consequences good? And nonetheless, I do
not find them strange coming from the pen of a Jesuit. For these venerable
fathers know how to try kings, without listening to them, and how to give, like
flotsam and jetsam, their kingdoms as prey for whoever can occupy them,
as they did with the late king. The sovereign courts do not behave in that fashion: they listen to the lawyers of the parties, but they do not believe them. And
especially for important cases, like this one: for their decision they go back to
their better and first judgment. That was done in this case. Arnauld and Dollé
were helped by their pleas about Barrière's tragic story;[4] the court did not want
to believe them, and very wisely so, because they had to see the law case against
him at Melun, by Lugoli,[5] in order to know what he was doing there. But where,
Jesuit,[6] is the sharp point of your spirit? You recognize this Parlement as being
composed of the greatest legal lights in the world. Moreover, having selected
the parties in the council, they moved ahead dispassionately; yet they suddenly turned away. You say he judged poorly, having based his decree on Châtel,
who had not accused you. The judges commit faults, either when they are lacking in judgment, or when their judgment is troubled by hatred, favor, or other
badly regulated passions. Neither the one nor the other were against you, as
you agree. It is the fault of us both. Your fault for wanting, by sophistries, and
with a hollow brain, to gobble up that decree. Mine, for wanting to give reasons

---

4   See Book 1, ch. 5 above.

5   See ch. 6 above.

6   For much of this paragraph, where Pasquier addresses the Jesuit, he uses the *tu* (thou) form
of the verb. Since he clearly was not the Jesuit's childhood friend, the *tu* almost certainly
expresses his disdain for the Jesuit.

for sustaining it. It should suffice for us that it is a decree; we must therefore stop there. In any trial, and especially in trials that are cut from this sort of fabric, God is in the midst of the judges, to inspire them. One person, who had heard the speeches in a trial and seen the documents, was preparing for absolution or for being declared guilty. But he changes his mind, owing to the opinion of the person who speaks just before he does; indeed, from time to time it happens that a single word from him gives rise to a new opinion in the person who is backing him up, although the first opinion-giver would not have thought of it. And when it comes to making a final decision (casting the bell, as they say in the trade), one gathers together a general opinion on which to build the decree. You think that Châtel's deed was the only piece that ruined you: you're mistaken. The court wisely debated the case in the council, in this way giving it to be understood that it did not want passion or precipitation, both of which are the stepmothers of Justice. This detestable act by one of your scholars suddenly steps in: the materials had been displayed for your condemnation: they are taken back while Châtel's case is being judged, and they judge it by the same means as they judge yours. His detestable Indignity awoke the fairness of the judges, who would have fallen asleep on your facts, if justice had not been awakened. And in all of this, there is nothing of the man, but there is a deliberate judgment by God, which must be trumpeted throughout the universe. It is certain that your college in Paris was the source and the seminary for all the misfortunes that we in France suffered during the recent Troubles. That was the planned rebellion; by it, maintained in everything and everywhere, your provincials, your rectors, your good fathers with the big collars were the first guides to this furrow, the first and the last persons to use this lovely merchandise. Your college was the rendezvous of those who have vowed the ruin of the state and the parricide of the king: things you were turning into trophies, by your sermons as well as your lessons. The upright persons who had the fleur de lis imprinted on their breasts, saw this tyranny; they sighed in their souls, for they did not dare give air to their sighs. Everything they said was directed to God, so that it would please him to have pity on them. God let you reign for five years and more, laying down the law to the people, the magistrates, the princes, in order to see whether, with time, there was some hope of improvement in you. No sooner had the king entered Paris than the just anger of the common people burst forth. The University of Paris stirred against you, took back the old procedures of the adjournment of 1564, a resumption that was founded on your new procedures and your unfortunate bearing. The case was pleaded by two courageous lawyers, Arnauld and Dollé, and it was listened to with wise patience rather than being immediately judged on the basis of the consequences. The fire and the anger of the plaintiffs could, with time, cool down, French-style. The judges did not get stirred up by the cases, only as much as they were pushed to do so. Otherwise, they would have wronged themselves, and one could say that they are petitioners, not judges. During this cooling-down, they forgot to judge the case: when Châtel unexpectedly stirred up the humors of both the judges and the parties. It was the hour for God's indignation: having for a long while temporized about your faults, he wanted Châtel to be a matchstick in the judges' hearts, in order to render justice, not so much against you as against him, and so that you would all serve as an excellent example for posterity. For, in order to accomplish that work, God permitted Châtel, who had been nurtured in your school, to get involved in putting into practice your holy lessons and exhortations against the king; not out in the fields, but in Paris, and that he should remain, not in a back corner of the city, but on the Île de la Cité, which is situated between the two other cities,[7] in a house situated next to a house with the door to the *Palais*, that is, the old lodging of our kings and of the sovereign justice of our France. This house belonged to his father, who was so unfortunate as not to reveal to the court the detestable advice given to his son, which he admitted knowing about. God chose that place at a good moment, in order to carry out the most exemplary punishment. For in cases of lèse majesté, the judges have an obligation to their sovereign prince: to raze the houses of the culprit and to erect an engraved memorial about everything that went on there. That is why that house was ordered torn down and why a pyramid was erected in its place, bearing a commemorative inscription, not only about Châtel's crime but also about the Jesuits' crime, the entire monument placed just opposite that great and royal *Palais*. So, our survivors will, in the future, know how indebted France is to the devout Society of Jesus. Was there ever, I won't say in France, I'll say in the world, a punishment more noteworthy than this one?

---

7   The two "cities" evoked here are parts of Paris: the Right Bank, home of royal palaces and wealthy royal officials; and the Left Bank where monasteries, the university, and various colleges were situated. Between the two, in the middle of the Seine River, was the Île de la Cité, site of the cathedral of Notre Dame and of the *Palais*, in which assembled the Parlement and its law courts. The Châtels apparently lived on the island.

Concerning the Pyramid Built in Front of the *Palais* of Paris, and the Decree Issued in Rome by the Magnificent Pasquin about the Reestablishment Being Sought by the Jesuits

THE LAWYER. "Oh, Marble (says the hypocritical Jesuit in his Very Humble Request, referring to the pyramid), what are you doing to a poor, innocent family, in order to show, centuries from now, the happiness of a great king, and the unhappiness of a great criminal?[1] Isn't your charge sufficiently just, without burdening yourself with defaming someone who hadn't done anything? But since you are telling outright lies, speak the language and tell the truth. Who etched on your spine the fact that they had pushed or advised a miserable Frenchman to assassinate the most Christian king of France? What testimony, what deposition, what assurance do you have, as you testify about him, give a deposition about him, and express assurance about what he is telling the world? Did you hear more, without ears, and did you see more, without eyes, than twenty-five thousand ears and just as many eyes could perceive in this carrying out of supreme justice, in the Place de Grève?[2] Are you talking more from a gay heart than this criminal dared say, forced to endure such severe torments?"

The force of someone's violent imagining is certainly great and terrible, producing prodigious effects not only in our souls, but even in our bodies. For we read that the son of Croesus, a mute, regained his speech when he saw that they wanted to kill his father. And Cippus, a king of Italy who had watched a bullfight with great apprehension, woke to find two horns on his forehead.[3] And Lucius Cossitius, who had wildly anticipated the pleasure he would experience with his bride, became a woman on his wedding night.[4] Alas! I greatly

---

1   Criticizing "the Jesuit" to his face, Pasquier returns to the *tu* form here.
2   The public square in the 4th arrondissement of Paris that since 1802 is called the Place de l'Hôtel de Ville. It was a site of public executions. In April 1792, the first guillotine was erected there.
3   Ovid, *Metamorphoses*, XV, 565–621. Michel de Montaigne (1533–92) used almost the same words when citing Ovid on Cippus, *Essays*, ch. 21, "Of the Power of the Imagination."
4   Pasquier inverts the sex change: Lucius Cossitius was transformed into a man on his wedding day (Sutto, 391n218, who refers to Pliny the Elder, *Natural History*, VII, iv).

© KONINKLIJKE BRILL NV, LEIDEN, 2021 | DOI:10.1163/9789004164062_059

fear that this honest-man Jesuit, looking at that pyramid, will see the general condemnation of him and his brethren, will turn to stone, as Niobe did when she saw her dead children.[5] For I can already see that he has lost the eyes of both his body and his spirit, bitterly informing the public of the innocence of his Society, and trying to persuade us that the decree was based solely on Châtel's act. Now come on! Since, with your forlorn senses, you don't know what the very walls are testifying to, and since you are speaking to a stone, I want a stone to answer you: a stone that is very antique and very authentic. That great and venerable Pasquin[6] in Rome, who matches you others in several ways. For just as you criticize kings and princes about some misinterpreted passages from Holy Scripture, since time immemorial Pasquin has criticized popes and cardinals, by the texts posted on him. Just as you, by your confessions, learn many things not only from the state but from private families, it is founded on the very old privilege of receiving information from all sides, by which he reveals things that were thought to be very secret. Seeing this mutual sympathy between you and him, I'm sure you'll believe him. For, Jesuit, don't think Pasquin didn't try that case in Rome, and didn't judge it in the council without mature deliberation; and don't think that, owing to your good reputation there, he didn't seek every means to have the decree nullified and to have the pyramid torn down, as he did for your reestablishment. But he labored in vain. Therefore, hear what he wrote to you in Italian, which I've translated into French as faithfully as I could. Perhaps you'll remain satisfied:

PASQUIN. Most Illustrious Father, I have read all the humble remonstrances and requests that you made to the most Christian King Henri IV, and likewise the memoranda that were given to Father Maggio in order to present him,[7] so that he can be reestablished. In which I took both great pleasure and great displeasure. Pleasure at seeing your choice of fine words; displeasure at seeing

---

5 Ovid, *Metamorphoses*, VI, 140–312.

6 Pasquin (or Pasquino) was a battered Hellenistic marble statue set up in the heart of Rome. People attached anonymous satirical texts to its base. According to Pasquier himself, Pasquin was Étienne Pasquier. A few years earlier, Richeome (calling himself Félix de la Grâce) published *La Chasse de Renard Pasquin* (Villefranche: Le Pelletier, 1603): Among the many appearances of the two characters are these remarks by Pasquin: "My name is Pasquin, but only when I speak; because when I write, I say *Monsieur Pasquier*, thinking to do him honor" (35). Pasquin also pokes fun at Pasquier's style: "Pasquin, who followed step by step in Pasquier's footprints, and who stole from him, word for word, several entire long sentences that are injurious to the Jesuits" (349). The mystery of Pasquin's appearance in the *Catechism* is perhaps solved: Pasquin is Pasquier himself.

7 Lorenzo Maggio (1531–1605), provincial of Austria and assistant for Italy, who visited both France and Germany. See Fouqueray, *Histoire de la Compagnie de Jésus en France*, 2:iv, 56–58, 120, 156–217.

how your father-ships were afflicted. If I am not mistaken, your principal goal is to have the pyramid demolished. For you would be reestablished in vain if that stone is not knocked down: it charges you with several crimes that you deem false and calumnious. Now, since it was a question of trying a stone, I guessed that a full knowledge of these facts was my task, exclusive of all other persons. And so that you will understand how diligent and just I was, I wanted to move on to examining this fact; and I remembered that your case had been pleaded twice, and that twice it had been adjourned: the first time in 1564, when you were asking to be received into the corps of the University of Paris; the second time in 1594, when the university was calling for your total banishment and expulsion from France. To be enlightened about the first, I wanted to see Pasquier's plea against you, and Versoris's plea in your favor, and also the last plea by du Mesnil, *avocat du roi*. All of them showed me that, at the time, it was not a question of the newness of your order, which contravened the ancient liberties of the Gallican Church. And since I wanted to inform my conscience more amply, here are a few mutinous spirits that you provided me in three books: the first book contains the bulls you obtained to your advantage; the second contains your Constitutions divided into ten parts; and the third is the Examen, or rather, if you want me to be more precise, the abridgment of them.[8] From them, I shall gather some passages previously unknown to me, a simple vow that your enemies say is full of fox-like subtleties and heresy, several extraordinary undertakings involving the *ordinaires* and the universities, a rich mendicancy about which you have taken a vow, and a blind obedience toward your superiors. As for the mendicancy of Our Holy Father, I shall not touch upon it: your principal bulls seem to me to have surprised the Holiness of the Holy See. Ha! (said I at the time) Who was that wicked person who let these books leave your colleges? He merits the gallows. There is no need to know the secrets of a devout family of religious; but there is a need to know how to speak to the common people and to make the desired remarks, to the scandal and the mockery of the entire order. But since the malefactor cannot be discovered, I think that the three books should be sent back to one of your colleges, and that the room should be turned over to four judges. It is not the first time that inanimate things were beaten with switches, to serve as an example. We know that the sea failed Xerxes, the wise king of Persia, who wanted to cross to Greece on a rope bridge; so Xerxes ordered that the sea be

---

8   For the Constitutions and the Examen, see *Constitutions of the Society of Jesus and their Complementary Norms*, 56–407 and 24–54. In addition, see the "Formulas" approved and confirmed by Paul III and Julius III, 3–16. Cf. Book II, ch. 3.

whipped.[9] By contrast, the Signoria of Venice, in order to flatter and re-pacify the sea, weds it every year on the feast of the ascension, and gives it a wedding ring.[10] And believe me, I was greatly perplexed when I compared the privileges of the Gallican Church with yours: it makes that law inviolable for me, although every law is uncertain and fluctuates according to variations in the weather and the seasons. Still, there is a very certain, fixed, and immutable law: that is, we must live according to the laws of the country in which we want to live. And seeing that your bulls and your standing are, in everything, and everywhere, contrary to the liberties of the Gallican Church, I have several major scruples, despite the gratification and the favor that I vowed to you.

Having read and reread all these documents about the first case decided in the council, I looked over the second plea, from 1594, which stirred up all the nerves of my spirit. For in that plea, it no longer was a question of your doctrine: it was a question of the assassination attempts that you directed against princes and princesses, and against the kingdoms in which you Jesuits dwell, especially France. A great thing, a dubious thing, a thing with very dangerous effects. That's why, for the duties of my position and the discharge of my conscience, I thought I should insert my own papers into this case, in a fashion that I hadn't been taught to do. For when I do things in that other fashion, I receive the packets that my vassals and subjects share with me, and I trust them merely on the basis of their reports. But here, the discourse has been totally different. Because, having read you book, which is so full of compassion and pity, I issued admonitions on all sides, *nemine dempto* [without exception], so that things can be revealed; and I awarded commissions for every nation (based on the permission I've been granted since antique times and throughout Christendom) in order to be informed, by letters and by witnesses, about what I think justifies you: issuing an order to all judges, whatever their rank, on pain of great and arbitrary fines, to send me the criminal and extraordinary cases that involved your brethren. After careful deliberation, your innocence

---

9   Xerxes I (c.519–465 BCE), known as Xerxes the Great, undertook an invasion of Greece in 480 BCE. Herodotus relates, in his *Histories*, that Xerxes built two bridges of papyrus and flax, over the harbor on the Hellespont. According to Herodotus, when the bridges were destroyed by a storm, Xerxes gave the straits three hundred whiplashes and branded it with red-hot irons as the soldiers shouted at the water. See *Encyclopaedia Britannica*, https://www.britannica.com/biography/Xerxes-I (accessed January 31, 2021).

10   "The ceremony of espousing the sea was first performed in 1177, when the Pope, on presenting the Doge Sebastian Ziani with a magnificent ring, accompanied the gift with the words: 'Take this as a token of the sovereignty which you and your successors shall exercise over this sea for ever.' In memory of this speech the Doge afterwards dropped a golden wedding-ring into the sea every year with imposing ceremonies" (F. Marion Crawford, *Gleanings from Venetian History* [London: Macmillan, 2018], 105).

having been demonstrated, this pyramid will be torn down, and the decree will go to the Inquisition. Just as, in the past, censures against you were issued by the Spanish Inquisition, a censure against you was issued by the Sorbonne in 1554.[11] For one must not be comfortably obstinate about your holy father-ships.[12] And what made me desire to do this even more, was your book, where I read, with extreme grief in my heart, about the ill treatment you received as a result of the decree; yet you admit that the court of the Parlement leads in knowledge, uprightness, and religiousness. And to tell you the truth, from the very start, here's a fleet of French, English, Scottish, Aragonese, Portuguese, Polish, Flemish, and Swedish people, who total three or four times more than I wanted. And since the voice of the common people is the voice of God, if one believes that commonplace, and if that's the consequence, I absolutely don't want to stop. But your book gives me a greater scruple than before: for to justify your actions, you say that, in 1593, at a general assembly called by your order in this city of Rome, your brethren were forbidden to become involved in the affairs of state. I could not really decipher that. In the future they are forbidden (I said) to get involved. This presupposes that they got involved in them in the past. I cannot get it into my head that these devout souls did that. Because the misfortune of this century is such that, in affairs of state, there is usually more impiety than religion, in order to conform to our affairs. And while I remained suspended in that uncertain fashion, someone whispered into my ear: No doubt about it, for the person who wrote the prohibitions for the Collège de Clermont in 1594 inserted the Latin article from beginning to end. I had some-one bring me the book, and I found that what the whisperer was saying was true. Someone else brought me Montaignes's book. See this passage (he said): in it, you'll find the motives behind our recent Troubles. And in that book, I found that Fathers Claude Mathieu and Émond Auger were once greatly cher-ished by King Henri III, and that he sometimes even invited them to ride in his coach. Then he added: Satan having tossed into the realm the apple of dis-cord, suspicions, and jealousies, affairs were altered and plans were changed, and they were the vinegar and gall of the wars we have witnessed. Since one never lacks commentaries, when this entire passage was read aloud, that per-son told me that only two words were needed in order to understand, and that this change was made by throwing out what those two blissful fathers received from the king, when he saw that they wanted to become involved in the affairs

---

11   See Book I, ch. 2 above.

12   "Father-ships," *paternités*: Pasquier uses this honorific term several times, doubtlessly to mock the professed Jesuits who call themselves "father."

of state. They behaved just like Narses the Eunuch,[13] who was ordered by the empress to spin with his distaff. He replied that he would coil a skein so tightly that neither she nor her husband would be able to untangle it. He did just that, when he introduced the Lombards into Italy. These two good religious, distanced from the king's good graces, wanted to show him that they knew another craft than simply reciting the book of Our Lady's hours.

And really, I shall frankly admit that I've never met folks with better consciences than you Jesuits, who no longer fear encountering the censures of Rome. First of all, there was Father Henri Sammier (the most frolicsome man possible), who declared that, as early as 1580 or 1581, I'm not lying, he had been sent by you to various countries, in order to gather news about the general revolt that you wanted to stir up against the king of France.[14] And since I maintained that this was neither true nor plausible, because at the time you had no reason to do that, he told me that if I didn't want to believe him, I should look at the extraordinary trial of William Parry, Englishman, who was executed on March 3, 1584, and there I would find at the end of a letter he wrote to the queen while he was a prisoner: "She would find that the king of France was being prevented from acting, when they should be helping him." Parry (Sammier told me) left England in 1582 and came to France, where he was suborned by our brethren to kill the queen of England and to stir up her state. And he objected that it would be difficult to do this, inasmuch as she would be helped by the king of France. We replied that if we did as much hard work for that king, he would be sufficiently prevented, without working to rescue someone else. This shows you that, from that time on, our warp and woof were ready to be interwoven. At the time, I did not have the official records of the lawsuit; but since then, the letter having been brought to me, I read it; and I found that what Sammier had told me was true. In good faith, he carried on regardless, and he confessed that he and Ross were sent to the king of Spain in 1584, and that Father Claude Mathieu was sent to Pope Gregory XIII, to learn from them how much money they wanted to contribute to defray the Holy League. To this Ross added: But that master monk is not telling you that he gently gave

---

13   Narses the Eunuch (c.480–574) was a Romanized Armenian who spent most of his life as a eunuch in the palace of the emperors in Constantinople. He was also a general, putting down a rebellion in 532, fighting the Ostrogoths, and consolidating power in Italy. See *Encyclopaedia Britannica*, https://www.britannica.com/biography/Narses-Byzantine-general (accessed January 31, 2021). This story is almost certainly legendary.

14   See ch. 11 above.

me bad luck.[15] For one night, when we were running together to deliver the post, he noticed that I was weary from the road and had fallen into a deep slumber. He had some post-horses brought to him, and he left me in the bed as payment; and he was so diligent that he almost finished our entire negotiation with the king of Spain, before I could take it up again.

Now, in order to bring this lawsuit to perfection, I had someone bring me the pleas of Arnauld, the university's lawyer, and those of Dollé, the lawyer for the curates of Paris. The reply to it was in the name of the Collège de Clermont. I also had them bring me François des Montaignes's book, *La Vérité défendue*, which refutes Arnauld; and some other pieces used in the case. I trusted Sammier as far as his facts were concerned; but as for Father Claude Mathieu, I didn't want his memory to be overloaded with someone else's confession. By this means, I had access to the literal proof, and I read the plea where Arnauld attacks him with alacrity. And I read the response in your plea, which goes like this: "Now, Arnauld first says that Claude Mathieu, who belongs to the same religious order as the said defendants, was the author and inventor of the League. The said defendants reply that Claude Mathieu, who had spent his whole life in their colleges, and with children, and who had lived as a scholar, lacked the judgment, the solace, the industry, the authority needed to make and to keep together a League that is so great and strong. And they said that although the aforesaid Mathieu worked to fortify it, as many others did in numerous states, he was not the author of it. Add to this the fact that he is merely one individual." Then, five or six lines later: "In the beginning, not a one of them knew what the aforesaid Mathieu was doing: and even if they had known, they would not have known how to prevent it, since he was their superior." Combining Arnauld's objection and this cold solution, it seemed to me that you agreed that we are obliged to you for these last Troubles. And while I was keeping my religious order more amply informed about the revolt that had taken place in Paris on January 7, 1589, even in the Sorbonne, up came a troop of several theologians, persons of honor and reputation, who told me that they truly had been called together to resolve things, and that all the older theologians were taking the opposite position, but not the young ones, most of whom had been scholars of the Jesuits of Paris. So that once the votes were counted, but not weighed,[16] the plurality of voices was accepted. Nonetheless, they did

---

15   This clearly is word-play: *moine* (monk) and *le moine* (the monk). *Bailler le moine* (to give someone a monk) means to bring him bad luck.

16   That is, if all votes are considered equal, the winner is determined by the number of votes (or "voices"). Votes can, however be "weighed," making one person's vote "heavier" than the vote of another. For example, the vote of a wise man can be worth more than (and is heavier than) the vote of a fool.

not dash to the rebellion at top speed: they wanted to postpone the effect of their conclusion, until it had been confirmed by the Holy See. But the next day, Father Jacques Commolet, Jesuit, rang the tocsin in Paris.[17] And from the annual letters of the Jesuits for 1589, I was able to learn, if not everything, at least a part of the above, and from their plea too. I ran to look at those letters, and in the ones for your college in Paris, I found: *Doctores Sorbonici, quoram magna pars discipuli nostri fuere.*[18] And in your plea: "It is certain that, for several years now, a good share of the bachelors of theology have studied with us." This made me suspicious that this conclusion was a lesson that had been discussed in your college from time to time. In the same letter, I read that although Gregory XIII had prohibited your brethren from attending processions, as soon as the rebellion ended, one of your brethren, in order to stir up the populace against its king, gathered three or four thousand children, whom he led in a procession throughout the city, followed by all sorts of persons. I read elsewhere that you sneaked the confraternity of Our Lady into Lyon,[19] and the confraternity of the Penitents, also called the Hieronymites, into Bourges, not in order to appease God's anger, but to provoke it against the late king. And as I was thumbing through your missives, here came Father Jacques Commolet (to whom I give that honorable preface),[20] with tears in his eyes, as if he were someone who can do what he wants with his eyes, and he declared to me that the day after this conclusion, he preached at the church of Saint-Merri; that the entire Sorbonne wanted to take up arms against the king; and that if some persons were opposed to that, it should not be thought strange, because there was a Judas in the company of Jesus, the most accomplished person who ever was. And from then on, the blindfolded common people of Paris ran to take up arms. For which he frankly confessed his fault: he had maintained that this resolution had been postponed at the good pleasure and the arbitration of the Holy See. In addition, the most noteworthy seigneurs of the Parlement having been imprisoned in the Bastille on the fifteenth of that month,[21] he had come to console them the next day; and for their consolation, he had preached to them solely about the tyranny of King Henri III, in order to incite them to

---

17   The *tocsin* is a way of ringing bells very intensely and rapidly, in order to sound an alarm.

18   The doctors of Sorbonne, whose majority had been our students.

19   The statutes were written by Auger. See Sutto, 397n233.

20   Another bit of mockery about Jesuits who call themselves fathers.

21   On November 15, 1591, the Leaguer Sixteen, who governed Paris, arrested and executed First President of the Parlement Barnabé Brisson, along with Magistrates Claude Larcher and Jean Tardif du Roi, for plotting against their regime. See Élie Barnavi and Robert Descimon, *La Sainte Ligue, le juge et la potence: L'Assassinat du Président Brisson (15 novembre 1591)* (Paris: Hachette, 1985).

rebellion; and he said that the person who had been their king no longer was their king. In addition, he said that as long as the Troubles lasted, he was a trumpet in the churches to shred not only the reputation of the former king but also the reputation of the king currently reigning; but that he had done this in common with the other preachers, which made it excusable. Montaignes did not deny this: he blamed it on the preachers' anger, when they are in the pulpit. Something unpleasant whispered in my ear: Watch out. For, what he calls anger, he would willingly say is the Holy Spirit, but he doesn't dare. I replied that he was troublesome and should be quiet, if he could. Father Bernard Rouillet went a step farther than what Commolet said he had done in Paris, and he admitted that, by his plots and sermons, he had removed the city of Bourges from obedience to the king.[22] But above all, what greatly pleased me was the revelation of Father Alexander Hay,[23] who was guiding me on this matter. FATHER HAY. Magnificent Lord Pasquin, since you recant in God's name and by virtue of the apostolic censures, I shall tell you what I know, both about our college in Paris and about myself in particular. Concerning the general: I will not hide from you the fact that, when the Troubles first broke out, we created a confraternity in our college in Paris, and to honor Our Lady, we named it the Congregation; and for that reason, it was called the Congregation of the Rosary, because the members were expected to wear a rosary and recite it every day. The membership of this congregation included all the devoted and zealous souls of our Holy League: Lord Mendoza, the ambassador of the Catholic king of Spain,[24] the Sixteen of Paris,[25] all their families,[26] and several other holy persons whose names I did not put in a register, for that was not my job. Our congregation met every Sunday in an upper chapel; all members were obliged to attend, unless they had some excuse. There, each of us made his confession on Saturday and received Communion on Sunday. After Mass, one of our fathers would preach and exhort the entire company to remain firm in the holy devotion that today is known in France as the Rebellion; since that

---

22   Bernard Roillet. See ch. 11 above.

23   See ch. 2 and 16 above. Cf. Thomas M. McCoog, S.J., "'Pray to the Lord of the Harvest': Jesuit Missions to Scotland in the Sixteenth Century," *The Innes Review* 53 (2002): 127–88.

24   Bernardino de Mendoza (*c.*1540–1604), Philip II's ambassador to France. See Jensen De Lamar, *Diplomacy and Dogmatism: Bernardino De Mendoza and the French Catholic League* (Cambridge, MA: Harvard University Press, 1964).

25   See Robert Descimon, *Qui étaient les Seize?: Mythes et réalités de la Ligue Parisienne (1585–1594)* (Paris: Mémoires des Sociétés historiques et archéologiques de Paris et de L'Ilede-France, 1983).

26   A reminder: *familles* (families) may well denote not only family members related by blood and marriage, but also their domestic servants. And Pasquier repeatedly treats the Jesuits as belonging to a "family," that is, a household.

name also pleases magistrates, I don't oppose it. After that, all the common people would leave, and the loftiest persons and the ones with the greatest authority would remain there, in order to work out the affairs of the Holy League. For a long time, Father Odon Pigenat presided there.[27] There, in a few words, you have what I can reveal to you about the general actions of our college. For as far as I myself am concerned, you should know that those who know me, call me Father Alexander Hay, Scot. For three or four years, during the Troubles, I taught the oldest students in our college; and to string together for you not everything, but a few noteworthy actions of my history, which will perhaps enlighten you about the other actions, I read to my students the invectives of Demosthenes against King Philip of Macedon.[28] In this I scarcely concurred with our good Father Commolet: for he, in churches, talked to his advantage about all the passages of the Old Testament that were against the Béarnais[29] (allow me to use that word in your Highness's presence, as we used to do in Paris). And so, I say Fy to those Philippics, which, I can tell you, were not so much school lessons as atrocious swearing at him, and which I enriched as I was ordered to do by a violent devotion on which I can never apply the brake. For I usually taught that a person who could kill him would be very happy; and that if he died while carrying out such a devout undertaking, he would go straight to paradise; and if his soul was sullied by some venial sins, he would nonetheless be exempted from the punishments of purgatory. And if God was afflicting Paris that much, let the Béarnais enter the city and pass through the Saint-Jacques gate. I swore publicly that I would throw myself from the highest window of our college, down onto him. On the day when the king first heard Mass at Saint-Denis, knowing that some of my scholars had been there, I chased them out of my class the next day, as if they had been excommunicated, and I forbade them to come back in until they had been absolved by one of our fathers. When people talked about peace, I ordered one of my scholars, who was far more advanced in literature than the others, to prepare to declaim in Greek on the subject of the miseries of France, and to deplore future calamities. It was self-evident that the declamation would sink all on its own. (As I told you, it was conference time, and each member of one party or the other was living only to see the parties reunited.)

---

27   See ch. 11 above.

28   He is referring to the *Philippics*, which date from 351–40 BCE. A philippic is a fiery, damning speech or tirade, delivered to condemn a particular political actor. The term is associated with Demosthenes of Athens (384–322 BCE), who opposed the imperialist ambitions of Philip of Macedon (382–336 BCE).

29   Pasquier wrote *le Biarnois*, which can only refer to Henri IV, native of the Béarn region. The epithet explicitly refuses to recognize him as king of France.

The scholar, without amusing himself with the specific points that I had told him to make, proposed to present only the broad subject: the wretchedness of France. He did his declaiming and began by talking about the misfortunes and miseries that the state was enduring as a result of the subjects' rebellion and disobedience, and that this was the chasm into which God permitted a people to fall when, after great patience, it wanted to experience iniquities that were not punished, and for which the people had long suffered. This scholar of mine showed that a prince's bad manners could not dispense his subjects from obeying him as they should. Something he proved by an infinity of examples, even though he had scorned everyone who had become convinced of the contrary. Seeing that he was not following the paths he had been given, and that he had chosen a different way, I lost patience with him and made him get out of the speaker's chair. I said several injurious things, calling him accursed and a heretic. When classes resumed after the surrender of the city of Paris to the man from Béarn, on that opening day, I saw one of my scholars, who had come to the college ahead of time. He wrote all over the classroom *Vive le Roi.* Long live the King. And as soon as I came in and saw this indignity, my anger turned to fury; and with a very rough voice, if not a frightening one, I began to say: *Qui ita infecit nostros parietes*?[30] And I said that if I learned who had written those fine scribbles (that's the very word I used), I would have him whipped by the president of the college and would have the scribbles erased that afternoon. I said that if someone came to smear the walls that way, I would make him feel just how disagreeable it was to me. I am telling you, magnificent Lord Pasquin, exactly what I did, and I am not at all afraid to tell you, for I am in this city of Rome, and I am not a subject of the Béarnais, because I am a born Scot. Even if I had been born French, I would still think that I should be pardoned for all this malevolence. For I have always had such a good conscience that, when I played games with my companions or others, I never did it for the money, but simply for *Pater noster's* and *Ave Maria's.*[31] And believe me, this merit toward God protected me from the Parlement of Paris, from which I was at some risk. And I can tell you that if my body or my spirit had been tortured, my body by questioning, or my spirit by ecclesiastical censures, I would have been done for.

PASQUIN. That is what I learned from Father Alexander [Hay], whom I found to be an Alexander the great among you other Jesuits, that is to say, a prince who can't be conquered. And after listening to him, I amused myself by making literal proofs. From your plea, I learned several things that seemed very unfavorable for you. For Arnauld and Dollé reproached your college in Paris as

---

30   "Who betrayed our walls thus?"
31   In other words, the loser would recite specific prayers for the winner.

being the Spanish meeting place, to debate together the business of the Holy Union. By your prohibitions, you are admitting that Ambassador Mendoza would come there on every feast day to hear Mass, and that you subsequently begged them to abstain, in order to remove all suspicion. That excuse seemed very vain to me: for one shouldn't beg someone to abstain from doing something that is honored at the time, if one believes what is commonly said. Also, the parties that were your adversaries objected to the fact that Odon Pigenat had been the captain of the Sixteen and had commanded in Paris, not only ordering ordinary magistrates around, but ordering the sovereign around. You agree with that: it is in both your plea and in Montaignes's book. True, you say that this was supposed to bring some soberness to their actions. While reading these two passages, each of us began to laugh, for we knew that although Pigenat was not in any way wise, he burned with fire and anger: and indeed, he since has become so odd that he is kept in a room, bound and gagged. In that same plea, I found this sentence: "They think the city of Paris is obligated to them, because during all the Troubles they never ceased teaching young people, there being at the time no other college in the university than theirs that was fully functioning." "Do you want me to tell you why?", asked a respected person. The principals of the other colleges had lowered their hands and, in their souls, were deploring the calamity that was causing the rebellion; but these principals were lifting their hands to heaven, as people do when they think they have obtained some victory in an undertaking. But above all, I found strange the letter that was sent to Spain: the bearer was Father Mathieu, the Jesuit, but it was intercepted by Sieur de Chazeron,[32] the governor of the Bourbonnais region. This letter was placed in my hands. This is its tenor:

> Sire, vostre Catholique Majesté nous ayant esté tant benigne, que de nous avoir fait entendre par le tres-religieux et reverend pere Mathieu, non seulement ses sainctes intentions au fait general de la Religion, mais particulierement ses bonnes affections et faveurs envers cette Cité de Paris.[33] And later: Nous esperons en brief que les armes de sa Saincteté, et de vostre Catholique Majesté jointes, nous delivreront de l'oppression de nostre ennemi, lequel nous a jusques à present et depuis un an et demi bloqué de

---

32   Gilbert de Chazeron (c.1550–1614), the king's lieutenant in the Bourbonnais region and a councilor of state, rallied to the cause of Henri IV in 1589. See Pierre-Germain Aigueperse, *Biographie ou dictionnaire historique des personnages d'Auvergne avec portraits*, 2 vols. (Clermont-Ferrand: Thibaud-Landriot, 1834), 1:173.

33   "Sire, your Catholic Majesty having been so kind as to have made us listen to the very religious and reverend Father Mathieu, not only his holy intentions on the general subject of Religion, but especially his good affections and favors toward this city of Paris."

toutes parts, sans que rien puisse entrer en cette Cité, que par hazard, ou
avecques la force des armes, et s'efforceroit de passer outre, s'il ne redoutoit
les garnisons qu'il a pleu à vostre Catholique, que les voeux et souhaits de
tous les Catholics sont DE VOIR VOSTRE CATHOLIQUE MAJESTE tenir
le Sceptre de cette Couronne, et regner sur nous, comme nous nous jettons
tresvolontiers entre ses bras, ainsi que de nostre Pere.[34] I won't give you
the rest of the letter, for you know it all too well: it talks of the marriage
with the Infanta. And lower, and to the side, is: *Le Reverend pere Mathieu*
present porteur, lequel nous a beaucoup edifies, bien instruit de nos affaires,
supplera au defaut de nos lettres envers vostre Majesté Catholique, laquelle
nous supplions humblement adjouter foy à ce qu'il en raportera.[35]

This letter stung me infinitely as far as your justifications are concerned, and I
wanted to see the reply you were making in your plea. *"Tenth* (said Arnauld) for
the year 1591. Monsieur de Chazeron intercepted letters to the king of Spain, to
ask for his daughter's hand, carried by Father Mathieu of the order of the said
defendants. They reply, having been corrected by the courts, that Arnauld is
misinformed. For the said Father Mathieu had died three years earlier at
Ancona in Italy, that is to say in 1588; and consequently, unless there is a greater
miracle than Saint Denis's miracle he cannot go back and forth to Spain. Then
he adds that this Mathieu was a Spanish Franciscan, in one of the four mendicant orders." I see that Montaignes gave a similar reply to one of the principal
persons of your order. This made me cry out against Arnauld: Oh, the unique
impudence of a lawyer, toward an innocent family! But someone near me
stopped me cold and said: Magnificent Signor Pasquin, run along softly, I pray
you. If there is any impudence, it comes from the Jesuits, or from their lack of
common sense. For Arnauld was very careful to say that Father Claude Mathieu
was not the bearer, it was another Jesuit whose name was similar to Father
Mathieu's. Let's read his plea: "When King Philip (he said) had admitted to his

---

34   "Briefly, we hope that the weapons of His Holiness and those of your Catholic Majesty,
      together, will deliver us from the oppression of our enemy, who up to the present and for
      a year and one-half, has blocked us on all sides, so that nothing can enter this City other
      than by chance, or by military force; and would try to assault it if it weren't for fear of the
      garrisons that it has pleased your Catholic Majesty to order for us. We can certainly assure
      your Catholic [Majesty] that the vows and wishes of every Catholic are TO SEE YOUR
      CATHOLIC MAJESTY hold the scepter of this crown, and to reign over us, as we very will-
      ingly throw ourselves into his arms, as with our father."

35   "Reverend Father Mathieu, the present bearer, who has been greatly edifying and who
      knows our affairs, will stand in the stead of our letters to your Catholic Majesty, whom
      we humbly beg to have faith in what he reports." Sutto, 401n246, points out that Claude
      Mathieu died in 1587, so this must refer to a Spanish monk.

Spanish garrison in Paris persons of the Jesuit persuasion and wanted a colorful title for what he was already holding by force, whom did he send if not Father Mathieu, the Jesuit, whose name was very similar to the name of the other Jesuit named Mathieu, who was the League's principal instrument in 1583? During the few days that this Mathieu stayed in this city, lodged in the college of the Jesuits, he had the letter written and signed there."[36] Just look (said this someone who was rejoicing despite me), just look at the inept sophistry of these messieurs. For in their plea to Arnauld, they make him say something that he never thought, but in fine terms they drew a distinction between the two Mathieus. So, claiming that it was a Spanish Franciscan named Mathieu is less plausible: because the four mendicant orders are not called fathers but brothers, and still less likely is the title reverends. Now, in that letter, the bearer is called Reverend Father Mathieu. Which clearly points out that since the letter was written in the name of the Sixteen *Anarques*[37] and Tyrants of Paris, of which Pigenat was the principal overseer, it came from the Jesuits' boutique, and they are the ones who composed it, just as they were its bearers. If you link the date of the letter, which is November 2, 1591, and the brutal cruelty that the Sixteen were exercising that same month, against the person who at the time was the head of the Parlement of Paris and two other noteworthy seigneurs[38] who were immediately captured and hanged, you will find that there is nothing in this whole negotiation that is not Jesuit. If all these learned documents and oral confessions do not content you, then read René de La Fon's book. There you will find that he admits that the Jesuits were the causes and reasons behind our recent Troubles, and the general ruination of all France. But inasmuch as this placard is very important to the subject under discussion, know that in two or three places in his plea, Pasquier said that if the Jesuit sect took root in France, it would produce a hot-bed of divisions between Christians and Catholics; and at the end of his plea,

---

36   See *Plaidoyé de M. Antoine Arnauld*, 16–17.

37   In French, *-arque* denotes a person of authority. That person can be a *monarque*, "monarch," that is, a "single ruler," (*mono-*). *Anarque*, "anarch," would therefore denote a person who rules over a state of anarchy. *Anarque* does not appear in DAF 1694. Related words do, however, appear in Cotgrave (1611): *anarche* was an adjective that describes something "without kingdome or command, without Prince, unruled"; the noun *Anarchie* denoted "an Anarchie; a commonwealth without a head; a confused state where one is as good as another; a want of government"; and the adjective *Anarchique*, meant "belonging to an Anarchie."

38   Claude Larcher (*c.*1521–91), counselor in the Grand Council, was captured by the League, taken to a courtroom, and hanged; Jean Tardif (?–1591), counselor at the Châtelet of Paris, met the same fate. See Mark Greengrass, *France in the Age of Henri IV: The Struggle for Stability* (London: Taylor & Francis, 2013), passim.

he protested that if this misfortune were to take place, the survivors would recognize that this century had not lacked men who, long in advance, foresaw the coming storm as from a lighthouse. In 1597, Monsieur Marion, *avocat du roi* in the Parlement of Paris, was pleading a case and added these words: "In which one can see a notable example of the two portents that God, when it pleases him, inspires in those he loves. The famous case judged thirty and more years ago, about the reception, not of their order, which was never approved in France, but of their college into the corps and privileges of the university, the wisest of that time, truly excellent when it comes to conjecturing the affairs of the world. It foresaw that, over time, they will light the torch of discord in the middle of the kingdom."[39] La Fon the Jesuit, thinking that this was a reference to Pasquier's plea, wanted to reply in such a fine fashion that I would very much regret not providing it for you here. "But who (he said) are the divine diviners who prophesized so well, so adroitly, and so appropriately about the Jesuits? Can we not prophesize about their names and their prophecies, even though the enthusiasm of these inspired spirits does not puff out our chests? Is Pasquier not one of them? And Marion, by the prophecies that he puts forth, does he not mark those that stand out as being by Pasquier? If my guess is right, Pasquier's plea turned me into a prophet. That plea, which was hidden for thirty years and was dug out three years ago, like an old idol loaded down with new placards, like a ridiculous Pasquin, spoke and prophesized backwards: what he did not know, or had not dared to say in 1564, came back from hell in 1594 and 1595; and, better informed about things that would happen in the future, he stated them like an oracle on a three-legged stool,[40] and I learned them from him. But the trouble will begin one day, when the plea is produced in its original form, in order to uncover the new postings attached to this plastered-up Pasquin; and on his back they will place the remuneration for his predictions." Oh! Great and worthy person! Who merits a statue placed in the central court of all their colleges, for having so bravely, not overwhelmed, but harassed the old enemy of their order. Has a man ever played with his pen and his spirit more appropriately? But I am not disappointed that, by attacking that poor old man with such courageous boasting, he is implying that he reworked his plea in 1594 and wrote a sort of prophecy about the things he had seen

---

39   Simon Marion, *Plaidoyez de Messire Simon Marion, Baron de Druy, cy-devant advocat en Parlement*, dernière édition (Paris: Pierre le Mur, 1629), 481–82.

40   At Delphi, various sybils (or Pythia) advised generals, kings, and commoners who came to ask questions. The Pythia sat on a three-legged stool, over a fissure in the ground from which vapors rose. These sweet-smelling vapors were known to produce visions and an exalted state of mind. See *Encyclopaedia Britannica*, https://www.britannica.com/topic/Pythia (accessed January 31, 2021).

happening in France since 1564. This upright man therefore admitted that all
the misfortunes of France come from the Jesuits. For that was the goal of
Pasquier's plea. As for me, I also realized that the Holy Spirit wanted to talk
through the mouth of that Jesuit. Oh! How great is the force of a Truth! It must
of necessity burst, no matter what artifices, pretenses, palliatives, hypocrisies,
and curtainings we use in order to disguise it. What, then, is more necessary
than you, great and venerable Pasquin, your spirit distilled by such diverse
researches, in order to know whether they were the authors and the guides of
our Troubles? Only this sole confession is needed, and it cannot be disavowed
by the general or the other superiors of that order, their *ordonnance* being that
way in the eighteenth article of the third part of their Constitutions: *Libri edi
non poterunt in lucem sine approbatione atque consensu praepositi Generalis,
qui eorum examinationem tribus committat.*[41] Do not think that, for something
of such great consequence, all the Jesuit books produced and in your possession were exposed to the light without the authorization and the statement of
their general, or of other superiors named by him to that end. Yet let us not
take as very truthful all their confessions concerning the Troubles, and especially the confession of René de La Fon. I thought so (I replied to this prattler),
yet I am not proud of it; but I am proud that this master-fool La Fon, coming
upon two names, compared Pasquier and Pasquin. All the more so since I do
not think there is a man alive, whoever he may be, who can compare him with
My-Highness-Me. You are telling the truth (the other replied), but if you know
who this Pasquier is, you will not be distressed: for the Jesuits fear him more
than they love him. And indeed, this is how I, Pasquin, behaved, in order to
shine some light on the first item in your accusation, which involves the recent
Troubles of France. The second item remains: it has to do with the attempted
assassinations, and the assassins, of kings, princes, and great seigneurs, who do
not favor your opinions. Now, just as I was about to examine this, one of your
agents brought me a book by Petrus Mathaeus, one of your agents, in his book
titled *Summa [constitutionum] summorum pontificum.*[42] Speaking about you
other messieurs with full honor and respect, he said: *Tyrannos aggrediuntur.*[43]
Some said that he said it out of hatred for the late King Henri III, who was
killed in 1589, which is the date when the book was first printed, at Lyon: and
your adversaries maintained that these words had been intentionally added

---

41   "And it will not be permissible to publish books without the approval and permission of
      the superior general, who will entrust the examination of them to at least three persons
      of sound doctrine and clear judgment about the field in question."
42   See ch. 9 above.
43   "They attack tyrants."

after the parricide of that king, whom you others were accustomed to call
Tyrant. On the other hand, your companions maintained in their plea, and by
Montaignes's book, that Mathaeus was not one of your brethren, so he could
not do something prejudicial to you. By that little stirrup in the human ear, I,
Pasquin, ordered Signor Marforio[44] to look over these pieces summarily and
immediately, and to give me a faithful report. He reported to me that, in truth,
Mathaeus was not a member of the Jesuit order, although he favored them all
out of proportion, whenever he talked about them. But that it was difficult to
judge whether his book had been printed before or after the death of King
Henri III. It's all one and the same (someone replied), for when praising them
for having waged war against the Tyrants, he meant either the beginning of the
Troubles, which at the time had broken out against that good king, or the murder that had been done to his person. Be it the one, or be it the other, they
could not offer an excuse, for they were praised for this beyond all measure, by
the person who had welcomed them so favorably in his book. In addition, the
Jesuits of Bordeaux were never willing to pray to God for the late king.
Montaignes agrees. And to show you that this Mathaeus supports only the general proposition of the Jesuits, I refer you to the *Aphorisms of Confession* by
their Father Emmanuel Sà, doctor of theology of their Society,[45] who, under
the heading "Princeps," maintains that a king can be deprived of his states by
his own people, if he does not do his duty. And under the heading "Tyrannus,"
he maintains that the prince who governs himself tyrannically, can be chased
away by his people, even if he has sworn perpetual obedience and fealty, if,
having been admonished, he does not wish to correct his actions. Submitting
all sovereign princes in this way to their abusive confessions, in order to make
idiots understand: idiots who behave uprightly in their positions, and the others who, not acting that way, can be forsaken. This proposition refers to the
proposition of *Mathaeus*, which they have since disavowed.

I have certainly not failed to whisper in your ear about the investigation of
you that was being pored over during this trial. Indeed, I can tell you that you
had some brave champions who have very effectively responded to the blows.

While this was going on, from various countries I was sent information
about special lawsuits against one person or another who had, at the Jesuits'

---

44   Marphurius, or Marforio, the river god, is one of the seven talking statues of Rome. He
      maintained a friendly rivalry with his most notable rival, Pasquin. Like Pasquin, Marforio
      was covered with satiric poetry poking fun at public figures. See Christopher J. Gilbert, "If
      This Statue Could Talk: Statuary Satire in the Pasquinade Tradition," *Rhetoric and Public
      Affairs* 18, no. 1 (2015): 79–112, https://doi.org/10.14321/rhetpublaffa.18.1.0079 (accessed
      January 31, 2021).

45   See Book II, ch. 19 above.

instigation, made an attempt, or wanted to make an attempt on the lives of princes: in England, the attempt by William Parry in 1584 and by Edward Squire in 1597.[46] In the Low Countries, the attempt by Balthasar Gérard in 1584,[47] and by Pierre Panne in 1598.[48] In France, the attempt by Pierre Barrière in 1593, and Jean Châtel in 1594.[49] Above all, I paused for a long time at the trial of Pierre Barrière, where I could see that the entire Jesuit order was extremely involved, especially Father Varade and Father Commolet. After that, came an infinity of young folks who, in order to unburden their consciences, declared that when they were scholars at the college of the Jesuits, they were continually being preached to about something else: the murder of the *Béarnais* (that's what they called the king of France now reigning). I finally cast an eye over Châtel's trial, which confirmed very amply everything that these young people had told me. For he was questioned by the court of the Parlement of Paris, about the assassination that he wanted to commit upon his king. Here the very words of his interrogation and his replies:

> "Inquired where he had learned this new theology? (which involved killing kings). Said he learned it by philosophy."
>
> "Questioned whether he had studied philosophy at the college of the Jesuits? Said Yes, and he did it under Father Gueret, with whom he was for two and one half years."
>
> "Inquired whether he had been in the Meditations Chamber, where the Jesuits place the greatest sinners, who saw in that chamber the portraits of several devils with diverse and frightful images, on the pretext of reducing them to a better life, in order to shake their spirits and push them, by that sort of admonition, to do some great thing? Said he had often been in that Meditations Chamber."
>
> "Inquired who had convinced him to kill the king? Said he had heard it in several places, that it must be considered a true maxim, that it was legal to kill the king, and that those who said that called him Tyrant."
>
> "Inquired whether the statements about killing the king were usual among the Jesuits? Said he had heard them say that it was legal to kill kings, and that he was outside the church and should not be obeyed, nor considered to be king, until the pope had absolved him."

---

46   See ch. 3 above.
47   See ch. 1 above.
48   See ch. 1 above.
49   See ch. 2 above.

"Once again questioned in the Great Chamber of the Parlement by messieurs the presidents and counselors of that chamber, and by the Tournelle, assembled, he gave the same replies, and notably he proposed and upheld the maxim that it was legal to kill kings, even the king who is reigning, who did not belong to the church, as he so stated, because he was not approved by the pope."

In truth, I see that this poor person, badly advised, does not point to any of your brethren who taught him that damnable lesson, but he pardons your order generally. And since I was amazed at that, this overseer of your actions, who was near me, said that one should not think it strange: all the more so because the Jesuits' lesson was a double one, when it came to having some prince assassinated. The first lesson was to promise a very sure paradise to the person who could carry out this masterpiece, and that he had to be killed inside a church, during divine services. The second lesson was that if the person committing the act was taken by surprise and placed into the magistrate's hands, in order to serve as an example, one ought, above all else, take care to avoid uncovering and revealing the names of those who had put him to work, on penalty of eternal damnation. And indeed, during Barrière's trial they found that these instructions had been given to him. True, not having been nurtured at the Jesuits' school, as Châtel was, he did not bring them up before his judges.

Having studied this trial, I looked over the trial of Robert Bruce, the Scots gentleman, who was denounced by Father William Crichton, Jesuit, for having been unwilling to assassinate Maitland, chancellor of the king of Scotland.[50] I learned the sources of all these Machiavelisms or Anabaptisms. Upon so doing, I was given your Constitutions, which order you to pay blind obedience to your superiors, and to follow their orders without backing off, as if the orders had come from the mouth of Jesus Christ. All together, they brought me the *Aphorisms of Confession* by your Emmanuel Sà, and also a book written by the principal of the seminary of Reims, by which they maintain that, in certain cases, subjects are permitted to kill their kings. And especially the book by Father Jean Guignard, one of our priests,[51] where he tried to prove not only that the late King Henri III, recently deceased, had been justly killed, but also that the same thing should be done to the king now reigning. His book states it in this manner: "That cruel Nero was killed by a person named Clément, and the pretend monk was dispatched by the hand of a real monk. This heroic act by Jacques Clément, as a gift from the Holy Spirit, called by

---

50   See ch. 1 and 2 above.
51   See ch. 18 above.

that name by our theologians, is rightly praised by Bourgoing, the prior of the Jacobins, a confessor and martyr.[52] The crown of France can and should be transferred to another family than the Bourbons: and the Béarnais, once he has converted to the Catholic faith, will be treated more gently than he deserves, if he is given the monkly crown in some nicely reformed monastery, so that he can do penance for all the ills he has wrought in France, and can thank God for giving him the grace to realize it before dying. And if he cannot be deposed without war, let them kill him." Those are the words in the book: not only are they scandalous, I dare say they are blasphemous, sprinkled with an infinity of other such words. Finally, I very diligently read your request to the king, which is full of fine little flourishes by which you condemn all these assassination attempts, as being forbidden by all laws, both divine and human. And as I was tormenting my spirit about these documents and wanted to get wrapped up in the decree of the Parlement of Paris, issued not only against Châtel but also against your Society, someone said to me: Remember that despite this decree, the old dice game of rebellion has remained imprinted on their souls. So, you shall see a Montaignes, Jesuit, celebrate a Jacques Commolet, a Claude Mathieu, a Hannibal du Coudret,[53] a Bernard Rouillet,[54] an Ambroise Varade.[55] And after Montaignes, comes his Monkey-La-Fon, who has made several others gamble, and who is notorious for having been a past master at teaching how to murder and stir seditions.

You shall see the *Book of Miracles* written by Richeome, their general for Aquitaine,[56] in which, among other things, he says that Our Lady of Le Puy worked several miracles during the Troubles, in order to preserve the city from its enemies, that is to say, from the king. For this city belonged to the other party. But as for the miracles that Saint Genevieve worked for the king, he is very careful not to discuss them. And yet they are very clear in three cases. The first was when the League wanted to go to Dieppe, and her reliquary was taken out; the second, when the Chevalier d'Aumale, on the night of the Feast

---

52   Edmond Bourgoing (?–1590) had a doctorate from the Faculty of Theology of Paris. He was the prior of the Dominicans of Paris and a renowned preacher in Nantes. He was executed in Tours. See Robert Harding, "Revolution and Reform in the Holy League: Angers, Rennes, Nantes," *The Journal of Modern History* 53, no. 3 (1981): 380–416, here 410–11.

53   See ch. 3 above.

54   See ch. 11 above.

55   See ch. 5 above.

56   Pasquier is mistaken. Perhaps he equated having books published at Bordeaux in 1599 (*Trois discours pour la religion catholique*) with being the "general" (the provincial?) for that province. Richeome was superior provincial of Lyon and assistant general to Acquaviva. See Book I, ch. 5.

of Saint Genevieve, attacked the city of Saint-Denis;[57] and the third, when the
reliquary was again taken out in May 1594, and a general procession was held
in order to oppose the king's forces. Nevertheless, all these vows, prayers, and
plans did about-faces, to the confusion of his enemies. For the king obtained a
great and unhoped-for victory near Dieppe: the Chevalier d'Aumale was killed
inside Saint-Denis, when he thought he had captured the city and his entire
company retreated. And finally, Paris was returned to the king two or three
days after the second display of the reliquary. Saint Genevieve is the tutelary
saint of Paris: the city of Paris belonged legitimately to the king, and he was
miraculously conserved by it in these three instances. Miracles that Richeome,
the great teller of tales, has been careful not to recount. It would be on his conscience, since it is in favor of the king. Moreover, see how Montaignes, in his
book called *La Verité défendue*, maintains that the pope can transfer kingdoms
from one hand to the other. A good and plausible proposition here in Rome,
but a scandalous one in France, even subject to corporal punishment. These
three books were printed after the decree of the Parlement. And from them
you learn of what the Jesuits' devotion for their king consists.

   All of that was communicated to me; and to tell the truth, the greater part
of these proofs come from your colleges. A very thorough inventory compiled
both for you and against you. I did not want to believe all on my own, so I
thought this lawsuit should be judged by others, along with me, others who
had long experience, and who were knowledgeable about such matters. Signor
Marforio was of the opinion that two great personages of France, should be
begged to join: Master Pierre de Cugnières,[58] who long ago had his seat and
jurisdiction in the diocese of Paris; and another person who, because he had
vowed perpetual mendicancy, lodged very long ago in front of the Hôtel-Dieu
hospital of Paris and who, owing to the strange austerity of his life, was called

---

57   Claude (1564–91), known as Chevalier d'Aumale, was the son of Claude de Lorraine, duke
      d'Aumale (1526–73). As the governor of Paris, he led the attack of the Leaguers against
      the royal forces camping at Saint-Denis on January 3, 1591 (feast of St. Genevieve), during
      which he was killed. See Book I, ch. 1 above.

58   Pierre de Cugnières (?–c.1355), also called Pierre de Coignet, was a jurist, a member of the
      king's council, a lawyer in the Parlement of Paris, and finally a president in the Chamber
      of Accounts (where Pasquier was the *avocat general*). He represented King Philip VI in
      disputes against the clergy and, at least according to legend, had caricatures of his face
      sculpted in various churches around France by way of clerical reprisal. Cotgrave, under
      his entry "Pierre du Coignet," says that it is "a Monkie-like Image of stone in our Ladies
      Church [Notre-Dame] at Paris, where it was a first set up, to the disgrace of that name, a
      great adversary unto the Clergie." See Liana Nissim and Alessandra Preda, eds., *Les lieux
      de l'Enfer dans les lettres françaises: Convegno internazionale di studi. Gargnano, Palazzo
      Feltrinelli 12–15 giugno 2013* (Milan: LED Edizioni Universitarie, 2014), 68.

the Abstainer.[59] I am writing them, and at my summons they arrive. I distribute the lawsuit to Signor Marforio, who looks at it with extreme diligence. We name a date for the judgment. Assembled as we are, I told the group that the pyramid was offending you tremendously, for it was a memorial and recalls forever what had gone on in France. I told them that it was a question of reestablishing you Jesuits, and at the same time knocking down that pyramid. For this reason, I begged them to cast off every passion, because our verdict would be solemnized forever by posterity. Marforio reports on this lawsuit very accurately, showing very clearly that he was not trained in this craft. And having read all the pieces, and seesawed back and forth, he finally wanted to be the first to give an opinion, as is customary for those who report on a lawsuit. I beg you, Signor Marforio, (I said to him) don't go any farther: let us honor our new guests. It is a question of suing a stone, and it seems to me that this honor really goes to Master Pierre, whom I beg to be willing to give his opinion first, and to remember that it is a question of reestablishing this great order of the Society of Jesus, which is so highly respected in Rome. Master Pierre did not have to be begged for very long: for he immediately stood up and said in a surly voice:

MASTER PIERRE. How long will these detestable hypocrites keep abusing our patience without being punished?[60] What? First the Jesuit was the firebrand of our recent Troubles, then his college in Paris was the firebrand, the general place for those who, speaking with deliberation, entered our France in order to get the upper hand: its classes, its trumpeting to scholars, to teach them about the parricides of kings, and about how his principal ministers have put weapons in the hands of several desperate souls, in order to assassinate our king. May they be so impudent today as to ask to be reestablished. That is to say, by oblique and indirect paths, to conduct the trial of this holy court of the Parlement of Paris, which was not, and never shall be blamed for the decrees it issues, if not that, as much as this sect is condemned, it never sent to the gibbet all its sidekicks who were in Paris. Because, for far fewer reasons, this great and venerable antique Senate of Rome condemned six hundred slaves to death for having killed their master in his own house, without knowing who did it. Master Pierre de Cugnières wanted to continue making his point, but I, Pasquin, stopped him short.

---

59   In the square before Notre-Dame, and near the entry door of the Hôtel Dieu hospital, there was a very old and massive statue of Aesculapius, the god of medicine. In one hand he held a book, and in the other a stick with a coiled serpent. The common people jokingly called him Master Pierre the Abstainer.

60   This is an imitation of the first sentence of Cicero's *Catiline Orations*: *Quo usque tandem abutere, Catilina, patientia nostra?*

PASQUIN. Come now, Master Pierre, come now. Little folk like you are usually angry. Remember that you aren't a lawyer in this trial, you're a judge. Master Pierre, who realized that he had failed, for this reason changed his tone.

MASTER PIERRE. Magnificent Signor Pasquin (he said to me), I humbly beg your Excellency to excuse the just anguish I feel for my country. Or, since it pleases you to honor me so greatly, letting me give my opinion first, I shall say, before going any farther, that this case is naturally in your jurisdiction: for wherever I turn, I see only stones.[61] Your Excellency, Signor Marforio, the venerable Abstainer, and I, we are stones. The pyramid is a stone, and even the Jesuits who want to be reestablished, are indubitably mad and innocent or, to be more accurate, they are real stones. Be that as it may, they lack the sense that stones have, insisting that the decree against them be retracted. No decree ever was more juridical than that one. And even if it were not, it can only be retracted by the usual legal pathways, which they are not taking. And even if they were to disregard all the essential formalities of the courts, people would want to put them back into the same state as before. So, what can they hope for from their trial, if not something worse? The only witnesses they need are the walls, to show that the French people have worn the hair shirt, carried the beggar's wallet, and done the penance for their misconduct, and that they have done so for five years. I push all the other proofs to the side. I am only having recourse to their books in order to condemn them. Antiquity teaches us that Mercury changed the shepherd Battus into a stone, owing to something perfidious that he had done:

> *Et me mihi perfidis prodis*
> *Me mihi prodis, ait, perivraque pectora vertit*
> *In durum silicem, qui nunc quoque dicitur*
> *Index.*[62]

Never has a Society been as perfidious as the Society of the Jesuits, against the king and against France. Pretending to favor them, Mercury sometimes plays with their pens, and even makes them repeat things uselessly. Having noticed their treachery, he wants all their books to be like the seeds of that stone *Index*,

---

61   Indeed, all the participants in this conversation are stones: that is, Marforio, Pasquin, and the Abstainer are all made stone (*pierre*), and Pierre is the baptismal name of both Cugnières and the Abstainer.

62   Ovid, *Metamorphoses*, II, 676–707: "'Liar, will you betray me to myself, telling me things to inform against me?' And he changed the perjured chest of Battus to solid flint, which is called, even now, the touchstone, and this old disgrace is linked to stone that has not merited the slur."

being the true indices and sure testimonies of their wickedness. I would be taking advantage of the time and of your leisure, if I strung them out, document by document. I shall be content to tell you that the things related to the Jesuits must be declared inadmissible. And to that end, I employ the decree that the Jesuit author[63] of the Very Humble Remonstrance and Request directed against his order. But as far as the general aspects of the case are concerned, since you are the sovereign of sovereigns on extraordinary matters, owing to an ancient privilege, I am of the opinion that you should use your absolute power, and add the following tail to the decree: Firstly, their house and their college shall be razed to the ground, just as the palace of the Bentivoglios,[64] formerly at Bologna la Grassa, was torn down, and only the ruins remain, known as *Il Guasto dei Bentivoglio*. Secondly, each and every one of the temporal possessions of the French Jesuits shall be sold, and the profits shall be used to buy back the royal domain that our king was forced to alienate in order to pay for the costs of the Troubles, of which the Jesuits were the authors.

Hearing this, we all began to act as if we were flabbergasted. For Master Pierre had understood the case in a totally different way than we had hoped, and a little murmur arose among us about that sale of property. MASTER PIERRE. Do not be astonished at my proposition. If you were raised in the law, as I was, this would not seem strange to you. Their possessions in France are under consideration, or their monasteries that they call houses, or their colleges. In the first case, they cannot sell, for their statutes prohibit it. In the second case, even less, because they have never been received and approved in France as true and legitimate colleges, capable of receiving legacies and alms, if not for everything they promised at the assembly of Poissy of 1561,[65] that is, to renounce all their vows and, like all the other colleges, reduce themselves to obeying their *ordinaires*. They have not yet done this, or they are not willing to do so. Consequently, we cannot and should not call them colleges. Now, if you look through the common and antique laws of the Romans, which we ought carefully to embrace, you will see that when the common law of a country does not contradict, when a will gives some property to a college, the legacy is good and valid, as long as the college is approved by the magistrate; but if it is not approved, the legacy must be converted in favor of another college, an approved one. The adjournment in 1564 kept the title

---

63   That is, Louis Richeome.

64   The palace of the Bentivoglios, tyrants of Bologna (the city is still nicknamed la Grassa, "the fat"), in Italy, was destroyed by a mob in 1507. The ruins were known as the *guasto*. See William E. Wallace, "The Bentivoglio Palace Lost and Reconstructed," *The Sixteenth Century Journal* 10, no. 3 (1979): 97–114.

65   See Book 1, ch. 5.

Jesuits uncertain: this title was judged totally against them in 1594, when they were ordered to leave France. Yet it is accurate to say, based on the event, that all the alms they had been given can be converted to another use, for the convenience of the public. The Jesuits have been the motives behind our Troubles. The Troubles have caused the alienation of the crown's domain, and they should consequently replace the alienated property. May they be the scorpions of France, and may France find, in their death, that new source of their venomous bites.[66] The Christian charity of which they boast being so full, the mendicancy of their order, a status about which they sound the trumpet, the needs of the state, the exemplary punishment: all this constrains them to be treated that way, for the unburdening of their consciences.

Having said this, MASTER PIERRE DU CUGNIÈRES stopped talking. He was not backed up by the Abstainer, his companion, nor was he backed up by his profound knowledge; he was backed up by the common rule of the suffering, who take consolation in having a few companions with the same afflictions. And he would very much have liked to see poor Jesuits, and abstainers like himself. Signor Marforio and I could not agree to this, so the trial was on the verge of a divided opinion. For we believed that this was a settlement worked out between the two French doctors, owing to which, after a few brief altercations, Marforio began speaking. MARFORIO: Of what use are all your decisions, *Recte quidem, sed quorsum quaeso tam recte?*[67] There are a lot of fine words here, sowed inappropriately: for you talk as if the Jesuits were enjoying all the possessions that have been given to them as alms. I inform you that they have sold almost everything and cashed it in. Their money is in diverse banks outside your kingdom, to serve them one day as a resource there, in case they find it convenient to give up your France. If they have any revenue it is in the form of benefices that they have integrated into their colleges; they are not part of the commerce of men. MASTER PIERRE. Are you telling me that they have sold them? On what basis could they have done so? With nothing more than the permission of their general, of whom we do not approve, or do not receive in France. Our laws are different when it comes to alienating the possessions of the church, or of religious communities. In a word, all these so-called alienations are null. I, Pasquin, broke my silence. PASQUIN. This overture goes a long way, and it could suddenly affect an infinity of persons, who can in no way contribute to this quarrel. If you do that, you will introduce chaos and

---

66   The scorpion was the symbol of both wisdom and self-destruction, because it was thought
        that the scorpion produced both venom and anti-venom. See Book I, ch. 5.

67   "I say not, but they are wisely handled, but to what end?"

confusion into your France. For this reason, I refer you to the antique law of our Romans: *Error communis facit jus.*[68]

Finally, having argued for a long while, we decided to leave things as they were: the pyramid would stay, and so would the Parlement's decree, with no innovations. PASQUIN. That's all I could get from my companions, although there were some bitter words from little Master Pierre, who whispered to me that he could see I was on the verge of dressing like a Jesuit, in order to maintain my status in this city of Rome, in my former splendor near splendid people. Of all these things I had wanted to warn your paternity, most-most reverend Father, as someone who is totally yours. Begging you no longer to talk publicly about your innocence, because some people are joking about it and the others are disdainful. It is a mud-hole that you should allow to go stagnant. For the more you stir it up, the more your affairs will stink. You yourself are the first and last judge of the condemnation of your order. I am referring specifically to you, who made a very humble request to King Henri IV, in which you recognize that the most barbaric of all barbaric people, is the one who attacks his king. And your Montaignes admits that he had joined up against his prince: that is the humor of a heretic. Put your hand over your heart and tell me whether this misfortune was not found in you other messieurs during France's recent Troubles. At least, issue orders that your brethren should no longer write, or that if they write, they will be wiser, on penalty of dooming your order.

68   "A common error makes law." That is, something that was illegal at first, having been repeated many times, is presumed to have acquired the force of usage. It therefore would be wrong to depart from it.

CHAPTER 21

On the Division That Seems to Exist between the Parlements of France Concerning the Jesuits, and How That Division Can Be Handled

THE LAWYER. Having ended this long speech, the Lawyer wanted to pause. This gave the Gentleman the opportunity to speak to him. THE GENTLEMAN. Hey, I really do praise your inventiveness at having that person play the roles of stones. For if men are silent, the stones must speak,[1] it being the doing of the Jesuits, as you have portrayed them; and you've proved it, not by vague and fluctuating proofs, but by very certain ones that even were gleaned from their books. But how can it be that, in this notoriety that is indeed permanent (permit me to borrow these expressions used by you, Messieurs-the-lawyers), there are some parlements that not only receive them but honor them, cherish them, and embrace them in their cities and jurisdictions? THE LAWYER. I was expecting you to ask that, and I would have brought it up myself if you had warned me. Don't think this strange: it's a hidden mystery of God, who hadn't withdrawn all his anger toward us, and who wants these messieurs to afflict us some other day. Nonetheless, don't think that it looks very much as if the other parlements will do this. Have you ever seen a New Testament with illustrations? When it comes to the Gospels, where Our Lord was tempted in the desert, Satan is depicted dressed as a monk. Some Lucianists[2] say that this shows that a monk's life is diabolical: but I think just the opposite. For, whoever painted the subject of the Temptation got the idea of putting that habit on the devil, and they did it for a good reason. Believing that this was a truly pious garment, they could think of no more prompt and assured way to surprise the conscience of upright persons. Now, after several masquerades, the devil wanted to shift to another time: transforming himself into Ignatius and his adherents, he would write that holy name Jesus and, speaking through the mouths of the Jesuits, he would not only promise the princes terrestrial kingdoms with which they will be invested (as Satan did with Our Lord), but he

---

1 This image is based on Luke 39–40: "Some of the Pharisees in the crowd said to him, 'Teacher, rebuke your disciples.' He said in reply, 'I tell you, if they keep silent, the stones will cry out!'"

2 Lucian of Samosata (120–c.180) was best known for his characteristic tongue-in-cheek style, with which he frequently ridiculed superstition, religious practices, and belief in the supernatural. His followers were known as "Lucianists." See *Encyclopaedia Britannica*, https://www.britannica.com/biography/Lucian (accessed January 21, 2021).

would also promise the kingdom of heaven to those who would carry out the ambush against the kings, their enemies. Here the devil wasn't fooled. For taking that great name, he first circumvented the sanctity of our popes, and of a succession of devout souls. And just as he is the spirit of division, isn't it strange that the Jesuits, his true and legitimate children, enjoy the same privilege as their father? They have introduced a schism between them and the prelates of France, between them and the universities, between the popes and the kings, between the popes and the other prelates. Now, if they are the cause of a new division between the parlements of France, all that remained was this final action that would make everything, everywhere, fulfill the prophecy of the Faculty of theology of Paris, which said, in its censure of 1554, *Multas in populo querelas, multas lites, dissidia, contentiones, aemulationes, variaque schismata inducit*.[3]

The Parlement of Paris, after mature and wise deliberations, banished them from its jurisdiction. A few other parlements keep them, despite the notorious assassination attempts of Barrière and Châtel on the king's person, and despite their being the first to undertake and direct our Troubles. As for me, seeing this dissention made me remember Henri II's apophtegme[4] directed at Pellisson,[5] president at Chambéry, who was downgraded by a decree of the Parlement of Dijon, owing to a denunciation by Tabouet,[6] the *procureur général*, and who suffered other indignities. Having later obtained letters of revision, and his case having been referred to the Parlement of Paris, he was reintegrated into his old social rank, and Tabouet was sentenced to an *amende honorable*, bare-headed and in his shirt, the rope around his neck. It was reported to the king how things had gone in the two parlements, to which he wisely replied that he admitted that all his judges were good and honorable folks, but that the ones at the Parlement of Dijon had judged according to their consciences, and those of the Parlement of Paris according to law and justice. I don't doubt that all the seigneurs of the other parlements were summoned to do this by their consciences, but there could be nothing cleaner and holier than what

---

3   "It caused many quarrels, controversies, discords, contentions, emulations, and many divisions in the nation."

4   *Apophtegme:* A memorable word or words having the value of a maxim; an aphorism.

5   Raymond Pellisson (1480–1556), master of requests, ambassador to Portugal, first president of the Senate of Chambéry during the brief period when France controlled Savoy. See François Léopold Marcou. *Étude sur la vie et les œuvres de Pellisson* (Paris: Didier, 1859).

6   Julien Tabouet (1500?–63), a jurist, historian, and writer; he was *procureur général* of the Senate of Chambéry. See "Registre du procès faict au parlement de Bourgonne (*sic*) à maistre Julien Tabouet, procureur général de Savoie, commencé le 1ᵉʳ septembre MCCCCC," http://patrimoine.bm-dijon.fr/pleade/ (accessed January 21, 2021).

was ordered by the Parlement of Paris. The others, I think, were pushed by the authority of the Holy See, which tolerates the Jesuits. That is no small advantage for them. Now, I don't want to fight them other than by that very same authority, and I beg them to agree to accept the very humble remonstrances that I intend to make to them, being assured that if it pleases them to listen to me, they'll find their own opinion condemnable. In the past, you've seen how, not once but twice, our Jesuits wanted to try to kill the king, for he belonged to a religion that opposed ours; but after he was reconciled with our church during a truce, he desired nothing as much as he desired a general reconciliation of all his subjects in his kingdom. They are greatly favored in Rome, as if they were ivy, which from the outside seems to be holding up the wall, but which is demolishing it inside. But if they had wanted to make no attack on the pope, I'm sure that their order would be abolished by a decree of that great and holy Consistory in Rome. At least, I note that this was done in similar cases, and for something less exemplary, but of greater consequence: the order of the Umiliati, whose story I am going to recount.

CHAPTER 22

How the Order of the Umiliati Was Suppressed by a Decree from Rome, and Why There Are More Arguments for Suppressing the Jesuits Than the Umiliati

THE LAWYER. Like the Jesuits, this order,[1] viewed from the outside, promised so much holiness and devotion that Cardinal Borromeo,[2] the archbishop of Milan, one of the most prudent counselors of our century, wanted to take it under his protective wing. Having noted that most of the religious, when set at liberty, turned to voluptuousness and debauches, this good prelate wanted to do something about it. Something that made a few indignant persons vow his death. In the city of Vercelli there was a guardian of this order named Girolamo Lignana, who with a few accomplices undertook the assassination.[3] And to facilitate their plan, they debated killing Brother Fabio Simonetta, who guarded the monastery's treasure at Milan, the order's chief place. This deliberation led them to decide to strangle him; but when they found him in church, praying and meditating, God didn't permit them to carry out their wicked plan, for some disagreement arose among them. Instead of doing that, they stole several gold and silver urns, which they turned into coins. This accomplished, Lignana went to see Donato Facia, one of their monastic brethren, a man who was determined to do evil. He was won over and corrupted by money, to kill Cardinal Borromeo. This respectable man, won over in that way, wanted to keep his word. So, waiting until the great holy man was praying to God in a

---

1   The order known as The Humiliati (*Umiliati*) or The Berrettini, appeared in Lombardy during the twelfth century. The early members were laymen closely linked to the wool trade and to the heretical movements of the time. They were recognized as a religious order (both male and female) in 1201. The masculine branch was suppressed in 1571 by Pius V. See Sotto, 415n287. Cf. *Catholic Encyclopedia*, https://www.newadvent.org/cathen/07543a.htm (accessed January 22, 2021). It is interesting to note that the suppression of this order was mentioned in the papal brief of the suppression of the Jesuits in 1773, *Dominus ac redemptor*, which suggests Pasquier's parallelism had long-term impact on anti-Jesuit rhetoric.

2   Cardinal Charles Borromeo (1538–84) was archbishop of Milan from 1564 to 1584. He recruited several Jesuits to run a newly founded seminary for his priests. The Jesuit Benedetto Palmio (mentioned by Pasquier in ch. 3 above) was Borromeo's confessor.

3   See "La Compagnia di Gesù negli stati della Casa di Savoia," *Civiltà cattolica* 70 (1919): 127–40, here 133.

chapel with his people, he suddenly shot a pistol at him, which by a great miracle from God damaged only his robe. Shortly after that, he was apprehended
by the law, along with Lignana: they were found fully guilty, were sent to the
gallows, and with one fell swoop of a hand, their order was totally suppressed
by Pius v in the full Consistory of Rome.

The Jesuits, as I'll show you later, say that it was a plot by the entire order
against Borromeo. That's an impudent lie, for there's no evidence that there
ever was a conspiracy, other than the conspiracy of Guardian Lignana, of the
priory of Saint Christopher at Vercelli, and a few individual monks. The order
of the Umiliati was distributed to several other monasteries that were scattered
throughout Italy, unbeknownst to the monks who had carried out this act. And
yet this single attack upon Cardinal Borromeo, which had no effect, was the
principal cause of the suppression of their order. If you compare this tale with
the tale of the Jesuits (I'm speaking to the seigneurs of the other parlements),
your consciences will blush from shame; for having made this great example
of the Umiliati, because one of them wanted to make an attempt on the life of
a single cardinal, whose death could not greatly prejudice the entire College
of Cardinals, and whom we allowed to live in our midst as the Jesuit sect does,
which we've seen make two attempts to assassinate our king, our king who
is unique in his kingdom, on whose life depends the repose and the general
safety of all his subjects: the principal king of all those who have reigned in
France for the last five hundred years.

I deem the rank of a cardinal to be very lofty in Rome, but not like the rank of
a king of France in his kingdom. There are several cardinals in Rome; in France
there's only one king. Among all the cardinals, I've always honored the memory
of Cardinal Borromeo; but I don't think that his death would have been of such
consequence throughout Italy (on that point I'll never be contradicted by any
living man), as the death of our great king would have been in this France.
And yet I'll carry on regardless. Someone will perhaps think that I'm too partial
about the Jesuits, seeing that, by his final confession, Barrière accused three
other religious from Lyon: a Carmelite, a Jacobin, and a Capuchin. It's necessary to chastise individuals who have committed a fault, and not focus solely
on the order as a whole (so say our Jesuits, in all four of the books they wrote,
books that have become known since the decree by the Parlement).

The crime is personal, and consequently the punishment follows only the
person of the criminal. I don't mean that, in cases that concern the state,
something that is unjust constitutes a good portion of justice. In the decima-
tion that took place in the old days among soldiers, when it was a matter of
chastising a regiment that had failed in its duty, the innocent died as quickly as
the guilty did; but nonetheless, never was justice more solemnized than it was

for maintaining a republic. Less, I might say, than what the great Tacitus said: "Habet aliquid ex iniquo omne magnum exemplum, quod in singulos utilitate publica rependitur."[4] I don't want to recall the opinion of one of the premier Roman jurists, who used to say that when it was a matter of the consequences of a sedition, it was necessary to strike while the iron was hot, beginning with executions, no matter who it was that fell under the magistrate's hand, and then conclude by doing the investigation. Here I don't want to quote for you the effect of all these maxims, although things that concern the life of a king shouldn't be stacked up, one example upon another, and no one else should be compared with him. And inasmuch as, in that sort of circumstance, some Roman Manlius[5] would think that a corps as a whole would suffer as a result of an individual's attempt to assassinate his king. But France wasn't given that option.

Indeed, as we've seen, no one attacked the entire Jacobin order when Jacques Clément, that Jacobin,[6] killed the late king; they attacked only him, and later his prior, who was drawn and quartered in Tours for having been its principal advisor. Inside the Jesuit sect, if there were only three or four who got mixed up in the craft of being an assassin, they would have to practice that common rule of chastising the delinquent and not letting it spread any further. But the vow to assassinate is as familiar to them as their four other vows. Be that as it may, without distancing ourselves from Barrière's tragedy, you'll find such a link in these affairs that, in addition to the individuals mentioned during the trial, the general body of their sect should necessarily be engaged. On the one hand, I see a Jesuit in Lyon who is very much involved. I see the murderer, who isn't sufficiently committed to his undertaking, come very deliberately to Paris to talk about it. But to whom does Aubri, the curate of Saint-André-des-Arts and the most seditious of the band, refer him? To the Jacobins, perhaps by chance, considering what went wrong in the last reign, or else to the Carmelites or the Capuchins. Nothing less. And so, wasn't he sure that, in their monasteries, assassination, even the assassination of a king, was approved. Where, then? He sends them back to those who were past masters in that art, to the house of the Jesuits, which they knew to be the assassins' general field of action.

---

4   Tacitus, *Annals*, xiv, xliv: "All great examples carry with them something of injustice – injustice compensated, as against individual suffering, by the advantage of the community."

5   Titus Manlius Torquatus, twice a dictator and three times a consul throughout the fourth century BCE, had his son decapitated for disobeying the order of the consuls during the campaign against the Latins and Campanians. See Andrew Drummond, "Manlius Imperiosus Torquatus, Titus," in *Oxford Classical Dictionary*, https://oxfordre.com/classics/view/10.1093/acrefore/9780199381135.001.0001/acrefore-9780199381135-e-3921 (accessed January 22, 2021).

6   See ch. 2 above.

Jesuits (I say) who, by the formulary of their confessions, know how to make strangely geometrical propositions for sins and merits. Killing a king of France could be a sin committed by a quartet: but to kill in order to give a king of Spain the upper hand, that could be a sin for eight. With merit surpassing sin by a great amount, murder was not only tolerable, it was very just. Was the curate deceived about this? Not really. For Barrière found Varade, rector of their college, who observed all the usual impieties in such affairs. He also found Commolet, who, working separately, subscribed to what Varade had told the council, and later gloried in it from his pulpit, without naming anyone. And yet, if there was only a single example, I'd be wrong to accuse their entire sect. But when you see that this same proposition was upheld by the Jesuits at the first assassination attempt against the late prince of Orange, at Antwerp, and then in the city of Trier,[7] where he was killed; at Douai, against Count Maurice, his son; in Venice, in Lyon, in Paris, against Queen Elizabeth of England in 1584; against her in Spain in 1597. In Scotland, against Chancellor Maitland;[8] in France first, and then in Paris, against our king in 1594, by one of their scholars, Châtel,[9] who face-to-face with his judges, was impudent enough to maintain that, in certain cases, it was permitted to kill one's king. If the dialecticians' rule is true, then several separate things that are brought together form something that is universal; so, I don't believe I can possibly be wrong when I maintain that the maxim about assassinating kings, princes, and great nobles is natural to them, as a residue of their vows. But why lie? For it's certain that they consented to the death of the late king, and that Guignard,[10] one of their brethren who has since been executed, wrote (as I've mentioned) a book intended to prove that this death was meritorious, and that the same thing should be done to the king who is reigning today. All this time, you've been hearing what I've been telling you while calling myself the Venerable Pasquin of Rome: this is something true, not something ridiculous. And among those books is the book on that subject written by the Jesuit who is the principal of the seminary at Reims. Since Arnauld objected to this in his plea, Montaignes was very careful to reply: for he's so involved in frivolous things that he didn't spare his pen. The conclusion of all this: in all their actions you see only advice to murder, which is why a fine wit in our France, having discovered a brief poem that reveals their unfortunate demeanor, finished it in this fashion:

---

7   See ch. 1 above.
8   See ch. 1 and 2 above.
9   See ch. 2 above.
10   See ch. 18 above.

A Gesis sunt indita nomina vobis,
Quae quia sacrilegi, Reges torquetis in omnes,
Inde sacrum nomen, sacrum sumpsistis et omen.[11]

After all that, one will say that the individuals must be punished, and not be attached to the entire religious order, which didn't consent. What idiot will believe that? I'll leave aside the way they've stirred up our state, in order not to take advantage of your time and your patience. I know that all the seigneurs in our parlements breathe only for the universal good of France. I hope they'll think about whether what I've said is true, or not. I don't want to use another rhetoric in order to induce them to share my opinion. And because I began this speech by the decree issued in Rome against the Umiliati, I'll return to that point in order to show you how impudent the Jesuits were about wanting to parry that blow.

11   Of *Gesum* comes your name. / A fatal tool that by sacrilege at kings you throw, / Whence your holy name and fortunes flow.

The Jesuits' Impudence in Order to Protect Themselves from the Decree of the Consistory of Rome, Issued against the Order of the Umiliati

THE LAWYER. In 1594, Arnauld was the first to remonstrate that the order of the Umiliati had been suppressed during our lifetime, and for less reason than the Jesuits; and he was followed by Marion, the *avocat du roi*. To be brief, both orders. That's the proposition that I still maintain today. Let's not flatter ourselves; let's see how this blow is fended off by the Jesuits. Montaignes wrote against Arnauld: "In order to take comfort in this feeble deposition, you cite as an example the Umiliati, who were suppressed in Italy. But the facts are very different. The reasons why the Umiliati were suppressed are stated in the bull: they did not follow the rules, they grumbled, they were imperious and incorrigible. That is because they were conspiring against their prelate, Borromeo, a protector and a reformer. He had made a deposition against the conspirators, and the conspirators had confessed their crime. You cannot say that about the Jesuits, or you would have said it." I agree with the Jesuit: there is nothing similar. For it was a matter of a simple prelate who had several companions. But in this case, it's a matter of a king who had no companions, and who is the true anointed of God. The conspirator at the Umiliati was punished, for he was captured; the Jesuit conspirator was not, for after the surrender of Paris, since nothing is impossible for them, they found a way to help him escape. In truth, that excuse of Montaignes's contained more prevarications than prohibitions. This is why wise La Fon denied it and contributed more tailoring and fabric to it than the other Jesuit did. "Concerning the Umiliati, François des Montaignes previously replied that they were folks who neglected everything, they had not studied literature, they followed no rules, they had no discipline, they were worldly, dissolute, scandalous, their houses were princely palaces, their bedchambers had gilded wainscoting, their cabinets were the cabinets of kings, their cloisters and galleries were full of lascivious paintings, their provost maintained a public whore, and all the inferior monks resembled their provost in humors and manners. They finally were convicted of conspiring as a small group and convicted of the attempted assassination of the person of their prelate, Cardinal Borromeo, who lived a holy life and was trying to reform them. Their case was closely scrutinized; their crimes were revealed,

not by a party but by the Holy Father, Pope Clement VIII, who has jurisdiction over such cases, and who sentenced them, not to leave Italy, but to live
among other religious who were pensioners and who had been deprived of
their possessions; some of them are still alive in Milan. And all of Milan is the
witness to this, along with the bull that talks about it." I had simply proposed
a comparison of the Jesuits and the Umiliati. But the impudence of that last
Jesuit made me eager to quarrel with him, before moving on. What sort of commentary is the one he's making about his companion, Montaignes? Where,
in either Montaignes or in the bull, does he find all the shame, the coyness,
and the irregularities that characterize him? Where's that group conspiracy
against Cardinal Borromeo? Where's the provost's prostitute? Was there only
one provost in that order? Didn't each priory have its own? What is that provost's name? It's a very fundamental privilege for a Jesuit: the farther he moves
ahead, the more he permits himself, and the more he promises us that we'll
feast, with impunity, on fibs, gibes, and impostures. Or to cut them away, in
case one offers oneself on a spit. I'll take them at their word: both refer us to the
bull of Pope Pius V: let's read it in full:

> PIUS EPISCOPUS servus servorum Dei, ad pertetuam rei memoriam.
> Quemadmodum sollicitus pater quem unicé carum educavit fillium, via
> salutis egressum revocare cupiens, primum hortatur, indulget, praetermit-
> tit, increpat, alia praeterea atque alia tentare non definit, dum quod expetit,
> modo aliquo consequatur, omnia denique expertus, cum nihil jam proficere
> intelligit, desperata prorsus salute, omnem de illo parentis animum ejicit,
> domo expellit, indignum existimans, qui parta haereditate fruatur: sic
> Romanus Pontifex, quem divina Majestas patrem et pastorem omnium
> Ecclesiae suae ordinum constituit sicubi quampiam sacrarum congregatio-
> num à regula, et vitae praescripto aberrare percipit, modo admonendo,
> modo corripiendo connititur, eam vel primis institutis restituere, vel certè,
> quo pacto emendatam in aliquo statu illis magis cohaeerenti continere:
> omnibus tandem ad illius sanitatem conquisitis magis cohaerenti conti-
> nere: omnibus tandem ad illius sanitatem conquisitis, ubi salutaria remedia
> fastidire, et viam iniquitatis obstinatius procedere, atque adeo in pravum
> indurescere animadevertit, ut potius confringi, quam corrigi possit, omni
> curatione rejecta, de ipsa removenda decernit, ne inveterati atque idomiti
> mali vis, in alias insurgat, eisque exitio sit futura. Quod (ut nostrum had in
> re studium flagrat) cum in plurimis, tum maximé in fratrum Humiliatorum
> familia enixe curavimus, nihil inexpertum relinquentes quin illa multis jam-
> pridem modis affecta, et si non protinus, certès accomoda rerum

moderatione directa ad pristinum institutum paulatim regrederetur. Etenim moderation directa ad pristinum institutum paulatim regrederetur. Etenim post quam dilectus filius noster Carolus, tituli sanctae Praxedis, presbiter Cardinalis Borrhomaeus, hujus Ordinis protector, et Apostolicae Sedis delegatus, animadevertens dictos Fratres in luxum jambridem effusos esse, multa de ratione cultus divini, de obedientia et vita, ut antea communi, deque modo recipiendorum et educandorum religiosorum providenter statuerat, intelligeremus eos, illa ceteraque, omnia regulae suae instituta, omnino aspernari vitamque omnium voluptatum varietate confertam ducere, ac praepositos, et qui ex eo ordine rerum administrationem habebant, bonam magnamque fructuum partem veluti propriam in vanitatibus mundanis turpitudinibusque flagitiosè profundere, innumeraque scelera commitere. Nos vias omnes quae illos in aperta hujusmodi pericula atque in commoda conjecerant, excindere conati, pleraque alia de ipsorum vita, moribus et proprietate regulae inimica, deque modo et tempore gubernandae cujusque praepositurae, nec non ratione administrationis bonorum, et dispensatione proventuum aliisque muneribus et officiis, ad prolapsi hujus status, et disciplinae regularis reparationem maximè conferentibus, edidimus, sperantes illa prosperos tandem successus dicto Ordini allatura. Sed obsistente bonarum rerum perturbatore plerique omnes (quoniam otio et desidia nimium assueverant) regulae instituta et emendationem abhorrentes, etsi statuta et praecepta nostra communi consensu palam acceptarunt, clam tamen quibus illa modis supprimerent comminiscentes, nefarias protestationes in occulto fecerunt, necessarios suos, et alios potentiorés laicos ad intestinas seditiones concitarunt, suasores praeterea et impulsores ad intimos summorum principum ministros dimiserunt, qui magnis praemiis et pollicitationibus eos pellicerent, in animos praedictorum principum inducere, ut nos ad illam rescindendam inclinarent, multaque alia de ea tollenda pravis artibus sunt conati, ut turpem illam et flagitiosam vitam suam retinerent, letalesque mundi voluptates sequerentur, inter quos non defuit, qui altius praecipitatus, etiam à Catholica fide ad Haereticos, et impia illorum dogmata declinarit. Quibus cognitis, omnium gravissimum impoenitentiae peccatum in eis animadvertimus, qui toties frustra correpti, in eadem obstinatione perdurare contendunt, non satis habentes talia attentare, nisi et iis qui inter ipsos qui posse putant, illis imprimis qui saluti eorum sedulo invigilant, exitium machinentur, illius stimulis concitati, qui scelestum Judam in funestum avaritiae morbum injecisse non contentus, etiam ad prodendum Dominum suum pecunia impulit. Hujus nimirum Spiritus nequissimi ductu, quondam Hieronimus Lignana praepositus praeposturae sancti Christophori. Vercellen et plures alii conscelerati hujus ordinis, in necem dicti Caroli Cardinalis propitiatoris sui conspirantes, ut pecuniam ad tantum nefas expeditam conficerent, de trucidando in primis dilecto filio Fabio Simoneta fratre dicti ordinis, proventuum praepositurae bredae Mediolanensis depositario, apud quem nummos invenire credebant, secreto convenerunt, inde ad Ecclesiam dictae praepositurae, in qua ipsum orantem, laqueo suffocare decreverant, profecti, sed inter se de modo aggrediendi, misericordia Salvatoris nostri, discordes, hoc conatu destiterunt, mutatoque consilio, sacra aurea et argentae furati sunt. Quibus clam venditis, seu pignori datis, praedictus Hieronimus quendam Donatum Faziam comprofessorem suum, apostatam, pacta pecunia induxit ut ipsum Carolum Cardinalem occideret, qui nacta loci et temporis opportunitate, in eum vesperi de more in sacello qui nacta loci et temporis opportunitate, in eum vesperi de more in sacello cum familia precantem, ut transverberaret sclopum glandibus confertum, igne admoto exoneravit, sed telorum parte ad vestes orantis exinanita, aliis utrinque in proximo violentia ictus defixit, innocentem Divina pietas salvum et incolumem conservavit. Quare ambo, et quidam alii hujus nefandi criminis participes postea capati poenas debitas persolverunt. Quando igitur familiam praedictam, nulli studio ad Ecclesiae Dei utilitatem proficienti incumbentem, nulli disciplinae Ecclesiasticae deditam, nullum omnino futurae virtutis specimen ostendentem, tam detestandis facinoribus infectam, tam atroci sacrilegio contaminatam, et praeterea impoenitentem atque incorrigibilem agnoscimus, omni de illa spe prorsus exclusa, ipsam tandem tollere constituimus, tanquam malam arborem fructus pessimos proferentem. Habita itaque cum fratribus nostris deliberatione matura, de illorum consilio, et nobis attributae potestatis plenitudine, extinguimus et abolemus ordinem praedictorum fratrum Humiliiatorum officium praepositi generalis ac provincialium, et quaecunque alia ministeria ordinis si suppressi, nec non omnia, et quaecumque statuta, consuetudines et decretal ejusdem, etiam juramento, confirmatione apostolica, vel alia quacumque firmitate munita, et pariter privilegia, et indulta generalia, et specialia, quorum omnium tenores ac si ad verbum insererentur, praesentibus habemus pro expressis, quibuscumque illa concepta sint formulis, nec non irritantibus aliis decretis, et vinculis roborata: Privamusque Generalem, ac caeteros omnes praepositos, et fratres omnes praeposituris dignitatibus, administrationibus, officiis et beneficiis Ecclesiasticis cum cura et sine cura, nec non domibus, conventibus et bonis immobilibus, mobilibus et se moventibus in Italia et ubicunque gentium constitutis, sacra quocunque, et communi supellectile, ac ipsorum

omnium usu, usufructa administratione ac possessione spirituali, et tempo-
rali, ac etiam jure et actione, sive per statuta nostra, sive alias quomodolibet
pertinente. Ac tollimus eis omnimodam facultatem, usum et auctoritatem
generalia et provincialia, et alia capitula de caetero celebrandi. Volumus
tamen ut omnes fratres qui nunc sunt, qui professionem regularem emise-
runt, deinceps in domibus et locis, quos eis cum victu, et aliis necessariis
proximè assignandos curabimus, omnino redigantur, ut ibi vitam ducant
regularem suae professioni conformem sub cura et visitatione ordinario-
rum locorum aut alterius, vel aliorum quos eis duxerimus delegandos, vel
juxta juris communis dispositionem transeant ad pares, vel strictiores ordi-
nis approbatos. Novitii vero et alii quicunque non professi, detracto
Religionis habitu ex professorum consortio, et domibus expellantur. Quibus
professoribus nominatim praecipimus atque interdicimus ne post hac
quemquam expulsorum, et omnino alium etiam voventem, ad professio-
nem, vel habitum admittant, nec novas domos, vel loca recipiant, vel
acquirant, quod si secus fiat, professio sit inanis, neminemque obliget,
neque in genere sic professum. Novarum domorum seu locorum receptiones
vel acquisitiones viribus et effectu careant, et contra facientes excommuni-
cationis sint sententia eo ipso innodati, a qua nullus nisi in mortis articulo
constitutus absolvi possit, absque Romani Pontificis licentia speciali.
Caeterum intendentes et cultui divino, et Ecclesiae ministris quamprimum
prospicere, omnes praeposituras, dignitates, personatus, administrationes,
officia, caeteraque beneficia Ecclesiastica, cum cura et sine cura, quae dein-
ceps secularia sint, per privationem praedictam, apud sedem Apostolicam
vacantia, nec non domos, conventus, loca supellectilem, bona, fructus, res,
actiones et jura supradicta, eorumque proprietatem et dominium nostrae et
dictae sedis liberae dispositioni specialiter et expresse reservamus.
Decernentes irritum et inane quicquid secus per praedictos, aut quoscu-
nque alios scienter vel ignoranter contigerit attentari. Voluimus autem ut
praesentium exempla notarii publici manu, et personae in dignitate
Ecclesiastica constitutae, sigillo obsignata, eandem illam prorsus fidem in
judicio et extra illud, ubique locorum faciant, quam ipsaemet praesentes
facerent, si essent exhibitae, vel ostensae. Nulli ergo, etc. Siquis autem, etc.
Datum Romae apud sanctum Petrum, Anno Incarnationis Dominicae 1577.
Idibus Februarii, Pontificatus nostri anno sexto.[1]

---

1 "Pope Pius, servant of the servants of God, in perpetual memory of this matter. As a careful father over that son whom he had brought up very tenderly, desirous to reclaim him,
when he has stepped out of the way of his salvation, first exhorts him, favors him, pardons

him, rebukes him, moreover, ceases not to try one thing after another, until he attained unto what he desired, & having at last made proof of all, when he sees nothing will do him good, utterly despairing of his recovery, casts off the affection of a father, and thrusts him out of doors, judging him unworthy to be his heir: So the bishop of Rome, whom the divine majesty had appointed to be a father and pastor of all the religious orders in his church, if he perceive any of these holy companies swerve from the rule and prescription of life they have undertaken, endeavors sometimes by admonition, sometimes by correction, to restore their ancient institution, or at least, by some kind of amendment, bring them in better order: After he had sought everything that may make for their good, when he saw them loathe all wholesome remedies, and stubbornly go on still in the way of wickedness, and perceived them to grow worse and worse, so that they may sooner be broken then mended, careless of all cure, he determined to remove them, lest the power of an inveterate and untamed evil overrun others, and destroy them. Which thing (because we are earnest in this point) both in many others, and especially in the company of the Humiliati, we have been very careful of, leaving nothing unattempted, but finding many flaws in them, so that if not altogether, yet in some convenient measure and moderation, they might by little and little, be fashioned to their first institution. For, after that our beloved Son Charles, of the title *sanctae Praxedis*, priest, Cardinal Borromeo, protector of this order, and delegate of the Apostolic See, of late perceiving the said friars to break out into riot, had providently set down many things, concerning the manner of God's worship, obedience, and common life, and of the manner of receiving and education of religious persons. We understood that they utterly despised both those, and all other rules of their own order, and lived very voluptuously, & that their governors, together with such as had any offices in the administration of their affairs, wickedly wasted a great part of the revenues (as if they had been their own) in worldly vanities and filthiness and committed innumerable sins.

We endeavored to cut off all those means that did cast them into so apparent dangers and inconveniences, took order for many things hurtful to their life and manners, and propriety of their rule and order, and for the manner and time of government in every one's commandment, and also for the managing their goods, & disposing of their revenues, and other places and offices, very profitable to repair the ruins of this decayed state and regular discipline, hoping that these things would in time to come bring good success to the said order. But the enemy of all good things resisting, almost all of them (because they had been too much inured to ease & idleness) detesting to live in order and to be amended, howsoever by common consent they outwardly accepted our laws and precepts, yet underhand they devised all the ways they could to suppress them. They held wicked conspiracies secretly, they stirred up their kindred and others of the laity that were mighty to sedition; they sent their brokers and agents, to the most intimate servants of mighty princes, to draw them by great rewards and promises, to work us by the aforesaid princes' means, to undo that we had done, and many others did they by evil practices attempt to this purpose, that they might continue their filthy and wicked course of life, & follow the deadly pleasures of this world, among whom was one that fell more high & headlong from the Catholic faith to heretics, and declined to their impious opinions.

Understanding these things, we found them guilty of impenitency, the greatest sin of all, who being so often reproved, strove to continue in the same obstinacy, not thinking it enough to have attempted these things, unless they contrived the destruction of such as were of authority among them, and chiefly did watch diligently over their own souls, provoked hereunto by him, who not contenting himself with plunging Judas into the grievous sin of covetousness, procured him also by money to betray his master. For by the enticement of this wicked spirit, Girolamo Lignana, once president of the house of Saint Christopher at Vercelli, and many other confederates of this order, conspiring the death of Charles the cardinal their protector, that they might have money to compass this heinous act, held a conventicle to murder first our beloved son Fabio Simonetta, a brother of the said order, treasurer of the revenues of Breda at Milan, thinking to furnish themselves with such coin as was in his keeping: thence determined they to go to the church of the said house, to strangle him there, as he was at his prayers, but (by God's mercy) disagreeing among themselves about the manner of the assault, they desisted from that, and changing their minds, they stole away the sacred gilt vessels of the church. Which being secretly sold, or pawned, the said Geronimo hired one Donato Facia, one of his brotherhood, an apostate, to murder Charles the cardinal, and he having spied his time & place, finding him at his prayers (as his manner was) with his household in a chapel in the evening shot of a pistol at him to strike him through, but disappointed of his purpose, some of the bullets were defeated by his garments while he prayed, others, by the violence of the blow, stuck nearby on either side of him: the innocent man by God's grace was preserved: wherefore both of them, with others that were partakers of this fact, were afterward beheaded.

Thus, when we saw this company grown unprofitable in the church of God, living in no order, showing no sign of amendment, infected with so grievous crimes, defiled with so cruel sacrilege, and furthermore impenitent and incorrigible, being out of all hope of their recovery, we have at last determined to root them out, like an evil tree that carries very bad fruit. Having therefore thoroughly deliberated with our brethren, by their advice, and by the absolute authority committed to us, we utterly extinguish and abolish the whole order of the said Friars Humiliati, the place of their general, and provincials, and all other offices of their order thus suppressed, and also all, and all manner of statutes, customs, and decrees of the same, howsoever they have been established by any oath, or apostolic confirmation, or any other warrant, and also all privileges and grants, both general & special, the tenors of all which, as if they were word for word here inserted, we take to be included by reference in these presents, whatsoever style or form they bear, confirmed with other decrees and clauses that may move us: And we deprive the general, and all other their governors, and brethren, of commandments, dignities, administrations, offices, and ecclesiastical benefices, with cure, & without cure, and also of their houses, convents, & goods immovable, movable, and self-moving, being in Italy or any other nation, of all holy things, and common household stuff, of the use of all and usufruct administration & possession spiritual and temporal, of right and action also, whether by our statutes, or any other way they appertain unto them. And we take from them all power and authority to hold from henceforth, any general, provincial, or other chapters. Yet we ordain, that all the brethren now remaining, who have made their regular profession, be from henceforth seated in such houses and places as we shall appoint, with things necessary for their maintenance: that there they may live according to their rule & profession, under the cure and visitation of the ordinaries of those places, or of some others, whom we shall appoint for that purpose; or else, that according to the direction of common law, they may transfer to some existing equivalent or stricter order.

As for the novices & others whatsoever not yet professed, their habit pulled over their ears, let them be expelled from the house and company of the professed. Which professed, we precisely command, & forbid, that from hence forth they never admit unto their profession or habit, any of them that are expelled, or any other that would be devoted to it: Neither shall they receive or purchase any new houses or places: if they do, the profession shall be

That is the complete bull, which I took from Matheus Toscanus's book titled *Summa constitutionum, et rerum in Ecclesia Romana gestarum à Gregorio nono usque ad Sixtum quintum.* He was a great friend of the Jesuits.[2] But what do you gather from that bull? That the Umiliati were drowning in voluptuous things. But there are none of the details invented by La Fon. More by specific terms than by their ploys and machinations, they stirred up troubles and seditions among the princes. *In occulto,* says the text, *necessarios suos et alios potentiores ad intestinas seditiones concitarunt.*[3] Isn't that a craft at which our reverend Jesuits are past masters? You won't find, in this bull, that the order of the Umiliati was accused of having assembled, as a body, to assassinate Cardinal Borromeo, their reformer, as the Jesuits conjecture. If it was an assembled body, that means that their general, the provincials of the order, the priors of their monasteries, had been part of the plot, or at the most, the majority of them had been. A circumstance that wouldn't have been omitted from the decretal about this great coup that Pope Pius v and the Holy Consistory of Rome were aiming at the entire order. For it indubitably played a decisive role in this suppression. And that's why the lying Jesuits rejected this condemnation of the entire order, which had been (as they put it) capitularily planned against Borromeo. Let's identify what is true and do it like children of Jesus Christ and not like children of Ignatius. The order of the Umiliati was defamed for the salaciousness with which it overflowed. Good Cardinal Borromeo had wanted to remedy this by a

void, and shall not bind the individual or the house so professed. All erections of such like new houses shall be of no force, and they that shall do contrary shall thereby incur the sentence of excommunication: from which none, unless it be upon the point of death, shall be absolved, without the special license of the bishop of Rome.

Furthermore, proposing to provide with all speed for the service of God, and the ministers of his church, we reserve by the aforesaid deprivation, all commands, dignities, administrations, offices, and other ecclesiastical benefices, with cure & without cure, which be hereafter secular, to the holy See, in their vacancy. And also, the houses, convents, places, household stuff, goods, fruits, substances, actions, and aforesaid rights, & their property and dominion, especially and expressly to the free disposition of our said See. Decreeing that to be void and of no effect, whatsoever shall happen to be wittingly or unwittingly attempted to the contrary, by the aforesaid friers or any other.

And we will, that the transcript of these presents, taken under the hand of a notary public, and sealed by an ecclesiastical person of dignity, shall be as authentic, in, or out of judgment, wheresoever they be drawn, as if these presents were exhibited and shown. [...]. Given at Rome in Saint Peter's Palace, in the year of the incarnation of our Lord, 1577, in the Ides of February, the sixth year of our pontificate."

2 This book was compiled by the Jesuit Pierre Matthieu. See ch. 9 above.

3 "They held wicked conspiracies secretly, they stirred up their kindred and others of the laity that were mighty, to sedition." In context, this seems to mean that they encouraged laypeople to lobby against Borromeo's reforms of their order.

general reform, but he had labored in vain. Although this was a very great fault, it wouldn't have gotten the order suppressed. That is a vice that blind nature makes easily slip into all sorts of persons, given how much she favored and has favored the multiplication of the human species. To the point that if one wanted to confront the different religious orders, where that evil sometimes abounds, even in those orders that are situated in the fields, in the woods, or on the river banks, far from the common people's prying eyes, we could say what wise Tacitus said: *Ut antea vitiis, ita tum demum legibus laboraremus*.[4] And it perhaps would be more scandalous to suppress them than to connive about such vices. What then? Who caused the suppression? Beyond all hope, God permits Lignana, prior of Vercelli, and a few other individuals who are irritated by this new reform, to conspire against Borromeo in the manner recounted in the bull. That calls to mind the general debauchery in the order, and how all of that, pell-mell together, caused the suppression; but principally it was an undertaking against Borromeo, which is laid out in detail, not lechery of the sort that La Fon has recounted.

Is there anything in this whole story that cannot be more appropriately applied to what was done and what went on against the Jesuits? They were notoriously defamed about the Troubles they ignited in France: and not only defamed, for they also triumphed and negotiated with foreigners to create a new king in this kingdom. Barrière's detestable deed was divulged everywhere in France: Commolet howled at the people to kill the king, even during the truce. As soon as the king entered Paris, all the people, and I mean from the humblest to the loftiest, demanded vengeance. The case was pleaded on behalf of the university; and since, when it came to judging, it had very often tried cases of consequence, by fearing that we would fail, we failed: we dragged things out; and in order not to fail, the case was adjourned. God willed that Châtel, the Jesuits' disciple, who had been infected with their damnable lessons, should strike the king with a knife; and having been captured, he looked at the full face of the law, and maintained that he had been able to do it justly. The atrociousness of this unfortunate deed, mingled with the other circumstances, led to the decree that was directed at the entire Jesuit order. I beg you to tell me: was the same Holy Spirit that operated during the suppression of the Umiliati in Rome, operating during the suppression of the Jesuits in Paris? The effects are the same, the procedures were the same, even though the names differed. And the sole difference involved two points: first, the Umiliati

---

4   The exact citation from Tacit (*Annal.*, III, 25) reads: "Ut olim flagitiis, sic nunc legibus laboramus" (As we were formerly by crimes, so we are now overburdened by laws). "Vitium" means fault, or vice in Latin.

were sinning by giving themselves over to voluptuousness; but that's a sin we learn from corrupted nature. And having brought about the Troubles, during which two hundred thousand people lost their lives, the Jesuits sinned against corrupted nature, and against the regulated good of us all. For there is nothing that nature abhors as much as it abhors death, which the Jesuits view as being cheap when others pay. And then, there's the other noteworthy diversity upon which I previously commented: because Lignana's attempt was aimed only at a cardinal, a cardinal whom I recognize as having been, in his profession, one of the holiest men of our century. A cardinal by whose death all the College of Cardinals would lose a great deal, a cardinal who nonetheless didn't cease to dwell in his former splendor and light. But Châtel's attack struck a king, the only one in the kingdom, a king whom everyone sees and should recognize as the most magnanimous and affable prince ever seen, and whose death, if the assassination attempt had succeeded, would have given birth to chaos, pell-mell, and to general confusion about everything in France. And we'll then favor them in some part of our kingdom? But because some persons, forgetting the past and not looking ahead to the future, let themselves be carried away by them, judging that they are the protectors of our Catholic religion, I'll show you now how the Jesuit sect brings just as much partiality and division to our church as Martin Luther's sect does. And in addition, there's nothing that the pope should fear so much, as prejudicial to his authority and splendor, as the Jesuits' general, despite a few contrary protestations that these messieurs express.

CHAPTER 24

The Jesuit Sect Is No Less Prejudicial to Our Church Than the Lutheran Sect Is

THE LAWYER. *Prima facie*, this proposition will seem paradoxical, but it is true. The compartments of the hierarchical order of our church have a certain conformity and similarity to the human body: the head makes royalty set all the other members to work, among which there are several noble parts (such as the heart, the liver, and the lungs), without which neither the head nor the entire body could subsist. And whoever removes the head to make it smaller, so that it can be distributed to the other noble parts; or whoever, to the contrary, removes some of the noble parts in order to give them to the head, that person removes the proportions and the symmetry that should exist among all the members: and he would ruin the entire body. Our hierarchy is like that. The head of the church is the pope, Our Holy Father; the noble parts beneath him are the archbishops, bishops, curates, and abbots; to that, I'll add kings and universities. As for the rest of the population, it represents the other members of the human body. Martin Luther was the first to offend the head, in order to introduce a form of aristocracy into our church, and to make all the bishops equal to the Holy See of Rome, in and within their dioceses. First the Lutheran sect, and then the Calvinist one, soared into the sky. A few years later came Ignatius of Loyola, who by a totally opposite proposition, defended the authority of the Holy See. But he did it at such a cost that he damaged our church just as much as he damaged the other church. Feigning to sustain Our Holy Father with better rewards than everyone else and attributing to him unaccustomed authority that worked to the disadvantage of the *ordinaires*, he and his religious successively obtained from one pope or another so many privileges, indults, and grants, to the disadvantage of all the prelates, monasteries, and universities, that by tolerating their living in our midst, you will erase the true face of our Catholic and Universal Church. Remember what I told you the day before yesterday, in the presence of the Jesuit: you'll find what I'm saying to be very true.

The difference, then, between Luther and Ignatius was that Luther troubled our church and armed himself against its head; but Ignatius was bumping up against the other noble parts. Becoming attached to extremes is a vice.[1] Virtue

---

1 Cf. William David Myers, "Ignatius Loyola and Martin Luther: A History and Basis of a Comparison," in *A Companion to Ignatius of Loyola: Life, Writings, Spirituality, and Influence*, ed. Robert A. Maryks (Leiden: Brill, 2014), 141–58.

is a mid-point between two extremes. Me, I believe that the true Catholic, Apostolic, Roman Church is the church that was active, starting with and after the passion of Our Savior and Redeemer Jesus Christ. That church was approved by all our ancient doctors of the church, the least of whom possessed more doctrine and Christian sentiment in their souls than Luther, than his followers, than Ignatius, and than all his friends. That's the church in which all good and faithful Christians must live and die. I'd willingly add that I'd prefer to fail with them, than to risk and wager my soul by enrolling myself with those newcomers; but that would involve speaking ill of such a high-level fabric. I'll therefore not say that I would love it better,[2] but I'll bravely say that I'll have less fear of failing. For if you say that the Jesuit is the true sword to repel the blows dealt by the Lutherans and the Calvinists, not only do I not think that, but I think the contrary: it's the principal way to confirm them in their erroneous opinions. I know that one of my friends who attended a Protestant sermon out of curiosity, not out of devotion, heard the minister shout to his faithful.

THE MINISTER. "My Christian brethren, God has viewed us with a pitying eye. While Martin Luther was powerful enough to fight the papacy with its banners deployed, Ignatius of Loyola gave us a great advantage: for he sapped the feet of the papacy, while feigning to support it. What finer means are there to subvert a republic than factiousness and internal divisions? And what else do the Jesuits and the Roman Church produce? Since that sect is its principal support, we've won the city. And at most, the head has to be infinitely ill if, in order to hold it up, by favoring a new sect we ruin the other noble parts. But what is causing this disarray? A Mission vow that is imaginary and in place of which the pope is the godfather of their quarrel. Let's therefore praise God, my friends, and let's say what Demea long ago said to Mitio, her brother, in the words of that comic poet: *Consumat, perdat, pereat, nihil ad me attinet.*"[3] These six or seven Latin words, when directed at the Holy See, are truly blasphemous. But they are unbridled licenses used in diverse ways by those who climb up into the pulpit to preach, and who attribute to the Holy Spirit all the faults coming from their anger. This unfortunate mismanagement in no way moved that minister, but it should greatly move the heart of every good Catholic, who wants to live and die in the Catholic, Apostolic, and Roman Church. We all share an interest in not letting these ministers triumph, and not letting their triumphs be founded on our Jesuits. See whether they have

---

2 *Aimer mieux*, "to love better," that is, "to prefer." Pasquier's point is subtle: he does not want to say "love," nor does he want to say "prefer" (*préférer* was however in use at the time, according to Cotgrave's dictionary of 1611.)

3 "Let him, if 'tis your pleasure, waste, destroy, and squander: it is no concern of mine," Terence, *The Brother* (*Adelphoe*), I, ii, 134.

some reason to say it. For among other peculiarities in the censure of our theologians in 1554, it said that the Jesuits would be seminaries for schisms and
divisions in our Christian Church, and that they were sooner introduced to the
ruin and desolation of that church, than to its edification. If I commit the fault
of saying that the Jesuit sect is no less prejudicial to the true church than the
Lutheran sect is, I'm not doing it without judgment, being guided on this by the
judgment of that venerable Faculty of Theology of Paris.

CHAPTER 25

Concerning the Noteworthy Undertaking of the Superior General of the Jesuits against the Holy See of Rome, and That There Is No New Sect That Eventually Can Be as Prejudicial to It

THE LAWYER. When the venerable Faculty of theology of Paris censured the Jesuit sect in 1554, it considered only the lesser orders, for both the temporal and the spiritual. But the faculty didn't go that far for things that involved the Holy See. And it would have been impossible, because at the time they couldn't consult all the Jesuits' bulls, nor their Constitutions. Now that God, by his holy grace, has enlightened us over time, I shall doubtlessly say that in the person of the general of the Jesuits, we see the image of Lucifer, who wanted to be a match with God, his creator. And Lucifer being a creature of the pope, not only presents himself as being similar, but also as having greater power and authority over his cohorts, than the pope has over the Universal Church. In Rome, they assert that they obey the pope absolutely, not only for the Mission but also for all other commands. And, under this pretext, they have obtained, and they obtain from one day to another, an infinity of extraordinary privileges to the disadvantage, and if I dare say so, to the shame of the archbishops, bishops, religious orders, universities, and the entire antique Catholic Church. Nonetheless, the truth is that, having two objects to revere, they show incomparably more honor for their general than they do for the Holy See.

Ignatius of Loyola, a Spaniard, born into a great and noble family, did not change his nature in order to change his life. Ribadeneyra tells us how Ignatius, on the brink of quitting his father's house, feigned a desire to see the duke of

Nájera.[1] Martín García,[2] Ignatius's older brother, doubted the truth of his words so he went to see him privately in his bedchamber and said to him: "Everything in you is great: spirit, judgment, courage, nobility, the favor of princes, the benevolence of the common people, prudence, experience in battle. Moreover, at an age when you are fresh and strong, you give great promise. What? Do you now want to disappoint our fine hopes, and take from our house the laurel wreaths that it expected to acquire, thanks to you, as you continue along the way that you have begun so fortunately? Although I'm older than you, you exceed me in authority. Brother, take care: I beg you not to do something that will not only rob us of all these fortunate hopes, but that can lead us to great dishonor. To this, (says Ribadeneyra) Ignatius replied with few words, saying that he wasn't forgetting either himself or his ancestors, and that he would take care not to be seen leaving his rank or ancestors, or obscuring their memory." These are promises to his brother that he certainly kept. For in that unhoped-for mutation in his life, he never stored petty ambitions away in his soul: but just a few changes of clothes and a pilgrimage to Jerusalem. Give a monkey

---

1   Antonio Manrique de Lara (1466–1535), second duke of Nájera and viceroy of Navarre (1516–21). See *Gran Enciclopedia de Navarre*, http://www.enciclopedianavarra.com/?page_id=13777 (accessed January 22, 2021). Ribadeneyra mentions this episode in his *Life*, ch. 3: "When he had gotten his health back to some extent, Ignatius prepared to travel under the pretext of visiting the Duke of Nájera with whom the Loyola household had a long-standing close connection. His real reason was to leave his home and his relatives (cf. Gen. 12:1). Martín García, his oldest brother and the head of the family, got wind of his intentions. Calling him aside into an inner room, he begged him not to go and destroy himself and his house. Rather he should think again and again about what a straight road to glory he had set out on, about what accomplishments he had achieved, and about how promising his mind and talents were. 'You have everything that it takes: talent, good judgment, spirit, noble heritage, influence with princes, popularity with the citizenry, military experience, prudence. And besides all of this, you are robust, in the prime of your life, and everyone expects great things from you. So, is this the way you are going to dash so many hopes, hopes that are so well-grounded and promising? Are you going to disappoint everybody? Are you going to rob our house of all those many honors that were your goals when you started down the path you took? Even though I am older, you still have the greater sway. Look, I am asking you, don't even *think* about doing anything that would not only deprive us and our house of the honor that we have been counting on, but even brand us with disgrace.' In reply, Ignatius briefly said that he was mindful of himself and of his forefathers, and that he would try hard not to seem to have fallen short of their mark or to have dimmed the luster of his house."

2   Martín García of Loyola was Ignatius's elder brother. In 1507, he became heir to their father's *mayorazgo* (primogeniture).

whatever clothes you please, he doesn't stop being a monkey: *Naturam expellas furca, tamen usque recurret. Coelum, non animum mutant, qui trans mare currunt.*[3]

Neither the plain habit that Ignatius wore anew, nor the pilgrimage overseas stopped in him that dash of generosity that he had brought with him from his mother's womb. As soon as he and his first six companions made their first vow at Montmartre, he had made himself their leader, without waiting for them to elect him. Something you will find in Maffei, who tells us that when, on the advice of his physicians, he was advised to take a change of air, owing to his long illness, as he headed to Spain, he left his companions behind with Pierre Favre, in whom he had great confidence: *Ceterum* (says Maffei) *nequid é suo discessu res parisiensis caperet detrimenti, primum commilitones ad perseverantiam ac fidem paucis adhortatus, Petrum Fabrum et annis et vcatione antiquissimum, illis praeposuit, cui interim obtemperarent.*[4] Thus at this time, he made himself preeminent over them. And all his later actions should remove all doubt. For it was he whom they promised to meet at Vincenza on a specific day, in order to discuss whether they would return to Rome, to set up their new sect, of which he was taking charge as their head. That was why he made sure that when a general for the order was elected, he could not miss holding that position; and before going any farther, he made sure that the general would exercise that charge for his entire life and would have absolute power over his religious.

Ergo sine controversia deligendum videri, cui omnes in terris, tanquam Christo parerent, cujus in verba jurarent, denique cujus sibi nutum ac voluntatem instar divini cujusdam oraculi ducerent. His ita constitutis deinceps quaesitum de hujus ipsius potestate, utrum certo dierum spatio definitam, an verò perpetuam esse oporteret: perpetuam esse placuit omnibus.[5]

Therefore (he said), it was decided, with no contention, that one would be elected whom all the others would obey on this humble earth, as if they were obeying Jesus Christ; they would do him faith and homage, and they would value his commands as if they came from a divine oracle. Now, things having been established, they discussed whether his power

---

3 "Drive nature out with a pitchfork, she'll come right back"; and "The change their sky, not their soul, who rush across the sea." Horace, *Epistles*, I, x, 24; and I, xi, 27.

4 "Lest the others might be harmed by his absence from Parisian affairs, after having exhorted his fellow soldiers to perseverance and faith he put Pierre Favre, the eldest both in years and in vocation, in command, whom they would obey in the meantime."

5 Maffei, Lib. 2, ch. 9.

would be fixed for a specific time, or whether it should be for life. And they decided it would be for life.

Since then, the order having been approved in Rome, and Ignatius having been elected general, the matter of absolute power arose. Having been raised amid weapons, not letters,[6] he introduced a tyrannical state into the Jesuit family; he wanted his will, and the wills of the generals who would succeed him, to be deemed absolutely good, just, and valuable. For although, at the time, they were pretending to pay similar obedience to the Holy See, on these grounds they were authorized in Rome, in everything, and everywhere. They were showing more obedience toward their general than toward the pope. I'll not say toward their general exclusively, but toward all the other superiors, such as their provincials and rectors: or more obedience to the mission vow than to blind obedience. I'll conclude now; and in so doing, I won't be repudiated by a dispassionate soul: the power to command that the pope and the general possess over the Jesuits is sovereign in every way, but it is incomparably more precise as far as their general is concerned.

This makes me believe that if the Holy See was ever breached, no sect could affect it adversely, except the Jesuits, as long as their general is in Rome. We exclaim about the Lutherans, and for good reason, since they were the first ones in our century to trouble the repose of the Catholic Church. But for all that, I don't consider them more dangerous for the Holy See than the Jesuits are. Some pedant or silly scholar will say that I'm heretical when I put forth that proposition. I don't think so but listen to my reason. All those whom, today, we in France say belong to the so-called Religion, or the Reformed Religion, or the New Religion, have no stable and permanent head over them. If they did have one, they would be contradicting the religion they profess, for they would have removed the primacy of the pope, in order to introduce another primacy over them. I've noticed that they live in an oligarchy, or else in an aristocracy. A person who, by his knowledge and his long experience, has some advantage over the other ministers, has a life-time authority that isn't transmitted to his successor when he dies. Moreover, they lack the external ceremonies without which the effects of a religion cannot easily operate in the hearts of simple people, for whom the eye gives rise to, or confirms an inner devotion. Among them, a person who is esteemed as a great minister never studied

---

6   This is a common myth. Ignatius was not a soldier but a knight. As such, he served the duke of Navarra to defend Pamplona in 1521—the only battle he ever participated in.

anything but Calvin's *Institutes*.[7] Or the works of Peter Martyr and a few other moderns.[8] So, I have no doubt that, in time, this sect will become lame all on its own. It would have been lurking behind every affair if the unfortunate ambitions of the Jesuits hadn't opposed the wise plans of the late king. I know full well that in saying this, I won't be welcome among the ministers; but I didn't make an effort to be welcomed. My sole ambition is to see our Apostolic, Catholic, and Roman Church observing the same discipline and dignity that it did in our grandparents' day. Conclusion: our kings being Catholic, as they necessarily must be if they want to reign, I fear nothing from the Huguenots of our France. Since we have to go where the devil drives us, they will be forced, over time, to leave the battlefield to the Holy See.

But I fear everything about the Jesuits, not only in France, but in Rome as well, because their regime aims only at establishing a tyranny over everyone, a tyranny that they will gain foot by foot, unless someone puts things in order. They have a general who is not elected at specific times (as the general of the Franciscans is) but who is perpetual, like the pope. They'll tell me that something similar is found among the Carthusians, and I agree.[9] But they are cloistered monks who lead a solitary life in their cloisters and have no business or communication with the outside world. People will add that there are several heads of orders, for example the orders of Cluny, Prémontré, and Grammond, who aren't elective, and who change little as long as they live. So be it. But they have inviolable statutes from their first institutions, to which they are limited, being unable to dispense with them to the detriment of their religious. That's not the case with our Jesuits: for them, nothing is as certain as the uncertainty of their Constitutions, which can be changed in the chapter, without seeking advice from the Holy See.[10] And likewise, when their general

---

7   *Institutio christianae religionis* (1536).

8   See Book 1, ch. 4 above.

9   Cf. "The Carthusian Order," in *The Catholics Encyclopedia*: "The prior of the Grande Chartreuse, who is elected by the monks of that house, is always the general of the order. He wears no insignia, but is the only one in the order who receives the title of 'Reverend Father', all other religious being known as 'Venerable Fathers'. The general chapter, which consists of the visitors and all the priors, meets annually, and receives the resignations of all the superiors of the order including the general. These it reinstates or removes at will."

10   Cf. *Exposcit debitum* (1550): "This superior general, with the council of his associates (with the majority of votes always having the right to prevail), shall possess the authority to compose constitutions leading to the achievement of this end which has been proposed to us. He shall also have the authority to explain officially doubts which may arise in connection with our Institute as comprised in this Formula. The council, which must necessarily be convoked to establish or change the Constitutions and for other matters of more than ordinary importance, such as the alienation or dissolution of houses and colleges once

is dealing with common matters, he does it by his sole authority. One knows how a lifetime or perpetual magistrate can make himself believed by those who hold their position for a specified time. In the first, General Congregation held by the Jesuits in 1558, Pope Paul IV intentionally sent Cardinal Pacheco[11] to them, to inform them that he wanted the generals to be elected for a set term, foreseeing the extraordinary splendor that could surge from this lifetime power; but worn down by their entreaties, he did what they wanted, although he notified them, via Cardinal Travensis,[12] that he thought perpetual power was better.

This general is perpetual, but all the dignities of his order are temporal. Beneath him are the provincials of the various provinces; under the provincials are the rectors, who have the particular authority over their houses and colleges, and consequently over the fathers, and over the spiritual and temporal coadjutors, and also over the approved scholars. As for the principals of the colleges, they are chiefly destined to keep an eye on the foreign scholars. These positions usually are triennial, but they can be prolonged or shortened, as the general wishes. He can dispose of temporal things without asking anyone's opinion but his own, and he has an infinity of prerogatives that aren't even granted to our bishops.

I'll restate, piece by piece, what I mean: the provincials are their bishops, the rectors are their curates. Just as, in the Languedoc region of southern France we call rectors those who elsewhere in France are called *curés*, curates. None of them (as I've pointed out) is perpetual, and they depend on the simple will of their general, who can appoint anyone he pleases. All the other dignities of Christianity do not compare with the dignity of Our Holy Father, yet when compared, the pope's dignity is less. For having provided someone with a bishopric, a curacy, or an abbey, his hands are tied in the future, and he cannot depose, with absolute power, those whom he himself has selected: they are not deposable *ad nutum*, on command, as Jesuit provincials and rectors

erected, should be understood (according to the explanation in our Constitutions) to be the greater part of the entire professed Society which can be summoned without grave inconvenience by the superior general."

11   Pedro Pacheco de Villena (1488–1560), a Spanish cardinal, was viceroy of Naples and bishop of Siguenza. He was made a cardinal in 1546. See John W. Padberg, "The General Congregations of the Society of Jesus: A Brief Survey of Their History," *Studied in the Spirituality of Jesuits* 6 (1974): 7.

12   Sutto, 430n308, identifies him as Giovanni Bernardino Scotti (?–1568), a Theatine, bishop of Piacenza, archbishop of Trani, and a judge on the tribunal of the Inquisition in Rome. He was made a cardinal in 1555. But more likely it was Cardinal Giovan Domenico de Cupis (1493–1553), the dean of the College of Cardinals, who had dealings with the Jesuits in Rome at that time. See Maryks, *Jesuit Order*, 89.

are. According to the antique canonical constitutions, Our Holy Father cannot grant bishops or abbots the power to alienate the temporal of their churches without full knowledge of the facts. In like manner, an assembly of the chapter is required, so that they can advise; and once consent has been granted, they go before the superior, who appoints a promoter[13] to act as *procureur* and defender of the church's possessions, in order to see whether or not the alienation is necessary. Their general can sell, pawn, alienate, dissipate the possessions of the Jesuit family, and he is accountable only to himself. And here is a tyranny that has no equivalent: having delegated some persons to sell and alienate, he can overthrow and annul everything they have done, even if they have not exceeded the limits of their assignment.[14] Our Holy Father does not assume for himself the authority to permit someone who has made a vow of poverty, chastity, and obedience, to receive inheritances and to possess temporal possessions privately; and even less does he permit that person to return to the world in order to marry, with the sole exception of kings and sovereign princes, when there is a very urgent need in their kingdoms. It is exactly the opposite in the Jesuit sect, when they take their first vow, which they call the simple vow. Aren't they giving more authority to their general than Our Holy Father gives to himself? I told you yesterday that, as far as the Missions are concerned, the general can send all his religious wherever he wishes, not only after the final vow, but after the first or the second. That is stated very clearly in the ninth part of their Constitutions, chapter 3, article 9.[15] Today I want to know from whom he gets that power, for the Holy See doesn't have it. Let's seek help from all the bulls of the Jesuit order. I know very well that in the bull of Paul III, 1549,[16] the general is permitted, like the pope, to send religious to diverse lands in order to propagate our faith; but that clause applies to the fathers who have been admitted to take the final solemn vow. For the Holy See's mission applies to them alone. It must therefore come from a special obligation that the other Jesuits have to their general. But where is it stated? Neither in the simple vow, nor in the first solemn vow, do they assume any obligation toward either the pope or their general, to make this mission vow, but simply to make the three substantial vows of the other religious orders.[17] Where, then, is that obligation hiding? It is hiding in the general's tyranny, and in their blind obedience. And

---

13   *Promoteur* (promoter): "a person who takes the principal care of a matter. It is especially said about the person who carries out the function of *procureur général* in a church court, or in an ecclesiastical assembly." DAF 1694.

14   *Constitutions*, IX, iii, 5, 6 (p. 361).

15   *Constitutions*, IX, iii, 9 (pp. 362–63).

16   In Paul III's *Licet debitum*. See Book II, ch. 3 above.

17   That is, of poverty, chastity, and obedience.

what gives one greatly to ponder, is that this same blind obedience is sworn by all of them, and it is promised to the pope, yet he does not exercise his power over missions, except for the fathers of the great and final vow. Whence comes this diversity? The answer is quick to find: to put it briefly, Our Holy Father does not have as much power over the Jesuits as their general does. He is their sovereign pope; he has usurped from them. And in their bizarre republic they recognize ours only by conduct.

Let's carry on, and let's see their other demeanors. They say that they received the law from the Holy See. To the contrary, I believe that they gave that law to the Holy See. Therefore, before the bull of 1540, there was no first foundation of their order: on their private authority, they carried on their monkey business before the Carthusians of Paris. Later they opened their schools to all comers and goers; and prior to obtaining permission in 1561, for forty-four entire years, they exercised their simple vow (which contravenes the constitutions of the church), until Gregory XIII gave them a safe-conduct.[18] And to the extent that, by surprise, they made our popes disposed not to contradict their splendors, that facility on the part of the Holy See opened up the means for their general to want to equal him.

Let's recognize, as ordered by God, that as soon as Our Holy Father is elected in the conclave, the cardinals kneel before him, reverence him, and kiss his hands. I don't think that honor should be given to anyone but the pope. The Jesuit general receives the very same kneeling and hand-kissing when he is elected.[19] And yet, I shan't be scandalized. For that is done in other monasteries, especially in public ceremonies. But to receive those ceremonies from others, that's not excusable. I won't go any farther for an example than Father Claudio Acquaviva, their current general. Having been elected in 1581, and all his religious having reverenced him, and having gone up to his bedchamber, *Inde pater* (says the first of the annual letters for that year) *cubiculum ascendens, eo die salutanti turbae omnis generis hominum, exosculandas manus praebuit.* That is to say: "From there, the father went up into his room, gave his hands to be kissed by all sorts of persons who came to salute him." What sort of new idolatry is that? It was done in plain sight, and the Jesuits boast about it. Isn't it like having a new pope in Rome, a pope who triumphs over the ancient papacy?

In our church, we have only one great head, whom we recognize above all the other prelates as being God's vicar. The general of the Jesuits, as if he were another pope, takes that same rank over his religious. All the vows that

---

18   See Book I, ch. 15 above.
19   *Constitutions*, viii, vi, 6.

the Jesuits make between his hands, call him the lieutenant of God.[20] I see little difference between a lieutenant and vicar of God. In one place in their Constitutions, a Jesuit's note calls him *Christi vicarium* [Christ's vicar]. They are so impudent: not only do they have their general take that title, but all their superiors use it with their inferiors: *Omnibus itidem commendatum sit ut multum reverentiae, et praecipue in interiore hominis, suis superioribus exhibeant, et Jesum Christum in eisdem considerent et revereantur.* "Let everyone also be enjoined to show great reverence for their superiors, especially in the interior of their souls, and that they revere them and recognize in them Our Lord Jesus Christ."[21]

Jesuit Montaignes, speaking of the obedience they vow to their general, does not disguise this matter: "If they promise to obey him (he says), it is in consideration of the fact that he is the vicar of God for the governing of the aforesaid Society." If he had written "vicar of Our Holy Father for the governing of this Society," it wouldn't have been adequate. For the Jesuits never lack fine appearances that are excerpted from the Holy Scripture and quoted out of context. So, to approve of this title that the general took, as a co-rival of the pope, they say: "Qui vos audit, me audit, et qui vos spern it me spernit."[22] David, speaking of the judges, said: "Vos dii estis, et Deus stetit in synagoga Deorum."[23] Saint Basil said that a prelate represents the person of Jesus Christ.[24] And Saint Gregory Nazianzen, addressing the emperor, said: "You hold the empire with Jesus Christ; with him you command on earth; you are God's image."[25] These allegations certainly are worthy of a Jesuit, to show that each person who commands someone else is a vicar of God. In stronger terms, I will assert something that I fetched up from their well. For when Popes Paul and Julius III, in their bulls

---

20   On two occasions the English translation of the *Constitutions*, 202, 206, done by the Institute of Jesuit Sources (1996), says that the general "holds the place of God" (part v, ch. 3, 3; and part v, ch. 4, iv, 2). "Lieutenant" of course means "place" + "holding." Hence Pasquier's comment to the effect that the two terms are virtually the same.

21   For these titles, see *Constitutions*, part 5, ch. 3, 3; part 5, ch. 4, 2; part 4, ch. 3, 2; and part 6, ch. 1, 2.

22   Luke 10:16. "And whoever rejects you rejects me. And whoever rejects me rejects the one who sent me."

23   "God takes a stand in the divine council, gives judgment in the midst of the gods." Ps. 82:1.

24   Pasquier refers here probably to Basil the Great's *Letters*, in which he discussed the character of priesthood. See Ioan Tulcan, "Sfin enia şi caracterul moral – condi ii ale preoţilor şi candidaţilor la preoţie, după epistolele Sfântului Vasile cel Mare," *Anuar*, serie noua, 2, no. 2 (2017): 73–86.

25   This model is usually associated with Eusebius of Caesarea (265–339). See Isabella Sandwell, *Religious Identity in Late Antiquity: Greeks, Jews and Christians in Antioch* (*Greek Culture in the Roman World*) (Cambridge: Cambridge University Press, 2009), 125.

of 1540 and 1550, speaking of their general, said: *In illo Christum velut praesentem agnoscant*,[26] was he intended to take that grand title over his brethren? Not really. But to use it just as we see it used at the Council of Trent: Our Lord, going up to heaven: *Sacerdotes sui ipsius Vicarios reliquit, tanquam praesides et judices, ad quos mortalia crimina deferantur, in quae Christi fideles inciderint*,[27] in order to give them absolution. Or in another place, when recommending the poor to persons holding benefices, he adds: *Memores eos qui hospitalitatem amant, Christum in hospitibus recipere*. That is to say, they should remember to be hospitable to the poor; and if they receive them as guests, they also receive Jesus Christ. Words that are proffered in order to stir up in us an abundance of piety, obedience, and charity: and not to form an Anabaptism like the one the Jesuits constructed upon these words: *Que l'on reconnoisse en leur General Jesu-Christ*.[28] That is what Jan van Leiden, king of the Anabaptists, wanted people to believe he was.[29]

But inasmuch as I've already discussed that amply, I'll be satisfied to tell you that, in taking that title of vicar of God over his religious, their general introduced a new schism between the pope and himself. And when, in order to defend that title, Montaignes and his suffragans make use of all the above-mentioned passages, falling (as the saying goes) from a low fever to a high one, by their subtle cunning they presented another schism, one with a more dangerous effect than the first one. All the more so since emperors, kings, and judges can each in his place usurp that title. And thus we fall at the feet of the archbishops and the bishops, whom we recognize in, and inside of, their dioceses, as being vicars of God. And without thinking about it, we fall into the heresy of the Lutherans, who want to reduce the power of Our Holy Father. And yet, they don't take that title, nor is it attributed to them. It is a title that belongs solely to the pope, a title that no good and faithful Christian can envy, and of which one must be jealous when confronted by those who want to put a shine on their splendor.

But have we gone blind? Some of us don't know that the bishops, in their positions, are true creations of God; and that, as such, starting with the days of the apostles, and on until today, they have been conserved until now. There isn't a single one of us who doesn't know that the Jesuits are the pope's new creatures. If there were subject and matter for taking the title "vicar of God,"

---

26   "They recognize in him the presence of Christ."

27   "Left behind him priests, his own vicars, as rulers and judges [Matthew 16:19, John 20:23], to whom all the mortal sins into which the faithful of Christ may have fallen" (session 14 of the Council of Trent that discussed the sacrament of penance).

28   "Let them recognize Jesus Christ in their general."

29   See ch. 1 above.

it should be the bishops, in the confines of their dioceses. But they don't take it, they modestly leave it for the pope. And the Jesuit who has no other honor than this, won't he use it in the same manner? From the Council of Trent, so celebrated in Rome, there are an infinite number of articles that prohibit bishops from doing many things in their dioceses, things that our Gallican Church deems to be well founded on ordinary law. They are ordered to be known as vicars of the Holy See: yet we permit the younger brothers of our church to have power over theirs, as vicars of God, and not as vicars of the Holy See? How can this be made to agree?

I'll add that usually we call cardinals *reverendissimi*, just as we call princes *illustrissimi*. Their general consistory doesn't enjoy that grand title. But the Society of Jesuits managed to get its foot into the Roman door, that is, to be called *illustrissimi*. This can be seen in Navarrus, the canonist.[30] *Advertendum est* (he says) *quod per solam gestionem habitus, per unum vel plures annos, in Illustrissimo Societatis Jesu ordine, non videtur fieri professio tacita.* "You must be careful (he says) that in the *Illustrissimus* order of the Society of Jesus, one is not thought to make a tacit profession in order to wear the habit." Navarrus was in Rome under Gregory XIII, and he was giving greater honor to those hypocrites than we do to the grand and venerable consistory of the cardinals, who are the ordinary advisors of the Holy See. When we write to bishops, we call them Reverend Fathers in God, and we think that, by doing this, we are honoring them sufficiently. Every Jesuit father of the great vow is given that title, as if he were a bishop. The letter about Father Mathieu, the Jesuit, that our Sixteen Parisian Tigers[31] sent to the king of Spain during the Troubles, calls him Reverend Father Mathieu in three places; and in most of the books that they wrote, two letters were added to the name: R.P., which denotes *Révérend Père*, Reverend Father. When we speak to Our Holy Father, we say *Votre Sainteté*, Your Holiness. When one speaks not only to the general or to another superior of this order but also to a simple Jesuit father, he would think you were mocking his splendor if you said *Votre Révérence*, Your Reverence. And we say that they aren't encroaching upon the authority of the Holy See? But why should we laugh when we encroach upon the authority of Our Lord Jesus Christ, to

---

30   See Book I, ch. 1 above. The citation is from Navarrus's, *De Regularibus commentarii quatuor*, commentary 4, n. 76. Cited in Francisco Suárez, *Tractatus de religione Societatis Jesu*, ed. Paul Guéau de Reverseaux (Brussels: Greuse, 1857), 146.

31   He is referring to the "Seize," that is, the leaders of the Holy League in Paris. Despite the name, derived from the fact that they represented the sixteen administrative districts of Paris, there were not actually sixteen of them. See ch. 11 above.

whom alone our church attributes apostles?[32] This, despite the fact that the general of the Jesuits is so impudent as to tolerate having all the fathers of his order who are in Portugal and in some parts of the Indies, be called his apostles. That doesn't mean that the pope is being pushed from his Seat,[33] nor Jesus Christ from his throne. That isn't being God's vicar, it's believing that one is God himself.

Circa 1503, when Ismail,[34] later called the Sophi, wanted, to disrupt the Levantine state, and take as a model the Ottoman emperors of Constantinople, he began by stirring up Mohammed's old religion, feigning that he wanted to change it from good to better, and to do it in a narrower way. He said that Mohammed (who never took a loftier title than prophet of God) had had a brother named Hali,[35] who, under his brother's banner, had introduced a more austere religion that Ismail was boasting about restoring. As part of this fine promise, he had Mohammed declared a prophet, and he changed the shape of the turban worn by his people, who began to reverence him as God's true image and to resolutely follow his orders. To the point that, on this pretext, he at first amassed a handful of folks, with whose help he first attacked some shacks; and later, in the manner of another new Mohammed, he swelled his army to such a point that he was followed by six thousand mounted men and footsoldiers, making all the Levant tremble. With these procedures that mingled religion and the state, and under the great and respected name of Sophi, he conquered an infinity of lands, from which his posterity profited. This comparison doesn't work in every detail, but if you look closely at everything that went on, and that goes on, you'll see that our Jesuits followed, and are following, in our Christianity, the same trails that Ismael did in his Mohammedism. Their prophet Ismail is the great Ignatius, who by his fabulous visions wanted to make people believe that, sometimes in daylight, and sometimes at night, he communicated with God the Father, with his Son Jesus Christ, with the Virgin Mary, with Saint Peter. And just as Ismail went back to Hali, Mohammed's purported brother, to find a new religion that sprouted from the old stalk, in

---

32   That is, Christ alone created the apostles, and thence their successors, the bishops. This is the Gallican view, as opposed to the papalist view that Christ delegated his authority to the papacy, which in turn subdelegates it to bishops.

33   Pasquier uses the word *Siège*, which means "seat." The Holy See is also a "seat," a *Sancta Sedes*. Indeed, Pasquier seems unable to repress this sort of joke.

34   Ismail I (1487–1524) founded the Safavid dynasty and ruled from 1501 to 1524 as Shah of Persia. See *Encyclopaedia Britannica*, https://www.britannica.com/biography/Ismail-I-shah-of-Iran (accessed January 22, 2021).

35   Ali ibn Abi Talib (601–661) was a cousin and son-in-law of Prophet Mohammed.

like manner Ignatius assumed the new name Jesuit, instead of the Christian word that is authorized by the apostles. We built a religion that had never been seen in the early days of our church. Ismail, under the new vow, changed the antique turban; Ignatius introduced a new monasticism in our very midst.[36] And he was very careful to have his followers wear the garments usually worn by monks.[37] In order to make himself great, Ismail mingled religion and the state. Ignatius and his men, didn't they do the same? Ismail and his successors ordered that they be reverenced by their followers. Ignatius did the same, and so did those who became generals after him; but they went farther, because the general of the Jesuits not only had his men reverence him, he also had it done by those who didn't belong to his sect but who were nonetheless infected by their superstitious hypocrisy. Ismail had people call him the prophet of God; the general says he is the vicar of God. By means of all these procedures and artifices, Ismail and his successors troubled the Mohammedan state. And we, in Rome, will we question everything related to the Jesuit Sophi? Anyone who doesn't mistrust him is not a true and legitimate child of the Holy See.

I beg you to conjure up a picture of their arrival and their progress. In the beginning, the Jesuits were content to total sixty: in three years, they had the door opened to all sorts of folks who wanted to be their supporters. After that, they preempted the *ordinaires* and the universities, and then the kings and their kingdoms. Finally, they aren't content with being like the bishops in their dioceses toward everyone who presents himself to them, but they make themselves still greater among their disciples than the popes are over us. Although one cannot base a certain judgment on future things, I nonetheless can say, and it is true, that when it involves the state, there are demonstrations to predict good or bad fortune, and these demonstrations are no less certain than the demonstrations of mathematics. When the popular government in Rome declined, a civil war was kindled in Gaul between two great factions: the Sequani and the Aedui, who aspired in various ways to a general princeship. The Aedui formed a confederation with the Romans and called upon them to help: Julius Caesar, who ever since his youth had no little ambition in his soul, was made governor for five years of the parts of Gaul that were on the nearer and the farther sides of the mountains.[38] With this, he was given four legions of armed men, paid for by the Republic. Since he was a great warrior, and at

---

36 The Jesuits were not founded as a monastic order. See Book I, ch. 15 above.

37 To the contrary, the Jesuit Constitutions did not prescribe a specific garb. See *Const.* [577] quoted in the discussion on this topic in Book II, ch. 1.

38 Pasquier uses the plural: *les Gaules*. Indeed, one can borrow Caesar's expression and say that Gaul was divided into three parts: Gallia Celtica, Belgica, and Aquitania. But one also spoke of "Nearer Gaul," that is, the northern part of the Italian peninsula, just south of

the same time directed his affairs so well, feigning to help the Aedui, he made all of Gaul pay tribute to the Roman people. In consideration of this, thanks to his friends' plotting, he often obtained special privileges. He even had, as an intermediary, Pompey the Great, the general, his son-in-law, who in addition to the marriage alliance, thought he was doing the right thing in promoting Julius Caesar's splendor. He lived very well in the city and was therefore very willingly followed. Wise Cato Uticensis,[39] seeing how everything was going, often shouted at him, saying that he was losing the Republic without thinking about it, and that he was tracing a tyrannical path to Caesar. He would experience this when it was too late to repent. What he had predicted, happened: and after several civil wars, the state fell to the family of Julius Caesar and his friends. God may want me to be a liar, but when I look at the history of our Jesuits, I'm very frightened. Martin Luther took direct offense at the authority of the Holy See: the Jesuits, linked to the state, didn't house any less ambition in their souls, beneath their simple cassocks, than Caesar did. They presented themselves to shore up the papacy, but they proposed an obedience so novel that, if I dared, I would willingly say that they form a third party between the true Catholic and the Lutheran. Caesar conquered the near and far Gauls by weapons. These Jesuits (if you are willing to believe them) conquered a part of the Indies by their prattling, thanks however to the kings of Portugal, in the places where they were all-powerful. As for our straying souls, I don't see that they worked great miracles in order to bring them to the bosom of the church. Caesar, as a reward for his victories, obtained several privileges from the Republic that had previously been given only to other lords. The Jesuits, talking about their imaginary conquests in unknown lands, obtained from the Holy See an infinity of indults that never before had been granted, except to them. Cato shouted about the privileges that Caesar would be ordered to give up when the Republic ended. The great Faculty of Theology of Paris declared, as early as 1554, that this sect would eventually be the desolation and ruin of our church: and a few foresighted spirits predicted that the church would one day trouble France, as it indeed did. Caesar changed the popular state into a tyranny consisting of him and his relations: how our Jesuits will end up toward the Holy See, that lies in God's hand. I am consoled by one thing, and no more, which is that this great Seat is built upon foundations that are far more solid

---

the Alps; and "Farther Gaul," roughly the France of today, situated north of the Alps. The Aedui and the Sequani both lived in Gallia Celtica-Farther Gaul.

39   Marcus Porcius Cato Uticensis (95–46 BCE), known as Cato the Younger, was a gifted orator. He is remembered for his moral integrity and his tenacity, especially during his long conflict with Julius Caesar. See *Encyclopaedia Britannica*, https://www.britannica.com/biography/Marcus-Porcius-Cato-Roman-senator-95-46-BC (accessed January 22, 2021).

than the foundations of the Roman Republic. But I'll also add that just as Our Lord Jesus Christ lodged his divinity in a human body in order to redeem us, as long as our great prelates lodge their holiness in themselves, everything will go well for them and for us: but if, in their holinesses they mingle indefinable traces of man, in order to think about preserving their splendor, they will be doomed; and they will, in the same way, doom our church.

CHAPTER 26

One Must Not Make It a Practice to Believe Our Jesuits' Promises, Because There Is No Faith and Law in Them, beyond the Faith and the Law That Depend on the Convenience of Their Affairs

THE LAWYER. Until now, you've been able to hear from me about the heresies, the Machiavellisms, and the Anabaptisms that are contained in the Jesuit sect, their assassinations, and the misfortunes they've brought to France and to wherever else they live. I won't sound retreat until tomorrow, but before doing that, I must skirmish again, to oppose the recovery they are obtaining against the decree of the Parlement of Paris, which was granted more by a just judgment of God than by men. Now, in that new pursuit, anyone who notes the time when they began to stir, and the authority of the person they are employing there, will judge them more worldly-wise than religious. I don't know whether they'll win in the end. For to tell the truth, the demands and the insistence that are their principal virtues, have great advantages over the Frenchman, who is naturally gall-less when one tickles his ears.[1] I'm sure that the memoirs of Maggio, the Jesuit, their delegate, are letting loose all sorts of fine promises by him, in order to attain what they want; but if they are ever reestablished, you can also be sure that they won't keep a single one of those promises. I'll prove this by an infinity of examples that I'll string out from the very beginning of their sect until today.

They had vowed themselves to God (as they say) in the church at Montmartre, in 1534, and they promised to go to Jerusalem to convert the Turks to Christianity.[2] On these grounds, they found themselves in Venice in 1537, debating whether they should leave after having received the blessings of Pope Paul III, by whom they had been well received, thanks to the intervention of several persons who were supporting them; and they were given

---

1 This sentence begins with the expression *être sans fiel* (to have no gall), that is, to show no rancor. It ends with an image from the Bible: 2 Tim. 4:3, "For the time will come when people will not put up with sound doctrine. Instead, to suit their own desires, they will gather around them a great number of teachers to say what their itching ears want to hear." The image of "itching ears," used this one time in the Bible, describes individuals who seek out doctrines that condone their own lifestyle, as opposed to the teachings of the apostles.

2 See Book I, ch. 12 above.

enough money to make the journey. Nothing was preventing their undertaking, other than the benevolence of a few lords whom they had met in Rome and under whose favor they promised to forge a sect that was more pliant. To excuse breaking their vows, they stressed that the paths were closed to them, owing to the war that they claimed was being waged between Venice and the Turks. Now, it's certain that, during the very year when they were approved, which was 1540, there were truces between the two countries, at first based on oaths; but there was also a full peace. So, what made them change their first plans? The convenience of their affairs, and nothing else.

In that same church at Montmartre, they had sworn not to undertake the conquest of lost souls, until they were doctors of theology. That was a promise made right in God's face. It was woven together and very reasonable. For along with the sincere conscience that they then had, they also needed knowledge of the effect of converting infidels. When they found their opportunity in Rome, did they have the patience to keep their promise? Nay, nay. They want their activities to be convenient, so they sought new advice.

These first two attempts made them masters at perfidy and at breaking faith, whenever an opportunity arose that looked as if it would advance their plans. At the Assembly of Poissy in 1561, they promised to renounce all their vows and to obey the usual discipline of the other colleges.[3] They have since renewed that promise before the full Parlement, after which they were received under the name Collège de Clermont in Paris, and nothing more, despite the fact that, they obtained bulls from Pope Pius IV that very same year that were contrary to all the ancient privileges of our universities, and that abolished some of them.

In 1564, when they presented their request to the Parlement to matriculate into the body of the university, forgetting the decrees of our Gallican Church that was confirmed by another decree, they had called themselves the Society of Jesus, a title they were forbidden to use. Pasquier having raised objections from the very start of the case, to the effect that the titles they had taken abolished the effect of their request, they renounced it through Versoris, their lawyer, saying that it had been issued in error by Pons Cogordan, who was the first and principal person to undertake the case. Cogordan himself disavowed it.[4]

In Rome, they obeyed the Holy See in everything, and they did it from blind obedience, as I showed you in their Constitutions. In France, if you believe them, solely on the basis of the mission vow, as you'll find their prohibition of

---

3   See Book I, ch. 5 above.
4   See Book I, ch. 4.

1594 for the Collège de Clermont, and Montaignes's book, and the very humble request that was presented to the king by an unnamed Jesuit.[5]

In Rome, they recognize the pope as the temporal and spiritual lord of all Christian princes. Otherwise, they would directly contravene all those extravagant decretals that lay down the law for all monarchs. That proposition is very familiar at the Roman Curia. Indeed, in the bulls issued for the publication of the Jubilee of 1600, Saint Peter and Saint Paul are called princes of the earth. In France, they are very careful not to be mistaken before the outside world. For in their plea of 1594, and in Montaignes's book, they maintain that the pope makes no claims over the temporal, other than what he has acquired in Italy over a long period of time. In his life of Ignatius, Ribadeneyra admits that the entire Jesuit order was praying to God specifically for the health of the late king of Spain.[6]

Read their books today: they don't know what to make of this peculiarity of praying for the king of Spain; but they generally pray for all the princes, under whose obedience they have established their residences. During the peak of our Troubles, no cardinal raised as many obstacles as did the dukes of Nevers,[7] and the Marquis of Pisani, who was sent by the king to Rome.[8] And there was the Cardinal of Toledo, a Jesuit.[9] When the Troubles were waning, no single individual worked harder to favor our affairs with His Holiness.

While our last troubles were going on, no one did as much evil as they did, if you believe the upright and honorable persons who were spectators at these tragedies. Read the very humble request and remonstrance that they presented to the king: there is nothing that this poor, innocent populace deems more abhorrent than what they previously adored. Legal practitioners say: "To manage something badly is to write good things about it."[10]

---

5   He is referring to Richeome's *Très humble remonstrance et requeste*, published anonymously (1598 and 1602).

6   Perhaps Pasquier refers here to the following passage from Book 11, ch. 18: "Day and night we ought to placate God with our prayers and wear him out with our requests that he watch over and keep safe and flourishing Philip the Catholic king as long as possible."

7   Louis (Ludovico) Gonzaga, duke of Nevers (1539–95), belonged to the League. He helped in the reconciliation between King Henri IV and the pope. See *DBI*, https://www.treccani .it/enciclopedia/ludovico-gonzaga_(Dizionario-Biografico) (accessed January 22, 2021).

8   See ch. 16 above.

9   Francisco de Toledo (1532–96), professor of theology and philosophy at the Roman College, was the first Jesuit cardinal. He played an important role in reconciling Henri IV and the pope. See *DHCJ*, 4:3807–8.

10   *À mal exploiter, bien écrit*: This saying refers to someone who fails at something, then writes about it, not as he did it, but as he should have done it.

Never did they put in doubt the way they mingled their holy devotions and the affairs of state, as they later made us realize. Seeing that our Troubles were on the decline, and that the king's affairs were prospering before our eyes, in 1593 they held a general assembly in Rome, where it was forbidden for them to become involved. And yet they have continued, since then, to make people believe that this was what they wanted.

But you may want a finer example than the one I'm going to talk about next. If you believe what they say, they abhor nothing so much as the Huguenot religion, and they censure books printed by Huguenots, even if they don't treat the religion as either good or evil. They categorically forbid their scholars to read those books. All the books are excommunicated for them. Oh, upright persons! But when they presented their request to the king, to be reestablished, they chose a Huguenot nobleman to be their advocate. By choosing him, they obliged him not to contradict them. These persons are part of the state and the time, and they think that everything is honest, Christian, and virtuous, as long as these things are useful to them. Long ago, when one talked about perfidious persons, one named the Carthaginians: and that led to the well-known saying: *Fides Punica*.[11] In like manner we today can say something similar about the Jesuits: *Fides jesuitica*. And we can attribute to them what Livy said about Hannibal: *Perfidia plusquam Punica, nihil veri, nihil sancti, nullus Deum metus, nullum jusjurandum, nulla religio.*[12]

A perfidy that is greater than Punic, nothing true, nothing holy, no fear of God, everything divides the parties, and every sense of religion is stepped on. They themselves, among their friends, use common words to glory in that perfidy. For if you were to ask them what a Jesuit is, *Quid est jesuita?* they would reply to you: *Omnis homo*, every man. Which means that these folks are as diverse as the chameleon, having as many colors as goals. That's certainly an accurate comparison, for the chameleon can't take on the color white, which in the Holy Scripture represents virtue. Shortly before the king's entry into Paris,[13] Father Alexander Hay, a Scot, saw that the activities of their League were declining greatly; and, with his heart overflowing, he happened to spew out these words in the midst of a large audience at the Collège de Clermont, where he was in charge of the oldest class. "Up until today, we've been Spaniards; from now on, we're obliged to be Frenchmen. It's all the same: we'll have to

---

11   *Fides Punica* (Punic faith) that is, treachery as the Romans saw it. Pasquier converts this to "Jesuit faith," that is, treachery according to the Gallican church.

12   "A perfidy worse than Punic, an utter absence of truthfulness, reverence, fear of the gods, respect for oaths, sense of religion," Livy, *The History of Rome*, XXI, iv, 9.

13   March 1594.

temporize until another season arrives. *Cedendum erit tempori* [It will be time to retreat]." Those are his very words.

And so that you won't think that this maxim comes from an ease of their consciences, with which they play for their own profit, good Father Ignatius taught them this dispensation, for which they have since created a special constitution. The other saintly fathers who founded various religious orders, established statutes and attached them (if those are the right words) to brass tables using diamond nails, so that they would perpetually be followed by their monks and religious. In the Jesuit sect, there is nothing so uncertain, as I said earlier. The bulls of Pope Paul III say:

> *Et quod possint constitutiones particulares, quas ad Societatis hujusmodi finem, et Jesu-Christi Domini nostri gloriam, ac proximi utilitatem conformes esse judicaverint, conderé: et tam hactenus factas, quam in posterum faciendas constitutiones, ipsas juxta locorum, temporum, et rerum qualitatem et varietatem mutare, seu in totum cassare, et alias de novo condere possint et valeant. Quae postea alteratae, mutatae. Seu de novo condita fuerint, eo ipso, Apostolicae sedis authoritate praefata, confirmatae censeantur, eadem Apostolica autoritate, de speciali gratia indulgemus.*

That they can issue (says Pope Paul III) special rules that they deem appropriate for use by the Society, to the glory of Our Lord Jesus Christ, and for the use of one's neighbor. And that those rules that have been issued, as explained later, can be changed, broken, and totally annulled, according to the variety and encounters of places, times, and things, and new ones established in their place. Which having been thus changed, revoked, or established anew, we want them confirmed by the authority of the Holy Apostolic See, and insofar as is necessary, by the same authority, we confirm them by special grace.

I've translated the passage word by word, but when the bull says, in Latin, that the Constitutions can be changed to fit the goals of the Society, that means for the manipulation and the advancement of the Society. From this general constitution, they distilled a special one that merits being known. The sixth part of their Constitutions, chapter 5, bears this title:

> *QUOD Constitutiones, peccati obligationem non inducunt.* It begins: *CUM exoptet Societas, universas suas Constitutiones, declarationes ac vivendi ordinum, omnino juxta nostrum institutum, nihil ultra in re declinando, observari: Optet etiam nihilominus suos omnes secures esse, vel certè*

adjuvari, ne in laqueum ullius peccati, quod ex vi constitutionum hujus-
modi, aut ordinationum proveniat, incidant, visum est nobis in Domino, ut
excepto expresso voto, quo Societas summo Pontifici pro tempore existente
tenetur, ac tribus aliis essentialibus, Paupertatis, Castitatis, et Obedientiae,
nullas Constitutiones, declarationes, vel ordinem ullum vivendi posse obli-
gationem ac peccatum mortale, vel veniale inducere. Nisi Superior ea in
nomine Domini Jesu Christi, vel in virtute obedientiae, juberet. And a bit
later: *Et loco timoris offensae, succedat amor et desiderium omnis perfectio-*
nis, et ut major Gloria et laus Christi creatoris ac Domini nostri consequatur.

Also, our Society desires that all its Constitutions and declarations and
its *ordonnances* for living should be observed in every regard according
to our Institute: wanting, nonetheless, all our Jesuits to be assured in their
consciences, or at least helped so that they will not fall into any sin that
could arise on account of the said Constitutions or *ordonnances*. We are
of the opinion that, by the grace of God, with the exception of the express
vow which our Society has made to Our Holy Father the pope, and with
the exception of the other three essential vows of poverty, chastity, and
obedience, no constitutions, declarations, or *ordonnances* for living can
induce any obligation involving mortal or venial sin, unless the superior specifically so orders, in the name of Christ our Lord, or by virtue
of obedience. So that, instead of fearing to sin, a love and a desire for
total perfection will enter their souls, and the glory of God will be more
exalted.

By the first article, they are permitted to change, and to change again, their
Constitutions for their good points and ease. By the second article, their
Constitutions are deemed indifferent as far as the soul is concerned. The Jesuit
can therefore break the rules without committing a mortal or a venial sin. This
is a law that their great legislator introduced, so that, for the honor and glory
of God, there would be fewer sinners in their Jesuit family. Oh, holy and conscientious souls! Souls who, in order to prevent their inferiors from sinning, let
their consciences break into a great gallop, in order to sin. Let's withdraw into
ourselves dispassionately, and let's consider the effects of these two propositions. The first is that no state is secure for its prince, unless it pleases monsieur
the Jesuit. The second is that no prince is sure of his person in his state. As
far as the first point is concerned, look again at everything that has gone on
for the past twenty-five or thirty years. There was no nation where, once they
were settled, they didn't want to become involved in the affairs of state. I think
of them as being such upright persons that it was owing to the permission

granted them by their tacit constitutions (which the ancient Romans called *Senatus–Consulta tacita*);[14] or if they did it on their private authority, the general was unworthy of his charge if he didn't chastise them for it. Later, in 1593, this was forbidden to them, when they realized that all their plans had turned to nothing. Let's suppose that more new Troubles arrive: these messieurs will break that last rule and will permit their brethren to become involved, as in the past. In every region where they dwell, doesn't this list of prohibitions give rise to a household disturbance? But what are their rules for such matters? That a tyrant can be killed; that a king who overrides the common laws of his country can be deprived of his crown by his people. That there are certain other cases for killing princes and seigneurs. Into what disarray will kings fall if, in order to make sure of their states, they are forced to be censured and examined by these hypocrites?

Let's look again at their new constitution of 1593. I not only want them to be prohibited from getting mixed up in affairs of state in general terms, but I also want them to be specifically prohibited from trying to kill princes. Are they obligated to obey? Not at all. All the more so since their lawgiver doesn't burden their consciences with it, unless, stating it directly, he forbids them by virtue of their blind obedience. And that's why neither Commolet, preaching after that last statute was issued, to the effect that a new Ehud was needed to kill our king; nor Walpole, providing instructions and poison to Squire to kill the queen of England, his lady, thought that he was sinning. Because in their consciences they believed that it was being done in God's honor, that he had to make a present of these two souls. The Anabaptist had only an absolute obedience that he owed to his superior. The Jesuit has two: one depends on his superiors, the other on his individual conscience, when he becomes convinced that what he is doing is for the glory of God and the advancement of his church.

---

14   "Julius Capitolinus speaks of a sort of *Senatus–Consulta*, not describ'd by any other Author; which he calls *Senatus-Consulta tacita*, and tells us that they were made in reference to affairs of great Secrecy, without the admittance of the very Publick Servants; but all the Business was done by the Senators themselves, after the passing of an Oath of Secrecie, 'till their Design shou'd be affected." See Basil Kennet, *Romae antiquae notitia: Or the Antiquities of Rome* (London: Knaplock, 1703), 104.

CHAPTER 27

Conclusion to the Third Book, about the Reestablishment of the Jesuits Who Had Been Chased Out

THE LAWYER. You will judge, by this (he continued) just how consequential is the reestablishment that they are seeking today with our king, since everything is indifferent to them, other than things that contribute to the debasing and degradation of their sect. Every lie, every bit of cheating, every fraud, every trumpery is, for them, full of piety, provided that it is done for the advancement of their sect. Twice God has miraculously protected our king from their hands. The king doesn't owe it to his prudence, although it is great; he owes it to divine providence. These miracles are lessons and warnings that neither he, nor the persons who are near him in order to advise him, should misuse. The more he takes that viewpoint, which he received as blessings from God, the more obligated he is to admit it in all humility. The Jesuits, past masters when it comes to entreaties, use the authority of a few great nobles in order to return to grace, despite the decree issued by the court of the Parlement of Paris. I most humbly beg the king to remember that these venerable hypocrites had no greater concern than to have him assassinated, not during the peak of our Troubles, but during the truce, a time when they wanted to see him return to the bosom of the church. That was where their preachers and their regents came together. I also humbly beg him to weigh the fact that his life depends on the repose of his subjects, and that the person who laments about the sea for no reason, and who has been rescued from two shipwrecks, nonetheless embarks for a third time. And finally, I beg him to consider what formerly happened in the kingdom of Portugal, and what happened to us so recently in this France. The person in Portugal who idolized this sect the most was King Sebastian, whom the Jesuits, his principal favorites, advised to set off to conquer another kingdom, where they thought he had been killed in a pitched battle. Yet he could never be found among the dead. A great pity for a king, if he died, to have no sepulcher: but a greater pity still, if he lives (as rumor has it) but no one today recognizes him.[1] It was quite different for our great King Henri. Ever since he drove the Jesuits from his fair city and his Parlement of Paris, God has sent him a general peace, both inside and outside his kingdom, and all the

---

1 See ch. 16 above.

resources for his affairs that he could or ought to want. These are not false or imaginary examples that I'm dangling before your eyes: there isn't a man who doesn't know them and who, by the same means, can't judge how this was a disgrace for the one and a blessing for the other. In this very humble request, which is not hypocritical, as the nameless Jesuit is, lies the fulfillment of my vows. And may God want my discourse to reach the king's ears. In that, I hope he will follow the advice of the Great Consistory of Rome, against the order of the Umiliati who, after having been driven out, were not reestablished. Yet its fault was far smaller toward the Holy See than the Jesuits' fault was toward the king. Assuring you, Messieurs, that there is nothing that leads me to quarrel with them, other than the general repose of our France. And on that, I call God as my witness, who clearly reads what is in my heart.

Thus did the Lawyer end his speech. Just as the opinions of men are diverse, we all were diversely touched in our souls by what he had outlined. Some were upset with the way their order had been dissected. Others left their mouths gaping, because they had never thought that there was so much shame, garbage, and modesty in that Society. And others were extremely indignant that these Jesuits were allowed to wander totally free in several parts of France. They judged that there had never been as much reason to chastise and suppress the Templars, as there was for these men. This was why the Jesuit, for the honor he owed his brethren, spoke to him: THE JESUIT. I don't know what wrong our Society has done you, nor what sort of tokens you received when you entered the field of combat against the Society. Well, I know that you never have small enemies in your head, and that you have to strike down an infinity of leaders (which is impossible) before you reach the top. Our Society is a veritable Senate,[2] like the one that was in Rome in the days of Pyrrhus,[3] king of Epirus, whose ambassadors reported having seen as many kings as senators. These ancient senators were called *Pères*.[4] We use the same term for ours. And just as those senators were the sinews of Ancient Rome, these senators are the sinews of the new Rome, I mean the papacy, which surpasses by a long

---

2 Pasquier's contemporaries often equated the Parlement of Paris and the Senate of ancient Rome.

3 Pyrrhus (*c.*318–272 BCE), a Greek, was king of Epirus. He was one of the strongest opponents of early Rome. His battles, although victories, left him with heavy losses: hence the term "Pyrrhic victory." See *Encyclopaedia Britannica*, https://www.britannica.com/biography/ Pyrrhus (accessed January 22, 2021).

4 *Patres conscripti* (conscript fathers), was a title given to Roman senators according to their age or because of the care they took of their fellow citizens. Those who constituted the ancient council of the republic, says Sallust, had bodies weakened by age, but their minds were fortified by wisdom and experience.

shot the vain splendor of the old Romans. Moreover, before attacking a corps such as ours, one must be very circumspect. Do you remember what happened to Minos, king of Crete, as a result of his brush with the Athenians?[5] THE LAWYER. That's where I'm waiting for them. For your Society isn't the Senate you say it is: it's a monster with one hundred times more heads than a hydra, against which I want to be another Gallic Hercules,[6] in order to massacre them. I want to ask one thing of you: if, when you are back in Rome, you want to report to your general (as I'm sure you will) about everything I've said, you'll present to him, on my behalf, this quatrain, which I'm sending him in the form of a thrown-down gauntlet:[7]

> If I've handled you otherwise than with a true point,
> You must, Jesuit, take revenge.
> But by telling me the opposite of what is expected
> If you possess truth, you'll do something strange.

We all began laughing, especially the Gentleman, who addressed him. THE GENTLEMAN. I won't permit you to disregard this. It's time to say *Hola*, no more of that. The meal will put an end to your quarrel. And if you'll do me the honor of believing me, everything said here will be forgotten. The law at my table is the law of Antiquity: *Odi memorem compotorem*.[8]

It would have been good (someone commented), if the Lawyer hadn't said all these words on an empty stomach.

With that, we stopped. Having dined, and our horses having been bridled, we thanked the Gentleman for the fine food he had been pleased to offer us, and he thanked us for the honor he claimed to have received from our visit. Now, there were six of us in our group: he kept the Lawyer at his house, saying that he wanted to pay a debt that he owed him, having not tended to it for a long while. As for the other five travelers, after crossing the mountains, three

---

5 According to myth, Minos exacted a tribute of youths from Athens; but when Theseus was sent as part of that tribute, he extracted Minos' daughter Ariadne from the Labyrinth and escaped with her (and the other Athenians). The matter did not end well for the Athenians either, though: the god Dionysus stole Ariadne during the return voyage and, in his distraction, Theseus neglected to use the signal that would have shown he was returning alive. Failing to see it, his father despaired and cast himself into the sea.

6 For *Hercules Gallois*, see Louis Lallemant, *The Spiritual Doctrine*, ed. and trans. Patricia M. Ranum (Chestnut Hill, MA: Institute of Jesuit Sources, 2016), 13–15.

7 Here the Jesuit guest is addressed with a scornful *tu*, that matches the thrown-down gauntlet. The "Gallic Hercules" prevailed not by strength but by eloquence.

8 "I hate a drinking companion who remembers," Johannes Sambucus, *Emblemata* (1564), "De oblivione et ferula Baccho dicata. Odi Memorem compotorem."

of them took the road to Venice, intending to sail to Jerusalem, in order to fulfill a vow to visit the Holy Sepulcher. The Jesuit and I set off for Rome, he to
give his brethren an account of his journey, and I not only to participate in the
Jubilee but also to see two great prelates, both of whom bear the name and title
of Father: Our Holy Father Pope Clement VIII, truly a father of concord and
union, having, thanks to the intervention of the wise Florentine Cardinal,[9] his
legate, brought peace between two great kings,[10] for which Christianity is infinitely obligated to him. The other is Father Claudio Acquaviva, general of the
Jesuits, the father, or to be more accurate, the living spring of discord, partiality, and division, like the person who had created those divisions in France by
eagerly pursuing his henchmen, to the general ruin of our state. May God see
to it that Saint Thomas Aquinas, from whose family he is said to have sprung,
will in the future teach him and his brethren the obedience and fidelity that a
subject should bear toward his king.

9   Alessandro Ottaviano de' Medici (1535–1605), pope under the name of Leo XI for less
        than a month in April 1605. See *Encyclopaedia Britannica*, https://www.britannica.com/
        biography/Leo-XI (accessed January 22, 2021).
10   In May 1598, the Peace of Vervins was signed by representatives of Henri IV of France
        and Philip II of Spain. See *Encyclopaedia Britannica*, https://www.britannica.com/place/
        France/Political-ideology (accessed January 22, 2021).

CHAPTER 28

On the Schism Recently Introduced by the Jesuits into the Catholic Church of England, Scorning the Authority of the Holy See, a Tragic Story That Is Full of Compassion and Pity

To captain ignatius
Father and premier
General of the
Jesuit Society.

Father Soldier, where is your helmet?
Take up again your sword and your dagger:
For this author is unmasking now
Your cheating and hypocritical vow.

∴

THE NARRATOR. I'd thought I would close this book with the above quatrain, a piece I wanted to put separately. But since the history of the Jesuits is endless, when it comes to furious undertakings, the recent misfortune that once again arose in our Church of England, means that I couldn't sound retreat, as I had planned. Our conversations were held in the house of an upright gentleman, early in 1600, when the Great Jubilee opened. At that time, the Lawyer advanced two points. First, the Faculty of Theology of Paris had, from 1554 on, predicted that this Jesuit sect would be a hothouse of schisms within our church. Second, he maintained, at the end of our talks, that despite the false semblances that the Jesuits were using, in order to appear to be the principal pillars of the Holy See, they nonetheless were, and shall be in the future, the principal pillars, and that events would one day make us wiser. Having heard tell about that second point, I judged that the reasons he laid out were talk, which couldn't be converted into a history, although I've learned the contrary since then. For as I was on the verge of having my dialogs printed, someone gave me two manifestos, sent by the English Catholic priests: the first was for

© KONINKLIJKE BRILL NV, LEIDEN, 2021 | DOI:10.1163/9789004164062_067

Our Holy Father the pope; the second was for messieurs the Inquisitors of the faith, whose seat is Rome, against the new schism introduced into England by the Jesuits, which scorns the Holy See, whose grand zealots they claim to be. A history that we didn't yet know existed, for it was only fulfilled after the above discussions. If I didn't share this with you, I'd be failing in my duty. And without a disguise, I also want it to come to the knowledge of the Holy See.

All of us know, and know it to our great regret, how afflicted our Catholic, Apostolic, Roman Church is in the kingdom of England. Since God never abandons his church, no matter what affliction it may be experiencing (the small boat that held Saint Peter was greatly agitated by the winds and the storms, but it did not sink), he does similar things in that country. A good number of Catholics survived this great deluge. In the midst of those survivors were several priests in disguise, who were ministering to them secretly. If they were so unfortunate as to be discovered, they would be confined to a little city in the Fens called Wisbech, and they were strongly guarded at the castle where, in the daytime, they had permission to stroll in the courtyard and communicate with one another; and at night they would be locked up in their bedchambers. Misfortune fell on forty of these Catholic priests: among them was Father Weston, a Jesuit.[1] Giving his ambition full rein, and not asking the jailor's permission, he began to show extraordinary superiority toward all his imprisoned companions, manipulating so artfully the consciences of a few of them that they became his followers. The others, incapable of tolerating this new and unaccustomed tyranny, opposed him. This spark lighted a great fire, because on the one hand the Catholic priests, subject to no man and at liberty, joined the latter; and Father Henry Garnet,[2] superior of the Jesuits, and a few of his supporters, joined the former. The quarrel between priests and Jesuits spread to Catholic lay persons, all of whom agreed to delay deciding on the basis of the arbitration of a great counselor, whom they all deemed suitable and who, when sentenced, was of the opinion that they should banish from their church these new supervisors about whom Weston had been so eager. To this, all the Catholics voluntarily acquiesced, even Garnet and all his associates.

This new dispute finally quieted down. The clergy wanted to reestablish the common discipline of our church; and instead of their suppressed bishops,

---

1   William Weston (1550–1615) entered the Society in 1575 and was vice-prefect of the English Jesuits. He was imprisoned at Wisbech for four years, and then at the Tower of London in 1559. Exiled to Spain, he taught theology at Seville. See *DHCJ*, 4:4028–29.

2   Henry Garnet (1555–1606) was professor of Hebrew at the Roman College, and superior of the province of England. Compromised in the Gunpowder Plot, he was executed in 1606. See Thomas M. McCoog, "Pre-suppression Jesuit Activity in the British Isles and Ireland," *BRPJS* 1, no. 4 (2019): 19 ff.

they introduced into each province a priest who would be the main supervisor of things spiritual. Certainly, a new honor, but a true image of the antique and apostolic church. This having been put into force, they elected those who shone above the others when it came to doctrine, prudent advice, and self-sufficiency. And yet it was ordered that everything should stop until the pope had exerted his authority. Was there ever a more meritorious plan, or one on which one could promise a more certain reestablishment of our English Church? Just as they were on the verge of informing Rome, the devil joined the party, in order to prevent it. But through whose ministry? The ministry of our holy and venerable Jesuits. And here's how. They communicated only by troubles and confusions, fearing that this ruling would keep each order within the limits of its duties; so they opposed it. Garnet had an intimate friend and confident named George Blackwell,[3] a priest who was not truly a professed Jesuit, but who was a Jesuit in his soul, and who knew something about fencing with his pen. At Garnet's instigation, he wrote a book dedicated to the late Cardinal Cajetan,[4] the protector of their nation in Rome, through whom he sent invectives at full speed, to oppose this new policy, maintaining that it was a plot especially organized by the clergy against the Jesuit family, which was a bulwark that sustained the English Catholic Church.[5]

Now, listen to the continuation of this history, for it merits being known. There is, in Rome, an English Jesuit father, Robert Parsons,[6] who took the Latin name Parsonus. And I, using a word more suitable to his manners, I call him Personatus, for he's the person who played as many different characters in England as there are religions. Brought up first in the old-fashioned way by his father and mother, he then became a Lutheran, and finally a Jesuit: but no matter what religion he was passing through, he perpetually had a disagreeable and turbulent soul. For this reason, our adversaries chased him from Oxford University, where he was of some rank. Hating this, and not wanting to remain a hunk of trash and laziness, he entered that holy Society, a real pasture in which to feed and exercise a seditious man like him, and for whom our adversaries lit fires of joy in their souls, assuring themselves that he would one day be a new household-troubler in our church. And in that state, he lived for some

---

3 George Blackwell (1547–1612) was archpriest to the secular clergy from 1598 to 1608. See, McCoog, "Pre-suppression Jesuit Activity," 27 ff.

4 Enrico Caetani (1550–99) was Cardinal Protector of England. Apparently, Blackwell did not publish any book of his. He died on December 13. See *DBI*, https://www.treccani.it/enciclopedia/enrico-caetani_(Dizionario-Biografico) (accessed January 22, 2021).

5 Here, again, Pasquier imitates French-style English pronunciation: "Anglesche."

6 Robert Persons or Parsons (1546–1610), was a major player in the Jesuit English mission. See McCoog, "Pre-suppression Jesuit Activity," passim.

time in England; but seeing that things weren't safe for him, he set off on the road to Rome, where he was made rector of the English Seminary; and in my conscience, I believe that there is no Jesuit more worthy of being the general after Acquaviva's death,[7] than he is. For he is accompanied by the principal perfections required for that position. Indeed, he looked good for the position being offered. As soon as Blackwell's book arrived, he circulated it around the city in order to improve, more and more, the reputations of the brethren around him. After that, he stirred up a new council: for seeing that their Jesuit, Weston, had been supplanted from the new tyranny that he was claiming, he bethought himself to erect that position anew and give it to Blackwell, the Jesuits' creature, who would have no power in that position other than by their approval. Acting the part of diverse personages, the Jesuits could play the same role in England. This he obtained by plots, not plots of Our Holy Father's but Cardinal Cajetan's plots. I'll say this, before moving on: if there was some vagueness about the new project of the English priests, to make their church a model for bishops, it was up to the pope to enlighten them about it, and to no one else, like a nail hammered into the general discipline of the church. Moreover, they shouldn't be condemned without being heard. That's the first lesson that God taught us, when he punished Adam and Cain. And the pope, who is his vicar over us, doesn't intend to do otherwise. One doesn't talk to him about it: and even less does one give the clergy the leisure to dispatch its deputies to Rome. But, by chance, Parsons obtained letters-patent from Cardinal Cajetan on March 18, 1598, by which, as protector of the nation, he erected and instituted an archpriesthood in England, which alone would have full power over the clergy. The archpriest would be assisted by twelve priests, six of whom he named, and the others would be selected at the discretion of the archpriest (this was a lean-to built in favor of the Jesuits). He gave that position to Blackwell, a man about whom he knew nothing, other than what Parsons had told him, and what he learned from several Jesuit tracts that he had learned about in the book. Was there ever so daring an undertaking against the Holy See as this one? Did a cardinal, pushed by a Jesuit, without summoning the parties concerned, turn upside-down, with a flourish of his pen, all the ancient discipline of the Catholic Church of England? And this wasn't done in France, Germany, Poland, or Sweden, but in the city of Rome, at Our Holy Father's feet, without speaking with him about it, as I shall later prove? What do you think a Jesuit can do when he is in a distant country? Well, you'll find the rest of the story even more prodigious.

---

7   Persons died in 1610, five years before Acquaviva did on January 31, 1615.

The letters-patent from the cardinal having been brought to him, Blackwell assembled the entire clergy, read the letters aloud, and, to make the letter stronger, also had a declaration read aloud that he claimed had been sent to him from Rome, by which he was very specifically ordered not to undertake these weighty affairs without the approval of Father Garnet and his circle. If ever people were astonished, it was these poor priests, when they saw that, contrary to their general conclusion, a new papacy was being introduced into their country, to the detriment of the old papacy of Rome; and it wasn't a papacy, it was a tyranny never before seen or known in our Catholic Church. Without having heard the letters read aloud, the ancient discipline of the bishops was being annulled: this discipline that they claimed to be bringing back into use among them, under the authority of the Holy See. In everything that was presented to them, they saw no decree from the pope. That's why, from that very moment on, they opposed the execution of these letters; and the only reasons they gave were that they didn't think this came from the pope, notwithstanding that, in the letters, the cardinal declared that what he was doing was done with the approval and authority of the Holy See. These words were stated precisely, but they weren't obliged to believe them, although they visibly represented his permission. They resolved to send two of their colleagues to Our Holy Father, to learn what he wanted. Blackwell and Garnet weren't willing to yield, maintaining that on pain of excommunication, this must be believed: the cardinal had declared it by his letters, just as if those letters were bulls *sub plombo*[8] of His Holiness. Owing to this contestation, the clergy sent Bishop[9] and Charnock,[10] very prudent priests with whom no upright man will ever repent at putting his conscience in a storeroom, when he wishes a reconciliation with God. Blackwell, indignant at this procedure, excommunicated everyone who opposed it, having been induced to do this by a book written by Lister,[11] a Jesuit, where he maintained that all those who wanted to have

---

8   A papal bull is an authoritative form of document issued by the pope. Attached to it is a *bulla*, or rounded lead seal.

9   William Bishop (1555–1624) was a student at Reims and at Rome. He was sent on a mission to England in 1581 and appointed a bishop of Chalcedon. Twice imprisoned, in 1603 he drafted the declaration of loyalty. See McCoog, "Pre-suppression Jesuit Activity," 41–42.

10   William Charnock was a professor at the English College in Rome and a missionary in England in 1587. See McCoog, *Society of Jesus in Ireland, Scotland, and England*, 186–88.

11   Thomas Lister (1559–1626?) was a doctor of law at the University of Pont-à-Mousson, a missionary in England, exiled in 1606, he was superior of the Oxford region in 1621. See McCoog, *Society of Jesus in Ireland, Scotland, and England*, passim. A partial transcription of this tract, *Adversus factiosos in ecclesia*, can be found in Thomas Graves Law, *A Historical Sketch of the Conflict between Jesuits and Seculars in the Reign of Queen Elizabeth* (London: David Nutt, 1889), 143–45.

recourse to the authority of the Holy See, to the detriment of the cardinal's declaration, were schismatics and disturbers of the peace of the church, and could therefore be excommunicated. In order to bring order to this new disorder, the principal priests of the clergy came to see Blackwell and begged him to confer with them. If they were unwilling, three of the principal Jesuit fathers should at least swear, on their holy orders, that they knew this to be the will of Our Holy Father. In which case, they offered to obey the letters without quibbling. But a deaf ear was turned to all that: Blackwell flatly refused their request, *sit pro ratione voluntas*.[12] They appealed to the Roman Curia about these fulminations and censures. Despite that appeal, Blackwood carried on regardless, and he suspended them *a divinis*,[13] in order to deprive them of their livelihoods.

Now, while things were going on in this fashion in England, the two deputized priests reached Rome, on December 11, 1598. Parsons, who had been notified of their departure, put some spies to work, who notified him of their arrival. By this means, under Cardinal Cajetan's authority, he led the *barrizel* and his policemen[14] to their inn, where they were taken prisoner; and he immediately turned them over to Parsons, who seized all their papers and instructions, and then put them in diverse prisons, so tightly guarded that no one could communicate with them. For four months they were not permitted to see anyone, and could not celebrate the divine service, or even attend it. While they were under guard, Parsons interrogated them: he chose as his record-keeper Tichborne,[15] a Jesuit priest, to whom he wrote whatever he pleased. In short, he was an informer, a jailer, and a judge, all mixed together. The atrociousness of the crime demanded an unusual procedure. For it was not a matter of

---

12   "My will stands in place of reason," Juvenal, *Satires*, VI, 223.

13   In canon law, suspension *a divinis* is defined in Canon 1333 as follows: "Can. 1333 §1. Suspension, which can affect only clerics, prohibits: 1/ either all or some acts of the power of orders; 2/ either all or some acts of the power of governance; 3/ the exercise of either all or some of the rights or functions attached to an office. §2. A law or precept can establish that a suspended person cannot place acts of governance validly after a condemnatory or declaratory sentence. §3. A prohibition never affects: 1/ the offices or the power of governance which are not under the power of the superior who establishes the penalty; 2/ the right of residence which the offender may have by reason of office; 3/ the right to administer goods which may pertain to the office of the person suspended if the penalty is *latae sententiae*; §4. A suspension prohibiting a person from receiving benefits, a stipend, pensions, or any other such thing entails the obligation of making restitution for whatever has been received illegitimately, even if in good faith."

14   The *barizel* or *barigel* (Italian, *barigello*) was the chief of police in certain Italian cities, notably Rome. His policemen were known as *sbirres*.

15   Henry Tichborne (1570–1606) entered the Society in Rome in 1587; he was prefect of studies at the English College, confessor, and professor of moral theology at the seminary of Seville, where he died. See McCoog *English and Welsh Jesuits*, 317.

knowing whether Cardinal Cajetan had done well by bringing new confusion to the English Church, which was moreover quite afflicted by our adversaries; it was a matter of knowing whether the pope had consented and had authorized it ever so little. This trial could be judged from one day to the next: they merely needed to present them to His Holiness. But no news about that. They were taken prisoner of the feast of Saint Thomas, 1598. On February 17, 1599, the *barrizel* and Parsons took them to Cajetan, for a trial in which he should have recused himself. For he was personally very much involved; and he was both judge and civil party. True, he chose Cardinal Borghese[16] to assist him. Several other persons also put in an appearance, purportedly attorneys for Blackwell: they began vomiting up insults at the two priests. But well attacked, well defended. For one of the two spoke for his companion, asserting that all this was calumny fabricated at Parsons's boutique, and assuring that they had no memoranda by Blackwell, which moreover they asked to see. The Jesuits prevented this, and the case was decided on the spot. For the cardinals saw that the two priests were innocent: their immediate release from prison was ordered. But Parsons didn't obey, and he kept them in prison, for no reason other than the fact that one of them had defended himself too daringly against Blackwell's attorneys. This is another great crime that truly was in the Jesuit republic, and that merited a cell or a dungeon. And they were kept prisoners in that state for two whole months, during which Parsons was solicited by letters from Blackwell and his supporters to provide information again. He finally sent information, by which an unidentified person made a deposition to the effect that he had heard someone tell two priests that one of the two prisoners, whose first and last names he gave, had known the mother and her daughter.[17] This was the deposition of a solitary man who could merely provide hearsay, which one must not however trust. But by his reply the prisoner went further, for with a strong voice he said that he had almost been taunted over this wickedness, and that, to the contrary, he was just like he was when he came from his mother's womb, and that if public modesty and uprightness permitted, he was ready to show it, by showing his person before all the physicians and surgeons one could choose. When he heard this, Parsons was de-horned, yet he wouldn't give up.

---

16   Camillo Borghese (1552–1621) became a cardinal in 1596. He reigned as Pope Paul v 1605–21. See *Encyclopaedia Britannica*, https://www.britannica.com/biography/Paul-V (accessed January 23, 2021) and John Hungerford Pollen, *The Institution of the Archpriest Blackwell: A Study of the Transition from Paternal to Constitutional and Local Church Government Among the English Catholics, 1595 to 1602* (New York: Longmans, Green, 1916), 42.

17   Pasquier does not say who these women are or what they are doing.

Nothing is impossible for the Jesuits: when they have undertaken some-thing, be it good or bad, they carry it out, guided by a firm opinion that they would find some patron in Rome, who would confess to everything they had done. They conducted themselves that way in teaching boys who opposed their first Institute: and that's what they did when carrying out their simple vow for forty years, and that's what they did in the present case. For, having violated the authority of the Holy See by Jesuit Parsons's entreaties to Cardinal Cajetan, they obtained a bull from Pope Pius IV dated April 11, 1599, confirming the cardinal's letters-patent. Having obtained this brief, Parsons had the two prisoners send letters to their brethren, saying whatever they pleased, and he readied his dispatch for England.

On the 27th of that month, the *barrizel* came to inform them of another sentence that, he said, had been decided by the cardinal, to the effect that the prisons should be opened for them; but they were expressly forbidden to return to England, Scotland, and Ireland, on pain of excommunication. This meant sending two innocent men to look for bread, as they did for a long while in this France, before being identified. And to tell the truth, I don't doubt that Parsons himself wrote that purported sentence, which in order to give vent to his barbarian fury, freed only one of the prisoners, and a few days later, the other, not wanting one companion to console the other along the road. Believe me: when a Jesuit bears his teeth at someone, his bite is more venomous than the bite of a mad dog.

The Catholic priests could oppose the fulmination of the bulls, as having been obtained by obreption and surprise; and they had not been read aloud. Yet as soon as the bulls were communicated, along with the missives of their delegates, they presented themselves before their new archpriest, asking him please to forget everything that had happened, for they previously had a just reason not to obey him; but now that they saw what His Holiness wanted, they promised full obedience in the future. To show that they shouldn't have obeyed Cajetan's letters, the letters stated that authorization by the Holy See was needed: besides, there is no law or chapter that obliges us to believe sim-ple narrative statements about an act that is prejudicial to us: merely reading the bull shows how it contradicts the letters. For the pope doesn't say that he permitted the cardinal to create anew, in England, the position of archpriest over the entire clergy, nor to confer it upon Blackwell; it confirms everything done by him, just as if it had been his command and apostolic *ordonnance*; the words are: *tanquam de mandato et ordine nostro*, "as if it were our own command and order." Those words should have ended this whole quarrel. Now, the archpriest, having listened to the clergy, received at first glance his excuse as payment, and he not only embraced them, but promised to see that those who were absent during this new disagreement, would return. But as soon as he spoke with the Jesuits, one could see a different face on him than before. He said that he had received a message from Rome by which the Catholic priests of England were declared schismatics, because they didn't want to obey and to trust Cajetan's letters; and that before receiving them for communion, they would have to expiate their faults in the hands of some confessors he would send, to do the penance that would be ordered.

Summoned, and asked how he had received this message, the archpriest replied: From the Jesuit fathers, Tichborne and Warford.[18] The former is Parsons's record-keeper, the latter is the person who gave Squire the advice and the poison for poisoning the queen of England, his natural lady. And he added to the above that he should immediately excommunicate, as needed, all those who didn't want to seek this penance. These poor priests, seeing that they were being ill-used in this way, had recourse to the Faculty of theology of Paris, as a true fountain from which everything is drawn that serves to enlighten our consciences. They sent a brief discourse about their disagreement, without naming either the kingdom or the persons, begging the faculty to please find a solution for this new excommunication. By its resolution of May 30, 1600, the faculty declared that in all this there was no fault on the part of the clergy, nor, therefore, was there a reason for censure. This message was presented to the archpriest: he forbade them, whether it was true or not, to make use of it, and he confirmed his first censures. They appealed this, adhering to their first appeals. But the more they implored the help of the Holy See, the more that new tyrant, who was the Jesuits' workmanship, stiffened against them. The Catholics came to look for the archpriest in London, in order to inquire earnestly on what he based those censures. He didn't want to see them or hear about them; and it's a very great pity that, among these afflicted priests, there was one who, having sold all his possessions, had for twenty-five years found whatever he could for all the poor Catholics of the English Church, and especially the prisoners: And who *pro tribunali olim* (reads the first manifesto) *cum patre Campiano martire productus, ac in summo vitae periculo, admiranda Dei bonitate, ex mortis faucibus ereptus; et in exilium missus: sed non multo post denuo rediens ad castra Dei, magna exinde laude, et praeclaris meritis, in*

---

18   William Warford (*c.*1560–1608) converted to Catholicism in 1582 and entered the Society in 1594. He was a missionary in England in 1591. He was professor at Valladolid, where he died. See McCoog, *Society of Jesus in Ireland, Scotland, and England*, 77.

Anglicana vixit Ecclesia.[19] The other prisoner,[20] who was one of the first nurslings born at the English Seminary in Rome, had been honored with the holy orders of priesthood by the late Pope Gregory XIII of sainted memory, in the church of Saint John Lateran, and for ten full years he had suffered in various prisons in England. He has since returned to Rome and was received and favorably welcomed by Our Holy Father, Pope Clement VIII. Since then, he is said to have been sent back to England by the pope, with his blessing, and with money to work in God's vineyard again. Soon after his arrival, he was chosen by the Catholics and the Jesuits, to end the disagreement caused by the usurped tyranny of Weston, the Jesuit. And by award by arbiters, to everyone's satisfaction the church was reduced to the same measures as before. These two buttresses of the church were entered into the catalog of the forbidden and the censured, despite their venerable age and prudence. That's not enough: for in order to take away from every Catholic, no matter what his rank, every means of appealing, they had to be strictly prohibited and forbidden to appeal to the Roman Curia in any way whatsoever, without having first received its permission to do so. Thus, our Catholic Church today remains fallow, as far as all those good father-confessors are concerned, who previously had experienced bad things and nonetheless did not experience such unfortunate persecution on the part of our adversaries, as those who today suffer because of that roaring lion who is led by Jesuit acrobats.

Until now, I have faithfully recounted to you this whole tragic story. Permit me to gather my wits. Where was this fierce tragedy performed? On the stage of the Catholic Church of England, which, for the past seventy years and more, has had its martyrs and confessors, in order to sustain our Catholic, Apostolic, Roman Church, no less zealous than our ancients who are so celebrated in our ecclesiastical history. Who were the poets who wrote the plays? Our holy and devout Jesuits, the sole resource of our Catholic Church. What was the plot being proposed? None other than that the poor Catholic priests, unable to endure the new disorder that was being introduced into their church, in eager pursuit of these blissful fathers, wanted to have recourse to the Holy See, the anchor of our last respite. Oh, the pitiful condition of our church! If this prodigious history isn't known in Rome, so that a remedy can be had. Will we therefore deem the Lawyer wrong when he maintained that, among all the

---

19   "Having been summoned earlier before the tribunal along with the martyr Fr. Campion, and by the wonderful goodness of God rescued from the jaws of death and sent into exile; but returning again not much later to God's fortress he lived from then on with great praise and outstanding merits in the Church in England."

20   Probably John Mush. See *ODNB*, https://doi.org/10.1093/ref:odnb/19669 (accessed February 1, 2021).

new sects, there wasn't a single one that, over time, encroaches as much upon the authority of the Holy See as this one does, while pretending to sustain it. And if it pleases you to see me divulge a sincere sorrow that is eating away at my soul, I'll tell you, as the conclusion of my book, and of this chapter, that the Jesuit sect is nothing other than the ruin of the papacy, under the authority of the papacy.

I have one more thing to say. You know that the Jesuits, in the way they live, mingle affairs of state and affairs of religion, and that in the kingdoms where they have become targets, they have long wanted to trouble the kingdom of England, sometimes stirring desperate men to make an attempt on the queen's life, and sometimes wanting to demonstrate, by books, that this kingdom belonged directly to a great prince who, during his lifetime, sought all these instructions and memoranda, in order to make himself the master. Believe this: the Jesuits are in a finer field today than ever before. For, by their new undertaking against the authority of the Holy See, the administering of the holy sacraments has been forbidden and banished. All those good English priests who were nurtured in our ancient Catholic religion, taught their people to live with a free conscience, under the authority of its natural and legitimate lady. But now, this religion is solely carried on by the Jesuits, and by their henchmen. I leave you to wonder how they have the means to surprise weak souls by their venomous confessions and to stir up new troubles, not only against the state but also against the queen's life. In this way, we will, in a short time, see three assassinations suddenly appear in England: one, has already come to pass against the Holy See, and the two others against the queen and her state.

• • •

Some Passages

Excerpts from the two manifestos on which this history was based.

In the first manifesto, addressed to Our Holy Father Pope Clement VIII, page 74.

> *Nos* (this is Blackwell's decree) *ex auctoritate nobis à sanctissimo Domino nostro commissa pronunciamus ac declaramus primas illas literas institutionis nostrae omnes Catholicos vere in Anglia obligasse* (*intelligit scilicet ante adventum Brevis Apostolici*), *eosque qui nostrae auctoritati scienter*

quovis modo repugnarunt (priusquam pateret ullo canonico diplomate ex mandato sanctitatis tuae fuisse institutam) verè inobedientes fuisse Sedi Apostolicae, et in nostrum officium per eandem Sedem institutum, fuisse rebelles.[21]

Deinde prohibet clericis, sub poenis suspensionis, et interdicti, et amissionis omnium facultatum, ipso facto incurrendis, et Laicis sub poena interdicti, nequis quovis modo, verbo vel scripto, directè vel indirectè praeteritam inobedientiam defendere praesumat.[22]

On page 75.

Tandem ut ipsimet et patribus Jesuitis, amplissimus semper pateat campus, tam ad desaeviendum liberè in fratres, quam ad quamlibet exercendam tyrannidem, eodem prohibet edicto NE QUIS SACERDOS sub poenis suspensionis à divinis, et amissionis omnium facultatum ullo modo suffragia, vel scripto, vel verbo danda ambiat, vel det ad quamcumque causam, quam antea secum, vel cum duobus Assistentibus suis non constet fuisse communicatam: Hoc edicto non aliud planè intendens, quàm omnes nobis praecludere vias appellationis ad sedem Apostolicam, in pressuris et aerumnis nobis ab illo illatis.[23]

And a bit later on the same page.

---

21 "With the authority entrusted to us by our most holy Lord we announce and declare that those first Letters concerning our Institute [the Society of Jesus] were truly obligatory on all Catholics in England (clearly he means before the arrival of the Apostolic Brief); and those who knowingly opposed our authority in any way (before it had been made clear that this had been set up by any canonical decree issued by your reverence) had been really disobedient to the Holy See and rebellious against our [Jesuit] authority set up by the same See."

22 "Further it prohibits any cleric, under pain of suspension and prohibition and loss of all faculties to be incurred ipso facto, and any lay person, under pain of interdict, who might presume to defend either directly or indirectly the past disobedience."

23 "Finally, in order that the widest possible scope may be available to himself and to the Jesuit fathers, so as to freely abuse the brethren and exercise any sort of tyranny, he forbids with this same decree that ANY PRIEST, under pain of suspension *a divinis* [from conducting religious services] and the loss of all faculties, should he seek support, by writing or word of mouth, on behalf of any cause, unless it is first established that this has been communicated beforehand to himself or to his two Assistants. With this decree he clearly had no other intention but to close off for us all appeal channels to the Apostolic See with regard to the pressures and hardships which might be imposed on us by him."

Nunquid hoc modo Jesuita sibi viam sternere possunt, ad facillime indu-cendum in Ecclesiam, vel errores, vel hereses, vel quaevis alia perniciosa si quicquid ipsis aut asserere, aut agere collibuerit, id potentia et authori-tate quasi Apostolica munitum cunctis obstrudatur: nec quicquam liceat, vel ipsorum ausibus refragari vel ad Petri Cathedram, omnibus Christianis salutis portum confugere, nisi ut ipsi velint qui tyrannidem exercent.[24]

But above all, let's listen to the poor common people deplore the wretched state to which they were reduced at one and the same time, in Rome and in England, when the two priests were prisoners.

Page 56.

Adversarii sub capitali poena nos prohibent in quibuscunque causis Ecclesiasticis ad sedem Apostolicam confugere seu appellare, Jesuitae et Arcipresbiter, in eandem nos sedem contumaces, rebelles et schismaticos dicunt, quod in dubiis non acquievimus, priusquam eandem sedem consul-eremus. Si igitur propter consimilia utrinque plectamur, qui Catholicorum optimo jure non verebitur ad praedictam sedem confugere?[25]

Page 57. Concerning the contentment in the souls of our adversaries, upon see-ing the great scandal and confusion introduced into our church by the Jesuits.

Eo certè majorem inde percipient malae mentis laetitiam, majorem accipi-unt occasionem subsannandi, calumniandique sacratissimam sedem, quod tuam Sanctitatem artificiosissime praeoccupatam perspexerint, atque abductam per eum ipsum hominem (he is referring to Parsons the Jesuit) *quem omnes heretici nostrates, cum adhuc hereticus aut schismaticus esset,*

---

24 "Therefore in this way the Jesuits can open a way for themselves by which they can more easily introduce into the Church either errors or heresies or any other sort of harmful ele-ment, if it should please them to assert something or act so, and they might impose this on all as if they were empowered Apostolically; and it might not be permissible for any-one to resist, either relying on one's own resources, or seeking refuge in the Chair of Peter, the port of safety available to all Christians, unless they themselves who were exercising this tyranny, were willing."

25 "Our enemies forbid us under pain of death to appeal or have recourse on any ecclesiasti-cal matter to the Apostolic See. The Jesuits and the Archpriest say that we are opposed, rebellious and schismatics with regard to that same See, because when doubts arise we do not acquiesce before we have consulted that same See. Therefore, if we are to bow down to both because of similar constraints, what Catholic will not quite rightly fear to have recourse to the aforesaid See?"

paulo antè quam Jesuita fieret ex Academia Auxoniensi, maximo omnium
plausu, et campanarum strepitu, non religionis causa, ut ipse vane jactat,
ejectum, sed quod summe deditus esset seditionibus, factionibus, et famo-
sis conscribendis libellis, quem post susceptum Religionis habitum, non
solum inter Catholicos, quin imo et inter homines sui ordinis, ob naturae
asperitatem (ut illustrissimi Alani verbis et judicio de eodem utamur) ob
immodicam naturae violentiam, et inquietum contentionis spiritum, sibi
transferendo, omnem navasse operam optime noverant.[26]

It's that great personage, Parsons, who, as I told you, turned upside-down the entire state of the Catholic Church of England: I deemed you worthy of one day being the general of the Jesuit order. See whether I'm not right.

On page 59, on the subject of our adversaries: *Illi jam certè cum cachinno dicere feruntur, Portus Anglicani egredientibus jam liberè pateant. Unus Parsonus plus terret ne Sacerdotes Romam petant, quàm ullae leges nostrae.*[27]

EVERYTHING I COPIED up to here comes from the first manifesto. The six or seven lines that follow are at the end of the second manifesto, addressed to the Inquisitors of the Faith.

Page 97.

SEDES APOSTOLICAE beneficia nobis erepta sunt: illa in nostra inju-
ria despecta est: Ecclesiasticae hierarchiae forma apud nos inversa est:
Authoritas ad voluntatis, non aequitatis norman exercita, cujus praetextu,
in Sacerdotes, sanctosque Christi Confessores vinctos in Domino saevitum

---

26   "Because of this, they certainly enjoy all the more evil-minded delight, and gain all the more opportunity to mock and calumniate the Most Holy See, as they see that your Holiness is preoccupied with such artifices and led astray by that same man (viz. the Jesuit, Robert Parsons), whom all our own heretical figures had known well when with the great applause of all and to the sound of bells he was expelled from Oxford University, while he was still a heretic or schismatic shortly before he became a Jesuit; and this not because of religion, as he himself boasts, but because he was much involved in sedition and factions and the writing of well-known pamphlets; also that after he took the religious habit he was known not only among Catholics but even among men of his order to have a harsh character (to quote from the words and opinion of the famous [Cardinal] Allen), inclined to excessive violence and an unquiet contentious spirit, who had zealously arranged for all the enterprise to be entrusted to him."

27   "Certainly, they are now said to proclaim with a guffaw, 'The doors are now wide open for Anglicans to leave. It is Parsons alone who terrifies priests from going to Rome more than any laws of ours.'"

est, ut in divinae laesae majestatis reos, et in Ecclesiae perduelles magis sae-
viri non potuerit.[28]

THE END

JESUITAS VERE
Esse concionatores,
et ideo in pristinum statum
restituendos. Ad Patrem
Jacobum Commolum, Jesuitam.

Concio. Romani dicta est furiosa Tribuni,
Quae rapit ad caedem seditione suos.
In cathedra stantum, rapida cum voce boares
Commole, te populus vidit et obstupuit.
Qui Regis caedem, Regni qui funera suades,
Qui varios motus hic et ubique cies:
Cujus in ore frequens furor est patriaeque ruina,
Haec est Jesitae concio sacra pii.
Cum tua parturiat civiles lingua procellas,
O Jesite Dei sancte Tribune vale.[29]

---

28   "The benefits of the Apostolic See have been torn from us. Now they are used contemp-
tuously for our harm. The hierarchical structure has been turned upside down among
us. Authority is used at somebody's whim, not for justice. With this pretext, there is violence against priests and against the holy confessors of Christ and servants in the Lord, so
that more savagery could not be found against criminals guilty of high treason before the
Divine Majesty and against traitors of the Church."

29   That Jesuits are right preachers, and therefore to be restored to their former place in Paris,
a scoffing epigram, written to Father Jacque Commolet the Jesuit:
The furious speech of a tribune of Rome,
Persuaded men to murder and commotion,
When roaring Commolet gave out his doom
In pulpit, people mus'd at his devotion:
He bid them kill their king, his realm annoys,
He stirred up many troubles everywhere,
Rage in his mouth his country to destroy,
This holy doctrine preached the Jesuit there.
And set his tongue doth civil tempests brew,
I bid this holy tribune here adieu.

AD HENRICUM QUARTUM
Franciae et Navarre
Christianissimum Regem.

Hoc te Epigramma puta, Magne ò Henrice docere
Quae de Jesuitis sint statuenda tibi.[30]

---

30   To *Henry* the fourth, the most Christian king of France and Navarre:
        Great Henry by this epigram is told,
        What course with Jesuits he ought to hold.

Index

Printed in the United States
by Baker & Taylor Publisher Services